Compensation

Fourth Edition Compensation

George T. Milkovich
Cornell University

Jerry M. Newman
State University of New York—Buffalo

With the assistance of Carolyn Milkovich

Homewood, IL 60430
Boston, MA 02116

© RICHARD D. IRWIN, INC., 1984, 1987, 1990, and 1993

All rights reserved. No part of this publication may be reproduced, stored in a retrieval system, or transmitted, in any form or by any means, electronic, mechanical, photocopying, recording, or otherwise, without the prior written permission of the publisher.

Senior sponsoring editor: Craig Beytien
Editorial coordinator: Lisa Brennan
Marketing manager: Kurt Messersmith
Project editor: Ethel Shiell
Production manager: Bette K. Ittersagen
Cover designer: Tara L. Bazata/Jeanne M. Rivera
Art coordinator: Mark Malloy
Compositor: J. M. Post Graphics, Corp.
Typeface: 10/12 Times Roman
Printer: R. R. Donnelley & Sons Company

Library of Congress Cataloging-in-Publication Data

Milkovich, George T.
　　Compensation / George T. Milkovich, Jerry M. Newman.—4th ed.
　　　　p.　　cm.
　　ISBN 0-256-10527-8
　　1. Compensation management.　I. Newman, Jerry M.　II. Title.
　HF5549.5.C67M54　1993
　　658.3′2—dc20　　　　　　　　　　　　　　　　　　92–27604

Printed in the United States of America

1　2　3　4　5　6　7　8　9　0　DOC　9　8　7　6　5　4　3　2

Preface

"The country's in a bind, but I'm cheerful and I'm chipper,
As I slash employee wages like a fiscal Jack the Ripper,
And I take away their health care and never mind their hollers,
And pay myself a bonus of a couple of million dollars."

Managing compensation is so fascinating that even comedians are getting into the act. Mark Russell's satire on executive pay confirms what everyone suspects: that pay, particularly one's own, is determined without apparent justice or reason.

We are in a period in which traditional approaches to pay determination are being increasingly questioned and scrutinized. Managers face economic pressures to improve productivity, boost the quality of products and services, and control labor costs. Social pressures stem from shifting employee expectations and continued government regulations. In light of these pressures, managers seek to better understand how to design and manage the compensation their employees receive. Traditional, often bureaucratic, approaches to pay are being reexamined. Different approaches—some new, some simply old goods in new wrappings—are being tried. Current approaches may be retained but are frequently better understood and managed after reexamination.

This process of creative reexamination is both a boon and a source of frustration for managers. On the positive side, managers have the opportunity to make decisions that dramatically affect their organizations. Pay decisions can be integrated into the entire strategic management process. Compensation policies can improve total quality, encourage employees to focus on satisfying customers, support equitable treatment of employees, and help achieve competitive advantage for an organization.

These opportunities can also be a source of frustration. Very simply, compensation can no longer be managed from a limited approach. Pursuit of the single, correct technique is futile. Viewing problems exclusively from a compensation perspective is also futile. Coordinating compensation decisions with other areas of human resource management is more likely to yield success.

When all is said and done, managing compensation remains an art. Like any art, not everything that can be learned can be taught. Not everything that is learned is done so consciously. Some managers of compensation seem more intuitive than others. They seem to be "naturals," like Wayne Gretsky. He knows how to put the hockey puck into the net but cannot always explain what he did right. Often what gets included in textbooks are the beliefs, examples, and tricks of the trade. Some of these are supported by related theory and research; many are not. Systematic knowledge is valued, and we have tried mightily to formalize it in this book. But please remember that managing compensation is not a science. The more we learn about this field, the more we appreciate that the less teachable parts of managing compensation are also valuable.

ABOUT THIS BOOK

The design of this book is largely based on four strategic choices involved in managing compensation. As the compensation model in Chapter 1 illustrates, these strategic choices include concerns for internal consistency, external competitiveness, employee contributions, and administration. Four sections in this book examine each of these strategic decisions and discuss the major compensation issues requiring resolution. These discussions are placed in the context of related theories, research, and state-of-the-art practices that can guide compensation decision making.

Additional chapters of this book cover employee benefits, government's influence on compensation, pay discrimination, compensation of special groups, and unions' role in pay administration. These are topics of continuing importance. First, costs of employee benefits are escalating rapidly, and employers are taking significant steps to contain those costs by modifying benefit programs. Employees are also increasingly able to choose various benefits tailored to their individual circumstances. Next, the government's role is considered in terms of its direct and indirect effects on pay. Directly, government is a regulator of pay decisions through legislation and the courts (e.g., minimum wage, pay discrimination, and comparable worth). Indirectly, through its fiscal and monetary policies (e.g., tax laws and stimulating the economy), the government affects the supply and demand for labor and, hence, compensation decisions. The changing yet critical role unions and special groups assume in compensation management is also examined in separate chapters and throughout the book.

Knowledge about international approaches to paying employees is increasingly important. Pay systems used in different cultures are examined throughout the book. Illustrations drawn from Japan, Germany, the United Kingdom, and others are used to help broaden your perspective to aid you in making more informed decisions.

This book undertakes three central tasks. The first is to examine the current theory and research related to managing compensation. This analysis is supported by extensive up-to-date references in each chapter.

The second task is to examine the changing state of compensation practice. Here we draw upon practices actually used by a wide variety of employers and consulting firms from around the globe. These practices illustrate new developments as well as established approaches to compensation decisions.

Finally, this book provides an opportunity for you to develop your own decision-making skills through a series of exercises based on actual experiences. These exercises apply concepts and techniques discussed in the chapters. A workbook with a more extensive case and computer applications is also available. Completing these exercises will help you develop skills readily transferable to future jobs and assignments.

ACKNOWLEDGMENTS

We relied on the contributions of many people in the preparation of this book. We owe a special, continuing debt of gratitude to our students. In the classroom, they motivate and challenge us, and as returning managers with compensation experience, they try mightily to keep our work relevant.

We appreciate the contributions of the many compensation professionals who shared their ideas and practices with us for this fourth edition. Some commented on early drafts of chapters; others shared details about particular problems and projects. Although we cannot hope to recognize all of them, the following are a few who went beyond the call of duty:

Jeanie Adkins   Mercer Meidinger Hansen
Robert Berg   Colgate Palmolive
Richard Blough   Outokumpu-American Brass
John Bronson   PepsiCo
Jim Curnow   3M
Shirley Currey   TRW
Bill Evans   General Electric
Joel Goldberg   RJR-Nabisco
Steven Gross   Hay
Michael Guthman   Hewitt
Doris Hauser   Office of Personnel Management
Kenjiro Ishihara   Toshiba
Steve Kumagai   IDS-American Express
John Markowski   Merck
David Ness   Medtronics
Steve O'Byrne   TPF&C
Bob Ochsner   Hay
Ray Olsen   TRW
Ronald Page   Hay
Larry Phillips   General Electric
Walt Read   Empire Blue Cross/Blue Shield
Robert Rusek   AT&T
Fumie Urashima   Johnson & Johnson–Japan
Dave Wessinger   Organization Resource Counselors

Cornell's Center for Advanced Human Resource Studies provided a forum for the interchange of ideas among human resource professionals and academics, including myself.

Several academic colleagues were also very helpful in the preparation of this and previous editions. The comments of the following were especially appreciated:

Ronald A. Ash   University of Kansas
David B. Balkin   University of Colorado, Boulder
Melissa Barringer   University of Massachusetts
David Belcher   San Diego State
Chris Berger   Purdue University
George Bohlander   Arizona State University
James T. Brakefield   Western Illinois University
Renae Broderick   Cornell University
Robert Cardy   Arizona State University
Michael D. Crino   Clemson University
Eric Cousineau   York University
John Delaney   University of Iowa
Donald Drost   California State—San Bernardino
John Fossum   University of Minnesota
Cynthia Fukami   University of Denver
Barry Gerhart   Cornell University
Luis Gomez-Mejia   Arizona State University
John Hannon   Purdue University
James C. Hodgetts   Memphis State University
Gregory S. Hundley   University of Oregon
Linda A. Krefting   Texas Tech University
Daniel J. Koys   DePaul University
Frank Krzystofiak   State University of New York—Buffalo
Michael Byungnam Lee   Georgia State University
Jay Liebowitz   Duquesne University
Thomas Mahoney   Vanderbilt University
Michael Moore   Michigan State University
Bonnie Rabin   Ithaca College
Robert Risley   Cornell University
Donald P. Schwab   University of Wisconsin
Susan Schwochau   University of Iowa
Michael Sturman   Cornell University
Glenn R. Thiel   Robert Morris College
Richard J. Ward   Bowling Green State University
Nathan Winstanley   Rochester Institute of Technology

Manuscript preparation by Amy Sabol and Hilde Rogers was always thorough and timely.

Contributions of Sarah Milkovich and Terrie, Erinn, and Kelly Newman to the authors' quality of life are unparalleled.

George T. Milkovich
Jerry M. Newman

Contents

3   Assessing Work   57

4   Evaluating Work: Job Evaluation, Skill-Based Plans, and Market Pricing   112

PART V

Compliance

13　The Government's Role in Compensation　459

14　Pay Discrimination　476

Strategic Issues and the Pay Model

Think of an employer, any employer—from Burlington Railroad to Ralph's Pretty Good Groceries—and consider the array of wages paid. Burlington's wages differ for different jobs ranging from locomotive engineers, to laborers on maintenance-of-way gangs, accountants, traffic clerks, and nurses. Similarly, Ralph's pays checkout clerks, produce department managers, and butchers.[1]

Why do some employers pay more (or less) than other employers? Why are different jobs within the same organization paid differently? And why do different workers doing the same work for the same employer receive different pay? How are these decisions made and who is involved in making them? And does any of this really matter? What are the consequences of these decisions for both the employer and the employee? These questions were so interesting to Mary Lemons, a Denver nurse, that she took her employer, the city of Denver, to court, alleging that it was illegal to pay Denver's tree trimmers (all men) more than its nurses (mostly women).[2] Compensation, whether it's your own or someone else's, is a fascinating topic.

Compensation managers are immersed in one of society's greatest challenges: the efficient and equitable distribution of the returns for work. As already noted, compensation decisions are many and varied. They include how much to pay people who perform both similar and different types of work; whether to use pay to recognize variations in employees' experience and/or performance; and how to allocate pay among cash and benefits and services. Such basic decisions must be made by every employer, no matter how large or small. Further, these decisions must be consistent both with society's changing values about what constitutes fair pay and with government regulations. Consequently, decisions about compensating people for the work they perform are increasingly critical.

This book is about the management of compensation. Its purpose is to give you the background required to make pay decisions.

COMPENSATION IN CONTEMPORARY SOCIETY

Perceptions of compensation vary. Some in *society* may see it as a measure of equity and justice. For example, a comparison of 1991 median weekly earnings of fully employed women ($265, or 73 percent) with that of men ($361) highlights apparent inequities in pay decisions, which many consider an indication of discrimination against women. To stockholders, executive pay is of special interest. Particularly befuddling was the pay of Robert Stempel, who made nearly $2.2 million in 1990, the same year his company, General Motors, lost $4.5 billion and announced the elimination of 74,000 jobs. Irate holders of stock in Fairchild, an aerospace firm, sued chief executive officer Jeffrey J. Steiner, charging that he "conducted a systematic scheme to loot" the company.[3] Others may see high pay as a cause of U.S. firms' inability to meet foreign competition. The fact that production workers in South Korea earn, on average, 21 percent ($3.23) of their U.S. counterparts' hourly pay ($15.39) is, to many consumers, the root of U.S. manufacturing competitive problems and is the reason companies are moving many jobs to

---

[1]Garrison Keillor, *Lake Wobegon Days* (New York: Viking Press, 1985).

[2]*Lemons* v. *City and County of Denver,* 620 F.2d 228 (1980).

[3]In an out-of-court settlement, Steiner agreed to cut his pay by $250,000 and forgo future bonuses and stock options.

other countries.[4] Some voters also see compensation, pensions, and health care for public employees as the cause of increased taxes. Public policymakers and legislators may view changes in average pay as guides for adjusting eligibility for social services (medical assistance, food stamps, and the like).

In contrast to the societal perspective, *employees* may see compensation as a return for services rendered or as a reward for a job well done. Compensation to some reflects the value of their personal skills and abilities, or the return for the education and training they have acquired. Benefits such as medical insurance, pensions, or wellness programs help protect employees and their dependents. The pay individuals receive for the work they perform is usually the major source of personal income and financial security, and hence a vital determinant of an individual's economic and social well-being. Employees, like stockholders, may also have more than a passing interest in the pay of their bosses. During the 1980s, CEO pay rose an average 212 percent, while the factory workers' pay increased by 53 percent. Stephen Wolf, head of United Airlines, collected $18.3 million in 1990, 1,200 times the starting pay of United's flight attendants, who hadn't had a raise in five years. Meanwhile, United's profits plummeted by 71 percent.

Managers also have a stake in compensation; they view it from two perspectives. First, it is a *major expense*. Competitive pressures, both internationally and domestically, force managers to consider the affordability of their compensation decisions. Studies show that in many enterprises labor costs account for more than 50 percent of total costs.[5] Among some industries, such as service or public employment, this figure is even higher. Recent studies report that labor costs as a percent of total costs vary even among individual firms within one industry. This has led many to conclude that compensation decisions can offer firms a competitive advantage.[6]

In addition to viewing compensation as an expense, a manager also views it as a possible *influence on employee work attitudes and behaviors*.[7] The way employees are paid may affect the quality of their work; their focus on customer needs; their willingness to be flexible and learn new skills, to suggest innovations and improvements; and even their interests in unions or legal action against their employer. This potential to influence employees' work attitudes and behaviors, and subsequently the productivity and effectiveness of the organization, is an important rationale for ensuring that compensation is managed fairly. These contrasting perspectives of compensation—societal, employee, and managerial, each with different stakes in compensation decisions—can account for

---

[4]*International Comparisons of Hourly Compensation Costs for Production Workers in Manufacturing, 1991,* Report 766 (Washington, D.C.: U.S. Department of Labor, Bureau of Labor Statistics, 1992).

[5]Luis Gomez-Mejia and David Balkin, *Compensation, Organization Strategy, and Firm Performance* (Cincinnati: South-Western Publishing, 1992).

[6]Luis Gomez-Mejia and Theresa Vukovich Wellbourne, "Compensation Strategy: An Overview and Future Steps," *Human Resource Planning* 11 (1988), pp. 173–189; Barry Gerhart and George Milkovich, "Employee Compensation," in *Handbook of Industrial and Organizational Psychology,* vol. 3, ed. M. D. Dunnette and L. Hough (Palo Alto, Calif.: Consulting Psychologists Press, 1992).

[7]George Milkovich and Renae Broderick, "Developing Compensation Strategies," in *Handbook of Wage and Salary Administration,* 3rd ed., ed. M. Rock (New York: McGraw-Hill, 1990).

the relevance of the topic. But these perspectives can also cause confusion if not everyone is talking about the same thing. So let's define what we mean by compensation.

FORMS OF PAY

Compensation, or pay (the words are used interchangeably in this book), is defined in the following terms:

> **Compensation** refers to all forms of financial returns and tangible services and benefits employees receive as part of an employment relationship.

Exhibit 1.1 shows the variety of forms of compensation. Pay may be received directly in the form of cash (e.g., wages, merit increases, incentives, cost-of-living adjustments) or indirectly through benefits and services (e.g., pensions, health insurance, paid time off). *Alternative rewards* are excluded from this definition, yet they affect employee behaviors. Recognition ceremonies, celebration of achievements, personal satisfaction from continually learning and successfully facing new challenges, working with great coworkers, and the like undoubtedly are an important part of the total returns people receive from their work. Such factors may be thought of as part of an organization's "total reward system" and are often coordinated with compensation.[8]

Programs that distribute compensation to employees can be designed in an unlimited number of ways, and a single employer typically will use more than one program. These pay delivery programs typically fall into four forms: base wage, merit pay, incentives, and employee services and benefits.

Base Wage.   Base wage is the basic cash compensation that an employer pays for the work performed. Base wage tends to reflect the value of the work itself and generally ignores differences in contribution attributable to individual employees. For example, the base wage for a word processor's work may be $12 an hour, but some individual operators may receive more because of their experience and/or performance. Some pay systems set base wage as a function of the skill or education an employee possesses; examples include engineers, scientists, and craft workers. Periodic adjustments to base wages may be made on the basis of changes in the overall cost of living or inflation, changes in what other employers are paying for the same jobs, or changes in experience/performance/skill of employees.

A distinction is often made between salary and wage, with *salary* referring to pay for those workers who are exempt from regulations of the Fair Labor Standards Act, and

---

[8]N. K. Sethia and M. A. Glinow, "Arriving at Four Cultures by Managing the Reward System," in *Gaining Control of the Corporate Culture,* ed. K. M. Saxton and R. Serpa (San Francisco: Jossey-Bass, 1991).

EXHIBIT 1.1   Forms of Compensation

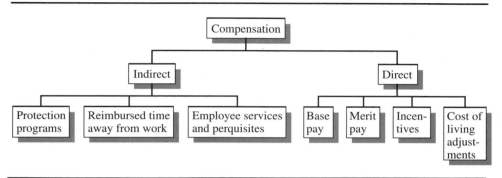

hence do not receive overtime pay.[9] Managers and professionals usually fit this category. We refer to such employees as *exempts*. Their pay would be calculated at an annual or monthly rate rather than hourly, because hours worked do not need to be recorded. In contrast, workers who are covered by overtime and reporting provisions of the Fair Labor Standards Act—*nonexempts*—usually have their pay calculated at an hourly rate referred to as a *wage*. Some employers, such as Hewlett-Packard and IBM, label all base pay as salary in an attempt to support a management philosophy that all employees are working as a team, rather than being divided into salaried and wage earners.[10]

Merit.   Merit pay rewards past work behaviors and accomplishments. Given as increments to the base pay, merit programs are commonly designed to pay different amounts (often at different times) depending on the level of performance. Thus, outstanding performers may receive a 10 to 12 percent merit increase nine months after their last increase, whereas a satisfactory performer may receive, say, a 6 to 8 percent increase after 12 or 15 months. According to surveys, 90 percent of U.S. firms reported using pay for performance.[11]

Incentives.   Incentives also tie pay directly to performance. Sometimes referred to as nontraditional compensation, incentives may be long or short term, and can be tied to the performance of an individual employee, a team of employees, a total business unit,

---

[9]Barry Gerhart and George Milkovich, "Organizational Differences in Managerial Compensation and Financial Performance," *Academy of Management Journal,* December 1990, pp. 663–90.

[10]*Employee Buy-In to Total Quality,* Report 974 (New York: The Conference Board, 1991); *Hewlett-Packard Personnel Policies and Guidelines.*

[11]Robert Heneman, *Merit Pay: Linking Pay Increases to Performance Ratings* (Reading, Mass.: Addison-Wesley, 1992); Robert Bretz, Jr., George Milkovich, and Walter Read, "The Current State of Performance Appraisal Research and Practice: Concerns, Directions, and Implications," *Journal of Management,* 1992; *Performance Appraisal Practice in Leading Companies* (Wyatt, 1991); George Milkovich and Alexandra Wigdor, *Pay for Performance* (Washington, D.C.: National Academy of Science, 1991).

or even some combination of individual, team, and unit. Usually very specific performance standards are used in short-term incentive programs. For example, at Union Carbide's Chemicals and Plastics Division, for every quarter that an 8 percent return on capital target is met or exceeded, bonus days of pay are awarded. A 9.6 percent return on capital means two extra days of pay for every participating employee for that quarter. Twenty percent return on capital means 8.5 extra days of pay. Performance results may be defined as cost savings, volume produced, quality standards met, revenues, return on investments, or increased profits; the possibilities are endless.

Long-term incentives are intended to focus employee efforts on longer range (multi-year) results. Top managers or professionals are often offered long-term incentives (e.g., stock ownership, bonuses) to focus on long-term organizational objectives such as return on investment, market share, return on net assets, and the like.[12] Some firms such as Merck grant shares of stock to selected "Key Contributors" who make outstanding contributions to the firm's success. And employee stock ownership (ESOP) plans in which all employees own shares of their employer are believed by some to motivate performance.[13]

Incentives and merit pay differ. Although both may influence performance, incentives do so by offering pay as an inducement. Merit, on the other hand, is a reward that recognizes outstanding past performance. The distinction is a matter of timing. Incentive systems are offered prior to the actual performance. Sales commissions are an example; an auto sales agent knows the commission on a Cadillac versus that on a Chevy prior to making the sale. Gainsharing is another example. Corning employees know the amount of the bonus they will receive if their plant exceeds its financial goals. Merit pay, on the other hand, typically is not communicated beforehand, and the amount of money to fund merit increases is usually not known very far in advance.

Merit and incentives are clearly related. Insofar as employees begin to anticipate their merit pay, it acts as an incentive to induce performance. Thus, anticipated rewards become incentives. Merit is typically based on individual performance; incentives may be based on the performance of an individual, team, or unit.

Perhaps the most important distinction is that merit pay usually adds into and permanently increases base pay, whereas incentives are one-time payments and do not have a permanent effect on labor costs. When performance declines, incentive pay automatically declines, too.

---

[12]*Executive Compensation: Principles and Guidelines for Roundtable Member Companies* (New York: Business Roundtable, 1992); David J. McLaughlin, "The Rise of a Strategic Approach to Executive Compensation," in *Executive Compensation: A Strategic Guide for the 1990s,* ed. Fred Foulkes (Boston: Harvard Business School Press, 1991); Geoffrey Colvin, "How to Pay the CEO Right," *Fortune,* April 6, 1992, pp. 60–69; M. C. Jensen and K. J. Murphy, "CEO Incentives: It's Not How Much You Pay, But How," *Harvard Business Review,* May–June 1990, pp. 138–53; Hewitt Associates, "Are Companies Starting to Rein In Long-Term Incentives?" *On Compensation,* February 1992; Graef Crystal, *In Search of Excess* (New York: W. W. Norton, 1991).

[13]Some believe greater stock ownership motivates performance; others argue that the link between individual job behaviors and the vagaries of the stock market are tenuous at best. See George Milkovich and Carolyn Milkovich, "Making Pay for Performance Work," *Compensation and Benefits Review,* September-October 1992.

Services and Benefits.   Employee services and benefits are the programs that include a wide array of alternative pay forms ranging from time away from work (vacations, jury duty), services (drug counseling, financial planning, cafeteria support), and protection (medical care, life insurance, and pensions). Because the cost of providing these services and benefits has been rising (for example, employers pay nearly half the nation's health care bills, and health care expenditures have been increasing at annual rates in excess of 15 percent), they are an increasingly important form of pay.[14] In a recent Gallup poll, people claimed they would require $5,000 more in extra pay to choose a job without pension, health care, and life insurance. Many employers now manage benefits as closely as they manage direct compensation.

These four pay forms make up the total compensation package paid to employees. The compensation manager is responsible for designing and managing all elements of pay/total compensation.

Returns in an Implicit Exchange

Taken literally, *compensation* means to counterbalance, to offset, to make up for. So compensation makes up for the effort an employee exerts on the employer's behalf. In this sense, pay is a "return" for services. But sometimes pay systems are referred to as *reward systems*. To some the distinction between rewards and returns is not very important. A reward is given for good performance. A return is given in exchange for something of value. But it's unlikely that employees see their pay as a reward. Rather, they are more likely to describe it as a return received *in exchange* for efforts and ideas given to an employer.

Exchange is the key. Some suggest that an implicit psychological contract is formed in the employment relationship.[15] Employees and employers, parties to this exchange, form ideas about their mutual obligations and returns. Compensation becomes part of that transaction. In some cases, employees form unions to negotiate more explicit terms of exchange.

Some forms of compensation clearly do act as rewards; merit increases are financial recognition of a job well done. Indeed, mounting evidence suggests that those forms of

---

[14]Nora Super Jones, "Politics and Employee Benefits: What to Expect in 1992," *Employee Benefit Notes,* January 1992, pp. 1–5; Jacque J. Sokolov, "National Health Care Reform: A Corporate Perspective," *Compensation and Benefits Management,* Spring 1992, pp. 1–6; "Proposed Health Care Reform," *On Health Care* (Hewitt Associates, 1992), pp. 10–11; G. F. Dreher, R. A. Ash, and R. D. Bretz, "Benefit Coverage and Employee Cost: Critical Factors in Explaining Compensation Satisfaction," *Personnel Psychology* 41 (1988), pp. 237–54; R. Feldman, M. Finch, and S. Cassou, "The Demand for Employment-Based Health Insurance Plans," *The Journal of Human Resources* 24 (1989), pp. 115–42; Jack Dolmat-Connell and Ken Cardinal, "Beyond Total Compensation: The Total-Cost Perspective," *Compensation and Benefits Review,* January–February 1992, pp. 56–60.

[15]Denise Rousseau, "New Hire Perceptions of Their Own and Their Employer's Obligations: A Study of Psychological Contracts," *Journal of Organization Behavior* 11 (1990), pp. 389–400.

pay that act as rewards may help organizations achieve competitive advantage. This research suggests that it may not be how much you pay but how you pay that matters.[16]

Expected Costs and Stream of Earnings

Up to this point compensation has been static, something paid or received at a moment in time. But compensation decisions have a temporal quality. Think about the manager who decides to make you a job offer—say $30,000. Look at that decision over time. Assume you stay with the firm an average of 5 years and receive 7 percent annual increases in each of those five years. You will be earning $39,324 in five years. The expected cost commitment of the decision to hire you turns out to be $224,279 ($30,000 base compounded by 7 percent for five years, plus benefits equal to 30 percent of base). But lest you rush out to purchase an $80,000 Range Rover, recognize that it will cost over $102,000 in five years, assuming 5 percent price increases every year.

   The point is that compensation can be both simple and involved. It is pay. It can be treated as a stream of future earnings, costs, or investment. It can include nonfinancial and psychological returns as in a total reward system. And it can take several forms: cash, benefits, and services. We turn now to a pay model that will serve as both a framework for examining current pay systems and a guide for much of this work.

A PAY MODEL

The pay model shown in Exhibit 1.2 contains three basic components: (1) the policies that form the foundation of the compensation system; (2) the techniques that make up much of the mechanics or technology of compensation management; and (3) the compensation objectives. Each of these components and the relationships among them are discussed in turn.

Compensation Objectives

Pay systems are designed and managed to achieve certain objectives. The basic objectives, shown at the right side of the model, include efficiency, equity, and compliance with laws and regulations. These objectives in the model are broadly conceived. The *efficiency* objective is typically stated more specifically: (1) improving performance, achieving total quality, focusing on customer needs and (2) controlling labor costs. Hewlett-Packard and Astra-Merck's compensation objectives are contrasted in Exhibit 1.3. Note the emphasis on performance and business success reflected in their objectives.

---

[16]Barry Gerhart and George Milkovich, "Employee Compensation," in *Handbook of Industrial and Organizational Psychology*, vol. 3, ed. M. D. Dunnette and L. Hough (Palo Alto, Calif.: Consulting Psychologists Press, 1992).

EXHIBIT 1.2   The Pay Model

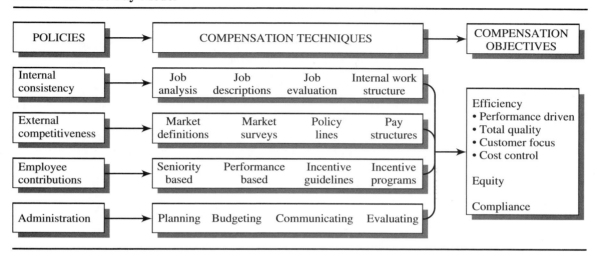

EXHIBIT 1.3   Comparisons of Pay System Objectives

Pay Objectives at Astra-Merck and Hewlett-Packard	
Astra-Merck	**Hewlett-Packard**
• Share commitment and responsibility; foster teamwork	• Help H-P continue to attract creative and enthusiastic people who contribute to its success
• Balance immediate and strategic interests	• Pay among the leaders
• Celebrate performance	• Reflect sustained relative contribution of unit, division, and H-P
• Promote fairness	• Be open and understandable
• Achieve simplicity	• Ensure fair treatment
• Be market competitive; pay at the 75th percentile of competitors	• Be innovative, competitive, and equitable

Equity is a fundamental theme in pay systems. Statements such as "fair treatment for all employees" or "a fair day's pay for a fair day's work" reflect a concern for equity. Thus, the equity objective attempts to ensure fair pay treatment for all participants in the employment relationships. The equity objective focuses on designing pay systems that recognize both employee *contributions* (e.g., offering higher pay for greater performance or greater experience or training) and employee *needs* (e.g., providing a "living wage," as well as fair procedures).

Procedural equity, often overlooked by both managers and researchers, is concerned with the processes used to make decisions about pay.[17] It suggests that the way a pay decision is made may be as important to employees as are the results of the decision. As an objective for a pay system, procedural equity helps ensure that employees, managers, and other relevant parties have a voice in the design of pay plans and an opportunity to voice any dissatisfaction with the pay received.

Compliance as a pay objective involves conforming to various federal and state compensation laws and regulations. As these laws and regulations change, pay systems often need to be adjusted to ensure continued compliance.

There are probably as many statements of pay objectives as there are employers. In fact, highly diversified firms such as TRW and General Electric, which compete in multiple lines of businesses, may have different pay objectives for different business units. Astra-Merck's and Hewlett-Packard's pay objectives in Exhibit 1.3 emphasize high-quality and innovative performance (productivity), competitiveness (costs—pay among leaders), ability to attract and retain quality people (productivity), and equity (employee communications, openness, and simplicity).

Establishing pay objectives involves several important decisions because these objectives serve several purposes. First, objectives guide the design of the pay system. Consider the employer whose objective is to reward outstanding performance. That objective will determine the pay policy (e.g., pay for performance) as well as the elements of pay plans (e.g., merit and/or incentives). Another employer may decide that its competitive advantage is best achieved by a flexible, continuously learning work force. This employer may decide that flexibility is best influenced through other personnel practices such as training and team-building techniques. A pay system with these objectives may stress market competitiveness with salaries that at least equal those of competitors and increases in pay that recognize increased skills or knowledge. The point is that different objectives guide the design of different pay systems.

Besides affecting the mechanics, objectives serve as the standards against which the success of the pay system is evaluated. If the objective is to attract and retain a highly competent staff, yet skilled employees are leaving to take higher paying jobs at other employers, the system may not be performing effectively. Although there may be many nonpay reasons for turnover and some turnover is probably desirable, objectives serve as a standard for evaluating the effectiveness of a pay system.

The Four Basic Policy Decisions

The pay model in Exhibit 1.2 rests on four basic policies that any employer must consider in managing compensation. The policy decisions shown on the left side of the pay model

---

[17]Daniel J. Koys, "Process Equity in Employee Compensation: Report to Survey Participants," Presentation at 1992 American Compensation Association Meetings, Anaheim, Calif.; Jerald Greenberg, "Looking Fair vs. Being Fair: Managing Impressions of Organizational Justice," in *Research in Organizational Behavior*, 12 ed. B. M. Staw and L. L. Cummings (Greenwich, Conn.: JAI Press, 1990); R. Folger and M. Konovsky, "Effects of Procedural and Distributive Justice on Reactions to Pay Raise Decisions," *Academy of Management Journal* 32, no. 1, pp. 115–30.

include (1) internal consistency, (2) external competitiveness, (3) employee contributions, and (4) administration of the pay system. These policies form the building blocks, the foundation on which pay systems are designed and administered. These policies also serve as guidelines within which pay is managed to accomplish the system's objectives. Taken together, they make up the compensation strategy of the organization.

Internal Consistency.   Internal consistency, often called *internal equity,* refers to comparisons among jobs or skill levels *inside* a single organization. The focus is on comparing jobs and skills in terms of their relative contributions to the organization's objectives. How, for example, does the work of the word processor compare with the work of the computer operator, the programmer, and the systems analyst? Does one require more skill or experience than another? Is the output from one valued more than the output from another? Internal consistency becomes a factor in determining the pay rates both for employees doing equal work and for those doing dissimilar work. In fact, determining what is an equitable difference in pay for people performing different work is one of the key challenges facing managers.

Determining equitable pay focuses on two dimensions:

1. The relative similarities and differences in the content of the work or the skills required.
2. The relative contribution of the work or skills to the organization's objectives.

The content of one set of tasks and behaviors (a job) is either equal to or different from another set of tasks and behaviors. A job's relative worth is based on its differing work content and its differing contribution to achieving the objectives of the organization. For example, the contribution of a systems analyst who designs a new inventory or production control system is typically considered to be greater than that of the programmer of the system. Similarly, one set of skills is either equal to or different from another set, and the relative value of each depends on its importance to the organization's achieving its objectives. Managers have several policy options; they can opt for many (or few) levels of work; they can select larger (or smaller) differences in pay rates among jobs, and they can place greater (or less) emphasis on what other employers are paying. In Exhibit 1.3, Astra-Merck is addressing internal consistency when it mentions teamwork and fairness. Hewlett-Packard also seeks to "ensure fair treatment."

Internal consistency policies affect all three compensation objectives. Equity and compliance with legislation are directly affected, while efficiency is affected more indirectly. As we shall see in Part I of the text, pay relationships within the organization affect employee decisions to stay (retention), to invest in additional training, or to seek greater responsibility. By motivating employees to choose increased training and greater responsibility, pay relationships indirectly affect the efficiency of the work force and hence the effectiveness of the total organization.

External Competitiveness.   External competitiveness refers to how an employer positions its pay relative to what competitors are paying. How much do other employers pay accountants, and how much do we wish to pay accountants in comparison to what other employers would pay them? Employers have several policy options. Recall that Astra-Merck's policy is to pay at the 75th percentile of competitors, while Hewlett-Packard's policy is to pay among the leaders. Some employers may set their pay levels higher than their competition, hoping to attract the best applicants. Of course, this assumes that someone is able to identify and hire the "best" from the pool of applicants. Another employer may offer lower base pay but greater opportunity to work overtime or better benefits than those offered by other employers. Or pay and benefits may be lower, but job security may be higher. The policy regarding external competitiveness has a twofold effect on objectives: (1) to ensure that the pay rates are sufficient to attract and retain employees—if employees do not perceive their pay as equitable in comparison to what other organizations are offering for similar work, they may be more likely to leave—and (2) to control labor costs so that the organization's prices of products or services can remain competitive. So external competitiveness directly affects both the efficiency and equity objectives. And it must do so in a way that complies with relevant legislation.

Employee Contributions.   The policy on employee contributions refers to the relative emphasis placed on performance. Should all such employees receive the same pay? Or should one programmer be paid differently from another if one has better performance and/or greater seniority? Or should a more productive team of employees be paid more than less productive teams? The degree of emphasis to be placed on performance and/or seniority is an important policy since it may have a direct effect on employees' attitudes and work behaviors and hence on improving efficiency and achieving equity. Employers with strong pay for performance policies are more likely to place greater emphasis on incentive and merit schemes as part of their pay systems. Astra-Merck seeks to "celebrate performance." Hewlett-Packard emphasizes performance at the unit, division, and companywide level.

Administration.   Policy regarding administration of the pay system is the last building block in our model. While it is possible to design a system that incorporates internal consistency, external competitiveness, and employee contributions, the system will not achieve its objectives unless it is administered properly. The greatest system design in the world is useless without competent administration. Administration involves planning the elements of pay that should be included in the pay system (e.g., base pay, short-term and long-term incentives), evaluating how the pay system is operating, communicating with employees, and judging whether the system is achieving its objectives. Are we able to attract skilled workers? Can we keep them? Do our employees feel our system is fair? Do they understand what factors are considered in setting their pay? Do they agree that these factors are important? Do employees have channels for raising questions and voicing complaints about their pay? How do the better performing firms, with better financial returns and a larger share of the market, pay their employees? Are the systems used by these firms different from those used by less successful firms? How does our labor cost per unit produced compare to that of our competitors? Such information is necessary to tune or redesign the system, to adjust to changes, and to highlight potential areas for further investigation. Hewlett-Packard's objectives include a plan designed to be "open and understandable." Astra-Merck hopes to "achieve simplicity."

Strategic Compensation: Balancing Consistency, Competitiveness, Contributions, and Administration

The balance or relative emphasis among the four basic policies becomes an employer's compensation strategy. Does it ever make sense to emphasize one policy over another? Some firms emphasize an integrated approach to all human resource (HR) management, and internal consistency of pay must fit that strategy. Other firms emphasize external competitiveness of pay and place less emphasis on internal consistency. Sometimes it makes sense to emphasize external competitiveness because the relationship of an employer's pay level to a competitor's pay level directly affects the ability to attract a competent work force, to control labor costs, and hence to compete with products or services. Yet ignoring internal consistency and employee contributions may increase an employer's vulnerability to lawsuits and may decrease employee satisfaction. If the person next to me is paid more than I am, there had better be a good reason for this differential. Internal pay differences can affect employees' willingness to accept a promotion, pay satisfaction, absenteeism, turnover, and interest in unionization.

Thus, all four—internal consistency, external competitiveness, employee contributions, and administration—are critical in the management of pay systems; achieving the desired balance among them is an important challenge in managing compensation. The policies determined for compensation should be consistent and fit the overall approach taken to managing HR.

Pay Techniques

The remaining portion of the model in Exhibit 1.2 shows the pay techniques. The exhibit provides only an overview since techniques are the topic of much of the rest of the book. Techniques tie the four basic policies to the pay objectives. Internal consistency is typically established through a sequence of techniques starting with job analysis. Job analysis collects and then evaluates information about jobs. Based on these evaluations, a job structure is built. A job structure depicts relationships among jobs inside an organization, based on work content and the jobs' relative contributions to achieving the organization's objectives. The goal is to establish a job structure that is internally equitable, because the equity of the pay system will affect employee attitudes and behaviors as well as the organization's regulatory compliance.

However, another approach to achieving internal consistency—knowledge-based plans—is receiving much attention. Polaroid has converted its entire organization to a knowledge-based plan. Polaroid starts with knowledge analysis—analyzing the knowledge required to perform the work. Then the knowledge applied by individuals is evaluated, and so on. The purpose remains the same: to help achieve the objectives of the pay system.

External competitiveness is established by setting the organization's pay level in comparison with what the competition pays for similar work. But who precisely is the "competition"? The pay level is determined by defining the relevant labor markets in which the employer competes, conducting surveys to find out what other employers pay, and using that information in conjunction with the organization's policy decisions to generate a pay structure. The pay structure influences how efficiently the organization is able to attract and retain a competent work force and to control its labor costs.

The relative emphasis on employee contributions is established through performance- and/or seniority-based increases, incentive plans, and salary increase guidelines. If an organization decides to pay employees on the basis of performance, it must have some way to evaluate employee performance and must adjust pay on the basis of that evaluation. Many organizations use some form of incentive plan to share their success with employees. These practices are all intended to have a significant effect on employee attitudes and behaviors, in particular the decisions to join, to stay, and to perform effectively. They are also designed to control costs.

Uncounted variations of these pay techniques exist; many are examined in this book. Such variations arise from the multitude of strategies organizations adopt to accomplish their objectives. Surveys have studied differences in compensation policies and techniques among firms.[18] While no single comprehensive analysis of the four major policy decisions has been reported, it is clear that the variations in compensation approaches arise from differences in the environments and natures of organizations and in the objectives they are trying to achieve with pay. Such variations may also be derived from the various strategies organizations adopt to accomplish their objectives.

STRATEGIC PERSPECTIVES

So far our discussion has highlighted the major views of compensation and the basic components of the pay model. Upcoming chapters will discuss the particulars of various techniques. But examining and dissecting techniques is so seductive that the mechanics of doing so become the focus, the ends in themselves for some compensation specialists. All too often, traditional pay systems seem to have been designed in response to some historical but long-forgotten situation or purpose. Questions such as "So what does this technique do for (to) us?" "How does this help achieve pay objectives?" and "Why bother with this technique?" are not asked.

So before proceeding to the particulars of pay systems, let us pause to consider some major strategic issues related to pay. The issues to which we will pay special attention include matching compensation to the organization's strategic and environmental conditions, its culture and values, the needs of its employees, and its union/management relationship.

Reflect the Organization's Strategies

All pay systems have a purpose. Answer the question, "For what do we want to pay?" and you'll begin to specify the objectives of the pay system. Some objectives are clearly identified, as in our pay model; others must be inferred from the actions of employers. A currently popular prescription found in almost every textbook and consultant's report

---

[18]David Balkin and Luis Gomez-Mejia, "Matching Compensation and Organization Strategies," *Strategic Management Journal* 11 (1990), pp. 153–59; Gomez-Mejia and Wellbourne, "Compensation Strategy"; most of the leading consulting firms also survey pay practices of firms.

is for managers to tailor their pay systems to support the organization's strategic conditions.[19]

The notion is seductive; the reasons offered seem persuasive. They are based on contingency notions. That is, differences in a firm's strategies should be supported by corresponding differences in personnel policies, including compensation policies. The underlying premise is that the greater the congruency, or "fit," between the organization conditions and the compensation system, the more effective the organization. Further, different pay system designs should be aligned with changes in strategic conditions.

Strategy refers to the fundamental direction of the organization. Strategies guide the deployment of all resources, including compensation. An example is PepsiCo's decision to acquire the independently owned and operated bottlers of Pepsi-Cola. Until then, PepsiCo, the overall corporation, was organized into several business units: Pizza Hut, Frito Lay, Taco Bell, and the soft drink unit Pepsi-Cola. Pepsi-Cola was manufactured and bottled by local, independently owned facilities throughout the United States and the world. The Pepsi-Cola unit focused on marketing the soft drink worldwide. PepsiCo shifted its business strategy and began to acquire these independent operators, thereby transforming the Pepsi-Cola unit into a manufacturing as well as marketing organization.

The decision by PepsiCo was strategic. It reflects a fundamental change in direction. Organization resources—financial, capital, and human—will need to be deployed in a manner consistent with the new direction.

As Exhibit 1.4 depicts, compensation systems can be designed to reinforce the business strategies adopted by organizations and to adapt to the competitive and regulatory pressure faced in the environment.

Reinforce Business Strategies

In the example above, PepsiCo corporate strategy for its Pepsi-Cola business unit shifted from marketing to manufacturing and marketing when it began to acquire the major bottling plants. As depicted in Exhibit 1.4, this shift to manufacturing has strategic human resources above and beyond compensation. Managers in the Pepsi-Cola business, for example, faced decisions about running bottling plants that included negotiating with unions, hiring and supervising production workers, learning how to design and manage employee teams, and the like. None of these decisions were faced when the unit's business focused on marketing. In sum, this overall strategy for managing human resources involves

---

[19]Robert C. Ochsner, "Strategic Compensation," *Compensation and Benefits Management,* Fall 1991, pp. 79–80; Mark Blessington, "Designing a Sales Strategy That Keeps the Customer in Mind," *Compensation and Benefits Review,* March–April 1992, pp. 30–42; George T. Milkovich, "A Strategic Perceptive on Compensation Strategy," in *Research in Human Resource Management,* ed. K. Rowland and G. Ferris (Greenwich, Conn.: JAI Press, 1988); George T. Milkovich and Renae Broderick, "Developing Compensation Strategies," in *Handbook of Wage and Salary Administration,* 3rd ed., ed. M. Rock (New York: McGraw-Hill, 1990); Marc J. Wallace, Jr., "Driving Competitive Advantage through Reward Design," Paper presented to Jacksonville Compensation Association, 1988; Jerry M. Newman, "Environment, Strategy and Internal Control Systems: Motivating Behavior in Boundary Occupations" (Working paper, SUNY Buffalo, 1989).

EXHIBIT 1.4   Strategic Perspective: An Illustration

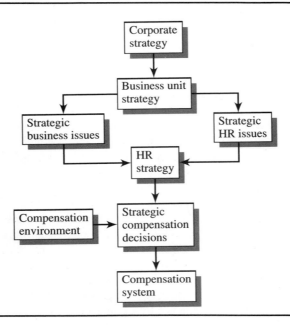

decisions about staffing, organization design, development, employee relations, and compensation. The critical compensation decisions facing managers can be considered in terms of the four basic policies in our pay model.

Consistency.   How should different levels of work be paid within each bottling plant? Should employee wages be based on the jobs performed or their abilities or skills to perform many different jobs? How large should the differences in pay be? And most importantly—so what? How do these decisions help Pepsi achieve its objectives?

Competitiveness.   How should each bottling plant pay in comparison to local wage rates? Should Pepsi-Cola have one nationwide set of rates, like AT&T pays its operators and technicians or General Motors pays its assemblers, or should rates be based on local comparable jobs? Again, so what? Do these decisions really matter in terms of PepsiCo's objectives?

Employee Contributions.   Should Pepsi-Cola employee pay increases be based on individual or team performance, on experience and seniority, on changes in the cost of living, on the facilities, or on Pepsi-Cola's performance? With 300,000 employees worldwide, Pepsi has become a behemoth. Pepsi wants each employee to "act like an owner, not a hired hand." Uh-huh! To attempt to sustain this "owner" idea, PepsiCo gave all 300,000 employees, from truck drivers to Pizza Hut workers, stock options. At current prices, the yearly options are equivalent to 10 percent of the base pay.

Administration.   What should the policy be toward the employee unions? How involved should employees be in the design of these pay systems? What role will each plant manager play in the design and management of pay systems? Will it be centralized at the business unit or decentralized to each plant?

Note in Exhibit 1.4 that the results of these four basic policy choices translate into the compensation system. Our point is that the techniques that make up the compensation system really translate the strategic policy choices into practice. And these strategic choices are critical to the business strategy for the particular business unit and the corporation.

"Fit" Environmental and Regulatory Pressures

Note in Exhibit 1.4 that the compensation environment also affects the compensation choices. Environment refers to a wide range of pressures, including competitive pressures from product and labor markets, pressures springing from changes in work force demographics, values and expectations, regulatory changes, and the like. In the case of Pepsi-Cola, its bottling business is very people intensive. Consequently, Pepsi-Cola managers expect that increasing work force diversity (e.g., with 52 percent of new entrants being women and increasingly single parents) will affect the forms of pay (child care, educational reimbursements, employee assistance programs) that will be necessary to attract and retain new workers.[20] And Pepsi managers probably do not expect to sit by passively while Congress considers whether to impose taxes on benefits paid to employees. Pepsi intends to shape the environment as well as be shaped by it.[21]

Public Not-For-Profit Sector.   Strategic decisions are also evident in governmental and public not-for-profit organizations. Examples include a university's desire for a winning football team, or a regional symphony orchestra's attempt to gain national recognition. Pay programs should also be tailored to facilitate the strategic directions of these organizations. The orchestra can offer a renowned conductor a share of the revenues gained from recording sales, or the university may increase funding for the coaching staff through a cut of the gate for that particular sport.

The common view is that business strategy and anticipated environmental pressures should affect the design of pay systems. But it can also be argued that historical pay decisions can affect subsequent business strategies. In many cases, efforts to adapt pay systems to shifts in strategic conditions are hindered by existing traditional pay policies and technologies. IBM and AT&T are both struggling to adjust their traditional pay plans to help them compete better in the new global markets.[22]

---

[20]Joseph Coates, *Future Work: Seven Critical Forces Reshaping Work and the Work Force in North America* (Washington, D.C.: J. F. Coates, 1991).

[21]J. S. Bronson, Presentation at 1992 Annual Meeting, Center for Advanced Human Resource Studies, Ithaca, New York; also PepsiCo Annual Report 1992.

[22]Bob Allen, "The 90s and Beyond—A Strategy for AT&T," Focus insert, *Fortune,* October 1991.

Managers should recognize that pay systems can be tailored to an organization's strategic conditions. In highly decentralized organizations such as PepsiCo, this can even mean that different subunits (Taco Bell, Frito Lay, Pizza Hut) may adopt different pay systems. It is also important to recognize that existing traditional pay systems may need to be changed as the organization's strategy changes.

Reflect the Organization's Culture and Values

Not only are pay programs related to strategic conditions and environment, they are also related to the organization's culture and values. The notions of culture and values are complex.[23] But the values underlying an employer's treatment of its employees can be reflected in its pay system. Some employers articulate their philosophies, such as those for AT&T and Honeywell, which are shown in Exhibit 1.5. These philosophies give us a sense of how these two firms treat employees and serve as guides for their pay systems. Note that Honeywell's principles (number 4) reflect its decentralized approach in which each business unit is responsible for its own pay system.

Pay is just one of many systems that make up an organization; its design is also partially influenced by how it fits with the other structures and systems in the organization.[24] A highly centralized and confidential pay system, controlled by a few people in a corporate unit, will not, according to this view, operate effectively in a highly decentralized and open organization.[25] Unfortunately, little research has been done directly on the relationship between pay systems and the culture and values of an organization. This may be because culture and values are ambiguous terms.

The importance of congruency between pay programs and other HR management processes can be illustrated with examples of recruiting, hiring, and promoting. The pay linked with a job offer or a promotion must be sufficient to induce acceptance. Some employers do not maintain significant pay differences between various skill levels and different levels of responsibility. Lack of adequate differences in pay diminishes the incentive for employees to take the training required to become more skilled or to accept the promotion to supervisor. The situation is reversed for many engineering and research jobs, where the pay for managerial positions induces people to leave engineering and research positions.

For managers of compensation, the key point to remember is that pay coexists with other systems in the organization. It must fit. An effective pay system cannot be designed without taking into account the nature of the organization, its business strategies, and other management systems.

---

[23]Kevin Sullivan, "Inventing the Future: New Approaches to Management, Compensation, and Learning at Apple Computer," *Employment Relations Today,* Winter 1991/92, pp. 417–24.

[24]Balkin and Gomez-Mejia, "Matching Compensation and Organization Strategies."

[25]L. R. Gomez-Mejia, "Structure and Process of Diversification, Compensation Strategy, and Firm Performance," *Strategic Management Journal,* October 1992; Renae Broderick, "Pay Policy and Business Strategy—Toward Measure of Fit" (Ph.D. dissertation, Cornell University, 1986).

EXHIBIT 1.5 Comparison of AT&T and Honeywell's Philosophies

AT&T Values

Help the Customer Succeed	Continuous Improvement	People	Integrity	Profit

To support customers' success, each of us will
• Interact with customers as a partner
• Know our customers' business
• Anticipate what is required for our customers' success
• Identify and know our value to our customer
• Develop creative/innovative ways to serve our customer
• Be responsive and flexible in providing quality products and services to our customers
• Provide value added solutions
• Provide unconditional customer satisfaction
	In the uncompromising pursuit of quality, we will make decisions based on data and will continuously
	• Measure and improve customer satisfaction
	• Improve the "value add" we provide our customers
	• Analyze and simplify our business process
	• Promote change as an opportunity to improve
	• Promote continuous learning
	• Evaluate our operations and perform only that which has value for the customer
	• Recognize no limits to improvement
		Each of us is important in determining the success of AT&T. Therefore, each of us
		• Is empowered and expected to act
		• Will treat each other with respect and dignity
		• Is expected to grow and achieve
		• Shares responsibility for the success of our customers and company
			Integrity and a high standard of ethics are fundamental in our business, community, and interpersonal relationships; therefore, each of us will
			• Make and keep commitments
			• Operate at the highest ethical standards
			• Act in a forthright and honest manner
			• Conform to the spirit and letter of the laws that govern our worldwide operations
				Sustained profitability is the ultimate measure of how well we serve our customers and is necessary to
				• Be a reliable partner and foster beneficial relationships with our
				   Customers
				   Investors
				   Communities
				   Vendors
				• Execute long-term plans
				• Provide opportunity for personal growth and reward

Honeywell's Philosophy and Principles

Philosophy

• Honeywell is one company, made up of different businesses. These businesses are united by a common set of values and by common technologies. Yet they differ in respect to their products and services, size, customers, locations, and competitors.

• The company's pay philosophy allows each individual business to design pay systems responding to that business's own requirements. It also means that each system must contain certain assurances of Honeywell employment. These assurances are expressed in four basic pay principles.

• In support of these objectives, four basic principles also apply to all Honeywell pay systems.

Principles

Fully Competitive	Fair Internally	Communicated	Business Responsibility
Pay must be fully competitive in the market, as defined by each business	Each individual's pay must be fair in relationship to the pay that other employees receive within the same Honeywell business	The communication must explain general pay principles, the specific pay system applicable, and the process used to determine individual pay levels under the system	Each Honeywell business has the basic responsibility for establishing and maintaining its own pay system

Employee Needs

Within some legally imposed limits, compensation can be delivered to employees in various forms already identified. The allocation of compensation among these pay forms to emphasize performance, seniority, entitlements, or the long versus short term can be tailored to the pay objectives of the organization. It can also be tailored to the needs of the individual employees.

The simple fact that employees differ is too easily and too often overlooked in designing pay systems. Individual employees join the organization, make investment decisions, design new products, assemble components, and judge the quality of results. Individual employees receive the pay. A major limitation of contemporary pay systems is the degree to which individual attitudes and preferences are ignored.[26] Older, highly paid workers may wish to defer taxes by putting their pay into retirement funds, while younger employees may have high cash needs to buy a house, support a family, or finance an education. Dual career couples who are overinsured medically may prefer to use more of their combined pay for child care, automobile insurance, financial counseling, or other benefits. Employees who have young children or dependent parents may desire dependent care coverage.[27]

Perhaps it is time to consider letting employees specify their own pay form (a choice that currently would meet with Internal Revenue Service disapproval and be a challenge to administer). Pay systems can be designed to permit employee choices. Flexible benefit plans are examples, and increasing numbers of employers are adopting them.[28]

Unions

Pay systems also need to be adapted to the nature of the union-management relationship.[29] Strategies for dealing with unions vary widely. The federal government formed a joint labor-management committee to examine how to strengthen the relationship between pay and performance for federal workers. At the other extreme, Caterpillar started hiring new, nonunion employees five months into a strike by the United Auto Workers. Between these extremes, hundreds of union contracts are negotiated each year with little fanfare or rancor.

Even though unions now represent only 15 percent of the civilian labor force in the United States union influence on the design and administration of pay systems is signif-

---

[26]R. D. Bretz, R. A. Ash, and G. F. Dreher, "Do People Make the Place? An Examination of the Attraction-Selection-Attrition Hypothesis," *Personnel Psychology* 42 (1989), pp. 561–81; K. Davis, W. F. Giles, and H. S. Field, *Benefits Preferences of Recent College Graduates,* Report 88-2 (Brookfield, Wis.: International Foundation of Employee Benefits Plans, 1988).

[27]Melissa Barringer, George Milkovich, and Olivia Mitchell, "Predicting Employee Health Insurance Selections in a Flexible Benefit Environment" (Working paper 91–21, Center for Advanced Human Resource Studies, Cornell University).

[28]Chapters 11 and 12 discuss benefits and their management in greater detail.

[29]Raymond E. Miles, "Adapting to Technology and Competition: A New Industrial Relations System for the 21st Century," *California Management Review,* Winter 1989, pp. 9–28; Charles Heckscher, *The New Unionism* (New York: Basic Books, 1988).

icant. Union preferences for different forms of pay (e.g., cost-of-living adjustments, improved health care) and their concern with job security affect pay system design. Historically, the allocation between wages and benefits was greatly affected by unions.[30] Unionized workers still have a greater percentage of their total compensation allocated to benefits than do nonunion workers.

In addition to affecting forms of pay, unions also play a role in administering pay. Most negotiated contracts specify pay intervals, minimum rates, and the basis for movement through a wage range. Some employers adopt the maintenance of union-free status as an objective of its pay system. Such systems usually are based on policies that include strong external competitiveness, internally consistent pay treatment to avoid feelings of inequitable treatment, emphasis on performance, and a fair and open administration of the compensation system. These policies often translate into rates that are at or above those for the market, merit pay, or an all-salaried work force, and great emphasis on communicating pay and benefit programs and on attitude surveys to monitor employee reactions.

Global Competition

Competitive pressures, particularly from international competitors, also affect pay decisions. During the mid-1980s, managers in U.S. firms felt pressures springing from the relatively higher wages paid in the United States compared to other countries. In 1985, hourly pay for production workers in West Germany was 74 percent of that of the U.S. worker, and a Korean worker received only 10 percent of the U.S. average wage. Responding to these pressures, U.S. employees accepted wage concessions, wage cuts, smaller pay increases, one-time lump sum increases that did not add into base pay, and health care deductibles.[31] By 1991 West Germany's hourly compensation exceeded that of the U.S. worker. Koreans earned 21 percent of U.S. workers' wages, and Japanese and Canadian wages were on a par with those in the United States. Caution should be exercised in interpreting these data, however, because government-provided benefits (health care in Canada and large layoff awards in West Germany) are not included. International wage comparisons vary considerably. Fluctuations in currency exchange rates also play a substantial role. Chapter 15 contains additional information on international labor costs.

Comparing pay between countries is often not the whole story, as Exhibit 1.6 illustrates. In comparison to Germany (excluding the former East Germany), the United States has relatively lower labor costs ($15.39 versus $24.36), longer work week (40 versus 37.6 hours), shorter vacation days (23 versus 42 days per year), and a longer work year (1,847 versus 1,499 days). These data, plus significantly lower tax rates, are some of the reasons BMW built a new facility in South Carolina rather than Dusseldorf, Germany.

---

[30]M. L. Weitzman and D. L. Kruse, "Profit Sharing and Productivity," in *Paying for Productivity,* ed. A. S. Blinder (Washington, D.C.: Brookings Institute, 1990).

[31]Bureau of Labor Statistics, Report 766 (Washington, D.C.: U. S. Department of Labor, 1992).

EXHIBIT 1.6 International Comparisons of Pay and Hours Worked

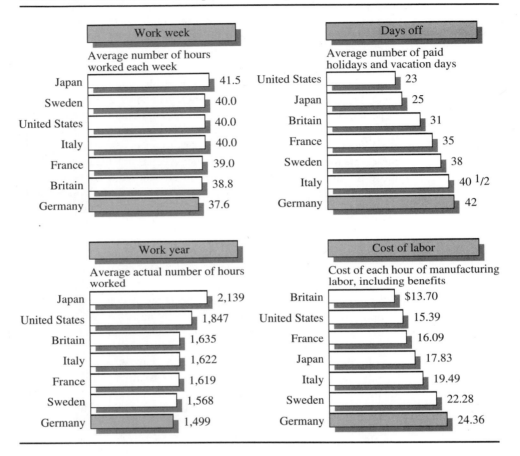

Differences in the actual pay systems among international competitors also cause U.S. managers to reconsider their pay systems.[32] Exhibit 1.7 describes Toshiba's pay system for its managers. Several items in the exhibit stand out. First, note that bonuses make up more than 78 percent of a Toshiba manager's pay.[33] These bonuses are paid at

---

[32]Jerry Bowles and Joshua Hammond, *Beyond Quality* (New York: G. P. Putnam, 1991); Hitoshi Kume, "The Quality Cultural Exchange," *Quality Progress,* October 1990, pp. 33–35; Charles Morris, *The Coming Global Boom: How to Benefit Now from Tomorrow's Dynamic World Economy* (New York: Bantam Books, 1990).

[33]Toshiba information from personal visit and discussion with Toshiba vice president for human resources, Tokyo, February 1992.

EXHIBIT 1.7   Toshiba's Managerial Compensation Plan

Pay Elements	Based On		Amount	Percent
1. Core salary (Geppo)	• Performance • Ability • Length of service		¥ 370,000	15%
2. Position and rank (Shokuseki-Teate)	• Performance		¥ 190,000	7%
		Sub Total	¥ 560,000	22%
3. Bonus* (Example)	• Performance • Ability • Toshiba profits		¥ 1,990,000	78%
Total cash compensation			**¥ 2,550,000**	**100%**

*Paid twice a year (December and June).

---

the end of the year, which offers a cash flow advantage to Toshiba. In addition, bonuses are not added into the employee's base pay, so they do not become fixed costs. Next, notice that Toshiba's managers' pay depends on their performance and is not as seniority-based as the business press in the United States would have us believe. The point is that no longer do U.S. managers simply face domestic competitors; they must become knowledgeable in how pay systems are designed by their global competitors.

More than 1,200 experts from 12 different countries were asked how organizations should use human resources to achieve competitive advantage in the 21st century.[34] Some of the results are summarized in Exhibit 1.8. The percentages refer to the amount of agreement among experts. In the United States, 87 percent of the experts agreed that "rewarding employees for customer service" was the top priority for achieving competitive advantage. Of the Germans, 96 percent judged that "identifying high potential employees early" was the highest priority; 85 percent of the Japanese agreed that "communicating business directions, problems, and plans" is a key action; and the Italian experts couldn't agree among themselves about what is important.

Also note that in the United States, four of the six actions the experts agreed upon were pay related (reward employees for customer service, reward employees for business/productivity gains, reward employees for innovation and creativity, implement pay systems promoting sharing). Clearly, U.S. experts see pay as having strategic value in achieving competitive advantage. Japanese experts agreed that only three actions were

---

[34]Based on data from an IBM/TPF&C Study, 1992. Half the experts were corporate executives, one fourth were consultants, and one fourth academics.

EXHIBIT 1.8 International Perspectives on Competitive Advantage

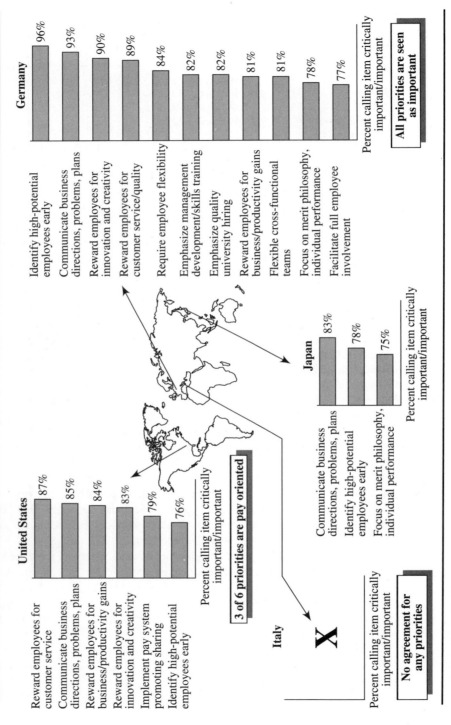

Germany

Priority	Percent
Identify high-potential employees early	96%
Communicate business directions, problems, plans	93%
Reward employees for innovation and creativity	90%
Reward employees for customer service/quality	89%
Require employee flexibility	84%
Emphasize management development/skills training	82%
Emphasize quality university hiring	82%
Reward employees for business/productivity gains	81%
Flexible cross-functional teams	81%
Focus on merit philosophy, individual performance	78%
Facilitate full employee involvement	77%

Percent calling item critically important/important

All priorities are seen as important

United States

Priority	Percent
Reward employees for customer service	87%
Communicate business directions, problems, plans	85%
Reward employees for business/productivity gains	84%
Reward employees for innovation and creativity	83%
Implement pay system promoting sharing	79%
Identify high-potential employees early	76%

Percent calling item critically important/important

3 of 6 priorities are pay oriented

Japan

Priority	Percent
Communicate business directions, problems, plans	83%
Identify high-potential employees early	78%
Focus on merit philosophy, individual performance	75%

Percent calling item critically important/important

Italy

X

Percent calling item critically important/important

No agreement for any priorities

NOTE: Priorities identified by 75 percent or more of surveyed managers.

critical for competitive advantage, and one was pay related: focus on merit pay philosophy and individual performance. Germans agreed on the largest number of actions, 11, and 4 of these were pay related.

Although consensus exists among international experts that pay systems are critical for achieving competitive advantage, significant cross cultural differences exist over the types of pay programs that are significant. The Japanese, for example, believe that individual merit pay is critical, whereas U.S. experts seem to favor more team- and group-based approaches.

Basic Premise: "Fit" Pays Off

The basic underlying premise of any strategic perspective is that if managers make pay decisions "fit" with the organization strategy and values, are responsive to its employees and union relations, and are globally competitive, then the organization is more likely to be successful. It would be nice to be able to say that this presumption has research as well as practical support. Unfortunately, little research has been conducted into the types of pay systems that fit different conditions and are related to performance. We do have some evidence beyond the promise and belief.[35] Research on executive pay reveals that firms with higher accounting profits paid their executives more. And top executive pay has also been linked to stockholder returns. Similarly, there is evidence that gain-sharing plans for manufacturing employees is related to improved employee work behaviors (e.g., reduced absenteeism, increased suggestions for productivity improvements, and lower unit costs). And the use of bonuses and stock options for managers, engineers, and other professional employees is also related to firm performance. But caution and more evidence are required in interpreting these results. It may be, for example, that organizations that are successful (higher profits, sales, or appreciating stock values) are better able to afford higher wages and offer incentives and stock options. Rather than the pay system affecting employee behaviors and organization performance, perhaps the reverse occurs: Employees' behaviors and organization performance cause changes in the pay system. In all likelihood, both happen.

At this point, you may be reminded of the definition of an academic—someone who takes something that works in practice (pay systems) and tries to make it work in theory. But the corollary is that if we can find out why some pay systems work in practice, then we can apply them in other settings, too.

BOOK PLAN

Compensation is such a broad and compelling topic that several books could be devoted to it. The focus of this book will be on the design and management of compensation systems. To aid in understanding how and why pay systems work, a pay model has been presented. This model, which emphasizes the key strategic policies, techniques, and objectives of pay systems, also provides the structure for much of the book.

---

[35]Barry Gerhart and George Milkovich, "Employee Compensation"; A. S. Blinder, ed., *Paying for Productivity.*

Strategic policy decisions form the crucial foundation of any pay system. The pay model identifies four basic policy decisions; the first three sections of the book examine each in detail. The first, internal consistency (Part I, Chapters 2 through 5), examines pay relationships within a single organization. What are the pay relationships among jobs and skills within the organization? What are the relative contributions of each job toward achieving the organization's goals? The linkage of pay decisions with the strategic and operating objectives of the organization, the need to establish internal equity, and the importance of ensuring the work relatedness of pay decisions are examined. Job analysis, job evaluation, and knowledge-based plans are the main techniques for achieving internally consistent pay. Developments and innovations in these techniques, some of them flowing from research efforts and some from organizations' responses to challenges they face, are discussed.

Part II (Chapters 6 and 7) examines external competitiveness—the competitive pay relationships among organizations—and analyzes the influence of market conditions. Pay policies reflect these conditions and are tailored to strategic objectives. Techniques include conducting pay surveys; updating survey data; establishing pay policy lines; and determining pay rates, ranges, and structures.

Once the compensation rates and structures are established, other issues emerge. How much should we pay each individual employee? How much and how often should a person's pay be increased and on what basis? Should employees be paid based on experience, seniority, or performance? Should pay increases be contingent on the unit's or the employee's performance? These are examples of employee contributions, the third building block in the model (Part III, Chapters 8, 9, and 10). Approaches that deliver pay to individual employees are designed with employee knowledge, skills, abilities, needs, preferences, performance, and seniority, as well as the presence or absence of unions, in mind. Recent theoretical and research developments related to motivational effects of pay, goal setting, and performance evaluation are examined in the light of the pay decisions that must be made by employers.

Part IV covers employee services and benefits (Chapters 11 and 12). While only two chapters are devoted to employee benefits, this does not imply that the design and management of benefits are unimportant. The opposite is true. Benefits have become so critical that a separate book is required. All we do here is discuss the major benefit forms, the challenges involved in designing and administering the benefit program, and how to tie benefits to the organization's strategic directions.

The government's role in compensation is examined in Part V, Chapters 13 and 14. The government affects compensation through its purchase of goods and services and its employment of a sizable segment of the work force. Additionally, pay practices must comply with legislation and court interpretations.

Managing the compensation system (Part VI, Chapters 15 through 17) includes planning, budgeting, evaluating, communicating, and providing for the special needs of certain groups (e.g., sales representatives, executives, unions).

Even though the book is divided into sections that are reflected in the pay model, that does not mean that pay policies and decisions are necessarily so discrete. All the basic policy decisions are interrelated, and together they form a major system designed to influence organization performance and employee behaviors. Throughout the book, our intention is to examine alternative approaches. Rarely is there a single "correct" approach; rather, alternative approaches exist or can be designed. The one most likely to be effective depends on the circumstances. We hope that this book will help you become better informed about these options and how to design new ones. Whether as an employee, a manager, or an interested member of society, you should be able to assess effectiveness and equity of pay systems.

SUMMARY

The model presented in this chapter provides a structure for understanding compensation systems. The three main components of the model include the objectives of the pay system, the policy decisions that provide the system's foundation, and the techniques that link policies and objectives. The following sections of the book examine in turn each of the four policy decisions—internal consistency, external competitiveness, employee contributions, and administration—as well as the techniques, new directions, and related research.

Two questions should constantly be in the minds of managers and readers of this text. First, "Why do it this way?" There is rarely one "correct" way to design a system or pay an individual. Organizations, people, and circumstances are too varied. But a well-trained manager can select or design a suitable approach.

Second, "So What?" What does this technique do for us? How does it help achieve our organization goals? If good answers are not apparent, there is no point to the technique. Adapting the pay system to meet the needs of the employees and to help achieve the goals of the organization is what this book is all about.

The basic premise of this book is that compensation systems do have a profound impact on a variety of individuals and objectives. Yet too often, traditional pay systems seem to have been designed in response to some historical but long-forgotten problem. The practices continue, but the logic underlying them is not always clear or even relevant.

REVIEW QUESTIONS

1. How do differing perspectives affect our perceptions of compensation?
2. Do you view pay as a reward or a return? Why?
3. How does the pay model help organize one's thinking about compensation?
4. What can a pay system do for an organization? For an employee?
5. How may the pay system be tied to organization strategy?
6. Under what circumstances would one of the three basic pay policies be emphasized relative to the other two? Try to think of a separate example for each basic pay policy.

YOUR TURN:
BERKELEY GRADUATE STUDENTS

Just two weeks before final exams began, students at a California campus had to cross picket lines to attend class during a two-day strike by graduate students.

Demanding that the university recognize them as employees, the students, most of them members of the Association of Graduate Student Employees, blocked or picketed at all the main entrances to the campus for two days. The association estimated that 2,000 people joined the blockade each day, including some full-time faculty members and undergraduate students.

The strike prompted many faculty members to cancel classes on the two days, and an informal survey of classes that were held indicated a marked drop in attendance.

Graduate students walking picket lines said they wanted the university to recognize their association as the official union of graduate student employees so that wage increases, tuition waivers, and other demands could be negotiated.

About 3,200 of the school's 9,000 graduate students are working for the university this semester. Most are either teaching assistants or research assistants.

Teaching assistants, working 20 hours a week, make between $1,063 and $1,265 a month, while research assistants working the same number of hours earn $917 a month. Striking graduate students said inflation, changes in the tax code, and the area's high cost of living make it difficult to live on these wages.

The state labor relations board ruled two weeks ago that teaching assistants and research assistants are not university employees for the purposes of collective bargaining. The decision reversed an earlier ruling by the board that the university must recognize the graduate student workers as employees who receive wages, not as students who receive financial aid. In a report issued with the ruling, the board said, "In cases of conflict between academic and employment considerations, academic considerations ultimately prevail."

A spokesman for the school said that although the university recognized the contributions of graduate student employees—who teach 38 percent of undergraduate courses—it would not recognize their association as a union.

"The collective-bargaining process is not the best way to deal with an educational program," a school spokesman said, adding that the university would explore other ways to negotiate with the students.[1]

Discussion Questions

1. Take the role of the students. Persuade your classmates that you are underpaid. Use the ideas and concepts discussed in this first chapter. What part of the pay model would you point to to buttress your argument? What strategic issue could you raise to counter the university's position?

2. Take the role of a university administrator. Persuade the students that your pay practices are appropriate. Frame your argument using the concepts in this chapter. State your objectives in setting rates for graduate students.

3. How would the above arguments differ if the university were a profit-making institution, that is, tuition from students were its only source of income?

---

[1]Adapted from an article in *The New York Times*, April 16, 1989, p. 43.

EXHIBIT I.1 The Pay Model

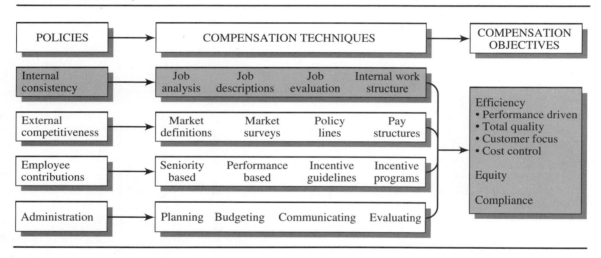

PART I Internal Consistency: Determining the Structure

Exxon employs a chief executive officer, chemical engineers, plant managers, nurses, market analysts, laboratory technicians, financial planners, hydraulic mechanics, accountants, guards, oil tanker captains, sailors, word processors, and so on. How is pay determined for all these different types of work? This question and the techniques employed to answer it lie at the heart of compensation management. Is the financial planner worth more than the accountant, or the mechanic more than the word processor? How much more? What procedures are used to set pay rates and who does it? Should the potential consequences of errors in the job, such as the disastrous Alaskan oil spill blamed on the captain of the *Exxon Valdez,* be considered in setting pay? How important are the characteristics of the employees—their knowledge, skills, abilities, or experience? How important are the characteristics of the work, the conditions under which it is done, or the value of what is produced? What about the employer's financial condition, or employee and union preferences?

Beyond understanding how pay is determined for different types of work, there are other critical questions in compensation management. Does how we pay employees make a difference? What are the purposes of paying the financial planner more than the accountant or the mechanic more than a word processor? Does the compensation system support Exxon's business strategy? Is Exxon better able to attract and retain the talent it needs? Do the procedures used to set pay support the way the work is organized and performed, such as the use of semiautonomous work teams in Exxon's Baytown, Texas, refineries? Or are the procedures bureaucratic burdens that hinder employee flexibility and teamwork? Does it matter whether employees are paid based on the jobs they are assigned versus the skills or knowledge they possess?

So two basic questions lie at the core of compensation management: (1) How is pay determined for the wide variety of work performed in organizations? (2) Does pay affect employees' attitudes and work behaviors and subsequently the success of the organization?

These questions are examined within the framework introduced in Chapter 1 and shown again in Exhibit I.1. This part of the book examines the framework's first strategic policy issue, internal consistency. In Chapter 2, the policy of internal consistency—what affects it and what is affected by it—is considered. Chapter 3 discusses various approaches to assess the similarities and differences in work content. Chapters 4 and 5 scrutinize job-based and skill-based approaches for determining internal pay structures.

CHAPTER 2 Defining Consistency

Chapter Outline

For the kingdom of heaven is like a householder who went out early in the morning to hire laborers for his vineyard. And having agreed with the laborers for a denarius a day, he sent them into his vineyard. And about the third hour, he went out and saw others standing . . . idle; and he said to them, "Go you also into the vineyard, and I will give you whatever is just." And again he went out about the vineyard, and about the ninth hour, and did as before. . . . But about the eleventh hour he went out and found others . . . and he said to them, "Go you also into the vineyard." When evening came, the owner said to his steward, "Call the laborers, and pay them their wages, beginning from the last even to the first." When the first in their turn came . . . they also received each his denarius. . . . They began to murmur against the householder, saying, "These last have worked a single hour, and thou hast put them on a level with us, who have borne the burden of the day's heat." But answering them, he said, "Friend, I do thee no injustice; take what is thine and go."[1]

Matthew's parable raises age-old questions about internal consistency and pay structures within a single organization.[2] Clearly, the laborers in the vineyard felt that those "who have borne the burden of the day's heat" should be paid more, perhaps because they had contributed more to the householder's economic benefit. According to the laborers, "fair pay" should be based on two criteria: the value of contributions and the time worked. Perhaps the householder was using a third criterion: an individual's needs without regard to differences in the work performed.[3]

But the householder seems to have overlooked other criteria, such as the way the work was organized and the relationship among the laborers. Perhaps they had organized into teams, with some members pruning the vines, others pulling weeds or tying the vines. Pay structures in contemporary compensation plans are typically designed by assessing how the work is organized and performed, its relative value, and the skills and knowledge required to perform it. This is done through procedures acceptable to the parties involved, for if the procedures used or the resulting pay structure is unacceptable to managers or employees, they'll probably murmur, too. Is tying more valuable than pruning? Today, murmuring may translate into turnover, unwillingness to try new technology, and maybe even a lack of concern about the quality of the grapes in the vineyard or the customer satisfaction with them.

This chapter examines the strategic policy of internal consistency in pay structures and its consequences for employees' behaviors and the organization's success.

INTERNAL CONSISTENCY AND THE PAY MODEL

Two basic concepts—internal consistency and pay structures—need to be clarified.

Internal consistency establishes equal pay for work of equal worth and acceptable pay differentials for work of unequal worth. But internal consistency involves more than the pay structure. Often called *internal equity,* a policy that emphasizes internal consistency places importance on the inner workings, relationships, and pressures found within an organization. Consequently, it includes concerns for the fairness of the procedures

---

[1]Matthew 20: 1–16.

[2]For an excellent history of the different standards for pay, see N. Arnold Tolles, *Origins of Modern Wage Theories* (Englewood Cliffs, N.J.: Prentice Hall, 1964).

[3]Several Japanese firms, Toshiba and Nissan for example, base a small portion of a worker's pay on the number of dependents. In the early 1900s, workers who were "family men" received a pay supplement in some U.S. firms as well.

> **Internal consistency** refers to the relationship between the pay structure and the design of the organization and the work. It focuses attention on the importance of designing a pay structure that supports the relationships and pressures internal to the organization: the organization's structure, the flow of work, and the similarities and differences in work and employees performing it.
>
> **Pay structure** refers to the array of pay rates for different work or skills within a single organization. It focuses attention on the levels, differentials, and criteria used to determine those pay rates.

used to establish the pay structure, as well as for the way the organization is designed and the flow of work.[4] Thus, managers must design procedures and establish pay structures that (1) assist managers and employees to achieve their organizational objectives, (2) are acceptable to employees and managers, and (3) are in compliance with laws and regulations.

PAY STRUCTURES AND THE PAY MODEL

Pay structures can be described on three dimensions: (1) number of levels, (2) pay differentials among levels, and (3) the criteria used to support the structure. Exhibit 2.1 shows a pay structure for engineers and scientists used at General Electric Aerospace Division. The six levels range from entry to fellows.

Levels

The essence of any pay structure is its hierarchical nature: the number of levels and reporting relationships. Pay structures typically reflect the organization structure and the flow of the work. Therefore, some are more hierarchical with multiple levels; others are flat with few levels. For example, another GE division, Plastics, employs a different technology from Aerospace. Plastics uses the five broad basic levels described in Exhibit 2.2 to array its jobs. These levels, labeled *career bands,* range from professional to executive. Obviously, managers in Aerospace have chosen to define the work more specifically than those in Plastics. Beyond the GE examples, the restructuring and de-layering announced by practically every major employer over the past few years typically reduce the number of reporting levels. Such actions are often accompanied by a redesign in the pay structure, since the structure supports the organization design.

---

[4]Joanne Martin and Joseph Harder, "Bread and Roses: Justice and the Distribution of Financial and Socioemotional Rewards in Organizations" (Research paper 1010, Stanford University, August 1988); and Jerald Greenberg, "Looking Fair vs. Being Fair: Managing Impressions of Organizational Justice," in *Research in Organizational Behavior* 12, ed. B. M. Staw and L. L. Cummings (Greenwich, Conn.: JAI Press, 1990).

EXHIBIT 2.1 Engineering Pay Structure at General Electric Aerospace Division

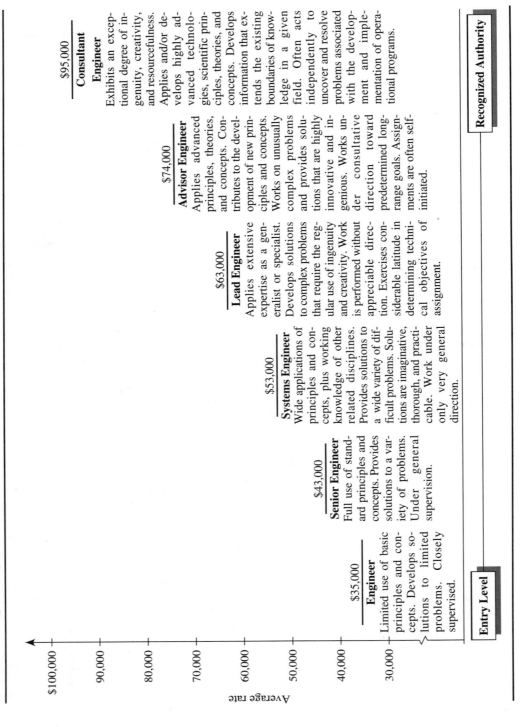

Average rate

$100,000
90,000
80,000
70,000
60,000
50,000
40,000
30,000

Entry Level

Recognized Authority

$35,000
Engineer
Limited use of basic principles and concepts. Develops solutions to limited problems. Closely supervised.

$43,000
Senior Engineer
Full use of standard principles and concepts. Provides solutions to a variety of problems. Under general supervision.

$53,000
Systems Engineer
Wide applications of principles and concepts, plus working knowledge of other related disciplines. Provides solutions to a wide variety of difficult problems. Solutions are imaginative, thorough, and practicable. Work under only very general direction.

$63,000
Lead Engineer
Applies extensive expertise as a generalist or specialist. Develops solutions to complex problems that require the regular use of ingenuity and creativity. Work is performed without appreciable direction. Exercises considerable latitude in determining technical objectives of assignment.

$74,000
Advisor Engineer
Applies advanced principles, theories, and concepts. Contributes to the development of new principles and concepts. Works on unusually complex problems and provides solutions that are highly innovative and ingenious. Works under consultative direction toward predetermined long-range goals. Assignments are often self-initiated.

$95,000
Consultant Engineer
Exhibits an exceptional degree of ingenuity, creativity, and resourcefulness. Applies and/or develops highly advanced technologies, scientific principles, theories, and concepts. Develops information that extends the existing boundaries of knowledge in a given field. Often acts independently to uncover and resolve problems associated with the development and implementation of operational programs.

36

EXHIBIT 2.2 **Managerial/Professional Job Levels at General Electric Plastics (GEP)**

Career Band	*Band Description*	*Developmental Objectives*	
Executive	Provides vision, leadership, and innovation to major business segments or functions of GEP	Ability to provide strategic direction and judgment that results in the global objectives of GEP being achieved	
Director	Directs a significant functional area or smaller business segment	Management:	Ability to provide direction and a global perspective to the management of a small business segment or significant functional area
		Individual Contributors:	Direct a project with broad business impact, drawing on others for completion of business objectives while holding accountability for end results
Leadership	Individual contributors leading projects or programs with broad scope and impact, or managers leading functional components with broad scope and impact	Management:	Ability to effectively manage diverse activities within a function and the resolution of decisions in the balanced best interests of the business
		Individual Contributors:	Ability to leverage in-depth technical knowledge in the achievement of business objectives
Technical/ managerial	Individual contributors managing projects or programs with defined scope and responsibility, or first tier management of a specialty area	Management:	Develop management skills and business perspective to effectively resolve cross-functional challenges
		Individual Contributors:	Ability to leverage specialized technical knowledge to achieve project or program results
Professional	Supervisors and individual contributors working on tasks, activities, and/or less complex, shorter duration projects	Ability to work independently on well-defined assignments or shorter term projects	

Differentials

The pay differences among levels are referred to as *differentials*. Pay structures typically pay more for work that requires more qualifications to perform, is performed under less-desirable working conditions, and/or whose input is more valued. The differential between a hamburger flipper ($5.00) and the front counter supervisor at McDonald's ($6.50) can be expressed as an absolute ($6.50 − $5.00 = $1.50) or as a percentage ([$6.50 − 5.00]/5.00 = 30%). Pay differentials of interest in managing compensation include those between adjacent levels in a career path, between supervisors and subordinates, between union and nonunion employees, and between executives and regular employees. For example, Michael Eisner, the chief executive officer of Disney, was paid $11.2 million in salary and annual bonus for his work in 1990.[5] His stock options for 1990 were valued at an additional $60.7 million, which brings the total for a single year to a breathtaking $72 million. Mr. Eisner's pay is a stunning contrast to the pay earned by Disney employees who perform as Mickey or Minnie Mouse. Mickey, Minnie, Pluto, and Goofy are all represented by the Teamsters and earn between $6.50 and $14.00 an hour. Such differentials may cause employees to murmur against executives just as the vineyard owner's laborers once did.

Criteria

Three criteria may be used to support the number of levels and size of the differentials that make up structures: the relative value or content of the work performed, the skills and knowledge required, and/or the performance or outcomes of the work.

Chapters 4 and 5 describe how to use these criteria in the actual design of structures. The criterion chosen can influence employee behaviors by describing what is required (i.e., promotion to increased work responsibilities, certification of greater skills, and/or improved performance) to get higher pay in the structure.

Egalitarian versus Hierarchical Structures

Pay structures can range from egalitarian at one extreme to hierarchical at the other. All pay structures contain some degree of hierarchy, but some have more than others. An egalitarian structure implies a belief that all workers should be treated equally. Some hold this belief as a matter of principle; others believe that more equal treatment will improve employee satisfaction, aid work team unity, and subsequently affect workers' performance.[6] Egalitarian structures have fewer levels and smaller differentials between adjacent levels and between the highest (CEO) and lowest paid workers.

By contrast, hierarchical structures are consistent with a belief in the value of recognizing differences in employee skills, responsibilities, and contributions to the organization. Hierarchical structures have more levels and greater differentials among them. Rather than leading to employee satisfaction, advocates of hierarchies believe that equal treatment will result in the more knowledgeable employees who perform more responsible jobs being unrecognized and unrewarded, which will cause them to leave the organization. Their departure will lower overall performance. So the case can be made for both egal-

---

[5]"How Do Executives Calculate Their Pay in 1990?" *Chief Executive*, December 10, 1991, pp. 26–30; "Developments in Industrial Relations," *Monthly Labor Review*, February 1991, pp. 49–51.

[6]E. E. Lawler III, "The New Pay," in *Current Issues in Human Resource Management*, ed. S. Rynes and G. Milkovich (Homewood, Ill.: Richard D. Irwin, 1986); G. Lodge and Richard E. Walton, "The American Corporation and Its New Relationships," *California Management Review*, Spring 1989, pp. 9–24; and Eric Cousineau and George T. Milkovich, "Pay Structures and the Effects on Firm Performance" (Working paper 89–15, Center for Advanced Human Resource Studies, Cornell University).

itarian and hierarchical structures. In this case, egalitarian structures actually hurt the organization.

How egalitarian or hierarchical should pay structures be? The size of the typical differential between CEOs and other employees has generated heated discussion. In the United States, the differentials between CEOs and operatives is 35 to 1, the highest among industrialized countries. In Japan, the differential is only 15 to 1. A number of writers have labeled the U.S. differentials excessive and raise concerns over fair treatment of employees.[7]

Yet egalitarian structures can cause problems, too. For example, Ben and Jerry's Homemade, a fast-growing purveyor of premium ice cream, maintains a spread of only 7-to-1 between its highest-paid and lowest-paid employee. (When the company started, the spread was only 5-to-1.) The relatively narrow range reflects the company's philosophy that the prosperity of its production workers and its management should be closely linked. But sometimes the narrow spread hurts the company's ability to recruit. For example, it could not find a qualified chief financial officer for what it was willing to pay. Its solution was to hire an accounting manager and provide backup support from a consultant two days a month.

An egalitarian structure is also more susceptible to *pay compression,* the narrowing of pay differentials between newly hired and employees at the next higher level. Compression can lead to a sense of inequity and increased turnover.[8]

So at what point does an egalitarian structure turn into a hiring or "compression problem" and a hierarchical structure into a "trust gap"? Theory and research do not yet provide much help finding the answers.[9] Absent hard evidence, opinions and beliefs abound. Many argue that egalitarian pay supports work teams and cooperative employee relations. They argue that more hierarchical pay structures reflect status, kill employee initiative, and crush creativity.[10] Unions also support egalitarian pay for political and solidarity reasons.[11] Others counter that properly designed hierarchies are more efficient

---

[7]Arne L. Kalleberg and James R. Lincoln, "The Structure of Earnings Inequality in the United States and Japan," *American Journal of Sociology,* vol. 94, supplement S121–S153; and Vladimir Pucik, "Revolution or Evolution: The Transformation of Japanese Personnel Practices" (Working paper, Center for Advanced Human Resource Studies, Cornell University).

[8]L. R. Gomez-Mejia and D. B. Balkin, "Effectiveness of Individual and Aggregate Compensation Strategies," *Industrial Relations* 28 (1989), pp. 431–45; and A. M. Konrad and J. Pfeffer, "Do You Get What You Deserve? Factors Affecting the Relationship between Productivity and Pay," *Administrative Science Quarterly* 35 (1990), pp. 258–85.

[9]Barry Gerhart and George Milkovich, "Employee Compensation: Research and Practice," in *Handbook of Industrial and Organizational Psychology,* 2nd ed., ed. M. D. Dunnette and L. M. Hough, (Palo Alto, Calif.: Consulting Psychologists Press, 1992).

[10]E. E. Lawler III, "Pay for Performance: A Strategic Analysis," in *Compensation and Benefits,* ed. L. R. Gomez-Mejia (Washington, D.C.: BNA, 1989); and R. M. Kanter, *When Giants Learn to Dance* (New York: Simon and Schuster, 1989).

[11]C. J. Berger, C. A. Olson, and J. W. Boudreau, "The Effect of Unionism on Job Satisfaction: The Role of Work Related Values and Perceived Rewards," *Organizational Behavior and Human Performance* 32 (1983), pp. 284–324; and P. Capelli and P. D. Sherer, "Assessing Worker Attitudes under a Two-Tier Wage Plan," *Industrial and Labor Relations Review* 43 (1990) pp. 225–44.

and support initiative and creativity.[12] They say that organizations need to be designed in terms of levels of accountability and skill required. Hierarchies offer incentives to obtain training, to take risks, and to excel.[13] Hierarchies support accountability and responsibility.

In practice, the answer to how the structure ought to look probably lies in how the work is organized. It can be organized around teams and cells or around individual performers. The pay structure should support the underlying organization structure. Obviously, this is a simplification. Think of any professional team sport—baseball, football, hockey—versus individual sports such as golf or bowling. Even in team sports, some positions are more valuable than others—a football team's quarterback, a basketball team's point guard and center. Consequently, these positions are paid more on average based on their relative value to the team's overall performance. So the team/individual distinction is easier to make in theory than in practice.

Distinguishing between Internal Consistency, External Competitiveness, and Employee Contribution Policies

Distinctions among internal consistency (what is the work worth relative to other work in the same organization?), external competitiveness (what are competitors paying relative to what we are paying for similar work?), and employee contribution (how much is this employee worth relative to other employees?) are also easier to make in a textbook than in the real world. Internal consistency refers primarily to the relationships among *jobs* within one employer. The comparison is *not* over pay differences between two individuals or between two firms; the worth of the work itself is determined with little regard to the individual who performs it. For example, the job of a word processor may be paid $10.50 per hour whether the employee doing the job holds a Ph.D. in journalism or is a vocational school graduate.

Separating internal consistency concerns from employee contribution and individual pay clearly oversimplifies the real world. In some work, particularly that requiring great responsibility and discretion, distinguishing the worth of the job from the individual does not make sense. A vice president whose work is designed around the qualifications and experiences of the individual performing it is one example. So although a policy of internal consistency deals primarily with *relationships among jobs inside a single or-*

---

[12]Elliot Jaques, "In Praise of Hierarchies," *Harvard Business Review,* January–February 1990.

[13]Ronald G. Ehrenberg and Michael L. Bognanno, "The Incentive Effects of Tournaments Revisited: Evidence from the European PGA Tour," Presentation at ILR-Cornell Research Conference on "Do Compensation Policies Matter?" Ithaca, N.Y., May 24, 1989; Edward Lazear and Sherwin Rosen, "Rank Order Tournaments as an Optimum Labor Contract," *Journal of Political Economy,* October 1989, pp. 41–64; Edward Lazear, "Pay Equality and Industrial Politics," *Journal of Political Economy,* June 1989, pp. 561–80; Sherwyn Rosen, "Prizes and Incentives in Elimination Tournaments," *American Economic Review,* September 1986, pp. 701–15; and Charles O'Reilly and Brian S. Main, "Comparisons: A Tale of Two Theories," *Administrative Science Quarterly,* June 1988, pp. 257–74.

ganization, equitable pay structures can be based directly on the skills of employees, as well as the jobs to which they are assigned.[14]

Comparisons of pay structures across organizations reveal significant differences. Some organizations pay the highest jobs 160 times the compensation of the lowest paid job.[15] In other organizations, the differences are considerably less (9 or 10 times). These observed differences raise questions about the design of internal pay structures. What factors influence or determine these structures? What are the consequences of different structures? Each question is considered in turn.

FACTORS INFLUENCING INTERNAL PAY STRUCTURES

The major factors that influence internal structures are shown in Exhibit 2.3. They include societal norms and customs; the economic conditions in which organizations operate; the culture, technology, policies, and objectives of a particular organization; and the particular characteristics of the work and the employees involved. The confluence of these pressures influences the design of pay structures.

EXHIBIT 2.3 Factors Influencing Internally Consistent Pay Structures

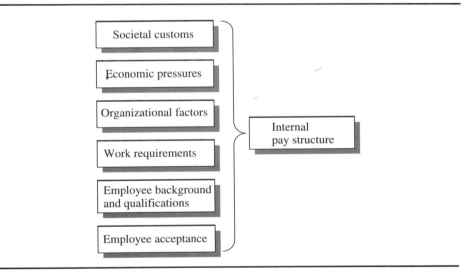

[14]E. E. Lawler III and G. E. Ledford, Jr., "Skill-Based Pay: A Concept That's Catching On," *Compensation and Benefits Review,* September 1985, pp. 54–61; and Fred Luthans and Marilyn L. Fox, "Update on Skill-Based Pay," *Personnel,* March 1989, pp. 26–32.

[15]Thomas A. Mahoney, *Compensation and Reward Perspectives* (Homewood, Ill.: Richard D. Irwin, 1979); Bonnie Rabin, "Executive Pay Dispersion: Measurement Issues and Evidence," (Paper presented at the 1989 Academy of Management Meetings, Washington, D.C., August 1989); and Graef S. Crystal, *In Search of Excess* (New York: W. W. Norton, 1991).

EXHIBIT 2.4   Theoretical Rationales for Internal Pay Structures

Theory		Factors Emphasized
Marginal productivity	$\longrightarrow$	Relative productivity of different jobs or skills
Human capital	$\longrightarrow$	Relative value of additional knowledge and experience
Resource dependency	$\longrightarrow$	Relative control over resources the organization depends upon
Institutional	$\longrightarrow$	Follow norms and mimic practices of other organizations
Internal labor markets	$\longrightarrow$	Norms and customs plus economic pressures Rules regulating employment relationship

---

Exactly how these factors interact is not well understood. No single theory accounts for all factors. Rather, a number of theories emphasize certain factors over others, and many ignore competing factors. No theory includes all the factors shown in Exhibit 2.3. Exhibit 2.4 catalogs some of the major theories that address internal pay structures. As we discuss the factors that influence pay structures, we will also look at these various theories.

Societal Factors

The historical role of societal conditions can be traced in various theories rationalizing pay differences.[16] These theories draw upon concepts from philosophy, sociology, economics, and psychology. Matthew's parable, for example, reveals an egalitarian policy: "the last even to the first," regardless of employee qualifications, working conditions, or hours worked. But this policy was not a hit with those workers who murmured against it.

Another approach to pay structures, the *just wage doctrine,* is attributed to attempts by 13th and 14th century artisans and craftsmen to take advantage of economic pressures. Nobles and landholders bid up the prevailing wages of skilled artisans, who were in relatively short supply following the devastation of the population by bubonic plague. The church and state responded by proclaiming a schedule of just wages. "Just" wages tended to reflect that society's class structure and were consistent with the prevailing notions of birth rights. Economic and market forces were explicitly denied as appropriate determinants of pay structures. Hence, some early compensation specialists employed concepts such as *societal norms, customs,* and *tradition* to design and justify pay structures. Present-day manifestations of the just wage doctrine can be seen in debates over minimum wage legislation and comparable worth, which also argue against economic forces as the sole determinant of pay structures.

Toshiba, the major international Japanese manufacturer, adheres to a combination

---

[16]See Tolles, *Origins of Wage Theory;* also see Jerald Greenberg, "Employee Theft as a Reaction to Underpayment or Inequity: The Hidden Cost of Pay Cuts," *Journal of Applied Psychology* 75 (1990), pp. 561–68.

of seniority and achievement in determining its internal pay structure. It would not only try to protect employees from the vagaries of external economic forces but would also counsel higher achieving younger employees to "wait; your turn will come" and to respect more senior employees. This is a societal custom with increasing appeal to the aging authors of this book.

Economic Factors

"Just wage" may have been a useful theory when the majority of people lived in feudal societies where wages were earned by only a few. The just wage concept preserved a privileged position in society for landowners and other small groups, including some skilled craftsmen. But the new commercial system developing in the 18th century, in Adam Smith's view, had the potential to make nations wealthy and also improve the welfare of the ordinary workers—if it would be allowed to operate unfettered by the customs and regulations of the past, including just wage. By the end of the 19th century, for the first time, the majority of people depended on wages for their livelihood. Smith advocated allowing supply and demand to be the main factors in setting wages. He ascribed to labor both exchange and use values. *Exchange value* is the price of labor (the wage) determined in a competitive market: in other words, labor's worth is whatever the buyer and seller agree on. *Use value,* on the other hand, is determined by the purpose for which the labor is used; in other words, the value to the employer of the goods or services labor produces. Exchange value is analogous to external competitiveness, whereas use value is related to internal equity.

But Smith did not address the issue of *how* supply and demand regulate wages. Accompanying the Industrial Revolution was a tremendous population surge and widespread poverty as people left the countryside for city life; this poverty contrasted sharply with the rising profits of employers. Theorists who observed these trends assumed that the supply of labor would constantly expand until there was just a bare minimum of subsistence for everyone. Ricardo, a 19th century businessman turned economist, theorized that the wages would always just equal the amount necessary to buy the goods the worker needed to live at a subsistence level. Any deviation from this equilibrium, for example, a wage increase, would bring about population changes that would reestablish the equilibrium, again at the subsistence level. This became known as the "iron law of wages."

On this foundation, Karl Marx built his theory of surplus value.[17] Under capitalism, he said, wages will always be based on exchange value and will provide only subsistent wage. But labor's use value is higher than its exchange value. The difference between exchange and use value produces a surplus that is being pocketed by the employer, when it should be paid to the worker, according to Marx.

These early theorists concentrated on the supply of labor to explain wages. But by the last half of the 19th century—not for the last time—reality disagreed with theory. Wages began to rise. So new theories were offered. Emphasis shifted to the demand for labor, and theorists argued that employers will pay a wage to a unit of labor that equals

---

[17]R. C. Tucker, ed., *The Marx-Engels Reader,* 2nd ed. (New York: W. W. Norton, 1978).

that unit's use value.[18] Unless a worker can produce a value equal to the value received in wages, it will not be worthwhile for the employer to hire that worker. This is consistent with the *marginal productivity theory* of wages. It says that work is compensated in proportion to its contribution to the organization's production objectives.

Accordingly, differences in the pay structure reflect differences in contributions associated with different work. In this view, work is compensated on the basis of worth to the employing organization, the volume of production or output associated with it, and the net revenue accruing to the organization from sale of the output. Marginalists assert that one job is paid more or less than another because of differences in productivity of the job and/or differences in consumer valuation of the output. Hence, differences in productivity provide a rationale for the internal pay structure. These views underlie many contemporary compensation practices.

Other economic factors such as supply and demand for specific skills also influence pay structures. Pay differences may reflect difficulties in recruiting and retaining employees for different jobs. University professors of accounting and engineering command higher salaries than do professors of history (particularly history of Yugoslavia and the Soviet Union), for example. Economic influences are discussed in more depth in Chapter 6, External Competitiveness.

Organizational Factors

The *technology* employed is a critical organizational factor influencing the design of pay structures.[19] Technology used in producing goods and services influences organizational structures, functional specialties, work teams, and departments. It influences the work to be performed and the skills required to perform it.

A case in point is the difference in the number of levels in the managerial pay structures at GE Aerospace (14 levels) versus GE Plastics (5 levels). The technology required to produce military hardware differs from that used to manufacture chemicals. Aerospace is more labor intensive (more than 50 percent of operating expenses are labor costs) than is Plastics (less than 20 percent); hence, different structures emerge.

The organization's *human resource policies* are another influence on pay structures. Policies in some organizations dictate using pay differentials as an incentive to induce employees to apply for higher-level positions (e.g., machinists to first-line supervisors). In other organizations, offering "management status" is considered a sufficient inducement, and little or no pay differential is offered. If pay differentials are designated as a key mechanism to encourage employees to accept greater responsibilities, then the pay structure must be designed to facilitate that decision.

Several organizational theories have been used to explain internal pay structures. *Resource dependency* theory says that the relative power of different jobs depends on

---

[18]Allan M. Cartter, *Theory of Wages and Employment* (Homewood, Ill.: Richard D. Irwin, 1959).

[19]M. Roznowski and C. Hulin, "Influences of Functional Specialty and Job Technology on Employees' Perceptual and Affective Responses to Their Jobs," *Organizational Behavior and Human Decision Processes* 36 (1985), pp. 196–208; M. H. Schuster, "Gainsharing: Current Issues and Research Needs" (Workshop, School of Industrial and Labor Relations, Cornell University, March 1990).

their ability to control resources the organization requires to achieve its objectives. For example, one study compared the pay structures of administrative jobs (directors of fund-raising, alumni affairs, admissions, community services, athletics, and student placement) in public and private universities.[20] Resource dependency theory predicts that those jobs that generated the university's financial resources would differ between public and private schools. As expected, jobs more critical to the objectives of each type of university did receive higher relative pay. For example, the chief development officer (e.g., fund-raiser) and directors of admissions and alumni affairs received higher relative pay in private universities' internal pay structures. But in public universities, the relative pay was higher for athletic directors, student placement, and community service directors. The point is that jobs differ in their importance to achieving organization objectives, and these differences affect the pay structure. The notion of resource dependency (i.e., relative importance to a firm's objectives) is similar to marginal productivity theory's productivity differences (i.e., relative contribution to objectives) as a basis for pay structures.

Institutional theory depicts organizations as simply following patterns exhibited by other organizations.[21] By extension, pay structures adopted by each employer would mimic accepted practice rather than be based on differences in productivity or power to procure key resources. Following fads is nothing new, even when it comes to designing pay structures; however, little empirical research supports mimicry as an important factor influencing pay structures. Nevertheless, it is not uncommon for executives to bring back "the answers" discovered at the latest conference. And surveys that benchmark the practices of the best companies facilitate others' copying those practices. Recent examples of such behaviors include the rush to "de-layer" organization structures, often with little regard to whether the de-layering makes sense for the organization or its employees.[22]

Both economic and organizational factors are combined in the notion of *internal labor markets.*[23] As depicted in Exhibit 2.5, internal labor markets refer to the rules and procedures that regulate the allocation of employees among different jobs within a single organization. Individuals tend to be recruited and hired only for specific entry level jobs and are later allocated (promoted or transferred) to other jobs. Because the employer competes in the external market for people to fill these entry jobs, their pay is tied to the external market. It must be high enough to attract a qualified pool of applicants. In contrast, pay for nonentry jobs (those staffed internally via transfer and promotions) is more heavily influenced by the organization's internal factors such as culture, norms,

---

[20]J. Pfeffer and A. Davis-Blake, "Understanding Organizational Wage Structures: A Resource Dependence Approach," *Academy of Management Journal* 30 (1987), pp. 437–55.

[21]L. G. Zucker, "Institutional Theories of Organization," *American Review of Sociology* 13 (1987), pp. 443–64; and D. Wazeter, "Determinants and Consequences of Pay Structures" (Ph.D. dissertation, Cornell University, 1991).

[22]Robert H. Guest, "Team Management under Stress," *Across the Board,* May 1989, pp. 30–35; Edgar H. Schein, "Corporate Teams and Totems," *Across the Board,* May 1989, pp. 12–17.

[23]Mark Granovetter, "Labor Mobility, Internal Markets, and Job Matching: A Comparison of the Sociological and the Economic Approaches," *Research in Social Stratification and Mobility* 5 (1986), pp. 222–27; Peter Doeringer and Michael J. Piore, *Internal Labor Markets and Manpower Analysis* (Lexington, Mass.: Heath-Lexington Books, 1971); and Paul Osterman, ed., *Internal Labor Markets* (Cambridge, Mass.: MIT Press, 1984).

EXHIBIT 2.5   Illustration of an Internal Labor Market

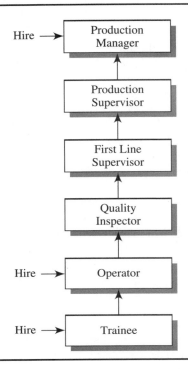

and/or contribution to the organization's success and less by external conditions.[24] In other words, external factors are dominant influences on pay for entry jobs, but the differentials for nonentry jobs tend to reflect the organization's economic objectives, culture, and traditions.

Expanding on this theme, internally equitable pay structures must also be designed to be congruent with the progression of jobs, or *career paths,* within an organization.[25] Higher pay is required for higher-level jobs to encourage employees to undertake the necessary training and gain the required experience to attain these jobs.

---

[24]David Pierson, "Labor Market Influences on Entry vs. Non-Entry Wages," *Nebraska Journal of Economics and Business,* Summer 1983, pp. 7–18.

[25]Lester C. Thurow, *Generating Inequality: Mechanisms of Distribution in the U.S. Economy* (New York: Basic Books, 1975); M. Roznowski and C. Hulin, "Influences of Functional Specialty and Job Technology on Employees' Perceptual and Affective Responses to Their Jobs," *Organizational Behavior and Human Decision Processes* 36 (1985), pp. 196–208; William D. Bridges and Robert L. Nelson, "Markets in Hierarchies: Organizational and Market Influences on Gender Inequality," *American Journal of Sociology* 95, no. 3 (1989), pp. 616–58; Peter Capelli and Wayne Cascio, "Why Some Jobs Command Wage Premiums: A Test of Career Tournament and Internal Labor Market," *Academy of Management Journal* 34, no. 4 (1991), pp. 840–68.

EXHIBIT 2.6   Simple Organization Chart

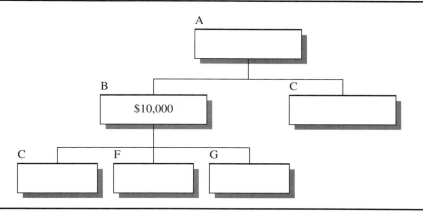

SOURCE: Illustrative organizational configuration from questionnaire, J. L. Kuethe and Bernard Levenson, "Conceptions of Organizational Worth," *The American Journal of Sociology,* November 1964, pp. 342–88. © The University of Chicago Press, 1964.

Employee Expectations

It is surprising that so little is known about employee expectations regarding pay differentials. Expectations, like beauty, may be in the eye of the beholder. For example, little research has been reported on whether different employee groups (older versus younger, line versus staff, men versus women, engineers versus personnel specialists, crafts versus office and clerical) hold different ideas about what constitutes fair pay differences among jobs.[26] In one study, business students and compensation administrators were asked to assign pay rates to organization charts (Exhibit 2.6).[27] One of the jobs was already assigned a pay rate to anchor the responses. The object of the study was to determine whether different groups would assign similar pay differentials. Business students and administrators did assign similar differentials. This finding led the researcher to suggest that a pay differential of approximately 30 percent is considered appropriate for the higher of two managerial organization levels and that the hierarchical level in the organization is the key determinant of judgments of equitable pay for managers.

Some research suggests that women have lower pay expectations and lower expectations about future pay than do similarly qualified men. For example, studies have reported substantial differences in the pay expectations of male and female MBA students,

---

[26]Jerald Greenberg and Suzy N. Ornstein, "High Status Job Titles as Compensation for Underpayment: A Test of Equity Theory," *Journal of Applied Psychology* 68, no. 2 (1983), pp. 285–97.

[27]Thomas A. Mahoney, "Organizational Hierarchy and Position Worth," *Academy of Management Journal,* December 1979, pp. 726–37.

with women reporting lower career entry and career peak pay expectations than similarly qualified men.[28]

But judgments about equitable differentials are probably a function of many things, including, apparently, the organization culture. For example, some believe that as organizations become more democratic, and as more employees are involved in decision making, salaries and benefits will become more equal. That is, the structure becomes more egalitarian; the size of differentials narrows.[29] Jaques asserts the existence of *societal-wide norms* of equitable pay.[30] He believes that most people would assign approximately the same pay differentials to various levels of work, based on commonly held beliefs of fairness in pay. Although research, limited though it is, lends support to the existence of pay norms among *similar* groups of employees (such as business students and administrators), little evidence supports Jaques' idea of universally held norms across a highly diverse society. And the number of lawsuits over what constitutes "fair" pay would seem to indicate that substantial disagreement exists. Nevertheless, even a diverse society may have norms regarding pay differences considered to be excessive as evidenced by the widespread criticism of the "excessive" difference between executive and regular employee pay in the United States, or Congress granting itself pay increases during economic recessions.

Mahoney points out that all of these explanations of pay structures have some validity and "in fact, likely are interrelated in the explanation of any specific pay structure."[31] Some pay structures may have been designed to reflect very rational economic reasons, that is, the technology, the differences in the type of work performed, and its relative contribution to the organization. Changes in pay structures may have arisen in response to economic factors such as skill shortages. Over time, the distorted differential became accepted as equitable and customary; efforts to change it were resisted as inequitable and destructive of social relationships within the organization. Thus, the pay structures established for organizational and economic reasons may be maintained for cultural or other reasons until another economic jolt overcomes the cultural resistance. Then a new set of norms are formed around the new structure.

EMPLOYEE ACCEPTANCE: A KEY TEST

In a classic article on pay structures, Livernash asserts that employees desire "fair" compensation.[32] He states that employees judge the fairness of their pay through com-

---

[28]S. M. Freedman, "The Effects of Subordinate Sex, Pay Equity, and Strength of Demand on Compensation Decisions," *Sex Roles* 5 (1979), pp. 649–58; B. Major, V. Vanderslie, and D. McFarlein, "Effects of Pay Received: The Conformatory Nature of Initial Expectations," *Journal of Applied Social Psychology* 14, no. 5 (1984), pp. 399–412.

[29]Jerome M. Rosow, "The Organization in the Decade Ahead," Conference sponsored by Work in America Institute, Scarsdale, N.Y., March 3–5, 1986.

[30]Elliot Jaques, *Equitable Payment* (New York: John Wiley, 1961).

[31]Mahoney, *Compensation and Reward Perspectives.*

[32]E. Robert Livernash, "The Internal Wage Structure," in *New Concepts in Wage Determination,* ed. G. W. Taylor and F. C. Pierson (New York: McGraw-Hill, 1957), pp. 143–72.

parisons with the compensation paid other jobs related in some fashion to their own jobs. He called such interrelated jobs *job clusters*. Accordingly, an important criterion for assessing the internal pay structure is its *acceptability to the employees involved*. Effectiveness of the pay structure depends on employee acceptance. Other factors (societal, economic, and organizational) also influence employee acceptance; but "workers' views about what constitutes an 'equitable' wage structure have an important role to play in the determination of wages."[33]

Distributive and Procedural Justice

The fairness of the procedures used to design and administer the pay structure constitutes procedural justice.[34] The actual results—the pay differences, the number of levels, and the criteria used in the structure—pertain to distributive justice: Are the actual pay differences distributed by the structure fair?

The distinction between procedural and distributive justice is important. Suppose you are given a ticket for speeding. *Procedural justice* refers to the process by which a decision is reached: the right to an attorney, the right to an impartial judge, and the right to receive a copy of the arresting officer's statement. *Distributive justice* refers to the fairness of the decision: guilty. Researchers have recently found that employees' perceptions of procedural fairness significantly influence their acceptance of the results; employees and managers are more willing to accept low pay if they believe the way this result was obtained was fair.[35] This research also strongly suggests that pay procedures are more likely to be perceived as fair (1) if they are consistently applied to all employees; (2) if employee participation and/or representation is included; (3) if appeals procedures are available; and (4) if the data used are accurate.

Based on the research on perceptions of procedural and distributive justice, Greenberg argues that employees' impressions can be managed.[36] In effect, he develops a case for marketing to employees and managers the pay structure and the procedures used to design it, just as one would market products or services to consumers. A campaign of public announcements, well-crafted brochures, videos, and articles in the company newsletter should be aimed at managing the belief that the pay structures and procedures are fair. Greenberg is careful to note that he does not condone manipulation—trying to sell an inequitable system. Rather, the emphasis is on employee perception, which should not be left to chance. If fair procedures and structures have been designed, a necessary step is to ensure that employees believe they are fair.

---

[33]P. Ryscavage and P. Helene, "Earnings Inequality in the 1980s," *Monthly Labor Review* 113, no. 12 (1990), pp. 3–16.

[34]Robert Folger and Mary Konovsky, "Effects of Procedural and Distributive Justice on Reactions to Pay Raise Decisions," *Academy of Management Journal,* March 1989, pp. 115–30; Jerald Greenberg, "Looking Fair vs. Being Fair: Managing Impressions of Organizational Justice," in *Research in Organizational Behavior,* vol. 12, ed. B. M. Staw and L. L. Cummings (Greenwich, Conn.: JAI Press, 1990).

[35]Folger and Konovsky, "Effects of Procedural and Distributive Justice."

[36]Greenberg, "Looking Fair vs. Being Fair."

CONSEQUENCES OF INTERNAL PAY STRUCTURES

But why worry about internal pay structure at all? Why not simply pay employees what it takes to get them to take a job and to stay? Why not simply let external market forces determine wages? The answers can be found in several situations. One is the presence of unique jobs that reflect organizational idiosyncracies. For example, the School of Veterinary Medicine at Cornell University has installed "windows" in the stomachs of several cows to study the animals' digestive processes. Laboratory technicians help install and maintain these windows and perform other equally exotic duties. Without similar jobs with other employers, it is difficult to determine the appropriate wage for such jobs. Other, more common illustrations of unique jobs may be found under titles such as "administrative assistant" or "research associate." The specific content of these jobs will vary with the technologies employed, the manner in which the work is designed, the skills and experiences of the particular incumbent, and so on. The pay for these unique jobs is typically set through comparison of the work with other internal jobs. So the existing internal pay structure provides a basis for arriving at a rate for unique jobs.

It is also possible that some jobs or skills are valued by a specific organization more or less than the rates reflected for that job in the market. For example, top-notch compensation specialists or accountants may have greater value to a compensation or accounting consulting firm than to heavy manufacturing companies. The consulting firm may pay higher-than-market rates for the greater contribution of the particular job to organization goals. Some genetics and engineering professors are leaving academia to design products for bio-tech firms—and become part of lucrative bonus pool and stock option plans that universities cannot match. Other examples of policies that emphasize internal consistency over market-determined external competitiveness can be found among public employers that have granted salary increases to clerical jobs held predominantly by women. The agreement of San Jose, California, with the American Federation of State, County, and Municipal Employees to raise the pay for office and clerical jobs relative to the pay for other city jobs is a case in point.[37]

The practical question is, Does any of this really matter? Recall the three dimensions of internal pay structures. What difference does the number of levels, the size of pay differentials between levels, and the criteria (job and skill based) make on the compensation system goals of efficiency, equity, and compliance? Exhibit 2.7 suggests some of the consequences of the internal pay structures.

Efficiency

Internal pay structures imply future rewards in a career; therefore, they may influence work force preparedness. The size of the pay differentials between the entry level in the structure and the highest level may induce employees to undertake the training and obtain the experience required for promotions. Human capital theorists suggest that pay differ-

---

[37]*Background Material on the San Jose Situation,* available from Comparable Worth Project, 488 41st Street, Oakland, CA 94609; and *Pay Equity: A Union Issue for the 1980s,* American Federation of State, County and Municipal Employees, 1625 L Street N.W., Washington, D.C. 20036.

EXHIBIT 2.7 Some Consequences of Pay Structure

Pay structure
- Undertake training
- Increase experience
- Reduce turnover
- Facilitate career progression
- Facilitate performance
- Reduce pay-related grievances
- Reduce pay-related work stoppages

---

entials serve as inducements for employees to invest in themselves by acquiring added knowledge, skills, and experience. Few workers bring fully developed work skills into the labor market. Usually, after obtaining an entry job, skills are acquired either formally or informally through on-the-job training. The incentive to acquire these skills is the pay differential among jobs requiring varying skill levels. According to this view, a computer design engineering job should pay more than a programming job. Without that pay difference, individuals are less likely to go through the education (and forgo earnings while in school) required to become an engineer. Similar logic can be applied to differentials between supervisors and production workers, which encourage employees to undertake more responsibilities. Pay differentials within organizations induce employees to remain with the organization, increase their experience and training, and seek greater responsibility.[38]

The highest salary paid for the top level in the structure also may influence individual decisions to accept an employment offer. According to one study, Pennsylvania school teachers compare job offers from competing school districts based on their career pay, the very top salary they could earn in each district's pay structure.[39] This contrasts with students who compare competing offers on the starting pay, rather than the top pay. It almost seems as if these teachers are intuitively considering the present value of a future stream of earnings. Perhaps private sector managers fail to emphasize the role of the pay structure in career advancement and future earnings potential.

Some economists argue that internal pay structures should be viewed as "tournaments." The premise is that the size of the differentials between levels in the structure affects the effort exerted by all employees. So if the CEOs earn significantly more than their subordinates and so on throughout the hierarchy, then each employee is more motivated. Note that this implies that the size of the differentials must be large enough

---

[38]Edward P. Lazear, "Severance Pay, Pensions, and Efficient Mobility," Working paper no. 854, National Bureau of Economic Research, Cambridge, Mass., February 1982.

[39]Wazeter, "Determinants and Consequences of Pay Structures."

to keep everyone motivated to stay in the tournament. The evidence for all this is mixed. One study of professional golfers reported the greater the differential between each level in the tournament prize structure, the better the scores per hole.[40] But contrary to some wishful thinkers, work in most organizations is probably not a round of golf, so the results may have limited applications.[41]

Equity

Several writers argue that employees' attitudes about the fairness of the pay structure affect their work behaviors. Livernash, for example, asserts that departures from an acceptable wage structure will occasion turnover, grievances, and diminished motivation.[42] Jaques argues that if fair differentials among jobs are not paid, individuals may harbor ill will toward the employer, resist change, change employment if possible, become depressed, and "lack that zest and enthusiasm which makes for high efficiency and personal satisfaction in work."[43]

Others, including labor unions, have long held the belief that more egalitarian pay structures support team workers, high commitment to the organization, and improved performance. But a recent study found that potential job candidates are more likely to accept job offers where pay is based on their individual efforts rather than group performance.[44]

Since employee judgments about pay structures are so important, we need to understand how employees make these judgments. Exhibit 2.8 shows the main determinants of whether an employee is likely to perceive pay as being equitable. The model, adapted from the distributive justice and inequity models, shows that employees' judgments about equity are based on comparisons.[45] A pay structure will be perceived as equitable or inequitable depending on whether the pay for job A compared to its requirements (education, experience), the work performed (task, behaviors, working conditions), and the value of contributions (to organization objectives and/or consumers) is congruent with the pay for job B relative to its requirements, work performed, contributions, and so on, through all jobs in the structure. However, very little research addresses the question of what factors influence employees' perceptions of the equity or fairness of pay structures per se.[46]

[40]M. L. Bognanno and R. G. Ehrenberg, "The Incentive Effects of Tournaments Revisited: Evidence from the PGA Tour," *Industrial and Labor Relations Review* 43 (1990), pp. 74–88.

[41]Gerhart and Milkovich, "Employee Compensation."

[42]Livernash, "Internal Wage Structure."

[43]Jaques, *Equitable Payment*, p. 123.

[44]Robert Bretz, Jr., and Tim Judge, "The Role of Human Resource Systems in Job Choice Decisions," Working paper no. 92–30, Center for Advanced Human Resource Studies, Cornell University, Ithaca, N.Y.

[45]E. E. Lawler III, *Pay and Organization Development* (Reading, Mass.: Addison-Wesley, 1981).

[46]B. Gerhart, "How Important Are Dispositional Factors as Determinants of Job Satisfaction? Implications for Job Design and Other Personnel Programs," *Journal of Applied Psychology* 73 (1987), pp. 154–62.

EXHIBIT 2.8   Perceived Equity of a Pay Structure

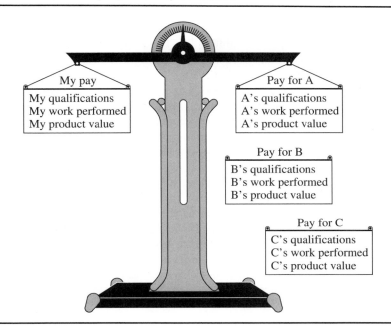

My pay
My qualifications
My work performed
My product value

Pay for A
A's qualifications
A's work performed
A's product value

Pay for B
B's qualifications
B's work performed
B's product value

Pay for C
C's qualifications
C's work performed
C's product value

Most of the research on employee attitudes toward pay has studied pay satisfaction. However, Heneman argues that pay satisfaction needs to be considered in terms similar to the four basic policy areas used in the pay model: satisfaction with the pay structure (internal consistency), with the pay level (external competitiveness), with individual pay (employee contribution), and with the administration of the pay system.[47] Recognizing that employee attitudes may be linked to each of the basic pay model components permits better analysis of specific aspects of the compensation system and employee satisfaction toward them. Lowering the external competitive position of pay may affect the satisfaction with the pay level, but may leave attitudes toward the pay structure unchanged.

Despite the fact that a great deal of research relating to pay satisfaction and dissatisfaction has been conducted, virtually no research has been directed toward understanding the consequences of *pay differences for different work*. Consequently, there is virtually no research evidence to help guide us in the design of pay structures that will yield positive employee attitudes.

[47]Herbert G. Heneman III, "Pay Satisfaction," in *Research in Personnel and Human Resources Management,* vol. 3, ed. K. M. Rowland and G. R. Ferris (Greenwich, Conn.: JAI Press, 1985), pp. 115–39.

Compliance

Certainly, all internal pay structures need to comply with government laws and regulations. In the United States, this includes legislation focusing on ensuring nondiscriminatory pay for women and minorities. The Canadian provinces have adopted pay equity legislation that prohibits pay structures that discriminate; the Social Charter of the European Community contains similar legislation. The regulatory influences on compensation management are examined in Chapters 13 and 14. At this point, it is enough to recognize that the design and administration of pay structures needs to comply with the regulations of the country in which the organization operates.[48]

So with virtually no research evidence to help guide the design and administration of internal pay structure, where does that leave us? What are the appropriate number of levels, the size of the differentials, and the criteria to advance employees through a structure? We believe the answers lie in understanding the factors discussed in this chapter: the norms and customs of the culture, the economic circumstances, and, perhaps most importantly, the nature of the work and employers. For example, narrow, egalitarian structures may be related to improving work force preparedness, satisfaction, and performance when the technology and the nature of the work requires cooperation and teamwork compared to more independent and autonomous situations. On the other hand, it is not difficult to think of examples in which very large pay differentials exist within highly successful (championship) teams (e.g., Michael Jordan and the Chicago Bulls; Andre Previn and the London Symphony).

SUMMARY

This chapter discusses what is meant by the strategic policy regarding internal consistency and how it affects employees, managers, and employers. *Internal consistency* refers to the pay relationships among jobs within a single organization. Although the potential consequences of internal pay structures are vital to organizations and individuals, little guidance has emerged from research concerning employee perceptions of internal pay structures.

Pay structures—the array of pay rates for different jobs within an organization—are shaped by societal, economic, organizational, and other factors. Employees judge a structure to be equitable on the basis of comparisons. The "ratio" of a job's relative pay to its relative requirements, work performed, and value of that performance is compared to the "ratio" for other jobs in the structure. Congruent ratios are believed to be equitable. Acceptance by employees of the relative pay differentials is the key test of an equitable pay structure.

Keep the goals of the compensation system in mind in the design and management of internal pay structures. There is widespread belief and considerable anecdotal evidence that differences in pay structures influence employees' attitudes and work behaviors and

---

[48]E. Groshen, "The Structure of Female/Male Wage Differentials: Is It Who You Are, What You Do, or Where You Work?" *Journal of Human Resources* 24, no. 3 (1991), pp. 458–72.

therefore the success of organizations. However, research to date offers little guidance regarding what the appropriate structure is in different situations.

REVIEW QUESTIONS

1. Why is internal consistency an important policy issue for the compensation system?
2. Discuss the factors that influence internal equity and pay structures. Based on your own experience, which ones do you think are the most important?
3. How would you go about trying to manage employees' impressions of the pay structure? Is this potentially destructive manipulation?
4. What is the "just wage" doctrine? Can you think of any present-day applications?
5. Explain how internal labor markets work.
6. What are pay structures most likely to affect?

You are the owner of Parcel Plus, a rapidly growing service that handles all a consumer's mailing needs. Bring in an item, and Parcel Plus will prepare it for shipping and make arrangements with UPS, air freight services, or overnight delivery services. Staff members will advise customers of options and costs.

Because more and more people are working out of their own homes, you have investigated the possibility of expanding service by offering pickup and delivery. Buying your own trucks would also allow handling larger packages that are outside the size and weight limitation set by UPS. Parcel Plus could pick up heavy shipments and take them to nearby larger cities for transfer to one of the nationwide trucking lines. This would help people who do not ship things on a regular basis and do not want to be bothered making the necessary shipping arrangements.

At present, Parcel Plus employs 10 people: 8 customer service representatives, an assistant manager, and a manager. The customer service representatives are paid between $5.50 and $6.50 per hour, depending on how long they have been employed. Both the assistant manager and the manager are former customer service representatives, and they are paid $8.50 and $10.00 per hour, respectively. You intend to create a new position, driver/customer service representative, and hire two new employees for this position. The job would consist of truck driving as needed and doing regular customer service-representative's duties when not driving. Since the pickup and delivery is a new service, you aren't sure what amount of time will be spent driving versus customer service work. The proportion spent driving will increase as the demand for this service increases. You feel that $6.50 per hour is a fair wage. But the first person who applied for the job, Carlos Sherman, said $6.50 was too low. "No self-respecting trucker would start at less than $8.50 an hour." You suspect that if you offer $7.50 per hour, he will take the job. Mr. Sherman seems physically strong enough to handle the job, even though he's had no trucking experience. When you shared this opinion with Corrianne Nation, the manager, she became quite upset. "If you hire someone off the street and pay $7.50 an hour, you better be sure no one else hears about it." You thought about this, but when no other job applicants seemed suitable, you decided to renegotiate with Mr. Sherman. You were just about to call him, when two customer service representatives came into your office. They got right to the point. "We think we all deserve a raise."

Discussion Questions

1. How should you handle the customer service representatives? Shall you give them an increase? If so, why, and how much? If not, why not? Present your case.

2. Shall you renegotiate with Mr. Sherman?

3. Is the amount of time on the job spent driving an important factor?

4. What additional information would you like to help you make your decision?

Chapter Outline

Three workers sit in front of computer keyboards, all of them nimbly pushing keys. But each of them is performing different work. Modern technology has made it possible for an engineer, a word processor, and a telephone operator all to perform very different jobs using the same tool, a computer. If pay is based on work performed, some way is needed to discover the differences and similarities among jobs. Observation is not enough.

What is required is information that will help ensure that compensation decisions are firmly based on identifiable similarities and differences in the work. Achieving some degree of internal consistency is one of the strategic policies, a basic building block, in our compensation model. Recognizing similarities and differences in the work within an organization is a key part of achieving internal consistency.

DIFFERENCES FORM THE INTERNAL PAY STRUCTURE

Differences in the work of an engineer, a word processor, and a phone operator at General Electric (GE) are fairly apparent, and the pay for these jobs reflects the relative value of these differences to GE.

Rather than these so obviously different jobs, consider instead the work in a single occupation at GE: engineering. How many different levels of work should be designed in an engineering pay structure? Currently, one GE division organizes it into six levels as described in Exhibit 3.1. However, these levels are undergoing change. The massive reordering of spending priorities by the Department of Defense, one of GE's prime customers, along with a significant shift in GE's marketing and product development strategy, has jolted GE into restructuring its engineering work and the way it is organized. Consequently, GE is considering four levels: merging the systems with the lead engineering position and the entry engineer and the senior positions. Each distinct level in GE's structure represents a major difference in the complexities of tasks—accountabilities and knowledge required to perform the work.

But a countervailing concern needs consideration. These structures represent career paths to employees.[1] They represent promotional opportunities, recognition, and rewards. Reducing the number of levels in a structure may also reduce opportunities for recognition and career growth. Toshiba, by comparison, already is down to four levels for its specialists and managers, as shown in Exhibit 3.2.

The point is that information about the actual work performed and the way it is designed is crucial for determining pay structures. This information helps ensure that the compensation decisions are firmly based on identifiable similarities and differences in the work. It is also essential input for designing career paths and promotional opportunities that are intended to reward increased knowledge and improved performance.

ALTERNATIVE CRITERIA FOR STRUCTURES

Pay system design traditionally begins with analyzing the work and building job structures that reflect the relationships among jobs within an organization. The criteria supporting

---

[1]Elliott Jaques, "In Praise of Hierarchies," *Harvard Business Review*, January–February 1990, pp. 11–35.

EXHIBIT 3.1   Engineering Pay Structure at General Electric Aerospace Division

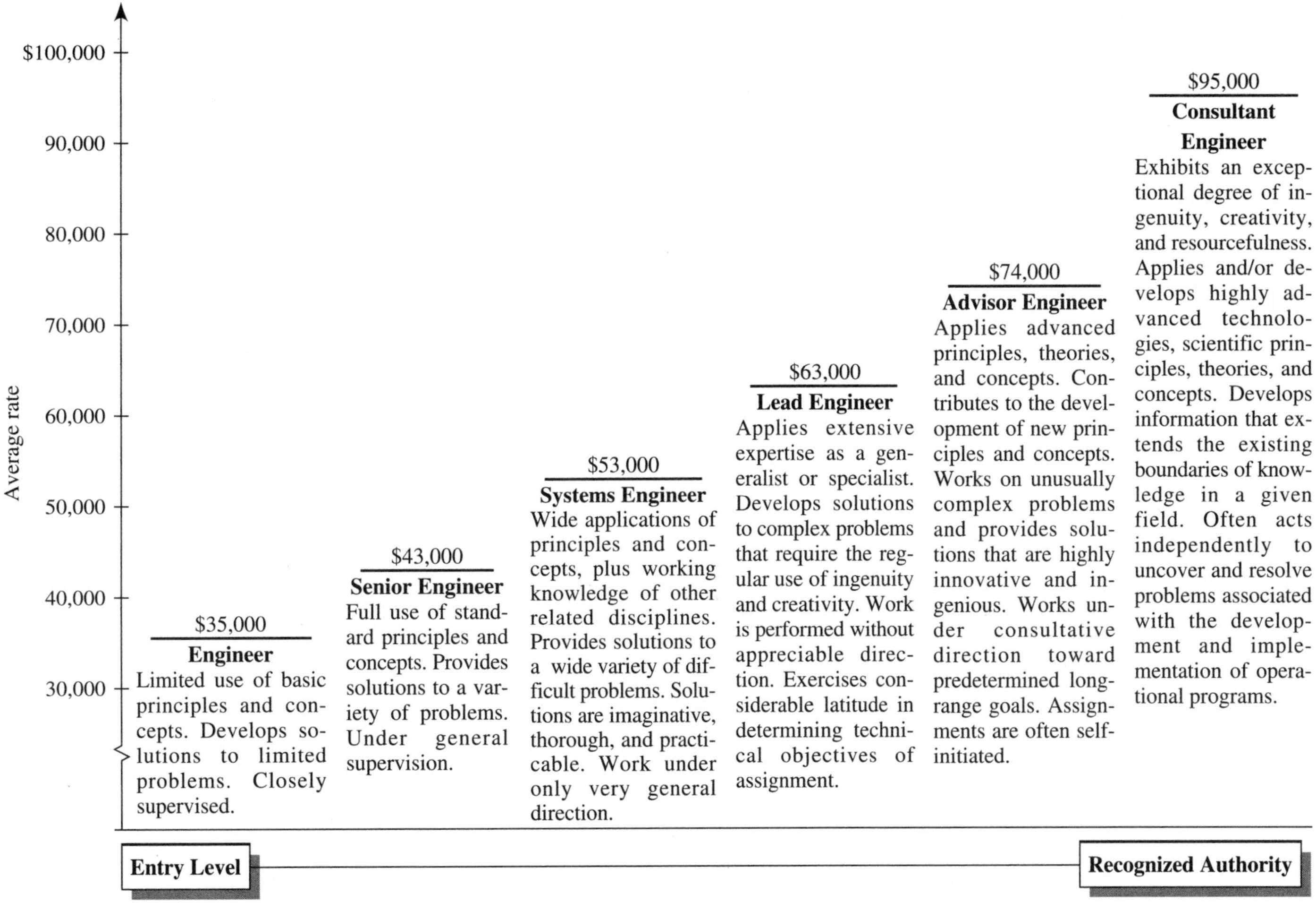

$100,000

90,000

80,000

70,000

60,000

50,000

40,000

30,000

Average rate

$35,000

Engineer

Limited use of basic principles and concepts. Develops solutions to limited problems. Closely supervised.

$43,000

Senior Engineer

Full use of standard principles and concepts. Provides solutions to a variety of problems. Under general supervision.

$53,000

Systems Engineer

Wide applications of principles and concepts, plus working knowledge of other related disciplines. Provides solutions to a wide variety of difficult problems. Solutions are imaginative, thorough, and practicable. Work under only very general direction.

$63,000

Lead Engineer

Applies extensive expertise as a generalist or specialist. Develops solutions to complex problems that require the regular use of ingenuity and creativity. Work is performed without appreciable direction. Exercises considerable latitude in determining technical objectives of assignment.

$74,000

Advisor Engineer

Applies advanced principles, theories, and concepts. Contributes to the development of new principles and concepts. Works on unusually complex problems and provides solutions that are highly innovative and ingenious. Works under consultative direction toward predetermined long-range goals. Assignments are often self-initiated.

$95,000

Consultant Engineer

Exhibits an exceptional degree of ingenuity, creativity, and resourcefulness. Applies and/or develops highly advanced technologies, scientific principles, theories, and concepts. Develops information that extends the existing boundaries of knowledge in a given field. Often acts independently to uncover and resolve problems associated with the development and implementation of operational programs.

Entry Level

Recognized Authority

59

EXHIBIT 3.2   Ranks and Positions at Toshiba

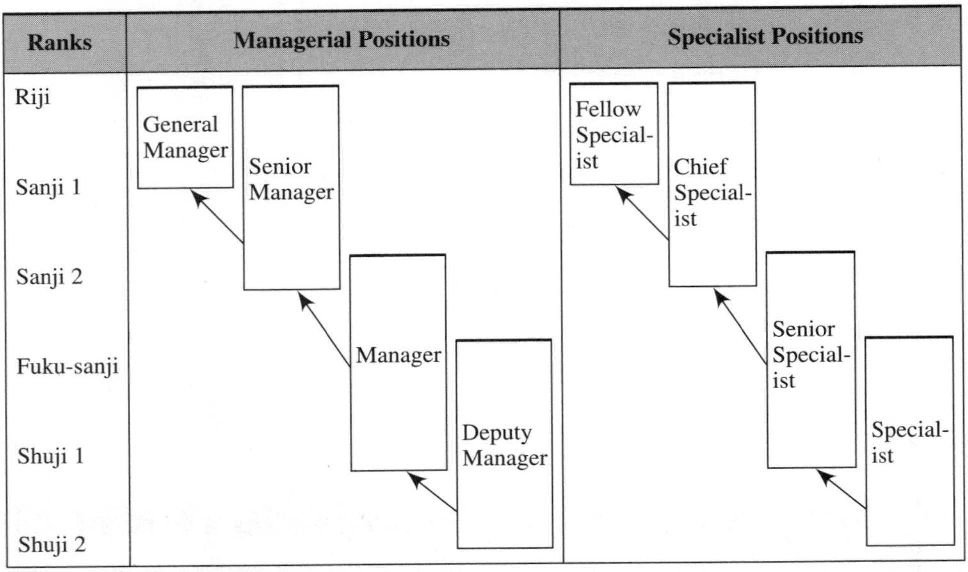

Ranks	Managerial Positions	Specialist Positions
Riji	General Manager / Senior Manager	Fellow Specialist / Chief Specialist
Sanji 1		
Sanji 2	Manager	Senior Specialist
Fuku-sanji		
Shuji 1	Deputy Manager	Specialist
Shuji 2		

NOTE: Arrow denotes promotion.

SOURCE: *Personnel Management in Toshiba* (Tokyo, Japan: Toshiba Corporation, 1991).

---

the structure is the *job* rather than the person doing the job. But as noted in the last chapter, and as Exhibit 3.3 shows, there are alternative criteria. Pay structures can be based on the skills and knowledge demonstrated by individuals, the performance results of their work, or the job content. Or even some combination of the three.[2] Knowledge-based structures are receiving increasing attention. Surveys report 5 to 15 percent of employers are using these structures or are considering using them.[3] However, job-based structures clearly remain the most common approach.[4] We will examine decisions involved in collecting information to design job-based structures (job analysis), and then we will examine the emerging approaches to skill-based pay structures.

---

[2]G. Ledford, "Three Cases on Skill-Based Pay: An Overview," *Compensation and Benefits Review*, March–April 1991, pp. 11–23.

[3]F. Luthans and M. L. Fox, "Update on Skill-Based Pay," *Personnel*, March 1989, pp. 26–31.

[4]Pay structures based primarily on performance regardless of the job or skills required are rare. Some sales and production plans that are straight incentive or piece rate are examples, but they usually include some form of job-based criteria also.

EXHIBIT 3.3   Possible Criteria for Internal Structures

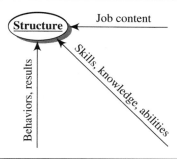

JOB ANALYSIS

Collecting information about jobs is known as *job analysis,* which can be defined as
follows:

> The systematic process of collecting relevant, work-related information related
> to the nature of a specific job.

The basic premise underlying job analysis is that jobs are more likely to be described,
differentiated, and valued fairly if accurate information about them is available.[5] Exhibit
3.4 shows that job analysis provides the underlying information for preparing job descriptions and evaluating jobs. Job analysis is a prerequisite for job-based pay structures.
It is input for describing and valuing work. Therefore it is highly related to the equity
and efficiency of the pay system.

Exhibit 3.4 also identifies the major decisions in designing a job analysis: (1) For
what purpose are we collecting job information? (2) What information should be collected?

---

[5]Particularly valuable sources of information on job analysis definitions and methods are U.S. Department
of Labor, Manpower Administration, *Handbook for Analyzing Jobs* (Washington, D. C.: U.S. Government
Printing Office, 1972); S. A. Fine and W. W. Wiley, *An Introduction to Functional Job Analysis,* Monograph
4 (Kalamazoo, Mich.: W. E. Upjohn Institute for Employment Research, 1971); E. J. McCormick, "Job and
Task Analysis," in *Handbook of Industrial and Organizational Psychology,* ed. M. D. Dunnette (Chicago:
Rand McNally, 1976), pp. 651–96; E. J. McCormick, *Job Analysis: Methods and Applications* (New York:
AMACOM, 1979); Stephen E. Bemis, Ann Holt Belenky, and Dee Ann Soder, *Job Analysis: An Effective
Management Tool* (Washington, D.C.: Bureau of National Affairs, 1983); Jai V. Ghorpade, *Job Analysis: A
Handbook for the Human Resource Director* (Englewood Cliffs, N.J.: Prentice Hall, 1988); and *Job Analysis*
(Winnipeg, Manitoba: Pay Equity Bureau, Manitoba Labour, 1989).

EXHIBIT 3.4 Determining the Internal Job Structure

Internal relationships within the organization →	**Job analysis** →	**Job descriptions** →	**Job evaluation** →	**Job structure**
	Collecting information about the nature of specific jobs	Summary reports that identify, define, and describe the job as it is actually performed	Comparison of jobs within an organization	An ordering of jobs based on their content or relative value

Some Major Issues in Job Analysis
- Analysis for what purpose
- What information to collect
- How to collect information
- Who should be involved
- Usefulness of results

---

(3) What methods should be used? (4) To what extent should the various parties be involved? (5) How useful for compensation purposes are the results?

WHY PERFORM JOB ANALYSIS?

An organization may perform job analysis for a number of reasons. They range from concerns for consistent treatment of employees to more specific uses in compensation and other personnel systems.[6]

Internal Consistency

For most people, the pay attached to their job is a matter of stunning importance. Therefore, pay decisions must be shown to be based on work-related logic and administered fairly. If an employer is not consistent in its treatment of its employees or cannot demonstrate the work-related logic of its pay, then it will be hard-pressed to explain its actions to employees or defend them in a lawsuit.[7] Although job analysis is not legally required, the data collected help managers construct a work-related rationale to communicate with employees and defend their decisions when challenged.

Compensation

There are two critical uses for job analysis in compensation: (1) to establish similarities and differences in the content of the jobs and (2) to help establish an internally equitable job structure. If jobs have equal content, then in all likelihood the pay established for them will be equal. If, on the other hand, the job content differs, then those differences

---

[6]J. R. Hackman and G. R. Oldham, *Work Redesign* (Reading, Mass.: Addison-Wesley, 1980).

[7]John Lacy, "Job Evaluation and EEO," *Employee Relations Law Journal* 7, no. 3 (1979), pp. 210–17.

are part of the rationale for paying jobs differently. Additional data, such as market rates paid by competitors and appropriate career paths, are also considered before any pay structure is determined.

Data collection procedures must gather sufficient detail to distinguish among jobs. Collection methods must be able to withstand challenges from both inside and outside the organization. Job analysis data become the key supports of an equitable pay structure. If the support is weak, the structure is vulnerable to challenge. Yet balance is required, since analysis in too great detail risks making the job analysis process too burdensome and costly.

Additional Uses of Job Analysis Data

Potential uses for job analysis are found in every major personnel function.[8] Often the type of job analysis data needed varies by function, as shown in Exhibit 3.5. For example, job analysis is used to identify the skills and experience required to perform the work, thereby clarifying hiring and promotion standards.[9] Training programs may be designed with job analysis data; jobs may be redesigned based on it.[10] In performance evaluation, both employees and supervisors look to the required behaviors and results expected in a job to help assess performance.

Rather than conducting a separate analysis for each application, some writers argue that a single, omnibus method can be designed to capture significant data for multiple uses (e.g., compensation and hiring).[11] After investing $300,000 to design an omnibus job analysis, J. C. Penney discovered that the data collected did not yield the pay structure expected.[12] The multiple uses simply did not materialize, maintenance costs exceeded expectations, and use of the analysis imposed too great a burden on line managers.

---

[8]R. A. Ash, E. L. Levine, and F. Sistrunk, "The Role of Jobs and Job-Based Methods in Personnel and Human Resource Management," *Research in Personnel and Human Resources Management* 1 (1983), pp. 45–84; Duane Thompson and Toni Thompson, "Court Standards for Job Analysis in Test Validation," *Personnel Psychology* 35 (1982), pp. 865–74; also see Chapter 4, George T. Milkovich and John Boudreau, *Personnel/Human Resource Management: A Diagnostic Approach,* 5th ed. (Homewood, Ill.: Richard D. Irwin, 1988).

[9]Robert M. Guion, "Recruiting, Selection, and Job Placement," in *Handbook of Industrial and Organizational Psychology,* ed. M. D. Dunnette (Chicago: Rand McNally, 1976); and D. P. Schwab, "Recruiting and Organization Participation," in *Personnel Management,* ed. K. M. Rowland and G. R. Ferris (Boston: Allyn & Bacon, 1982), pp. 105–30.

[10]Hackman and Oldham, *Work Redesign;* R. W. Griffen, A. Welsh, and G. Moorhead, "Perceived Task Characteristics and Employee Performance: A Literature Review," *Academy of Management Review* 6 (1981), pp. 655–64; J. M. Nicholas, "The Comparative Impact of Organizational Developments on Hard Criteria Measures," *Academy of Management Review* 7 (1982), pp. 531–42; R. W. Griffen, *Task Design, an Integrative Approach* (Glenview, Ill.: Scott, Foresman, 1984); and Ramon J. Aldag, Steve H. Barr, and Arthur P. Brief, "Measurement of Perceived Task Characteristics," *Psychological Bulletin* 90, no. 3 (1981), pp. 413–31.

[11]Ronald C. Page "The Use of Job Content Information for Compensation and Reward Systems," Paper presented at Academy of Management Meetings, August 1982; and Debra Suhadolnik, Clark Miller, and Ronald Page, *FOCUS Job Analysis/Evaluation System* (Minneapolis, Minn.: Control Data Business Advisors, 1986).

[12]*J. C. Penney General Management Position Questionnaire* (New York: J. C. Penney Company, 1985); *Management Position Description* (Palo Alto, Calif.: Hewlett-Packard, 1983); *3M Management Position Description Questionnaire* (St. Paul, Minn.: 3M, 1985); and *Superior Oil Job Analysis Questionnaire* (Houston, Tex.: Superior Oil Company, 1982).

EXHIBIT 3.5   Personnel Functions, Job Analysis Information, and Results

| | Job Analysis | | |
Function	Information		Result
Recruitment and selection	Required skills, abilities, and experience	→	Selection and promotion standards
Training and development	Tasks, behaviors	→	Training programs
Performance appraisal	Behavior standards or expected results	→	Performance appraisal criteria
Job design and organization development	Tasks, expected results	→	Organization structure
Compensation	Tasks, abilities, skills, behaviors	→	Similarities and differences in the work; job descriptions

---

Employee and manager acceptance of data collected is important and easily overlooked.[13] For example, the analyst may believe that behavioral descriptions adequately describe a job (e.g., coordinate advertising campaigns with marketing group plans), but the jobholders may believe that greater emphasis on the scope of contact (e.g., works with outside clients, prepares reports for vice president of marketing) or the financial responsibility (e.g., budgetary control and approvals) more accurately describes the jobs. No matter how well the rest of the compensation system is designed and administered, if jobholders are dissatisfied with the initial data collected, they are less likely to be satisfied with the resulting structure.

The key issue for managers is still to ensure that the data collected serve the purpose of making compensation decisions and are acceptable to the employees involved. As the flowchart in Exhibit 3.4 indicates, collecting job information is only an interim step, not an end in itself.

WHAT DATA TO COLLECT?

Recommendations on the types of data to collect can range from the job title (word processor I, receptionist, executive secretary) to the frequency (daily, twice daily, as needed) with which specific tasks (answer the phone or open the mail) are performed. Generally, a good job analysis collects sufficient information to adequately identify, define, and describe a job.[14]

---

[13]Luis R. Gomez-Mejia, Ronald C. Page, and Walter W. Tornow, "A Comparison of the Practical Utility of Traditional, Statistical, and Hybrid Job Evaluation Approaches," *Academy of Management Journal* 25, no. 4 (1982), pp. 790–809.

[14]Sidney Gael, *Job Analysis* (San Francisco: Jossey-Bass, 1983); Bemis, Belenky, and Soder, *Job Analysis: An Effective Management Tool;* and Jesse T. Cantrill, "Collecting Job Content Information through Questionnaires," and Thomas S. Roy, Jr., "Collecting Data through Interviews and Observations," both in *Handbook of Wage and Salary Administration,* 2nd ed., ed. Milton L. Rock (New York: McGraw-Hill, 1984).

Identifying a Job.   Data that identify a job include its title, the number of people in the organization who hold this job, and the department in which the job is located. Good job titles will provide information and will not obfuscate. Job families may have similar titles, but titles should be consistent with work level; similar sounding titles at different levels can be confusing. The job may be further identified by number of incumbents, whether or not it is exempt from the Fair Labor Standards Act, where it is located (department, work site), and job number, if any is used.

Defining a Job.   Data here reflect the purpose of the job, why it exists, and how it fits in with other jobs and with overall organization objectives. End results that flow from the satisfactory performance of this job are typically included.

For managerial jobs, statistics on the size of the budget, accountability, and reporting relationships with subordinates and other managers are frequently included. Financial and organizational data are needed to locate a job in the organization. So "defining" may have multiple aspects; what positions and departments are supervised, what functions are the responsibility of this position, and budget and financial responsibilities.

Describing a Job.   There are lists upon lists of suggested data to be gathered to describe a job. Exhibit 3.6 is typical. Notice that there are two main categories of data to describe jobs; those that are job based (content and work characteristics), and those that are employee based (knowledge, prior experience). These two categories are clearly delineated in some of the earliest work on job analysis, which has been refined into functional job analysis.

Functional Job Analysis

The U.S. Department of Labor's (DOL) work on job analysis may be the strongest single influence on job analysis practice in the United States.[15] Certainly, anyone contemplating undertaking job analysis for the first time would be well advised to consult the *Handbook for Analyzing Jobs*. They are also well advised to realize the commitment of resources and personnel required to undertake job analysis as prescribed in the *Handbook*.

The *Handbook* suggests categorizing data as (1) actual work performed (job data) and (2) worker characteristics (employee data). It further refines work performed into three categories:[16]

1. What the worker does in relationship to *data, people,* and *things*.
2. The methods and techniques employed.
3. The materials, products, subject matter, and/or services that result.

---

[15]U.S. Department of Labor, *Handbook for Analyzing Jobs*.

[16]U.S. Civil Service Commission, *Job Analysis: Developing and Documenting Data* (Washington, D.C.: Bureau of Intergovernmental Personnel Programs, 1973); Sidney Fine, *Functional Job Analysis Scales: A Desk Aid* (Kalamazoo, Mich.: Upjohn Institute for Employment Research, 1973); Fine and Wiley, *Introduction to Functional Job Analysis*.

Exhibit 3.6   Typical Data Collected for Job Analysis

Data Related to Job

Job content/context factors

Duties	Communications network
Functions	Output (e.g., reports, analyses)
Tasks	Working conditions
Activities	Time allocation
Performance criteria	Roles (e.g., negotiator, monitor, leader)
Critical incidents	

Work characteristics

Risk or exposure	Dependence/independence
Constraints	Pattern or cycle
Choices	Time pressure
Conflicting demands	Fragmentation
Origin of activities	Sustained attention
Expected/unexpected	Time orientation (short or long)

Data Related to Employee

Employee characteristics

Professional/technical knowledge	Managerial skills
Prior experience	Bargaining skills
Manual skills	Leadership skills
Verbal skills	Consulting skills
Written skills	Human relations skills
Quantitative skills	Aptitudes
Mechanical skills	Values
Conceptual skills	Style

Interpersonal relationships

Internal	External
Boss	Suppliers
Other superiors	Customers
Peers	Regulatory
Subordinates	Consultants
Other juniors	Professional/industry
	Community
	Union/employee group

Functional job analysis (FJA), widely used in the public sector, emphasizes the worker and relates what the worker does to the goals and objectives of the organization. Although few private sector employers use it, all practices reflect FJA's influence.[17]

Most researchers subdivide worker characteristics into two groups, one concerned with the worker's behavior on the job, and the other with the underlying abilities required to make such behavior possible.[18]

---

[17]Ron Ash, "Job Elements for Task Clusters: Arguments for Using Multi-Methodological Approaches to Job Analysis and a Demonstration of Their Utility," *Public Personnel Management Journal,* June 1982, pp. 80–90.

[18]Robert J. Harvey, "Job Analysis," in *Handbook of Industrial and Organizational Psychology,* ed. M. D. Dunnette and L. M. Hough (Palo Alto, Calif.: Consulting Psychologists Press 1991).

So we essentially have three categories of information to consider: work data (what tasks are done), worker data (what behaviors occur), and ability data (what abilities underlie the behaviors and task performance). These categories can be confusing because they all look at the same thing—a worker doing a job—and take different approaches to describe what is happening. Perhaps some examples will clarify the differences.

Task (or Work) Data

Task data involve the elemental units of work, subparts of a job, with emphasis on the purpose of each task. An excerpt from a job analysis questionnaire that collects task data is shown in Exhibit 3.7. The inventory describes communication in terms of actual tasks,

EXHIBIT 3.7   Communications: Task-Based Data

1. Mark the circle in the "Do This" column for tasks that you currently perform.
2. At the end of the task list, write in any unlisted tasks that you currently perform.
3. Rate each task that you perform for relative time spent by marking the appropriate circle in the "Time Spent" column.

   Please use a No. 2 pencil only and fill all circles completely

Time spent in current position

Do This / Very small amount / Much below average / Below average / Slightly below average / About average / Slightly above average / Above average / Much above average / Very large amount

PERFORM COMMUNICATIONS ACTIVITIES

Obtain technical information.

421. Read technical publications about competitive products.
422. Read technical publications to keep current on industry.
423. Attend required, recommended, or job-related courses and/or seminars.
424. Study existing operating systems/programs to gain/maintain familiarity with them.
425. Perform literature searches necessary to the development of products.
426. Communicate with system software group to see how their recent changes impact current projects.
427. Study and evaluate state-of-the-art techniques to remain competitive and/or lead the field.
428. Attend industry standards meetings.

Exchange technical information.

429. Interface with coders to verify that the software design is being implemented as specified.
430. Consult with co-workers to exchange ideas and techniques.
431. Consult with members of other technical groups within the company to exchange new ideas and techniques.
432. Interface with support consultants or organizations to clarify software design or courseware content.
433. Attend meetings to review project status.
434. Attend team meetings to review implementation strategies.
435. Discuss department plans and objectives with manager.

for example, "read technical publications" and "consult with co-workers." The other distinguishing characteristic is the emphasis on output, or objective of the task; for example, "read technical publications to keep current on industry" and "consult with co-workers to exchange ideas and techniques." Task data reveal the actual work performed and its purpose or outcome.[19]

Behavioral Data

This data approach describes jobs in terms of the behaviors that occur. Exhibit 3.8 shows such behavioral observations, again concerned with "communications." This time, the questions focus on verbs that describe the human behavior (e.g., advising, negotiating, persuading). Exhibit 3.8 is from the Position Analysis Questionnaire (PAQ).[20] The PAQ groups work information into seven basic factors: information input, mental processes, work output, relationships with other persons, job context, other job characteristics, and general dimensions. With the PAQ, similarities and differences among jobs are described in terms of these seven factors, rather than in terms of specific aspects unique to each job.[21] The communications behavior in Exhibit 3.8 is part of the "relationships with other persons" factor. Let us compare the PAQ's approach to communications to the task inventory's approach in Exhibit 3.7. Item 105 on the PAQ: "Nonroutine information exchange (the giving and/or receiving of *job-related* information of a nonroutine or unusual nature)" is probably similar to item 430 on the task inventory: "Consult with co-workers to exchange ideas and techniques." Both are getting at the same aspect of work, by different approaches. But lest you think Exhibit 3.7 offers the beauty of simplicity, note that item 431 lists "consult with members of other technical groups . . . to exchange new ideas and techniques" and item 432 lists "interface with support consultants to clarify . . . design." In fact, the task inventory from which Exhibit 3.7 is excerpted contains 250 items and covers only systems and analyst jobs, whereas the behavioral data in Exhibit 3.8 are from an inventory of 194 items, whose developers claim it can be used to analyze *all* jobs. New task-based questions need to be designed for each new set of jobs, whereas behaviors, at least as defined in the PAQ's seven factors, may be applied across all jobs.

---

[19]Ramon J. Aldag, Steve H. Barr, and Arthur P. Brief, "Measurement of Perceived Task Characteristics," *Psychological Bulletin* 90, no. 3 (1981), pp. 415–31; and Page, "The Use of Job Content Information."

[20]Much of the developmental and early applications of the PAQ was done in the 1960s and 1970s. See, for example, McCormick, *Job Analysis* (New York: AMACOM, 1979); McCormick, "Job and Task Analysis"; McCormick et al., *A Study of Job Characteristics and Job Dimensions as Based on the Position Analysis Questionnaire* (West Lafayette, Ind.: Occupational Research Center, Purdue University, 1969); P. R. Jeanneret and R. C. Meacham, "A Study of Job Characteristics and Job Dimensions as Based on the Position Analysis Questionnaire (PAQ)," *Journal of Applied Psychology* 56 (1972), pp. 347–68; and Mecham et al., *The Use of Data Based on the Position Analysis Questionnaire* (West Lafayette, Ind.: Occupational Research Center, Purdue University, 1969). The PAQ is distributed by the University Book Store, 360 West State St., West Lafayette, IN 47906. For more recent discussions, see *PAQ* Newsletter 1990 and 1991.

[21]R. C. Mecham, E. J. McCormick, and P. R. Jeanneret, *Technical Manual for the Position Analysis Questionnaire (PAQ) System* (Logan, Utah: PAQ Services, 1977).

EXHIBIT 3.8 Communications: Behavioral-Based Data

Section 4   Relationships with Other Persons

This section deals with different aspects of interaction between people involved in various kinds of work.

Code Importance to this Job (1)	
N	Does not apply
1	Very minor
2	Low
3	Average
4	High
5	Extreme

4.1   Communications

Rate the following in terms of how *important* the activity is to the completion of the job. Some jobs may involve several or all of the items in this section.

4.1.1   Oral (communicating by speaking)

99 ____   Advising (dealing with individuals in order to counsel and/or guide them with regard to problems that may be resolved by legal, financial, scientific, technical, clinical, spiritual, and/or other professional principles)

100 ____   Negotiating (dealing with others in order to reach an agreement or solution, for example, labor bargaining, diplomatic relations, etc.)

101 ____   Persuading (dealing with others in order to influence them toward some action or point of view, for example, selling, political campaigning, etc.)

102 ____   Instructing (the teaching of knowledge or skills, in either an informal or a formal manner, to others, for example, a public school teacher, a machinist teaching an apprentice, etc.)

103 ____   Interviewing (conducting interviews directed toward some specific objective, for example, interviewing job applicants, census taking, etc.)

104 ____   Routine information exchange: job related (the giving and/or receiving of *job-related* information of a routine nature, for example, ticket agent, taxicab dispatcher, receptionist, etc.)

105 ____   Nonroutine information exchange (the giving and/or receiving of *job-related* information of a nonroutine or unusual nature, for example, professional committee meetings, engineers discussing new product design, etc.)

106 ____   Public speaking (making speeches or formal presentations before relatively large audiences, for example, political addresses, radio/TV broadcasting, delivering a sermon, etc.)

4.1.2   Written (communicating by written/printed material)

107 ____   Writing (for example, writing or dictating letters, reports, etc., writing copy for ads, writing newspaper articles, etc.; do *not* include transcribing activities described in item 4.3, but only activities in which the incumbent creates the written material)

4.1.3   Other Communications

108 ____   Signaling (communicating by some type of signal, for example, hand signals, semaphore, whistles, horns, bells, lights, etc.)

109 ____   Code communications (telegraph, cryptography, etc.)

SOURCE: E. J. McCormick, P. R. Jeanneret, and R. C. Mecham, *Position Analysis Questionnaire,* copyright © 1969 by Purdue Research Foundation, West Lafayette, Ind. 47907. Reprinted with permission.

While the developers claim simplicity some evidence suggests that the PAQ's seven factors are simply too generally defined for pay purposes.[22] These functions seem to emphasize similarities in the jobs and are less sensitive to differences. Recall that the ability to distinguish among jobs is a key requirement of any job analysis. Nevertheless, employers do use both task inventories and the PAQ behavior inventories to analyze jobs and establish pay structures.

Abilities Data

Abilities data capture the knowledge and skills a worker must possess to satisfactorily perform the job. One taxonomy that includes (1) psychomotor abilities, (2) physical proficiency abilities, and (3) cognitive abilities forms the foundation for the ability-based job analysis.[23] AT&T, in conjunction with the Communication Workers of America (CWA) and other unions, developed a set of 16 abilities required in nonmanagerial work at AT&T, shown in Exhibit 3.9.[24] "Expression" and "comprehension," the first two factors, probably correspond most closely to the communication aspect we looked at with task and behavior data. Exhibit 3.10 excerpts AT&T's measurement of comprehension abilities required on the job. Note that the behavioral descriptors used to anchor the scales for oral comprehension (e.g., "understand a McDonald's hamburger commercial," "understand instructions for a sport," and "understand a lecture on navigating in space") are not work-specific but are drawn from daily life outside the job. The AT&T–CWA project was not put into practice; yet it is noteworthy because it represents an early effort at developing a skill-based approach to designing pay structures. We will discuss this approach later in this chapter.

The "communication" scales shown in Exhibits 3.7, 3.8, and 3.10 illustrate the differences in task, behavior, and ability data. They vary in the way they describe a job. Thus, it is not surprising the varying approaches to job analysis may yield different results. One study examined seven supervisory jobs in a chemical processing plant using all three types of job analysis data.[25] Using the same statistical procedures on all three

---

[22]E. T. Cornelius III, T. J. Carron, and M. M. Collins, "Job Analysis Models and Job Classification," *Personnel Psychology* 32 (1979), pp. 693–708; also see R. W. Lissitz, J. L. Mendoza, C. J. Huberty, and V. H. Markos, "Some Ideas on a Methodology for Determining Job Similarities/Differences," *Personnel Psychology* 32 (1979); and JoAnn Lee and Jorge Mendoza, "A Comparison of Techniques Which Test for Job Difference," *Personnel Psychology* 34 (1981), pp. 731–48.

[23]E. A. Fleishman, *Structure and Measurement of Physical Fitness* (Englewood Cliffs, N.J.: Prentice Hall, 1964); Fleishman, "Toward a Taxonomy of Human Performance," *American Psychologist* 30 (1975), pp. 1017–32; Fleishman, "Evaluating Physical Abilities Required by Jobs," *The Personal Administrator* 24 (1979), pp. 82–92; Fleishman "On the Relation between Abilities, Learning, and Human Performance," *American Psychologist* 27 (1972), pp. 1017–32.

[24]Ken Ross, "Occupational Job Evaluation Study" (Basking Ridge, N.J.: AT&T, 1983); and Ronnie J. Staw and Lorel E. Foged, "The Limits of Job Evaluation to Achieve Comparable Worth," Paper presented at Atlantic Economic Conference, Montreal, Canada, October 11–14, 1984.

[25]Cornelius et al., "Job Analysis Models"; and Jack E. Smith and Milton D. Hakel, "Convergence among Data Sources, Response Bias, and Reliability and Validity of a Structured Job Analysis Questionnaire," *Personnel Psychology* 32, no. 4 (1979), pp. 677–92.

EXHIBIT 3.9   AT&T–CWA Job Analysis Factors: Abilities-Based

---

1. *Expression* is speaking and/or writing in words, sentences, or numbers so others will understand. It is measured in terms of the complexity of the information being expressed as well as the comprehension ability of the receiver of the information.

2. *Comprehension* is understanding spoken and/or written words, sentences, or numbers. It is measured in terms of the complexity of the information being received as well as the quality of the information being received.

3. *Fact Finding* is obtaining or selecting pertinent information through observation, research, or questioning. It includes organizing and combining different pieces of information into meaningful order to identify a problem. It does not include the application of this information to solve the problem. An unknown is the key element in fact finding.

4. *Systems Reasoning* is making decisions that involve the selection and application of appropriate business resources or usage of relevant facts to solve identified problems or to achieve a desired result. This is based on knowledge and understanding of products and services, materials, policies, practices, and procedures.

5. *Mathematics* is the selection and application of mathematical methods or procedures to solve problems or to achieve desired results. These systems range from basic arithmetic computations to the most complex statistical techniques or other applications such as occur in physics or engineering problems.

6. *Adaptability* is the need to adapt one's behavior to changing or unusual circumstances to achieve a desired result. This includes changes in personal interactions or work situations.

7. *Persuasion* is influencing the behaviors or actions of others. The changes in others' behaviors or actions may not be observed immediately.

8. *Mental Demand* is mental effort associated with attending to or performing a task in the presence of distractions or work frustrations. Distractions and work frustrations arise from boredom, overlapping demands, exacting deadlines and output standards, lack of latitude to adapt behavior, discouraging circumstances, repeated unsuccessful attempts, and nonemployee controlled work flow.

9. *Physical Demand* is physical effort associated with activities such as handling weights, repetition of work motions, maintenance of difficult work positions, or exposure to unpleasant surroundings.

10. *Safety Skills* measures the adherence to prescribed safety and personal security practices in the performance of tasks involving exposure to hazard or risk in the work environment.

11. *Electrical/Electronic Knowledge* is the knowledge and application of the principles of electricity, electronics, electronic logic, and integrated transmission technologies such as lasers and fiber optics. This includes understanding of circuits, their component parts and how they work together, and understanding the output from devices or meters that register or display information related to these systems.

12. *Mechanical Knowledge* is the knowledge and application of principles of how mechanical equipment such as gears, pulleys, motors, and hydraulics works. It includes the operation, repair or maintenance of systems. It *does not* include knowledge of tools and their uses.

13. *Tools and Uses* is the knowledge, appropriate selection and application of hand tools, office machines, mechanical and electrical tools (test sets). This does not include keyboard devices.

14. *Graphics* is reading, interpreting and/or preparing graphic representations of information such as maps, plans, drawings, blueprints, diagrams, and timing/flow charts. It includes the preparation of visual artwork.

15. *Coding* is reading and/or writing and interpreting coded information. Codes may be identified by the fact that the ideas or concepts they represent may be translated, expanded, or expressed in English.

16. *Keyboard Skills* is the operation of keyboard devices such as typewriters, data terminals, calculators, and operator equipment.

EXHIBIT 3.10   Communications: Abilities-Based Data

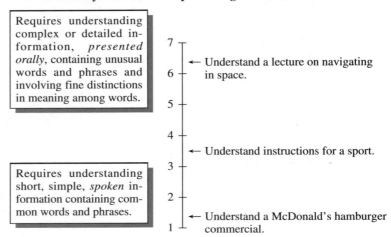

ORAL COMPREHENSION
This is the ability to understand spoken English words and sentences.

Requires understanding complex or detailed information, *presented orally*, containing unusual words and phrases and involving fine distinctions in meaning among words.

7

6 ← Understand a lecture on navigating in space.

5

4

3 ← Understand instructions for a sport.

Requires understanding short, simple, *spoken* information containing common words and phrases.

2

1 ← Understand a McDonald's hamburger commercial.

---

data sets, they found that different sets yielded different results. In other words, the type of data collected will affect the results. This research provides sound advice for the compensation professional: The purpose of the analysis dictates the nature of the data to collect. Thus, if you intend to design training programs, according to Exhibit 3.5, you'll need to collect task and behavioral data. If developing a pay structure, then all three types of data may be useful.

Other research has identified another factor that affects the results of job analysis: the level of analysis.

Level of Analysis

The nature of the data collected can be considered in terms of a hierarchy, shown in Exhibit 3.11. Some items of the hierarchy are the same as the types of data we just discussed. In the hierarchy, tasks represent a grouping of elements or behaviors into a basic accomplishment or duty. For example, elements such as "gathering time cards and using calculators to multiply hours worked by hourly wage" are combined into a task, "calculating employee wages for time cards." Moving up the hierarchy, tasks are grouped into positions that constitute different individuals performing the same group of tasks in a particular organization. In the illustration in Exhibit 3.11, there are three individuals who hold a Bookkeeper I job in firm A. Jobs similar across several firms (bookkeeper,

---

EXHIBIT 3.11   Levels of Analysis

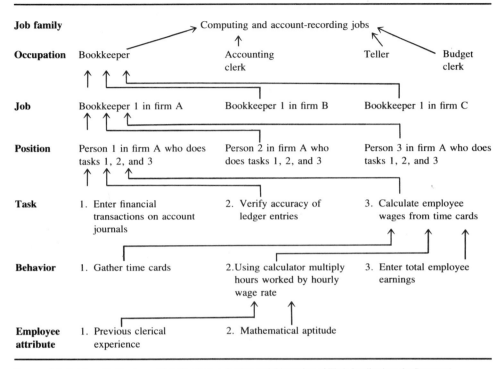

Job family		Computing and account-recording jobs		
Occupation	Bookkeeper	Accounting clerk	Teller	Budget clerk
Job	Bookkeeper 1 in firm A	Bookkeeper 1 in firm B	Bookkeeper 1 in firm C	
Position	Person 1 in firm A who does tasks 1, 2, and 3	Person 2 in firm A who does tasks 1, 2, and 3	Person 3 in firm A who does tasks 1, 2, and 3	
Task	1. Enter financial transactions on account journals	2. Verify accuracy of ledger entries	3. Calculate employee wages from time cards	
Behavior	1. Gather time cards	2. Using calculator multiply hours worked by hourly wage rate	3. Enter total employee earnings	
Employee attribute	1. Previous clerical experience	2. Mathematical aptitude		

SOURCE: Adapted from K. Pearlman, "Job Families: A Review and Discussion of Their Implications for Personnel Selection," *Psychological Bulletin* 87 (1980), pp. 1–28. Copyright 1980 by the American Psychological Association. Adapted by permission of the author.

accounting clerk, teller) are in turn considered to belong to an occupation. Occupations could be grouped into a job family such as a "computing and account recording job family."

What does all this have to do with making pay decisions? The level or unit of analysis chosen may influence the decision of whether the work is similar or dissimilar. At the occupation level, bookkeepers, tellers, and accounting clerks are considered to be similar; yet at the job level, these three are considered dissimilar. Hence, the specificity of the work information to be collected is a critical decision. An analogy might be looking at two grains of salt under a microscope versus looking at them as part of a serving of french fries. If job data suggest that jobs are similar, then the jobs must be paid equally; if jobs are different, they can be paid differently. Whether or not jobs are substantially similar has been a main focus of much discrimination litigation and thus takes on financial meaning beyond concerns for internal consistency.

GENERIC JOBS: FLEXIBILITY VERSUS COSTS AND BENEFITS OF JOB ANALYSIS

In practice, the amount and detail of information collected for job analysis vary considerably. Most employers use position or job level data, arguing that all the detailed data on tasks and behaviors are not necessary when determining wages. Further, if job analysis is required, then people and resources are required to undertake it. The time and expense to collect data are unjustified in comparison to the benefits received. A growing number of employers are increasing flexibility by reducing the number of separate job classifications used. New United Motors Manufacturing, Inc. (NUMMI), a joint venture between General Motors and Toyota, went from 120 separate jobs to four levels of technicians to perform all the tasks necessary to assemble automobiles.[26] The result is broad, generic descriptions that cover a large number of related tasks akin to the occupation level in Exhibit 3.11. Two employees working in the same broadly defined jobs may be doing entirely different sets of related tasks. But for pay purposes, they are doing work of equal value. Employees working in very broadly defined jobs can easily be switched to other tasks that fall within the broad range of the same job, without the bureaucratic burden of making job transfer requests and wage adjustments. Thus, employees can more easily be matched to changes in the work flow. However, such broad, generic descriptions of work leave employers open to challenge regarding potential inequities. At what point is work similar or different for pay purposes?

On the other hand, narrowly defined jobs leave employers (or taxpayers) footing the bill for unneeded employees, as in Philadelphia, where it takes three city employees to change a light bulb. Thanks to that city's union contracts, a building mechanic removes the light panel, an electrician replaces the bulb, and a custodian cleans up any dust and debris. For employees to perform work out of their job descriptions requires extra pay.

So where does this leave us? What data should be collected and what level of analysis should be used? There is no clear-cut answer. It depends on the situation and the resources available. But the more specific and detailed the data, the more likely they are to capture differences in the work and adequately describe the work content. Whether such detailed information is worth the expense involved depends on the circumstances in the organization. Clearly, detailed data may justify pay differences to a skeptical judge presiding over a pay discrimination suit. Yet more broadly defined jobs with generic titles and descriptions offer increased flexibility in work assignments. But paying equally for substantially different work may eventually lead to employee dissatisfaction. Herein lies one of the continual challenges to compensation managers.

---

[26]John F. Krafcik, "High Performance Manufacturing: An International Study of Auto Assembly Practice" (Working paper, International Motor Vehicle Program, MIT, January 1988); Haruo Shimada, "The Perceptions and the Reality of Japanese Industrial Relations," in *The Management Challenge: Japanese Views*, ed. L. Thurow (Cambridge, Mass.: MIT Press, 1985); and John Paul MacDuffie, "The Japanese Auto Transplants: Challenges to Conventional Wisdom," *ILR Report*, Fall 1988, pp. 12–18.

HOW CAN THE DATA BE COLLECTED?

After having decided on the purpose, level, and the nature of the data, the next major decision is the method(s) of collecting it. A wide variety of methods exists; the most common ones are described in Exhibit 3.12. We will combine these methods into two basic types: conventional and qualitative.

Conventional Methods

A common data collection method involves an analyst using a questionnaire to interview job incumbents and supervisors. The questionnaires and interviews are structured to achieve a uniform response format. The approach requires considerable involvement of employees and supervisors, which increases their understanding of the process, provides an opportunity to clarify their work relationships and expectations, and increases the likelihood that they will accept the results. Usually, an analyst translates the data collected

---

EXHIBIT 3.12   Data Collection Methods

Method	*Descriptions*	*Characteristics*
Questionnaire	Using standardized form, jobholders and/or supervisors describe the work. Data can be gathered either through mailed survey or through individual interview.	Variations include combining questionnaire with individual or group interview. As with all questionnaires, responses may be incomplete or difficult to interpret, a limitation minimized by combining with interviews. Standard format eases mathematical analysis. Interviews, however, may be time consuming, and become more difficult with workers at multiple locations.
Checklist	Jobholders and/or supervisors check items on a task inventory that apply to their particular job. Check list can be tailor-made or purchased.	Depends on recognition rather than recall. Cheap, easy to administer and analyze. However, care must be taken that all significant aspects of work are included in the list.
Diary	Jobholders record activities as they are performed.	Has the advantage of collecting data as events occur, but it is often difficult to obtain continuous and consistent entries. Obtained data is not in a standardized format.
Observation	Analyst records perceptions formed watching the work being done by one or more jobholders.	The absence of preconceived structures or artificial constraints can lead to richer data. Each job can be studied in any depth desired. However, validity and reliability of data can be a problem, and the relative emphasis of certain work aspects is dependent on the acuteness of the analyst's perceptions. Also, the observation of employee behavior by an analyst influences it.
Activity sampling	Observations are made at random intervals.	
Activity matrix	Respondents identify time spent in relation to tasks and products or services.	Data collected is amenable to quantitative analysis, and is highly adaptable to other human resource management needs; however, another job analysis procedure must be used initially to develop the matrix.
Critical incidents	Behaviorally oriented incidents describe key job behaviors. Analyst determines degree of each type of behavior present or absent in each job.	Analysis clearly based on concrete behavior. Scales require some expertise to develop.

to a summary job description sheet. Often, both incumbents and supervisors are given an opportunity to modify and approve the job description; this helps ensure its acceptance. In some cases the preparation of these description sheets is left to the supervisors and incumbents, and the analyst role becomes one of trainer/facilitator. The analysts are trained (either formally or through trial and error) in verbal style and form to ensure that description sheets are uniform. Some trainers go so far as to specify "correct" verbs and adjectives to use.[27] Appendix 3–A contains a step-by-step procedure for conducting a conventional job analysis plus a conventional job analysis questionnaire.

Conventional methods place considerable reliance on the analyst's abilities to understand the work performed and to translate it. Certain safeguards, such as multiple approvals (by supervisors and incumbents), may help minimize the difficulties inherent in translating the results of questionnaires and personal discussions into an accurate representation of the job.

In a review of job analysis, McCormick points out that "of the various deficiencies of conventional job analysis procedures, probably the sharpest criticism is that the typical essays of job activities *are not* adequately descriptive of the jobs in question." After granting the positive contribution of obtaining work-related data through conventional methods, he observes in an artful understatement,"They probably ha[ve] not generally benefitted from . . . systematic, scientific approaches."[28] Another critic is more direct: "conventional job analysis . . . [is] floundering in a morass of semantic confusion."[29]

Reducing subjectivity in job analysis is the primary goal of quantitative job analysis. The critical advantages of quantitative job analysis over conventional approaches are that quantitative analysis lends itself to statistical analysis, is documentable and quantifiable, and *may* be more objective. Additionally, a computerized job analysis offers the promise of relieving much of the drudgery of collecting and translating job data, though to date that promise has not been realized.

Quantitative Methods

Inventories are the core of all quantitative job analysis. Inventories, illustrated in Exhibits 3.7, 3.8, and 3.10, are questionnaires in which tasks, behaviors, and abilities are listed. Each item is assessed, usually by both job incumbents and supervisors, in terms of time spent, importance to the overall job, and/or learning time.[30] Systematic assessment doc-

---

[27]R. T. Henderson, *Compensation Management,* 4th ed. (Reston, Va.: Reston Publishing, 1985).

[28]McCormick, "Job and Task Analysis."

[29]Quoted in Robert Harvey, "Job Analysis," *Handbook of Industrial and Organizational Psychology*, vol. 2, ed. M. D. Dunnette and L. Hough (Palo Alto, Calif.: Consulting Psychologists Press, 1992).

[30]J. E. Morsh, "Job Analysis in the United States Air Force," *Personnel Psychology* 17, no. 17 (1964), pp. 7–17; J. E. Morsh, M. Joyce Giorgia, and J. M. Madden, "A Job Analysis of a Complex Utilization Field—The R&D Management Officer" (Personnel Research Laboratory, Aerospace Medical Division, Air Force Systems Command, 1965); J. N. Mosel, "The Domain of Worker Functions as a Partially Ordered Set," Paper presented at American Psychological Association Meetings, Philadelphia, 1963; and A. J. Siegel and D. G. Shultz, *Post-Training Performance Criterion Development and Application: A Comparative Multidimensional Scaling Analysis of the Task Performed by Naval Aviation Electronics Technicians at Two Job Levels* (Wayne, Pa.: Applied Psychological Services, 1964).

uments decisions and results, and the resulting data can be subjected to further statistical analysis.

Usually a compensation manager must decide whether to buy a commercially available, predeveloped inventory or to develop a quantitative inventory tailored for a specific organization.[31] Not surprisingly, consulting firms stand ready to offer predeveloped plans as well as the experience and analytical skills necessary to design a tailored plan. More details on some of these plans may be found through the references.[32]

Without question, the PAQ is the best known and most generally used quantitative job analysis.[33] Exhibit 3.8 is an example.

The Position Information Questionnaire (PIQ) is an example of a questionnaire designed specifically to collect job information to support compensation decisions. A copy is included as Appendix 3–B. Developed by TPF&C with the assistance of its clients at Bank of America, 3M, and Campbell Soup, PIQ is similar to products of several consulting firms (e.g., Wyatt and Hay). PIQ is clearly more structured and systematic than the conventional approach shown in Appendix 3–A. However, it is not designed to serve other purposes of job analysis such as hiring or training decisions.[34]

Predeveloped inventories offer the advantage of having been pretested, which avoids substantial expense and lead time required in inventory design. But a major limitation of most of these predeveloped plans is that they are not tailored to particular job families or organizations. Consequently, their questions may be too general to be useful in identifying differences in specific jobs.

Tailoring a Plan

Rather than adopting an existing inventory, some employers opt to tailor one to their specific work and conditions. Several consulting organizations market technical expertise to assist these employers.

However, development costs of custom-designed inventories may exceed the returns. Our experience is that employers using quantitative job analysis usually opt to modify

---

[31]R. E. Christal and J. J. Weissmuller, *New Comprehensive Occupational Data Analysis Programs (CODAP) for Analyzing Task Factor Information,* AHFRL Interim Professional Paper 7R-76-3 (Lackland Air Force, Tex.: Air Force Human Resources Laboratory, 1976); and M. H. Trattner, "Task Analysis in the Design of Three Concurrent Validity Studies of the Professional and Administrative Career Examination," *Personnel Psychology* 32 (1979), pp. 109–19. Contact the Personnel Research Division of the Human Resources Laboratory, Lackland Air Force Base, Texas, for more information on CODAP.

[32]Information on custom-designed quantitative job analysis plans can be obtained from TPF&C, New York, Minneapolis, San Francisco, and other locations; Personnel Decisions Research Institute, Minneapolis; Sibson & Co., Chicago, and other locations; and Wyatt & Company, New York, Detroit, San Francisco, and other locations.

[33]Information on the PAQ is available from PAQ Services, P.O. Box 3337, Logan, Utah 84321, (801) 752-5698.

[34]The reader interested in additional predeveloped approaches should read Robert Harvey, "Job Analysis," in *Handbook of Industrial and Organizational Psychology,* vol. 2. Other approaches include Executive Checklist (Excel) Position Description Questionnaire (PDQ). Few have been used for compensation decisions, however.

existing predeveloped approaches to fit their situation. The 3M modification of PIQ is an example.[35]

Computerized Analysis

Computer-assisted job analysis ranges from using optical scanners to enter data, to scoring responses, to generating generic job descriptions. The promise of computerized job analysis is that it reduces the demands of a highly labor intensive activity—job analysis—and permits employees and line managers to complete job analysis and descriptions. Most major consulting firms have job description software. However, the promise of automated systems has yet to be fully realized. Some managers are not sufficiently computer literate to handle the "friendly" software. Automation often requires more highly trained employees to achieve its full advantage.[36]

WHO IS INVOLVED IN JOB ANALYSIS?

Some employers view the job analyst as an entry-level position and adopt the "learn-by-doing" approach: Analyzing work provides a thorough introduction to the company, and after 6 to 12 months, the analyst is ready for a new job assignment. In spite of real-world practice, most textbook writers continue to insist that the analysis should be done by someone who is thoroughly familiar with the organization, its work flow, and its policies and objectives.[37]

Who Collects the Data?

The choice of who collects the data is usually among an analyst, the supervisors, and/or the jobholders.[38] Some firms require the supervisor to perform the analysis, since supervisors are assumed to be knowledgeable, and their involvement may help increase their understanding of exactly what their subordinates do. Obvious shortcomings of this arrangement include the possibility of limited knowledge of the actual tasks, skills, and behaviors required on the job. The authors' experience suggests that the employees actually performing the work need to be involved in the process as a way to ensure accuracy and acceptability of resulting pay structures. But not everyone agrees; Brandt says that job descriptions written by incumbents are unsatisfactory because they don't use the proper

---

[35]For an excellent example and guide to developing a tailored inventory, see Walter W. Tornow, "An Integrated Approach to Job Analysis and Job Evaluation," Paper presented at Conference on Job Analysis, Institute of Industrial Relations, University of California, Berkeley, 1979. Also see Harvey, "Job Analysis."

[36]For an up-to-date inventory of available software, see Richard Franzreb, ed., *The Personnel Software Census* (Roseville, Calif.: Advanced Personnel Systems, 1990); and *Compensation Software* and *Benefit Software*, both published by the American Compensation Association, Scottsdale, Ariz.

[37]Harvey, "Job Analysis," pp. 105–6.

[38]R. Harvey and J. Lozada-Larson, "Influence of Amount of Job Descriptive Information on Job Analysis Rating Accuracy," *Journal of Applied Psychology* 73 (1988), pp. 457–61.

words to facilitate comparisons among jobs. He even argues against incumbent approval of a proposed job description, saying this is a prerogative of management.[39]

Regardless of who collects the data, some training in the process seems to be a requirement.[40] In the absence of more research, publicly available materials from the Department of Labor may be of value in developing training programs.

Who Provides the Data?

The decision on the source of the data (jobholders, supervisors, and/or analyst) hinges on how to ensure consistent, accurate, and acceptable data.[41] Expertise about the work resides with the jobholders and the supervisors; hence, they are the principle sources. For key managerial/professional jobs, supervisors "two levels above" have also been suggested as valuable sources since they may have a more cosmic view on how jobs fit in the overall organization. In other instances, subordinates and employees in other jobs that interface with the job under study are also involved. The number of incumbents per job from which to collect data probably varies with the stability of the job. An ill-defined or changing job will require either the involvement of more respondents, or a more careful selection of respondents. Obviously, the more people involved, the more time-consuming and expensive the process.

Finally, the support of top management is absolutely essential. They must be alerted to the cost and time-consuming nature of job analysis. Some of the questions for top management include:

- Does top management understand what is involved in performing job analysis?
- Does management understand the risks involved in making pay structure decisions without collecting data on the work performed?
- Have all the time and cost considerations been explored? Are they understood and approved?
- Is it understood that changes may be recommended as a result of the analysis? Has the potential nature of these changes been discussed prior to undertaking job analysis?

The vital importance of employee and operating management involvement has been repeatedly emphasized. This involvement may take several forms, ranging from active participation in describing their own and/or subordinates' work to serving on compensation task forces or committees directly responsible for the design and development of job analysis procedures. Even those employees not directly involved need to be kept informed

---

[39]Alfred R. Brandt, "Describing Hourly Jobs," in *Handbook of Wage and Salary Administration,* ed. M. Rock (New York: McGraw-Hill, 1984).

[40]Harvey, "Job Analysis."

[41]Samuel B. Green and Thomas Stutzman, "An Evaluation of Methods to Select Respondents to Structured Job-Analysis Questionnaires," *Personnel Psychology,* Autumn 1986, pp. 543–64; and Edwin T. Cornelius III, Angelo S. DeNisi, and Allyn Blencoe, "Expert and Naive Raters Using the PAQ? Does It Matter?" *Personnel Psychology* 37 (June 1984), pp. 453–64.

as to the purposes and progress of all the activity. Employees will guess at the purpose of this work, and it seems only sound compensation practice to help make it an educated guess. Top managers will constantly question the expenses associated with what appears to be another burdensome personnel practice.

IS JOB ANALYSIS USEFUL?

Job analysis is the Rodney Dangerfield of managing compensation: It gets no respect.[42] It is time-consuming, expensive, and difficult to relate to the bottom line. Yet without it, the work relatedness of pay structures is open to challenge and difficult to ensure.

Job analysis procedures, whether conventional or quantitative, involve a high degree of judgment. It is important to consider the comparative usefulness of job analysis methods, particularly in terms of their reliability, validity, acceptability, and costs.

Reliability

Reliability is the consistency of the results obtained. Are the results (whether the work is similar or dissimilar) the same regardless of who is involved (supervisors, incumbents, analysts, consultants) and what methods are used?

Several studies have compared employee-supervisor agreement on work content.[43] They present a mixed picture of the reliability of job analysis. Employees and supervisors often differ in how they view the distribution of time among tasks, the skills required to perform the work, and the difficulties of the tasks performed. In one study, employees did not report 30 percent of the tasks supervisors said were part of their jobs.[44] Obviously, employees and supervisors have different views of the job content. Different analysts using the same quantitative methods on the same jobs tend to get the same results. However, even job incumbents may have different perceptions and definitions of the same work. For example, employees who have been on the job a long time may change it by adopting shortcuts and new routines.[45] All these factors may influence the job analysis results.

---

[42]Harvey, "Job Analysis."

[43]Other examples of early studies include H. H. Meyer, "Comparison of Foreman and General Foreman Conceptions of the Foreman's Job Responsibility," *Personnel Psychology* 12 (1959), pp. 445–52; A. P. O'Reilly, "Skill Requirements: Supervisor-Subordinate Conflict," *Personnel Psychology* 26 (1973), pp. 75–80; J. T. Hazel, J. M. Madden, and R. E. Christal, "Agreement between Worker-Supervisor Descriptions on the Worker's Job," *Journal of Industrial Psychology* 2 (1964), pp. 71–79.

[44]Robert Harvey, "Incumbent vs. Superior Perception of Jobs," Presentation at SIOP Conference, Miami, 1990.

[45]Charles A. O'Reilly III and David F. Caldwell, "The Impact of Normative Social Influence and Cohesiveness on Task Perceptions and Attitudes: A Social Information Processing Approach," *Journal of Occupational Psychology* (September 1985), pp. 193–206; D. Caldwell and C. A. O'Reilly III, "Task Perceptions and Job Satisfaction: A Question of Causality," *Journal of Applied Psychology* 67, no. 3 (1982), pp. 361–69; Kenneth N. Wexley and Stanley B. Silverman, "An Examination of Differences between Managerial Effectiveness and Response Patterns on a Structured Job Analysis Questionnaire," *Journal of Applied Psychology* 63, no. 5 (1978), pp. 646–49.

Conventional job analysis does not usually lend itself to formal reliability analysis because of the narrative and unstructured output. This imprecision and obscure structure make reliability a serious issue for conventional methods. But even quantitative methods have problems. The high reliability measures attributed to the PAQ, for example, are probably the result of inadequate statistical analysis. The high number of "does not exist (as part of this job)" responses may yield false statistics that paint an overly optimistic picture of the questionnaire's reliability.[46] With such mixed results, it is important that whatever method is adopted should be used independently by several people (analysts, supervisors, subordinates) and that any differences should be investigated and resolved.

Consistent (reliable) job information does not necessarily mean that it is accurate, comprehensive, or free from bias. To find out whether the results are accurate, we need to consider their validity.

Validity

Research on how to estimate the validity of job analysis is particularly difficult, since there is almost no way to show the extent to which the results are accurate portraits of the work. In the most recent extensive review of job analysis research, Harvey concludes, "Taken together the evidence . . . paints a troubling picture regarding the reliability and validity of job analysis."[47] The most promising approach may be to examine the convergence of results among multiple sources of job data (analysts, incumbents, supervisors) and multiple methods. A common approach to attempt to increase accuracy of job analysis is to require both the job holder and the manager to "sign off" on the results. Although getting the parties mutually to sign off on the results may reflect their acceptance, it may also reflect their desire to get rid of the analyst and get back to performing the job rather than analyzing it.

Acceptability

Employee acceptability of data collected is important and easily overlooked. No matter how well the rest of the compensation system is administered, if jobholders are dissatisfied with the initial data collected and the process for collecting it, they are not likely to believe that the results are internally equitable.

Conventional job analysis is not always well accepted by the parties involved because of its potential for subjectivity. One writer says, "We all know the classic procedures. One (worker) watched and noted the actions of another . . . at work on (the) job. The actions of both are biased and the resulting information varied with the wind, especially the political wind."[48] But the acceptability of quantitative job analysis is also mixed.

---

[46]For an example of the statistical analysis on PAQ results, see R. D. Arvey, S. E. Maxwell, R. L. Gutenberg, and C. Camp, "Detecting Job Differences: A Monte Carlo Study," *Personnel Psychology* 34 (1981), pp. 709–30.

[47]Harvey, "Job Analysis," p. 114.

[48]E. M. Ramras, "Discussion," in *Proceedings of Division of Military Psychology Symposium: Collecting, Analyzing, and Reporting Information Describing Jobs and Occupations,* 77th Annual Convention of the American Psychological Association, Lackland Air Force Base, Tex., September 1969, pp. 75–76.

Control Data's Executive Position Questionnaire, developed over a four-year period, ran into several problems, which led most managers to refuse to use it.[49] The difficulities included:

1. *Employee/manager understanding.* The statistical methods used were difficult to understand, so many managers were unable to communicate the results to employees.

2. *Behaviorally oriented versus "scope" data.* Analyzing work in terms of work behaviors, omitting "scope" data (e.g., size of budgets, total payroll, contribution to organization objectives) caused managers to believe that the questionnaire did not accurately analyze their jobs.

3. *Abstract and ambiguous factors.* The data collected were perceived to be too abstract and ambiguous. Results were considered too subjective and open to personal interpretation.

Practicality

Researchers recognize the necessity of judging the usefulness of job analysis methods according to the purpose of the analysis.[50] A group of researchers asked 93 experienced job analysts to compare a number of job analysis methods on their utility for 11 different organization purposes.[51] The researchers concluded that the effectiveness and practicality of each method varied with the purpose. The PAQ was among those rated highest for the purpose of creating job structures. The usefulness of the results obtained is probably the most important criterion on which to judge alternative approaches to job analysis.

There are very few data publicly available on costs of various approaches to job analysis.[52] Our own experience with custom-designed quantitative job analysis plans suggests about 24 months from design through installation, plus significant time commitments from participating managers who serve on task forces. Considerable time and money are required for any job analysis, with or without computer assistance.[53]

The practical utility of quantitative job analysis, with its relatively complex procedures and analysis, remains in doubt for compensation purposes. Some advocates get so taken

---

[49]Gomez-Mejia et al., "A Comparison of the Practical Utility of Traditional, Statistical, and Hybrid Job Evaluation Approaches."

[50]Ronald A. Ash and Edward L. Levine, "A Framework for Evaluating Job Analysis Methods," *Personnel* 57, no. 6 (November–December 1980), pp. 53–59; E. L. Levine, R. A. Ash, and N. Bennett, "Exploratory Comparative Study of Four Job Analysis Methods," *Journal of Applied Psychology* 65 (1980), pp. 524–35; and R. A. Ash, E. L. Levine, and F. Sistrunk, "The Role of Jobs and Job Based Methods in Personnel and Human Resources Management," *Research in Personnel and Human Resources Management* 1 (1983), pp. 45–84.

[51]Edward L. Levine, Ronald A. Ash, Hardy Hall, and Frank Sistrunk, "Evaluation of Job Analysis Methods by Experienced Job Analysts," *Academy of Management Journal* 26, no. 2 (1983), pp. 339–48.

[52]Frank Krzystofiak, Jerry M. Newman, and Gary Anderson, "A Quantified Approach to Measurement of Job Content: Procedures and Payoffs," *Personnel Psychology,* Summer 1979, pp. 341–57.

[53]J. N. Gambardella and W. G. Alvord, "Ti-CODAP: A Computerized Method of Job Analysis for Personnel Management" (Prince Georges County, Md., April 1980).

with their statistics and computers that they ignore the role that human judgment must continue to play in job analysis. As Dunnette states,

> I wish to emphasize the central role played in all these procedures by human judgment. I know of no methodology, statistical technique or objective measurement that can negate the importance of, nor supplement, rational judgment as an important element in the process of deriving behavior and task information about jobs and of using that information to develop or justify human resources programs.[54]

Quantitative and more systematic approaches to job analysis do not remove the judgment; they only permit us to become more systematic in the way we make it.

JOB DESCRIPTIONS

The data collected in job analysis must be put into a form that is usable by employees and managers. Often that form is the job description. A job description identifies, defines, and describes the job as it is being performed. As with job analysis, textbooks extol the multiple uses of job descriptions—in career development, replacement charting, performance evaluation, and employment planning, among others. However, one study reports that more than 40 percent of the respondents in a 77-company survey made little use of job descriptions for purposes other than wage administration.[55] That study also found little or no apparent correlation between the character of the job description and its intended usage or the size or type of company involved.

The job description typically contains three sections, which roughly correspond with the purposes of identifying, defining, and describing the job. Recall that these were the categories delineated in deciding what data to collect in job analysis. Exhibits 3.13 and 3.14 are typical job descriptions of a nurse's position, albeit 100 years apart. The job description should indicate the major duties of this jobholder, the specific work performed, how closely supervised this job is, and what controls limit the actions of the jobholder. In addition to describing the tasks performed, the training and experience required to perform them may also be included here, or in a separate section called *job specifications*. The description should provide an accurate "word picture" of the job.

Managerial Jobs

Describing managerial jobs poses special problems. Managers frequently do not perform a prescribed set of duties. Instead of specific tasks with specific outcomes, they have broad accountability for the accomplishment of results that help the organization attain its objectives. For example, a marketing vice president is broadly responsible for moving goods from their site of manufacture to the consumer in a profitable manner. A further

---

[54]M. D. Dunnette, L. M. Hough, and R. L. Rosse, "Task and Job Taxonomies as a Basis for Identifying Labor Supply Sources and Evaluating Employment Qualifications," in *Affirmative Action Planning,* ed. George T. Milkovich and Lee Dyer (New York: Human Resource Planning Society, 1979), pp. 37–51.

[55]Brandt, "Describing Hourly Jobs."

EXHIBIT 3.13   Job Description for Nurse, 1992

Job Title

Registered Nurse

Job Summary

Accountable for the complete spectrum of patient care from admission through transfer or discharge through the nursing process of assessment, planning, implementation, and evaluation. Each R.N. has primary authority to fulfill responsibility for the nursing process on the assigned shift and for projecting future needs of the patient/family. Directs and guides patient teaching and activities for ancillary personnel while maintaining standard of professional nursing.

Relationships

Reports to: Head Nurse or Charge Nurse.
Supervises: Responsible for the care delivered by L.P.N's, nursing assistants, orderlies, and transcribers.
Works with: Ancillary Care Departments.
External relationships: Physicians, patients, patients' families.

Qualifications

Education: Graduate of an accredited school of nursing.
Work experience: Critical care requires one year of recent medical/surgical experience (special care nursing preferred),
                   medical/surgical experience (new graduates may be considered for noncharge positions).
License or registration requirements: Current R.N. license or permit in the State of Minnesota.
Physical requirements: A.   Ability to bend, reach, or assist to transfer up to 50 pounds.
                         B.   Ability to stand and/or walk 80 percent of 8-hour shift.
                         C.   Visual and hearing acuity to perform job-related functions.

Responsibilities

1.   Assesses physical, emotional, and psycho-social dimensions of patients.
     Standard: Provides a written assessment of patient within one hour of admission and at least once a shift. Communicates
                 this assessment to other patient care providers in accordance with hospital policies.
2.   Formulates a written plan of care for patients from admission through discharge.
     Standard: Develops short and long term goals within 24 hours of admission. Reviews and updates care plans each shift
                 based on ongoing assessment.
3.   Implements plan of care.
     Standard: Demonstrates skill in performing common nursing procedures in accordance with but not limited to the
                 established written R.N. skills inventory specific to assigned area. Completes patient care activities in an
                 organized and timely fashion, reassessing priorities appropriately.

NOTE: Additional responsibilities omitted from exhibit.

difficulty in describing managerial jobs is the expectation that the individuals will change the jobs. Therefore, the format for describing these jobs must be adjusted to adequately describe such work. In addition to sections that identify, define, and describe the job, the following additions are usually made to managerial job description in a format similar to the one used in Exhibit 3.15.

1.   *Dimensions*. Provides statistics on the size of the payroll, budget, and number of people supervised. This is an expanded version of the identification section.

EXHIBIT 3.14 Job Description for Nurse, 1887

In addition to caring for your 50 patients each nurse will follow these regulations:

1. Daily sweep and mop the floors of your ward, dust the patient's furniture and window sills.
2. Maintain an even temperature in your ward by bringing in a scuttle of coal for the day's business.
3. Light is important to observe the patient's condition. Therefore, each day, fill kerosene lamps, clean chimneys, and trim wicks. Wash the windows once a week.
4. The nurse's notes are important in aiding the physician's work. Make your pens carefully, you may whittle nibs to your individual taste.
5. Each nurse on day duty will report every day at 7 A.M. and leave at 8 P.M. except on the Sabbath on which day you will be off from 12:00 noon to 2:00 P.M.
6. Graduate nurses in good standing with the director of nurses will be given an evening off each week for courting purposes, or two evenings a week if you go regularly to church.
7. Each nurse should lay aside from each pay day a goodly sum of her earnings for her benefits during her declining years, so that she will not become a burden. For example, if you earn $30 a month you should set aside $15.
8. Any nurse who smokes, uses liquor in any form, gets her hair done at a beauty shop, or frequents dance halls will give the director good reason to suspect her worth, intentions, and integrity.
9. The nurse who performs her labors and serves her patients and doctors faithfully and without fault for a period of five years will be given an increase by the hospital administration of five cents a day, provided there are no hospital debts that are outstanding.

---

2. *Nature and scope.* Identifies how the position fits into the organization, the composition of the supporting staff (e.g., assistant director of personnel, director of development) and the key issues to be handled by the person in this job. This is similar to the definition section previously discussed.

3. *Accountabilities.* Delineates the broad end results this position seeks to attain. For example, the personnel vice president in Exhibit 3.15 has final responsibility for providing "a wage, salary, and benefits program which is both internally equitable and externally competitive." How this responsibility will be carried out is unclear, since the job description does not list a compensation director reporting to this position. We have taken the liberty of sending the vice president a copy of this book to help overcome the oversight.

Writing the Job Description

Great detail exists on how to write job descriptions, including specific definitions of verbs. Vague terms (e.g., "many" or "relatively easy") or those with a variety of meanings (e.g., "takes care of," or "handles") are frowned upon. This is not the place for polished prose, or even complete sentences. English majors need not apply, since a smooth-flowing writing style may make the crucial information harder to pick out, thus discouraging use of the description.

To ensure equitable comparisons of content across jobs, jobs are typically described in a standardized manner, not only in format but also in choice of words. For example, "supervises" is not the same as "directs," "facilitates," or even "leads."

EXHIBIT 3.15   Sample Position Description for a Manager

TITLE:	Vice president personnel	**DATE:**	
INCUMBENT:		**ANALYST:**	
REPORTS TO:	Chairman and CEO	**APPROVALS:**	

ACCOUNTABILITY OBJECTIVE

This position is accountable for assuring the continuing availability of acceptable levels of human resources (both quantity and quality) for the company. This is accomplished by selecting, training, and compensating the employees in a manner which helps to create a positive working environment.

DIMENSIONS

Personnel budget: $3MM	Total co. payroll: $12–14MM
Personnel dept. payroll: $350M	Personnel supervised: 3 direct
	51 indirect

NATURE AND SCOPE

This position along with the VP Control, VP Branches and VP Operations reports to the chairman and CEO. Reporting to the incumbent is a staff of three: the assistant director of personnel, the director of training, and the director of development.

The personnel department's subdivisions include employment, training, compensation and benefits, and record keeping, covering approximately 6,000 hourly rated employees and 250 senior executives.

Labor relations and contract negotiations with the seven unions working at the store are a significant responsibility for the incumbent. Although the actual time involved in contract negotiations may appear minimal, the implications and consequences of the contracts themselves are felt throughout the year. The incumbent also directs personnel activities which ensure the company's compliance with EEOC, and department of labor regulations.

The Vice President assures the completion of his acountabilities through his direction of the following functions:

Assistant director of personnel – Supervises all branch personnel directors, the record room and benefits. Administers the employment and record keeping function for the downtown store. Assures the proper functioning of the wage and salary program and the publication of the in-house newspaper.

Director of development – Responsible for recruiting, placement and career ladder movement of all junior executives (generally assistant, buyer, and above). This includes maintaining and developing an effective college relations program as well as administering the storewide executive training program.

Director of training – In addition to the rank and file orientation program, initial and retraining programs, the director administers the training programs run by the branch store training managers and the five downtown training representatives.

In addition to ensuring coordinated personnel effort, company-wide, the vice president works closely with the division level organization on matters concerning executive recruiting, placement, and compensation and the participation of corporate executives on intrastore committees. This position is also personally in charge of senior executive training and aids in productivity reviews.

Because of the wide corporate scope of this position, the incumbent finds a portion of time must be devoted to working with various racial or ethnic groups, fund raising, community service, and participating on external committees such as the State Retail Merchants Association, College Advisory Boards, etc.

PRINCIPAL ACCOUNTABILITIES

1. A wage, salary and benefits program which is both internally equitable and externally competitive.
2. Union contracts which fairly and equitably reflect the desires of company management, while maintaining effective working relationships with union personnel.
3. A trained and motivated personnel department staff capable of carrying out the objectives assigned.
4. Identified and available executive and junior executive talent sufficient for corporate growth and maintenance of current operations.

(Additional accountabilities omitted from exhibit.)

Although it is necessary to be brief, the description also needs to be accurate. One organization goes so far as to suggest writing a first draft of unlimited length, ensuring inclusion of all necessary detail. The first draft then is reviewed to eliminate all words and sentences that do not contribute to meaning. A length of two to three pages for managerial jobs, fewer for nonmanagerial jobs, is usually considered long enough to be accurate without being unwieldy. The attractiveness of computer-generated job descriptions becomes clear as one begins to write a job description.

Accuracy of job descriptions can have effects beyond the compensation system. Accurate job descriptions can also affect union/management relations. For example, disputes may arise if workers feel they are performing work that belongs to a higher level, higher paid job. Problems can also arise if job descriptions are not kept current or are not changed as the jobs change. Changes in technology, physical location, product line, strategic direction, and even key personnel can precipitate job changes.

SKILL ANALYSIS

As we pointed out in Exhibit 3.13, skill or knowledge is one of the alternative criteria for an internal pay structure. Skill-based structures pay employees based on what they have demonstrated they know, rather than what particular *job* they are doing.[56] Generally, skill-based plans can be grouped into two types:

1. *Knowledge based,* which link pay to depth of knowledge related to *one job* (e.g., scientists and teachers).
2. *Multiskill based,* which link pay to the number of *different jobs* (breadth) an employee is certified to do (e.g., related production jobs).[57]

These plans are known by several names. Skill-based, knowledge-based, competency-based, and applied knowledge are some of the many terms used to describe them. For simplicity, this book will use the term skill-based plans.

Knowledge Based: Depth.   Basing pay structures on knowledge possessed by individual employees is not new. The pay structures for your elementary or high school teachers have long been based on their knowledge as measured by education level. A typical teacher's contract specifies a series of steps, with each step corresponding to a level of education. A bachelor's degree in education is step one, and is the minimum required for hiring. To advance a step to higher pay requires additional education. For example, an additional 9 semester hours of coursework earns an increase of $225 in Ithaca, New

[56]E. E. Lawler III and G. E. Ledford, Jr., "Skill-Based Pay" (Working paper 84–18, Los Angeles Center for Effective Organizations, University of Southern California); Nina Gupta, G. Douglas Jenkins, Jr., and William Curington, "Paying for Knowledge: Myths and Realities," *National Productivity Review,* Spring 1986, pp. 107–23; T. P. Schweizer, "Pay-for-Knowledge Systems: An Alternative Approach to Compensation," *Proceedings of the Southwest Academy of Management,* 1986, pp. 159–63; and H. Tosi and L. Tosi, "What Managers Need to Know About Knowledge-Based Pay," *Organization Dynamics* 14, no. 3 (1986), pp. 52–64.

[57]Fred Luthans and Marilyn L. Fox, "Update on Skill-Based Pay," *Personnel,* March 1989, pp. 26–32.

York. The result can be that two teachers may receive different pay rates for doing essentially the same job—teaching English to high school juniors. The pay is based on the knowledge of the individual doing the job (measured by number of college credits) rather than job content. The presumption is that teachers with more knowledge are more effective and more flexible—able to teach seniors, too.

Multiskill Based: Breadth.   As with the teachers, employees in a multiskill system earn pay increases by acquiring new knowledge, but the knowledge is specific to a range of related jobs.[58] An example from Borg Warner illustrates the system. Borg Warner assembles drive chains for automobile transmissions. Exhibit 3.16 shows its job hierarchy. Previously, 7 different jobs were involved in the assembly process, starting with stackers, and moving up through packers, assemblers, and riveters. When Borg Warner switched to a skill-based pay system, these 7 jobs were reorganized into three broad categories: Cell Operators A, B, and C. Cell Operator C is an entry-level position. Once Operator Cs are able to satisfactorily demonstrate that they have mastered the stacker through measurer jobs, they become eligible to train for the Operator B jobs. With each job mastery comes a pay raise. Operator Bs can be rotated among any of the jobs for which they have demonstrated mastery, including C-level jobs. An Operator B can do all the jobs required, including stacking, and still receive Operator B pay. Operator As can also do all jobs, plus they assume responsibility for scheduling and supervising teams. The advantage to Borg Warner is work force flexibility and hence lower staffing levels.

The multiskilled system differs from the knowledge-based system of engineers or teachers in that the job responsibilities assigned to an employee in a multiskill system

EXHIBIT 3.16   Borg Warner Automotive Assembly Classifications

	Pay System	
	Job Based	Skill Based

Chain stacker
Packer
Cleaner
Ultrasonic inspector
Measurer
Assembler
Riveter
Leadership, Supervisory
  and Scheduling
  Responsibilities
	Skill C (stacker–measurer)	Skill B / Skill A

---

[58]Nina Gupta et al., *Exploratory Investigations of Pay-for-Knowledge Systems* (Washington, D.C.: U.S. Department of Labor, Bureau of Labor-Management Relations and Cooperative Programs, 1986).

can change drastically over a short period of time. Whereas teachers and engineers increase the *depth* of their skills on the same basic job, employees in multiskill systems emphasize increased *breadth* of skills so that employees can perform a variety of jobs. Pay is based on the highest level of individual skill mastery. Typically, training and evaluation systems are established to ensure that individuals have adequately mastered the skills for which they are being paid, and that those skills are maintained.

Skill-based structures are currently enjoying a great deal of favorable attention. The idea of basing pay increases on improving employee skills is very appealing. Applications are most common among small- to medium-size facilities (under 400 employees), especially where a continuous process technology is used. A recent survey found that on average about 30 percent of the work force in the facility is included in a particular plan. To date, few plans include clerical employees, and managerial/supervisory employees are almost never included.[59]

Skills Information

If pay structures are to be based on the skills required to perform the work, some way is needed to discover different types of skills to define different work related to levels of it.

The parallels to job analysis should be obvious.

Skill analysis is a systematic process of collecting information about the knowledge or skills required to perform work in an organization.

The basic premise is that blocks of skill required are more likely to be described, certified, and valued fairly if accurate work-related data about them are available. Exhibit 3.17 identifies the major decisions in designing a skill analysis: (1) What information should be collected? (2) What methods should be used? (3) Who should be involved? (4) How useful are the results for pay purposes?

These are exactly the same decisions managers face in job analysis. However, skill analysis in compensation is so new that very little research exists to offer guidance. Currently, the state of practice must be culled from a few case studies describing applications in a handful of manufacturing facilities.[60]

Polaroid has launched the most ambitious effort to date. The work of all its 8,000 employees from the CEO to operatives, including patent attorneys, financial analysts, and

---

[59]G. Douglas Jenkins, Jr., Gerald E. Ledford, Jr., Nina Gupta, and D. Harold Doty, *Skill-Based Pay* (Scottsdale, Ariz.: American Compensation Association, 1992).

[60]Gerald E. Ledford, Jr., "Three Case Studies of Skill-Based Pay: An Overview," *Compensation and Benefits Review,* March–April 1991, pp. 11–23. Pages 23–77 of this issue contain case studies of applications at General Mills, Northern Telecom, and Honeywell.

EXHIBIT 3.17   **Determining the Internal Skill-Based Structure**

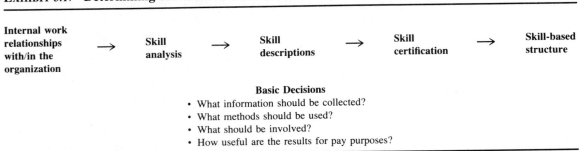

Basic Decisions
- What information should be collected?
- What methods should be used?
- What should be involved?
- How useful are the results for pay purposes?

EXHIBIT 3.18   **AKP Level Evaluation Categories at Polaroid**

- **Depth of functional knowledge**—the level and complexity of knowledge required for the assignment.
- **Breadth of functional knowledge**—the variety of skills and knowledge required for the assignment.
- **Communication/interface**—the skills required to exchange and present information (verbally or in writing), and to work with others inside or outside the company.
- **Leadership and responsibility**—the skills required to organize, direct, and motivate other employees, and the scope and impact of the assignment's leadership role.
- **Administrative skills**—the knowledge required to interpret and apply company policies and procedures, and to organize and analyze data for planning, budgeting, scheduling, and other such tasks.

secretaries is being analyzed under Polaroid's new Applied Knowledge Plan (AKP). More than 2,000 specific types of knowledge or skill have been identified by employee teams. They are now attempting to subgroup these skills into the five AKP level evaluation categories shown in Exhibit 3.18. One of the difficulties in such a major project is the sheer diversity of skill required in a complex contemporary business. So, for example, how specific (or general) should "depth of functioning knowledge" and "breadth of functional knowledge" be? Note the parallels to the level of analysis issue discussed in job analysis. The challenge is to describe the blocks of knowledge sufficiently specific to support pay differences and reward employees' efforts to increase their knowledge or skill. Once again, too detailed an analysis risks becoming unnecessary and burdensome.

What Information to Collect?

Skill or knowledge blocks are the different types of knowledge required to perform the work. There is virtually no systematic guidance about general blocks to look for in the compensation literature. However, reinventing the wheel is not required. Competencies, knowledge, skills, and abilities have long been studied in psychology and education. The military and others have devoted considerable resources to identifying work-related knowledge, skills, and abilities (KSAs) for use in selection, placement, and training. A national task force on work force preparedness recently identified the five competencies, resources, interpersonal, information, systems, and technology, defined in Exhibit 3.19, as essential to improve the quality of the labor force.

Case studies are also a source of ideas about skill blocks. Each site appears to use different blocks; a General Mills production plant divided the production process into four basic blocks with different levels within each block. For example, the Technical Knowledge block has three levels: (1) limited ability to operate without direction, (2) partial proficiency, and (3) full competency. Northern Telecom used different blocks for each of three functions: engineering, technician, and support. Dresser Rand uses general skills and applies them across product lines. There are obvious similarities between these skill blocks and the factor "abilities required to perform the work" that we discussed under job analysis.

Methods to Use/Whom to Involve?

To date, virtually no attention has been focused on alternative methods (e.g., focus groups, interviews, questionnaires) available to collect skill-based information. Teams of employees and managers groping their way and muddling through seems to be the approach. This has obvious advantages—high participation and commitment—and equally obvious problems—limited perspective on possible future changes, overreliance on stereotypes, and so on. But our experience has generally shown employee teams to be extremely knowledgeable, highly committed, and fully understanding of the logic underlying the resulting pay structure, which is often more than can be said about conventional job analysis methods.

Advantages of Skill-Based Pay Structures

Clearly, the flexibility in scheduling and the leaner staffing that results are the overwhelming advantages offered by skill-based pay structure. The results reported in case studies, admittedly written by the designers and advocates, offer support. These reports list results ranging from improved productivity, quality, attendance, safety ratings, employee satisfaction, and turnover.

Disadvantages of Skill-Based Systems

Exhibit 3.20 contrasts job versus skill-based structures. It points out that no system is perfect. The skill-based system has potential limitations, in addition to its advantages.

EXHIBIT 3.19   Five Competencies Identified by National Task Force on Work Force Preparedness

---

Resources: Identifies, organizes, plans, and allocates resources.
  A. *Time*—Selects goal-relevant activities, ranks them, allocates time, and prepares and follow schedules.
  B. *Money*—Uses or prepares budgets, makes forecasts, keeps records, and makes adjustments to meet objectives.
  C. *Material and facilities*—Acquires, stores, allocates, and uses materials or space efficiently.
  D. *Human resources*—Assesses skills and distributes work accordingly, evaluates performance, and provides feedback.

Interpersonal: Works with others.
  A. *Participates as member of a team*—contributes to group effort.
  B. *Teaches others new skills.*
  C. *Serves clients/customers*—works to satisfy customers' expectations.
  D. *Exercises leadership*—communicates ideas to justify position, persuades and convinces others, responsibly challenges existing procedures and policies.
  E. *Negotiates*—works toward agreements involving exchange of resources, resolves divergent interests.
  F. *Works with diversity*—works well with men and women from diverse backgrounds.

Information: Acquires and uses information.
  A. *Acquires and evaluates information.*
  B. *Organizes and maintains information.*
  C. *Interprets and communicates information.*
  D. *Uses computers to process information.*

Systems: Understands complex interrelationships.
  A. *Understand systems*—knows how social, organizational, and technological systems work and operates effectively with them.
  B. *Monitors and corrects performance*—distinguishes trends, predicts impacts on system operations, diagnoses deviations in systems' performance, and corrects malfunctions.
  C. *Improves or designs systems*—suggests modifications to existing systems and develops new or alternative systems to improve performance.

Technology: Works with a variety of technologies.
  A. *Selects technology*—chooses procedures, tools, or equipment including computers and related technologies.
  B. *Applies technology to task*—understands overall intent and proper procedures for setup and operation of equipment.
  C. *Maintains and troubleshoots equipment*—prevents, identifies, or solves problems with equipment, including computers and other technologies.

The most important disadvantage is that it can be come expensive if not properly managed. As you might expect, the majority of employees whose pay is based on skill mastery want the necessary training to move to the top of the pay ladder as fast as possible. But if all employees are earning top pay rates, an employer may experience higher labor costs than its competitors and will therefore be at a price disadvantage in marketing its products. There are several ways to avoid this situation: set starting pay slightly below competitors, or control the rate at which employees can move up in skill mastery. A skill system requires that higher wage rates must be offset by a smaller work force or greater pro-

EXHIBIT 3.20   Skill-Based Compared to Job-Based Structures

	Job Based	Knowledge Based
Pay structure	Based on job performed	Based on skills possessed by the employee
Managers' focus	Job carries wage Employee linked to job	Employee carries wage Employee linked to skill
Employee focus	Job promotion to earn greater pay	Skill acquisition to earn greater pay
Procedures required	Assess job content Value jobs	Assess skills Value skills
Advantages	Pay based on value of work performed	Flexibility Reduced work force
Limitations	Potential personnel bureaucracy Inflexibilities	Potential personnel bureaucracy Cost controls

ductivity, or the organization's labor costs will become a significant competitive disadvantage.

In addition to higher pay rates and training costs, skill-based plans may become as complex and burdensome as job-based approaches. To date, little research on the effectiveness of skill-based structures exists beyond the already cited case studies. Although these accounts are valuable, no evidence examines the lingering belief that traditional job-based structures, properly designed and managed, are equally effective.

Additionally, questions still remain about the system's compliance with the Equal Pay Act. If a member of a protected group is doing the same job as a white male, but being paid less for it (because of a difference in skill mastery), does this violate the equal pay/equal work standard specified in the legislation?[61] Later chapters (13 and 14) discuss this and other pay legislation at length.

SUMMARY

Fairness of the pay structure within an organization is one of the hallmarks of a sound compensation system. The compensation manager faces several decisions when designing an equitable pay structure. One of the first is a policy decision—how much to emphasize the importance of an internally consistent and equitable pay structure. Some emphasize market pricing over internal consistency. Whatever the choice, it needs to support the organization's overall human resource strategy.

---

[61]G. V. Barrett, "Comparison of Skill-based Pay with Traditional Job Evaluation Techniques," *Human Resource Management Review* 1, 1991, pp. 97–105.

Next, managers must decide whether job and/or individual employee characteristics will be the basic unit of analysis supporting the pay structure. This is followed by deciding what data need to be collected, what method(s) will be used to collect it, and who should be involved in the process.

A key test of an equitable pay structure is acceptance of results by managers and employees. The best way to ensure acceptance of job analysis results is to involve employees as well as supervisors in the process. At the minimum, all employees should be informed of purposes and progress of the activity.

If almost everyone agrees about the importance of job analysis for equitable compensation, does that mean everyone does it? Of course not. Unfortunately, job analysis can be tedious and time-consuming. Often the job is given to newly hired compensation analysts, ostensibly to help them learn the organization, but perhaps there's also a hint of "rites of passage" in such assignments.

Alternatives to job-based structures such as skill-based systems are being experimented with in many firms. The premise is that basing structures on the skill required will encourage employees to become more flexible, and fewer of them will be required for the same level of output. Nevertheless, job content remains the conventional criterion for structures.

This completes our discussion of job analysis. The next step is to take the resulting job descriptions and evaluate the jobs according to their contributions to the organization goals. This is the subject of the next chapters.

REVIEW QUESTIONS

1. Distinguish between job-based and skill-based structures. Compare their relative advantages and disadvantages.
2. What does job analysis (and skill analysis) have to do with internal consistency?
3. Describe the major decisions involved in job analysis.
4. Distinguish among task, worker, and abilities data.
5. What is the critical advantage of quantitative approaches over conventional approaches to job analysis?
6. How would you decide whether to use job-based or knowledge-based structures?

EXHIBIT 3A.1 General Procedures for Conventional Job Analysis

Step	Things to Remember or Do
1. Develop preliminary job information	a. Review existing documents in order to develop an initial "big-picture" familiarity with the job: its main mission, its major duties or functions, work flow patterns. b. Prepare a preliminary list of duties which will serve as a framework for conducting the interviews. c. Make a note of major items which are unclear, or ambiguous or that need to be clarified during the data-gathering process.
2. Conduct initial tour of work site	a. The initial tour is designed to familiarize the job analyst with the work layout, the tools and equipment that are used, the general conditions of the workplace, and the mechanics associated with the end-to-end performance of major duties. b. The initial tour is particularly helpful in those jobs where a first-hand view of a complicated or unfamiliar piece of equipment saves the interviewee the thousand words required to describe the unfamiliar or technical. c. For continuity, it is recommended that the first level supervisor-interviewee be designated the guide for the job-site observations.
3. Conduct interviews	a. It is recommended that the first interview be conducted with the first-level supervisor who is considered to be in a better position than the jobholders to provide an overview of the job and how the major duties fit together. b. For scheduling purposes, it is recommended that no more than two interviews be conducted per day, each interview lasting no more than three hours.
Notes on selection of interviewees	a. The interviewees are considered subject matter experts by virtue of the fact that they perform the job (in the case of job incumbents) or are responsible for getting the job done (in the case of first-level supervisors). b. The job incumbent to be interviewed should represent the *typical* employee who is knowledgeable about the job (*not* the trainee who is just learning the ropes *nor* the outstanding member of the work unit). c. Whenever feasible, the interviewees should be selected with a view towards obtaining an appropriate race/sex mix.
4. Conduct second tour of work site	a. The second tour of the work site is designed to clarify, confirm, and otherwise refine the information developed in the interviews. b. As in the initial tour, it is recommended that the same first-level supervisor-interviewee conduct the second walk-through.
5. Consolidate job information	a. The consolidation phase of the job study involves piecing together into one coherent and comprehensive job description the data obtained from several sources: supervisor, jobholders, on-site tours, and written materials about the job. b. Past experience indicates that one minute of consolidation is required for every minute of interviewing. For planning purposes, at least 5 hours should be set aside for the consolidation phase. c. A subject matter expert should be accessible as a resource person to the job analyst during the consolidation phase. The supervisor-interviewee fills this role. d. Check your initial preliminary list of duties and questions—all must be answered or confirmed.
6. Verify job description	a. The verification phase involves bringing all the interviewees together for the purpose of determining if the consolidated job description is accurate and complete. b. The verification process is conducted in a group setting. Typed or legibly written copies of the job description (narrative description of the work setting *and* list of task statements) are distributed to the first-level supervisor and the job incumbent interviewees. c. Line by line, the job analyst goes through the entire job description and makes notes of any omissions, ambiguities, or needed clarifications. d. Collect all materials at the end of the verification meeting.

Job Analysis Report

Date _2-23-90_

Job Analyst _C. Davis_

1. Job Title _Executive Secretary_

2. Department _General Headquarters_

3. No. incumbents _2_   Interviewed _2_

4. Relation to other jobs:

   Promotion: From _Secretary-D_   To _Executive Secretary_

   Transfer: From _Administrative Assistant_   To _Executive Secretary_

   Supervision received _From President and/or Chairman of the Board._
   Works under minimal supervision.

   Supervision given _Regularly to other clerical personnel._

5. Summary of Job:

   Personal Secretary to President and/or Chairman of the Board. Performs variety of secretarial and clerical duties including transcribing dictation, filing, routing mail, as well as answering telephone and written inquiries. Exercises discretion in handling confidential and specialized information, screening telephone calls and letters, arranging meetings, and handling inquiries during superior's absence.

6. Equipment used: Typewriter, word processor, dictaphone and telephone.

Working conditions:

   Hazards (list): N/A

   Work space and quarters: Office environment

Noise exposure: None

Lighting: Good

Temperature: Regulated office environment

Miscellaneous: —

Job training:

A. Required experience: (include other jobs)
Four years of secretarial-stenographic experience or the equivalent.

B. Outside educational courses:

	Time in semesters/quarters
Vocational courses: Typing, stenography	2 semesters
High school courses: Graduate	6-8 semesters
College courses:	None
Continuing education required:	None

C. In-house training courses:

	Time in months
Courses: Basic and Advanced Word Processing	1/2 month

Task Statement Worksheet

Task Statement: Opens and organizes mail addressed to superior.

1. Equipment used —

2. Knowledge required Must be well versed on superior's responsibilities, how superior's job fits into overall organization.

3. Skills required —

4. Abilities required Discretion. Organization skills.

5. Time spent and frequency of task performance (hourly, daily, monthly)
   Time varies by assignment. Weekly frequency.

6. Level of difficulty/consequence of error
   Relatively difficult, little effect of error.

Task Statement: Establishes, maintains, and revises files.

1. Equipment used Typewriter, word processor.

2. Knowledge required Understanding of organization and responsibilities of superior.

3. Skills required Typing and word processing, filing.

4. Abilities required Ability to organize and categorize information.

5. Time spent and frequency of task performance (hourly, daily, monthly)
   One hour spent daily.

6. Level of difficulty/consequence of error Relatively easy, but moderate to serious consequences if information mishandled.

APPENDIX 3–B
EXAMPLE OF QUANTITATIVE JOB ANALYSIS: THE POSITION INFORMATION QUESTIONNAIRE

Position Information Questionnaire

Introduction

The 3M Position Information Questionnaire (PIQ) is a key part of 3M's job evaluation process. Job evaluation involves a comparison of jobs in relation to other 3M jobs. Job evaluation is a systematic way to help management classify jobs and pay for work appropriately.

The PIQ collects information about the work you do. It takes into account what 3M considers to be most important in the work that you perform. The PIQ asks questions about:

- **Skills/Knowledge Applied**
- **Complexity of Duties**
- **Impact on Business**
- **Working Conditions**

It will take some time for you to complete the PIQ, but it will be time well-spent. 3M needs the information to properly understand your job and its responsibilities. Your supervisor will give you enough time during normal working hours to complete the PIQ.

Suggestions For Completing The PIQ

Before you begin to write . . .

1. Read through the entire questionnaire.

2. Think about what you do in your work - daily, weekly, and monthly. What are the most important things you do?

3. Make a few notes to yourself, either on a separate sheet of paper or in the margins of the PIQ, outlining the key points you will make on each question.

 Note: If you are unsure about the meaning of a certain question, contact your supervisor, your Human Resources Manager, or call Compensation for assistance.

Then, fill out the questionnaire . . .

1. Begin completing the questions when you feel that you are familiar with the PIQ and have thought through each question.

2. When you have finished filling out the PIQ, put it aside for a day or two. Then reread it to see if you have forgotten anything. Add any additional points you may want to make.

 Important Points to Keep In Mind

 - Since the PIQ is used to describe many jobs, you will probably find questions that do not apply to your job. Do not be concerned about this. What is important is that you find the appropriate places to explain the key parts of your job. If not, there is space for additional comments at the end of the PIQ.

 - The PIQ, and 3M's job evaluation process, considers many aspects of your work. Do not try to explain everything about your job in any one question. You should be able to make each point you feel is important. Again, use the space for additional comments at the end of this document if necessary.

When you have finished the questionnaire . . .

1. Return the completed PIQ to your supervisor who will review it for consistency and completeness. He/she will discuss any possible changes with you.

2. You and your supervisor must sign the last page of the PIQ.

3. Your supervisor will send the completed PIQ to your Human Resources Manager in St. Paul.

Remember . . .

The PIQ is not used to measure your performance on your job. It is not used for performance appraisal. The focus is on the nature of the work that you do, the job's duties and requirements, **not** your performance or personal characteristics.

Obtaining information about what employees do in their work is an important step in defining relationships between jobs and in establishing a competitive pay program. This information helps 3M maintain appropriate relationships between jobs inside 3M, and analyze the competitiveness in pay between 3M jobs and similar jobs outside 3M.

Your input and efforts in completing the PIQ are important. Thank you for participating in this process.

I. Job Overview

Job Summary	What is the main purpose of your job? (Why does it exist and what does the work contribute to 3M?)
	   Examples: To provide secretarial support in our department by performing office and administrative duties.
	        To purchase goods and services that meet specifications at the least cost.
	        To perform systems analysis involved in the development, installation, and maintenance of computer applications.
	Hint: It may help to list the duties first before answering this question.

		Percentage of Time Spent (Total may be less than but not more than 100%)
Duties and Respon-sibilities	What are your job's main duties and responsibilities? (These are the major work activities that usually take up a significant amount of your work time and occur regularly as you perform your work.) In the spaces below, list your job's five most important or most frequent duties. Then, in the boxes, estimate the percentage of time you spend on each duty.	
	1.	
	2.	
	3.	
	4.	
	5.	

II. Skills/Knowledge Applied

Formal Training or Education	What is the level of formal training/education that is needed to start doing your job?
	   Example: High School, 2 Year Vo-Tech in Data Processing, Bachelor of Science in Chemistry.
	In some jobs, a combination of education and job-related experience can substitute for academic degrees.
	   Example: Bachelors Degree in Accounting **or** completion of 2 years of general business courses plus 3 - 4 years work experience in an accounting field.

	What additional training, certification program, or licensing requirement is needed in order to start doing your job? Example: CPR training, state certification in boiler operation, licensing for pharmacists.
Experience	In addition to the formal training/education or equivalent experience you stated was necessary, how many months or years of previous job-related experience are needed to start doing your job.? Note: "None" can be a correct answer. For example, there is typically no previous work experience required for a new college graduate hired as a beginning engineer.
	Months: Years: ☐ None
Skills/ Compet- encies	What important skills, competencies, or abilities are needed to do the work that you do? (Please give two examples for each skill area you identify.)
	A. Coordinating Skills (such as scheduling activities, organizing/maintaining records)
	Are coordinating skills required? ☐ Yes ☐ No If yes, give two examples of specific skills needed
	Example #1
	Example #2
	B. Administrative Skills (such as monitoring financial data, interpreting policies and procedures)
	Are administrative skills required? ☐ Yes ☐ No If yes, give two examples of specific skills needed
	Example #1
	Example #2
	C. Analytical Skills (such as drawing conclusions from statistical data, examining alternative methods)
	Are analytical skills required? ☐ Yes ☐ No If yes, give two examples of specific skills needed
	Example #1
	Example #2
	D. Engineering Skills (such as identifying process control needs, defining capital equipment requirements, designing product testing systems)
	Are engineering skills required? ☐ Yes ☐ No If yes, give two examples of specific skills needed
	Example #1
	Example #2
	E. Communication Skills (such as handling inquiries, composing standard correspondence)
	Are communication skills required? ☐ Yes ☐ No If yes, give two examples of specific skills needed
	Example #1
	Example #2

	F. Influencing Skills (such as presenting project concepts, negotiating contracts, convincing others, dealing directly with customer)
	Are influencing skills required? ☐ Yes ☐ No If yes, give two examples of specific skills needed
	Example #1
	Example #2
	G. Computer Skills (such as systems analysis, software development, evaluation of computer hardware capabilities)
	Are computer skills required? ☐ Yes ☐ No If yes, give two examples of specific skills needed
	Example #1
	Example #2
	H. Creative Art Skills (such as writing feature articles, developing video productions, designing packaging, evaluating creative work)
	Are creative art skills required? ☐ Yes ☐ No If yes, give two examples of specific skills needed
	Example #1
	Example #2
	I. Vocational Skills (such as operating laboratory equipment, fixing machinery or equipment, testing and diagnosis against standards)
	Are vocational skills required? ☐ Yes ☐ No If yes, give two examples of specific skills needed
	Example #1
Skills/	Example #2
Compet-	**J. Basic Leadership Skills** (such as instructing, assigning work, maintaining flow of work, overseeing program implementation)
encies	Are basic leadership skills required? ☐ Yes ☐ No If yes, give two examples of specific skills needed
	Example #1
	Example #2
	K. Advanced Leadership Skills (such as creating group vision, coaching, directly supervising others, deciding the best allocation of resources, directing and controlling projects)
	Are advanced leadership skills required? ☐ Yes ☐ No If yes, give two examples of specific skills needed
	Example #1
	Example #2
	L. Manual Skills (such as sorting materials, filing, operating a lift truck, mixing ingredients, operating a keyboard)
	Are manual skills required? ☐ Yes ☐ No If yes, give two examples of specific skills needed
	Example #1
	Example #2
	M. Mechanical Skills (such as designing component parts, installing machinery, drafting blueprints)
	Are mechanical skills required? ☐ Yes ☐ No If yes, give two examples of specific skills needed
	Example #1
	Example #2

	N. Short-Term Planning Skills (such as preparing annual budgets, projecting inventory requirements)
	Are short-term planning skills required? ☐ Yes ☐ No If yes, give two examples of specific skills needed
	Example #1
	Example #2
	O. Long-Term Planning Skills (such as developing a division strategic plan, planning new product introductions) **Note:** Include only planning that extends beyond one year.
	Are long-term planning skills required? ☐ Yes ☐ No If yes, give two examples of specific skills needed
	Example #1
	Example #2
	P. Mathematical Skills (such as calculating unit costs, computing percentages, measuring proportions)
	Are mathematical skills required? ☐ Yes ☐ No If yes, give two examples of specific skills needed
	Example #1
	Example #2
Skills/ Compet- encies	**Q. Scientific Skills** (such as interpreting experimental results, product research and development, solving product technical problems)
	Are scientific skills required? ☐ Yes ☐ No If yes, give two examples of specific skills needed
	Example #1
	Example #2
	R. Software/Word Processing Skills (such as creating spreadsheets, updating sales data base, utilizing word processor to prepare correspondence, utilizing electronic mail)
	Are software/w. proc. skills required? ☐ Yes ☐ No If yes, give two examples of specific skills needed
	Example #1
	Example #2
	S. Other Special Skills Describe any other special skills, trades, or talents required for your job
	Most Critical Skills Of all the skills you named in the preceding section, which are the most important to the work that you do? In order of importance list the letter codes as used above. Example: 1. C, 2. P, 3. B, 4. R for Analytical, Mathematical, Administrative, and Software/Word Processing Skills
	1._____ 2._____ 3._____ 4._____

III. Complexity of Duties

Structure and Variation of Work	How processes and tasks within your work are determined, and how you do them are important to understanding your work at 3M. Describe the work flow in your job. Think of the major focus of your job or think of the work activities on which you spend the most time.
	1. From whom/where (title, not person) do you receive work?
	2. What processes or tasks do you perform to complete it?
	3. What are typical outputs?
Problem Solving and Analysis	Each job at 3M encounters problem situations, but jobs vary in how solutions are sought and found. Give three examples of problems you must solve in your work on a regular (e.g., daily, weekly, monthly) basis:
	1.
	2.
	3.
	Give an example of a particularly difficult problem that you face in your work.
	Why does it occur?
	How often does it occur?
	What special skills and/or resources are needed to solve this difficult problem?
	Within your work unit, is anyone else able to help solve the problem? Explain.
Creativity and Innovation	In which parts of your job can you be creative and innovative, to introduce new ideas or better ways to do things? Give examples; please be specific. Examples: Finding new uses for an existing product, modifying methods for tracking information, changing procedures to cut 3M shipping costs.

IV. Impact on Business

<table>
<tr>
<td rowspan="5">Indepen-
dence/
Nature
of Work
Review</td>
<td>Review of work can occur in different ways; for example, by direct supervision, by computer through built-in checks and balances, or by customers.
Who (title, not person) reviews your work?

 </td>
</tr>
<tr>
<td>What is the reviewer looking for?
   Examples: Accuracy of work, getting the job done on time, results of specific projects, accomplishment of broad objectives.

 </td>
</tr>
<tr>
<td>Is all your work reviewed, or does the review focus more on the end result? Explain.

 </td>
</tr>
<tr>
<td>When you come upon situations that do not fit established policies, procedures or practices, what do you do?
   Examples: Refer all questions to supervisor, consult with a more experienced co-worker, make a decision and have it approved.

 </td>
</tr>
<tr>
<td rowspan="5">Types of
Decisions
Made</td>
<td>Give three examples of the types of decisions you regularly make on the job.
   Examples: Directing a telephone call to the right person, determining the content of a new report, allocating work among those you supervise, approving proposed projects.

1.

2.

3.</td>
</tr>
<tr>
<td>If decisions in your job were not made properly, what kinds of errors would be likely to occur?
   Examples: Inaccurate calculations, misfiling documents, losing data.

 </td>
</tr>
<tr>
<td>What would be the likely results of such errors?
   Examples: Costly build-up of inventory, significant time loss, delayed production, loss of customer.

 </td>
</tr>
<tr>
<td>What would need to be done to correct the error or errors? Who would be involved?

 </td>
</tr>
</table>

Restricted Information	What types of 3M restricted information do you see or learn about on your job? 　Examples: Proprietary processes, trade secrets, costs, human resource-related information.
	How often do you see or use this information? ☐ Regularly　☐ Occasionally　☐ Rarely　☐ Not at all
	In the normal course of doing your job, how often might you have the chance to disclose restricted information? ☐ Frequently　☐ Occasionally　☐ Once in a while　☐ Not at all　Give an example of how disclosure might happen.
	What would be the impact if restricted information were disclosed? 　Examples: Damage to an important division objective, internal dissatisfaction.

Working With Others	This section asks about the level and purpose of your contacts with others while doing your job. In describing the purpose of your contacts, try to use key words such as give, receive, or exchange information, discuss, explain, convince, or persuade.

Internal Contacts

List the titles of other 3M jobs outside your immediate work unit with which you have **regular, work-related** contact. Describe the purpose and nature of the contacts.

Title Examples: Division Accountant 　　　　　Purchasing Agent	**Purpose/Nature** Discuss pricing strategy Explain invoice price discrepancy

External Contacts

List the titles and, if appropriate, companies/agencies outside 3M with which you have **regular, business-related** contacts. Describe the purpose of the contacts. List customers as a category, not by individual names.

Title/Company/Agency Examples: Customers 　　　　　University of Minnesota	**Purpose/Nature** Explain product features Discuss research contract

	Multinational/Global Responsibilities
	Do you have contacts with individuals or companies, including 3M subsidiaries, in countries other than the United States?
	☐ Yes ☐ No ➜ If no, go to next section
	If yes, what is the nature of these contacts? Examples: Telephone conversations, transmitting information, consultations, monitoring plan implementation.
	What percent of time is spent dealing with non-US individuals or companies?
	☐ Greater than 50% ☐ 25 - 49% ☐ 10 - 24% ☐ Less than 10%
Working With Others (cont.)	**Language Skills**
	Do you need to speak, read or write any language other than English to perform your work?
	☐ Yes ☐ No ➜ If yes, what are these languages, in order of importance?
	1. 2. 3.
	Explain how these other languages are on the job. Examples: To explain 3M policies, to take notes in meetings.

	Some 3M jobs are **accountable** for money management - either income, expenses, assets, or a combination of these. These are typically jobs with leadership, supervisory, or management responsibility. **Note:** To help you decide whether or not you should complete this section, ask yourself this question: "Am I held directly responsible for producing income, controlling expenses, or managing or safeguarding assets?" If your answer is no, enter "4" on each of the lines under the "Impact" column. Otherwise, continue.
	How does your job directly affect 3M's revenue, expenses or assets?

	Directions:
	1. Estimate the dollar amount(s) for which you are accountable on an annual basis.
	2. Use the impact scale to describe your accountability.
	3. Briefly describe the nature of your financial responsibility in the space provided.
	   Examples: Recommends and monitors spending of advertising budget, approves inventory levels that meet requirements,
	         minimizes investment in accounts receivable.

Financial Respon-sibility	**Impact Scale**
	1 - Overall control or managerial responsibility
	      (Establishes objectives, approves activities)
	2 - Important role in effective management
	      (At liberty to implement approved activities)
	3 - Participative or advisory role in planning/implementation
	4 - No responsibility

	Note: A "0" dollar amount followed by a "4" on impact is an acceptable answer.

	Annual Dollars	Impact	Description
Revenue	$		
Expense	$		
Assets	$		

Work Direction	This section is only for jobs that include responsibility for the work of others. This responsibility can be very limited (example: allocating work), very broad (example: hiring, terminating, merit rating), or indirect (example: leading task forces). ☐ If your job does not have any of these responsibilities, check this box and proceed to the next section. Otherwise, continue. Please list the number of people for whom you do any of the following; then provide the titles of jobs supervised. **Note:** Do not report intermittent or occasional supervisory duties. Examples of what not to list include: process engineers supervising production workers during test runs, filling-in for an absent supervisor or manager, singular (non-repeating) leadership of a task force or short-term project.

Type of Work Direction Provided	Number of People	
	Exempt	NonExempt
Direct supervision of others (conduct performance appraisals, make hiring decisions) Titles of jobs:		
Work direction of employees who are not direct reports (assign or allocate work, oversee corporate or divisional program) Titles of jobs:		
Frequent team leadership (task forces, project teams) Titles of jobs:		
Frequent direct supervision of non-3M employees (contract workers, consultants) Titles of jobs:		
Other (explain) Titles of jobs:		

V. Working Conditions

This section examines each job in terms of physical demands and environmental factors.

Work Position	What percentage of each day do you spend in these work positions? Your responses should total 100%.	
	Nonconfined sitting (free to move about at will)	%
	Confined sitting (cannot readily move about)	%
	Standing or walking	%
	Crouching, crawling, climbing, or other non-sitting, non-standing positions	%
Activity Summary	Approximately what percentage of your work time do you spend on: (Total need not equal 100%. Give examples.) **Examples**	
	Section A — Finger/hand manipulation	%
	Section A — Lifting/carrying/pushing/pulling	%
	Approximately what percentage of your work time do you spend on: (Total should equal 100%. Give examples)	
	Section B — Mental concentration	%
	Section B — Visual concentration	%

Risk Exposure	Describe any risk of injury to which you may be exposed while on the job. State the percentage of the work day you are exposed, assuming normal safety precautions are taken. State the possible consequence if an accident were to occur. Then, check the degree of attention required to minimize risks.

Risk Description & Possible Consequence Example: Chemical spill may require medical care but disability unlikely 5%	**%**	**Precaution Required**
		☐ Ordinary care and attention
		☐ Safety rules, training or protective equipment
		☐ Special skill/high level alertness

Environmental Comfort Level	Describe any noises, odors, drafts, dust, temperature extremes, special clothing or other discomforts associated with your job. State the approximate percentage of the work day you are exposed.

	%
	%

VI. General Comments

General Comments	What percentage of your job duties do you feel was captured in this questionnaire? ☐ 0 - 25% ☐ 26 - 50% ☐ 51 - 75% ☐ 76 - 100%
	What aspect of your job was not covered adequately by this questionnaire?

Important

Review your PIQ to make sure that you have not overlooked any important information.

When you have finished, give the PIQ to your supervisor/manager. He or she will discuss any possible changes with you. Finally, both you and your supervisor must read and sign below.

We have jointly reviewed and discussed the responses to this questionnaire and believe that they are representative of the position being described.

Employee Signature	Date
Supervisor/Manager Signature	Date

Note: Employee signature is not required where the supervisor/manager has completed the PIQ for a newly-created job.

YOUR TURN:
JOB ANALYSIS

1. Use the job analysis questionnaire in Appendix 3–A to describe a specific job you presently hold or have held in the past. This can be a part-time job or volunteer work for which you were not paid. Be sure to put your name on the questionnaire.

2. After you have completed the questionnaire, pick a teammate (or the instructor will assign one) and exchange completed questionnaires with your teammate.

3. Write a job description for your teammate's job. Does the questionnaire give you sufficient information? Is there additional information that would be helpful?

4. Exchange descriptions. Critique the job descriptions written by your teammate. Does it adequately capture all the important job aspects? Does it indicate which aspects are most important?

5. Save the description. We will examine it again in a later case.

Evaluating Work: Job Evaluation, Skill-Based Plans, and Market Pricing

---

Chapter Outline

My 14-year-old daughter absolutely refuses to go shopping with me. She's embarrassed by my behavior. (Can you imagine that?) The last time I took her to the mall to help her pick out (and pay for) sneakers, I spent most of my time interrogating the assistant store manager about how he was paid—more precisely, how his pay compared to that of the stock clerks, the manager, and regional managers. My daughter claims I do this everywhere I go. *Compensationitis,* she calls it. And I know it's contagious, because a colleague of mine grills his seatmates on airplanes. He's learned the pay rates for performers versus the understudies in the touring company for the musical *Cats.*

The next time you go to the supermarket, check out the different types of work there: store manager, produce manager, front-end manager, deli workers, butchers, stock clerks, checkout people, bakers—the list is long, and the work surprisingly diverse. How does any organization go about valuing work? Specifically, what techniques does it use, and does the technique really matter? But be careful—compensationitis is contagious, and it can embarrass your friends and relations.

The next two chapters discuss techniques used to value work. The end result is an internally consistent pay structure that will be acceptable to employees and aid the organization in being successful. Three basic techniques are examined: (1) job evaluation, (2) skill-based plans, and (3) market pricing. This chapter first discusses various perspectives on job evaluation and some of the key decisions in the process. Establishing the purposes and choosing among alternative methods of job evaluation are discussed. Next, it does the same for skill-based approaches and market pricing. Chapter 5 continues the discussion by focusing on the importance of achieving commitment and involvement of employees, as well as evaluating the usefulness of these techniques.

JOB-BASED STRUCTURES: JOB EVALUATION

Recall from our model the techniques used to design job-based structures. Everything focuses on jobs. The results of job analysis serve as input for evaluating jobs and establishing a job structure. Job evaluation involves the systematic evaluation of the job descriptions that result from job analysis. The evaluation is based on many factors: content of the work, skills required to perform the work, value of the work to the organization, the culture of the workplace, and external market forces. The potential to blend internal and external market forces represents both a major contribution of job evaluation and a source of controversy. This will become evident as we discuss the variety of definitions and decisions that surround job evaluation.

DIFFERING PERSPECTIVES

Perspectives on job evaluation are as diverse as the blind men's elephant. Job evaluation simultaneously includes (1) distinctions between content and value of the work, (2) linking the content of the work with the external market, and (3) aspects of measurement and administration.

Content and Value

The usual end result of job evaluation is a hierarchy of jobs or groups of jobs in the organization. Perspectives vary on whether these hierarchies are based on the jobs' content, and their value, or on some combination of both. *Job content* refers to the skills required, the degree of responsibilities assumed, and so on. The *value* of jobs refers to their relative contributions to organization goals, to their external market rates, or to some other agreed-upon rates set through collective bargaining or other negotiated process.

A structure based on comparing the relative content of jobs may differ from one based on relative value. This occurs, for example, when the relative value of the work performed is more (or less) in one organization than in another. The value of a compensation specialist to a firm whose earnings are generated through sales of manufactured goods or engineering expertise may differ from the value of that specialist to a consulting firm whose revenues come through the sale of compensation expertise. The skills are similar, yet their relative value differs for each organization.

Linking Content with the External Market

Some see job evaluation as a mechanism that links job content with the external market rates. Livernash observed, "The fundamental character of job evaluation is the integration of market wage rates and job content factors." Schwab concurs: "As practice, it [job evaluation] serves the important administrative function of linking external and internal labor markets. . . . No alternative procedure has been proposed that better performs this function."[1]

In this view, the structure resulting from job evaluation does not completely reflect the job's relative value unless it incorporates external market influences. Consequently, certain aspects of job content (e.g., skills required, magnitude of responsibilities) take on value based on their relationship to market wages. Because higher skill levels or willingness to undertake greater responsibility usually commands higher wages in the labor market, then skill level and degree of responsibility become useful criteria in job evaluation for establishing differences in pay among jobs. If some aspect of job content, such as working conditions, were not related to wages paid in the external labor market, then it would not be included in the job evaluation. Accordingly, since job content obtains value through the external market, it makes little sense to assert that content has an intrinsic value outside of its worth in the external market. It is job evaluation's role to integrate job content with external market forces.

But not everyone agrees. Bellak, in describing the Hay job evaluation plan (perhaps the most widely used plan among large corporations), states that the "measures are independent of the market and encourage rational determination of the basis for pricing

---

[1]Donald P. Schwab, "Job Evaluation and Pay Setting: Concepts and Practices," in *Comparable Worth: Issues and Alternatives,* ed. E. Robert Livernash (Washington, D.C.: Equal Employment Advisory Council, 1980), pp. 49–77.

job content."[2] For Bellak, job evaluation establishes the relative values of jobs based on their content, independent of a link to the market.

"Measure for Measure" versus "Much Ado about Nothing"

Some researchers believe that job evaluation takes on the trappings of measurement (objective, numerical, generalizable, documented, and reliable). If it is viewed as a measurement instrument, then job evaluation can be judged according to technical standards. Just as with employment tests, the reliability and validity of job evaluation plans can be compared.[3]

Those involved in actually making pay decisions have a different view. They see job evaluation as a process to help gain acceptance of pay differences among jobs, an administrative procedure through which the parties become involved and committed. Employees, union representatives, and managers can haggle over the relative worth of jobs—"the rules of the game."[4] As in sports contests, we are more willing to accept the results if we believe the rules of the game, in this case job evaluation, are fair.[5]

As an administrative procedure, job evaluation invites give and take. Consensus building often requires active participation by all those involved. Job evaluation even involves negotiations among managers of different units or functions within a single organization.

Livernash summarizes:

> Job evaluation is not a rigid, objective, analytical procedure. Neither is it a meaningless process of rationalization. If a group of people with reasonable knowledge of certain jobs rate (evaluate) them, there will be frequent small differences of opinion, some major differences as well, but also a high degree of general agreement. The application of group judgment through the rating process normally produces an *improved pay structure, but extreme attitudes as to the accuracy of ratings are difficult to defend.*[6]

---

[2]Alvin O. Bellak, "Comparable Worth: A Practitioner's View," in *Comparable Worth: Issue for the 80's,* vol. 1 (Washington, D.C.: U.S. Civil Rights Commission, 1985); and Ronnie J. Steinberg, "Identifying Wage Discrimination and Implementing Pay Equity Adjustments," in *Comparable Worth: Issue for the 80's,* vol. 1.

[3]Howard W. Risher, "Job Evaluation: Validity and Reliability," *Compensation and Benefits Review,* January–February 1989, pp. 22–36.

[4]George T. Milkovich, "Compensation, Equity, and Job Evaluation in the 1980's," *Proceedings of the Symposium of Job Evaluation and Equal Employment Opportunity* (New York: Industrial Relations Counselors, 1979); and George T. Milkovich and Charles J. Cogill, "Measurement as an Issue in Job Analysis and Job Evaluation," in *Handbook of Wage and Salary Management,* ed. Milton Rock (New York: McGraw-Hill, 1984). Also see Howard Risher, "Job Evaluation: Mystical or Statistical?" *Personnel* 55, no. 5 (September/October 1978), pp. 23–36; John Gaito, "Measurement Scales and Statistics: Resurgence of an Old Misconception," *Psychological Bulletin* 87, no. 3 (1980), pp. 564–67.

[5]Robert Folger and Mary Konovsky, "Effects of Procedural and Distributive Justice on Reactions to Pay Raise Decisions," *Academy of Management Journal,* March 1989, pp. 115–30; Jerald Greenburg, "A Taxonomy of Organizational Justice Theories," *Academy of Management Review* 12 (1987), pp. 9–22; and E. A. Lind and T. R. Tyler, *The Social Psychology of Procedural Justice* (New York: Plenum Press, 1988).

[6]E. Robert Livernash, "Internal Wage Structure," in *New Concepts in Wage Determination,* ed. George W. Taylor and Frank C. Pierson (New York: McGraw-Hill, 1957).

The following definition seems to include many of the nuances attributed to job evaluation.

Job evaluation is a systematic procedure designed to aid in establishing pay differentials among jobs within a single employer.

MAJOR DECISIONS

The major decisions involved in the design and administration of job evaluation are depicted in Exhibit 4.1. They include (1) establish the purpose(s) of job evaluation, (2) decide whether to use single or multiple plans, (3) choose among alternative approaches, (4) obtain the involvement of relevant stakeholders, and (5) evaluate its usefulness. The first three of these decisions are discussed in this chapter; the remaining two are covered in the next.

Establish the Purpose

Why bother with job evaluation? Because it aids in establishing a pay structure that is internally equitable to employees and consistent with the goals of the organization.

More specific purposes of job evaluation often include the following:

- Help integrate pay with a job's relative contributions to the organization.
- Establish a workable, agreed-upon pay structure.
- Assist employees to adapt to organization changes by improving their understanding of job content and what is valued in their work.
- Simplify and rationalize the pay relationships among jobs and reduce the role that chance, favoritism, and bias may play.
- Aid in setting pay for new, unique, or changing jobs.
- Reduce and resolve disputes and grievances over pay differences among jobs.
- Support other human resource programs such as career planning and training.

However, no one has studied the effects of formal job evaluation on any of these objectives.[7] Since they guide the design and administration of job evaluation, objectives need

---

[7]George Thomason, *Job Evaluation: Objectives and Methods* (London: Institute of Personnel Management, 1980); R. C. Smyth and M. J. Murphy, "Job Evaluation by the Point Plan," *Factory Management and Maintenance,* June 1946; Paul T. Stimmler, "The Job Evaluation Myth," *Personnel Journal,* November 1966, pp. 594–96; Douglas S. Sherwin, "The Job of Job Evaluation," *Harvard Business Review* 35 (1957), pp. 63–71; M. S. Viteles, "A Psychologist Looks at Job Evaluation," *Personnel,* May 1941; Herbert G. Zollitsch and Adolph Langsner, *Wage and Salary Administration* (Cincinnati, Ohio: South-Western, 1970); Howard Risher, *Job Evaluation Revisited* (New York: William M. Mercer, 1982); and R. F. Milkey, "Job Evaluation after 50 Years," *Public Personnel Review,* January 1960.

EXHIBIT 4.1   Determining an Internally Consistent Job Structure

---

**Internal consistency:
Work relationships
within the
organization** $\longrightarrow$ **Job analysis** $\longrightarrow$ **Job descriptions** $\longrightarrow$ **Job evaluation** $\longrightarrow$ **Job structure**

Some Major Decisions in Job Evaluation
- Establish purpose of evaluation
- Decide whether to use single or multiple plans
- Choose among alternative approaches
- Obtain involvement of relevant stakeholders
- Evaluate plan's usefulness

---

to be specified. But initially—established objectives too often get lost in complex procedures and bureaucracy that sprout around job evaluation. Job evaluation sometimes seems to exist for its own sake, rather than as an aid to achieve goals.

Lawler derides job evaluation, saying it "emphasizes control and focuses on carefully prescribed and described activities. It supports a top down, control oriented, bureaucracy."[8] These criticisms have validity when job evaluation is used for its own sake rather than as an aid to achieve the objectives listed above. Similar criticisms have been leveled at skill-based approaches, especially by managers who have extended experience with them. Recently, a vice president at General Mills lamented that the skill-based approach at one of its facilities was more bureaucratic and technically complex than the job evaluation plan it replaced.[9] So an organization is best served by establishing its objectives for the process and using them as a constant yardstick to evaluate the usefulness of these techniques.

Single versus Multiple Plans

Once the objectives of job evaluation are established, it is necessary to decide which jobs are going to be evaluated. Rarely will an employer evaluate all jobs in the organization at one time. More typically, related groups of jobs, for example, production, engineering, or marketing, will receive attention.

Many employers design different evaluation plans for different types of work. They do so because they believe that the work content is too diverse to be adequately evaluated using the same plan. For example, production jobs may vary in terms of working conditions and the physical, manipulative skills required. But engineering and marketing

---

[8]E. E. Lawler, "What's Wrong with Point-Factor Job Evaluation," *Compensation and Benefits Review,* March-April 1986, pp. 20–28.

[9]G. V. Barrett and D. Doverspike, "Another Defense of Point-Factor Job Evaluation," *Personnel,* March 1989, pp. 33–36.

jobs do not vary on these factors, nor are those factors particularly important in engineering or marketing work. Rather, other factors such as technical knowledge and skills and the contacts with customers may be relevant. Including factors that are relevant to only a portion of the jobs can make a plan unwieldy and decrease its usefulness.

The decision about single versus multiple plans is also important in the comparable worth controversy. The issue is whether the jobs usually found within a single firm can be adequately evaluated by a single plan or whether several plans are required to measure job characteristics adequately.[10] Advocates argue that an operational definition of comparable worth hinges on the application of a single evaluation system across all job families, both to rank order and to set salaries.[11] Yet to define universal factors in such a way that they accurately evaluate all obs within a single employer and at the same time remain acceptable to all parties imposes a burden on a single plan.[12] This issue is examined again in Chapter 14, Pay Discrimination.

Rather than using either universal factors or entirely unique factors for each type of work, some employers, notably Hewlett-Packard, use a core set of common factors and another set of factors unique to particular occupational or functional areas (finance, manufacturing, software and systems, sales). Their experiences suggest that unique factors tailored to different job families are more likely to be acceptable to employees and managers and easier to verify as work related than are generalized universal factors.

Choose among Methods

Four fundamental job evaluation methods are in use: ranking, classification, factor comparison, and point method. Uncounted variations of these methods exist. According to a survey of job evaluation practices reported in Exhibit 4.2 the point method is by far the most commonly used method. The following sections examine each of the methods and provide examples of some adaptations. All of the methods assume that an accurate job analysis has been translated into useful job descriptions.

RANKING

Ranking simply orders the job descriptions from highest to lowest based on a definition of relative value or contribution to the organization's success. Our experience suggests

---

[10]Donald J. Treiman and Heidi J. Hartmann, eds., *Women, Work and Wages: Equal Pay for Jobs of Equal Value* (Washington, D.C.: National Academy Press, 1981); and D. Treiman, ed., *Job Evaluation: An Analytic Review,* Interim Report to the Equal Employment Opportunity Commission (Washington, D.C.: National Academy Press, 1981).

[11]Helen Remick, *Comparable Worth and Wage Discrimination* (Philadelphia: Temple University Press, 1984). See also Karin Allport, "Equal Pay for Equal Work? Of Course," *Across the Board* 17, no. 10 (October 1980); and James T. Brinks, "The Comparable Worth Issue: A Salary Administration Bombshell," *Personnel Administrator,* November 1981, pp. 37–40.

[12]Legislation in Ontario, Canada, requires single plans for each bargaining unit with an employer. Thus, a single employer could have three plans if the Teamsters Union represented one occupation, and the Sheetmetal Workers Union another. An additional plan is required for employees who are not in a bargaining unit. *Pay Equity Implementation Series* (Toronto, Ontario, Canada: The Pay Equity Commission, 1989).

EXHIBIT 4.2   Methods Used in Job Evaluation

	Executive/ Managers	Scientists/ Engineers	Customer Reps	Exempt Staff	Clerical Employees	Hourly Employees
Ranking	22.6	14.0	15.6	20.3	20.8	16.3
Point	49.9	37.8	44.6	55.6	56.2	36.4
Factor comparison	11.5	9.3	10.1	12.1	11.3	7.4
Other	6.4	3.8	4.7	5.4	6.1	9.9

SOURCE: Reprinted by permission of the American Compensation Association from *Report on the 1987 Survey of Salary Management Practices,* 1988.

EXHIBIT 4.3   Alternation Ranking

Jobs		Rank
Number	Title	Most Valued
1	Shear operator	Master welder
2	Electrician	Electrician
3	Punch press operator	
4	Master welder	
5	Grinder	
6	Receiving clerk	Receiving clerk
		Least Valued

---

that it is common in small to medium-sized firms. Ranking is the simplest, fastest, easiest to understand and explain to employees, and the least expensive method, at least initially.

Two ways of ranking are usually considered: alternation ranking and paired comparison. Alternation ranking involves ordering the job descriptions alternately at each extreme. Exhibit 4.3 illustrates the method. Agreement is reached among evaluators on which job is the most valuable, then the least valuable. Evaluators alternate between the next most valued and next least valued, and so on, until all the jobs have been ordered. For example, evaluators agreed that the job of master welder was the most valued of the six jobs listed in the exhibit, and receiving clerk the least valued. Then they selected most and least valued from the four remaining jobs on the list.

The paired comparison method compares all possible pairs of jobs using a matrix, as shown in Exhibit 4.4. The higher-ranked job is entered in the cell. Starting at the top left cell and moving to the right, each pair of jobs is compared. For example, of the shear operator and the electrician, the electrician is ranked higher. Of the shear operator and the punch press operator, the shear operator is ranked higher. When all comparisons have been completed, the job with the highest total number of "most valuable" rankings

EXHIBIT 4.4   Paired Comparison Ranking

	Electrician	Punch press operator	Master welder	Grinder	Receiving clerk
Shear operator	E	S	M	S	S
Electrician		E	M	E	E
Punch press operator			M	P	P
Master welder				M	M
Grinder					G

Total favorable comparisons:

Shear operator: 3

Electrician: 4

Punch press operator: 2

Master welder: 5

Grinder: 1

Receiving clerk: 0

Resulting ranks:

Master welder

Electrician

Shear operator

Punch press operator

Grinder

Receiving clerk

becomes the highest ranked job, and so on. Alternation ranking and paired comparison methods may be more reliable (produce similar results consistently) than simple ranking.

Caution is required if ranking is chosen. The criteria or factors on which the jobs are ranked are usually so poorly defined, if they are specified at all, that the evaluations can become subjective opinions that are difficult, if not impossible, to explain and justify in work-related terms. Further, evaluator(s) using this method must be knowledgeable about every single job under study. The numbers alone turn what should be a simple task into a formidable one—50 jobs require 1,225 comparisons; and as organizations change, it is difficult to remain knowledgeable about all jobs. Some organizations try to overcome this difficulty by ranking jobs within single departments and merging the results. However, without greater specification of the factors on which the rankings are based, merging ranks is a major problem. Even though ranking appears simple, fast, and inexpensive, in the long term it may be more costly. The results are difficult to defend, and costly solutions are often required to overcome the problems created. However, in simplified structures, with fewer, broad generic jobs (e.g., Colgate-Palmolive's four levels of technicians), ranking is appealing.

CLASSIFICATION

The classification method is not even listed in the survey data shown in Exhibit 4.2. In spite of this omission, classification methods are widely used by public sector employers.[13]

---

[13]*Modernizing Federal Classification: An Opportunity for Excellence* (Washington D.C.: National Academy of Public Administration, July 1991).

The classification method involves slotting job descriptions into a series of classes that cover the range of jobs. Classes can be conceived as a series of carefully labeled shelves on a bookshelf. The labels are the class descriptions that serve as the standard against which the job descriptions are compared. Each class is described in such a way that it captures sufficient work detail yet is general enough to cause little difficulty in slotting jobs.

The classes may further be labeled by the inclusion of benchmark jobs that fall into each class. Benchmark jobs are defined as reference points having the following characteristics:

- The contents are well-known, relatively stable over time, and agreed upon by the employees involved.
- The jobs are common across a number of different employers. They are not unique to a particular employer.
- They represent the entire range of jobs being evaluated.
- They are accepted in the external labor market for setting wages.

Writing class descriptions can be troublesome when jobs from several occupations or job families are covered by a single plan. Although greater specificity of class definition improves the reliability of evaluation, it also limits the variety of jobs that can easily be classified. For example, class definitions written with sales jobs in mind may make it difficult to slot office or administrative jobs and vice versa. You can see the difficulty by examining the class definitions from the federal government's 18-class evaluation system (see Exhibit 4.5). The point of using benchmark jobs is to anchor the comparisons for each job class. Anchoring the classes in this way has the advantage of illustrating the typical job in a class.

In practice, the job descriptions not only are compared to the standard class descriptions and benchmark jobs but also to each other, to ensure that jobs within each class are more similar to each other than to adjacent classes. The final result is a series of classes with a number of jobs in each. The jobs within each class are considered to be equal (similar) work and will be paid equally. Jobs in different classes should be dissimilar and may have different pay rates.

The Federal Government's General Schedule

Although classification is more complex than ranking, it still is relatively inexpensive to develop and simple to install and understand. Probably the best known example is the Office of Personnel Management's General Schedule (GS), with 18 "grades" (classes)[14] (Exhibit 4.5). The GS system is *not* based on related subject matter of work (e.g.,

---

[14]The federal system utilizes the terms *grades* and *classes* differently than does this book. We have previously avoided referring to *job grades* because of possible confusion with *pay grades,* discussed in Chapter 7. However, the federal government refers to the results of its classification as *grades,* rather than *classes.* In the GS system, a series of *classes* links jobs of similar work (e.g., Clerk Typist Class I, Clerk Typist Class II).

EXHIBIT 4.5   Examples of General Schedule Descriptions for the Federal Government's Job Classification Method

---

Grade General Schedule 1 includes all classes of positions the duties of which are to be performed, under immediate supervision, with little or no latitude for the exercise of independent judgment, (1) the simplest routine work in office, business, or fiscal operations, or (2) elementary work of a subordinate technical character in a professional, scientific, or technical field.

Grade-General Schedule 5 includes all classes of positions the duties of which are (1) to perform, under general supervision, difficult and responsible work in office, business, or fiscal administration, or comparable subordinate technical work in a professional, scientific, or technical field, requiring in either case (A) considerable training and supervisory or other experience, (B) broad working knowledge of a special subject matter or of office, laboratory, engineering, scientific, or other procedure and practice, and (C) the exercise of independent judgment in a limited field; (2) to perform, under immediate supervision, and with little opportunity for the exercise of independent judgment, simple and elementary work requiring professional, scientific, or technical training equivalent to that represented by graduation from a college or university of recognized standing but requiring little or no experience; or (3) to perform other work of equal importance, difficulty, and responsibility, and requiring comparable qualifications.

Grade-General Schedule 9 includes all classes of positions the duties of which are (1) to perform, under general supervision, very difficult and responsible work along special technical, supervisory, or administrative experience which has (A) demonstrated capacity for sound independent work, (B) thorough and fundamental knowledge of a special and complex subject matter, or of the profession, art, or science involved, and (C) considerable latitude for the exercise of independent judgment; (2) with considerable latitude for the exercise of independent judgment, to perform moderately difficult and responsible work, requiring (A) professional, scientific, or technical training equivalent to that represented by graduation from a college or university of recognized standing, and (B) considerable additional professional, scientific, or technical training or experience which has demonstrated capacity for sound independent work; or (3) to perform other work of equal importance, difficulty, and responsibility, and requiring comparable qualifications.

Grade-General Schedule 13 includes all classes of positions the duties of which are (1) to perform, under administrative direction, with wide latitude for the exercise of independent judgment work of unusual difficulty and responsibility along special technical, supervisory, or administrative lines, requiring extended specialized, supervisory, or administrative training and experience which has demonstrated leadership and marked attainments; (2) to serve as assistant head of a major organization involving work of comparable level within a bureau; (3) to perform, under administrative direction, with wide latitude for the exercise of independent judgment, work of unusual difficulty and responsibility requiring extended professional, scientific, or technical training and experience which has demonstrated leadership and marked attainments in professional, scientific, or technical research, practice, or administration; or (4) to perform other work of equal importance, difficulty, and responsibility, and requiring comparable qualifications.

---

accounting jobs); rather, level of difficulty distinguishes the various classes.[15] Most jobs are in 15 grades; the top 3 have been combined with a "supergrade" that covers senior executives. Employees in these top 3 grades are eligible for bonuses and special stipends based on performance. Collapsing or "banding" the top three classes into one "supergrade" provides flexibility by making it easier to move people at this level among different

---

[15]GAO Report to the Chairman, Subcommittee on Federal Services, Post Office, and Civil Service, *Observations on the Navy's Personnel Management Demonstration Project* (May 1988).

agencies in order to best utilize these particular employees' skills and meet different agency needs.[16]

The Federal Classification Act of 1923 provided an early impetus for job classification in the federal government. Classification and the job descriptions provided the basis for internal consistency and a uniform job terminology, which allowed centralized financial control. The argument at the time was that the law made better, more efficient government a possibility.[17] (Not a reality, only a possibility.)

Subsequent legislation further refined and expanded the use of the classification method. Currently, the Factor Evaluation System (FES) uses nine factors to classify approximately 1 million nonsupervisory general schedule positions. These factors are listed in Exhibit 4.6. With the plan, jobs as diverse as conservationist in the Agriculture Department, border patrol officer in Immigration, and account auditor in the Internal Revenue Service are placed in the same GS level. Each factor also receives point values that reflect the factor's importance in a job. The sum total of the factor ratings equals the job's total worth. The Factor Evaluation System gives managers three potential comparisons to guide their evaluation of a job: the general class description, the factor comparisons, and the benchmark jobs that anchor each class.

EXHIBIT 4.6   Factor Evaluation System: Nine Factors, with Subfactors

Knowledge required by the position
1. Nature or kind of knowledge and skills needed
2. How the knowledge and skills are used in doing the work

Supervisory controls
1. How the work is assigned
2. The employee's responsibility for carrying out the work
3. How the work is reviewed

Guidelines
1. The nature of guidelines for performing the work
2. The judgment needed to apply the guidelines or develop new guides

Complexity
1. The nature of the assignment
2. The difficulty in identifying what needs to be done
3. The difficulty and originality involved in performing the work

Scope and effect
1. The purpose of the work
2. The impact of the work product or service

Personal contacts

Purpose of contacts

Physical demands

Work environment

---

[16]Ibid., p. 10.

[17]Paul A. Katz, "Specific Job Evaluation Systems: White Collar Jobs in the Federal Civil Service," in *Handbook of Wage and Salary Administration,* ed. Milton Rock (New York: McGraw-Hill, 1984), pp. 14/1–14/10; and Steven W. Hays and T. Zane Reeves, *Personnel Management in the Public Sector* (Boston: Allyn and Bacon, 1984).

The Factor Evaluation System is not the only job evaluation system within the federal government.[18] The government's approach seems to be similar to that of private industry: pick, choose, and adapt, according to specific needs.

Many states and other governmental units use variations of the classification system, too. In addition, classification is applied to a wide variety of private sector jobs. High-technology and defense-related businesses have frequently developed four to six job classes for engineers. However, the differences among classes in this setting are often more related to experience or "years-since-degree" than to differences in work done by engineers (see Exhibits 4.6 and 4.7).

Flexibility: Balancing Control and Chaos

Classification plans afford flexibility to adapt to changing conditions. Sufficient vagueness usually exists in the class descriptions to permit reinterpretation of classes and benchmark jobs as the situation requires.[19] Thus, the introduction of new technology or restructuring of operations may be accommodated by these inherent flexibilities.

This flexibility may be very attractive to managers coping with increased competitive pressures and the need to restructure the work. Many employers have slashed the number of classes to increase responsiveness and flexibility.[20] At Colgate-Palmolive's Ohio facilities, all plant jobs are grouped into only four job classes. Rather than use diverse job descriptions, all workers are known as technicians or associates. The same actions have been taken by Corning at its Blacksburg, Virginia, plant, by M&M Mars in its New Jersey plants, and by many others.

However, the lack of detailed, work-related evaluations cuts two ways—generic classes and vague descriptions such as "associates" or "technicians" may not provide sufficient work-related evidence to justify pay decisions.[21] This lack of detail clearly avoids bureaucracy—managers are "free to manage." But it also reduces control and may increase the likelihood of equal pay lawsuits or make it harder to placate disgruntled employees who believe the work they do is misvalued.

Some balance between chaos and control is required. Prior to the widespread use of job evaluation, employers in the 1930s and 1940s had irrational pay structures—the legacy of decentralized and uncoordinated wage-setting practices. Pay differences were a major source of unrest among workers. American Steel and Wire, for example, had more than

---

[18]The following report summarizes different approaches: *Modernizing Federal Classification: An Opportunity for Excellence* (Washington D.C.: National Academy of Public Administration, 1991). Also see Edward B. Shils, "A Perspective on Job Measurement," in *Handbook of Wage and Salary Administration,* ed. Milton Rock (New York: McGraw-Hill, 1984), pp. 8/1–8/14; P. Katz, "Specific Job Evaluation Systems," in *Job Evaluation and Pay Administration in the Public Sector,* ed. Harold Suskin, (Chicago: International Personnel Management Association, 1977); and Hays and Reeves, *Personnel Management in the Public Sector.*

[19]Thomas H. Patten, Jr., *Pay, Employee Compensation and Incentive Plans* (New York: Free Press, 1977).

[20]Edgar Schein, "Corporate Teams and Totems," *Across the Board,* May 1989, pp. 12–17. Also see, in that same issue, Robert H. Guest, "Team Management under Stress," pp. 30–35, and Paul Chance, "Redefining the Supervisor's Role," pp. 36–37.

[21]Elliot Jaques, "In Praise of Hierarchies," *Harvard Business Review,* January–February 1990.

100,000 pay rates.[22] Employment and wage records were rarely kept before 1900; only the foreman knew with any accuracy how many workers were employed in his department and the rates they received. Foremen used wage information to play favorites by varying the day rate or assigning favored workers to jobs where piece rates were loose. What's the point? History suggests that when flexibility without guidelines exists, chaotic and irrational pay rates too frequently result. Removing inefficient bureaucracy is important, but balanced guidelines are necessary to ensure that employees are treated fairly and that pay decisions are guided by the system's objectives.

FACTOR COMPARISON

In the factor comparison method, jobs are evaluated based on two criteria: (1) a set of compensable factors and (2) wages for benchmark jobs. The two criteria are combined to form a job comparison scale, which is then applied to nonbenchmark jobs. However, the method's complexity limits its usefulness. It is the least popular of the conventional methods listed in the survey in Exhibit 4.2.

Although several versions of factor comparison exist, the basic approach involves the following steps:

1. *Conduct job analysis.* As with all job evaluation methods, information about the jobs must be collected and job descriptions prepared. However, the factor comparison method differs from others in that it requires that jobs be analyzed and described in terms of the compensable factors used in the plan. Benge, Burk, and Hay prescribed five factors: mental requirements, skill requirements, physical factors, responsibility, and working conditions.[23] Exhibit 4.7 contains definitions of these five factors. The developers consider these factors to be universal—able to evaluate all jobs in all organizations. However, there is latitude in the specific definition of each factor among organizations.

2. *Select benchmark jobs.* The selection of benchmark jobs is critical since the entire method is based on them. Benchmark jobs (also called *key jobs*) serve as reference points. The characteristics of benchmark jobs are specified on page 121. In factor comparison, the requirements for a benchmark job are even more specific: they must cover the entire range of each factor. For example, if a compensable factor is mental requirements, benchmark jobs must cover the full range of mental requirements that exists in the job group being evaluated.

---

[22]Thomas Schlereth, *Victorian America: Transformations in Everyday Life* (New York: Harper Collins, 1991); Sanford M. Jacoby, "Development of Internal Labor Markets," in *Internal Labor Markets,* ed. P. Osterman (Cambridge, Mass.: MIT Press, 1984), pp. 23–70.

[23]Eugene J. Benge, Samuel L. H. Burk, and Edward N. Hay, *Manual of Job Evaluation* (New York: Harper & Row, 1941). See also Eugene J. Benge, "Using Factor Methods to Measure Jobs," in *Handbook of Wage and Salary Administration,* ed. Milton R. Rock (New York: McGraw-Hill, 1972); Edward N. Hay, "Four Methods of Establishing Factor Scales in Factor Comparison Job Evaluation," *Personnel,* September 1946, pp. 115–24; and Edward N. Hay, "Characteristics of Factor Comparison Job Evaluation," *Personnel* 22, no. 6 (1946), pp. 370–75.

EXHIBIT 4.7   Universal Factor Definitions Used in Factor Comparison Method

1. **Mental requirements—either the possession of and/or the active application of the following:**
   A. (Inherent) mental traits, such as intelligence, memory, reasoning, facility in verbal expression, ability to get along with people, and imagination.
   B. (Acquired) general education, such as grammar and arithmetic; or general information as to sports, world events, etc.
   C. (Acquired) specialized knowledge such as chemistry, engineering, accounting, advertising, etc.

2. **Skill:**
   A. (Acquired) facility in muscular coordination, as in operating machines, repetitive movements, careful coordinations, dexterity, assembling, sorting, etc.
   B. (Acquired) specific job knowledge necessary to the muscular coordination only; acquired by performance of the work and not to be confused with general education or specialized knowledge. It is very largely training in the interpretation of sensory impressions. Examples:
      (1) In operating an adding machine, the knowledge of *which key* to depress for a subtotal would be skill.
      (2) In automobile repair, the ability to determine the significance of a certain knock in the motor would be skill.
      (3) In hand-firing a boiler, the ability to determine from the appearance of the firebed how coal should be shoveled over the surface would be skill.

3. **Physical requirements:**
   A. Physical effort, as sitting, standing, walking, climbing, pulling, lifting, etc.; both the amount exercised and the degree of the continuity should be taken into account.
   B. Physical status, as height, weight, strength, and eyesight.

4. **Responsibilities:**
   A. For raw materials, processed materials, tools, equipment, and property.
   B. For money or negotiable securities.
   C. For profits or loss, savings or methods' improvement.
   D. For public contact.
   E. For records.
   F. For supervision.
      (1) Primarily the complexity of supervising *given* to subordinates.
      (2) Also, the degree of supervision *received*.
         To summarize the four degrees of supervision:
            Highest degree—gives much—gets little
            High degree—gives much—gets much
            Low degree—gives none—gets little
            Lowest degree—gives none—gets much

5. **Working conditions:**
   A. Environmental influences, such as atmosphere, ventilation, illumination, noise, congestion, fellow workers, etc.
   B. Hazards—from the work or its surroundings.
   C. Hours.

The exact number of benchmarks required varies; some rules of thumb have been suggested (15 to 25), but the number depends on the range and diversity of the work to be evaluated.

3. *Rank benchmark jobs on each factor.* Each benchmark job is ranked on each compensable factor (Exhibit 4.8). In our example, a job family consisting of

six jobs is first ranked on mental requirements, then on experience, and so on. The approach differs from the ranking plan in that each job is ranked on *each factor* rather than as a "whole" job.

4. *Allocate benchmark wages across factors.* Once each benchmark job is ranked on each factor, the next step is to allocate the wages paid for each job to each factor. Essentially this is done by a compensation committee that decides how much of the wage rate for each benchmark job is associated with mental demand, how much with physical requirements, and so on across all compensable factors. For example, in Exhibit 4.9, of the $5.80 per hour paid to the punch press operator, the committee has decided that the job's mental requirements equal $.80, experience/skill is worth $.80, physical factors account for $2.40, supervision accounts for $1.10, and other responsibilities are worth $.70 an hour in this job. The total $5.80 is allocated among the compensable factors. This process is repeated for each of the benchmark jobs.

EXHIBIT 4.8 Factor Comparison Method: Ranking Benchmark Jobs by Compensable Factor

Benchmark Job	Mental Requirements	Experience/ Skills	Physical Factors	Supervision	Other Responsibilities
A. Punch press operator	6	5	2	4	4
B. Parts attendant	5	3	3	6	1
C. Riveter	4	6	1	1	3
D. Truck operator	3	1	6	5	6
E. Machine operator	2	2	4	2	5
F. Parts inspector	1	3	5	3	2

NOTE: Rank of 1 is high.

EXHIBIT 4.9 Factor Comparison Method: Allocation of Benchmark Job Wages across Factors

Benchmark Job	Current Wage Rate ($/hour)		Mental Requirements $		Experience/ Skills $		Physical Factors $		Supervision $		Other Responsibilities $
A. Punch press operator	5.80	=	.80	+	.80	+	2.40	+	1.10	+	.70
B. Parts attendant	9.60	=	2.15	+	2.35	+	1.90	+	.60	+	2.60
C. Riveter	13.30	=	2.50	+	3.10	+	2.45	+	4.50	+	.75
D. Truck operator	8.50	=	3.40	+	3.20	+	.60	+	.80	+	.50
E. Machine operator	11.80	=	3.60	+	2.90	+	1.75	+	2.90	+	.65
F. Parts inspector	11.40	=	4.50	+	2.20	+	1.20	+	2.50	+	1.10

After the wage for each job is allocated among that job's compensable factors, the dollar amounts for each factor are ranked as shown in Exhibit 4.10. The job that has the highest wage allocation for mental requirements is ranked 1 on that factor, next highest is 2, and so on. Separate rankings are done for the wage allocated to each compensable factor. In the example in Exhibit 4.10, parts inspector has more of its wages allocated to mental requirements than does any other job, so this job receives the highest rank for that factor.

We now have two sets of rankings, which are shown in Exhibit 4.11, the first ranking (Exhibit 4.8) reflects the relative presence of each factor among the benchmark jobs. The second ranking reflects the proportion of each job's wages that is attributed to each factor (Exhibit 4.10). The next step is to see how well the two rankings agree.

EXHIBIT 4.10   Ranking Wage Allocations

	Factors									
	Mental Requirements		*Experience/ Skills*		*Physical Factors*		*Supervision*		*Other Responsibilities*	
Benchmark Job	*$*	*Rank*	*$*	*Rank*	*$*	*Rank*	*$*	*Rank*	*$*	*Rank*
A. Punch press operator	.80	6	.80	6	2.40	2	1.10	4	.70	4
B. Parts attendant	2.15	5	2.35	4	1.90	3	.60	6	2.60	1
C. Riveter	2.50	4	3.10	2	2.45	1	4.50	1	.75	3
D. Truck operator	3.40	3	3.20	1	.60	6	.80	5	.50	6
E. Machine operator	3.60	2	2.90	3	1.75	4	2.90	2	.65	5
F. Parts inspector	4.50	1	2.20	5	1.20	5	2.50	3	1.10	2

NOTE: Rank of 1 is high.

EXHIBIT 4.11   Comparison of Factor and Wage Allocation Ranks

	Mental Requirements		*Experience/ Skills*		*Physical Factors*		*Supervision*		*Other Responsibilities*	
Benchmark Job	*Factor Rank*	*Wage Rank*	*Factor Rank*	*Wage Rank*	*Factor Rank*	*Wage Rank*	*Factor Rank*	*Wage Rank*	*Factor Rank*	*Wage Rank*
A. Punch press operator	6	6	5	6	2	2	4	4	4	4
B. Parts attendant	5	5	3	4	3	3	6	6	1	1
C. Riveter	4	4	6	2	1	1	1	1	3	3
D. Truck operator	3	3	1	1	6	6	5	5	6	6
E. Machine operator	2	2	2	3	4	4	2	2	5	5
F. Parts inspector	1	1	3	5	5	5	3	3	2	2

5. *Compare factor and wage allocation ranks.* The two rankings are judgments based on comparisons of compensable factors and wage distributions. They agree when each benchmark is assigned the same location in both ranks. If there is disagreement, the rationale for each ranking must be reexamined. Both are judgments, so some slight "tuning" may bring the rankings into line. If agreement cannot be achieved, then the job is no longer considered a benchmark and is removed. Exhibit 4.11 reveals that the two rankings of benchmarks in our illustration agree on all factors except experience/skills, and so the decisions that went into ranking this factor need to be reexamined to see if the ranks can be brought into agreement.

6. *Construct the job comparison scale.* A job comparison scale slots benchmark jobs into a dollar scale for each factor based on the amount of pay assigned to each factor. In Exhibit 4.12, the punch press operator is slotted as $.80 under mental requirements, the parts attendant at $2.15, and so on. These slottings correspond to the wage allocations shown in Exhibit 4.9.

7. *Apply the scale.* All the nonbenchmark jobs are now slotted into the scales under each factor at the dollar value thought to be appropriate. This is done by comparing the factors in the job descriptions of nonbenchmark jobs with the scaled factors. Consider the mental requirements for the nonbenchmark job stocker. The evaluator reads the stocker job description and examines the first compensable factor mental requirements. After examining the job descriptions for punch press operator and parts attendant, the evaluator decides the mental requirements for stockers lie between these two jobs, and slots the stocker at $1.40 for mental requirements. The same procedure is carried out for each of the other factors. To calculate the wage rate for the stocker, the dollar values assigned on the job comparison scale for all the factors are simply added. The rate for the stocker is $7.40 (mental requirements = $1.40, experience = $2.60, physical demands = $1.00, supervisor = $1.40, and other responsibilities = $1.00).

After reading this discussion on factor comparison, it's easy to understand why only about 10 percent of employers using formal job evaluation use this approach. The method is complex, difficult to explain to dissatisfied employees and managers, and requires continuous updating. As the agreed-upon wage rates of the benchmark jobs change, the relationships among the jobs may change, and the allocation of the wages among the factors must be readjusted.

But note that the factor comparison approach represents a significant change from simple ranking and classification. First, the criteria for evaluating jobs, the compensable factors, are made explicit. Second, the use of existing wage rates of benchmark jobs systematically links external market forces with internal, work-related factors. Third, in the factor comparison approach, we see the use of a scale of degrees of worth (dollars) for each compensable factor. These three features—defining compensable factors, scaling the factors, and linking an agreed-upon wage structure with the compensable factors— are the basic building blocks on which point plans are based.

EXHIBIT 4.12   Job Comparison Scale

$ Value	Mental requirements	Experience/ skills	Physical demands	Supervision	Other responsibilities
.00					
.20					
.40					Truck operator
.60			Truck operator	Parts attendant	Machine operator / Riveter
.80	Punch press operator	Punch press operator		Truck operator	Punch press operator
1.00			STOCKER		STOCKER
.20			Parts inspector	Punch press operator	Parts inspector
.40				STOCKER	
				Parts inspector	
.60			Machine operator		
.80			Parts attendant		
2.00	Parts attendant				
.20		Parts inspector / Parts attendant			
.40	Riveter		Punch press operator / Riveter		
.60		STOCKER			Parts attendant
.80					
3.00		Machine operator / Riveter		Machine operator	
.20		Truck operator			
.40	Truck operator				
.60	Machine operator				
.80					
4.00					
.20					
.40	Parts inspector			Riveter	
.60					
.80					
5.00					

POINT METHOD

Like factor comparison, designing a point system is rather complex and often requires outside assistance by consultants. But once designed, the plan is relatively simple to understand and administer. Point methods have three common characteristics: (1) compensable factors, with (2) factor degrees numerically scaled, and (3) weights reflecting the relative importance of each factor. Appendix 4–A provides factor definitions and weights for a plan used for manufacturing jobs.

In point methods, each job's relative value, and hence its location in the pay structure, is determined by the total points assigned to it. A job's total point value is the sum of the numerical values for each degree of compensable factor that the job possesses. In the illustration in Exhibit 4.13, the point plan has four factors: skills required, effort required, responsibility, and working conditions. There are five degrees of each factor. In addition to factor definitions, the evaluator will be guided by benchmark jobs and/or written descriptions that illustrate each degree of every factor.

Additionally, factors may be weighted. For example, in Exhibit 4.13, the skills required item carries a greater weight (40 percent of the total points) for this employer than does working conditions (10 percent of the total points). Thus, a job's 240 total points may result from two degrees of skills required (2 × 40 = 80), three each of effort required (3 × 30 = 90) and responsibility (3 × 20 = 60), and one of working conditions (1 × 10 = 10); (80 + 90 + 60 + 10 = 240). Weighting reflects the relative value of a factor to an employer.

Once the total points for all jobs are computed and a hierarchy based on points established, then jobs are compared to each other to ensure that their relative locations in the hierarchy are acceptable.

EXHIBIT 4.13   The Point Method: Factors, Weights, and Scaled Degrees

Factors			*Degrees*			*Weight of this Factor*
Skills required	1	2	3	4	5	40%
Effort required	1	2	3	4	5	30
Responsibility	1	2	3	4	5	20
Working conditions	1	2	3	4	5	10

Example: Job X

			Degrees			×	*Weight*	=	*Points*
Skills required	1	②	3	4	5	×	40%	=	80
Effort required	1	2	③	4	5	×	30	=	90
Responsibility	1	2	③	4	5	×	20	=	60
Working conditions	①	2	3	4	5	×	10	=	10
									240

Points for Job X = 240

DESIGNING THE POINT PLAN

Exhibit 4.14 illustrates the steps in the design of a point plan. As with all job evaluation plans, the first step is job analysis. The next steps are to choose the factors, scale them, and establish the factor weights. The end product of the design phase is a job evaluation plan that can be used to evaluate all other jobs.

Conduct Job Analysis

Information about the jobs to be evaluated is the cornerstone of all job evaluation. Although ideally, all jobs will be analyzed, the relevant work content—the behaviors, tasks performed, abilities/skills required, and so on—of a representative sample of jobs forms the basis for deriving compensable factors.

Choose Compensable Factors

Compensable factors play a pivotal role in the point method. In choosing factors, an organization must decide the following: "What factors are valued in these jobs? What factors will be paid for in this work?" One company's scale for measuring the factor decision making is shown in Exhibit 4.15. It has three dimensions: (1) the risk and complexity (hence the guidelines available to assist in making decisions), (2) the impact of the decisions, and (3) the time that must pass before the impact is evident.

Compensable factors should possess the following characteristics:

Work Related.   Compensable factors must demonstrably reflect the actual work performed. Some form of documentation (i.e., job descriptions, job analysis, employee and/or supervisory interviews) must support the factors. Work-related documentation of factors helps gain acceptance by employees and managers, is easier to understand, and can withstand a variety of challenges to the pay structure. For example, managers may argue that the salaries of their subordinates are too low in comparison to those of other employees, or that the salary offered to a job candidate is too low. Union leaders may face questions from members about why one job is paid differently from another. Allegations of pay discrimination may be raised. Employees, line managers, union leaders, and compensation managers must understand and be able to explain why work is paid differently or the same. Differences in factors that are obviously work related provide that rationale. Properly selected factors may even diminish the likelihood of the challenges arising.

EXHIBIT 4.14   Steps to Design a Point Plan

---

1. Conduct job analysis.
2. Choose compensable factors.
3. Establish factor scales.
4. Derive factor weights.
5. Prepare evaluation manual.
6. Apply to nonbenchmark jobs.

EXHIBIT 4.15   Example of a Compensable Factor Definition: Decision Making

---

Compensable Factor Definition: Evaluates the extent of required decision-making and the beneficial or detrimental effect such decisions would have on the profitability of the organization. Consideration is given to the:
  • Risk and complexity of required decision-making
  • Impact such action would have on the company

What type of guidelines are available for making decisions?

_____1. Few decisions are required; work is performed according to standard procedures and/or detailed instructions.

_____2. Decisions are made within an established framework of clearly defined procedures. Incumbent is only required to recognize and follow the prescribed course of action.

_____3. Guidelines are available in the form of clearly defined procedures and standard practices. Incumbent must exercise some judgment in selecting the appropriate procedure.

_____4. Guidelines are available in the form of some standard practices, well-established precedent and reference materials and company policy. Decisions require a moderate level of judgment and analysis of the appropriate course of action.

_____5. Some guidelines are available in the form of broad precedent, related practices and general methods of the field. Decisions require a high level of judgment and/or modification of a standard course of action to address the issue at hand.

_____6. Few guidelines are available. The incumbent may consult with technical experts and review relevant professional publications. Decisions require innovation and creativity. The only limitation on course of action is company strategy and policy.

What is the impact of decisions made by the position?

_____1. Inappropriate decisions, recommendations or errors would normally cause minor delays and cost increments. Deficiencies will not affect the completion of programs or projects important to the organization.

_____2. Inappropriate decisions, recommendations or errors will normally cause moderate delays and additional allocation of funds and resources within the immediate work unit. Deficiencies will not affect the attainment of the organization's objectives.

_____3. Inappropriate decisions, recommendations or errors would normally cause considerable delays and reallocation of funds and resources. Deficiencies will affect scheduling and project completion in other work units and, unless adjustments are made, could affect attainment of objectives of a major business segment of the company.

_____4. Inappropriate decisions, recommendations or errors would normally affect critical programs or attainment of short-term goals for a major business segment of the company.

_____5. Inappropriate decisions, recommendations or errors would affect attainment of objectives for the company and would normally affect long-term growth and public image.

The effectiveness of the majority of the position's decisions can be measured within:

_____1. One day.   _____4. Six months.
_____2. One week.   _____5. One year.
_____3. One month.   _____6. More than a year.

SOURCE: Jill Kanin-Lovers, "The Role of Computers in Job Evaluations: A Case in Point," *Journal of Compensation and Benefits* (New York: Warren Gorham and Lamont, 1985).

Business Related.   Compensable factors need to be consistent with the organization's culture and values, its business directions, and the nature of the work. Any changes in the organization or its directions may necessitate changing factors. For example, both 3M and TRW recently included multinational responsibilities, as shown in Exhibit 4.16, as a factor in their managerial job evaluation plans. The factor is defined in terms of the

---

EXHIBIT 4.16 Compensable Factor Definition: Multinational Responsibilities

---

This factor concerns the multinational scope of the job. Multinational responsibilities are defined as line or functional managerial activities in one or several countries.

---

1. **The multinational responsibilities of the job can best be described as:**
   A. Approving major policy and strategic plans.
   B. Formulating, proposing, and monitoring implementation of policy and plans.
   C. Acting as a consultant in project design and implemention phases.
   D. Providing procedural guidance and information on well-defined topics.
   E. Not applicable.

2. **Indicate the percentage of time spent on multinational issues:**
   A. >50%
   B. 25–49%
   C. 10–24%
   D. <10%

3. **The number of countries (other than your unit location) for which the position currently has operational or functional responsibility:**
   A. More than 10 countries
   B. 5 to 10 countries
   C. 1 to 4 countries
   D. Not applicable

---

type of responsibility, the percent of time devoted to international issues, and the number of countries covered. In both firms, strategic business plans call for increased emphasis on international operations, which already account for more than 40% of revenues. Consequently, the business-related logic is to ensure that the compensable factors include international responsibilities in the work. Another example: Burlington Northern revised its job evaluation plan to omit the factor number of subordinates supervised. Although many plans include a similar factor, Burlington Northern decided that a factor that values increases to staff runs counter to the organization's objective of reducing the work force size. With the increased concern for customer centered behavior, some organizations have included responsive to customers as a compensable factor. Major shifts in the business strategy or values are not daily occurrences, but when they do occur, the factors need to be reexamined to ensure that they are consistent with the new directions.

Acceptable to the Stakeholders.   Acceptance of the pay structure by managers and employees is critical. This is also true of compensable factors used to slot jobs into the pay structure. To achieve acceptance of the factors, all the relevant parties' viewpoints need to be considered.

An example illustrates the point. A senior manager refused to accept a job evaluation plan unless the factor working conditions was included. The compensation specialist, a recent college graduate, demonstrated through statistical analysis that working conditions did not vary enough among 90 percent of the jobs under study to have a meaningful effect on the resulting pay structure; statistically, working conditions did not affect the results. The manager rejected these data, pointing out that the compensation professional had never worked in the other 10 percent of the jobs, which were in the plant's foundry. The manager knew that working conditions were important to the foundry employees. To get the plan and pay decisions based on it accepted, the compensation specialist redesigned the plan to include working conditions. In sum, compensable factors need to be work related, business related, and acceptable.

Approaches to Choosing Factors

There are two basic ways to select and define factors: adapt factors from an existing standard plan, or custom design a plan. In practice most applications fall between these two. Standard plans often are adjusted to meet the unique needs of a particular organization, and many custom-designed plans rely heavily on existing factors.

Adapting Factors from Existing Plans.   Although a wide variety of factors is used in standard existing plans, the factors tend to fall into four generic groups: skills required, effort required, responsibility, and working conditions. These four were used more than 50 years ago in the National Electrical Manufacturers Association (NEMA) plan and are also included in the Equal Pay Act (1963) to define equal work.[24]

Many of the early points plans, such as those of National Metal Trades Association (NMTA) and NEMA, and the Steel Plan, were developed for nonexempt manufacturing and/or office jobs. Since then, point plans have also been applied to managerial and professional jobs. The Hay Guide Chart-Profile Method, used by 5,000 employers worldwide (130 of the 500 largest U.S. corporations), is perhaps the most widely used. The three Hay factors—know-how, problem solving, and accountability—and an example of the guide charts are included in Appendix 4–B.[25]

Factors are usually chosen by a task force or job evaluation committee made up of key decision makers (or their representatives) from various functions (or units, such as finance, operations, engineering, and marketing). Joint union-management development of compensable factors is common. Dresser Rand and the electrical workers union, and Borg-Warner and the machinists' union are two examples. Not only is increased employee acceptance of a jointly developed plan likely, but employees provide valuable expertise, since they are usually the most knowledgeable about the actual work performed.

---

[24]Helen Baker and John M. True, *The Operation of Job Evaluation Plans* (Princeton, N.J.: Princeton University, Industrial Relations Section, 1947); William Gomberg, "A Collective Bargaining Approach to Job Evaluation," *Labor and Nation,* November–December 1946, pp. 46–53; L. Cohen, "Unions and Job Evaluation," *Personnel Journal,* May 1948, pp. 7–12; Boris Shiskin, "Job Evaluation: What It Is and How It Works," *American Federationist,* July–September 1947, p. 213–22; William Gomberg, *A Labor Union Manual on Job Evaluation* (Chicago: Roosevelt College, Labor Education Division, 1947).

[25]Hay Associates does not define its guide chart-profile method as a variation of the point method. Whether it is a point method or factor comparison is less important than recognizing that it is a widely used plan that combines characteristics of both methods.

Custom-Designed Factors.   Although modifying factors borrowed from standard plans remains a common approach, several employers have custom designed their own plans. Typically, they begin with a task force or committee representing key figures from management.[26] Compensable factors are identified by answering two basic questions:

1. What in the nature of work should we value and pay for?
2. Based on our operating and strategic objectives, what should we value and pay for in this work?

Factors may be solicited through focus groups of large numbers of employees, or through selective interviews with key employees. J. C. Penney involved more than 5,000 of the 15,000 managers whose jobs would eventually be covered by a job evaluation plan in focus groups. A compensation committee combined the lists of factors suggested by the focus groups, refined the factor definitions, and eliminated overlapping factors. In the end, six compensable factors were approved by top management: decision making impact on the company's objectives, communications, supervision and management, knowledge requirements, internal customers, and external customers. Two additional factors, stress and employee development, were eliminated after further discussions with the executive management. Penney decided that these two factors were difficult to quantify and tended to be a function of the person, not the job (i.e., what I find stressful, you may find energizing). Since the compensable factors were suggested by such a cross section of the managers, there's little question of their acceptability to those same managers when used to determine pay structures.

Obviously, custom-designing factors is time-consuming and expensive. The argument in favor of it rests on the premise that these factors are more likely to be work related, business related, and acceptable to the employees involved.

Several consulting firms adopt a more selective approach to soliciting factors. Early in the design of the point plan, key executives and senior managers are interviewed to collect information on a variety of issues.[27] Questions can cover what the executives see as inequities in current practices, their views on the firm's value system, and future business directions.

Establish Factor Scales

Once the factors are chosen, scales reflecting the different degrees within each factor are constructed. Each degree may also be anchored by the typical skills, tasks, and behaviors taken from benchmark jobs that illustrate each factor degree. Exhibit 4.17 shows NMTA's scaling for the factor of knowledge.

A major problem in determining degrees is to make each degree equidistant from

---

[26]Charles Fay and Paul Hempel, "Whose Values? A Comparison of Incumbent, Supervisor, Incumbent-Supervisor Consensus and Committee Job Evaluation Ratings" (Working paper, Rutgers University, 1991).

[27]Jill Kanin-Lovers and Michael L. Davis, "Selecting and Defining Job Evaluation Factors," *Journal of Compensation and Benefits*, January–February 1988, pp. 1–38.

EXHIBIT 4.17   Illustration of Factor Scaling from National Metal Trades Association

---

1. Knowledge

This factor measures the knowledge or equivalent training required to perform the position duties.

1st Degree
Use of reading and writing, adding and subtracting of whole numbers; following of instructions; use of fixed gauges, direct reading instruments and similar devices; where interpretation is not required.

2nd Degree
Use of addition, subtraction, multiplication and division of numbers including decimals and fractions; simple use of formulas, charts, tables, drawings, specifications, schedules, wiring diagrams; use of adjustable measuring instruments; checking of reports, forms, records and comparable data; where interpretation is required.

3rd Degree
Use of mathematics together with the use of complicated drawings, specifications, charts, tables; various types of precision measuring instruments. Equivalent to 1 to 3 years applied trades training in a particular or specialized occupation.

4th Degree
Use of advanced trades mathematics, together with the use of complicated drawings, specifications, charts, tables, handbook formulas; all varieties of precision measuring instruments. Equivalent to complete accredited apprenticeship in a recognized trade, craft or occupation; or equivalent to a 2-year technical college education.

5th Degree
Use of higher mathematics involved in the application of engineering principles and the performance of related practical operations, together with a comprehensive knowledge of the theories and practices of mechanical, electrical, chemical, civil or like engineering field. Equivalent to complete 4 years of technical college or university education.

---

the adjacent degrees (interval scaling). The following criteria for determining degrees have been suggested: (1) limit to the number necessary to distinguish among jobs, (2) use understandable terminology, (3) anchor degree definition with benchmark job titles, and (4) make it apparent how the degree applies to the job.[28] Using too many degrees makes it difficult for evaluators to accurately choose the appropriate degree. This, in turn, reduces the acceptability of the system.

Some plans employ two-dimensional grids to define degrees. For example, in the Hay Plan (see Appendix 4–B), degrees of the factor know-how are described by four levels of managerial know-how (limited, related, diverse, and comprehensive) and eight levels of technical know-how (ranging from professional mastery through elementary vocational). An evaluator may select among at least 32 (4 × 8) different combinations of managerial and technical know-how to evaluate a job.

---

[28]David W. Belcher, *Compensation Administration*, 3rd ed. (Englewood Cliffs, N.J.: Prentice Hall, 1974).

Derive Factor Weights

Once the degrees have been assigned, the factor weights must be determined. Different weights reflect differences in importance attached to each factor by the employer. For example, the National Electrical Manufacturers Association plan weights education at 17.5 percent; another employer's association weights it at 10.6 percent; a consultants' plan recommends 15.0 percent; and a trade association weights the same factor at 10.1 percent.

There are two basic methods used to establish factor weights: *committee judgment* and *statistical analysis*. In the first, members of the compensation committee or, in some rare cases, groups of employees are asked to allocate 100 percent of value among the factors. Some structured decision process such as delphi or other nominal group technique may be used to facilitate consensus.[29]

Statistical Approach

Statistical approaches are not new. The basic approach was developed more than forty years ago.[30] The weights are statistically derived in such a way as to correlate as closely as possible to pay rates that are agreed upon by the parties involved. Typically, those rates are the agreed-upon pay structure for benchmark jobs. By statistically analyzing an agreed-upon pay structure for benchmark jobs on the factor degrees assigned to each job, a set of weights is derived that will produce total job evaluation scores that will closely match the agreed-upon pay structure.

Most major consulting firms use this approach to establish both factor weights and scales. Although each firm's model and computer software are proprietary, as best we can judge, the basic approaches are similar statistically. Basically, they derive factor weights and scales that best fit a criterion pay structure.

Choosing the Criterion Pay Structure.   The choice of the criterion is a critical decision since the factor weights and degrees are modeled to reproduce it. Several options are available: (1) current wage rates paid by the firm for benchmarks. This criterion is used when the firm simply wants a job evaluation plan that will reproduce the current structure or (2) competitive rates paid in the labor market for benchmark jobs. The premise in this case is that the firm wants to set its pay structure to match the structure found in the labor market at a particular time.

---

[29]Andre L. Delbecq, Andrew H. Van de Ven, and David H. Gustafson, *Group Techniques for Program Planning: A Guide to Nominal Group and Delphi Processes* (Glenview, Ill.: Scott, Foresman, 1975); and D. D. Robinson, O. W. Wahlstrom, and R. C. Mecham, "Comparison of Job Evaluation Methods: A 'Policy-Capturing' Approach Using the PAQ," *Journal of Applied Psychology* 59, no. 5 (1974), pp. 633–37.

[30]Paul M. Edwards, "Statistical Methods in Job Evaluation," *Advanced Management,* December 1948, pp. 158–63; and J. L. Otis and R. H. Leukart, *Job Evaluation: A Basis for Sound Wage Administration* (Englewood Cliffs, N.J.: Prentice-Hall, 1954). See also Eugene J. Benge, "Statistical Study of a Job Evaluation Point System," *Modern Management,* April 1947, pp. 17–23; Kermit Davis, Jr. and William Sauser, Jr., "Effects of Alternative Weighting Methods in a Policy-Capturing Approach to Job Evaluation: A Review and Empirical Investigation," *Personal Psychology* 44 (1991), pp. 85–127.

Some people object to using market rates since they may not be linked to the firm's business strategy. Still others object because they believe wage rates for some jobs, that is, those held predominantly by women, are artificially depressed due to historical gender discrimination.[31] Duplicating the existing pay structure, whether within the firm or in the market, perpetuates this discrimination, they say. Other possible criteria include (3) the rates for jobs held predominantly by men (on the grounds that they are the best estimates of bias-free rates) and (4) wage rates that have been negotiated with employees through collective bargaining.

The statistical approach is often labeled as *policy capturing* to contrast it with the committee judgment approach. Both approaches are policy capturing; only the policy or criterion captured may vary and the method used to capture that policy may vary (statistical versus judgmental).

Often the initial results of either the committee judgment or statistical approach for deriving factor weights and degrees may not be completely satisfactory. The job evaluation results and the agreed-upon pay structure may not agree. Several procedures are commonly used to overcome this disagreement. First, the sample of benchmark jobs is often changed by adding or deleting jobs. Second, the factor degree assigned to each benchmark job may be adjusted. Third, the pay structure serving as a criterion may be adjusted. And, finally, the weighting scheme may be adjusted. Thus, a task force beginning with exactly the same factors and degrees could end up with very different job evaluation plans, depending on the specific benchmark jobs, the pay structure chosen as the criterion, and the method used to establish the weights.

How Many Factors?   A remaining issue to consider is how many factors should be included in the plan. Some factors may have overlapping definitions or may fail to account for anything unique in the criterion chosen. We have already noted that factors must often be included to ensure the plan's acceptance. More than 40 years ago, researchers demonstrated that a few factors will yield practically the same results as many factors. Three to five factors explained most of the variation in the job hierarchy. In one study, a 21-factor plan produced the same job structure that could be generated using only 7 of the factors. Further, the jobs could be correctly slotted into classes using only 3 factors. Yet the company decided to keep the 21-factor plan because it was "accepted and doing the job."

---

[31]Donald J. Treiman, "Effect of Choice of Factors and Factor Weights in Job Evaluation," in *Comparable Worth and Wage Discrimination,* ed. H. Remick (Philadelphia: Temple University Press, 1984), pp. 79–89; Susan L. Josephs, "Equal Pay and Comparable Worth: Collective Bargaining Approaches" (Ohio State University); Winn Newman, "Pay Equity Emerges as a Top Labor Issue in the 1980s," *Monthly Labor Review,* April 1982, pp. 49–51; MacNeill/Lehrer Report, "Wage Discrimination," Library 1287, Show 6047 (New York: Educational Broadcasting Corporation, September 2, 1980); Richard Arvey, "Sex Bias in Job Evaluation Procedures," *Personnel Psychology* 39 (1986), pp. 315–35; and Steve O'Byrne, *TPF&C Report on Statistical Methodology for the Weighted Job Questionnaire* (New York: TPF&C, 1988); and J. E. Laughlin, "Comment on 'Estimating Coefficients in Linear Models: It Don't Make No Never Mind,'" *Psychological Bulletin* 8 (1978), pp. 247–53.

Combining Factor Scales and Weights. To translate weights and factor scales into actual job points, the maximum number of points to be used in the system is first divided among the factors according to their weights. The points for each factor are then attached to that factor's scale. For example, if the knowledge factor scaled in Exhibit 4.17 is weighted 20 percent in a 500-point system, then a total of 100 points is assigned to this factor, and each of the five degrees of knowledge is worth 20 points; for example, fourth degree $= 4 \times 20 = 80$ points.

Single-Factor Systems

Single-factor job evaluation systems have been proposed by some researchers. They all appear to focus on measuring the amount of discretion an employee has in a job. The most widely known is Jaques's Time Span of Discretion (TSD).[32] Each job comprises tasks, and each task has an implicit or explicit time before its consequences become evident. Jaques defines TSD as "the longest.period of time in completing an assigned task that employees are expected to exercise discretion with regard to the pace and quality of the work without managerial review."[33] Jaques asserts that TSD is distinct from job evaluation in that it represents measurement (of time units) rather than subjective judgment. But judgment is still required to assess the time.

The premise underlying these single-factor approaches is that the job content or value content is unidimensional.[34] Perhaps the major complaint about single-factor plans is from employees who are not convinced that one factor can adequately represent the entire domain of their work.

---

[32]Elliot Jaques, *Equitable Payment* (London: Heinemann, 1970); T. T. Paterson, *Job Evaluation*, vol. 1 (London: Business Books Ltd., 1972); A. W. Charles, "Installing Single-Factor Job Evaluation," *Compensation Review*, First Quarter 1971, pp. 9–21; Jay R. Schuster, "Job Evaluation at Xerox: A Single Scale Replaces Four," *Personnel*, May/June 1966, pp. 15–23; Lee A. Chambliss, "Our Employees Evaluate Their Own Jobs," *Personnel Journal* 29, no. 4 (September 1950), pp. 141–42; Thomas J. Atchison, *A Comparison of the Time-Span of Discretion, A Classification Method of Job Evaluation and a Maturity Curve Plan as Methods of Establishing Pay Differentials for Scientists and Engineers Using Perceived Equity as a Criterion* (Doctoral dissertation, Graduate School, University of Washington, Seattle, 1965); T. T. Paterson, *Job Evaluation*, vol. 2 (London: Camelot Press Ltd., 1972); Elliott Jaques, *Time Span Handbook* (London: Heinemann, 1964), *Measurement of Responsibility* (London: Heinemann, 1972), and "Taking Time Seriously in Evaluating Jobs," *Harvard Business Review*, September/October 1979, pp. 124–32. See also Michael E. Gordon, "An Evaluation of Jaques' Studies of Pay in the Light of Current Compensation Research," *Personnel Psychology* 4 (1969), pp. 369–89; Paul S. Goodman, "An Empirical Examination of Elliott Jaques' Concept of Time Span," *Human Relations* 20 (1967), pp. 155–70; T. O. Kvalseth and E. R. Crossman, "The Jaquesian Level-of-Work Estimators: A Systematic Formulation," *Organizational Human Performance* 11 (1974), pp. 303–15; J. M. M. Hill, "A Note on Time-Span and Economic Theory," *Human Relations*, November 1958, pp. 373–80.

[33]Jaques, *Equitable Payment*, p. 10.

[34]T. T. Paterson and T. M. Husband, "Decision-Making Responsibilities: Yardstick for Job Evaluation," *Compensation Review*, Second Quarter 1970, pp. 21–31; T. T. Paterson, "The Link between Pay and Decision-Making," *International Management*, December 1977, pp. 14–16; N. H. Cuthbert and J. M. Paterson, "Job Evaluation: Some Recent Thinking and Its Place in an Investigation," *Personnel Management*, September 1966, pp. 152–62; Dov Elizur, *Job Evaluation* (Hants, England: Gower Publishing, 1980) (Distributed in North America by Renouf/USA, Brookfield, Vt.); and Dov Elizur, "Facets of Work Values: A Structural Analysis of Work Outcomes," *Journal of Applied Psychology* 69, no. 3 (1984), pp. 379–89.

Exhibit 4.18   Determining the Internally Consistent Skill-Based Structure

Internal consistency: Work relationships within the organization	→	Skill analysis	→	Skill certification	→	Skill-based structure

Some Major Decisions in Skill Assessment and Certification
- Establish the purpose of a skill-based plan
- Determine the skill blocks and levels
- Establish certification methods
- Obtain involvement and commitment of stakeholders
- Evaluate the plan's usefulness

SKILL-BASED STRUCTURES

Internal pay structures do not need to be based on jobs; rather, they can be based on skill. The second technique for valuing work, the skill-based method, focuses on the skill or skills required to perform the work. Hence, work is analyzed to determine the skill required. The skill required serves as input to certify whether employees possess the required skill. Employees are paid based on the required knowledge or skills they possess rather than the jobs they perform or whether they actually use the knowledge in their work.

MAJOR DECISIONS

Even with the renewed interest in how to design and manage skill-based structures, there is as yet no well-established, agreed-upon approach. However, we can identify the major decisions involved in designing a skill-based plan. They are depicted in Exhibit 4.18 and include the following:

1. Establish the purpose of a skill-based plan.
2. Determine the skill blocks and levels.
3. Establish certification methods.
4. Obtain involvement and commitment of stakeholders.
5. Evaluate the plan's usefulness.

As with job evaluation, the first three of these decisions are discussed in this chapter, and the remaining two are covered in the next. An example of Borg-Warner's skill-based plan is found in Appendix 4–A.

Establish the Purpose

Under skill-based plans, employees are paid for the skill they are capable of using rather than the jobs they are performing. The key objectives for a skill-based plan include the following:

- Provide employees with incentives to learn additional skills and knowledge.
- Remove job barriers: "It's not in my job description."
- Establish a workable, agreed-upon pay structure.
- Integrate employees' pay with continuous learning to help the organization compete.
- Explain/reduce disputes in terms of skill differences.
- Help ensure that the pay structure supports other human resource programs such as training and career planning.[35]

Polaroid developed its Applied Knowledge Plan as part of a strategy to "build a learning based environment."[36] It established the following three purposes:

- Ensure the knowledge and skills to keep Polaroid at the leading edge of technology and business practices.
- Ensure continual improvement in our ability to cope with technological change and improve the speed with which new products and services are delivered to market.
- Focus on continually improving quality, customer orientation, and performance.

How well skill-based approaches achieve such objectives is virtually unexamined. However, both General Mills and Honeywell do report positive effects on employee attitudes toward work and pay at two of their facilities.[37]

Determine Skill Blocks and Levels

Skill blocks, as noted in Chapter 3, are different types of skill required to perform the work. Just as with compensable factors used in job evaluation, skill blocks should be (1) derived from the work to be performed, (2) focused on developing a highly flexible work force, and (3) understood and acceptable to the stakeholders involved.

Skill levels are simply the degrees within a particular block of skill. For example, the General Mills plan has three levels within each block. The levels reflect the proficiency of the employee. In the technical skill block, the three levels include (1) limited abilities to apply principles, (2) partially proficient, and (3) fully competent. Borg-Warner's skill-based evaluation plan (see Appendix 4–A) uses levels of each skill block, similar to degrees of a compensable factor in a job evaluation plan.

A skill-based plan for technicians at FMC is shown in Exhibit 4.19. The plan has three skill blocks: (1) foundation, (2) core electives, and (3) optional electives. The levels within the core elective block are calibrated by points assigned to each specific skill. The

---

[35]Richard Bunning, "Models for Skill-Based Pay Plans," *HR Magazine*, February 1992, pp. 62–64.

[36]*The Polaroid Pay Plan Manual* (Cambridge, Mass.: Polaroid Corporation, 1991).

[37]Gerald E. Ledford, Jr., "Three Case Studies on Skill-Based Pay: An Overview," *Compensation and Benefits Review*, March–April 1991, pp. 11–23.

EXHIBIT 4.19 Technician Skill-Based Structure

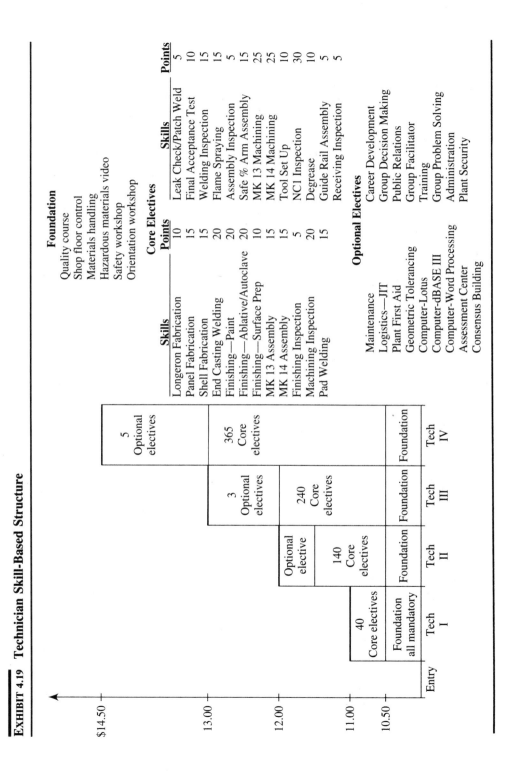

Foundation

Quality course
Shop floor control
Materials handling
Hazardous materials video
Safety workshop
Orientation workshop

Core Electives

Skills	Points	Skills	Points
Longeron Fabrication	10	Leak Check/Patch Weld	5
Panel Fabrication	15	Final Acceptance Test	10
Shell Fabrication	15	Welding Inspection	15
End Casting Welding	20	Flame Spraying	15
Finishing—Paint	20	Assembly Inspection	5
Finishing—Ablative/Autoclave	20	Safe % Arm Assembly	15
Finishing—Surface Prep	10	MK 13 Machining	25
MK 13 Assembly	15	MK 14 Machining	25
MK 14 Assembly	15	Tool Set Up	10
Finishing Inspection	5	NC1 Inspection	30
Machining Inspection	20	Degrease	10
Pad Welding	15	Guide Rail Assembly	5
		Receiving Inspection	5

Optional Electives

Maintenance	Career Development
Logistics—JIT	Group Decision Making
Plant First Aid	Public Relations
Geometric Tolerancing	Group Facilitator
Computer-Lotus	Training
Computer-dBASE III	Group Problem Solving
Computer-Word Processing	Administration
Assessment Center	Plant Security
Consensus Building	

Chart (wage rates):

- $14.50
- 13.00
- 12.00
- 11.00
- 10.50

	Entry / Tech I	Tech II	Tech III	Tech IV
	Foundation all mandatory	Foundation	Foundation	Foundation
	40 Core electives	140 Core electives	240 Core electives	365 Core electives
		Optional elective	3 Optional electives	5 Optional electives

technician pay structure has five rates ranging from an entry rate of $10.50 per hour to a Technician IV rate of $14.50 per hour. The three skill blocks are described as follows:

- *Foundation.* This block includes a quality seminar, videos on materials handling and hazardous materials, a three-day safety workshop, and a half-day orientation. All foundation competencies are mandatory and must be certified to reach the Technician I rate ($11).
- *Core electives.* These are necessary to the facility's operations (e.g., fabrication, welding, painting, finishing, assembly inspection). Note that each skill is assigned a point value. A total of 40 points (of 370) must be certified, in addition to the foundation competencies to reach Technician II ($12 per hour).
- *Optional electives.* These are additional specialized competencies ranging from computer applications to team leadership and consensus building. One optional elective must be certified to reach Technician III.

A fully qualified Technician IV (e.g., certified as mastering foundations, 365 points core electives, and five optional electives) is able to perform all work in a cell at the facility. Technician IV earns $14.50 per hour and can be assigned to any task, Technician III earns $13 per hour and can handle more tasks than Technician II, and so on.

The FMC approach should look familiar to any college student: required courses, required electives, and optional electives. There is a minor difference, of course—FMC employees get paid for passing these skills, whereas college students pay their schools to take courses!

Certification Methods

How should employees be certified that they possess the skill and are able to apply it? Who should be involved in the process? Practice varies widely. Some organizations use successful completion of courses to verify certification. Elementary and secondary school teachers get pay increases for completing additional college courses. Other organizations use peer review, on-the-job demonstrations, and tests for certification. This is similar to the traditional craft approach (i.e., apprentice, journeyman, and master). Still others require successful completion of formal courses, plus time on the job. Northern Telecom uses a preassessment meeting between supervisor and employee to discuss skill accomplishments and goals and training needs. Subsequently, a certification committee made up of employees and supervisors examines employees to determine whether they can be certified in the skills. Honeywell's plan calls for evaluating employees during the six months after they have learned the skills. Again, supervisors and peers are used in the certification process.[38]

This whole approach to certification may be fraught with potential legal vulnerabilities if employees who fail to be certified challenge the process. At this point, very little

---

[38]G. Douglas Jenkins Jr., Gerald E. Ledford Jr., Nina Gupta, and D. Harold Doty, *Skill-Based Pay* (Scottsdale, Ariz.: American Compensation Association, 1992).

attention has been devoted to assessor training or validating the certification process. On the face of it, just as employment tests used for hiring and promotion decisions are vulnerable to regulatory pressures, so too are certification procedures used to determine pay increases. Clearly, there is a need to ensure that procedures are work related and bias free.

MARKET PRICING

The third technique for valuing work differs markedly from job evaluation and skill-based approaches. Market pricing involves setting pay structures almost exclusively by relying on rates paid in the external market.

Employers following such an approach typically match a large percentage of their jobs with market data and collect as much market data as possible. Opting for market pricing may reflect an emphasis on external competitiveness and a deemphasis on internal consistency, the relationships among jobs within the firm. Organizations that fill large proportions of their job vacancies with new hires from the outside may become market pricers. The potential problems with market pricing stem from giving up internal consistency among jobs to the vagaries of the external market and therefore to competitors' decisions. In effect, market pricing lets competitors determine an employers' internal pay structure.

EXHIBIT 4.20   Market Pricing at Pfizer

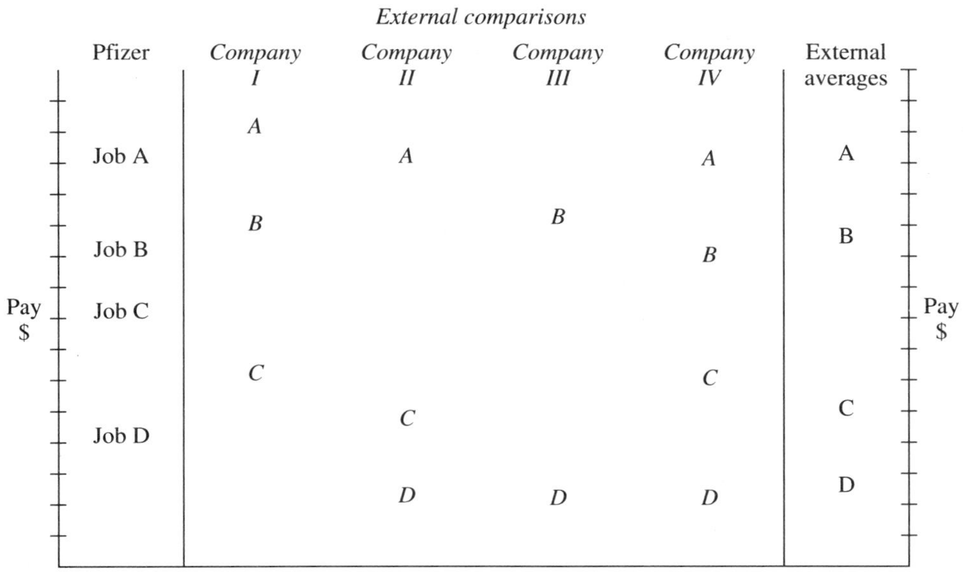

Market pricers often use the ranking method to determine the pay for jobs unique to their firms. Often called *Rank to Market,* it involves first determining the competitive rates for positions for which external market data are available and then blending the remaining (nonbenchmark) jobs into the pay hierarchy.

At Pfizer, for example, job analysis results in written job descriptions. This is immediately followed by labor market analysis and market pricing for as many jobs as possible. Exhibit 4.20 shows Pfizer's pay comparisons with comparable jobs at surveyed companies. After that, the internal job relationships are reviewed to be sure they are "reasonable in light of organization needs." The final step is pricing those jobs not included in the survey. These remaining jobs are compared to the survey positions "in terms of their total value to Pfizer." This internal evaluation seeks to ensure consistency with promotion opportunities and to properly reflect cross-functional job values (e.g., production versus clerical jobs).

SUMMARY

The differences in the rates paid for different jobs affect the ability of managers to achieve their business objectives. Differences in pay matter. They matter to employees, because their willingness to take on more responsibility and training, to focus on quality of products, and to be flexible enough to adapt to change all depend at least in part on how pay is structured for different levels of work. Differences in the rates paid for different jobs also influence how fairly employees believe they are being treated. Unfair treatment is ultimately counterproductive.

So far we have examined three basic approaches for determining how to design pay differences for different work: job evaluation, skill-based plans, and market pricing. All three need to be understood as procedures used to help design an internal pay structure that is based on the work, will help achieve the business objectives, and is acceptable to the key stakeholders.

Since it has been widely used for more than 40 years, job evaluation has evolved into many different forms and methods. Consequently, wide variations exist in its use and how it is perceived. This chapter discussed some of the many perceptions of the role of job evaluation and reviewed the criticisms leveled at it. No matter how job valuation is designed, its ultimate use is to help design and manage a work-related, business-focused, and agreed-upon pay structure.

We also examined the emerging state of practice of the skill-based plans. Skill-based pay structures clearly signal that continuous learning is valued, at least to the top rate in the structure. Finally, the market pricing approach was also examined.

At this point, we have examined three alternative approaches to valuing work. In the next chapter, we look at ensuring the involvement of the relevant parties, administering these plans, and evaluating their usefulness.

REVIEW QUESTIONS

1. Distinguish among job evaluation, skill-based plans, and market pricing.
2. What do these three approaches have to do with a policy of internal consistency?

3. How does the concern over flexibility, control, and chaos relate to these three approaches?

4. What are the pros and cons of using multiple plans within an organization?

5. Why are there so many definitions of job evaluation? What would you emphasize in a definition? Why?

6. You are the manager of 10 employees. Everyone becomes very suspicious and upset upon receiving a memo from the personnel department saying jobs are going to be evaluated. How will you reassure the employees?

APPENDIX 4–A
FACTOR WEIGHTS AND DEFINITIONS IN BORG-WARNER'S SKILL-BASED PLAN

FACTOR 1: BASIC KNOWLEDGE

1st Degree (22 points).   Ability to read, write, add and subtract basic mathematics, interpret and complete simple instructions.

2nd Degree (47 points).   Knowledge of higher mathematical calculations such as basic decimal and fractional equations, ability to read and follow semicomplicated written instructions and to use basic measuring equipment.

3rd Degree (72 points).   Knowledge of a variety of manufacturing skills, specific training, work experience equivalent to trade school or high school, ability to read semicomplicated measuring equipment, graphics, technical or written reports.

4th Degree (111 points).   Extensive specific skills training in a specialized field; equivalent to one–two years of college or vocational (technical) training or master trade certificate.

FACTOR 2: ELECTRICAL/ELECTRONIC SKILLS

Application of the principles of electricity, electronic logic, and integrated transmission technologies such as lasers. This includes understanding of circuits, their component parts, and how they work together.

1st Degree (7 points).   Operational knowledge of electrical/electronic equipment without understanding the electrical/electronic principles on which the equipment operates.

2nd Degree (15 points).   Operational knowledge of electrical/electronic equipment with understanding the electrical/electronic principles on which the equipment operates.

3rd Degree (23 points).   Application of principles of electronic circuitry and appropriate wiring procedures.

4th Degree (37 points).   Application of principles of miniaturized electronic circuits and digital and analog transmission concepts.

FACTOR 3: MECHANICAL SKILLS

The application of mechanical knowledge of how/why mechanical equipment works. It includes the operation, repair, or maintenance of machinery/mechanical systems.

1st Degree (5 points).   This includes the use of basic mechanical ability to operate/adjust single or multiple pieces of mechanical or electromechanical equipment. It includes, but is not limited to, such elements as clearing jams and setting feed speeds and/or pressure changes.

2nd Degree (12 points).   This includes all elements of 1st Degree basic mechanical ability, with the exceptions that the incumbent is required to have the skills to perform preventive maintenance, disassemble/reassemble specific components, change tools, and the like.

3rd Degree (25 points).   Perform servicing and procedural repair activities on mechanical systems/machinery as the primary function.

4th Degree (31 points).   Apply advanced principles of mechanical skills to repair, rebuild, service to a close tolerance level of fit.

5th Degree (37 points).   Perform sophisticated diagnostic and repair activities on complex mechanical or electromechanical machinery/systems.

FACTOR 4: GRAPHICS

Reading, interpreting, and/or preparing graphic representations of information, such as maps, plans, drawings, blueprints, diagrams, schematics, and timing/flowcharts.

1st Degree (5 points).   Understand basic blueprints and/or prepare rough sketches.

2nd Degree (12 points).   Understand more complex blueprints and/or prepare simple graphic information.

3rd Degree (25 points).   Understand complex, technical graphic representations of information and/or prepare technical graphics.

4th Degree (31 points).   Prepare and/or interpret complex, technical graphic representations of a wide range of information.

5th Degree (37 points).   Develop, prepare, and/or interpret highly complex, sophisticated graphic representations.

FACTOR 5: MATHEMATICAL SKILLS

The selection and application of mathematical methods or procedures to solve problems or to achieve desired results.

1st Degree (8 points). Simple arithmetic computations involving addition, subtraction, multiplication, or division.

2nd Degree (15 points). Computations involving decimals, percentages, fractions, and/or basic statistics.

3rd Degree (23 points). Computations involving algebra (e.g., solving for an unknown) or geometry (e.g., areas, volumes).

4th Degree (38 points). Computations involving the use of trigonometry (properties of triangles and circles including sine, cosine, and tangent functions), logarithms and exponents, and advanced statistics.

FACTOR 6: COMMUNICATION/INTERPERSONAL SKILLS

This factor measures the scope and nature of relationships with others.

1st Degree (28 points). Little or no contact with others. Relationships involve providing and/or receiving information or documents.

2nd Degree (56 points). Some contact with others. Relationships often require explanation or interpretation of information.

3rd Degree (84 points). Substantial contact with others. Relationships usually involve discussions with stakeholders or recommendations on issues regarding policies, programs, and so on. Impact is considerable and may be limited to individual departments/programs.

4th Degree (140 points). Extensive contact with others. Relationships usually include decisions in a broad sense and will affect several areas within the manufacturing unit.

FACTOR 7: SAFETY SKILLS

This factor measures the requirements for adherence to prescribed safety and personal security practices in the performance of required tasks. These safety and personal security practices are generally required to minimize exposure to hazard or risk in the work environment.

1st Degree (10 points). Perform work in accordance with a few simple safety procedures to minimize potential for injury.

2nd Degree (40 points). Perform work in accordance with several specific safety procedures to minimize potential for injury.

3rd Degree (80 points).   Perform work in accordance with a wide range of safety procedures to minimize some potential for injury.

4th Degree (100 points).   Perform work in a highly variable environment where safety principles and procedures need to be tailored to deal with unforeseen hazards to minimize high potential for serious injury.

FACTOR 8: DECISION MAKING/SUPERVISION REQUIRED

This factor measures the degree of decision making required without being checked by others, and the degree to which immediate supervisor is required to outline the procedures to be followed and/or the results to be attained on the job.

1st Degree (36 points).   Limited decision making by the incumbent. Progress of work is checked by others most of the time, and/or 60–90 percent of activities are defined by other than the incumbent.

2nd Degree (89 points).   Routine decision making based on specific criteria. Progress of work is often checked by others, and/or 40–60 percent of activities are defined by other than the incumbent.

3rd Degree (112 points).   Significant decision making based on established guidelines and experience. Progress of work is checked by others some of the time, and/or 25–40 percent of activities are defined by other than the incumbent.

4th Degree (180 points).   Extensive decision making based on broad policies, procedures, and guidelines. Progress of work is seldom checked by others, and/or less than 25 percent of activities are defined by other than the incumbent.

APPENDIX 4–B
HAY GUIDE CHART PROFILE

THE HAY GUIDE CHART

ILLUSTRATIVE

HAY GUIDE CHART–PROFILE METHOD
OF POSITION EVALUATION

INDUSTRIAL

Know-How
DEFINITIONS

DEFINITION: Know-How is the sum total to every kind of skill, however acquired, required for acceptable job performance. This sum total which comprises the overall "savvy" has 3 dimensions — the requirements for:

1 Practical procedures, specialized techniques, and scientific disciplines.

2 Know-How of integrating and harmonizing the diversified functions involved in managerial situations occurring in operating, supporting, and administrative fields. This Know-How may be exercised consultatively (about management) as well as executively and involves in some combination the areas of organizing, planning, executing, controlling and evaluating.

3 Active, practicing, face-to-face skills in the area of human relationships (as defined at right).

MEASURING KNOW-HOW: Know-How has both scope (variety) and depth (thoroughness). Thus, a job may require some knowledge about a lot of things, or a lot of knowledge about a few things. The total Know-How is the combination of scope and depth. This concept makes practical the comparison and weighing of the total Know-How content of different jobs in terms of: "How much knowledge about how many things."

3 HUMAN RELATIONS SKILLS

1. BASIC: Ordinary courtesy and effectiveness in dealing with others.

2. IMPORTANT: Understanding, influencing, and/or serving people are important, but not critical considerations.

3. CRITICAL: Alternative or combined skills in understanding, selecting, developing and motivating people are important in the highest degree.

KNOW-HOW

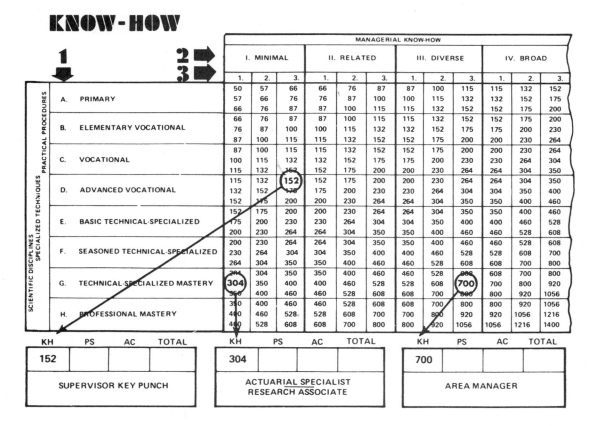

Problem Solving
DEFINITIONS

DEFINITION: Problem Solving is the original, "self-starting" thinking required by the job for analyzing, evaluating, creating, reasoning, arriving at and making conclusions. To the extent that thinking is circumscribed by standards, covered by precedents, or referred to others, Problem Solving is diminished, and the emphasis correspondingly is on Know-How.

Problem Solving has two dimensions:

1 The thinking environment in which the problems are solved.

2 The thinking challenge presented by the problem to be solved.

MEASURING PROBLEM SOLVING: Problem Solving measures the intensity of the mental process which employs Know-How to (1) identify, (2) define, and (3) resolve a problem. "You think with what you know." This is true of even the most creative work. The raw material of any thinking is knowledge of facts, principles and means; ideas are put together from something already there. Therefore, Problem Solving is treated as a percentage utilization of Know-How.

PROBLEM SOLVING

		THINKING CHALLENGE					
		1. REPETITIVE	2. PATTERNED	3. INTERPOLATIVE	4. ADAPTIVE	5. UNCHARTED	
A.	STRICT ROUTINE	10% 12%	14% 16%	19% 22%	25% 29%	33% 38%	A
B.	ROUTINE	12% 14%	16% 19%	22% 25%	29% 33%	38% 43%	B
C.	SEMI-ROUTINE	14% 16%	19% 22%	25% 29%	33% 38%	43% 50%	C
D.	STANDARDIZED	16% 19%	22% 25%	29% (33%)	38% 43%	50% 57%	D
E.	CLEARLY DEFINED	19% 22%	25% 29%	33% 38%	43% 50%	57% 66%	E
F.	BROADLY DEFINED	22% 25%	29% 33%	38% 43%	50% 57%	(66%) 76%	F
G.	GENERALLY DEFINED	25% 29%	33% 38%	43% 50%	(57%) 66%	76% 87%	G
H.	ABSTRACTLY DEFINED	29% 33%	38% 43%	50% 57%	66% 76%	87% 100%	H

KH	PS	AC	TOTAL
152	50		

SUPERVISOR KEY PUNCH

KH	PS	AC	TOTAL
304	200		

ACTUARIAL SPECIALIST RESEARCH ASSOCIATE

KH	PS	AC	TOTAL
700	400		

AREA MANAGER

Accountability
DEFINITIONS

DEFINITION: Accountability is the answerability for action and for the consequences thereof. It is the measured effect of the job on end results. It has three dimensions in the following order of importance.

1 FREEDOM TO ACT — the degree of personal or procedural control and guidance as defined in the left-hand column of the chart.

2 JOB IMPACT ON END RESULTS — as defined at right.

3 MAGNITUDE — indicated by the general dollar size of the area(s) most clearly or primarily affected by the job.

2 IMPACT OF JOB ON END RESULTS

Indirect:

REMOTE: Informational, recording, or incidental services for use by others in relation to some important end result.

CONTRIBUTORY: Interpretive, advisory, or facilitating services for use by others in taking action.

Direct:

SHARED: Participating with others (except own subordinates and superiors), within or outside the organizational unit, in taking action.

PRIMARY: Controlling impact on end results, where shared accountability of others is subordinate.

ACCOUNTABILITY

	(1) VERY SMALL OR INDETERMINATE				(2) SMALL				(3) MEDIUM				(4) L	
	R	C	S	P	R	C	S	P	R	C	S	P	R	C
A. PRESCRIBED	10	14	19	25	14	19	25	33	19	25	33	43	25	33
	12	16	22	29	16	22	29	38	22	29	38	50	29	38
	14	19	25	33	19	25	33	43	25	33	43	57	33	43
B. CONTROLLED	16	22	29	38	22	29	38	50	29	38	50	66	38	50
	19	25	33	43	25	33	43	57	33	43	57	76	43	57
	22	29	38	50	29	38	50	66	38	50	66	87	50	66
C. STANDARDIZED	25	33	43	57	33	43	57	76	43	57	76	100	57	76
	29	38	50	(66)	38	50	66	87	50	66	87	115	66	87
	33	43	57	76	43	57	76	100	57	76	100	132	76	100
D. GENERALLY REGULATED	38	50	66	87	50	66	87	115	66	87	115	152	87	115
	43	57	76	100	57	76	100	132	76	100	132	175	100	132
	50	66	87	115	66	87	115	152	87	(115)	152	200	115	152
E. DIRECTED	57	76	100	132	76	100	132	175	100	132	175	230	132	175
	66	87	115	152	87	115	152	200	115	152	200	264	152	200
	76	100	132	175	100	132	175	230	132	175	230	304	175	230
F. ORIENTED DIRECTION	87	115	152	200	115	152	200	264	152	200	264	350	200	264
	100	132	175	230	132	175	230	304	175	230	304	400	230	304
	115	152	200	264	152	200	264	350	200	264	350	460	264	350
G. BROAD GUIDANCE	132	175	230	304	175	230	304	400	230	304	400	528	304	400
	152	200	264	350	200	264	350	460	264	350	460	(608)	350	460
	175	230	304	400	230	304	400	528	304	400	528	700	400	528
H. STRATEGIC GUIDANCE	200	264	350	460	264	350	460	608	350	460	608	800	460	608
	230	304	400	528	304	400	528	700	400	528	700	920	528	700
	264	350	460	608	350	460	608	800	460	608	800	1056	608	800
I. GENERALLY UNGUIDED	304	400	528	700	400	528	700	920	528	700	920	1216	700	920
	350	460	608	800	460	608	800	1056	608	800	1056	1400	800	1056
	400	528	700	920	528	700	920	1216	700	920	1216	1600	920	1216

KH	PS	AC	TOTAL
152	50	**66**	268

SUPERVISOR KEY PUNCH

KH	PS	AC	TOTAL
304	200	**115**	619

ACTUARIAL SPECIALIST RESEARCH ASSOCIATE

KH	PS	AC	TOTAL
700	400	**608**	1708

AREA MANAGER

PROFILES   CHECK EVALUATION JUDGEMENT

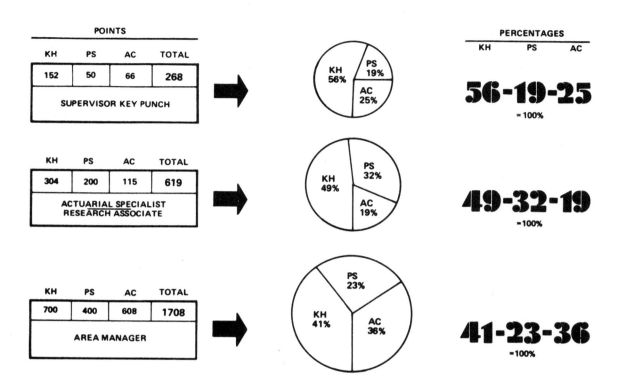

POINTS			
KH	PS	AC	TOTAL
152	50	66	268
SUPERVISOR KEY PUNCH			

KH 56% PS 19% AC 25%

PERCENTAGES
KH   PS   AC

56-19-25
= 100%

KH	PS	AC	TOTAL
304	200	115	619
ACTUARIAL SPECIALIST RESEARCH ASSOCIATE			

KH 49% PS 32% AC 19%

49-32-19
=100%

KH	PS	AC	TOTAL
700	400	608	1708
AREA MANAGER			

PS 23% KH 41% AC 36%

41-23-36
=100%

Borg-Warner (BW), a 600-person facility, manufactures the world's highest-quality timing and drive chains. These chains, similar in concept to the chain on a bicycle, are used in car and light truck transmissions. General Motors, Ford, and BMW use BW as the primary supplier of drive chains for their vehicles. Honda and Toyota also order BW chains, although these Japanese manufacturers also produce their own chains. For the last 10 years, BW's chains have had a worldwide reputation for quality, but their consumers pay a premium price for BW's product.

Recently, the quality differential between chains manufactured by foreign competitors, primarily the Japanese and South Koreans, and BW has narrowed. And foreign-produced chains are lower priced. Although BW remains the "supplier of choice" for its major customers, its management is concerned about its ability to remain competitive.

The Advanced Engineering Unit developed a series of changes for the current manufacturing process. These changes have the potential to vary the quality of chains depending on the customers' specifications. For example, some high performance cars such as GM's Corvette and BMW's 500 and 700 series all demand tight tolerances. In contrast, the tolerances for chains in other product lines such as light trucks and standard cars are looser.

Beyond these changes in the current manufacturing process, Advanced Engineering is working with IBM to develop a computer–integrated manufacturing (CIM) technology. The CIM project will introduce even greater changes to the current manufacturing process.

The first series of technological changes is ready for implementation in the plant now. The CIM technology will be ready in two to three years.

Modifying the BW manufacturing process is inevitable in light of foreign competition and advances in technology. The general manager at the BW facility is ready and eager to move on the first set of changes and has increased the research budget allocated to Advanced Engineering's CIM project.

The general manager also assembled a task force, including an industrial engineer, a member of the advanced engineering group, a production supervisor, and you. Your mission is to develop an implementation process for the first series of changes to position BW for the future. The task force assembled the following information.

BACKGROUND

- It is clear that flexibility is going to have to be a permanent feature of life at BW. Examples include changing technology, using just-in-time inventory systems, increasing variability in customers' orders in terms of chain quality specification and volume orders, and obtaining increasing competitive quality and pricing from competitors.

- The human resource philosophy and practices at BW currently emphasize the importance and dignity of the individual employee, team work, and employee participation. This philosophy is reflected in BW's practices. For example, BW's top managers meet with all employees in groups of 50–60 each to report the facility's financial condition, its future business prospects, and answer any questions employees may wish to raise. These group meetings with the "brass," held on company time, are well attended and lively.

Current Compensation

Employee compensation includes profit sharing (based on the facilities' profit performance and paid annually), benefits that match those of U.S. competitors, plus a competitive base pay. Two critical jobs also have individual incentive schemes. Base pay is determined by conventional job analysis and evaluation plans that define each job's duties and tasks and evaluate them using four factors: skill, effort, responsibility, and working conditions. Thus, the base pay employees receive is based on the *job* they hold. Based on attitude surveys and other feedback, employees seem very satisfied with the job evaluation results and the pay relationships among different jobs.

Incentive Pay

Only two jobs, chain assembler and riveter, have incentives. The incentive is a standard piece rate plan with the standard based on the industrial engineering department's time studies. Employees report that these standards are fair; they have remarked, however, that the existing plans emphasize quantity produced rather than quality. Chain quality is controlled through two jobs, ultrasonic tester and inspector/repairer.

Work Flow and Structure

The facility's current work flow and job structure are described in Exhibit 1. Note that bringing the chain parts from inventory to the assembly line is performed by employees in the stacker job. Automatic assemblers operate machines that assemble the chains, chain measurers operate equipment that measures and cuts chains to appropriate lengths, and riveters hook up and perform the final assembly of the chain. Next, the chains are prepared by the chain cleaner and oiler to undergo quality control inspection by the ultrasonic tester. A defective chain goes

to the repairer job and, once reassembled, it is re-routed to the ultrasonic tester. Finally, chains that meet BW's quality standards are prepared for shipment by the chain packer.

Current and Proposed Structure

The task force is considering converting the *job-based structure* to one based on employees' *knowledge or skill* required to perform the work. Exhibit 2 compares the current job structure and pay rates to the proposed skill-based structure. Note that BW currently requires seven jobs (10 employees) for each assembly group. With the proposed technological changes in the manufacturing process, each "manufacturing cell" will require three basic skills levels; A, B and C. Skill C basically incorporates the skills and knowledge required to perform five current jobs (stacker, cleaner, and oiler, ultrasonic tester, repairer, and chain stacker). Skill B includes those skills currently involved in assembler and riveter, in addition to all the skill C jobs. Finally, skill A will include *all* the skills and knowledge required in all seven jobs plus some supervisory and team leadership skills. Employees who attain the level of skill A will be able to perform any tasks in the team, and they will assume some of the leadership, coordination, and scheduling tasks formerly performed by first-level supervision.

The ideal mix of skills required for each new cell is not clear, but the task force anticipates that five

EXHIBIT 1   Current Work Flow and Structure

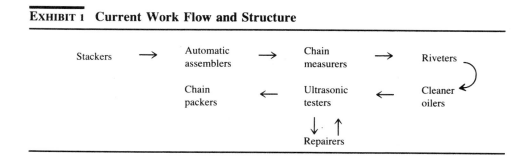

EXHIBIT 2   Current Job-Based Pay Structure and Proposed Skill-Based Structure
---

	Current—Job Based		
Hourly Pay Rate	*Employees*	*Job Classification*	*Proposed Skill Based*
6.50	1	Chain Stacker	
6.60	2	Chain Packer	
6.60	1	Cleaner/Oiler	Skill C
6.75	1	Ultrasonic Tester	Skill B
6.80	1	Chain Repairer	
11.65*	2	Chain Assemblers/Measurers	
10.50*	2	Riveters	
			Skill A

*Average hourly rate earned under current piece rate incentive plan.

---

to seven employees will be required to produce the same volume of chains as the current manufacturing groups. At the minimum, one employee must have obtained each level of skill and a minimum of five employees would be required for a cell to operate.

Discussion Questions

1. What are the major advantages and limitations of internal pay structure based on skills? What are *the key differences between the two approaches* (job evaluation and job-based structures compared to skill-based structures)?

2. What rates of pay for each skill level do you recommend? What is the rationale for your proposal? Will you keep the individual incentive schemes for skill B?

3. How would you go about introducing the skill-based approach to employees? What are some key issues involved in the actual implementation of such an approach? Based on the information provided, discuss whether you would recommend the proposed skill-based plan. What are the costs of each approach? Has the task force considered all the implications of a skill-based approach (e.g., training programs and skill evaluation procedures required)? What, if anything, will be done with any surplus employees? Finally, what two or three pieces of additional information should the task force gather and how would you recommend it use the information to aid its decision making?

Your state is enjoying economic growth. Tax revenues are up, but so is the workload for government employees. Recently there have been increasing complaints about pay. Some employees believe that their salary is out of line in comparison to the amount received by other employees. As a first step, the state personnel director hired you to perform job analysis and write job descriptions. The results are shown below. Now a job structure is needed.

1. Divide into teams of four to six students each. Each team should evaluate the eight jobs and prepare a job structure based on its evaluation. Assign titles to each job, and list your structure by title and job letter.

2. Each team should describe the process the group went through to arrive at that job structure. Job evaluation techniques and compensable factors used should be described, and the reasons for selecting them should be stated.

3. Each team should give each job a title and put its job structure on the board. Comparisons can then be made among job structures of the various teams. Does the job evaluation method used appear to affect the results? Do compensable factors chosen affect the results? Does the process affect the results?

4. Evaluate the job descriptions. What parts of them were most useful? How could they be improved?

Job A

Kind of Work. Directs a large and complex fiscal management program in a large state department, agency, or institution. Provides technical and supervisory financial support to carry out policies and programs established by the department head. Serves as the chief liaison to activity managers to ensure coordination of their activities in planning with the accounting division. Maintains a close working relationship with the finance agency controller to ensure compliance with budgetary and financial planning requirements of the Department of Finance. Considerable latitude is granted employee in this class for developing, implementing, and administering financial methods and procedures. Typically reports to a high-level department manager with work reviewed through periodic conferences and reports.

Principal Responsibilities

- Directs all accounting functions of the department, agency, or institution so that adequate financial records and fiscal controls are maintained.

- Provides supervisory and high professional skills for the financial operations of the department consistent with the appropriate state and federal laws and regulations so that state and federal funds are utilized and expanded in the most efficient and effective manner.

- Provides coordination with other state and federal agencies relating to financial matters so that the department head and agency controller are informed as to matters pertaining to policies, procedures, and programs that may have an effect on the financial operation of the department.

- Develops authorized department budgets and financial plans, goals, and objectives for review and approval by the agency controller and the department head so that maximum use will be made of financial resources.

- Consults with and advises the department head, managers, supervisors, and the agency controller on financial policies and procedures, organizational changes, and interpretation of financial data and reports to ensure efficient and effective fiscal management.

Job B

Kind of Work.   Keeps financial records where the accounts are relatively complex or assists higher-level accountants and accounting technicians when the accounts are complex and extensive.

Receives direction from higher-level accounting personnel in the form of a review of work for accuracy and completeness. In some cases, may provide lead work direction to account clerks or clerical personnel engaged in the bookkeeping operation. Prepares relatively simply reports, makes preliminary analyses of financial conditions for use by other employees, and implements minor procedural and transactional changes in the fiscal operation. Emphasis is on bookkeeping procedures and the smooth transition of fiscal operations.

Principal Responsibilities

- Maintains the financial records of a moderate-sized department according to established procedures and makes adjustments to the records as directed.
- Prepares special analytical data for use by others in preparing budget requests or other reports.
- Approves and processes travel, account, invoice, and claim documents for payment.
- Codes and records all receipts and disbursement of funds.
- Reviews encumbrance or liquidation documents for accuracy and conformity with procedures and expedites financial transactions.
- Accesses or inputs information to the statewide accounting system.
- Investigates errors or problems in the processing of fiscal transactions and recommends changes in procedures.
- Issues purchase orders.
- Provides lead work direction to other bookkeeping and clerical employees.
- Performs related work as required.

Job C

Kind of Work.   Serves as section chief or top assistant to an accounting director or other high-level fiscal management officer in a moderate or large-sized state department. Directs the activities of an accounting or fiscal management section consisting of several subsections or assists the supervisor with the supervision of a very large and complex accounting operation. Works closely with the chief fiscal officer in formulating fiscal policies and independently establishes new accounts in payroll procedures to accomplish the department's program. Considerable independence of action is granted the employee, with work reviewed through reports and conferences.

Principal Responsibilities

- Prepares and administers the department budget, confers with operating officials on projected needs, and devises methods of adjusting budgets so that agency programs may be carried on efficiently and effectively.
- Provides technical accounting assistance and guidance to operational accounting units within a large or medium-sized agency so that operating procedures and staff skills will be upgraded on a continuing basis with resultant improvement in quality and reduction in cost.
- Produces special accounting plans, reports, and analyses involving complex accounting methods and principles as a basis for decision making by the chief fiscal officer and the department head.
- Constructs and maintains the department's accounting structure and cost accounting capabilities so the department can conform to legislative intent, meet state and federal regulatory requirements, and provide the department with reporting capabilities.
- Assists in the coordination and ongoing analysis and control of fiscal matters relevant to satellite institutions under departmental supervision.

Job D

Kind of Work.   Maintains a large and complex system of accounts. Serves as a section chief in the finance division of a very large department, maintains large state-federal or state-county accounts, and oversees a major statewide accounting function in the Department of Finance. Responsible for coordinating and supervising the various phases of the accounting function. Responsibility extends to the development of procedure and policies for the work involved. Supervises a staff of account clerks, accounting technicians, and accounting officers.

Principal Responsibilities

- Provides regular budget review so that program managers have adequate funds to be effective.

- Conducts financial analysis for economical and equitable distribution or redistribution of agency resource.

- Prepares long- and short-range program recommendations for fiscal action so that agency policies are consistent.

- Plans and directs the computerization of systems applied to fiscal services to ensure efficient operation.

- Develops and defines accounting office procedures to ensure the efficient delivery of fiscal services.

- Reviews and analyzes cost accounting computer output to ensure proper documentation of projected cost as required by federal policy and procedures.

- Prepares and supervises the preparation of federal budgets and grant requests, financial plans, and expenditure reports so that they accurately reflect needs and intent of the agency.

- Develops accounting and documentation procedures for county welfare departments so that state and federal auditing and reporting requirements are met.

- Establishes and maintains a financial reporting system for all federal and other nonstate funding sources so that all fiscal reporting requirements are adhered to on a timely and accurate basis.

- Assists grantee agencies in proper reporting procedures under federal grant programs so that requirements for reimbursement may be made on a timely basis.

- Determines the statewide indirect costs so that all state agencies are allocated their proportionate share of indirect costs.

- Supervises the review and processing of all encumbrance documents submitted to the Department of Finance so that necessary accounting information is recorded accurately and promptly in the accounting system.

Job E

Kind of Work.   Keeps financial records when the accounts are relatively simple, or assists others in assigned work of greater difficulty where accounting operations are more complex and extensive. The work involves a combination of clerical and bookkeeping responsibilities requiring specialized training or experience. Receives direction from higher-level accounting personnel in the form of detailed instructions and close review for accuracy and conformance with law, rules, or policy. Once oriented to the work, employee may exercise independent judgment in assigned duties.

Principal Responsibilities

- Maintains complete bookkeeping records independently when scope, volume, or complexity is limited or maintains a difficult part of an extensive bookkeeping operation.
- Codes and records all receipts and disbursement of funds.
- Prepares travel, account, invoice, and claim documents for payment.
- Reviews encumbrance or liquidation documents for accuracy and conformity with procedures and expedites financial transactions.
- Prepares financial information of reports and audits, invoices, and expenditure reports.
- Keeps general, control, or subsidiary books of accounts such as cash book appropriation and disbursement ledgers and encumbrance records.
- Accesses or inputs information to the statewide accounting system as directed.
- Performs related tasks as required.

Job F

Kind of Work.   Performs varied and difficult semiprofessional accounting work within an established accounting system. Maintains a complex set of accounts and works with higher management outside the accounting unit in planning and controlling expenditures. Works with higher-level employees in providing technical fiscal advice and service to functional activities. Receives supervision from higher-level management or accounting personnel. May provide lead work to lower-level accounting, bookkeeping, or clerical personnel.

Principal Responsibilities

- Assists the chief accounting officer in the preparation of all budgets to ensure continuity in financial operations.
- Prepares and assembles the biennial budget and coordinates all accounting functions for a small department according to overall plan of department head and needs expressed by activity managers.
- Maintains cost coding and allocation system for a major department to serve as a basis for reimbursement.
- Provides accounting and budgetary controls for federal, state, and private grants including reconciling bank statements and preparing reports on the status of the budget and accounts.
- Evaluates the spending progress of budget activities, ensures that budgetary limits are not exceeded, and recommends or effects changes in spending plans.
- Provides technical services to divisions of an agency in the supervision of deposits, accounts payable, procurement, and other business management areas.
- Performs related work as required.

Job G

Kind of Work. Performs professional accounting work as the fiscal officer of a small department, institution, or major division, or as an assistant to a higher-level accountant in a large fiscal operation. Work involves providing a wide range of accounting services to professional and managerial employees. Assists in the development and maintenance of broad fiscal programs. Regularly performs complex fiscal analysis, prepares fiscal reports for management, and recommends alternative solutions to accounting problems. May supervise account clerks, accounting technicians, or clerical employees engaged in the fiscal operation. Receives supervision from a higher-level accountant, business manager, or other administrative employee.

Principal Responsibilities

- Helps administrative employees develop budgets to ensure that sufficient funds are available for operating needs.
- Monitors cash flow to ensure minimum adequate operating balance.
- Produces reports so that management has proper fiscal information.
- Submits reports to federal and state agencies to ensure that financial reporting requirements are met.
- Analyzes and interprets fiscal reports so that information is available in useful form.
- Instructs technicians and clerks in proper procedures to ensure smooth operation of accounting functions.
- Investigates fiscal accounting problems so that adequate solutions may be developed.
- Recommends and implements new procedures to ensure the efficient operation of the accounting section.
- Interprets state laws and department policies to ensure the legality of fiscal transactions.

Job H

Kind of Work. Performs semiprofessional accounting work within an established accounting system. Responsible for maintaining accounting records on a major set of accounts, preauditing transactions in a major activity, or handling cash receipts in a major facility, and for classifying transactions, substantiating source documents, balancing accounts, and preparing reports as prescribed. Responsible for recognizing errors or problems in the fiscal transactions of an agency and recommending alternative solutions for consideration by other staff. Must regularly exercise initiative and independent judgment and may provide lead-work direction to account clerks or clerical employees engaged in the fiscal operation. Receives supervision from an accounting technician, senior business managers, or professional accountant.

Principal Responsibilities

- Controls expenditures so they do not exceed budget totals and prepares allotment requests in the agency's budgetary accounts.
- Processes encumbrance changes of expenditures authorization and adjusts budget as necessary and desired.
- Reconciles department accounting records with the statewide accounting system and records documents so that funds may be appropriated, allotted, encumbered, and transferred.
- Authorizes reimbursement for goods and services received by a major department.
- Develops and maintains a system of accounts receivable, including issuance of guidelines for participants and preparation of state and federal reports.
- Provides daily accounting on loans receivable or financial aids for a major college.
- Audits cost vendor statements for conformity within departmental guidelines.
- Reconciles the payroll disbursements by payroll period for a major organization and prepares spending reports by AID.
- Supervises cash accounting unit and prepares reports on receipts and deposits.
- Performs related work as required.

Evaluating Work: Administration

American Telephone & Telegraph Co. (AT&T) for years had little competition in its business. Its local operating companies petitioned state commissions for rate changes that more often than not were granted. Prices for phone services were calculated on some sense of "adequate return on investment," profits generated by improved technology in long distance lines were used to hold down charges for local service. But antitrust lawsuits led to the breakup of AT&T. AT&T kept its long distance lines unit, its manufacturing unit (Western Electric), and its research arm (Bell Labs). They were integrated into two major business sections: regulated (long distance calls) and unregulated (information technologies, such as computers and switching equipment). Other subsidiaries and operating companies became completely separate business entities. For the first time, AT&T faced direct competition in both its regulated and unregulated businesses. The company became free to compete in the communications/information industry, and it transformed its basic business directions. Its objectives and business strategy changed, and, as a result, its compensation system also changed. AT&T redesigned its managerial pay structures, permitting each business unit to determine whether job evaluation, skill-based plans, or market pricing best suited its situation. The management job evaluation plan at AT&T was redesigned to include compensable factors that more accurately reflected the new competitive environment. The company asked, "What is it we want to pay for?" and it got a different set of answers than it did under its previous totally regulated environment. As a result of the changing business strategies and technological improvements, the work at nonmanagerial levels also has changed. More work involves information processing. Even the telephone is changing. Has anyone not had the experience of calling a business whose phone is answered by a computer that delivers the message, "If you wish to place an order, press 1. If you wish to inquire about an order, press 3. If you wish, etc., etc., etc.," to be greeted at the end by a dial tone?

For AT&T managers, the balance shifted from emphasis on government and public relations to increasing market share and profitability. While the job evaluation plans retained a "skills-required" factor, the nature of the required skills was redefined and reweighted to reflect more accurately the changing environment, technologies, and strategies. At Bell South, the job evaluation plan now reflects movement into new business ventures such as Hispanic yellow pages, cellular phones, and building services. So it is with other employers: the system for evaluating work must be designed and administered in a manner consistent with the organization's strategies and objectives.

The underlying premise, covered throughout this book, is that compensation decisions need to help the organization achieve competitive advantage.

We began our discussion of evaluating work in the previous chapter. We examined three basic approaches: job evaluation, skill-based plans, and market pricing. Also recall what the last three chapters are all about: designing and managing the internal pay structures that help the organization treat employees fairly. The major decisions already discussed include (1) determining the purpose of evaluating work, (2) deciding whether to use single or multiple plans, and (3) choosing among alternative approaches. This chapter discusses the remaining decisions: (4) ensuring the involvement of key stakeholders and (5) evaluating the usefulness of the plans and resulting structure.

WHO SHOULD BE INVOLVED?

Who should be involved in evaluating work? The choice is usually among compensation managers, operating managers, and/or jobholders. Regardless of the approach, if it is to aid managers and if ensuring high involvement and commitment from employees is important, those managers and employees with a stake in the resulting structures need to be involved.

Committees, Task Forces, and Teams

A common approach to understanding pay decisions and gaining their acceptance is the use of committees, task forces, and teams.[1] Membership in these groups seems to vary among firms. All of them typically include representatives from key operating functions, and many include nonmanagerial employees. In some cases, the group's role is only advisory; in others, it designs the evaluation approach and approves all major changes. Some go so far as to prescribe roles for members similar to those shown in Exhibit 5.1.

The Design Process Matters

Case studies of the knowledge-based approaches emphasize the importance of identifying key stakeholders to champion the approach internally.[2] In the case studies, the champions or advocates tend to be line managers. The design teams focus on achieving employee and manager ownership of the results. This is an uncommon practice in the design of

EXHIBIT 5.1   Roles of Evaluation Group Members

Leader	*Members*	*Facilitator*	*Expert*
• Understand evaluation plan	• Understand evaluation plan	• Understand evaluation plan	• Clarify job analysis data
• Listen	• Listen	• Listen	• Provide additional information
• Keep the group moving	• Discuss facts and assumptions	• Ask questions to facilitate objectives	• Serve as an adviser
• Encourage participation	• Analyze information objectively	• Make suggestions on group process	• Can be a temporary "voting" member
• Prevent individuals from dominating	• Ask questions	• Help group reach a consensus	
• Express own opinion	• Formulate and express opinion	• Can be a full committee member	
• Encourage consensus	• Encourage and reach consensus	• Maintain documentation	
	• Commit to participation and timetable		

SOURCE: Jill Kanin-Lovers, "Using Committees to Evaluate Jobs," *Journal of Compensation and Benefits* (New York: Warren Gorham and Lamont, 1986).

---

[1] Jill Kanin-Lovers, "Using Committees to Evaluate Jobs," *Journal of Compensation and Benefits*, July–August 1986.

[2] Gerald E. Ledford, Jr., "Three Case Studies on Skill-Based Pay: An Overview," *Compensation and Benefits Review*, March–April 1991, pp. 11–23.

job evaluation and market pricing plans, and may help explain the growing popularity of knowledge-based plans.

Procedural equity, discussed in Chapter 2, is highly related to employee involvement and acceptance. Research strongly suggests that attending to the equity of the design process and the approach chosen (job evaluation, knowledge-based plan and market pricing) rather than focusing solely on the results (the internal pay structure) is likely to achieve employee and management commitment, trust, and acceptance of the results.[3] And achieving procedural equity is related to the design process and who participates.

Ledford reports improved employee attitudes toward their pay at both the General Mills and Honeywell sites following the use of high employee involvement in the design of knowledge-based plans.[4] These results need to be treated with a tad of caution. The reported improvement in attitudes may have been due to high involvement or the knowledge-based plan or to any number of other factors not controlled, including the attention and interest paid to employees, or the possibility that employees believe they will get higher pay under the new plans. Research does show that higher pay is related to higher satisfaction with pay—no great surprise.[5]

The absence of participation may make it easier for employees and managers to imagine ways the structure might have been rearranged to their personal liking. Crepanzano and Folger observed ". . . if people do not participate in decisions, there is little to prevent them from assuming that things would have been better, 'if I'd have been in charge.' "[6] Additional research is needed to ascertain whether the payoffs from increased participation offset potential costs (time involved to reach consensus, potential problems caused by disrupting current perceptions, etc). For example, the involvement of both operating managers and compensation professionals raises the potential for conflict due

---

[3]One of the key findings of a National Academy of Science report that examined virtually all research on pay was that the process used to design pay plans is vital to achieving high commitment. Also, see Edward E. Lawler III and J. Richard Hackman, "Impact of Employee Participation in the Development of Pay Incentive Plans: A Field Experiment," *Journal of Applied Psychology* 53, no. 6 (December 1969), pp.467–71; D. E. Ewing, *Freedom Inside the Organization* (New York: E. P. Dutton, 1978); Carl F. Frost, John W. Wakely, and Robert A. Ruh, *The Scanlon Plan for Organization Development: Identity, Participation, and Equity* (East Lansing: Michigan State Press, 1974); E. E. Lawler III, "Creating High Involvement Work Organizations, in *Perspectives on Organizational Behavior,* 2nd ed., ed. J. R. Hackman, E. E. Lawler III, and L. W. Porter (New York: McGraw-Hill, 1982); K. C. Sheflen, E. E. Lawler III, and J. R. Hackman, "Long-Term Impact of Employee Participation in the Development of Pay Incentive Plans: A Field Experiment Revisited," *Journal of Applied Psychology* 55 (1971), pp. 182–86; E. A. Locke and D. M. Schweiger, "Participation in Decision Making: One More Look," *Research in Organization Behavior* (Greenwich, Conn.: JAI Press, 1979); J. F. Carey, "Participative Job Evaluation," *Compensation Review,* Fourth Quarter 1977, pp. 29–38; and G. J. Jenkins, Jr., and E. E. Lawler III, "Impact of Employee Participation in Pay Plan Development," *Organizational Behavior and Human Performance* 28 (1981), pp. 111–28.

[4]Ledford, "Three Case Studies."

[5]Herbert Heneman III, "Pay Satisfaction," in *Research in Personnel and Human Resources Management,* vol. 3, ed. K. M. Rowland and G. R. Ferris (Greenwich, Conn.: JAI Press, 1985), pp. 115–39; Barry Gerhart and George Milkovich, "Employee Compensation," in *Handbook of Industrial and Organizational Psychology,* vol. 3, ed. M. D. Dunnette and L. Hough (Palo Alto, Calif.: Consulting Psychologists Press, 1992).

[6]R. Crepanzano and R. Folger, "Referent Cognitions and Task Decision Autonomy: Beyond Equity Theory," *Journal of Applied Psychology,* September 1989, pp. 17–23.

to their differing perspectives. Operating managers wish to gain greater flexibility that will allow them to funnel more pay to key individuals. The compensation manager, aware of the difficulties caused by perceptions of favoritism and bias, wishes to ensure consistent treatment for all employees. Note the difference in focus. The manager has operating objectives to achieve, does not want to lose key individuals, and views compensation as a mechanism to help accomplish this. The compensation manager, on the other hand, adopts an organization-wide perspective and focuses on ensuring that the system is managed consistently and fairly for all employees.

Unions' Stake

To what extent should unions be involved? Management probably will find it advantageous to include union representation as a source of ideas and to help promote acceptance of the results. For example, union-management task forces participated in the design of new evaluation systems for both a Borg-Warner facility and the federal government.[7] Their roles involved mutual problem solving. But other union leaders believe that philosophical differences prevent their active participation.[8] They take the position that collective bargaining yields more equitable results than does job evaluation or skill-based plans. In other cases, jobs are jointly evaluated by union and management representatives, and disagreements are submitted to an arbitrator. So the extent of union participation varies. No single union perspective exists on the value of active participation in the process, just as no single management perspective exists.

Union involvement with the current wave of skill-based plans is relatively new. Our experience with the employees' unions at Dresser Rand and Colgate-Palmolive suggests that in a reasonably trusting relationship, union officials make significant contributions in design and administration.

ADMINISTERING THE PLAN

Our previous chapter led us through the technical decisions involved in evaluating work. The output of the technical phase is typically a manual to assist in applying the plan. The manual becomes the "yardstick" for the plan. It contains information on the plan and a description of the method. Compensable factors are defined and enough information is provided to allow the user to recognize varying degrees of each factor. Skill blocks and levels and certification procedures are detailed in the manual. Information needs to be detailed enough to permit accurate and rapid application of whatever approach is used.

Appeals/Review Procedures

No plan anticipates all situations. It is inevitable that some jobs will be incorrectly evaluated, or at least employees and managers may suspect incorrect evaluation. Or some

---

[7]*Modernizing Federal Classification: An Opportunity for Excellence* (Washington D.C.: National Academy of Public Administration, 1991).

[8]Mike Burns, *Understanding Job Evaluation* (London: Institute of Personnel Management, 1978).

individuals may believe that a skill level should have been certified. Consequently, the manual needs to contain review procedures to handle such cases and to help ensure procedural equity.[9] Often the compensation manager handles reviews, but increasingly, peer or team reviews are being used. Very occasionally, these take on the trappings of formal grievance procedures (e.g., documented complaints and responses, levels of approval, and so on). The problems may also be handled by managers and the employee relations generalists through informal discussions with employees.

Training

Once the manual is complete, those who will be applying the methodology require training in its proper use. These employees may also need background information on the entire pay system and how it relates to the overall human resource strategies and the organization's business strategy.

Approval and Certification Processes

When the evaluations are completed, approval by higher levels of management is usually required. The particular approval process differs among organizations; Exhibits 5.2 and 5.3 are examples. The approval process serves as a control. It helps ensure that any changes that result from evaluating work are consistent with the organization's operations and directions.

EXHIBIT 5.2   Job Evaluation Process

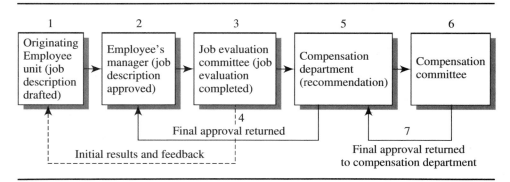

9Donna Blancero-Moran, "Employee Dispute Resolution Systems: Determinants and Consequences" (Ph.D. thesis, Cornell University, 1991); R. Folger and M. A. Konovsky, "Effects of Procedural and Distributive Justice on Reactions to Pay Raise Decisions," *Academy of Management Journal*, March 1989, pp. 115–30; J. Greenberg, "Reactions to Procedural Injustice in Payment Distributions: Do the Ends Justify the Means?" *Journal of Applied Psychology* 72 (1987), pp. 55–61; and R. Folger and J. Greenberg, "Procedural Justice: An Interpretative Analysis of Personnel Systems," in *Human Resources Management*, vol. 3, ed. K. M. Rowland and G. R. Ferris (Greenwich, Conn.: JAI Press, 1985), pp. 141–83.

EXHIBIT 5.3   Skill Assessment Process

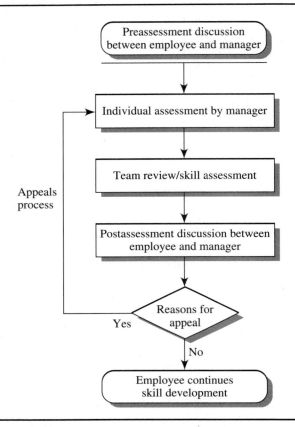

SOURCE: Peter Leblanc, "Skill Based Pay Case #2: Northern Telecom," *Compensation and Benefits Review*, March-April 1991, p. 50.

Communication

Employee and managerial understanding and acceptance of the process requires communication. Either through brochures, movies, information sessions, or other communication devices, the goals of the system, the stakeholders' roles in it, and the final results need to be explained to all employees. Employees have a right to know what a system does for (to?) them.

Final Result: Internal Structure

The final result of the administration phase is a hierarchy of work. This hierarchy translates the employer's internal consistency policy into practice. Exhibit 5.4 shows four hypo-

EXHIBIT 5.4   Resulting Internal Structures—Job and Skill Based

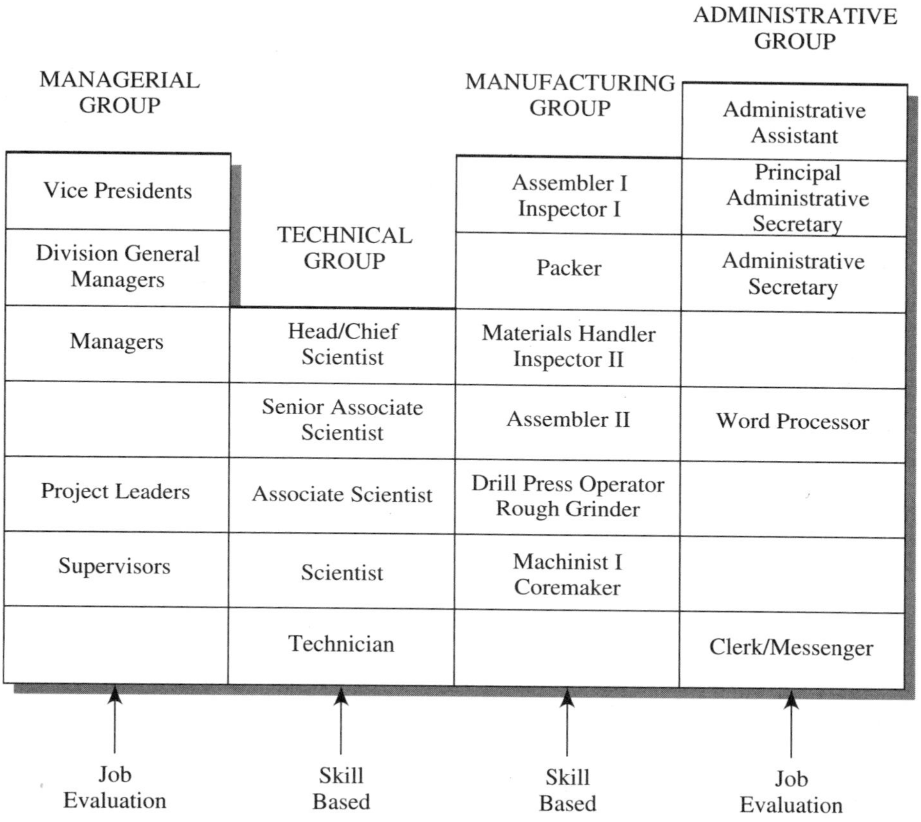

MANAGERIAL GROUP	TECHNICAL GROUP	MANUFACTURING GROUP	ADMINISTRATIVE GROUP
			Administrative Assistant
Vice Presidents		Assembler I Inspector I	Principal Administrative Secretary
Division General Managers		Packer	Administrative Secretary
Managers	Head/Chief Scientist	Materials Handler Inspector II	
	Senior Associate Scientist	Assembler II	Word Processor
Project Leaders	Associate Scientist	Drill Press Operator Rough Grinder	
Supervisors	Scientist	Machinist I Coremaker	
	Technician		Clerk/Messenger
↑ Job Evaluation	↑ Skill Based	↑ Skill Based	↑ Job Evaluation

thetical job structures within a single evaluation. These structures were obtained via different approaches to evaluating work. The jobs are arrayed in hierarchies within four basic functions: managerial, technical, manufacturing, and administration. The managerial and administrative structures were obtained via a point job evaluation plan, and technical and manufacturing work via two different skill-based plans; the manufacturing plan was negotiated with the union. The point of the exhibit is to illustrate the results of evaluating work: structures that are consistent with the policy of internal consistency. Organizations commonly have multiple structures derived through multiple approaches. Consistency in such cases may be interpreted as consistency within each functional group or unit. Although some employees in one structure may wish to compare the procedures used in another structure with their own, the underlying premise in Exhibit 5.4 and in practice is that internal consistency is most influenced by fair and equitable treatment of employees doing similar work in the same skill group.

Once the structure or structures are established, managers must ensure that they remain internally consistent and equitable. This requires seeing that jobs and skills that employees believe are incorrectly evaluated are recertified and reevaluated (e.g., appeals/review procedures) and that new jobs or those that experience significant changes get reevaluated. Under skill-based plans employees often are required to be recertified, since the work they perform may not require them to use all the skills for which they were certified. Airplane pilots, for example, must go through an emergency landing simulation every 12 months, since the airlines' objective is to ensure that such crucial skills are not actually demonstrated on the job with any frequency. Similarly, the introduction of new skill requirements and the obsolescence of previous skill requires recertification. At its Ome facility in Tokyo, Toshiba requires all team members to recertify their skills every 24 months. Those who fail to pass previously certified skills have the opportunity to retrain and attempt to recertify before their pay rate is reduced. However, the pressure to keep up-to-date and avoid obsolescence is intense.

EVALUATE USEFULNESS

The usefulness of any management system is a function of how well it accomplishes its objectives. Job evaluation, skill-based plans, and market pricing are no different; they need to be judged in terms of their objectives. In the previous chapter, we noted that pay structures are intended to influence a wide variety of employee behaviors, ranging from staying with an employer to investing in additional training and willingness to take on new assignments. Consequently, the structures ought to be assessed in terms of their ability to affect such decisions. Unfortunately, little of this type of research is done.[10] There is virtually no evidence beyond individual experience and the prescriptions of pay pundits to offer guidance on when to use job evaluation, skill-based plans, or market pricing. Further, no evidence exists regarding how well alternative pay structures accomplish their objectives. The opportunities for such evaluation abound, since so many organizations are restructuring, and therefore redesigning their pay structures. Most frequently, internal structures are compared to what other employers are doing rather than to whether they aid the organization in achieving competitive advantage.

Skill-based approaches have been the subject of virtually no research beyond the case studies already discussed. The case studies are valuable because they describe practices. But more work evaluating alternatives and effects is needed.[11]

On the other hand, the job evaluation *procedures,* rather than the resulting *structures,* have been extensively researched. In general, these efforts focus on job evaluation as a measurement device: its reliability, its validity, the costs included in its design and implementation, and its compliance with laws and regulations. Let us review some of the work that has been reported.

---

[10]Sandra M. Emerson, "Job Evaluation: A Barrier to Excellence?" *Compensation and Benefits Review,* January–February 1991, pp. 38–51; Richard Bunning, "Models for Skill-based Pay Plans," *HR Magazine,* February 1992, pp. 62–64.

[11]G. Douglas Jenkins, Jr., Gerald E. Ledford, Jr., Nina Gupta, and D. Harold Doty, *Skill-based Pay* (Scottsdale, Ariz.: American Compensation Association, 1992).

Reliability: Do Different Evaluators in Different Circumstances Obtain Different Results?

Any evaluation involves substantial judgment. *Reliability* refers to the consistency of results obtained under different conditions. For example, to what extent do different evaluators produce similar results? Few employers or consulting firms report the results of their studies. However, several research studies by academics present a mixed picture; some report relatively high consistency (different evaluators assign the same jobs the same total point scores), whereas others report lower agreement on the values assigned to each specific compensable factor.[12] Some evidence also reports that evaluators' background and training may affect reliability.[13] An evaluator's affiliation with union or management appears to have little effect.

Using evaluators who are familiar with the jobs appears to enhance reliability.[14] This result lends support to the practice of involving employees in the evaluation process. One study reports that results obtained through a group consensus process were similar to those obtained by independent evaluators or an average of individual evaluators' results.[15]

---

[12]Several studies on the reliability of job evaluation plans have been reported. Four reviews provide useful overviews: R. D. Arvey, "Sex Bias in Job Evaluation Procedures," *Personnel Psychology,* Summer 1986, pp. 315–35; D. P. Schwab, "Job Evaluation and Pay Setting: Concepts and Practices," in *Comparable Worth: Issues and Alternatives,* ed. E. R. Livernash (Washington, D.C.: Equal Employment Advisory Council, 1980), pp. 49–78; R. J. Snelgar, "The Comparability of Job Evaluation Methods," *Personnel Psychology* 36 (1983), pp. 371–80; and R. M. Madigan, "Comparable Worth Judgments: A Measurement Properties Analysis," *Journal of Applied Psychology* 70 (1985), pp. 137–47. Other references include G. Satter, "Method of Paired Comparisons and a Specification Scoring Key in the Evaluation of Jobs," *Journal of Applied Psychology* 33 (1949), pp. 212–21; R. Richardson, *Fair Pay and Work: An Empirical Study of Fair Pay Perception and Time Span of Discretion* (Carbondale: Southern Illinois University Press, 1971); D. Doverspike and G. Barrett, "An Internal Bias Analysis of a Job Evaluation Instrument," *Journal of Applied Psychology* 69, no. 4 (1984), pp. 648–62; P. Ash, "The Reliability of Job Evaluation Rankings," *Journal of Applied Psychology* 32 (1948), pp. 313–20; D. J. Chesler, "Reliability and Comparability of Different Job Evaluation Systems," *Journal of Applied Psychology* 32 (1948), pp. 465–75; D. Doverspike, A. M. Carlisi, G. V. Barrett, and R. A. Alexander, "Generalizability Analysis of a Point-Method Job Evaluation Instrument," *Journal of Applied Psychology* 68 (1983), pp. 476–83; C. H. Anderson and D. B. Corts, *Development of a Framework for a Factor Ranking Benchmark System of Job Evaluation,* TS-73-3 (Washington, D.C.: U.S. Civil Service Commission, Personnel Research and Development Center, 1973); R. D. Arvey, S. E. Maxwell, and L. M. Abraham, "Reliability Artifacts in Comparable Worth Procedures," *Journal of Applied Psychology* 70, no. 4 (1985), pp. 695–705; T. Naughton, "Effects of Female-Linked Job Titles on Job Evaluation Ratings," *Journal of Management* 14, no. 4 (1988), pp. 567–78; Vandra Huber, "Comparison of Supervisor-Incumbent and Female-Male Multidimensional Job Evaluation Ratings," *Journal of Applied Psychology* 76, no. 1 (1991), pp. 115–21.

[13]C. H. Lawshe, Jr., and P. C. Farbo, "Studies in Job Evaluation: 8. The Reliability of an Abbreviated Job Evaluation System," *Journal of Applied Psychology* 33 (1949), pp. 158–66; Francis D. Harding, Joseph M. Madden, and Kenneth Colson, "Analysis of a Job Evaluation System," *Journal of Applied Psychology* 5 (1960), pp. 354–57; F. G. Moore, "Statistical Problems in Job Evaluation," *Personnel,* September 1946, pp. 125–36; Marvin G. Dertien, "The Accuracy of Job Evaluation Plans," *Personnel Journal,* July 1981, pp. 566–70.

[14]J. M. Madden, "The Effect of Varying the Degree of Rater Familiarity in Job Evaluation," *Personnel Administrator* 25 (1962), pp. 42–45; R. E. Cristal and J. M. Madden, *Effect of Degree of Familiarity in Job Evaluation* (Lackland Air Force Base, Tex.: Personnel Laboratory, Wright Air Development Division, 1960).

[15]D. P. Schwab and H. G. Heneman III, "Assessment of a Consensus-Based Multiple Information Source Job Evaluation System," *Journal of Applied Psychology,* 71 (1986), pp. 354–56.

Group consensus is widely used in practice. Each evaluator makes a preliminary independent evaluation. Then, meeting as a job evaluation committee, evaluators discuss their results until consensus emerges.

Although all this research is interesting, it fails to address a key issue: to what extent does the degree of reliability of job evaluation influence pay decisions and employees' attitudes and work behaviors? Only two studies have directly addressed this issue. Madigan examined three different job evaluation plans: a guide chart method similar to the Hay Guide Charts presented in the Appendix 4–B, the Position Analysis Questionnaire discussed in Chapter 3, and a custom-designed point plan using six factors (knowledge, experience, interpersonal skill, and supervisory, decision-making, and fiscal responsibilities). Although he found high consistency among raters, when he examined the impact of the results from different plans on actual pay decisions, he found significant differences. For example, when different evaluators used the custom-designed point plan, their pay recommendations for the jobs agreed in only 51 percent of jobs. The differences in results translated into a range of ± 160 evaluation points, which meant significant pay differences for affected employees. Madigan points out that by traditional academic standards, the reliability of these three methods was acceptable. However, managers and affected employees probably wouldn't agree. (Nor would academics if it were their pay.) Madigan observes, "The assessment of potential error . . . in job evaluation must go beyond reliability estimates to include the estimates of impact of pay decisions."[16]

Validity: Do Results Depend on the Method?

The choice among evaluation approaches depends on the circumstances and objectives faced. Does it make any difference? Do the results obtained differ?

Validity refers to the degree to which an evaluation method yields the desired results. The desired results can be measured several ways: (1) the hit rate (percentage of correct decisions it makes), (2) convergence (agreement with results obtained from other evaluation plans), and (3) employee acceptance (employee and manager attitudes about the evaluation process and the results).[17]

Hit Rates: Agreement with Predetermined Benchmark Structures.

The hit rate approach focuses on the ability of the job evaluation plan to replicate a predetermined, agreed-upon job structure. The agreed-upon structure, as we discussed in the last chapter, can be based on several criteria. The jobs' market rates, or a structure negotiated with a union or a management committee, or rates for jobs held predominantly by men, or some combination of these are all examples. Exhibit 5.5 shows the hit rates for a hypothetical

---

[16]Madigan, "Comparable Worth Judgments."

[17]Validity can also be reflected in the R^2 and standard error of estimate generated via regressing benchmark job's wages on compensable factors. R^2 alone is insufficient because it reflects only the strength of the relationship. The error terms are also important, since they reflect the precision with which job grade and pay decisions can be made. Hit rates, in a general sense, capture the R^2 and standard error information. For an early discussion of validation and job evaluation, see William M. Fox, "Purpose and Validity in Job Evaluation," *Personnel Journal* 41 (1962), pp. 432–37.

EXHIBIT 5.5   Illustration of Plan's Hit Rate as a Method to Judge the Validity of Job Evaluation Results

---

Total jobs: 49

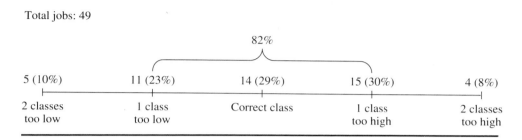

job evaluation plan. The agreed-upon structure has 49 benchmark jobs in it. This structure was derived through negotiation among managers serving on the job evaluation committee. The job evaluation plan placed only 14 (29 percent) of the jobs into their current (agreed-upon) pay classes and came within ± one pay class or 82 percent of the jobs in the agreed-upon structure. In a study conducted at Control Data Corporation, the reported hit rates for six different plans ranged from 49 to 73 percent of the jobs classified with ± 1 class of their current, agreed-upon classes.[18] Madigan and Hoover applied two job evaluation plans to 206 job classes for the state of Michigan.[19] Their hit rates ranged from 27 to 73 percent, depending on the scoring method used.

Is a job evaluation plan valid (i.e., useful) if it can correctly place only one third of the jobs? As with so many questions in compensation, the answer is "It depends." It depends on the alternative approaches available, on the costs involved in designing and implementing these plans, and on the magnitude of errors involved in missing a "direct hit." If, for example, being within ± 1 pay class translates into several hundred dollars in pay, then employees probably aren't going to express much confidence in the "validity" of this plan. If, on the other hand, the pay difference between ± 1 class is not great *or* the plan's results are treated only as an estimate to be adjusted by the job evaluation committee, then its validity (usefulness) is more likely.

Convergence of Results.   Evaluation plans can also be judged by the degree to which different plans yield similar results. The premise is that convergence of the results from independent methods increases the chances that the results, and hence the methods, are valid. Different results, on the other hand, point to lack of validity. We again turn to Madigan's report on the results of three job evaluation plans (guide chart, PAQ, and

---

[18]L. R. Gomez-Mejia, R. C. Page, and W. W. Tornow, "A Comparison of the Practical Utility of Traditional, Statistical, and Hybrid Job Evaluation Approaches," *Academy of Management Journal* 25 (1982), pp. 790–809.

[19]R. M. Madigan and D. J. Hoover, "Effects of Alternative Job Evaluation Methods on Decisions Involving Pay Equity," *Academy of Management Journal,* March 1986, pp. 84–100.

point plan).[20] He concludes that the three methods generate different and inconsistent job structures. An employee could have received up to $427 per month more (or less), depending on the job evaluation method used.

Another study applied three variations on a point plan to 15 jobs from three different job families: blue collar, clerical, and professional/technical. Although all three plans gave similar results, none of them matched the employer's rankings in any of the job groups. The authors conclude that the methods were reliable, but not necessarily valid or correct, because all three of them ranked a police officer higher than a detective.[21] Readers of detective fiction know that detectives rank higher than police officers. A Dalgleish beats an Inspector Lestrade any day.[22]

Another study of five different weighting variations used on two different plans found that the weighting of factors can affect the results, and that weighting makes the most difference when the compensable factors are independent (i.e., not much overlap in what they measure).[23]

These results are provocative. They are consistent with the proposition that job evaluation, as traditionally practiced and described in this and other textbooks, is not a measurement procedure. This is so because it fails to consistently exhibit properties of reliability and validity. However, it is important to maintain a proper perspective in interpreting these results. Few compensation managers consider job evaluation a measurement tool in the strict sense of that term. More often, it is viewed as a procedure to help rationalize an agreed-upon pay structure in terms of job and business-related factors. As such, it becomes a process of give and take, not some immutable yardstick. This perspective leads us to a third criteria used to judge the validity of a job evaluation plan: acceptance among the parties involved.

Acceptability.   Acceptance by the employees and managers involved remains a key test of any evaluation plan. A recurring theme in this book is that the usefulness of pay techniques must include employee and manager acceptance.

Several devices are used to assess and improve acceptability. An obvious one is the inclusion of a *formal appeals process,* discussed earlier. Employees who believe their jobs are incorrectly evaluated should be able to request reanalysis and/or skills reevaluation. Most firms respond to such requests from managers, but few extend the process to all employees, unless those employees are represented by unions who have negotiated a grievance process. No matter what the outcome from the appeal, the results need to be explained in detail to anyone who requests reevaluation.

---

[20]Madigan, "Comparable Worth Judgments"; also see Doverspike and Barrett, "Internal Bias Analysis," and Richardson, *Fair Pay.*

[21]Judith Collins, "Job Evaluation" (Working paper, University of Arkansas—Little Rock, 1992).

[22]Dalgleish is the hero of several novels by P. D. James; Inspector Lestrade is frequently bested by Sherlock Holmes in stories by Arthur Conan Doyle.

[23]Kermit Davis, Jr., and William Sauser, Jr., "Effects of Alternative Weighting Methods in a Policy-Capturing Approach to Job Evaluation: A Review and Empirical Investigation," *Personnel Psychology* 44 (1991), pp. 85–127.

EXHIBIT 5.6   Illustrations of Audit Indexes

A. **Overall indicators.**
   1. Ratio of number of current descriptions to numbers of employees.
   2. Number of job descriptions evaluated last year and previous year.
   3. Number of jobs evaluated per unit.
      (*a*) Newly created jobs.
      (*b*) Reevaluation of existing jobs.

B. **Timeliness of job descriptions and evaluations.**
   1. Percent of total jobs with current descriptions.
   2. Percentage of evaluation requests returned within 7 working days, within 14 working days.
   3. Percentage of reevaluation requests returned with changed (unchanged) evaluations.

C. **Workability and acceptability of job evaluation.**
   1. Percentage of employees (managers) surveyed who know the purposes of job evaluation.
   2. The number of employees who appeal their job's evaluation rating.
   3. The number of employees who receive explanations of the results of their reevaluation requests.

A second method of assessing acceptability is to include questions about it in *employee attitude surveys*. Questions can assess perceptions of how useful evaluation is as a management tool. Another method is to *audit* how the plan is being used based on a series of measures of use. Exhibit 5.6 lists examples of indexes used by various employers. These indexes range from the percentage of employees who understand the reasons for evaluation to the percentage of jobs with current descriptions, to the rate of requests for reevaluation. Acceptability is a somewhat vague test of the job evaluation—acceptable to whom is an open issue. Clearly, managers and employees are important constituents because acceptance makes it a useful device. But as we will discuss in the chapter on pay discrimination (Chapter 14), others outside the firm also have a stake in job evaluation and the pay structure.

Costs

Two types of costs associated with evaluation can be identified: (1) design and administration costs and (2) labor costs that result from pay structure changes occasioned by evaluation. The labor cost effects will be unique for each application. Little recent data have been published on design and administration costs. Winstanley offers a rule of thumb of 1 to 3 percent of covered payroll as the cost for traditional job evaluation.[24] Recent experience suggests that costs can range from a few thousand dollars for a small organization to more than $500,000 in consultant fees alone for major projects in large firms. This does not include the costs of the compensation professionals, managers, and employees involved. Little cost data for skill-based plans have been published.

---

[24]Based on one of N. Winstanley's many welcome notes to us about the real world of compensation management.

Gender Effects in Evaluation

Much attention has been directed at job evaluation as both a potential source of bias against women and as a mechanism to reduce bias.[25] Although Chapter 14 presents an extended discussion of pay discrimination, it has been widely speculated that job evaluation is susceptible to gender bias. To date, three ways that job evaluation can be biased against women have been studied.[26] Unfortunately, no studies of gender effects in skill-based plans exist.

Jobholder's Gender.   Direct bias occurs if jobs held predominantly by women are undervalued relative to jobs held predominantly by men, simply because of the jobholder's gender. Evidence does not support the proposition that the gender of the jobholder influences the evaluation of the job. One study found no effects when it varied the gender of jobholders using photographs and recorded voices.[27] Another study reported a slight bias in favor of female-linked *job titles* (e.g., orderly vs. nurses aide). The evaluators received extensive training in potential gender bias; hence, they may have "bent over backwards" to avoid it.[28] Simply telling evaluators that varying proportions of men and women performed the jobs made no difference.[29]

However, specific compensable factors may be biased for or against gender-segregated jobs.[30] A study found that those compensable factors related to job content (contact with others and error in judgment) did reflect bias, but others pertaining to employee requirements (education and experience required) did not.[31] Two job descriptions were evaluated. The female-linked title, executive secretary, was reportedly undervalued on the job content factors. However, the author concludes "that the job evaluation procedures

[25]D. J. Treiman and H. I. Hartmann, eds., *Women, Work and Wages: Equal Pay for Jobs of Equal Value* (Washington, D.C.: National Academy of Sciences, 1981); H. Remick, *Comparable Worth and Wage Discrimination* (Philadelphia: Temple University Press, 1984); and R. G. Blumrosen, "Wage Discrimination, Job Segregation, and Title VII of the Civil Rights Act of 1964," *University of Michigan Journal of Law Reform* 12, no. 3 (1979), pp. 397–502.

[26]This discussion is adapted from D. Schwab and R. Grams, "Sex-Related Errors in Job Evaluation: A 'Real-World' Test," *Journal of Applied Psychology* 70, no. 3 (1985), pp. 533–59; and Arvey, "Sex Bias in Job Evaluation Procedures."

[27]Richard D. Arvey, Emily M. Passino, and John W. Lounsbury, "Job Analysis Results As Influenced by Sex of Incumbent and Sex of Analyst," *Journal of Applied Psychology* 62, no. 4 (1977), pp. 411–16; Carol T. Schreiber, "Job Evaluation and the Minority Issue," Paper presented at Industrial Relations Counselors Symposium, Atlanta, September 1978, pp. 14–15; J. Goodman and J. Morgan, "Job Evaluation without Sex Discrimination," *Personnel Management* 11, no. 10 (October 1979), pp. 158–67; Catherine M. Meek, "Auditing Your Job Evaluation Plan—A Case Study," *EEO Today,* Spring 1979, pp. 21–27.

[28]Michael K. Mount and Rebecca A. Ellis, "Investigation of Bias in Job Evaluation Ratings of Comparable Worth Study Participants," *Personnel Psychology,* Spring 1987, pp. 85–96.

[29]R. Grams and D. Schwab, "An Investigation of Systematic Gender-Related Error in Job Evaluation," *Academy of Management Journal* 28, no. 2 (1985), pp. 279–90.

[30]Gerald V. Barrett and Dennis Doverspike, "Another Defense of Point-Factor Job Evaluation," *Personnel,* March 1989, pp. 33–36.

[31]Arvey, "Sex Bias in Job Evaluation Procedures."

appear to perform their intended purpose; to array jobs in a hierarchy based on job requirements."[32]

The psychological literature identifies a common tendency to make stereotypical assumptions, usually to the detriment of women when compared to men. Perhaps by calling out the job-related criteria for making judgments, job evaluation is able to avoid this bias.[33]

Wages Criteria Bias.   The second potential source of bias affects job evaluation indirectly, through the current wages paid for jobs. In this case, job evaluation results may be biased if the jobs held predominantly by women are incorrectly underpaid. Treiman and Hartmann argue that women's jobs are unfairly underpaid simply because women hold them.[34] If this is the case and if job evaluation is based on the current wages paid, then the job evaluation results simply mirror any bias in the current pay rates. Considering that many job evaluation plans are purposely structured to mirror the existing pay structure, it should not be surprising that the current wages for jobs influence the results of job evaluation. In one study, 400 experienced compensation administrators were sent information on current pay, market, and job evaluation results. They were asked to use this information to make pay decisions for a set of nine jobs. Half of the administrators received jobs linked to men (e.g., more than 70 percent of job holders were men—security guards) and the jobs given the other half were held predominantly by women (e.g., more than 70 percent of job holders were women—secretary II). The results revealed that (1) market data had a substantially larger effect on pay decisions than did job evaluations on current pay data and (2) the jobs' gender had no effect.[35] This study is a unique look at several factors that may affect pay structures. If market rates and current pay already reflect gender bias, then these biased pay rates could work indirectly through the job evaluation process to deflate the evaluation of jobs held primarily by women.[36] Clearly, the criteria used in the design of evaluation plans are crucial and need to be business and work related.

Evaluator's Gender.   The third possible source of gender bias in evaluation flows from the gender of the individual evaluators. Some argue that male evaluators may be less

---

[32]Naughton, "Effect of Female-Linked Job Titles on Job Evaluation Ratings."

[33]L. A. Krefting, P. K. Berger, and M. J. Wallace, Jr., "The Contribution of Sex Distribution, Job Content, and Occupational Classification to Job Sextyping," *Journal of Vocational Behavior* 13 (1978), pp. 181–91; and L. A. Krefting, P. K. Berger, and M. J. Wallace, Jr., "Sextyping by Personnel Practitioners," Paper presented at Academy of Management national meetings, San Francisco, 1978.

[34]Treiman and Hartmann, *Women, Work and Wages.*

[35]S. Rynes, C. Weber, and G. Milkovich, "The Effects of Market Survey Rates, Job Evaluation, and Job Gender on Job Pay," *Journal of Applied Psychology* 74 (1989), pp. 114–23; and D. Doverspike and G. Barrett, "An Internal Bias Analysis of a Job Evaluation Instrument," *Journal of Applied Psychology* 69 (1984), pp. 648–62.

[36]Grams and Schwab, "Investigation of Systematic Gender-Related Error in Job Evaluation."

favorably disposed toward jobs held predominantly by women. However, research finds no evidence that the job evaluator's gender affects the results.

Several recommendations seek to ensure that job evaluation plans are bias free.[37] Such recommendations include the following:

1. Define the compensable factors and scales to include the content of jobs held predominantly by women. For example, working conditions should include the noise and stress of office machines and the repetitive movements associated with the use of word processors.

2. Ensure that factor weights are not consistently biased against jobs held predominantly by women. Are factors usually associated with these jobs always given less weight?

3. Apply the plan in as bias-free a manner as feasible. Ensure that the job descriptions are bias free, exclude incumbent names from the job evaluation process, and train women as evaluators.

Some writers see job evaluation as the best friend of those who wish to combat pay discrimination. Without a properly designed and applied system, "employers will face an almost insurmountable task in persuading the government that ill-defined or whimsical methods of determining differences in job content and pay are a business necessity."[38] On the other hand, some lawyers recommend that employers avoid job evaluation on the grounds that the results will lead to lawsuits. This issue will be discussed again in the chapter on pay discrimination.

RESEARCH ON SKILL-BASED PLANS

At the risk of pointing out the obvious, all issues concerning job evaluation also apply to skill-based plans. For example, the acceptability of the results of skill-based plans can be studied from the perspective of measurement (reliability, validity) and administration (costs and returns). The various points in skill certification at which errors and biases may enter into judgment (e.g., different views of skill-block definitions, potential favoritism toward team members, defining and assessing skill obsolescence) and whether skill block points and evaluators make a difference all need to be studied. A cynic might observe that one reason that skill-based plans seem to be increasing in popularity is that they have yet to take on all the administrative and regulatory baggage to which job evaluation has been subjected.

---

[37]Remick, *Comparable Worth and Wage Discrimination:* Helen Remick, "Strategies for Creating Sound, Bias-Free Job Evaluation Plans," Paper presented at Industrial Relations Counselors, Inc., Symposium on Job Evaluation and EEO, September 15 and 17, 1978, Atlanta. Also see David J. Thomsen, "Eliminating Pay Discrimination Caused by Job Evaluation," *Personnel,* September–October 1978, pp. 11–22; John Lacy, "Job Evaluation and EEO," *Employee Relations Law Journal* 7, no. 3 (1979), pp. 210–17; and Pay Equity Bureau, *Pay Equity: Equality at Work, Book 3: Interpretation and Wage Adjustments* (Winnipeg, Manitoba: Pay Equity Bureau, 1989).

[38]Marsh W. Bates and Richard G. Vail, "Job Evaluation and Equal Employment Opportunity: A Tool for Compliance—A Weapon for Defense," *Employee Relations Law Journal* 1, no. 4 (1984), pp. 535–46.

MICROCOMPUTERS AND JOB EVALUATION

Several compensation consulting firms offer computer-based job evaluation plans. Their software does everything from analyze the job analysis questions and provide computer-generated job descriptions, to predict the pay classes for each job. Some caution is required because "computer assisted" does not equate with more efficient, more acceptable, or cheaper evaluations. In a survey of more than 1,000 U.S. organizations, 76 percent of respondents currently are not using computer assistance in the job evaluation process.[39] However, approximately 30 percent said they are "considering" using some form of computer assistance. Complaints voiced about job evaluation are that it takes too much time; it's a burdensome bureaucracy; it involves too many people to ensure perceived equity; and the accuracy, objectivity, and usefulness of the results remain in question. The primary advantages seen for computer-aided job evaluation according to its advocates include the following:

- Alleviation of the heavy paperwork and tremendous time saving.
- Marked increase in the accuracy of results.
- Creation of more detailed databases.
- Opportunity to conduct improved analysis.[40]

But even with the assistance of computers, job evaluation remains a subjective process that involves substantial judgment. Computers may help reduce the bureaucratic burden that job evaluation often becomes, and it may even help make the process more systematic—but judgment awaits.

SUMMARY

This section of the book started by examining pay structures within an organization. The importance placed on internal consistency in the pay structures was the basic policy issue addressed. We pointed out that the basic premise underlying a policy that emphasizes internal consistency is that internal pay structures need to be tailored to be consistent with the organization's business strategy and its values, the design of the work flow, and a concern of fair treatment of employees. Internal equity, the work relationships within a single organization, is an important part of a policy of internal consistency. Equitable structures, acceptable to the stakeholders involved, affect satisfaction with pay, the willingness to seek and accept promotions to more responsible jobs, the effort to undertake additional training, and the propensity to remain with the employer; they also reduce the incidence of pay-related grievances.

The techniques used to help establish internally consistent structures typically include job evaluation, skill-based plans, and market pricing. Although viewed by some as

---

[39]Fred Crandall, "Micro Computer Use on the Rise in Job Evaluation," *American Compensation Association News,* February 1986, p. 6. A full copy of the report is available from Sibson & Company, 101 N. Wacker Drive, Suite 705, Chicago, IL 60606.

[40]Robert A. Rheaume and Warren W. Jones, "Automated Job Evaluations That Consolidate What Employees Do," *Computers in Personnel,* Summer 1988, pp. 39–45.

bureaucratic burdens, these techniques can aid in achieving the objectives of the pay system when they are properly designed and administered. Without them, our pay objectives of improving competitiveness and equity are more difficult to achieve.

We have now finished the first part of the book. In it, you were introduced to strategic perspectives on compensation, the key policy issues in compensation management, and the model that provides a framework for the book. Compensation management requires adapting the pay system to support the organization strategies, its culture and values, and the needs of individual employees. We examined the first basic policy issue, internal consistency of the pay structure. We discussed the techniques used to establish consistency as well as its effects on compensation objectives. The next section of the book focuses on the second major policy issue in our pay model, external competitiveness.

REVIEW QUESTIONS

1. What are the pros and cons of having employees involved in compensation decisions?
2. Thinking back on the earlier chapters of job and knowledge analysis and work evaluation, including job evaluation and skill certification, what forms can employee involvement take?
3. Why does the process used in the design of the internal pay structure matter? Distinguish between the process used to design and administer the structure and the techniques or mechanics used.
4. If you were a compensation manager, how would you recommend that your company evaluate the usefulness of its job evaluation or skill-based plans?
5. What are the sources of possible gender bias in job evaluation?
6. How can compensation managers and employees ensure that job evaluation or skill-based plans are bias free?

YOUR TURN:
DISCRIMINATORY JOB FACTORS

The chart below is taken from a United Kingdom Equal Opportunities Commission report. It deals with gender bias in job factors and describes some factors that, in the opinion of commission members, strongly favor males or females, weakly favor males or females, or are neutral.

1. Use this chart to analyze the job descriptions in Exhibits 3.13, 3.14, and 3.15 (nurse and personnel vice president). For each description, list any factors that appear to

   a. Strongly favor males.
   b. Weakly favor males.
   c. Be neutral.
   d. Weakly favor females.
   e. Strongly favor females.

   What is your overall assessment of the possibility of gender bias in these descriptions?

2. In the same way, analyze the job description you and your teammate prepared following Chapter 3. Is there a gender bias?

EXHIBIT 1 Gender-Biased and Gender-Neutral Job Factors Cited by United Kingdom Equal Opportunities Commission

	Favors Male Jobs		Neutral	Favors Female Jobs	
	Strongly	Weakly		Weakly	Strongly
Factors with a time dimension	Length of service Experience	Age Qualifications Education Knowledge Breadth of know-how	Trained period Level of skill Depth of know-how		
Factors with a seniority dimension		Responsibility for cash or assets Discretion Responsibility Effect of decisions Supervision of subordinates Accountability Decision making Planning	Confidential data/ information		
Factors with a relationship dimension			Safety of others Cooperation Supervising Creating new business Communication Coordination Personal appearance Expression	Contacts: internal/ external Human relations responsibility Public relations responsibility Accuracy	Caring

(continued)

EXHIBIT 1 (concluded)

	Favors Male Jobs			Favors Female Jobs	
	Strongly	*Weakly*	*Neutral*	*Weakly*	*Strongly*
Factors with a physical activity dimension	Heavy lifting Physical hazards Spatial ability Unpleasant working conditions	Technical expertise Responsibility for equipment Physical skills Physical effort Responsibility for standards Operational knowledge Knowledge of machinery, tools, and materials	Safety of others Stamina Responsibility for materials Versatility Procedural know-how Fatigue	Monotony Visual concentration Scanning and location of details	Dexterity Typing keyboard skills
Factors with a mental activity dimension		Numerical calculation Knowledge Numerical ability Mathematical reasoning Problem solving	Initiative Originality Ingenuity Judgment Mental effort Complexity of job Planning Verbal comprehension Verbal expression	Concentration Memory Information ordering	
Factors with a sensory activity dimension		Differentiating sounds	Differentiating tastes Differentiating smells Visual concentration Aesthetic appreciation Tactic sensitivity Artistic/Musical creativity		

EXHIBIT II.1 The Pay Model

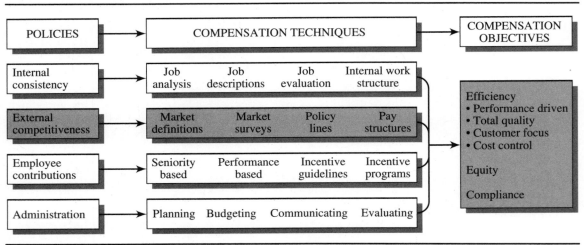

PART II External Competitiveness: Determining the Pay Level

The objective of Part II is to discuss the way employers position their pay relative to the way other employers who compete in the same labor and product markets pay. Exhibit II.1 shows that the external competitiveness policy fits into the total pay model. It represents the second of the four major policy decisions in the model.

An employer's pay level helps determine its external competitiveness. Three pure policy alternatives exist: to lead competitors' pay, to match it, or to lag below it. But variations exist. Employers may tie pay to the firm's financial success through bonuses. When profits are high, pay may lead that offered by other firms. When profits are weak, no bonuses are paid and the pay may be less than that offered by others. Another variation is to become the "employer of choice" by emphasizing the total returns in addition to pay, such as employment security, training, status of a highly respected employer, or challenging projects. In practice, some employers use different policies for different units and/or job groups, and there are many different ways to put these policies into practice.

How a company positions its pay relative to its competitors depends on three major factors: (1) labor conditions, stemming from competition in the labor market or labor union demands; (2) product market conditions that affect the organization's financial vitality and, in turn, what the organization can afford to pay; and (3) the strategic and operating objectives that the organization has established.

External competitiveness translates into practice when the company establishes a pay level. The pay level has a twofold effect on pay objectives: (1) it directly affects the employer's operating costs (i.e., labor costs) and (2) it directly affects the employer's ability to attract and maintain a stable and qualified work force. Consequently, the policies and practices related to external competitiveness are among the most critical in compensation management.

In Chapter 6, the major factors affecting external competitiveness policies, consequences of these policies, and theories and research related to them are discussed. Chapter 7 discusses the decisions and techniques that translate an employer's external competitiveness policy into pay level and pricing the structures discussed in Part I.

Chapter Outline

Every year employers make job offers to students graduating with master's degrees in HR management. In 1992, offers ranged from $35,000 to $50,000 per year, with the most common around $45,000. Early in the recruiting season, students attributed this range to differences among themselves: grade point average, courses taken, interviewing skills, and analytical and interpersonal abilities. But after some students rejected initial offers, employers extended the same offer to other students. Why were the offers not changed when extended to different students with different qualifications? The better students seemed to get more offers rather than all the higher offers. If an individual's qualifications do not explain differences in offers, what does? Location had an effect: firms in San Francisco and New York City made higher offers. The nature of the work also had some effect: jobs in employment paid a little less than jobs in compensation and labor relations. (Now aren't you glad you didn't drop this course?) A major difference in job offers was related to the industry to which the different firms belonged. Pharmaceuticals, brokerage houses, and petroleum firms tended to offer more than consumer products, insurance, banking, and heavy manufacturing firms. In fact, several studies report stable industry effects over time; the relatively high-paying industries such as autos and pharmaceuticals of 70 years ago continue to be relatively high-paying today; low wage industries such as education (ouch!) and insurance continue to be lower paying.[1]

What determines these differences in pay levels, and what effects do these differences have on organization performance and employee work behavior? This chapter examines these two questions.

EXTERNAL COMPETITIVENESS AND THE PAY MODEL

In practice, policies regarding external competitiveness translate into the employer's pay level. It is important to understand the two concepts.

> *External competitiveness* refers to the pay relationships *among* organizations—the organization's pay relative to its competitors.

[1]Richard H. Thaler, "Interindustry Wage Differentials," *The Winner's Curse* (New York: Free Press, 1992); William T. Dickens and Lawrence F. Katz, "Inter-Industry Wage Differences and Industry Characteristics," in *Unemployment and the Structure of Labor Markets,* ed. K. Lang and J. Leonard (Oxford, England: Basil Blackwell, 1987); William T. Dickens and Lawrence F. Katz, "Inter-Industry Wage Differences and Theories of Wage Determination," (Working paper 2271, National Bureau of Economic Research, Cambridge, Mass., 1987); Alan B. Krueger and Lawrence H. Summers, "Reflections on the Inter-Industry Wage Structure," in *Unemployment and the Structure of Labor Markets*, ed. K. Lang and J. Leonard (Oxford, England: Basil Blackwell, 1987); Alan B. Krueger and Lawrence H. Summers, "Efficiency Wages and the Inter-Industry Wage Structure," *Econometrica,* March 1988, pp. 259–93; and Summer Slichter, "Notes on the Structure of Wages," *Review of Economics and Statistics* 32 (1950), pp. 80–91.

Pay level refers to an *average* of the array of rates paid by an employer. It focuses attention on (1) the costs of human resources to the employer and (2) the use of pay to attract and retain employees.

The heart of the concept of external competitiveness is its relative nature: comparisons with other employers. Although pay is a primary component of external competitiveness, other components include the mix of various forms of pay (i.e., use of bonuses, benefits), career opportunities, challenging assignments, or financial stability of the organization.

Pay level decisions have a significant impact on most organizations' total expenses. Other things being equal, the higher the pay level, the higher the labor costs. Furthermore, the higher the pay level relative to what competition pays, the greater the relative costs to produce similar products. So it would seem that the obvious conclusion is to set the minimum pay level possible.

However, other things are rarely equal. For example, a high pay level may make it easier to attract and retain a qualified work force.[2] High-wage employers should not have to train or recruit as extensively as low-paying ones.[3] Yet evidence suggests that high-wage employers also expend greater efforts on recruiting.[4] This dichotomy is explained by the greater selectivity in hiring that is made possible by the large number of applicants attracted by the high wages. If better applicants are hired, then greater productivity may offset the higher labor costs per employee—fewer, more productive employees are the result. So a decision to set a high pay level can also be justified. In fact, employers do set different pay levels. That is why there is no single "going rate" in the labor market for a specific job.

No Single "Going Rate."   As graduating students discover each year, the rates paid for similar jobs and skills vary among employers.[5] An array of rates exists. Notice that in Exhibit 6.1 the salary paid by firms participating in this survey for word processors varies from $6.14 per hour to $12.40 per hour. The average rate paid by employers ranges from $8.24 per hour to $10.53 per hour. Although some of this difference may be attributable

---

[2]S. L. Rynes and A. E. Barber, "Applicant Attraction Strategies: An Organizational Perspective," *Academy of Management Review,* 1990; and Margaret L. Williams and George Dreher, "Compensation System Attributes and Applicant Pool Characteristics," *Academy of Management Journal,* August 1992.

[3]H. J. Holzer, "Wages, Employer Costs, and Employee Performance in the Firm," *Industrial and Labor Relations Review* 43 (1990), pp. 147S–164S.

[4]S. L. Rynes, "Compensation Strategies for Recruiting," *Topics in Total Compensation* 2 (1987), pp. 185–96.

[5]*College Placement Council Salary Survey* is published quarterly by the College Placement Council, Bethlehem, Penn. It reports starting salary offers to college graduates as collected by college placement offices. Data are reported by curriculum, by functional area, and by degree. It is one of several sources employers may use to establish the offers they extend to new graduates.

EXHIBIT 6.1 **Salary Survey Results**

Word Processing Operator, Lead

Duties

Assumes responsibility for directing work flow through the word processing center or cluster and provides administrative support to principals to improve overall productivity. Uses word processor to type high-priority and confidential work.

High school graduate or equivalent, plus three years of word processing experience required.

Job Title: Word Process Operator III	*Company Code*	*Minimum Rate*	*Mid Rate*	*Maximum Rate*	*Average Rate*	*Employee Population*
	D	$9.34	$10.88	$12.40	$10.53	1
	Y	$8.23	$ 9.69	$11.14	$10.53	1
	E	$8.53	$10.07	$11.60	$10.17	3
	YY	$8.71	$10.14	$11.56	$10.01	1
	B	$7.66	$ 9.59	$11.49	$ 9.37	2
	N	$7.69	$ 9.62	$11.55	$ 9.37	14
	W	$6.68	$10.07	$11.51	$ 9.05	1
	XX	$7.72	$ 9.07	$10.89	$ 9.02	12
	OO	$6.19	$ 8.05	$ 9.90	$ 8.57	2
	Q	$7.22	$ 9.63	$11.46	$ 8.49	3
	MM	$6.38	$ 7.99	$ 9.59	$ 8.29	2
	G	$6.14	$ 7.59	$ 9.05	$ 8.24	1
	R	$6.94	$ 8.55	$10.14	$ 8.24	3
Straight average		$7.49	$ 9.31	$10.94	$ 9.25	46
Weighted average		$7.56	$ 9.31	$11.08	$ 9.15	

SOURCE: Dallas Area Electronics Survey. Survey sponsors: Recognition Equipment, Rockwell International, Collins Radio Group, and Texas Instruments, Inc.

---

to such factors as experience and seniority within the firm, much of it also reflects different pay levels among different employers.

Even within a single industry, a wide variation in pay levels exists. A survey of aerospace firms (reported graphically in Exhibit 6.2) indicates that the top-paying firm paid more than 21 percent above the average pay in its market, and the bottom one paid more than 13 percent below the overall average pay of all 21 firms.[6] Despite this wide variation in pay levels, about 70 percent of the firms were within about 10 percent (plus or minus) of the average.

Even more interesting is the fact that the firms in this survey exhibited different competitive positions for different job families. For example, Company S, which was 10.5 percent *below* market overall, paid its sales and marketing people almost 40 percent *above* market for those positions, but its CEO 30 percent below market. Company J, 2.6 percent above market overall, paid its CEO 7 percent above market and its marketers 3 percent above the market. So Company J's internal pay relationships more closely mirrored the market than did those of S.

---

[6]Ken Foster, "An Anatomy of Company Pay Practices," *Personnel*, September 1985, pp. 67–71.

EXHIBIT 6.2 **Relationship of Company Pay Scales to Market Average**

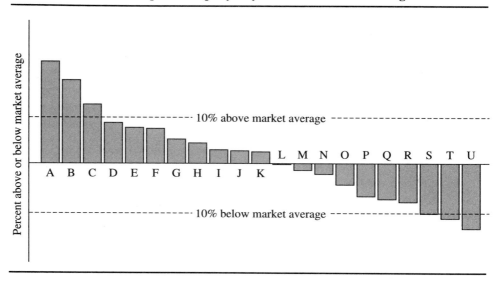

Although it is risky to infer different competitive policies from these data, it is clear that different employers in the same industry adopt different policies and practices regarding external competition and pay levels.[7] The next section discusses the theories and research related to understanding these differences.

FACTORS INFLUENCING EXTERNAL COMPETITIVENESS

The factors that affect the pay level and consequently external competitiveness are grouped in Exhibit 6.3. They include the pressures exerted by (1) competition in labor markets for workers with sought-after skills and abilities; (2) competition in product and service markets, which affects the financial condition of the firm; and (3) characteristics unique to each organization and its work force, such as its business strategies, and the productivity and experience of its work force. These factors act in concert to influence pay levels set during the design and administration of pay systems.

---

[7]George Milkovich, "Compensation Systems in High Technology Companies," in *Human Resource Management in High Technology Firms*, ed. A. Kleingartner and C. S. Anderson (Lexington, Mass.: Lexington Books, 1987), pp. 103–14; Barry Gerhart and George T. Milkovich, "Organizational Differences in Managerial Compensation and Financial Performance," *Academy of Management Journal* 33 (1990), pp. 63–91; and Barry Gerhart and George Milkovich, "Employee Compensation: Research and Practice," in *Handbook of Industrial and Organizational Psychology*, 2nd ed., M. D. Dunnette and L. M. Hough (Palo Alto, Calif.: Consulting Psychologists Press, 1992).

EXHIBIT 6.3   Factors Influencing Pay Level

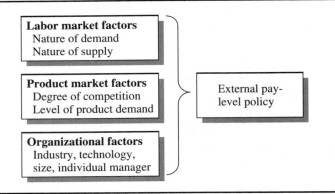

LABOR MARKET FACTORS

Economists describe two basic types of markets: the quoted price and the bourse. Stores that label each item's price or ads that list a job opening's starting wage are examples of *quoted price markets*. Buying at a flea market or haggling over the terms and conditions in professional athletes' contracts are examples of *bourses*. Graduating students usually find themselves in a quoted market, though some haggling over terms may occur.[8] Both types of market involve an exchange between buyers (the employers) and sellers (the workers). College recruiting, want ads, and employment agencies facilitate the exchange of information about jobs and skills. If the inducements offered by the employer and the skills offered by the worker are acceptable to both parties, a contract is executed. The contract may be formal, such as those made with unions, professional athletes, and executive officers, or informal, with an implied understanding or a brief letter. The result of the workings of the labor market is the allocation of employees to job opportunities at specified pay rates.

How Markets Work

Four basic assumptions underlie economic analysis of markets.

1. Employers always seek to maximize profits.
2. Human resources are homogenous and therefore interchangeable; a business graduate is a business graduate is a business graduate.
3. The pay rates reflect all costs associated with employment (e.g., holidays, benefits, and training).

---

[8]Barry Gerhart and Sara Rynes, "Determinants and Consequences of Salary Negotiations by Male and Female MBA Graduates," *Journal of Applied Psychology* 76, no. 2 (1991), pp. 256–62; and Kathryn Bartol and David Martin, "When Politics Pays: Factors Influencing Managerial Compensation Decisions," *Personnel Psychology* 43 (1990), pp. 599–614.

4. The markets faced by employers are competitive; so there is no advantage for a single employer to change them.

Although these assumptions oversimplify reality, they provide a framework for understanding labor markets.

Compensation managers often refer to the "market": "Our pay levels are based upon the market," "We pay competitively with the market," or "We are market leaders." Understanding how markets work requires analysis of the demand and supply of labor. The demand side looks at *employers'* hiring behavior: how many employees they seek and what they are able and willing to pay. The supply side looks at the *workers*: their qualifications and the pay they are willing to accept in exchange for their services. Exhibit 6.4 shows a simple illustration of demand for and supply of business graduates. The vertical axis represents pay rates from $20,000 a year to $70,000 a year. The horizontal axis is the number of business graduates in the market, ranging from 100 to 1,000. Demand is the sum of all employers' hiring requirements for business graduates at various pay levels. The higher the salaries, the lower the demand will be. Thus, the demand line slopes downward. The supply of business graduates is the sum of all business graduates

EXHIBIT 6.4   Supply and Demand for MBAs in the Short Run

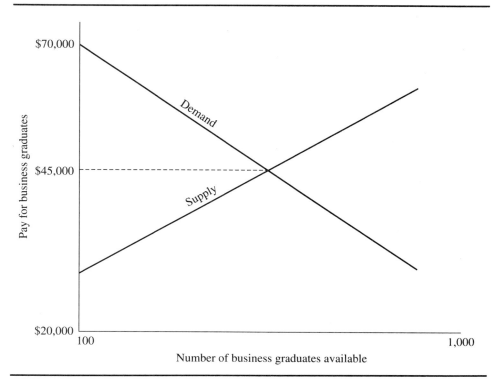

who would be interested and available for jobs at different pay levels. As pay rates rise, more graduates become interested and available, so the supply line slopes upward. The pay rate at which the demand and supply intersect is called the *market-determined rate*. In this illustration, the market-determined rate for business graduates is $45,000. The pay level for business graduates in the market is $45,000, determined by the interaction among *all* employers and *all* business graduates.

Labor Demand

So if $45,000 is the market-determined rate for business graduates, how many business graduates will a specific employer hire? The answer requires an analysis of labor demand. In the near term, when an employer cannot change technology or capital and natural resources, its level of production can change only if the level of human resources (HR) employed, its labor demand, is changed. Under such conditions, a single employer's demand for labor coincides with the marginal product of labor.

The *marginal product of labor* is the additional output associated with the employment of one additional human resources unit, with other factors held constant.

The *marginal revenue of labor* is the additional revenue generated when the firm employs one additional unit of human resources, with other factors held constant.

Marginal Product

Assume that two business graduates form a consulting firm that provides services to 10 clients. They hire a third and add 5 more clients. The marginal product (the change in output associated with adding additional units of labor) of employing the third business graduate is 5. But the marginal product of a fourth hire may not be the same as the marginal product of the third. In fact, adding a fourth business graduate generates only 4 new clients. This diminishing marginal productivity results from the fact that each additional worker has a progressively smaller share of the other factors of production with which to work. In the short term, other factors of production (e.g., office space, computer services) are fixed. As more business graduates are brought into the firm, the marginal productivity must eventually decline.

Marginal Revenue

Now let's look at marginal revenue. Marginal revenue is the money generated by the sale of the marginal product, the additional output associated with the employment of one additional HR unit. In the case of the consulting firm, it's the revenues generated by each additional business graduate. If the graduate's marginal revenue exceeds its costs of $45,000, profits are increased by the additional hiring. Conversely, if marginal revenue is less than $45,000, the employer would lose money on the last hire but could increase profits by reducing labor. Recall that our first assumption is that employers seek to maximize profits. Therefore, the employer will continue to employ additional graduates until the marginal revenue generated by that last hire is equal to the expenses associated with employing that worker. Remember that other potential costs such as office space, computer services, and so on, will not change in the short run. Hence, the level of demand that is consistent with profit maximization is that level at which the marginal revenue of the last hire is equal to its marginal costs.

Exhibit 6.5 shows the model at both the level of the market and of a single employer. The model at the left is the same supply and demand model from Exhibit 6.4. Recall that pay level ($45,000 for business graduates) is determined by the interaction of all employers' demand for all MBAs. The individual employer is a wage "taker" rather than wage "maker." The right side of the exhibit shows supply and demand at the level of the individual employer. The market has determined the pay rate ($45,000), and at that rate, the individual employer can hire as many business graduates as desired. Supply is now a horizontal line representing an unlimited supply of graduates (assumption 4, no single employer is large enough to influence the market). The supply and demand lines intersect at 20; that is, for this employer, the marginal revenue of the 20th graduate is $45,000. The marginal revenue of the 19th graduate is more than $45,000, and the marginal revenue of the 21st graduate is less than $45,000. So the employer will hire 20 business graduates.

EXHIBIT 6.5 Supply and Demand at the Market and Individual Employer Level

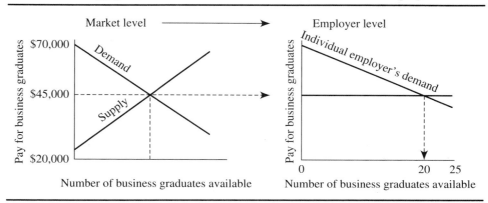

Every employer who uses the marginal product model must do two things: (1) determine the pay level set by market forces and (2) determine the marginal revenue generated by each potential new employee. These two pieces of information will permit the employer to decide how many people to hire.

Although this model of labor supply and demand provides a valuable analytical framework, it has a number of limitations when applied to managing compensation. The first is that managers have no idea what the marginal revenue or marginal costs of employees are. The second is that the model's assumptions oversimplify the real world. For example, the assumed degree of competition among buyers and sellers does not exist, nor are factors of production homogeneous, nor are all firms profit maximizers (some maximize market share, long-term profits, and so on).

A third objection is operationalizing pay. The model implies that individuals are paid according to some function of their productivity times the market price of their product. Unfortunately, the real world is not so simple; problems include the following:

1. Placing a value on the goods or services each individual employee produces.
2. Determining individual values on products and services that are produced through joint efforts of different workers with a variety of talents. Think about this the next time you are in any establishment: the local supermarket, the symphony hall, or even your college. It should be clear that labor is heterogeneous, not homogeneous.
3. Factoring out the contributions of other resources (capital and raw materials) in the production process.

Since measuring marginal product and marginal revenue directly is difficult, managers often use other factors that they believe produce value in their organizations. In the last two chapters, we discussed compensable factors and skill blocks. When the compensable factors define what organizations value in work, job evaluation based on these factors assesses the job's contribution to organization goals. Thus, in a sense, job evaluation results may be a proxy for marginal revenue product. However, compensable factors are usually defined as input (skills required, problem solving required, responsibilities), not as the value of the output for each job.

Marginal productivity concepts may be relevant to establish the maximum pay rates for jobs or to link the size of pay increases to performance. For example, the highest pay rates or performance payments should not exceed the marginal revenue product, or how much can be received for what the employee produces. But as we'll see in the next chapter, managers rarely make such a direct link between an individual's pay and the value of what is produced. Managers may have a "feel" for the link between maximum pay and what the organization can afford, but links to marginal revenue product are theoretical only. As to linking performance to pay, any gains from such a link must be traded off against the cost of measuring, or even estimating, performance.[9] If output from a job is easily measurable, then calculating marginal revenues and linking it to pay may

---

[9]Charles Brown, "Firms' Choice of Method of Pay," *Industrial and Labor Relations Review* 40 (1990), pp. S165–S182.

be possible. But for most work, the requirement of having easily measured output and placing a value on it simply cannot be met.

Labor Supply

The labor supply curve in Exhibit 6.4 represents different numbers of employees available at different pay rates. Like demand, the exact shape of the line representing the supply of labor depends on the assumptions. In perfectly competitive markets, an individual employer faces a horizontal (or elastic) supply; that is, the market determines the price, and the individual employer can hire all the employees it wants, at that price. (See the right side of Exhibit 6.5.) This model assumes that many workers are seeking jobs, that they possess accurate information about all job openings, and that no barriers to mobility (discrimination, licensing provisions, or union membership requirements) among jobs exist.

As in the analysis of labor demand, these assumptions greatly simplify the real world. As the assumptions of the model change, so do the supply curves. An upward-sloping curve, as shown on the left of Exhibit 6.5, means that as pay increases, more people are willing to take a job. But if unemployment rates are low, an employer's offer of higher pay may be matched quickly by competitors, leaving the employer with a higher pay level but no increase in supply. For example, when Giant Foods raised its hourly pay 50 cents above the minimum wage in the Chicago area, Wendy's and Burger King quickly followed suit. The result was that the supermarket was paying more for the employees it already had but was still shorthanded. An employer who dominates the local labor market, such as Corning Glass in Corning, New York, may also find that raising wages doesn't necessarily attract more applicants. Under full-employment conditions, a dominant employer has relatively few sources from which to attract new applicants. Any increase in employment requires that additional applicants must be induced to enter the labor supply, perhaps from schools, retirement, or more distant areas. Similarly, local applicants have very few job alternatives and may have to commute to distant areas if they are rejected by the dominant employer. A dominant employer has relatively wide latitude in determining pay levels, since few local labor market competitors exist. However, once the local labor supply is exhausted, small increases in the pay levels may not attract more applicants. The supply curve, although sloping upward, may take on the shape of a "step" function and may require large pay increases to attract additional people. Although many firms prefer to lower the job requirements and hire less-skilled workers, any pay savings may be offset by increased training expenses. Small employers competing with a single dominant employer often must match the dominant employer's pay level or offer other advantages to obtain sufficient labor. So although pay is not the sole determinant of labor supply, it is an important factor. Just as two blades of a scissors are required to cut cloth, both supply and demand together determine economic outcomes in the labor market.

MODIFICATIONS TO THE DEMAND SIDE OF THE LABOR MARKET MODEL

Keeping in mind that the labor market is composed of *all* the buyers (employers) and *all* the sellers (employees), the demand side focuses on employers' behavior regarding hiring.

EXHIBIT 6.6   **Labor Demand Theories and Implications**

Theory	*Prediction*	*So What?*
Compensating differentials	Work with negative characteristics requires higher pay to attract workers.	Compensable factors must capture these negative characteristics.
Efficiency wage	Above-market wages will improve efficiency by inducing employees to work better.	Staffing programs must have the capability of selecting the best employees; work must be structured to take advantage of employees' greater efforts.
Signaling	Pay policies signal the kinds of behavior the employer seeks.	Pay policy must accurately reflect the employer's strategy and objectives.

But as we move from *all* the employers to individual employers, we see that employers do not limit themselves to behaviors predicted by economic models. A "market-determined wage" doesn't allow for what one economist called "idiosyncratic" wage effects—the great variation in pay levels that actually exists. Three modifications to the classic economic model address the pay level behavior of individual employers: compensating differentials, efficiency wage, and signaling. (See Exhibit 6.6.) Generally, these modifications seek to explain why employers pay differently and why pay rates may be above or below "market."

Compensating Differentials

More than 200 years ago, Adam Smith argued that individuals consider the "whole of the advantages and disadvantages of different employments" and make decisions based on the alternative with the greatest "net advantage."[10] If a job has negative characteristics, that is, if the following apply, then employers must offer higher wages to compensate for these negative features.

1. More time and expense are necessary to acquire the skill and experience required to perform the work.
2. Job security is tenuous.
3. Working conditions are disagreeable.
4. Chances of succeeding on the job are lower.

These "compensating differentials" explain the presence of various pay rates in the market.

Differences in employers' pay levels result from actual (though perhaps unobserved) differences in both jobs and employees. For example, differences in chances for pro-

---

[10]Thomas A. Mahoney, *Compensation and Reward Perspectives* (Homewood, Ill.: Richard D. Irwin, 1979), p. 123.

motion, opportunities to gain experience and training, flexible work schedules, and co-workers and supervising relationships as well as location and ease of commuting to and from work all enter into differences among employers. The level of pay necessary to attract and retain employees becomes part of this broader array of differences among employers. If employers wish to increase the number and/or quality of people willing to accept employment, they must raise the pay level to offset advantages of other alternatives.

Compensating differentials assume that all employers are wage takers; that is, they must pay the market-determined wage rate if they are to operate efficiently. However, the market-determined rate varies among employers because of all the other noncompensation job attributes that must be factored in. Although the notion is appealing, it is hard to document, due to the difficulties in measuring and controlling all the factors that go into a net advantage calculation.

Another modification to demand theory, efficiency wage, challenges the basic assumption of the employer as wage taker.

Efficiency Wage Theory

This theory states that many employers maximize profits by paying above-market wages. These employers are not wage takers. Instead, the higher wages they offer allow them to become more profitable by inducing employees to be more efficient.[11] Efficiency is increased in a number of possible ways.

1. Attracting higher-quality applicants.
2. Lowering turnover.
3. Increasing worker effort.
4. Reducing "shirking" (what economists say when they mean "screwing around").
5. Reducing the need to supervise employees.

Notice that the first four mechanisms assume that the same number of employees will be hired, even at higher rates. The additional costs are offset by increased productivity. Only the last mechanism, reduced supervision, opens the possibility of increasing efficiency by hiring fewer employees. So basically, efficiency increases by hiring better employees or motivating average employees to work harder. The underlying assumption is that pay level determines effort—again, an appealing notion but difficult to document. Few employees, including Lee Iacocca, believe that they are overpaid.

There is some research on efficiency wage. One study of high school graduates correlated higher wages with longer tenure in the job.[12] So perhaps turnover was reduced. However, few companies evaluate their recruiting programs well enough to show that

---

[11]A. B. Krueger and L. H. Summers, "Efficiency Wages and the Inter-Industry Wage Structure," *Econometrica* 56 (1988), pp. 259–93.

[12]Holzer, "Wages, Employer Costs, and Employee Performance."

higher wages did in fact allow them to choose superior applicants.[13] Although high pay attracts more qualified applicants, it also attracts people with poor qualifications and motivations. So an above-market wage does not always guarantee a more productive work force. It also requires superior selection and recruiting programs.

Does an above-market wage allow an organization to operate with fewer supervisors? Some research evidence says "yes." For example, a study of hospitals found that those that paid high wages to staff nurses employed fewer nurse supervisors.[14] However, the researchers did not speculate on whether the higher wages attracted *better* nurses or caused *average* nurses to work harder. Also, we don't know whether the higher wages allowed the hospital to operate more efficiently (i.e., reduce overall nursing costs).

A variation on the notion that an above-market wage induces workers to increase efforts (rationale 3) is the *fair-wage model.*[15] This model says firms will pay above-market wages whenever employees' perceived fair wage exceeds competitive wage. The model predicts that employees of high-profit industries will perceive that fairness requires the firm to pay more and so the firm will do so. The model does explain why secretaries and janitors in high-wage industries (i.e., petroleum) are paid more than secretaries and janitors doing the same tasks in other industries (i.e., education). Unfortunately, many secretaries and janitors in low-wage industries also perceive that fairness requires their employers to pay more, but they don't. And some professors who write compensation textbooks always seem to perceive that fairness requires their publishers to pay more, but they don't.

Signaling

Another variation on the demand model seeks to explain the variability in employees' pay levels, including paying wages that may be *below* the market.[16] *Signaling theory* says that employers may deliberately design pay policies as part of a strategy that signals to both prospective and current employees what kinds of behaviors are sought. A policy of paying below the market for base pay yet offering generous bonuses or training

---

[13]S. L. Rynes and J. W. Boudreau, "College Recruiting in Large Organizations: Practice, Evaluation, and Research Implications," *Personnel Psychology* 39 (1986), pp. 729–57.

[14]Erica Groshen, "Why Do Wages Vary Among Employees?" *Economic Review* 24 (1988), pp. 19–38; E. Groshen and A. B. Krueger, "The Structure of Supervision and Pay in Hospitals," *Industrial and Labor Relations Review,* February 1990, pp. 134S–46S.

[15]R. W. Rice, S. M. Phillips, and D. B. McFarlin, "Multiple Discrepancies and Pay Satisfaction," *Journal of Applied Psychology* 75 (1990), pp. 386–93; R. Thaler, "Interindustry Wage Differentials;" Lawrence F. Katz and Lawrence H. Summers, "Industry Rents and Industrial Policy," Brookings Papers on Economic Activity (forthcoming); Assar Lindbeck and Dennis Snower, "Cooperation, Harassment, and Involuntary Unemployment: An Insider-Outsider Approach," *American Economic Review,* March 1988, pp. 167–88; George Akerlof, Andrew Rose, and Janet Yellen, "Job Switching and Job Satisfaction in the U.S. Labor Market," Brookings Papers on Economic Activity (forthcoming); and R. Thaler, *The Winner's Curse* (New York: Free Press, 1992).

[16]Allison Barber, "Pay as a Signal in Job Choice" (Graduate School of Business Administration, Michigan State University); J. M. Barron, J. Bishop, and W. C. Dunkelberg, "Employer Search: The Interviewing and Hiring of New Employees," *The Review of Economics and Statistics* 67 (1985), pp. 43–52.

opportunities sends a different signal, and presumably attracts different applicants, than a policy of paying market wage without bonus tied to performance. For example, an employer who combines low base with high bonuses may be signaling that employees are expected to be risk takers. The proportion of people within the organization who are eligible for bonuses signals the extent to which the reward system is geared to all employees (versus managers only). One theorist suggests that in the absence of complete and accurate information about the job, applicants make inferences about nonmonetary job attributes (colleagues, job assignments, etc.) based on what they know about an employer's relative pay level. If this is so, then pay level signals a whole raft of information, both intended and unintended, accurate and inaccurate.[17]

Signaling works on the supply side of the model, too, as suppliers of labor signal to potential employers. Individuals who are better trained, have higher grades in relevant courses, and/or have related work experience signal to prospective employers that they are likely to be better performers. Presumably they signal with the same degree of accuracy as employers. So both investments in human capital (degrees, grades, experience) and pay decisions about level (lead, match, lag) and mix (higher bonuses, benefit choices) act as signals and presumably help employees and organizations to exchange information.

MODIFICATIONS TO THE SUPPLY SIDE OF THE LABOR MARKET MODEL

Turning to the supply side of the model, the question changes: What affects worker behavior? We'll discuss three theories shown in Exhibit 6.7: reservation wage, human capital, and job competition.

Reservation Wage

Economists are renowned for their linguistic creativity and their great sense of humor. So many of them describe pay as "noncompensatory."[18] What they mean is that job seekers have a reservation wage below which they will not accept a job offer, no matter how attractive the other job attributes. If pay does not meet their minimum standard, no other job attributes can compensate (i.e., noncompensatory) for this inadequacy. Other theorists go a step further and say that some job seekers—satisfiers—take the first job offer they get when the pay meets their reservation wage. If pay truly is "noncompensatory," then it's hard to understand why "below-market" wages continue to exist. Let us look at several theories that provide a little more leeway in the variability of pay rates.

Human Capital

The theory of human capital, perhaps the most influential economic theory for explaining pay differences, is based on the premise that higher earnings flow to those who improve

---

[17]M. A. Spence, "Job Market Signalling," *Quarterly Journal of Economics* 87 (1973), pp. 355–74.

[18]C. Brown, "Firms' Choice of Method of Pay," *Industrial and Labor Relations Review*, February 1990, pp. S165–S182.

EXHIBIT 6.7   Labor Supply Theories and Implications

Theory	*Prediction*	*So What?*
Reservation wage	Job seekers will not accept jobs whose pay is below a certain wage, no matter how attractive other job aspects.	Pay level will affect ability to recruit.
Human capital	The value of an individual's skills and abilities is a function of the time and expense required to acquire them.	Higher pay is required to induce people to train for more difficult jobs.
Job competition	Workers compete through qualifications for jobs with established wages.	As hiring difficulties increase, employers should expect to spend more to train new hires.

---

their productive abilities by investing in productive capabilities (e.g., education, training, experience).[19] The theory depends on the assumption that people are in fact paid at the value of their marginal product. Improving productive abilities by investing in training and even in one's physical health will increase one's marginal product. The value of an individual's skills and abilities is a function of the time, expense, and resources expended to acquire them. Consequently, jobs that require long and expensive training (engineering, physicians) should receive higher pay levels than jobs (clerical work and even elementary school teaching) that require less investment. According to this logic, the time and expenses associated with acquiring the skills restrict entry into occupations. Increasing the pay level for these occupations will induce people to overcome the barriers. So as pay level increases, the number of people willing to overcome barriers increases, which creates an upward-sloping supply.

Research does support the relationship between years of education and experience and earnings, although some evidence suggests that carrying this to a ridiculous extreme (i.e., getting a Ph.D.) is not as sound an investment as getting a bachelor's and/or master's degree.

Job Competition

Job competition theory is somewhat similar to human capital theory in that both imply that a decreased labor supply is associated with higher costs for the employer. The human capital theory says these higher costs are the result of higher pay levels. The job competition model says the higher costs take the form of additional training expenses that the employer must bear.[20]

---
[19]Gary S. Becker, *Human Capital* (Chicago: University of Chicago Press, 1975); Barry Gerhart, "Gender Differences in Current and Starting Salaries: The Role of Performance, College Major, and Job Title," *Industrial and Labor Relations Review* 43 (1990), pp. 418–33.

[20]Barron, et al., "Employer Search."

The job competition model asserts that workers do not compete for pay in labor markets. Rather, pay for jobs is "quoted" or established, and workers compete through their qualifications for the job opportunities. A pool of applicants develops for every opportunity. Individuals in the pool are ranked by prospective employers according to the skills, abilities, and experience required for the job. As the employer dips further and further into the applicant pool, individuals require more training and are less productive, even though they receive the same wage. Accordingly, the total costs (pay plus training) associated with each additional unit of labor in the pool increases as the market demand increases.

Job competition and human capital theories both imply that prospective employees signal their value through their training and educational attainments. Employers receive the signals and use them to rank the candidates. Then they choose which applicants to hire. But in fact, 90 percent of jobs are filled by an employer making a single job offer to one out of many applicants. This is consistent with job competition theory. An employee choosing from a number of offers, the scenario described at the beginning of this chapter, rarely occurs, normally only upon college graduation. After that, most jobs are filled by an employer deciding among candidates and making an offer to a single individual, then another, until one accepts.

A number of additional factors affect the supply of labor available to an employer. Geographic barriers to mobility among jobs, union requirements, lack of information about job openings, the degree of risk involved, and the degree of unemployment also have an influence on labor market conditions.

PRODUCT MARKET FACTORS

Any organization must, over time, generate enough revenue to cover expenses, including compensation. It follows that an employer's pay level is constrained by its ability to compete in the product/service market. So the product market affects external competitiveness and pay level by determining what the organization can afford to pay.

The degree of competition and product demand are the two key product market factors. Both affect the ability of the organization to change the prices it charges for its products and services. If prices cannot be changed without decreasing sales and thereby losing income, then the ability of the employer to set a higher pay level is constrained.

Although the labor market conditions put a floor on the pay level required to attract sufficient employees, the product market puts a lid on the maximum pay level that an employer can set. If the employer pays above the maximum, it must either pass on the higher pay level through price increases or hold prices fixed and allocate a greater share of total revenues to cover labor costs.

For many years, U.S. automakers solved this affordability dilemma by passing on increased pay levels in the form of higher car prices. Although competition among the "Big Three" automakers existed, they all passed on the pay increases. But then, a 1970s gasoline shortage (induced by oil-producing nations) changed the nature of product demand almost overnight. Suddenly, everyone wanted less expensive cars that got good gas mileage. U.S. automakers couldn't profitably produce such cars, but Japanese automakers could. At the same time, the total demand for cars actually declined, because the oil shortage slowed the entire economy. Both of these factors constrained the U.S. auto firms' ability to change the pay level. In response, some autoworkers took pay cuts, accepted smaller wage increases, and agreed to job redesign intended to improve productivity. Publicly available data suggest that General Motors' direct labor costs still account for about 25 percent of total costs, compared to the 15 to 20 percent experienced by Toyota and Honda in their U.S. plants. The wage rates are equal, but because of design differences in both products and plants, the Japanese transplants require fewer direct labor hours per car.

So the nature of the product demand and the degree of competition in the industry influence the pay level and the ability to change it over time. An employer's ability to finance higher pay levels through price increases depends on the product market conditions. Employers in highly competitive markets such as aspirin manufacturers will be less able to raise prices without loss of revenues. At the other extreme, single sellers of a product such as Merck with its patented drugs that reduce cholesterol will be able to raise prices.

Other factors besides the product market conditions affect pay level. Some of these have already been discussed. The productivity of labor, the technology employed, the level of production relative to plant capacity available, and the extent of nonhuman resource expenses all affect ability to pay. These factors vary more *across* than *within* industries. In other words, the technologies employed and consumer preferences may vary among auto manufacturers, but the differences are relatively small when compared to the technologies and product demand of auto manufacturers versus the oil or banking industry. These across-industry differences permit firms to adopt different pay levels.

Since the pay level directly affects operating costs, it must be set with an eye on both competitors' costs and what the organization can afford to pay. Hence, the product market conditions set the maximum beyond which the organization will be unable to competitively price its goods and services. Labor market conditions set the minimum pay level to attract and retain a pool of qualified workers. Set the pay level too low and managers will have trouble attracting and holding employees. Set the pay level too high and the employer's ability to sell products will be affected.

ORGANIZATION FACTORS

Although product and labor market conditions create a range of possibilities within which managers may set the pay level, other organizational factors such as the type of industry and organization size also influence pay level decisions.[21]

---

[21]Erica L. Groshen, "Sources of Intra-Industry Wage Dispersion: How Much Do Employers Matter?" *Quarterly Journal of Economics*, August 1991, pp. 869–84.

Industry

The industry in which an organization chooses to compete dictates the particular technologies it employs. Labor-intensive industries, such as education and services, tend to be lower paying than are industries whose technologies are less labor-intensive, such as petroleum and pharmaceuticals. The importance of qualifications and experience tailored to particular technologies is often overlooked in theoretical analysis of labor markets. But machinists and millwrights who build diesel locomotives for General Motors in LaGrange, Illinois, have very different qualifications from those machinists and millwrights who build airplanes for Boeing in Seattle, Washington.

Some of these industry differentials result from custom. Almost 40 years ago, Dunlop noted that Boston coal truck drivers were paid wage rates of about 75 percent of those of oil truck drivers.[22] Furthermore, these industry effects are remarkably stable over time. A 1950 study found stable patterns between 1923 and 1946. A more recent study compared executive pay data from the 1930s with similar 1970s data for U.S. and British firms.[23] After adjusting all data to 1981 dollars, the industries that paid high in the 1930s also paid high in the 1970s. In fact, industry wage patterns are consistent internationally, too, especially among developed, market-based countries.[24] As Exhibit 6.8 shows, correlations between industry wages in the United States and those in Canada, France, Japan, Germany, Korea, Sweden, and the United Kingdom all exceed 0.80. A high correlation indicates a relatively similar pattern of industry wage differences (i.e., high-wage industries in the United States, such as automobile manufacturing and petroleum, are also high-wage industries in other developed, capitalist countries; low-wage industries in the United States, such as educational services and shoe manufacturing, are also low-wage industries in other countries). But we must also remember the data shown in Exhibit 6.2. Not only do pay levels for the same job differ by industry, but they also differ among employers within the same industry and the same geographic location.

Employer Size

There is some evidence that large organizations tend to pay more than small ones. For example, a study of manufacturing firms found that firms with 100 to 500 workers paid 6 percent higher wages than did smaller firms; firms of more than 500 workers paid 12 percent more than did the smallest firms. The study controlled for differences in worker characteristics.[25] A comparison of executive pay data from the 1930s and 1970s found that today's correlation between organization size and pay level relationship existed in the 1930s, too.

---

[22]John Dunlop, "The Task of Contemporary Wage Theory," in *New Concepts in Wage Determination*, ed. George W. Taylor and Frank C. Pierson (New York: McGraw-Hill, 1957).

[23]Peter Kostiuk, "Firm Size and Executive Compensation," *Journal of Human Resources*, XXV–I, pp. 91–105.

[24]Krueger and Summers, "Reflections on Interindustry Wage Structures."

[25]Wesley Mellow, "Employer Size and Wages," *Review of Economics and Statistics* 64, no. 3 (August 1982), pp. 495–501.

EXHIBIT 6.8   International Correlations with U.S. Wages for Manufacturing Jobs, 1982 (Logs)*

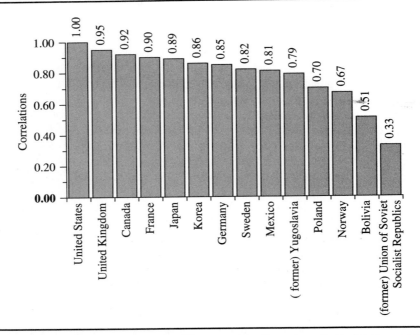

*Log scales measure ratios rather than actual dollar differences, and therefore are less subject to distortion caused by magnitude of flat dollar differences.
SOURCE: Alan B. Krueger and Lawrence H. Summers, "Reflections on the Inter-Industry Wage Structure," in *Unemployment and the Structure of Labor Markets,* ed. Kevin Lang and Jonathan S. Leonard (Oxford: Basil Blackwell, 1987).

Individual Manager

Most economic models make heroic assumptions about how individual employees react to different pay levels. Rational behavior, or optimizing expected value, is the basic assumption of individual behavior. As we have discussed, higher levels of pay are presumed to elicit less "shirking," more investment in education and experience, greater effort, and so on. The image springs to mind of a calculator generating present values of a stream of expected payoffs among an array of options. But only one of our colleagues actually behaves that way. The rest seem to behave differently. Nonrational is a more apt descriptor; some even border on irrational.

Behavioral decision models also offer insights into how managers make pay level decisions. Two such devices individuals use to make decisions are *representativeness* and *anchoring*. They often lead to nonrational decisions.[26]

---

[26]A. Tversky and D. Kuhneman, "Framing of Decisions and the Psychology of Choice," *Science*, January 1981, pp. 453–58.

Representativeness refers to how a particular event represents the entire population. For example, let's say that a manager's top-performing employee recently took a higher-paying job in another city. The manager assumes the problem is that the competitor's pay level is higher. But what if the employee left to follow a job-changing spouse? The manager relies on one recent and very salient event, even though the cause of that event may have been unique and therefore not indicative of a pay problem in that firm.

Anchoring refers to decision makers who focus on the first objective data provided and make only small adjustments from this position. For example, the manager who lost the employee to a competitor's higher pay will assume that the competitor's rate is the going rate in the market and will be loathe to deviate from it. The rate serves as an anchor regardless of how accurately the employee reported it or how or whether the job is even the same.

Both representativeness and anchoring in behavioral decision models attempt to capture how managers actually make decisions rather than presuming a rational model.

RELEVANT MARKETS

Up to this point, we've examined labor market, product market, and organization factors that influence the pay level. Next, we focus on relevant markets. Although the notion of a single homogeneous labor market may be an interesting analytical device, it does not mirror reality. Rather, each organization operates in many labor markets, each with unique demand and supply configurations. A major task for managers is to define the markets that are relevant for pay purposes and to establish the appropriate pay level in these markets. The three factors usually used to determine the relevant labor markets are the occupation (qualifications required), the geography (willingness to relocate and/or commute), and the other employers that directly compete in the same product market.

Occupations

The skills and qualifications required in an occupation are important because they tend to limit mobility among occupations. Qualifications include licensing and certification requirements as well as training and education. Accountants, for example, would have difficulty becoming a dentist—though I recently visited a dentist who should have been an accountant.

Geography

Qualifications interact with geography to further define the scope of the relevant labor markets. Degreed professionals (accountants, engineers, physicians) are typically recruited nationally. Technicians, craftspeople, and operatives are usually recruited regionally, and office workers, locally. However, the geographic scope of a market is not fixed. It changes in response to workers' willingness to relocate or commute certain distances. This propensity to be mobile in turn may be affected by personal and economic circumstances as well as the employer's pay level. Configurations of local markets are even shaped by the availability of convenient public transportation. Furthermore, the geographic limits may not be the same for all in a broad skill group. All accountants do not operate in a national market; some firms recruit them regionally, others locally.

Product Market Competitors

In addition to the occupation and its geography, the industry in which the employer competes, the product market, also affects the relevant labor markets by relating the qualifications required to particular technologies, and focusing on the costs for labor and the organization's ability to compete.

How do employers choose their relevant market? Surprisingly little research has been done on this issue. But if the markets are incorrectly defined, the estimates of other employer's pay rates may be incorrect and the pay level inappropriately established. One study divided the process of collecting pay rates into two decisions.[27]

1. Which companies to request data from.
2. Whose data to use and how to weight it.

The first decision is based on known characteristics of the companies: industry, union status, location, size, and hiring practices. But whose data are actually used depends on the quality of the data received. (See Chapter 7 for more specifics.)

Whose data are weighted most heavily in defining the relevant market, the product market competitors' or the labor market competitors'? The data of product market competitors are likely to receive greater weight when the following factors apply:

1. Labor costs are a large share of total costs.
2. Product demand is elastic (i.e., responsive to price changes; that is, people won't pay $2.50 for a bottle of Leinenkugel; they'll have a Budweiser instead).
3. Supply of labor is inelastic (i.e., not responsive to changes in pay).
4. Employee skills are specific to the product market and will remain so. (Recall the Boeing millwrights. However, if Boeing begins to emphasize small twin-engine planes, the product market comparisons become less important.)

On the other hand, labor market comparisons will be more important if the following are true:

1. The organization is having difficulty attracting and retaining employees.
2. Recruiting costs are higher.[28]

In summary, we have discussed the economic and behavioral theories that offer some help in understanding the variations in pay levels we observe among employers' comparisons. Next, we focused on relevant markets, a key concept that captures the blending of the factors in the labor and product market and the organization. But so what? How,

---

[27]Chockalingam Viswesvaran and Murray Barrick, "Decision Making Effects on Compensation Surveys: Implications for Market Wages" (Working paper, University of Iowa, 1991).

[28]Gerhart and Milkovich, "Employee Compensation."

in fact, do managers set pay level policy, and what difference does it make? In the remainder of this chapter, we will discuss those two issues.

COMPETITIVE PAY POLICY OPTIONS

There are three conventional pay level policies: to lead, to meet, or to follow competition. How do managers choose a policy? A 1948 survey of 63 firms revealed that the most important factors in setting pay level policies were rates paid by other employers in the area or industry and union pressures. The least important factors were the firm's financial position and company profits. A Conference Board survey of 280 firms in 1978 and 1983 reports a shift in the importance of factors.[29] As shown in Exhibit 6.9, industry patterns remained the most important factor in 1978, just as they had 30 years earlier. But industry

EXHIBIT 6.9 **The Relative Importance of Factors Used to Set Wage Objectives in Corporations in 1978 and 1983**

Rank	1978	1983
1	Industry patterns	Productivity or labor trends in this company
2	Local labor market conditions and wage rates	Expected profits of this company
3	Expected profits of this company	Local labor market conditions and wage rates
4	Productivity or labor cost trends in this company	Industry patterns
5	Consumer price index increases	Consumer price index increases
6	Influence of this settlement on other wage settlements or nonunion wage levels, or both	Internal (company) wage patterns (historical)
7	Potential losses from a strike	Influence of this settlement on other settlements or nonunion wage levels, or both
8	Internal (company) wage patterns (historical)	Internal (company) benefit patterns (historical)
9	Internal (company) benefit patterns (historical)	Potential losses from a strike
10	Major union settlements in other industries	National labor market conditions and wage rates
11	National labor market conditions and wage rates	Major union settlements in other industries

NOTE: The sample comprised 197 major U.S. corporations, which, in both 1978 and 1983, ranked factors used in setting company wage objectives, with 1 being the most important factor and 11, the least important.
SOURCE: Audrey Freedman, *The New Look in Wage Policy and Employee Relations* (New York: The Conference Board, 1985).

---

[29]*The New Look in Wage Policy and Employee Relations* (New York: The Conference Board, 1983).

EXHIBIT 6.10   Probable Relationships between External Pay Policies and Objectives

Policy	Compensation Objectives				
	Ability to Attract	*Ability to Retain*	*Contain Labor Costs*	*Reduce Pay Dissatisfaction*	*Increase Productivity*
Pay above market (lead)	+	+	?	+	?
Pay with market (match)	=	=	=	=	?
Pay below market (lag)	−	?	+	−	?
Variable pay	?	?	+	?	+
Employer of choice	+	+	+	−	?

---

patterns dropped to fourth place in 1983, whereas a firm's specific financial situation and its productivity or labor costs and expected profits (ability to pay) were listed as the most important. Union-related factors, rated extremely important in the 1948 study, were among the least important in the more recent Conference Board studies. Consequently, although the factors considered in setting pay level may be stable, their relative importance may vary over time. A study of the factors used in the 1990s is needed. What difference does the competitive pay policy make? The basic premise is that the competitiveness of pay will affect the organization's ability to achieve its compensation objectives, which in turn will affect the organization's performance. The probable effects of alternative policies are shown in Exhibit 6.10.

Pay with Competition (Match)

Given the choice to match, lead, or lag, the most common policy is to *match* rates paid by competitors.[30] Managers historically justify the "matching" policy for three reasons: (1) failure to match competitors' rates would cause employee dissatisfaction, (2) lower rates would limit the organization's ability to recruit, and (3) management was somehow obligated to pay prevailing rates. Nonunionized companies frequently try to lead or at least match competition to discourage unionism.[31] However, a firm's actual pay policy may differ from its stated policy, depending on which surveys and statistics are used, whether or not all forms of compensation are considered (base pay, incentives, benefits, etc.) and how well jobs are matched across competitors.[32] A pay with competition policy

---

[30]C. Weber and S. Rynes, "Effects of Compensation Strategy on Job Pay Decisions," *Academy of Management Journal*, March 1992, pp. 86–109.

[31]P. D. Lineneman, M. L. Wachter, and W. H. Carter, "Evaluating the Evidence on Union Employment and Wages," *Industrial and Labor Relations Review* 44 (1990), pp. 34–53.

[32]Gerhart and Milkovich, "Employee Compensation"; J. J. Chrisman, C. W. Hofer, and W. R. Boutton, "Toward a System of Classifying Business Strategies," *Academy of Management Review* 13 (1988), pp. 413–28.

tries to ensure that an organization's wage costs are approximately equal to those of its product competitors and that its ability to attract people to apply for employment will be approximately equal to its labor market competitors. This policy avoids placing an employer at a disadvantage in pricing products or in maintaining a qualified work force. But it may not provide an employer with a competitive advantage in its labor markets. Most classical economic models, those relying on competitive markets and marginal productivity concepts, would predict that employers would meet competitive wages.

Lead Policy

A lead policy maximizes the ability to attract and retain quality employees and minimizes employee dissatisfaction with pay. Or a lead policy may offset less attractive features of the work. Military combat pay is a classic example. The relatively high pay offered by brokerage firms that offsets the lack of employment security is another. These are an illustration of Adam Smith's notions of net advantage.

We have already observed that sometimes an entire industry can pass high pay rates on to consumers if pay is a relatively low proportion of total operating expenses or if the industry is highly regulated. But what about specific firms within a high-pay industry? For example, if Chevron or Exxon adopts a pay leadership position in their industry, do any advantages actually accrue to them? If all firms in the industry have similar technologies and operating expenses, then the lead policy must provide some competitive advantage to Chevron or Exxon that outweighs the higher costs.

Does a lead policy really permit the employer to select the best of the applicant pool? Assuming that the employer is able to select the most qualified from this pool, does this higher quality talent translate into greater productivity, lower unit labor costs, improved product quality, and increased innovation? A 1990 study estimated that approximately 50 percent of higher wage costs were offset by benefits in recruiting and training.[33] Although the number of assumptions required for this analysis limits confidence in the precision in the estimate, a number of researchers have linked high wages to ease of attraction, reduced vacancy rates and training time, and better-quality employees. A study of government employees found that as wages increase, both the quality and quantity of applicants also increased.[34] Research also suggests that increasing pay levels reduces turnover and absenteeism. One study found no evidence that pay level affected an organization's return on assets (ROA).[35] However, this study found that the use of variable forms of pay (bonuses and long-term incentives) was linked to a higher ROA.[36]

---

[33]J. J. Chrisman, C. W. Hofer, and W. R. Boutton, "Toward a System of Classifying Business Strategies."

[34]A. B. Krueger, "Efficiency Wages,"; M. B. Tannen, "Is the Army College Fund Meeting Its Objectives?" *Industrial and Labor Relations Review* 41 (1987), pp. 50–62; Hyder Lakhani, "Effects of Pay and Retention Bonuses on Quit Rates in the U.S. Army," *Industrial and Labor Relations Review* 41 (1988), pp. 430–38.

[35]B. Gerhart and G. Milkovich, "Organizational Differences in Managerial Compensation and Financial Performance," *Academy of Management Journal* 33 (1990), pp. 663–91.

[36]Variable pay is discussed in Chapters 8 through 10. *Variable* indicates that the pay increase (bonus) is not added to base pay; hence, it is not part of fixed costs but is variable, since the amount may vary next year.

The problem with much pay level research is that it focuses on base pay and ignores bonuses, incentives, and other nonbase payments; yet base pay represents only a portion of compensation. Indeed, many managers seem increasingly convinced that they get more bang for the buck by allocating dollars away from base pay and into variable forms that more effectively shape employee behavior.[37]

There are possible down sides to a lead policy. If an employer leads only when hiring new employees but does not adjust wages of current employees, these more experienced employees may murmur against the employer just as those vineyard laborers did in Matthew's parable referred to in Chapter 3. (See Chapter 7 for a discussion of compression.) Also, because relatively higher pay makes recruiting easier, it may mask other job attributes that may contribute to high turnover later on (e.g., lack of challenging assignments, or hostile colleagues).[38]

Lag Policy

Setting a lag pay policy to follow competitive rates may hinder a firm's ability to attract potential employees. However, if pay level is lagged in return for the promise of higher future returns (i.e., stock ownership), as in a high-tech startup firm, such promise may increase employee commitment and foster teamwork, which, according to some, will increase productivity. Anderson Consulting, a software and systems firm, tells college recruits that its starting offers are lower than its competitors but that successful performers will make more than competitors within two to four years. Clearly, Anderson runs a risk of not being able to attract highly qualified talent. But the promise of the bigger carrot seems to attract enough good students, especially in a down economy. Thus, a lag policy's effect on hiring and motivating employees is not clear. Additionally, it is possible to lag competition on pay but to lead on other aspects of rewards (e.g., challenging work, desirable location, outstanding colleagues).

Although lower pay levels probably contribute to turnover, pay may be only one of many factors influencing an employee to quit.[39] For example, alternative jobs available and length of service undoubtedly play a role. It is unclear how dissatisfied employees must be with pay before they will actually leave. Our experience suggests that individuals seem to vary in their tolerance for relatively lower pay, given other returns and rewards.

Match, lead, and lag are the conventional policy options. Some employers adopt nonconventional policies; two examples are offering *variable pay* and becoming the *employer of choice.*

---

[37]The Conference Board, *Variable Pay: New Performance Rewards*, Research Bulletin 246 (New York, 1990).

[38]Rynes, "Compensation Strategies."

[39]Raymond A. Noe, Brian D. Steffy, and Alison E. Barber, "An Investigation of the Factors Influencing Employees' Willingness to Accept Mobility Opportunities," *Personnel Psychology*, Autumn 1988, pp. 559–80; Richard Ippolito, "Why Federal Workers Don't Quit," *Journal of Human Resources* 22, no. 2 (1987), pp. 281–99; Alan Krueger, "The Determinants of Queues for Federal Jobs," *Industrial and Labor Relations Review*, July 1988, pp. 567–81; Timothy W. Lee and Richard Mowday, "Voluntarily Leaving an Organization: An Empirical Investigation of Steers and Mowday's Model of Turnover," *Academy of Management Journal*, December 1987, pp. 721–43.

Variable Pay

Under a variable pay policy, higher earnings through profit sharing or incentive pay are offered if the firm's performance is strong. Union Carbide's Chemicals and Plastic Division offers employees the opportunity to earn a bonus of up to 40 days' pay if the Division's operating profits exceed certain targets ($280 million in 1990). However, Carbide repositioned its base pay to 5 percent below its usual "match" in the market position. So, in effect, Carbide lags the market by 5 percent but pays a bonus that yields a slight lead position when the company has a good year. This competitive position has several potential effects. The variable pay policy is intended to focus employee attention on the firm's financial performance and motivate productivity improvements. Its effects on turnover and ability to attract probably depend on individual employees. Some employees may want to share the gains and risks inherent in a business. Others may prefer greater certainty in their pay increases. The effect on costs is a little more certain. The 5 percent lag reduces labor costs. The variable pay controls labor costs as a percentage of corporate income.

Employer of Choice

An *employer of choice* policy is more complex than the other options. Basically, it embeds a firm's external competitive position as part of the entire set of HR policies offered. The competitive policy may be to offer challenging work, employment security, and pay that in some sense fits these other policies. For example, IBM leads its competitors with its extensive training opportunities, employee assistance programs, and the like. But it meets or even follows with its cash compensation. A competitor such as Apple Computer may lead with pay but lag on the extensive nonfinancial aspects of employment. IBM's competitiveness policy views pay as part of the total pattern of HR policies.

In summary, adopting a competitive pay policy is akin to establishing a niche in the market. Unfortunately, there is little evidence of the consequences of these different options. It is not known whether the effects of pay level on the financial performance of a firm, its productivity, or its ability to attract and retain employees is sufficient to offset the effects on payroll costs. Nor is it known how much of a pay level variation makes a difference; will 5 percent, 10 percent, or 15 percent be a noticeable difference? Although lagging competitive pay could have a noticeable reduction in short-term labor costs, it is not known whether this gain is accompanied by a reduction in the quality and performance of the work force. Similarly, we simply do not know the effects of the variable pay or employer of choice options. It may be that an employer's pay level will not gain any competitive advantage; however, the wrong pay level may put the organization at a serious disadvantage.

So where does this leave the compensation manager? In the absence of convincing evidence, the least-risk approach is to set the pay level to match competition, though some employers set different policies for different skills. They may adopt a lead policy for skills that are critical to the organization's success, a match policy for less critical skills, and a lag policy for jobs that are easily filled in the local labor market. TRW, a large, highly decentralized firm, allows its different business units to establish a variety of pay level policies. Some of these differences reflect different industries in which the units operate (financial services, automotive- and defense-related units). Other differences reflect varying labor market conditions (high unemployment in Cleveland versus lower unemployment in Phoenix) and business strategies (cost-plus defense contracts versus the highly competitive auto parts supplier market). Other diversified firms also encourage each of its business divisions to set its pay level policies independently. An obvious concern with such decentralization is to achieve some degree of control and uniformity of policies, at least at the corporate level. However, specifying a pay-level policy does not make it so. Evidence exists of a sizable discrepancy between what managers believe is their pay level and what is the actual pay level. When asked to define their target pay level, one study of compensation managers found only a 0.50 correlation between their responses and their actual relative pay levels. Interestingly, none of the companies reported that it paid below the median. Once again, the Lake Woebegon phenomenon (all the children are above average) prevails.

CONSEQUENCES OF PAY LEVEL DECISIONS

Earlier we noted that the degree of competitiveness of the pay level has two major consequences: (1) its effect on operating expenses and (2) its effect on employee attitudes and work behaviors. These consequences, shown in Exhibit 6.11, have been discussed throughout this chapter. All we will do here is to note again that the competitive policy and the pay level are key decisions that affect the performance of the organization. The pay level directly affects the compensation objectives of efficiency, equity, and compliance.

Efficiency

Wages paid represent an expense, so any decision that affects their level is important. A variety of theories makes assumptions about the effects of relative pay levels on an

EXHIBIT 6.11   Some Consequences of Pay Levels

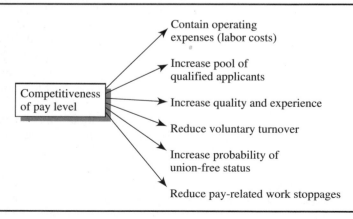

Competitiveness of pay level

- Contain operating expenses (labor costs)
- Increase pool of qualified applicants
- Increase quality and experience
- Reduce voluntary turnover
- Increase probability of union-free status
- Reduce pay-related work stoppages

organization's effectiveness. Some believe that lead policies diminish shirking, permit hiring better-qualified applicants, and so on. Yet other models (e.g., free markets and marginal productivity) point to matching competitors. Virtually no research evidence guides managers in which policy yields the most efficient results under different circumstances. Pay level indirectly affects revenues through the quality of the work force induced to join and the productivity and experience levels of those who stay. Reduction in turnover of high performers, increased experience levels, increased probability of remaining union free, and reduction of pay-related grievances and work stoppages are examples of the work behaviors presumed to be affected by pay level decisions.

Equity

Employees' sense of fair treatment regarding pay is clearly affected by the level of their pay. As noted in Chapter 2, satisfaction with pay is directly related to the pay level: more is better.[40] But as with most things, the relationship between pay and equity is more complex. Employees' sense of pay equity also is related to how others are paid and how they expected to be paid. A friend of ours at Stanford told us that if all but one of the faculty in the Stanford Business School got $1 million and that one person received $1 million plus $1, the others would all be murmuring against the dean and asking for an explanation.

Compliance

It's not enough to say that an employer must pay at or above the legal minimum wage. Provisions of prevailing wage laws and equal rights legislation must also be met. In fact, we will return to the subject of market wages again when we discuss pay discrimination in Chapter 14. From a practical perspective, the manager of the pay system must consider all these factors. From a research perspective, disentangling the relationship among pay level decisions and employee behaviors and organization performance is difficult. We do know that pay level decisions are related to firm performance in the case of the top executives, managerial and professional employers. We also know that the pay mix (ratio of bonuses and long-term incentives to base pay) appears to be more important than the overall pay level. And we know that relative pay level affects the organization's ability to recruit and retain employees. However, the links between pay levels and many of the behaviors listed in Exhibit 6.9 remain to be studied.

    Before we proceed, let us reemphasize that the major reason we are interested in the external competitiveness policy and the pay level is that they have profound consequences on the organization's objectives. Theories and practical experience support this belief. As we have also noted, very little research exists to guide us in making pay level decisions. We have clearly established that differences among organizations' competitive policies and pay levels exist. We have examined the factors that determine these differences.

---

[40]H. G. Heneman III, "Pay Satisfaction," *Research in Personnel and Human Resource Management* 3 (1985), pp. 115–39.

What remains to be better demonstrated are the potential effects that different policies will have.

No matter the external pay policy, it needs to be translated into practice. The starting point is measuring the market through use of a salary survey. For this, we turn to the next chapter.

SUMMARY

The pay model used throughout this book emphasizes four strategic policy issues: consistency, competitiveness, contributions, and administration. Policies regarding these four issues need to be designed to achieve specific pay objectives. This section is concerned with external competitiveness, or pay comparisons among organizations. Does Apple Computer pay its accountants the same wage that Virginia Electric and Power pays its accountants? Probably not. Different companies pay different rates; the average of the overall array of rates in an organization constitutes the pay level. Each integrated job structure or career path within the organization may have its own pay level and competitive position in the market. To achieve the objectives stipulated for the pay system, the pay level must be properly positioned relative to competitors. The next chapter considers the decisions involved and the variety of techniques available to implement decisions.

REVIEW QUESTIONS

1. Distinguish policies on external competitiveness from policies on internal consistency. Why is external competitiveness so important?
2. What factors influence an organization's external competitiveness?
3. What does marginal revenue product have to do with pay?
4. What pay level does the efficiency wage theory predict? Does the theory accurately predict organization behavior? Why or why not?
5. How do behavioral decision models modify the conventional economic perspective on pay levels?
6. What are the consequences of a lead and/or lag policy?
7. How does the notion of reservation wage fit with the notion of compensating differentials?

YOUR TURN:
COOK COUNTY ROAD AND BRIDGE

On Tuesday, February 18, in the middle of a snow-storm, the 16 members of the Road and Bridge Department of Cook County, Minnesota, filed notice that they intended to strike. The members, represented by Local 49, International Union of Operating Engineers, operate the trucks, graders, and other equipment used to maintain the roads and bridges and plow the snow.

Since 1986, when a one-year wage freeze was imposed, Road and Bridge employees have received smaller pay increases than other county employees. This was done to comply with Minnesota's pay equity law. The county commissioners determined that Road and Bridge pay was out of line with that of other county employees. In an effort to even things out, pay increases for Road and Bridge have been smaller, according to the personnel director for the county.

In 1987 and 1988, when other county employees received a 1 percent pay increase, Road and Bridge workers received a one-time payment of $250 each. This payment did not add to their base pay. In 1989 and 1990, while other county employees got a pay increase of 3 percent, Road and Bridge got 2.5 percent. The following year, other county employees got 48 cents an hour, Road and Bridge got 3 percent, or about 37 cents an hour.

Exhibit 1 lists what the 16 Road and Bridge employees earned in the most recent year. The figures are taken from actual payroll records; the employees have a 40-hour work week and get paid time and one half for overtime. The figures include overtime.

In addition, the county pays $239 per employee a month for Blue Cross insurance. The employee pays $60. The county also contributes 4.48 percent of gross pay to the Public Employees Retirement Association for pension benefits, plus Social Security (6.2 percent of gross pay), Medicare (1.45 percent), and long-term disability insurance (1.12 percent).

EXHIBIT 1 How Much Are Road and Bridge Workers Paid?

Engineering Technician	$33,044
Maintenance Worker III	30,315
Engineering Technician	30,122
Maintenance Worker III	29,270
Maintenance Worker II	28,869
Maintenance Worker III	28,860
Maintenance Worker II	28,393
Engineering Technician	28,271
Maintenance Worker II	27,764
Maintenance Worker II	27,587
Maintenance Worker III	27,474
Maintenance Worker II	25,982
Maintenance Worker II	25,966
Maintenance Worker II	25,905
Mechanic	25,221
Maintenance Worker II	24,968

Discussion Questions

1. Analyze the pay structure in the department. Do you see any potential problems?

2. What are the county's total labor costs for Road and Bridge?

3. Do you think the $250 flat payment was a good idea? Why or why not? How do you think it affected labor costs? The pay structure? Organization effectiveness?

4. How should the county respond to the strike threat? Remember, this is February, and it's snowing. Winter tourism is becoming an increasingly important business as more and more people are discovering the joys of dog sledding. Tourists need to be able to get to

the dogs. On the other hand, the rush hour in February still consists of one logging truck driving through town, and the county is strapped for funds. The state is still giving you heat on your comparable worth adjustments, and is cutting back on grants for other mandated social services (e.g., medicaid, aid to families with dependent children).

5. The jobs whose salaries were raised to comply with the comparable worth law included the police dispatcher, the clerk of court, the sales clerk in the county liquor store, and several secretaries. How will your recommendation for Road and Bridge affect these employees? What action, if any, do you recommend the county take concerning these employees? What will you tell these employees?

Chapter Outline

The desired position in compensation is to be above the market—equal to or better than.

Our pay philosophy is to be, on the average, better than average.

The Policy for pay and benefits is to be in the top 10 percent.

The company pays a slight premium in its nonunion plans over the wages paid in the general geographic area for similar work at union plants.

The pay policy, an unwritten one, is to be competitive with the area. We use our own surveys. We check midpoints, and while the policy is to pay slightly above, in practice we pay at the midpoint. The salaried employees are below midpoint and the hourly people are at the midpoint.

Our goal is to be in the 65th percentile nationally.[1]

The above statements refer to different organizations' policies regarding the competitive positions of their pay. *Competitive position* refers to the comparison of the compensation offered by one employer relative to that paid by its competitors in its product/service markets and labor markets. In the last chapter, we discussed the factors that influenced these policies. The level and types of the compensation that competitors offer—base salary, incentive potential, types of benefits—are critical. Labor market factors include the supply of qualified workers and the demand for these workers from other firms. Organizational factors such as the employer's financial condition, technology, work force demographics, productivity, and the influence of unions may also affect a firm's competitive pay policies. In this chapter, we examine how managers use these factors to design their organization's pay levels and structures.

MAJOR DECISIONS

The major techniques and decisions involved in setting externally competitive pay and designing the corresponding pay structures are shown in Exhibit 7.1. They include (1) establishing the employer's external pay policy; (2) determining the issues to be addressed in a survey; (3) designing and conducting surveys; (4) interpreting and applying survey results; (5) designing ranges, flat rates, and/or incentives; and (6) adjusting the structure to balance internal and external considerations and employee contributions. The first decision, establishing the external pay policy, was discussed in the previous chapter. The approaches associated with the remaining decisions are discussed in the rest of this chapter. As you read through the chapter, you will become aware that each new decision may cause an employer to revise previous decisions. The process may be better described as circular than linear. For example, the use of incentives (decision 5) may cause the employer to revise its external policy or decide that a specialized survey is needed to determine what types of incentives other employers are using. Or a firm may discover that it is losing employees to competitors who offer child care. As information changes, policy decisions may change.

---

[1]Fred K. Foulkes, *Personnel Policies in Large Nonunion Companies* (Englewood Cliffs, N.J.: Prentice Hall, 1980).

EXHIBIT 7.1 **Determining Externally Competitive Pay Levels and Structures**

| External competitiveness: Pay relationships among organizations | → | Policy determination | → | Market definition | → | Conduct pay surveys | → | Draw policy lines | → | Competitive pay levels and structures |

Some Major Decisions in Pay Level Determination
- Determine pay level policy
- Define purpose of survey
- Design and conduct survey
- Interpret and apply results
- Design ranges, flat rates, incentives

WHY CONDUCT A SURVEY?

Surveys provide the data for setting the pay policy relative to competition and translating that policy into pay levels and structures.

> A *survey* is the systematic process of collecting and making judgments about the compensation paid by other employers.

Most firms conduct or participate in several different pay surveys. Some writers claim that large employers participate in up to 100 surveys in a single year, although data from only a few surveys are used to make compensation decisions.[2]

An employer will conduct or participate in a survey for a number of reasons: (1) to adjust the pay level in response to changing external pay rates, (2) to establish or price the pay structure, (3) to analyze personnel problems that may be pay related, or (4) to attempt to estimate the labor costs of product market competitors.

Adjust Pay Level

Most organizations make adjustments to employees' pay on a regular basis. Such adjustments can be based on cost of living, performance, seniority, or simply the overall upward movement of pay rates among competitors. Market surveys provide information on pay rates among other employers. Periodic changes in overall rates must be known

---

[2]Milton Rock and Lance Berger, eds., *The Compensation Handbook*, 3rd ed. (New York: McGraw-Hill, 1991).

to maintain or adjust a firm's pay level in relationship to its competitors in the relevant market.

Adjust Pay Structure

As noted in Chapter 4 on job evaluation, some firms go directly from job descriptions to market pricing and deemphasize job evaluation. Under such an approach, the pay structure depends heavily on the data obtained from market surveys. Many employers also use market surveys to validate their own job evaluation results. For example, job evaluation may place data processing jobs at the same level in the job structure as some secretarial jobs. But if the market shows vastly different pay rates for the two types of work, most employers will recheck their evaluation process to see whether the jobs have been properly evaluated. Some may even establish a separate structure for the data processing work. Thus, the job structure that results from job evaluation may not match the pay structure found in the external market. Reconciling these two pay structures is a major issue. As with so much of compensation management, informed judgment based on the organization's specific circumstances and objectives is required.

Pay-Related Personnel Projects

Information from a specialized survey may shed light on a pay-related problem. For example, an employer experiencing abnormally high turnover among good performers may survey prime competitors. Many special studies are used to appraise the starting salary offers or current pay practices for targeted groups, for example, patent attorneys, retail sales managers, or chemical engineers. Survey data may also be used to justify pay differences among men and women in discrimination lawsuits. Employers have successfully argued that the difference in pay between nurses and craft workers is due to pay differences found in the external market for these skills. This argument rests on the defensibility of the market data collected through wage surveys. Consequently, managers need to ensure that their surveys will withstand legal challenges.[3]

Estimate Competitors' Labor Costs

Some firms, particularly those in highly competitive businesses such as microcomputer, auto, or specialty steel production, use salary survey data in their financial analysis of competitors' product pricing and manufacturing practices. Industry-wide labor cost estimates are reported in the Employment Cost Index (ECI), one of four types of salary surveys published regularly by the Department of Labor. The ECI measures quarterly changes in employer costs for employee compensation. It allows a firm to compare its average costs to an all-industry or specific-industry average. However, this comparison

---

[3]Sara L. Rynes and G. T. Milkovich, "Wage Surveys: Dispelling Some Myths about the 'Market Wage,' " *Personnel Psychology,* Spring 1986, pp. 71–90.

has limited value, since industry averages may not reflect relevant competitors, and the ECI gives undue weight to unionized firms.[4]

Survey results serve as crucial input for decisions that ultimately affect a firm's compensation objectives of efficiency, equity, and compliance. An employer's labor costs and the competitiveness of its products can be affected by conclusions drawn from survey data. Because their results are so significant to the organization, surveys must be designed and managed carefully. A first step to ensure careful management is to identify the key issues the employer seeks to resolve in the survey.

DEFINING THE RELEVANT MARKET

In Chapter 6, we pointed out that for most employers *one* market rarely exists; rather, employers compete in many labor markets. The relevant market depends on the purpose of the survey. To make decisions about pay levels and structures or to estimate competitors' labor costs, the relevant labor market includes those employers with whom an organization competes for employees. Although a statistician may design a survey to sample a broad population, salary surveys are typically designed to capture a narrower population of employers (i.e., the competition). As we observed in Chapter 6, competitors forming the relevant markets are typically defined by the following:

1. Employers who compete for the same occupations or skills required.
2. The geographic distance employees are willing to commute (or relocate).
3. Employers who compete with the same products.

So the definition of relevant labor market will vary, depending on the purpose of the survey and the particular jobs and skills being examined.

Exhibit 7.2 shows how qualifications interact with geography to define the scope of relevant labor markets. As the importance of the qualifications and the complexity of qualifications increase, the geographic limits also increase. Competition tends to be national for managerial and professional skills, but local or regional for clerical and production skills. However, these generalizations do not always hold true. In areas with high concentrations of scientists, engineers, and managers (e.g., Boston, Dallas, or Palo Alto), the primary market comparison may be regional, with national data used only secondarily. Exhibit 7.3 translates these generalities into policy for a pharmaceutical manufacturer. For top managerial jobs, national surveys of companies with sales between $1 billion to $4 billion are used. For research jobs, only data from pharmaceutical industry firms are used. For clerical jobs, local data from a wide range of industries and organization sizes are used.

In major metropolitan areas, the relevant market may be further restricted by commuting times and patterns.[5] But the amount of time people are willing to commute varies

---

[4]Thomas Stone and Sarosh Kuruvilla, "The Wage Comparison Process in a Local Labor Market" (Working paper, University of Iowa, 1988).

[5]Stone and Kuruvilla, "The Wage Comparison Process in a Local Labor Market."

TABLE 7.2   Relevant Labor Markets by Geographic and Employee Groups

	Geographic Scope	Employee Groups/Occupations					
		Production	Office and Clerical	Technicians	Scientists and Engineers	Managerial Professional	Executive
R E L E V A N T	*Local:* Within relatively small areas such as cities or MSAs (Metropolitan Statistical Areas) (e.g., Dallas metropolitan area)	Most likely	Most likely	Most likely			
L A B O R	*Regional:* Within a particular area of the state or several states (e.g., oil producing region of southwestern U.S.)	Only if in short supply or critical	Only if in short supply or critical	Most likely	Likely	Most likely	
M A R K E T	*National:* Across the country				Most likely	Most likely	Most likely
	International: Across several countries				Only for critical skills or those in very short supply	Only for critical skills or those in very short supply	Some-times

EXHIBIT 7.3   Labor Market Competitors

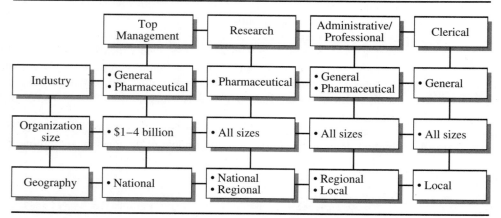

SOURCE: Jane A. Bjorndal and Linda K. Ison, *Mastering Market Data* (Scottsdale, Ariz.: American Compensation Association, 1991).

by locale as well as by personal and economic circumstances. Tokyo's 90-minute train rides and Los Angeles' 90-minute traffic jams are legendary. Further, managers can influence the willingness of people to commute with actions other than setting higher pay levels. For example, a firm may lobby the local transit authority for convenient bus routes and schedules or may sponsor company-owned vans and car pooling programs. One New York City department store chain buses 160 workers from Brooklyn to its suburban stores during busy holiday seasons so that the stores will have an adequate supply of sales personnel.

From the perspective of cost control and ability to pay, including competitors in the product/service market is crucial.[6] The pay rates of product/service competitors will affect both costs of operations and financial condition (e.g., ability to pay). However, this becomes a problem when the major competitors are based in countries with far lower pay rates, such as China or Mexico. In fact, the increasingly international character of business has spawned interest in global survey data, particularly for managerial and professional talent.[7]

Some writers argue that if the skills are tied to a particular industry, as underwriters, actuaries, and claims representatives are to insurance, it makes sense to define the market on an industry basis.[8] If accounting, sales, or clerical skills are not limited to one particular industry, industry considerations are less important. But this position ignores financial objectives of the employer. Pricing labor competitively with others who offer similar products and services is necessary to achieve the organization's financial objectives. Within these product/service market constraints, occupational and geographic factors come into play. Additionally, a firm's size (number of employees, total revenues, and assets) reflects its market dominance. If one firm dominates and becomes a "wage maker" rather than a "wage taker," a survey that omitted that firm would not accurately capture the market.

EEO Considerations

A final consideration in determining the relevant market relates to equal employment opportunity (EEO). As noted earlier, market data are frequently used in pay discrimination litigation to explain pay differentials.[9] If market data are to serve as criteria to explain

---

[6]Barry Gerhart and George Milkovich, "Employee Compensation," in *Handbook of Industrial and Organizational Psychology*, 2nd ed., ed. M. D. Dunnette and L. M. Hough (Palo Alto, Calif.: Consulting Psychologists Press, 1992).

[7]*Expatriate Compensation Survey* (Organization Resource Counselors) and *International Benefit Guidelines* and *Compensation Benefits Survey* (William M. Mercer) are just some of the surveys conducted annually. Most major consulting firms offer international survey.

[8]Felicia Nathan, "Analyzing Employers' Costs for Wages, Salaries, and Benefits," *Monthly Labor Review*, October 1987, pp. 3–11.

[9]*Kouba and EEOC* v. *Allstate Insurance Company*, 1982, 691 F. 2d 873; and *Briggs* v. *City of Madison*, W.D. Wisc. 1982, 436 F. Supp. 435. Also see *In the Matter of Boston Survey Group*, Mass. Superior Court, Docket No. 56341, August 2, 1982; and Rynes and Milkovich, "Wage Surveys: Dispelling Some Myths."

and justify pay practices, the definition of the relevant markets and the survey methodology must be defensible. This means that procedures and decisions must be

1. *Documented.* An organization's policies regarding external wage comparisons are specified, and actions taken in conducting surveys are consistent with these policies.
2. *Business related.* Firms competing with similar products/services are included.
3. *Work related.* Employers of similar skills within similar geographic areas are included. Caution should be exercised here since some employers, by virtue of the nature of their product market or pressure from their unions, may be able and/or willing to pay more. For example, Price Waterhouse may be willing to pay its accountants in Chicago more than Marshall Field department store pays its Chicago accountants, since accountants are more critical to generating revenues to Price Waterhouse than they are to Marshall Field.

How Many Employers?

There are no firm rules on how many employers to include in a survey.[10] Large firms with a lead policy may exchange data with only a few (6 to 10) top-paying competitors. A small organization in an area dominated by two or three employers may decide to survey only smaller competitors. National surveys conducted by consulting firms may include more than 100 employers. Clients of these consultants often stipulate special analyses that report pay rates by selected industry groups, geographic region, and/or pay levels (e.g., top 10 percent).

Who Should Be Involved?

In most organizations, the responsibility for managing the survey lies with the compensation manager. But since the pricing of human resources (HR) has a powerful effect on profitability, operating managers and employees need to be involved, too. A recurrent theme in this text has been the need to get user acceptance through involvement in procedure design. This point is valid when selecting compensable factors to use in job evaluation, certifying skills under skill-based structure, and pricing. Including managers and employees on task forces or surveying employees to discover what firms they use for pay comparisons makes sense.

Outside consulting firms are often used as third-party protection from possible "price-fixing" lawsuits. Suits have been filed alleging that the exchange of survey data violates Section 1 of the Sherman Act, which outlaws conspiracies in restraint of trade. One court interpreted the Sherman Act to find survey participants guilty of price-fixing if the overall effect of the information exchange is to interfere with competitive prices and artificially

---

[10]Chockalingam Viswesvaran and Murray Barrick, "Decision-Making Effects on Compensation Surveys: Implications for Market Wages" (Working paper, University of Iowa, 1991).

hold down wages. Another case involved the Boston Survey Group, a 34-member association, that exchanged data on wages for a variety of clerical jobs. The survey reported the salaries of individuals in each job classification surveyed; each participating firm's information was clearly identified by company name, and the results were reported by industry group. A consent decree agreed to by the Boston Survey Group and the Massachusetts State Attorney General's office stipulates the following:

- The data will no longer be identified by company names.
- Only aggregated information will be reported; salaries of individual employees will not be published.
- No data will be published on a per industry basis.
- Data will not be reported if fewer than 10 people are in a job.
- Members may choose to allow their employees to see the aggregated survey results for their own jobs.

Hiring a third party instead of managing the survey internally buys legal protection at the cost of control over the decisions that determine the quality and usefulness of the data. The consent decree prohibiting exchange of industry data eliminated the ability to make industry or product market comparisons. This might not be important in clerical jobs, but industry groups are important when making comparisons for wages for other skills and jobs. For example, a Hewlett-Packard marketer's job is probably more similar to that of an AT&T Information Systems marketer than it is to a Union Carbide marketer. If the skills in question are generalized and thus transferrable, then industry data can safely be ignored. However, industry data are crucial from a competitive market perspective. Further, if the skills are highly specialized (e.g., semiconductor designer), then they may be industry specific and therefore not available across industries.

Make or Buy?

The decision to retain outside expertise or design one's own survey includes a complex set of trade-offs. The availability of staff time and talent and the desire to control the quality of analysis and results are often given as reasons to tailor one's own survey. On the other hand, consulting firms offer a wide choice of ongoing surveys covering almost every job family and industry group imaginable.

Purchasing Criteria.   Opinions about the value of consultant surveys are rampant; research is not. Do Hay, Mercer, Executive Compensation Services, TPF&C, or MCS's 777 surveys of managerial pay yield significantly different results? Can these various surveys successfully withstand pay discrimination litigation? Many firms select one survey as their primary source and use others to cross-check or "validate" the results. Professional consultants who design employment tests for applicant selection report the test's performance against a set of measurements (reliability, validity, etc.). Analogous standards for pay surveys have not yet evolved. Issues of sample design and statistical inference are seldom considered. Some employers routinely combine the results of several surveys and weight each survey in this composite according to the quality of the data reported.[11] Yet little systematic study of differences in market definition, participating firms, types of data collected, analysis performed, and/or results is available.

Publicly Available Data.   The Bureau of Labor Statistics (BLS) is a major source of publicly available pay data. It publishes industry wage studies, the National Survey of Professional, Administrative, Technical, and Clerical Pay (PATC), the Employee Benefits Survey, local area wage surveys (AWS), and the Employment Cost Index (ECI), the measure of changes in employee compensation costs discussed earlier. In addition, most states and even some counties provide pay data to the public.

Exhibit 7.4 illustrates the nature of the BLS data. The data are inexpensive and readily available. Public sector employers seem to use BLS data more often than do private sector employers. Some private firms track the rate of change in BLS data and the ECI as a cross-check on other surveys and to examine geographic differentials for various nonexempt jobs (e.g., file clerks in Chicago versus file clerks in Durham, North Carolina).

EXHIBIT 7.4   Example of BLS Survey Data

Weekly earnings of office workers in establishments employing 500 workers or more in Chicago, Ill., July 1992.

Occupation and Industry Division	Number of Employees	Average Weekly Hours	Weekly Earnings ($)		
			Mean	*Median*	*Middle Range*
Secretarial and Keyboarding Operations					
Secretaries	2,148	39.5	472.50	466.50	413–524
Nonmanufacturing	6,146	39	476	461	407–523
Trans and utilities	735	39.5	508	502	439–562.5
Secretaries I	711	38.5	404	393.5	336–487.5
Nonmanufacturing	614	38.5	399.5	384	336–487.5
Secretaries II	1,230	39	413.50	407	376–444
Nonmanufacturing	983	39	416.5	410	379.5–444
Secretaries III	3,666	39	453.50	452	408–490
Manufacturing	1,127	39.5	454	454	411–494
Nonmanufacturing	2,539	39	453	451	408–488
Trans and utilities	166	39.5	493	483	401.5–555
Secretaries IV	2,083	39	531.50	530	484–580
Manufacturing	480	39.5	516	522	480–569.5
Nonmanufacturing	1,603	39	536	534	487.5–585.5
Trans and utilities	282	39	511.5	512.5	457–562.5

[11]L. S. Hartenian and N. B. Johnson, "Establishing the Reliability and Validity of Wage Surveys," *Public Personnel Management* 20, 3 (1991), pp. 367–83.

WHICH JOBS TO INCLUDE?

A general guideline is to keep things as simple as possible. Select as few employers and jobs as necessary to accomplish the purpose. The more complex the survey, the less likely employers are inclined to participate unless the survey results are important to them also. There are several approaches to selecting jobs for inclusion.

Benchmark Jobs Approach.   Benchmark jobs share the following characteristics:

- The contents are well-known, relatively stable, and agreed upon by the employees involved.
- The supply and demand for these jobs are relatively stable and not subject to recent shifts.
- They represent the entire job structure under study.
- A sizable proportion of the work force is employed in these jobs.

Typically, only benchmark jobs are included in surveys. Descriptions of the benchmark jobs are included in the survey so that participants can match the survey job with the correct job in their organization.

Some employers also use the percentage of incumbents who are women and men as a defining characteristic of a benchmark job to try to ensure that the benchmarks are free of possible employment discrimination.

Generally, the approach is to ensure that benchmark jobs represent all key functions and levels in the organization. In Exhibit 7.5, this would mean identifying benchmarks for as many of the 16 levels and five functions (production, maintenance, services, laboratory, and office) as possible. Selecting a benchmark job from each level ensures coverage of the entire work domain for these functional areas. Including the entire domain of work and jobs held by large numbers of employees helps ensure the accuracy of the work relatedness of decisions based on survey results.

Global Approach.   Rarely do several organizations have identical jobs. This is particularly true in organizations that emphasize semiautonomous teams or continuously adapt jobs to meet changing conditions. The global approach may be better suited to survey pay levels in these situations.

EXHIBIT 7.5   Representative Benchmark Jobs

Job structures

	1	2	3	4	5	6	7	8	9	10	11	12	13	14	15	16
Office	X		X		X	X		X								
Lab			X	X	X		X									
Services			X			X		X								
Maintenance				X						X			X		X	
Production	X	X			X		X		X		X	X		X		

NOTE: X = benchmark job.

EXHIBIT 7.6 Frequency Distribution—All Engineers, All Companies

YEARS SINCE BS (columns 0–37)

MONTHLY SALARY — Totals by salary band:

Monthly Salary	Total
6950 - OVER	40
6825 - 6949	9
6700 - 6824	12
6575 - 6699	14
6450 - 6574	31
6325 - 6449	24
6200 - 6324	42
6075 - 6199	43
5950 - 6074	44
5825 - 5949	63
5700 - 5824	70
5575 - 5699	95
5450 - 5574	97
5325 - 5449	102
5200 - 5324	116
5075 - 5199	151
4950 - 5074	173
4825 - 4949	178
4700 - 4824	180
4575 - 4699	210
4450 - 4574	192
4325 - 4449	232
4200 - 4324	216
4075 - 4199	290
3950 - 4074	281
3825 - 3949	262
3700 - 3824	255
3575 - 3699	234
3450 - 3574	205
3325 - 3449	193
3200 - 3324	176
3075 - 3199	174
2950 - 3074	155
2825 - 2949	174
2700 - 2824	189
2575 - 2699	158
2450 - 2574	172
2325 - 2449	116
2200 - 2324	48
UNDER 2200	29

Summary rows by Years Since BS:

Yrs	TOTAL	MEDIAN	MEAN	STD DEV
0	62	2458	2433	110
1	120	2455	2447	170
2	142	2553	2564	243
3	117	2703	2711	275
4	105	2728	2752	289
5	87	2804	2854	344
6	116	2976	3008	388
7	167	3195	3199	428
8	165	3295	3332	479
9	131	3429	3434	491
10	139	3455	3501	513
11	166	3658	3665	583
12	145	3688	3698	527
13	154	3908	3924	673
14	193	4005	4041	678
15	221	4089	4189	699
16	187	4186	4209	729
17	170	4188	4239	798
18	174	4304	4421	791
19	164	4422	4466	856
20	179	4429	4476	932
21	148	4432	4438	861
22	183	4512	4637	951
23	170	4503	4502	807
24	168	4524	4583	839
25	137	4595	4638	859
26	128	4630	4685	819
27	119	4551	4629	826
28	131	4762	4741	897
29	124	4439	4659	979
30	111	4655	4821	1097
31	109	4585	4657	929
32	103	4682	4738	965
33	89	4762	4851	1010
34	74	4950	4826	1011
35	91	4637	4772	943
36	82	5012	4899	887
37	354	4748	4850	963
TOTAL	5425	4035	4090	1051

SOURCE: Organization Resources Counselors, Inc., New York.

232

With a global approach, the rates paid to every individual employee in an entire skill group or function (e.g., all chemical engineers, or all computer scientists) are used. Exhibit 7.6 shows external market data for engineers with bachelor's degrees. Exhibit 7.7 translates those data into percentiles. So a survey user can determine rates paid to engineers (Exhibit 7.6) as well as the rate's relationship to years since degree (YSD) (Exhibit 7.7). Because of this relationship to years since degree, the curves in Exhibit 7.7 are often referred to as *maturity curves*. A global approach simply substitutes a particular skill (represented by a B.S. in engineering in the example) and experience or maturity (YSD) for detailed descriptions of work performed.

EXHIBIT 7.7 **Percentile Curves: Years since First Degree versus Monthly Salary—All Engineers, All Companies**

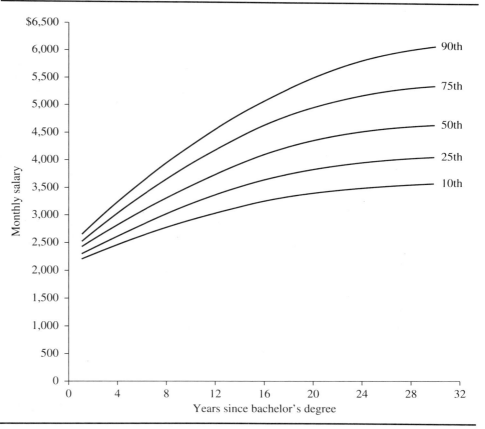

SOURCE: Organization Resources Counselors, Inc., New York.

Low-High Approach.   If an organization is using skill-based structures or generic job descriptions, it may not be able to match jobs with competitors who use a traditional job-based approach. Job-based market data must be converted to fit the skill-based structure. The simplest approach is to identify the lowest- and highest-paid benchmark jobs for the relevant skills in the relevant market and to use the wages for these jobs as anchors for the skill-based structures. Work at various levels within the structure can then be slotted between the anchors. For example, Exhibit 7.8 shows the skill-based system at Borg-Warner, discussed in Chapter 3. Since the structure begins with unskilled labor, market rates for entry-level unskilled labor would anchor the low end of the structure. Market rates for team leaders would anchor the high end. On a graph with wage rates on the y-axis and the structure on the x-axis, a line can be drawn connecting the rates for the anchors. Wage rates for the rest of the structure can then be slotted on this line. For example, if the entry market rate is $8 per hour and the rate for team leaders is $28 per hour, then the rate for operator Bs can be somewhere between $8 and $28 per hour.

The usefulness of this approach depends on how well the extreme benchmark jobs match the organization's work, and whether they really do tap the entire range of skills. Hanging a pay system on two pieces of market data raises the stakes on the accuracy of those data.

Benchmark Conversion Approach.   This approach to matching survey jobs requires an employer to apply its plan to value the benchmark jobs provided in the survey and to compare those results with internal results. If an organization uses job evaluation, then its job evaluation system is applied to the benchmark jobs, and job evaluation points are assigned to these jobs. If an organization uses skill-based pay, then skill points can be assigned to the survey jobs. The magnitude of difference in skill points or job evaluation points provides a guideline for making similar adjustments in the market data collected for the survey job.

EXHIBIT 7.8   Borg-Warner Job Structure with Traditional and Skill-Based Pay System

	Pay System	
	Job Based	*Skill Based*
Chain checker		
Stacker		
Cleaner	Skill C	
Ultrasonic inspector		Skill B
Chain packer		
Assembler		Skill A
Riveter		
Leadership, supervisory and		
scheduling responsibilities		

So, the real issue is to ensure that the jobs or skill groups included in the survey provide data that will be useful. Depending on the purpose of the survey, either the benchmark approach, the global approach, the low-high approach, or the benchmark conversion approach can help.

WHAT INFORMATION TO COLLECT?

Three basic types of data typically are requested: (1) information about the nature of the organization, (2) information about the total compensation system, and (3) specific pay data on each incumbent in the jobs under study. Exhibit 7.9 lists the basic data elements and the logic for including them.

EXHIBIT 7.9 **Data Elements to Consider for Surveys and Their Rationale**

Basic Elements	Examples	Rationale
Nature of Organization		
Identification	Company, name, address, contact person	Further contacts
Financial condition	Assets, sales, profits (after taxes)	Indicates nature of the product/service markets, the ability to pay, size, and financial viability
Size	Profit centers, product lines	Importance of specific job groups to business success
	Total number of employees	Impact on labor market
Structure	Organizational charts	Indicates how business is organized and how important managerial jobs are
Nature of Total Compensation System		
Cash forms used	Base pay, pay increase schedules, long- and short-term incentives, bonuses, cost of living adjustments, overtime and shift differentials	Indicate the mix of compensation offered, used to establish a comparable base
Noncash forms used	Composition of benefits and services, particularly the degree of coverage and contributions to medical and health insurance and pensions	
Incumbent and Job		
Date	Date effective	Need to update rates to current date
Job	Match generic job descriptions	Indicates degree of similarity with survey's key jobs
	Number of employees supervised and reporting levels describe scope of responsibilities	
Individual	Years since degree, education, date of hire	Indicates training and tenure of incumbents
Pay	Actual rates paid to each individual, total earnings, last increase, bonuses, incentives	

EXHIBIT 7.10   **Total Annual Remuneration Comparison for a Specific Job**

	Companies										
	A	B	C	D	E	F	G	H	[I]	J	K
Cash compensation	$100	$110	$120	$130	$150	$155	$170	$210	$250	$255	$260
Benefits and perquisites	40	45	65	60	75	77	50	35	72	25	30
Total excluding stock options	140	155	185	190	225	232	220	245	322	275	290
Stock options	–0–	–0–	40	45	50	70	80	60	75	–0–	–0–
Total including stock options	$140	$155	$225	$235	$275	$302	$300	$305	$297	$275	$290

SOURCE: Justin Brisk, William M. Mercer, Incorporated.

No survey includes all the data that will be discussed. Rather, the data collected depend on the purpose of the survey and the jobs and skills included. Since no standards or guidelines on what to collect have been developed, managers must rely on their expertise and experience to make that decision.

Organization Data.   This information assesses the similarities and differences among survey users. Financial information, size, and organization structure are usually included. Surveys of executives and upper-level positions include more detailed financial and reporting relationships data. The logic for including these additional data is that compensation for these jobs is more directly related to the organization's financial performance. More often than not, the financial data are simply used to group firms by size expressed in terms of sales or revenues.

EXHIBIT 7.11   **Company Positioned at the Specified Quartile Break**

	Q1	Q2	Q3	(Company I + Q3)%
Cash compensation	C (120)	F (155)	I (250)	100%
Benefits and perquisites	H (35)	G (50)	I (72)	100%
Total excluding stock options	C (185)	E (225)	J (275)	117%
Stock options	D (45)	H (60)	I (75)	100%
Total including stock options	C (225)	J (275)	F (302)	131%

SOURCE: Justin Brisk, William M. Mercer, Incorporated.

Total Pay System Data.   All the basic forms of pay need to be covered in a survey to assess the similarities and differences in the entire pay packages and to accurately assess competitors' practices.[12] For example, more and more employers offer various forms of team awards and incentives along with the base pay. Some employers roll these awards into the base pay, others do not, and still others roll only a percentage of them into employees' base pay. Inconsistent reporting (or not reporting) of these awards will distort the data. For example, company I in Exhibit 7.10 may target itself to be at the third quartile among a selected comparison group for cash compensation, benefits and perquisites, and stock options. But because they surveyed cash compensation, benefits, and stock options separately, company I ends up being the highest payer in the group. When all three pay elements are added together, company I is 31 percent above its targeted position (Exhibit 7.11).

It is particularly difficult to include *all* the pay forms in detail. For example, including details on benefits such as medical coverage deductibles, flexible benefit options, and even vacation policies quickly makes a survey too cumbersome to be useful. Methods to handle this problem range from a brief description of a benchmark package to including only the most expensive and variable benefits or asking for an estimate of total benefit expenses as a percentage of total labor costs. Some estimate of total compensation is needed to assess the entire compensation package offered by competitors. The approach in Exhibit 7.12 combines a benchmark value for base salary, short- and long-term incentives, benefits, and perquisites.

Incumbent Data.   The most important data in the survey are the *actual* rates paid to each incumbent. Total earnings, hours worked, date and amount of last increase, and

---

EXHIBIT 7.12   A Total Compensation Analysis

Job X	*Benchmark X in the Market*
Base salary	Base salary
Short-term incentives value	Short-term incentives value
Long-term incentives value	Long-term incentives value
Benefits value	Benefits value
+ Perquisites value	+ Perquisites value
= Total compensation value for Job X	= Total compensation value for comparable jobs in the market

SOURCE: Jack Dolmat-Connell and Ken Cardinal, "Beyond Total Compensation: The Total-Cost Perspective," *Compensation and Benefits Review*, January–February 1992, pp. 56–60.

---

[12]*Managing Total Remuneration* (New York: William M. Mercer, Inc., n.d.); Jack Dolmat-Connell and Ken Cardinal, "Beyond Total Compensation: The Total-Cost Perspective," *Compensation and Benefits Review*, January–February 1992, pp. 56–60.

bonus and incentive payments are included. However, the usefulness of each element needs to be balanced against the cost of trying to collect it.

Enough data must be available to appraise the match between the benchmark jobs in the survey and jobs within each company. Some personal data on incumbents (e.g., tenure on job, educational degrees) are also included to facilitate matching. The degree of match between the survey's benchmark jobs and each company's jobs is assessed by various means. Hay Associates, for example, has installed the same job evaluation plan in many companies that participate in their surveys. Consequently, jobs in different organizations can be compared on their total job evaluation points and the distribution of points among the compensable factors. Other surveys simply ask participants to judge the degree of match, using a scale similar to the following one.

Please check (   ) degree to which your job matches the benchmark job described in the survey:

My company's job is

Of moderately less value	( )
Of slightly less value	( )
Of equal value	( )
Of slightly more value	( )
Of moderately more value	( )

Still other survey designers periodically send teams of employees familiar with the benchmark jobs to visit each participating organization to discuss the matches. Many public agency and trade association surveys simply rely on each participant to match the benchmark jobs as closely as possible. The BLS has perhaps the most rigorous job-matching process. It includes site visits and detailed job analysis.

International Data.   International competition requires international pay comparisons. Most large consulting firms conduct international surveys. Exhibit 7.13 is an example of TPF&C's report on cash remuneration practices in 20 countries. International surveys raise additional issues of comparability because legal regulations and tax policies, as well as customs, vary among countries. For example, because of tax reasons, Korean executives rarely receive incentive pay. Some South American countries mandate cost of living adjustments, which makes the timing of the survey data collection crucial. Exhibit 7.14 gives an idea of the type of background information on benefits in more than 60 countries that Mercer provides its clients. Companies with worldwide locations use local surveys for jobs filled locally and international surveys for top executive and managerial jobs.

EEO-Related Data.   To date, no surveys collect data specifically for EEO purposes. Since market data are frequently important in explaining pay differences between men and women, length of time to fill vacancies may give a more accurate picture of labor market conditions. For example, the fact that the city of Madison had difficulty attracting public health sanitarians to fill job vacancies was an important factor for the court that

EXHIBIT 7.13   Example of International Survey Data Reported by Compensation Consulting Firm

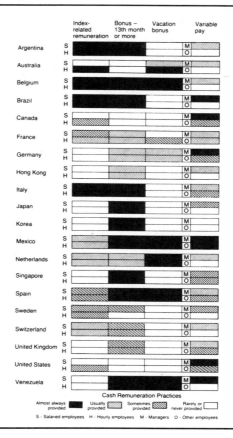

examined the pay differences between sanitarians (predominantly men) and nurses (predominantly women).[13]

Accuracy of Data.   Despite the acceptance of courts of market data as legal justification for salary differentials, the whole area of collection, analysis, and interpretation has not been subject to the same scrutiny as hiring practices and testing. Whether it should have been is another question. Certainly, a sound, business-related rationale for every step in the process is important. But fine distinctions using data that are extremely general may be faulty. Some survey data profile a general guide to assess the adequacy of the whole

[13]*Briggs* v. *City of Madison* 1982 W.D. Wisc. 436 F Supp. 435.

EXHIBIT 7.14   International Benefit Data

Kenya

Three factors combine to provide a more fertile climate for employee benefit plans development than exists in most non-industrialized African countries—a capitalist economy, relative political stability since independence in 1963 (in spite of the attempted coup in 1982), and the British origins of most of the country's institutions.

South Korea

The spectacular and consistent levels of economic growth which were seen in Korea during the 1970s and 1980s eased in 1989, with a disappointing growth rate of around 7 percent. Many argue that this reduction in growth is a result of the transition from a less-developed cheap labour economy to a more mature environment.

Indeed, the era of cheap hard-working labour is drawing to a close as workers demand a suitable reward from this growth. Union pressure for wage increases, shorter working hours, and better working conditions has intensified with established foreign companies being the target for some extreme and occasionally violent industrial action. Minimum wages increased by some 15 percent in 1989 with average wages increasing by up to 20 percent.

South Korea continues to develop its welfare system. Following the implementation of the National Pension Scheme in 1988, 1989 saw the extension of the National Medical System to everyone. The next issue on the agenda is the possible introduction of unemployment insurance in the 1990s.

Egypt

During 1989, the Egyptian government pursued its commitment to act to rectify the country's economic problems. Inflation was reduced below the 30 percent plus of recent years and the level of unemployment has remained stable. Investment laws were revised with the intention of stimulating the private sector. Of particular interest to foreign investors is the introduction of a Debt Equity Conversion Scheme. Steps were taken to liberalize foreign exchange controls and regulations. A favourable exchange rate against hard currencies helped the buoyant tourism sector and the continued development of manufacturing is expected to benefit the industrial sector.

SOURCE: *1990 International Benefit Guidelines* (William M. Mercer Consultants).

---

pay structure, but not necessarily pay of specific jobs. Other surveys are designed to price specific jobs, and still others to assess only the rate of change in the rates paid. The purpose of the survey needs to be kept in mind when judging the accuracy of the data.

How to Collect the Data?

Two basic methods are used to collect pay data: interviews (in person or by phone) and mailed questionnaires. The purpose of the survey and the extensiveness of the data required usually determine the method. Special studies or double-checking results is often performed through phone interviews. Mailed questionnaires are probably most common. The Bureau of Labor Statistics (BLS), the most experienced wage surveyor of all, uses extensive field interviews. Some organizations use field visits every second or third year to hold down costs and time requirements.

Many aspects of pay surveys have been ignored by researchers. Little can be said about the effects of different formats in the accuracy of the data obtained. Little is known about ensuring comparability of job matches or benefit packages. We don't know how representative surveys are of some markets. The same lack of research plagues the analysis of survey results.

INTERPRET AND APPLY SURVEY RESULTS

To discover how survey data are actually analyzed, Belcher interviewed 34 compensation professionals. He reports:

> Every organization uses its own methods of distilling information from the survey; uses different surveys for different purposes; and uses different methods for company surveys. I could find no commonality in these methods of analysis by industry, by firm size, or by union presence. For example, some did nothing except read the entire survey, some emphasized industry data, others geographic competitors (commuting distances), some made comparisons with less than five competitors, some emphasized only large firms, others throw out the data from large firms.[14]

Diversity rules in analyzing survey data. We hope diversity reflects the flexibility of managers who adjust their analysis to deal with a variety of circumstances. We worry that diversity reflects a lack of business- and work-related logic; such approaches will not be able to withstand close critical scrutiny.

Verify Data

If no standard approach exists, how should analysis proceed? Exhibit 7.15 suggests a number of ways to assess the quality and accuracy of data from each company. Unusual patterns raise flags for further checking. Maximums higher than the patterns, use of broad bands, atypical minimums, use of awards, and out-of-the-ordinary reporting relationships are identified.

A common first step is to check the accuracy of the job matches. Job descriptions will be included with the survey data. However, even descriptions that match perfectly do not indicate how various companies value the same jobs, or their pay policies in reference to that job.

Exhibit 7.16 reports a survey provided by Organization Resources Counselors, Inc., for participants in its Salary Information Retrieval System. This particular survey report was prepared for company P844, a pharmaceutical firm, and reports wages for a business applications programmer/analyst position. We will use this report to illustrate a survey analysis. Examining the number of employees in each company shows that two clusters of wages seem to exist at $39,894 and at $46,000–47,000. Such clustering might raise questions with an analyst. Fortunately, the survey report provides assistance. A modifier key with which to assess the goodness of fit of job description is in the upper left corner of Exhibit 7.16. The careful analyst will notice that one company, E017, employs by far the largest number of people whose salaries we are analyzing: 297 in MCS2-business,

---

[14]Letter from D. W. Belcher to G. T. Milkovich, in reference to D. W. Belcher, N. Bruce Ferris, and John O'Neill, "How Wage Surveys Are Being Used," *Compensation and Benefits Review,* September–October 1985, pp. 34–51.

EXHIBIT 7.15   Checking for Inconsistencies in Survey Data

Survey Position: Applications Development Unit Head

| Company Number | Title | Reports to | Staff Size | Formal Salary Range | | | Base Salary | Incentive | |
				Min.	Mid.	Max.		Amount	Target %
3	Project manager	Director, Systems	20	52,100	65,150	78,200	83,300*	8,796	10
6	Manager, MIS	Director, Systems	16	36,000†	—	72,000	69,208	Not elig.	—
2	Manager, tech. services	Director, MIS	8	39,416	50.232	61,048	56,000	Not elig.	—
5	Applications area manager	VP, Information Systems	11	44,750	56,000	67,200	55,950	5,610	15
7	Systems dept. unit head	Director, Systems & Programming	15	51,900‡	52,400	62,900	51,135	7,850	18
1	Programming manager	Director, Information Systems Development	12	45,840	57,300	68,760	47,333	500§	10
4	Senior applications systems analyst‖	Manager, Applications Area	2	38,500	50,050	61,600	42,600	2,200	5

*The base pay is higher than the range maximum and is also significantly higher than the survey data pattern. Check the match.
†This company uses broad banding (salary ranges at this level are typically at 50% or 60% spread from minimum to maximum, not 100%). Use these data with discretion.
‡The minimum is too high (should be 41,900).
§Incentive amount paid is well below target; this may be a partial year award or an "atypical" award. Check these data.
‖This title and reporting relationship may indicate the matched position is reported at least one level too low for a match; also, the staff size may indicate lower job level. Check and/or remove the match.

SOURCE: James R. McMahon and Janice S. Hand, *Measuring the Marketplace* (Scottsdale, Ariz.: American Compensation Association, 1991).

earning an average of $39,894. But this same company E017 also reports data on 125 people in job MCS-3, earning an average of $46,359. What effect does this second job have on the survey results? Clearly, Company E017 distinguishes between these two jobs, and pays them differently. Should both be included here in the same report? Should all the data from Company E017 be discarded? Most surveys report only one job match per company, but most surveys also provide little information to assess the strength of that match. The three lines at the bottom of Exhibit 7.16 (pp. 244–45) disaggregate the salary data according to the goodness of the match.

Leveling. If the job description is similar but not identical, and the survey data are not disaggregated by closeness of match, the data may be weighted according to the match. This technique is called *survey leveling*.[15] Based on a scale such as the one shown on

---

[15]Bruce Ellig, ed., *Compensation and Benefits: Design and Analysis* (Scottsdale, Ariz.: American Compensation Association, 1985).

p. 238, if the job in the survey has more responsibility, some analysts adjust the survey data (e.g., multiply it by 0.8) to bring its pay closer in comparability to the employer's job. Conversely, the survey data could be adjusted upward. For example, if you believed that your accountants had slightly more responsibility than the survey job description indicated, you might multiply the $20,800 average salary in the survey by 110 percent and use the result, $22,880, instead. Leveling is another example of the use of judgment in the survey analysis process. It clearly leaves the objectivity of the decisions open to challenge.

Typical Analysis

Becoming familiar with the actual data in a survey is a necessary first step to assessing its accuracy and usefulness. In order to do so, we need to review some simple statistics. We will use the data in Exhibit 7.16 to illustrate some possible analyses.

Frequency Distribution.   Arranging the data from lowest to highest and then tallying the entries allows construction of a frequency distribution. When extensive data are to be analyzed, they are usually grouped into intervals. The frequency table in Exhibit 7.17 on page 246 displays the salary data from Exhibit 7.16 in intervals of $2,500. The data are then readily converted to a histogram, or frequency distribution, also shown in the exhibit. The histogram helps visualize the information in the survey and may highlight nonconformities. For example, the one salary above $55,000 may be considered an outlier—an extreme that falls outside the majority of the data points. Whether or not to include outliers is a judgment call.

Histograms can vary in their shape. Unusual shapes require further analysis to assess the usefulness of the data. They may reflect problems with job matches, widely dispersed pay rates, or employers with widely divergent pay policies. If the data look reasonable at this point, one wag has suggested that it is probably the result of two large, offsetting errors.

Central Tendency.   The vast amount of information contained in a survey must be reduced to a single number that represents the market wage for programming analysts. The arithmetic average, or mean, is the most widely used, calculated by adding all the numbers in the group and then dividing by the number of numbers. The "simple average" for this survey is $45,216, calculated by adding all the actual average salaries (e.g., $32,283 + $36,574, + $39,097, etc.) and dividing by 32, the number of positions. (*Note:* Data from the company for which the report was prepared are *not* included in any of these calculations.) This calculation of mean, or arithmetic average, gives equal weight to every *company* in the survey. The programmer wage paid by company G002, which has only one individual in that position, counts as much as the wage paid by E017, which has 297 programmers. An alternative is a **weighted mean**, or weighted average, which gives equal weight to *each individual employee's* wage. Each company's mean wage is weighted by the number of people in that company who occupy that job. For example, let's simplify

EXHIBIT 7.16 Survey Report Prepared by Compensation Consulting Firm

Job: PROGRAMMING / ANALYST-BUSINESS APPLICATIONS

Modifiers: A = Stronger match
B = Exact match
C = Weaker match

Prepared for company P844 Lomeli Pharmaceuticals

Co #	Modifiers	Job Title	No. of Inc.	Actual Salaries			Range Min.	Mid Pt.	Range Max.	% Sp	Total Comp.
				Avg.	Low	High					
E067	B	Prog/Analyst Sr	2	$36,283	$36,108	$36,400	$28,246	$35,351	$42,456	50	$37,735
E008	C	SR Data Proc Analyst	5	36,574	31,682	39,719	28,654	39,719	50,785	77	38,242
P023	B	Programmer Analyst Sr	13	39,079	35,817	43,854	28,654	41,787	54,920	92	39,079
D032	B	Mgmt Syst Analyst Bus	2	39,079	37,914	40,185	35,235	44,262	53,289	51	39,079
E009	B	Prog/Analyst Bus	8	39,634	35,280	43,008	32,659	42,403	52,147	60	39,634
E017	B	MCS 2—Business	297	39,894	32,206	51,076	32,905	44,204	55,502	69	39,894
G002	B	Princ Business Prog	1	40,588	40,588	40,588	35,548	44,083	52,617	48	40,588
P019	B	Prog/Analyst Sr	12	41,292	36,108	49,096	35,235	46,679	58,123	65	41,292
E231	B	Prog Analyst Sr	3	41,731	36,960	44,284	32,363	42,107	50,507	56	43,400
E111	C	Prog Analyst Sr	3	42,040	38,707	46,502	32,363	41,442	50,520	56	42,072
P221	B	Prog/Analyst III	1	42,537	42,537	42,537	34,648	44,352	54,055	56	42,537
E008	B	ADP Analyst	4	43,621	39,020	48,339	30,401	44,087	57,774	90	43,621
E035	B	Sr Sys Analyst Gen	22	43,908	30,240	53,978	37,632	47,040	56,448	50	43,908
→ P844	B	Systems Dev Spec III	3	43,962	41,879	47,376	31,073	44,392	57,711	86	43,962
A012	B	Info Syst Prog/Analyst	9	44,844	40,069	48,863	37,448	48,717	59,987	60	47,535
K215	B	Computing Analyst Sr	7	45,019	34,944	49,397	34,827	44,437	53,988	55	45,019
E020	B	Prog/Analyst Sr	1	45,194	45,194	45,194	40,185	51,804	63,423	58	45,194
E015	C	Prog Analyst II	4	45,267	43,680	49,504	35,002	43,739	52,474	50	45,267

Code		Title	Incumbents							
C026	B	Sr Syst Analyst	13	45,651	40,669	53,697	34,832	55,664	60	45,651
E003	B	Prog/Analyst Sr	6	45,709	42,067	49,392	35,750	53,625	50	45,709
E017	A	MCS 3—Business	125	46,359	36,865	57,075	35,992	59,230	65	46,359
E111	B	Prog/Syst Analyst Sr	3	46,502	45,696	47,712	36,395	56,891	56	46,502
B110	B	Prog Analyst III	103	46,784	38,707	57,388	38,707	58,060	50	46,784
F007	A	Sr Prog/Analyst	24	47,026	33,358	59,068	38,545	61,676	60	47,026
P112	B	Sr Porg/Analyst	1	47,980	47,980	47,980	36,288	56,672	56	47,980
E009	A	Prog Analyst Business	10	48,249	44,634	55,009	37,094	59,808	61	50,179
S037	B	Mgmt Syst Analyst Sr	2	48,339	47,349	49,271	34,361	57,075	66	48,339
E034	B	Analyst Bus Syst Sr	1	50,086	50,086	50,086	35,351	59,754	69	50,086
Q154	A	Prog Analyst Sr	1	50,435	50,435	50,435	40,127	60,977	52	50,435
E231	A	Prog Analyst Staff	4	53,128	49,929	59,404	40,992	63,947	56	53,128
Q018	A	Info Syst Analyst Sr	4	53,424	52,241	54,888	36,624	63,705	74	53,424
E015	B	Prog Analyst I	1	54,104	54,104	54,104	37,564	56,318	50	54,104
P005	B	Sr MIS Spec	1	56,551	56,551	56,551	38,321	61,268	60	56,511
		26 companies								
		Total incumbents	696							
		Company P844 average	**3**	**43,962**	**41,879**	**47,376**	**31,073**	**57,711**	**86**	**43,962**
		Market weighted average	693	43,199	41,491	49,205	34,920	56,898	63	43,285
		Market simple average		43,216			35,280	56,365	60	45,511
		Market arithmetic average midpoint						46,000		
		Median		45,230	40,328	49,329	35,450	56,650	58	45,459
		Low		36,283	30,240	36,400	28,246	42,456	48	37,735
		High		56,551	56,551	59,404	40,992	63,947	92	56,551
		3 companies matching modifier C	12	40,839	38,023	45,241	32,006	51,260	60	41,533
		23 companies matching modifier B	513	42,035	41,139	47,955	34,937	55,677	59	42,097
		6 companies matching modifier A	168	46,920	44,577	55,980	38,229	61,557	61	47,036

SOURCE: Adapted from Organization Resources Counselors, Inc., New York.

EXHIBIT 7.17   Frequency Distribution of Survey Data

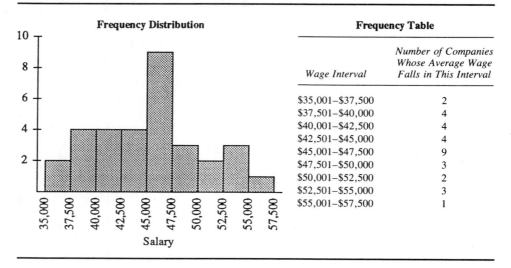

Wage Interval	Number of Companies Whose Average Wage Falls in This Interval
$35,001–$37,500	2
$37,501–$40,000	4
$40,001–$42,500	4
$42,501–$45,000	4
$45,001–$47,500	9
$47,501–$50,000	3
$50,001–$52,500	2
$52,501–$55,000	3
$55,001–$57,500	1

by assuming that only three companies participated in this survey. The calculation for weighted average is shown below.

Company	Number of People Holding This Job		Average Wage		
E067	2	×	$36,283	=	$ 72,566
E00B	5	×	$36,574	=	182,070
PO23	13	×	$39,079	=	508,027
Total	20			=	$ 762,663

1. Multiply the number of job holders for each company by the average wage in that company.
2. Add these numbers ($762,663) and divide by the total number of people in all the companies (20).

The answer, $38,133, is the weighted mean wage for the programmers in this sample. For the total 696 incumbents included in Exhibit 7.16, the weighted average wage is $43,199. A weighted average gives a more accurate picture of actual labor market conditions, since it better recognizes the size of the supply and demand.

An alternative measure of central tendency frequently used is the *median*. Median is the middle number of numbers arranged in either increasing or decreasing order. If the sample contains an even number of entries, the median is the arithmetic average of the two middle numbers after ranking. What is the median wage in Exhibit 7.16? (Remember to omit the data for company P844 in this calculation.)

Although mean is by far the most common measure of central tendency, outliers (extreme values) can distort it. Therefore, some analysts calculate more than one central tendency measure to compare to the scatter plot and/or frequency distribution before deciding which one best represents "market wage."

What difference does all this make? Central tendency measures summarize all the survey responses into a single wage for each job. Although the frequency distribution shows all the wages, central tendency gives just one. Therefore, the analyst must choose the wage measure that gives the most accurate description of the survey data.

Dispersion

The distribution of rates around a measure of central tendency is called *dispersion*. **Standard deviation** is probably the most common statistical measure of dispersion, although its use in salary surveys is less common. Standard deviation refers to how far from the mean each of the items in a frequency distribution is located. In the frequency distribution based on data in Exhibit 7.16, the standard deviation from the mean is $5,029, which means that 68 percent of the salaries lie within $\pm$ 1 standard deviation or between $43,403 and $47,029. Information about dispersion gives the analyst a better idea of the relationship between the central tendency measure and the frequency distribution.

Quartiles and Percentiles.   Quartiles and percentiles are the most common measure of dispersion used in salary survey analysis. Recall from the introduction to this chapter that one organization's policy was to "be in the top 10 percent," and another's was "to be in the 65th percentile nationally." A 65th percentile means that 65 percent of all companies' pay rates are at or below that point, and 35 percent are above. To calculate quartiles, arrange the measures from lowest to highest. Exhibit 7.16 already has done this. Recall that the median separates the measures into two equal groups. If the measures are separated into four groups, each group contains 25 percent of the measures, and the numbers that separate the groups are called *quartiles*. There are three quartiles (first, second, and third) for any set of scores. The second quartile always corresponds to the median. To say that a measure is in the fourth quartile means that it falls anywhere above the point of separation between the third and fourth quartile. Exhibit 7.18 shows the survey data with quartiles and percentiles marked.

Percentiles separate scores into 100 equal groups, and the points of separation mark the percentiles. What percentile corresponds to the median? Exhibit 7.7 shows the 10th, 25th, 50th, 75th, and 90th percentile curves for engineers' salaries. Ten percent of all engineers in the survey receive salaries below the 10th percentile; 90 percent receive salaries above that line. Quartiles correspond to the 25th (Q1), 50th (Q2), and 75th (Q3) percentiles.

The survey report in Exhibit 7.16 also includes range information and indicates whether the programming analysts receive any bonus or incentive compensation. All these issues will be explained in later chapters.

EXHIBIT 7.18   Quartiles and Percentiles

$36,283	←	**Minimum**	**$45,267**	←	**Quartile 2, 50th Percentile**
36,574			45,651		
39,079			45,709		
39,079	←	**10th Percentile**	46,359		
39,634			46,502		
39,894					
40,588			46,784		
41,292			47,026		
41,731	←	**Quartile 1**	47,980		
42,040			**48,249**	←	**Quartile 3**
42,537			48,339		
43,621			50,086		
43,908			50,435		
44,844			53,128		
45,019			**53,424**	←	**90th Percentile**
45,194			54,104		
			56,551	←	**Maximum**

Where Do We Go from Here?

We have discussed some of the ways to analyze survey data for a job. We looked at ways to calculate central tendency and to visualize the data to assess how "good" they are and how well the central tendency measure reflects the survey data. However, a survey rarely focuses on a single job. Rather, data are gathered for any number of different jobs. These jobs may be related (e.g., computer programmers, computer programming analysts, and computer operators), or they may cover a broader range of work. If the purpose of the survey is to set pay rates for a number of jobs with respect to the market, a way is needed to combine data from all the surveyed jobs. A market pay line does this by summarizing rates of the various jobs found in the market. But before further reviewing more mechanics, it is useful to step back a moment and reconsider what we are trying to accomplish with surveys. The objective is to design pay structures that employees believe are fair and equitable and that will help accomplish management's objectives.

COMBINE INTERNAL STRUCTURE AND EXTERNAL WAGE RATES

Two components of the pay model are emerging, and their relationship to each other is depicted in Exhibit 7.19.

- An *internally consistent structure* has been developed and is shown on the horizontal axis in Exhibit 7.19. For this illustration, our structure consists of jobs A through P, with P being the most complex job in this structure. Jobs B, D, F, G, H, J, M, and P are benchmark jobs that have been matched in a survey. Job M is the programmer analyst.
- External wage rates paid by relevant competitors for those benchmark jobs, as measured by the survey, are shown on the vertical (y) axis. The purpose of the survey is to assist the organization to address external competitiveness, much as job analysis addressed internal consistency.

EXHIBIT 7.19   Combining Internal Structure with External Wage Rates

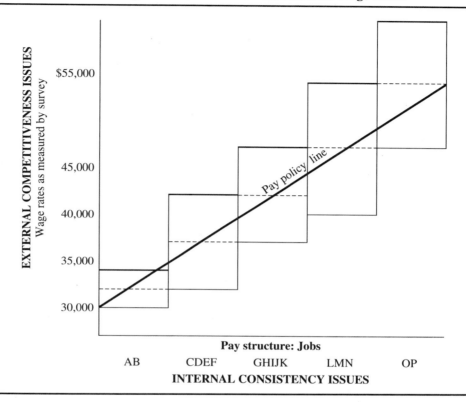

These two components—internal consistency and external competitiveness—come together in the pay structure. The pay structure has two aspects. One is the actual pay policy line, which reflects market rates adjusted to the job structure and pay level policy decisions of the organization. The second is pay ranges, which build flexibility into the structure.

Getting from where we are now—wage rates for a number of benchmark jobs—to an actual pay policy line requires only three easy steps.

1. *Construct a market pay line.* Recall the frequency distribution calculated for the programmer job M (Exhibit 7.17). If frequency distributions are calculated for all the benchmark jobs B, D, F, H, M, and P, then it is a simple step to transfer all the distributions onto the graph in Exhibit 7.20, where the employer's job structure (job evaluation points) is the x-axis and wage rates are on the y-axis. The frequency distributions are at right angles to the x- and y-axes, similar to a topographic map. (*Note:* For clarity, only four distributions are shown on the exhibit.) Summarizing the data from all these distributions into a market pay line may be as simple as drawing a line that connects the means,

EXHIBIT 7.20   **Constructing a Market Pay Line**

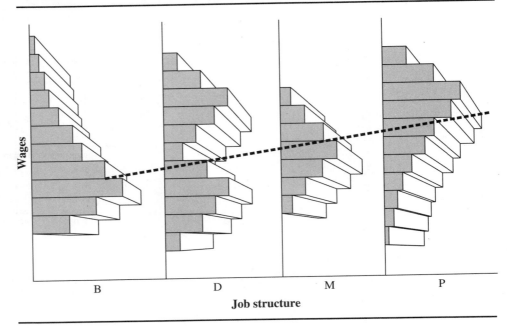

percentiles, or other measures of central tendency of the distributions, as in the exhibit. A straight line or a curve is most useful, even though midpoints for some jobs may not fall on this line. Exactly where this line is drawn will reflect the employer's pay policy. Lines may be drawn to represent various percentiles in the distributions of job rates (e.g., a 60 percent line would indicate that 60 percent of market rates fall below this line). A market line may be drawn freehand on the basis of simple inspection of the data, or statistical techniques, such as regression analysis, may be used. Regression fits a line that minimizes the variance of observations around it. The appendix to this chapter provides additional information on regression. The result is a statistically more accurate market pay line that summarizes the distribution of going rates in the market.

Comparing going rates to the employer's rates will show the competitiveness of the current pay rates. Comparisons may be made across job families or by individual jobs. Exhibit 7.21 shows a comparison based on "market index," which is the actual salary divided by the market rate. The market index for personnel representatives is 86%, or $19,600 (average salary of the four personnel representatives) divided by $22,700 (the market rate for personnel representatives). This low ratio may be the result of deliberate policy choices by the employer (e.g., lag the market for HR positions), the nature of the job, (e.g., personnel reps quickly get promoted into other jobs), or the survey data (e.g., personnel reps in the survey had greater responsibilities). It's up to the analyst to decide whether the variance from the market is explainable and acceptable. A market index can

EXHIBIT 7.21 Using the Market Index to Determine Competitiveness of Current Pay

Grade	Job Title	Number of Employees	Average Actual Salary	Market Rate Composite	Market Index
1	Personnel representative	4	$19,600	$22,700	86%
3	Senior compensation analyst	2	25,700	28,000	92
4	Security supervisor*	1	33,000	33,500	99
5	Manager, Training*	1	41,000	39,500	104
6	Director, Human Resources*	1	45,000	44,000	102
				Overall market index (Human Resources):	94%
1	Accounting assistant	10	20,000	21,000	95%
2	Accountant	6	24,000	24,500	98
3	Accounting supervisor*	3	31,500	30,000	105
5	Internal auditor	1	38,000	38,000	100
6	Controller*	1	48,000	45,000	107
				Overall market index (Finance):	99%
1	LPN	25	22,000	20,000	110%
2	Registered nurse	100	29,500	27,000	109
3	Nursing instructor	10	34,500	30,500	113
3	Nurse supervisor*	5	38,000	35,000	109
6	Director, Emergency Room*	1	47,500	38,500	123
				Overall market index (Nursing):	110%
1	Programmer	6	21,000	26,500	79%
2	Data entry supervisor*	4	23,500	25,500	92
4	Systems analyst	2	30,000	32,000	94
5	Manager, Computer Operations*	1	38,000	36,500	104
6	Director, MIS*	1	47,500	46,000	103
				Overall market index (MIS):	90%

*Overall market index for management: 104%
Overall market index for nonmanagement: 108%

SOURCE: Jane Bjorndal and Linda Ison, *Mastering Market Data* (Scottsdale, Ariz.: American Compensation Association, 1991).

also be computed for an entire department. To do so, each salary would be weighted by the number of employees (e.g., [4 × $19,600] + [2 × $25,700] + [1 × $33,000] . . . divided by 9) to calculate the average actual salary for the department. This average salary would then be divided by the market average (e.g., $22,700 + $28,000 + $33,500 . . . divided by 5) to get the overall market index for the human resource management department.

2. *Update the survey data.* The comparisons with the market pay line give the analyst information on the competitiveness of the current pay. The next step is to update or "age" the market data for comparisons at a future time period.

Because they reflect decisions of employers, employees, unions, and government agencies, wages paid by competitors are constantly changing. And competitors adjust their wages at different times. Universities typically adjust to match the academic year. Unionized employers adjust to correspond to dates negotiated in labor agreements. Many employers adjust each employee's pay on the anniversary of the employee's date of hire. Even though these changes do not occur smoothly and uniformly throughout the year, as a practical matter it is common practice to assume that they do. Therefore, a survey that requires three to six months to collect, code, and analyze data is probably outdated before it is available. Consequently, the data are usually updated to forecast the competitive rates for the future date when the pay decisions will be implemented.

The amount to update (often called *aging* or *trending*) is based on several factors, including historical trends in the market economic forecasts, prospects for the economy in which the employer operates, consumer price index, and the manager's judgment, among others.

Exhibit 7.22 uses the survey data for the programmer's wage to illustrate updating. In the example, the pay rates collected in the survey were in effect at point A, January 1 on the *current year*. Because this company's stated policy is to "match at the 60th percentile," the figure at A ($45,709) is the 60th percentile of the frequency distribution of the market rates for the programmer's job. The compensation manager will use these data for pay decisions that will go into effect at C, which is January 1 of the *plan year*. Assume that pay rates have been increasing by approximately 5 percent annually. If we assume that the future will be like the past, then the market data are multiplied by 1.05,

EXHIBIT 7.22   Updating Survey Data

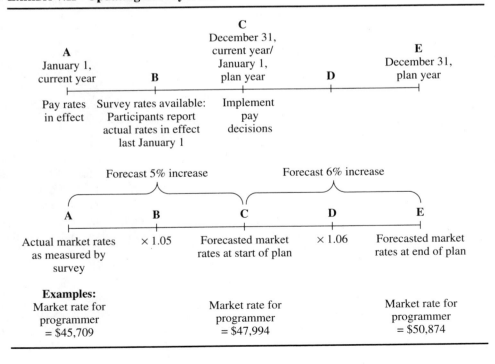

or 105 percent, to account for the rise in pay that is expected to occur by the end of the *current year*. The programmer's $45,709 this past January 1 is updated to $47,994, the amount at C, by the end of the *current year*.

To estimate what the market rates will be by the *end* of the *plan* year (point E), a judgment is made about the rate of increase expected during the plan year and survey results are updated again on the basis of this judgment. In Exhibit 7.22, the 6 percent increase by the end of the plan year may be based on an expected increase in demand for the particular skills included in this survey. By the end of the plan year, the assumption is that the market will have increased by a factor of 1.113 (1.05 × 1.06 = 1.113), or 11.3 percent beyond the programmer rate A collected in the survey. So the survey data are projected into the future by multiplying by 1.113, or 111.3 percent.

3. *Translate pay level policy into practice.* Exhibit 7.23 shows the practical results of updating. Because an individual company typically adjusts its pay level only once per period, its pay will be at the same point at both the beginning and end of the plan year, represented by the horizontal line A_1A_2 in the exhibits. But whether an organization

EXHIBIT 7.23 Putting Pay Level Policy into Practice

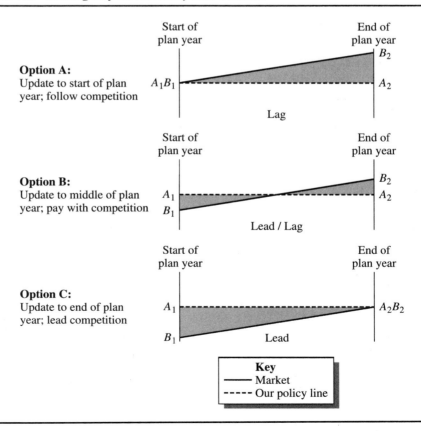

updates to the end of the current year (point C, programmer rate = $47,994), the end of the plan year (point E, programmer rate = $50,874), or someplace in between (point D) depends on its pay level policy and how it puts that policy into practice. If the company chooses a market rate comparison consistent with its pay level policy (60th percentile), updates survey data to the end of the current year/start of the plan year (programmer rate = $47,994), and keeps this rate in effect throughout the plan year, the company will actually be lagging the market, option A, since it matches its desired market pay level only at the beginning of the plan year. The market rates continue to rise throughout the year; the company's rates do not. The shaded area in option A depicts the lag that grows as market competitors adjust their rates throughout the year.

To lead competition, option C, an employer can age market data to the *end* of the plan year (point E, programmer = $50,874), then pay at this rate throughout the plan year. Aging the market data to a point halfway through the plan year (point D in Exhibit 7.22), a technique called *lead/lag,* will produce the line shown in option B. The original survey rates are updated to the end of the current year plus half the projected amount for the plan year (1.05 × 1.03 = 1.0815; programmer = $49,434).

We have oversimplified this discussion by omitting other possible mechanics. For example, some companies lead by matching the competitor's 75th percentile; others match only a few top-paying competitors. The point is that pay level policy and actual practice may not coincide, depending on how the policy is translated into practice.

DESIGN PAY RANGES

So far we have constructed a line that reflects market pay rates and projected those rates into the future in a way that reflects the organization's pay level policy. All this is part of designing a pay structure that will reflect the organization's policies on internal consistency and external competitiveness. The next step is to design pay ranges.

Why Bother with Ranges?

The wide variation of market rates paid for similar jobs and skills reflects two *external* pressures:

1. Quality variations (skills, abilities, experience) among individuals in the external market (e.g., company A has stricter hiring requirements for its buyer position than does company B, even though job descriptions are identical).
2. The recognition of differences in the productivity-related value to employers to these quality variations (e.g., buyers for Neiman-Marcus are accountable for different results than are buyers for Wal-Mart).

In addition to these external differences in rates, an organization's internal pay policy may call for differences in rates paid to employees on the same job. A pay range exists whenever two or more rates are paid to employees in the same job. Hence, internal pay ranges reflect the following *internal* pressures:

1. The intention to recognize individual performance variations with pay (e.g., buyer A makes better, more timely decisions for Neiman-Marcus than does

buyer B, even though they both hold the same job and have the same responsibilities).

2. Employees' expectations that their pay will increase over time.

From an internal consistency perspective, the range reflects the approximate differences in performance or experience the employer wishes to pay for a given level of work. From an external competitiveness perspective, the range also acts as a control device. A range maximum sets the lid on what the employer is willing to pay for that work; the range minimum sets the floor.

Not all employers use ranges. Skill-based plans establish single *flat rates* for each skill level regardless of performance or seniority. And many collective bargaining contracts establish single flat rates for each job (i.e., all Senior Machinists II receive $14.50 per hour regardless of performance or seniority). This flat rate is often set to correspond to some midpoint on a survey of that job.

Constructing Ranges

Designing ranges is relatively simple. Three basic steps are typically involved.

1. *Develop grades.* A *grade* is a grouping of different jobs that are considered substantially equal for pay purposes. Grades enhance an organization's ability to move people among jobs within a grade with no change in pay. In Exhibit 7.24 the horizontal axis is the job structure with the jobs now slotted into grades.

The question of which jobs are substantially equal and therefore slotted into one grade requires the analyst to reconsider the original job evaluation results. Jobs in the same grade may have approximately the same job evaluation points (e.g., within 20 or 30 points in a 500-point job evaluation plan). Each grade will have its own pay range, and all the jobs within the grade have that same range. Jobs in different grades (e.g., jobs C, D, E, and F in grade 2) should be dissimilar to those in other grades (grade 1 jobs A and B) and will have a different range.

Although grading permits flexibility, they are difficult to design. The objective is for all jobs that are similar for pay purposes to be placed within the same grade. If jobs with relatively close job evaluation point totals fall on either side of grade boundaries (e.g., in Exhibit 7.24, jobs E, F, and G have point totals within 30 points of each other, but E and F are in one grade, and G is in another), the magnitude of difference in salary treatment may be out of proportion to the magnitude of difference in job content. Resolving such dilemmas requires an understanding of the specific jobs, career paths, and the flow of work in the organization.

Grouping jobs depends on how the work is organized, traditions in the workplace, and the career paths in the organization. Some grouping may have already occurred through use of an egalitarian job structure (Chapter 3) or a classification job evaluation plan (Chapter 4). To the list of factors considered for grouping we now add the results of the survey data, particularly the pay differentials that are established between the grades. There is no "correct" number of job grades. Designing the grade structure that "fits" each organization involves trial and error until one seems to fit the best without too many problems.

EXHIBIT 7.24   **Developing Pay Grades**

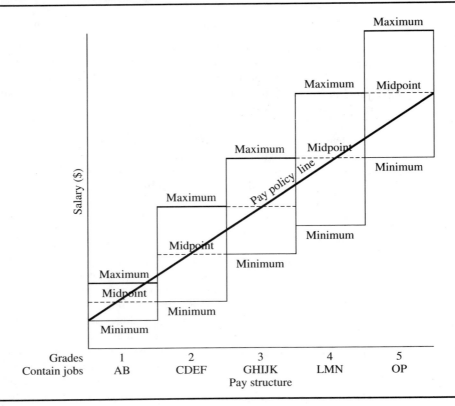

2. *Establish ranges (midpoint, minimum, and maximum).* The midpoints for each range are usually set to correspond to the competitive pay level established earlier. The point where the pay policy line crosses each grade becomes the midpoint of the pay range for that grade. The midpoint of the range is often called the *control point*. It specifies the pay objective for a fully trained employee who is satisfactorily performing a job within that grade. It also reflects the competitive position in the relevant market.

The desired range spread is based on some judgment about how the ranges support career paths, promotions, and other organization systems.[16] Range spreads seem to vary between 10 to 120 percent. Top-level management positions commonly have range spreads of 60 to 120 percent; entry to mid-level professional and managerial positions, between 35 to 60 percent; office and production work, 10 to 25 percent. The underlying logic is that wider range spreads in the managerial jobs are designed to reflect the greater opportunity for individual discretion and performance variations in the work.

---

[16]John D. England and David A. Pierson, "Salary Ranges and Merit Matrices: The Time Targeting Approach," *Compensation and Benefits Review*, January 1992, pp. 36–46.

Another, perhaps better basis on which to determine the desired range spread is what makes good sense for the particular employer. Surveys usually provide data on both the actual maximum and minimum rates paid, as well as the ranges established by policy. Some compensation managers use the actual rates paid, particularly the 75th and 25th percentiles in the survey data, as their maximums and minimums. Others examine alternatives to ensure that the proposed spread includes at least 75 percent of the rates in the survey data. Still others establish the minimum and maximum separately. The amount between the minimum and the midpoint can be a function of the amount of time it takes a new employee to become fully competent. Jobs quickly learned may have minimums much closer to the midpoints. The maximum becomes the amount above the midpoint that the company is willing to pay for sustained performance on the job. In the end, range spread is based on judgment that weighs all these factors.

Once the midpoint (based on the pay policy line) and the range spread (based on judgment) are specified, minimums and maximums are calculated:

$$\text{Minimum} = \text{Midpoint} \div [100\% + (1/2 \text{ range spread})]$$
$$\text{Maximum} = \text{Minimum} + (\text{Range spread} \times \text{Minimum})$$

For example, with a range spread of 30 percent, and a midpoint of $10,000,

$$\text{Minimum} = \$10,000 \div (1 + 0.15) = \$8,695$$
$$\text{Maximum} = \$8,695 + (0.30 \times \$8695) = 8695 + 2609 = \$11,304$$

Note that these formulas assume symmetrical ranges (i.e., equal distance above and below the midpoint).

3. *Degree of overlap.* If A and B are two adjacent pay grades, with B the higher of the two, the degree of overlap is defined as

$$100 \times \frac{\text{Maximum rate grade A} - \text{Minimum rate grade B}}{\text{Maximum rate grade A} - \text{Minimum rate grade A}}$$

What difference does overlap make? Consider the two extremes shown in Exhibit 7.25. The high degree of overlap and low midpoint differentials in Figure A indicate small differences in the value of jobs in the adjoining grades. Such a structure results in promotions (title changes) without much change in pay. On the other hand, in Figure B, few grades and ranges result in wider range midpoint differentials and less overlap between adjacent ranges, and permit the manager to reinforce a promotion (movement into a new range) with a larger pay increase. At some point, the differential must be large enough to induce employees to seek and/or accept the promotion or to undertake the necessary training required. However, there is little research to indicate how much a differential is necessary to influence employees to take on additional responsibilities or invest in training.

Broad Banding

Figure C collapses the number of salary grades within the structure into only a few broad grades (or bands) with much wider ranges. This technique, known as *broad banding,*

EXHIBIT 7.25   Range Overlap

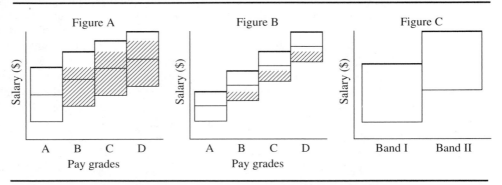

consolidates as many as four or five traditional grades into a single band with one minimum and one maximum. Because the band encompasses so many jobs of differing values, a range midpoint is usually not used.[17]

Redesigned organizations that eliminated levels of managerial jobs, or that merged, downsized, or restructured, often find that broad banding provides flexibility to define job responsibilities more broadly. Astra-Merck, for example, uses five broad bands for its entire structure with titles ranging from contributor to executive. However, if a system is not carefully monitored, broad bands can permit all employees to float to the maximum pay, which for many jobs in the band is much higher than market value. Recall from Exhibit 7.15 that broad banding was one of the "flags" that called for discretion in using survey data from a particular company. Many companies that use broad banding have found that managers tend to build in "shadow" grades; that is, they divide a broad band into smaller units. Although this seems to defeat the purpose of the broad band, the managers apparently feel ownership of the system, since they disassemble the broad band to meet their needs.

An issue related to ranges is the size of pay differentials between supervisors and the employees they supervise. A supervisory job would typically be at least one pay range removed from the jobs it supervises. Although a 15 percent pay differential has been offered as a rule of thumb, large range overlap, combined with possible overtime or incentive pay available in some jobs but not in supervisory jobs, could make it difficult to maintain such a differential. On the other hand, some argue that differentials are counterproductive if they force good technical talent (i.e., engineers) to become managers solely because managers command higher incomes. So the organization culture, the work, and the objectives of the compensation system will determine the structure of the pay ranges.

---

[17]"Questions and Answers on Broad Banding," *On Compensation* (Hewitt Associates, 1991).

BALANCING INTERNAL AND EXTERNAL PRESSURES: ADJUSTING THE PAY STRUCTURE

Establishing the pay ranges for work reflects a balance between competitive pressures and pressures for internal consistency and fairness. Up until now, we have tended to make a distinction between the job structure and the pay structure. A *job structure* orders jobs on the basis of total job evaluation points or the levels of skill required to perform them. The *pay structure,* on the other hand, is anchored by the organization's pay policy line, which is set using the market rates paid for benchmark jobs.

Reconciling Differences

The problem with using two methods (market surveys versus job evaluation or skill-based plans) to create a structure is that they are likely to result in two different structures. The order in which jobs are ranked on internal and external factors may not completely agree. Differences between market structure and rate and job evaluation rankings warrant a review of the basic decisions in evaluating and pricing that particular job. This may entail a review of the job analysis, the job description, and the evaluation of the job, or the market data for the job in question. Often this reanalysis solves the problem. In cases in which discrepancies persist, experienced judgment is required. Sometimes survey data are discarded; sometimes benchmark job matches are changed.

One study of how differences are actually reconciled found that managers weigh external market data more heavily than internal job evaluation data. In light of all the judgments that go into internal evaluation, market data may be considered to be more objective when differences arise.

Sometimes differences arise because a shortage of a particular skill has driven up the market rate. But reclassifying a market-sensitive job (one in which a supply-and-demand imbalance exists) into a higher salary grade, where it will remain long after the imbalance has been corrected, will create additional problems in the long term. Creating a special range that is clearly designated as market responsive may be a better approach. However, caution is advised. Decisions made on the basis of expediency undermine the integrity of the pay system.

Locality Pay

Many employers have historically maintained one national pay structure for their managerial-professional work force and separate schedules tied to local pay rates for their blue collar and clerical employees. The federal government's general schedule (GS), discussed in Chapter 4, provides guidelines for uniform pay rates across the United States. The federal government is one of the largest employers, with some of the most diverse jobs, in the world. More than three million employees work in jobs ranging from swine herders (Agriculture Department) to astronauts (NASA) to law enforcement (Treasury Department). But costs of living and variations in external structures in different locations make it difficult to recruit and transfer employees paid on a national schedule. For example, data in Exhibit 7.26 indicate how market structures vary between Los Angeles and

EXHIBIT 7.26   Rank Ordering Comparison of Salaries for Two Cities

	Los Angeles		Cincinnati	
	Median Salary	*Rank*	*Median Salary*	*Rank*
Janitor, porter	$10,400	1	$ 8,840	1
Switchboard/Receptionist	16,198	2	14,560	2
Material handling laborer	18,241	3	20,196	10
Key entry operators	18,304	4	15,210	3
Order clerk	18,720	5	18,122	9
Shipper	20,592	6	15,288	4
Receiver	20,592	7	17,846	7
Drafter	21,632	8	23,322	11
Payroll clerk	21,918	9	17,472	6
Warehousers	22,110	10	18,705	8
Word processors	22,464	11	16,120	5
Truckdriver tractor/trailer	30,264	12	27,248	12
Computer programmer	35,932	13	28,340	13
Tool and die makers	36,254	14	32,302	14
Computer systems analyst	42,016	15	36,608	15

SOURCE: Cincinnati, Los Angeles Area Wage Surveys (1989), Bureau of Labor Statistics.

Cincinnati. In Los Angeles, word processors are the fifth highest of the 15 benchmark jobs surveyed. But Cincinnati word processors are fifth from the bottom.

The FBI documented the problems with a single structure. In New York City, starting salaries for FBI agents were 40 percent less than those for New York City detectives. An FBI agent transferred from Omaha to Boston faced living costs 56 percent higher. In response, the Federal Employee Pay Comparability Act of 1990 (FEPCA) seeks to close any gap between federal employees and those workers employed by local or state government as well as private industry.[18] The act phases in wage adjustments when rates differ from local market rates by more than 5 percent. However, pay differences based on local and regional data may also cause dissatisfaction and lack of cooperation across locations. Omaha FBI agents may feel underpaid if Boston-area agents make more money. In addition, wages for private sector employees may be partially determined by performance differences, whereas the General Schedule makes no allowances for performance differences. And the local structure may change much faster than the federal government can adjust.

---

[18]Paul Hempel, Charles Fay, Philip Bobko, and Howard Risher, "Locality Differences in the Structure of Wages: Implications for Federal Pay Reform" (Working paper, Institute of Management and Labor Relations, Rutgers University, 1991); *Strengthening the Link between Pay and Performance*, Report of the Pay-for-Performance Labor-Management Committee, George T. Milkovich, chairman (Washington, D.C.: Office of Personnel Management, November 1991).

Compression

Compression problems are one result of an imbalance between external competitive pressures and internal consistency. Compression results when wages for those jobs filled from outside the organization are increasing faster than the wages for jobs filled from within the organization.[19] As pay differentials among jobs become very small, the traditional pay structure becomes compressed. An example is an employer with a large number of jobs at or near the minimum wage. Whenever Congress legislates an increase in the minimum wage, or labor market conditions necessitate raising entry-level wages, the employer must decide whether to shift the entire wage structure upward to maintain differentials, or to narrow it. Either decision can be costly, in dollars and/or employee dissatisfaction.

Compression is also an issue in professional work (engineers, lawyers, professors) when new graduates command salaries almost equal to those of professionals with three to five years of experience. A study of business school professors found that a decision to boost faculty quality by paying premium salaries for the best new assistant professors available backfired, because rates for the rest of the faculty were not also increased.[20] Dissatisfaction among older faculty led to the rapid loss of the best professors, who were able to find other jobs. With only the less-marketable professors remaining, the overall faculty quality declined. (The older the authors of this text get, the more importance we attach to studies that recommend raising salaries for older professors.)

Certain compensation practices can also inadvertently narrow the differentials among jobs to cause compression. For example, wide range overlap between adjacent job grades may mean that a job perceived to be harder to do actually pays very little more than a job that is clearly easier. Another example is across-the-board pay increases, with the same dollar amount going to all employees. The technique has an egalitarian appeal, but it also reduces differentials. Employers can minimize compression problems to some extent by utilizing internal employees to fill vacancies as much as possible, thereby reducing exposure to the external market. Chapter 15, Managing the System, discusses ways to monitor the pay structure to identify possible compression problems. But compensation practices never cease to amaze us. What is compression to some may be egalitarian (smaller pay differences among jobs) to others. So when does compression become egalitarian? The cynic in us says when it's not our pay that is being compressed.

In sum, the process of balancing internal and external pressures is a matter of judgment, made with an eye to the objectives established for the pay system. Deemphasizing internal pay relationships may lead to feelings of inequitable treatment among employees. These in turn may reduce employees' willingness to share new ideas on how

---

[19]Thomas J. Bergmann, Marilyn A. Bergmann, Desiree Roff, and Vida Scarpello, "Salary Compression: Causes and Solutions," *Compensation and Benefits Management,* Fall 1991, pp. 7–16; W. C. Lawther, "Ways to Monitor (and Solve) the Pay Compression Problem," *Personnel,* March 1989, pp. 84–87.

[20]Luis R. Gomez-Mejia and David B. Balkin, "Causes and Consequences of Pay Compression: The Case of Business Schools" (Working paper, Management Department, University of Florida, Gainesville, November 1984); David Balkin, "Compensation Strategy for Firms in Emerging and Rapidly Growing Industries," *Human Resource Planner* 11, no. 3 (1988), pp. 207–14.

to improve the work or improve the product's quality. Inequitable internal pay relationships may also lead employees to seek other jobs, file grievances, form unions, go out on strike, or refuse to take on increased job responsibilities. Neglecting external pay relationships, however, will affect both the ability to attract job applicants and the ability to hire those applicants who match the organization's needs. External pay relationships also influence the organization's labor costs and hence its ability to compete in the product/service market.

SUMMARY

This chapter has detailed the basic decisions and techniques involved in setting pay levels and designing pay ranges. Most organizations survey other employers' pay rates to determine competitive rates paid in the market. An employer using the survey results considers how it wishes to position its pay in the market: to lead, to match, or to follow competition. This policy decision may be different for different business units and even for different job groups within a single organization. Pay policy is translated into practice by setting pay policy lines that reflect the employer's competitive policy and serve as reference points around which pay ranges are established.

The use of ranges is a recognition of both external and internal pressures. No single "going rate" for a job exists in the market; an array of rates exists. This array results from variations in the quality of employees for that job and differences in employer policies and practicies. It also reflects the fact that employers differ in the value they attach to the jobs and qualifications. Internally, the use of ranges is consistent with variations in the discretion present in jobs. Some employees will perform better than others; some employees are more experienced than others. Pay ranges permit employers to value and recognize these differences with pay.

Let us step back for a moment to review what has been discussed and preview what is coming. We have examined two components of the pay model. A concern for internal consistency meant that job analysis and perhaps job descriptions and job evaluation were used to determine a job structure. A concern for external competitiveness required policy determination, survey design and analysis, setting the pay policy line, and designing pay ranges. The next part of the book is concerned with employee contributions—paying the individuals who perform the work. This is perhaps the most important part of the book. All that has gone before is a prelude, setting up the pay levels and pay structures within which individual employees are to be paid.

REVIEW QUESTIONS

1. Which competitive pay level policy would you recommend to an employer? Why? Does it depend on circumstances faced by the employer? Which ones?
2. How would you design a survey for setting pay for welders? How would you design a survey for setting pay for financial managers? Do the issues differ? Will the techniques used and the data collected differ? Why or why not?
3. What factors determine the relevant market for a survey? Why is the definition of the relevant market so important?

4. In what situations would you recommend your employer use benchmark jobs in a survey? When would you recommend a skill-based or job valuation approach?

5. What do surveys have to do with pay discrimination?

6. Why are pay ranges used? Does their use assist or hinder the achievement of internal consistency? External competitiveness?

7. You are the compensation manager for Lomeli Pharmaceuticals, and you directed the survey reported in Exhibit 7.16. Analyze the results. Specify which measure(s) gives the best representation of the market wage for programming analysts. Make the case that Lomeli's pay for its systems development specialist is too high. Make the case that it's too low.

APPENDIX
REGRESSION ANALYSIS

Using the mathematical formula for a straight line,

$$y = a + bx$$

where

y = dollars
x = job evaluation points
a = the y value (in dollars) at which
x = 0 (i.e., the straight line crosses the y-axis)
b = the slope of the line

If $b = 0$, the line is parallel to the x-axis and all jobs are paid the same, regardless of job evaluation points. Using the dollars from the market survey data and the job evaluation points from the internal job structure, solving this equation enables the analyst to construct a line based on the relationship between the internal job structure and market rates. An upward sloping line means that more job evaluation points are associated with higher dollars. The market line can be written as

Pay for job A $= a + (b \times$ Job evaluation points for job A)
Pay for job B $= a + (b \times$ Job evaluation points for job B), etc.

The issue is to estimate the values of a and b in an efficient manner, so that errors of prediction are minimized. This is what "least squares" regression analysis does.

For many jobs, particularly high-level managerial and executive jobs, job evaluation is not used. Instead, salaries are related to some measure of company size (sales, volume, operating revenues) as a measure of responsibility through the use of logarithms. In such situations, x and y are converted to logarithms (in base 10), and the equation for a straight line becomes

$$\log y = a + b(\log x)$$

where

x = sales or revenues (in millions of dollars)
y = current compensation (in thousands of dollars)

Example

Given sales and compensation levels for a sample of jobs, assume that

$a = 1.7390$
$b = 0.3000$

Using the equation log y = 1.7390 + 0.3000 (log x), one can calculate the current market rate for the chief executive in a company with sales of $500 million.

1. First, set $x = 500$, that is 500,000,000 with six zeros dropped.
2. Log $x = 2.6990$.
3. Multiply log x by 0.3000, which is the coefficient of the variable log x in the given equation. This results in a value of 0.8997.
4. Add to 0.8097 the constant in the equation, 1.7390. The result, 2.5487, is the value of log y.
5. The chief executive's total current compensation is the antilog of log y, which is 354.

Read in thousands of dollars, it is $354,000.

$$\begin{aligned}
\text{Equation: log } y &= 1.7390 + 0.3000 \text{ (log } x) \\
x &= \$500,000,000 = 500 \\
\log x &= 2.6990 \\
\log y &= 1.7390 + 0.3000 \ (2.6990) \\
\log y &= 1.7390 + 0.8097 \\
\log y &= 2.5487 \\
\text{antilog } y &= 354 \\
y &= \$354,000
\end{aligned}$$

Your Turn:
Comparing Faculty Salaries

Cornell University is frequently ranked as one of the top universities in the country. It is by far the largest employer in Ithaca, New York. Cornell is organized into two colleges, statutory and endowed. The statutory college includes the Agricultural, Human Ecology, and Industrial and Labor Relations Schools. The statutory colleges are considered a public university. About one-third of their budget is provided by New York state, and their tuition is comparable to other state-supported universities. The endowed schools—the arts and sciences, engineering, and architecture—are private. Tuition is on a level with Harvard, Princeton, and Yale. The following article by David Folkenflik recently appeared in the *Cornell Daily Sun*.

Cornell Faculty Salaries Remain Uncompetitive with Top Colleges[1]

Cornell professors received pay raises commensurate with the national university average for the past school year and slightly above the rate of inflation, but salary levels continue to lag behind comparable institutions, according to faculty and top administrators.

Many University officials believe the salary levels may prove to be a source of difficulty for the University in its quest to recruit and retain top faculty.

"We see that, on average, we pay about 10 percent below the marketplace," said the dean of the College of Arts and Sciences.

Figures released by the Financial Policy Committee indicate that the University has become less competitive for faculty salaries in relationship with Ivy League schools and other "peer institutions"—for both endowed and statutory colleges.

"In the early 80s, the endowed colleges of Cornell (were) ranked tenth" in faculty salaries among top four-year private universities, said Ronald D. Ehrenberg, a member of the financial policy committee. "Now, in the private part of the University, we're just not competitive," he said.

The tables released by another committee member peg Cornell's endowed schools as the 16th highest paying private institution, behind not only top-ranked Harvard and Stanford Universities, but Columbia University, the University of California at Berkeley, and the Massachusetts Institute of Technology.

Cornell's State University of New York (SUNY) units, however, are in an even worse position than their endowed counterparts, Ehrenberg said.

Professors at the state colleges—the College of Agriculture and Life Sciences, the School of Industrial and Labor Relations, the College of Veterinary Medicine and the College of Human Ecology—receive yearly percentage increases commensurate with faculty at other SUNY schools, but start with lower base salaries.

Average raises from the year before last for full faculty in the endowed colleges worked out to 6.2 percent; for associate professors, 7.1 percent; and for assistant professors, 7.7 percent, according to the figures released by the IPA. The figures for the pay hikes cover only continuing faculty members eligible for the IPA survey, and include raises caused by promotions.

"If you go on the figures, we're competing with second-echelon institutions" rather than Ivy League schools and other top universities, said one financial policy committee member.

Discussion Questions (Use Spreadsheet Software, if Available)

1. Using graph paper, chart the salaries reported in Exhibit 1. Put the three jobs—assistant pro-

---

[1]Adapted from an article by David Folkenflik that appeared in the *Cornell Daily Sun* on May 1, 1989, p. 1.

fessor, associate professor, and full professor—on the x-axis. Put salary levels on the y-axis. Connect the points to make a pay line for each comparison. You should then have four lines on your chart, one connecting the salary levels at All Public Universities, another connecting the salary levels at Cornell (Statutory), etc. Differentiate your lines by using either color or different combinations of dots and dashes. Label the lines.

2. How is Cornell defining its relevant market? Do you agree with its distinction? Add a fifth line, the average salary at Cornell line, by combining data from Cornell (Statutory) and Cornell (Endowed), and calculating an average. Should the other jobs at Cornell be compared against similar markets? For example, should office, clerical, and technicians in the endowed schools be compared to rates paid in other endowed schools? Or should different markets be used for different groups of jobs?

3. What is Cornell's pay level when compared to the market? Does it matter whom they compare to?

4. The cost of living in Ithaca, New York, is relatively low in comparison to the Boston area (Harvard, MIT), New York City (Columbia), and California (Stanford, Berkeley). Does this matter? Should it matter to managers designing and administering the Cornell pay system?

5. Why do you think Cornell (Endowed) gives different percentages to full, associate, and assistant professors? What effect will such a policy have on the slope of their pay lines? What effect will it have on average pay? What effects do you think it may have on professors' attitudes and behaviors and subsequently on the university's effectiveness?

6. Assume that Cornell (Endowed) will give these same percent increases next year. Calculate the new salaries after the raises are granted. Based on this, what future problems may Cornell anticipate?

7. If you are familiar with spreadsheet software, project the salary increases for all comparisons three years and five years into the future using a computer. Graph the resulting salaries, and compare the slope and relative positions of the lines in five years with the present. Did anything change? If so, what are the implications of this result?

8. Exhibit 2 shows the same salary comparisons for 1991–92. How do actual salaries compare to the projections based on the older data? Did Cornell change any of its decisions?

EXHIBIT 1   Faculty Salaries 1988–89

	All Public Universities		Cornell (Statutory)		All Private Universities		Cornell (Endowed)	
	Salary	*1-yr. Increase*	*Salary*	*1-yr. Increase*	*Salary*	*1-yr. Increase*	*Salary*	*1-yr. Increase*
Full professor	$54,240	5.9%	$57,100	8.3%	$64,800	6.3%	$62,800	6.2%
Associate professor	39,570	5.7	43,600	8.4	43,680	6.1	44,000	7.1
Assistant professor	33,400	6.1	35,100	8.2	36,650	7.1	37,700	7.7

Information Courtesy of IPA and the American Association of University Professors.

EXHIBIT 2   Faculty Salaries 1991–92

	All Public Universities	*Cornell (Statutory)*	*All Private Universities*	*Cornell (Endowed)*
Full professor	$61,950	$63,400	$76,890	$74,900
Associate professor	45,090	49,800	51,700	52,000
Assistant professor	38,030	41,000	43,630	46,000

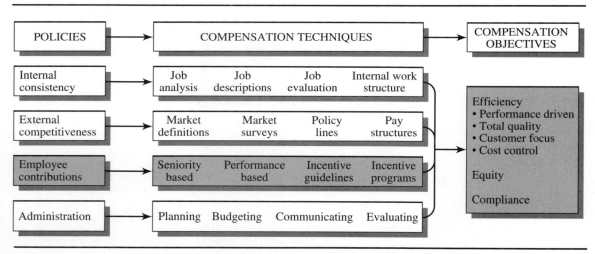

EXHIBIT III.1   The Pay Model

| POLICIES | COMPENSATION TECHNIQUES | COMPENSATION OBJECTIVES |

| Internal consistency | Job analysis | Job descriptions | Job evaluation | Internal work structure |

| External competitiveness | Market definitions | Market surveys | Policy lines | Pay structures |

| Employee contributions | Seniority based | Performance based | Incentive guidelines | Incentive programs |

| Administration | Planning | Budgeting | Communicating | Evaluating |

Efficiency
• Performance driven
• Total quality
• Customer focus
• Cost control

Equity

Compliance

PART III Employee Contributions: Determining Individual Pay

Thus far we have concentrated on two components of the pay model (Exhibit III.1). Internal consistency and the practices to ensure it—job analysis and job evaluation—provide guidance relating jobs to each other in terms of the content of the work and the relative contributions of the jobs to the organization's objectives. External competitiveness, or comparisons with the external labor market, raises issues of proper survey definitions, setting policy lines, and arriving at competitive pay levels and equitable pay structures. This part of the book deals with a third critical dimension of the pay system design and administration—paying individual employees performing the job.

How much should one employee be paid relative to another when they both hold the same jobs in the same organization? If this question is not answered satisfactorily, all prior efforts to evaluate and price jobs may have been in vain. For example, the compensation manager determines that all systems analysts should be paid between $28,000 and $36,000. But where in that range is each individual paid? Should a good performer be paid more than a poor performer? If the answer is yes, how should performance be measured and what should be the differential reward? Similarly, should the systems analyst with more years' experience (i.e., higher seniority) be paid more than a co-worker with less time on the job? Again, if the answer is yes, what is the trade-off between seniority and performance in assigning pay raises? As Exhibit III.1 suggests, all of these questions involve the concept of employee contribution. For the next three chapters we will be discussing different facets of employee contribution.

Chapter 8 considers how pay affects performance. In particular, two questions are addressed: First, *should* pay systems be designed to affect performance? Second, *can* pay systems be designed to affect performance? Many of the answers to these questions come from theories of motivation and empirical research evaluating strategies to motivate employees in the workplace.

Chapter 9 focuses on more subjective performance measurement systems and their relationship to compensation in general and pay increases in particular.

Chapter 10 looks at pay systems that attempt to increase productivity and lower costs. In these times of productivity stagnation, such incentive systems are becoming increasingly attractive to organizations.

Chapter Outline

The Little Red Hen: A Productivity Fable
Once upon a time there was a little red hen who scratched about the barnyard until she uncovered some grains of wheat. She turned to other workers on the farm and said: "If we plant this wheat, we'll have bread to eat. Who will help me plant it?"

"We never did that before," said the horse, who was the supervisor.

"I'm too busy," said the duck.

"I'd need complete training," said the pig.

"It's not in my job description," said the goose.

"Well, I'll do it myself," said the little red hen. And she did. The wheat grew tall and ripened into grain. "Who will help me reap the wheat?" asked the little red hen.

"Let's check the regulations first," said the horse.

"I'd lose my seniority," said the duck.

"I'm on my lunch break," said the goose.

"Out of my classification," said the pig.

"Then I will," said the little red hen, and she did.

At last it came time to bake the bread.

"Who will help me bake the bread?" asked the little red hen.

"That would be overtime for me," said the horse.

"I've got to run some errands," said the duck.

"I've never learned how," said the pig.

"If I'm to be the only helper, that's unfair," said the goose.

"Then I will," said the little red hen.

She baked five loaves and was ready to turn them in to the farmer when the other workers stepped up. They wanted to be sure the farmer knew it was a group project.

"It needs to be cleared by someone else," said the horse.

"I'm calling the shop steward," said the duck.

"I demand equal rights," yelled the goose.

"We'd better file a copy," said the pig.

But the little red hen turned in the loaves by herself. When it came time for the farmer to reward the effort, he gave one loaf to each worker.

"But I earned all the bread myself!" said the little red hen.

"I know," said the farmer, "but it takes too much paperwork to justify giving you all the bread. It's much easier to distribute it equally, and that way the others won't complain."

So the little red hen shared the bread, but her co-workers and the farmer wondered why she never baked any more. [From *Federal News Clip Sheet,* June 1979.]

The first seven chapters of this book focused on determining the worth of jobs, both from an organization's perspective (job evaluation) and in the eyes of competitors (salary surveys). The result typically is a salary range that leaves room for discretion to pay different amounts to incumbents of the same job. We shift, therefore, from the value of jobs to the value of people in jobs. Both issues influence pay. Some experts, though, argue that individual salary determination has greater potential to influence an organization's success than any of the prior chapter discussions of job worth and pay level for jobs.[1] Is this true? The answer probably depends on whether compensation, in the form of individual salary determination, can be used in motivating employees to achieve their potential. To unlock this potential, we first look at the different perspectives on what it takes to motivate employees.

COMPENSATION AND EMPLOYEE MOTIVATION

If compensation managers could discover why behavior occurs and why it is directed toward one of countless possible goals, considerable progress could be made in improving

---

[1]B. Gerhard and G. Milkovich, "Organizational Differences in Managerial Compensation and Financial Performance," *Academy of Management Journal* 33 (1990), pp. 663–91.

employee job performance. Consider, for example, two operatives who work side by side on an assembly line in an automotive plant. One of the workers makes the appropriate welds in a timely fashion as cars pass on the assembly line. The other expends considerable energy in finding ways to "beat the system": missing welds and welding coat hooks to internal parts of the car, which is discovered only when the owner complains about an "irritating rattle." Both of these employees work on the same line, with similar environments; each receives the same pay and works the same hours. Yet obviously the behavior of each is directed to entirely different goals.

Each of the theories discussed below sheds some light on this and countless other motivation problems experienced in the real world. The approach taken will be to discuss these theories as they may bear on job performance. Again, particular emphasis will be placed on the role pay assumes in the motivation-performance link.

Content Theories.   Content theories can be distinguished by their emphasis on *what* motivates people rather than *how* people are motivated. The key variable in most of these theories is different types of need. It has been speculated that psychologists have enumerated several hundred needs that are thought to motivate people.[2]

The two most well-known content theories are those by Maslow[3] and by Herzberg, Mausner, and Snyderman[4] (referred to as the *Herzberg Theory*). Maslow's theory is based on a hierarchy of five needs (Exhibit 8.1), each assumed to motivate behavior in varying degrees. Maslow argues that lower-level needs in the hierarchy are prepotent: People's behavior is directed toward satisfying their physiological needs and those of their families. After obtaining a job that ensures consistent satisfaction of that need, the security need becomes dominant. Behavior is then directed toward obtaining physical and emotional security. Higher-order needs become progressively more important as lower-order needs are satisfied.

One of the major problems with this approach is that it is extremely difficult to identify which needs are prepotent at any given time. Without this information, it is virtually impossible to determine how a work environment should be structured to improve performance. For example, research indicates that needs vary by age, geographic location (urban/rural), socioeconomic status, and gender, to name a few. There is even speculation that the needs of the general population have been shifting over time toward a greater concern for such higher-level needs as autonomy and self-actualization.[5]

In comparison, Herzberg's theory is very similar to Maslow's.[6] He argues that two types of factors are present across organizations: hygienes and motivators. Hygiene factors include such things as company policy and administration, supervision, salary,

---

[2]Edward Lawler III, *Pay and Organizational Effectiveness: A Psychological View* (New York: McGraw-Hill, 1971).

[3]Abraham Maslow, *Motivation and Personality* (New York: Harper & Row, 1954).

[4]F. Herzberg, B. Mausner, and B. Snyderman, *The Motivation to Work* (New York: John Wiley, 1959).

[5]Theodore Roszak, *The Making of a Counter Culture: Reflections on the Techno-Cratic Society and Its Youthful Opposition* (Garden City, N.Y.: Doubleday, 1969).

[6]Herzberg et al., *The Motivation to Work.*

EXHIBIT 8.1   Maslow's Hierarchy of Needs

1. Physiological needs	Need for food, water, and air
2. Safety needs	Need for security, stability, and the absence from pain, threat, or illness
3. Social needs	Need for affection, belongingness, love
4. Esteem needs	Need for personal feelings of achievement or self-esteem and also a need for recognition or respect from others
5. Self-actualization needs	Need to become all one is capable of becoming, to realize one's own potential or achieve self-fulfillment

---

interpersonal relations, and working conditions. Motivators are represented by opportunities for advancement, achievement, responsibility, and recognition. In essence, it might be argued that Maslow's theory has gravitated in the same direction as Herzberg's. If, in fact, most lower-order needs are generally satisfied in our affluent society, then individual needs that are prepotent in Maslow's framework include esteem and self-actualization.[7] As conceived by Maslow, these needs are very similar to Herzberg's conception of advancement, achievement, and recognition. Since these factors are prepotent, they assume responsibility for a great deal of the goal direction of individuals. In Herzberg's terms, they become the motivators, the factors that can lead to job satisfaction if met by the organization. The one major difference that can be inferred from these two theories is the function assumed by pay. As already indicated, numerous studies have shown that pay can serve to satisfy, to some extent, Maslow's needs. In contrast, Herzberg's work is often interpreted as if he argued that pay is solely a hygiene factor. Pay is necessary at sufficient levels to thwart job dissatisfaction, but it is not appropriate for motivating behavior. In fact, this assessment is not correct. Although Herzberg's theory can be attacked on a number of grounds, it is inappropriate to assume Herzberg relegated pay to the status of only a hygiene factor.[8] The original work by Herzberg also demonstrated that pay takes on significance as a source of satisfaction when it is perceived as a form of recognition or reward. In this context, pay provides feedback to an employee in the form of recognition for achievement.

It is apparent from this summary of content theories that pay can serve to satisfy needs and impact on motivation. This discussion, however, has been silent on the mechanism by which this occurs. In fact, this is a general criticism of content theories. Although it is apparent that pay can motivate behavior, one category of which is job performance, it is not at all clear *how* organizations can use pay to achieve this goal. In the following discussion of process theories of motivation, emphasis is placed on explaining the mechanisms that lead to motivation.

Process Theories.   Process theories of motivation focus on how people are motivated. They certainly recognize the role of content theories in examining the types of needs and

---

[7]Roszak, *The Making of a Counter Culture*.

[8]R. J. House and L. A. Wigdor, "Herzberg's Dual-Factor Theory of Job Satisfaction and Motivation: A Review of the Evidence and a Criticism," *Personnel Psychology* 20 (1967), pp. 369–90.

reinforcers that are part of the motivational process, but they also attempt to explain how this process operates.

In explaining how motivation operates, some theories prominently mention the importance of rewards, including compensation. Others, although presumably acknowledging some role for compensation, focus on other factors that affect individual motivation.

Operant conditioning theory and expectancy theory both grant a prominent role to rewards (e.g., compensation). Pay motivates job performance to the extent that merit increases and other work-related rewards are allocated on the basis of performance.

Much of the operant conditioning literature focuses on the types of reinforcement schedules that best motivate high performance. Do workers respond better when rewards are based on their individual performance, or when their work units' success is the major determinant of rewards? Is a continuous reinforcement schedule (after each performance unit) motivationally superior to a variable reinforcement schedule? A summary of these findings is included in Chapter 9.

Of even more interest to researchers over the past two decades has been the utility of the expectancy, or VIE, theory. VIE is an acronym for valence, instrumentality, and expectancy. Borrowing from earlier works,[9] Campbell and Pritchard present an excellent composite picture of the variables important in a VIE model.[10] Exhibit 8.2 summarizes this model.

The key variable to be explained in this model is effort level. According to Exhibit 8.2, effort level depends on three factors: (1) expectancy, (2) valence, and (3) instrumentality. *Expectancy* is viewed as a subjective probability estimate made by an individual as to whether a specific level of effort will result in task accomplishment. For example, if you were to have a test on the subject matter of this chapter tomorrow, what do you think the probability of getting an A would be if you studied hard for five hours tonight? In an organizational context, employees would assess whether or not they could accomplish specific assignments made by their supervisor. These probabilities are assessed in numbers between .00 and 1.00. As the probability of a goal accomplishment rises (approaches 1.00), the probability of expending a specific amount of effort rises.

The second factor in the model is *goal valence*. How much does an individual value (i.e., what is the anticipated satisfaction from) task accomplishment? To link Maslow's hierarchy of needs with this model, a task that satisfies a need that is prepotent would have a relatively high valence. Carrying the earlier illustration further, if you did not place a high value on earning an A in tomorrow's exam, even though it was within your capability (i.e., high expectancy), you would be less likely to expend the necessary effort. From an individual's perspective in an organization, consider a reward of a promotion offered for successful accomplishment of a lengthy and difficult task. Most supervisors

---

[9]V. H. Vroom, *Work in Motivation* (New York: John Wiley, 1964); G. Graen, "Instrumentality Theory of Work Motivation: Some Experimental Results and Suggested Modifications," *Journal of Applied Psychology* 53, no. 2 (1969), pp. 1–25; L. W. Porter and E. E. Lawler III, *Managerial Attitudes and Performance* (Chicago, Ill.: Dorsey Press, 1968); John P. Campbell and Robert Pritchard, "Motivation Theory in Industrial and Organizational Psychology, in *Handbook of Industrial and Organizational Psychology,* ed. Marvin Dunnette (Chicago: Rand McNally, 1976), pp. 63–130.

[10]Campbell and Pritchard, "Motivation Theory."

Exhibit 8.2   A Composite Expectancy-Valence Model

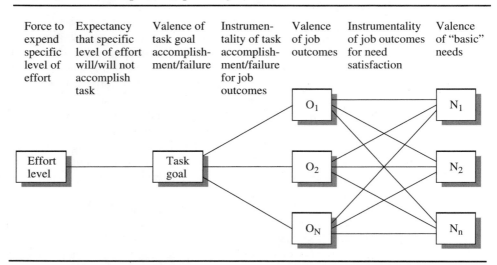

| Force to expend specific level of effort | Expectancy that specific level of effort will/will not accomplish task | Valence of task goal accomplishment/failure | Instrumentality of task accomplishment/failure for job outcomes | Valence of job outcomes | Instrumentality of job outcomes for need satisfaction | Valence of "basic" needs |

NOTE: For purposes of simplicity, this schematic portrays only one level of effort and one level of success on one task goal. A similar set of relationships exists for alternative levels of effort and alternative tasks or alternative levels of success.

SOURCE: John P. Campbell and Robert Pritchard, "Motivation Theory in Industrial and Organizational Psychology," in *Handbook of Industrial and Organizational Psychology*, ed. Marvin Dunnette (Chicago: Rand McNally, 1976). Copyright © 1976, Marvin D. Dunnette. Reprinted by permission of John Wiley & Sons, Inc.

offering this promotion would assume that subordinates would value highly this type of reward. Some employees, though, are content with their existing job responsibilities and do not want to assume more job responsibility. The low valence attached to this reward may lead to lower effort expenditure, a disappointment to supervisors who assume that their employees hold consistent values.

Normally, completion of a task is not considered to have value in and of itself. In one sense, this is correct. Most people associate work in organizations with the rewards that can be obtained from successful completion of that task. Actually, though, a reasonably large body of literature indicates that tasks can offer intrinsic rewards that occur simply because of performance and completion of the tasks.[11] So a task goal can have a valence attached to it. More traditionally, though, people think about the rewards that result from task accomplishment, the so-called extrinsic rewards (e.g., pay, promotion) because they are outcomes resulting from performance of the task. It is in this linkage

[11] See, for example, McNaly Csikszentmihalyi, "Play and Intrinsic Rewards," *Journal of Humanistic Psychology* 4 (1979), pp. 16–22; A. Bandura, *Social Learning Theory* (Englewood Cliffs, N.J.: Prentice Hall, 1977); E. Deci, "Notes on the Theory and Metatheory of Intrinsic Motivation," *Organizational Behavior and Human Performance* 15 (1975), pp. 130–45.

in which the third component, *instrumentality,* becomes important. Assuming that an employee accomplishes a task, what is the probability that a desired outcome or reward will result? If it is estimated that the subjective probability of obtaining a reward given task accomplishment is 1.00, then an employee is more likely to expend the necessary effort to start this sequence in motion. Instrumentality, as was true for expectancy, is expressed as a subjective probability varying between .00 and 1.00. Carrying the example with the test grade one step further, students might attempt to estimate the probability that earning an A on an exam tomorrow will result in an A for the entire course. Or, going even further, they might estimate the probability that obtaining an A in this course will lead to a good job offer. It is not a coincidence, for example, that finance majors probably expend more effort on obtaining As in their finance courses. They view these courses as more relevant to their chosen career goals. When students talk about course relevance in this context, they are expressing judgments that are considered instrumentalities in this model.

You will notice that the model in Exhibit 8.2 carries the idea of valences and instrumentalities out beyond the first-level outcomes and their attached valences. In fact, this is a reasonable expression of reality that also portrays the role of pay in this model as it affects motivation. As Opsahl and Dunnette have noted, pay can serve as an *instrument* (this term is derived from the word *instrumentality* taken from the model).[12] Consider the manager who obtains a pay raise for an employee who performs well. By itself, the pay raise may have no value. However, it can have a high instrumentality. Pay can be used to purchase goods that have a high valence. Given sufficient money, the subjective probability that money can be used to buy a wide variety of desired goods is quite high (i.e., high instrumentality).

Note: This chain of events was triggered by a manager who established the pay-for-performance link. At least from an employee's perspective, *pay for performance* is partially an issue of instrumentality: "If I perform at the *desired* level considered excellent by my company, what is the probability I will be rewarded in turn with a corresponding pay increase?" Involved in this question is whether or not the company is viewed as paying for performance (i.e., allocating pay raises differentially to employees based on level of performance). This is just one of several questions that will be addressed after discussing the last two theories relevant to the pay-for-performance issue.

Equity Theory. There has been some question about whether this theory is really a distinct theory or whether it can be subsumed under VIE theory.[13] Since equity theory plays such an important role in compensation, though, separate discussion is included here.

---

[12]R. L. Opsahl and M. D. Dunnette, "The Role of Financial Compensation in Industrial Motivation," *Psychological Bulletin* 66 (1966), pp. 94–118.

[13]Lawler, *Pay and Organizational Effectiveness;* Campbell and Pritchard, "Motivation Theory."

Although a number of models deal with the equity concept, two have generated sufficient research or intriguing potential to warrant discussion.[14] Adams argues that individuals compare their inputs and outcomes to those of some relevant other person in determining whether they are equitably (fairly) treated.[15] Stated another way, the comparison process can be expressed as a comparison of ratios:

$$O_p/I_p \text{ compared to } O_o/I_o$$

where

O_p, O_o = Outcomes of person (p) or other (o)

I_p, I_o = Inputs of person (p) or other (o)

This model suggests that people compare the rewards they receive, relative to the inputs they must make to receive those rewards, to the same ratio for some relevant other. If the two ratios are not equal, the consequence is motivation to reduce the "perceived" inequity. A key in this explanation is the word *perceived*. The inequity could result because some individuals evaluate and classify as inputs and outcomes factors that other individuals might consider irrelevant. For example, a physically attractive salesperson might consider attractiveness a relevant input and expect to be compensated more than a less attractive individual, other things being equal. Yet the organization may consider this an irrelevant input, pay the two individuals equally, and never realize that the person views such pay as an inequitable exchange. Correspondingly, a supervisor might evaluate an outcome that a subordinate is not even aware exists as relevant. As an example, consider a supervisor who keeps a particular employee informed of information about company activities affecting the employee's job. Potentially, the supervisor could view this as a reward, treating the subordinate as a member of the "in" group, privy to information not disseminated to other subordinates.[16] If this is not perceived as a reward by the subordinate, although the supervisor views it as a reward for above-average performance, feelings of inequity may result.

The impact that inequity may have on motivation and subsequent performance is pointed out by Adams.[17] Granted, inequity is viewed in this theory as a source of motivation. However, the consequences do not necessarily bode well for improved performance. As Adams notes, people can (1) cognitively distort their or another's inputs

---

[14]G. C. Homans, *Social Behavior: Its Elementary Forms* (New York: Harcourt Brace Jovanovich, 1961); E. Jaques, *Equitable Payment* (New York: John Wiley, 1961); M. Patchen, *The Choice of Wage Comparisons* (Englewood Cliffs, N.J.: Prentice Hall, 1961); J. S. Adams, "Wage Inequities, Productivity, and Work Quality," *Industrial Relations* 3, no. 1 (1963), pp. 9–16, and "Injustices in Social Exchange," in *Advances in Experimental Social Psychology*, vol. 2, ed. L. Berkowitz (New York: Academic Press, 1965), pp. 267–99.

[15]Ibid.

[16]Fred Dansereau, G. Graen, and W. Haga, "A Vertical Dyad Linkage Approach to Leadership within Formal Organizations: A Longitudinal Investigation of the Role Making Process," *Organizational Behavior and Human Performance* 13 (1975), pp. 46–70.

[17]Adams, "Injustices in Social Exchange."

and/or outcomes, (2) attempt to change their or another's inputs and/or outcomes, (3) change the comparison person, or (4) reduce their involvement in the exchange relationship. Several of these consequences have negative implications for performance. For example, consider a union that represents all blue collar workers in a firm. If non-unionized clerical workers do not receive raises commensurate with those obtained by unionized workers, one possible outcome could be efforts by clerical workers to form their own union. This is particularly true if clerical workers use the unionized blue collar workers as relevant others and perceive that rewards for the two groups are out of balance, given inputs. In this case, disgruntled clerical workers could view unionization as a way to improve outcomes and reestablish equity.[18]

The role money plays in equity theory is quite evident. Money is only one of many outcomes that are evaluated in the exchange relationship. But since money is one of the most visible components, and frequently one of the easiest to modify, it becomes extremely important.

The second equity model of interest here was formulated by Elliot Jaques.[19] From Jaques's perspective, feelings of inequity do not depend on the existence of a relevant other whose ratio of input to outcomes differs from the target person's ratio. Rather, Jaques suggests that the relevant equity comparison is an internal standard. Presumably, individuals have some internal standard of fairness based on accumulated past experiences against which current conditions are compared to determine fairness of, for example, current pay. From a compensation administrator's perspective, this can cause problems. A well-constructed and administered job evaluation system may reduce feelings of inequity in comparison with what other persons in the company may be receiving. If an internal standard is employed, however, any experiences in other organizations become relevant. This requires a compensation administrator to be equitable with respect to practices of other organizations. (*Note:* Adams's equity theory does not preclude a relevant other who is external to the organization. Consequently, the same implications could be inferred for this theory. However, it has been speculated that the relevant other is more likely to be a coworker than someone outside the firm.)

Most of the research relating equity theory to performance has stimulated inequity by either underpaying or overpaying individuals for tasks and then recording the impact on performance. At best the research has had mixed support.[20]

Social Information Processing Theory.   Recall that need theories focus on internally generated needs. People behave in ways to lessen needs. Social information processing (SIP) theory counters need theory by focusing not on internal, but rather on external,

---

[18]Chris Berger, Craig Olson, and John Boudreau, "The Effects of Unions on Work Values, Perceived Rewards, and Job Satisfaction," Paper presented at the National Academy of Management meetings, August 1980.

[19]Jaques, *Equitable Payment.*

[20]L. Dyer and D. Schwab, "Personnel/Human Resources Management Research," in K. Rowland and G. Ferris, eds., *Research in Personnel and Human Resources Management* (Greenwich, Conn.: JAI Press), pp. 7–30.

factors that motivate performance.[21] According to SIP theory, workers pay attention to environmental cues (e.g., performance levels of coworkers, goals imposed by supervisors) by cognitively processing this information in a way that may alter personal work goals, expectancies, and perceptions of equity.[22] In turn, this influences job attitudes, behavior, and performance. By far the strongest evidence that external factors influence motivation comes from the goal-setting research of Locke and associates.[23] A review of this literature indicates that the vast majority of studies on goal setting find a positive impact of goal setting on performance. Workers assigned "hard" goals consistently do better than workers told to "do your best."[24]

Notice that nothing in this discussion of SIP theory has suggested a role for compensation in the motivational process. Part of the reason may be that researchers are divided on whether compensation has additive, interactive, or independent influences on goal setting. Locke and associates suggest that pay affects performance only by affecting the level of goals or individual commitment to achieving goals already established.[25] A second perspective views goal setting and compensation as independent.[26] Positive, or negative, influences of goal setting or compensation on performance are not enhanced or diminished by their joint presence. Countering this argument of independence, a third line of research argues that the joint presence of incentives and goal-setting conditions has a negative effect on performance.[27] Perhaps the best summary, though, is to admit that we still do not know enough about the motivational and cognitive processes that lead goal setting and compensation to trigger higher performance.[28] The next section explores this relationship between pay and performance.

PAY FOR PERFORMANCE: THE POSITIVE EVIDENCE

"Is pay the answer?" Can employee motivation and performance be affected by devising different pay strategies? The answer to this question depends on the answer to three subquestions: (1) Is money important to individuals? (2) Do people believe pay increases should be based on performance? (3) Do companies tie pay to performance so that performance improves?

---

[21]Terence R. Mitchell, Miriam Rothman, and Robert C. Liden, "Effects of Normative Information on Task Performance," *Journal of Applied Psychology* 70, no. 1 (1985), pp. 48–55.

[22]Ibid.

[23]Edwin A. Locke, Karyll N. Shaw, Lise M. Saari, and Gary P. Latham, "Goal Setting and Task Performance: 1969–1980," *Psychological Bulletin* 90 (1981), pp. 125–52.

[24]Ibid.

[25]Locke et al., "Goal Setting and Task Performance."

[26]R. D. Pritchard and M. I. Curtis, "The Influence of Goal Setting and Financial Incentives on Task Performance," *Organizational Behavior and Human Performance* 10 (1973), pp. 175–83; J. R. Terborg and H. E. Miller, "Motivation, Behavior, and Performance: A Closer Examination of Goal Setting and Monetary Incentives," *Journal of Applied Psychology* 63 (1978), pp. 29–39.

[27]J. Mowen, R. Middlemist, and D. Luther, "Joint Effects of Assigned Goal Level and Incentive Structure on Task Performance: A Laboratory Study," *Journal of Applied Psychology* 61 (1981), pp. 598–603.

[28]Donald J. Campbell, "The Effects of Goal-Contingent Payment on the Performance of a Complex Task," *Personnel Psychology* 37 (1984), pp. 23–40.

Is Money Important to Individuals?

Some evidence indicates that employers may place too much reliance on money as a reward for performance. In one study, applicants rated salary only ninth of 18 different types of rewards affecting job attractiveness.[29] Compounding this problem, evidence indicates that when applicants become employees, managers overestimate the importance of pay to them.[30] By attaching too much importance to money as a motivator, supervisors may become disillusioned when money fails to motivate better performance. This failure results in a general condemnation of pay as a motivator. In reality, however, it may be more advantageous not to view money as the supreme motivator, but rather as one of the numerous factors in the work environment that affect employee motivation.

For example, it appears that one of the other factors affecting employee motivation is *the way that rewards are distributed*. There is strong evidence that employees are concerned not only about fairness in the amount of rewards they receive (distributive justice), but also in the means used to distribute those rewards (procedural justice).[31] Employees who perceive that they are being treated fairly in the way rewards are distributed (as opposed to the actual amount they receive) exhibit more trust in their supervisors and greater commitment to their organization.[32] Making efforts to allocate rewards in ways that are perceived as being fair seems to have positive payoffs! When we discuss design of compensation systems at the end of this chapter, we will discuss in greater detail ways to be fair.

Should Pay Increases Be Based on Performance?

Given that money can satisfy at least a subset of basic needs, the question now becomes whether salary increases should be based on level of performance. Substantial evidence exists that management and workers alike believe pay should be tied to performance.

Dyer et al. asked 180 managers from 72 different companies to rate nine possible factors in terms of the importance they should receive in determining size of salary increases.[33] As Exhibit 8.3 indicates, workers believed that the most important factor for salary increases should be job performance. Following close behind is a factor that presumably would be picked up in job evaluation (nature of job) and a motivational variable (amount of effort expended).

---

[29]Barry Posner, "Comparing Recruiter, Student, and Faculty Perceptions of Important Applicant Job Characteristics," *Personnel Psychology* 34 (1981), pp. 329–37.

[30]F. A. Heller and L. W. Porter, "Perceptions of Managerial Needs and Skills in Two National Samples," *Occupational Psychology* 40 (1966), pp. 1–13.

[31]Robert Folger and Mary Konovsky, "Effects of Procedural and Distributive Justice on Reactions to Pay Raise Decisions," *Academy of Management Journal* 32 (1989), pp. 115–30; Jerald Greenberg, "A Taxonomy of Organizational Justice Theories," *Academy of Management Review* 12, no. 1 (1987), pp. 9–12.

[32]Folger and Konovsky, "Effects of Procedural and Distributive Justice on Reactions to Pay Raise Decisions," *Academy of Management Journal* 32 (1989), pp. 115–130; G. Greenberg, "Reactions to Procedural Injustice in Payment Distributions: Do the Means Justify the Ends?" *Journal of Applied Psychology* 72 (1987), pp. 55–61.

[33]L. Dyer, D. P. Schwab, and R. D. Theriault, "Managerial Perceptions Regarding Salary Increase Criteria," *Personnel Psychology* 29 (1976), pp. 233–42.

EXHIBIT 8.3   **Mean Ratings of Criteria That *Should Be* Used to Determine Size of Salary Increases**

Criteria	Mean Rating
1. Level of job performance	6.23
2. Nature of job	5.91
3. Amount of effort expenditure	5.56
4. Cost of living	5.21
5. Training and experience	5.15
6. Increases outside organization	4.64
7. Budgetary considerations	4.53
8. Increases inside organization	3.69
9. Length of service	3.31

SOURCE: L. Dyer, D. P. Schwab, and R. D. Theriault, "Managerial Perceptions Regarding Salary Increase Criteria," *Personnel Psychology* 29 (1976), pp. 233–42. © 1976, Personnel Psychology, Inc.

Two other studies support these findings.[34] Both college students and a second group of managers ranked job performance as the most important variable in allocating pay raises. Once we move away from the managerial ranks, however, other groups express a different view of the pay-performance link. The role that performance levels should assume in determining pay increases is less clear-cut for blue collar workers.[35] As an illustration, consider the frequent opposition to compensation plans that are based on performance (i.e., incentive piece-rate systems). Unionized workers prefer seniority rather than performance as a basis for pay increases.[36] Part of this preference may stem from a distrust of subjective performance measurement systems. Unions ask, "Can management be counted on to be fair?" In contrast, seniority is an objective index for calculating increases. Some evidence also suggests that women might prefer allocation methods not based on performance.[37]

Finally, we have to ask the question whether merit pay should be a fixture in organizations in which cooperation and team participation are stressed. Does merit pay breed intragroup rivalries, so that efforts to build team cohesion may be subverted? At least one study raises such fears. Employees who worry that merit pay may increase

[34]John Fossum and Mary Fitch, "The Effects of Individual and Contextual Attributes on the Sizes of Recommended Salary Increases," *Personnel Psychology* 38 (1985), pp. 587–603; F. Hills, K. Scott, S. Markham, and M. Vest, "Merit Pay: Just or Unjust Desserts," *Personnel Psychology* 32, no. 9 (1987), pp. 53–59.

[35]Opinion Research Corporation, *Wage Incentives* (Princeton, N.J.: Opinion Research Corporation, 1946), and *Productivity from the Worker's Standpoint* (Princeton, N.J.: Opinion Research Corporation, 1949); L. V. Jones and T. E. Jeffrey, "A Quantitative Analysis of Expressed Preferences for Compensation Plans," *Journal of Applied Psychology* 48 (1963), pp. 201–10.

[36]D. Koys, T. Keaveny, and R. Allen, "Employment Demographics and Attitudes that Predict Preferences for Alternative Pay Increase Policies," *Journal of Business and Psychology* 4 (1989), pp. 27–47.

[37]B. Major, "Gender, Justice and the Psychology of Entitlement," *Review of Personality and Social Psychology* 7 (1988), pp. 124–48.

competition and reduce cooperation believe that increases *should not* be tied to performance.[38]

Much of the discontent with performance-based plans may be a reaction to the specific type of plan and the way it is administered. Often opposition to incentive pay arises because employees believe that they cannot trust the company to administer incentive schemes properly.[39] From these data, it appears that there is some belief among *employees* that pay should be based on performance, particularly if the company can be trusted to administer the performance-based plan effectively.

From an organization's perspective, we can ask the same question: *Should* pay be based on performance? Assume that a company does tie pay to performance. What are the payoffs? One school of thought argues that designing reward systems to meet employee expectations can increase job satisfaction.[40] In turn, this increase in job satisfaction may lower both absenteeism and turnover, and increase job performance. Estimates place the savings to a company from an increase of just one half of a standard deviation in job satisfaction at more than $25,000 in today's dollars.[41]

Do workers, in fact, perform better when they receive pay tied to level of performance? No less authority than the church believes so! Starting in 1986, priests at the Episcopal Church of Newark were paid according to performance. Raises were awarded when parish growth occurred and when the priests gave high-quality sermons. Are there any hard data to support this belief in pay for performance?

Numerous studies indicate that tying pay to performance has a positive impact on employee performance.[42] Unfortunately, many of these studies are flawed. For example, to argue that the link between pay and performance is important, it seems crucial to determine whether performance improves (declines) after this link is established (eliminated). One review of pay-for-performance studies indicated that only 6 of 22 studies looked at performance levels subsequent to the implementation or removal of a merit pay plan.[43] On the encouraging side, though, 4 of these research efforts concluded that pay for performance works.

---

[38]Koys et al., "Employment Demographics."

[39]Lawler, *Pay and Organizational Effectiveness,* p. 61.

[40]Edward Lawler, "Pay for Performance: A Strategic Analysis," in L. R. Gomez-Mejia, ed., *Compensation and Benefits* (Washington, D.C.: Bureau of National Affairs, 1989).

[41]Philip Miruis and Edward Lawler, "Measuring the Financial Impact of Employee Attitudes," *Journal of Applied Psychology* 62, no. 1 (1977), pp. 1–8.

[42]George Green, "Instrumentality Theory of Work Motivation," *Journal of Applied Psychology* 53, no. 2 (1965), pp. 1–25; L. Porter and E. Lawler, "Managerial Attitudes"; D. P. Schwab and L. Dyer, "The Motivational Impact of a Compensation System on Employee Performance," *Organizational Behavior and Human Performance* 9 (1973), pp. 215–25; R. D. Pritchard, D. W. Leonard, C. W. Von Bergen, Jr., and R. J. Kirk, "The Effects of Varying Schedules of Reinforcement on Human Task Performance," *Organizational Behavior and Human Performance* 16 (1976), pp. 205–30; Donald Schwab, "Impact of Alternative Compensation Systems on Pay Valence and Instrumentality Perceptions," *Journal of Applied Psychology* 58 (1973), pp. 308–12.

[43]R. Heneman, "Merit Pay Research," *Research in Personnel and Human Resource Management* 8 (1990), pp. 203–63.

One recent article summarizes the reasons that a company should pay for performance as follows.[44] First, money can serve as an effective motivator of performance for employees. Following from this motivation increase, a good merit program tying pay to performance will then improve productivity, reduce costs, and increase competitiveness.[45] Second, superior employees resent automatic increases. As in the example of the Little Red Hen in the beginning of this chapter, working harder than other workers for the same level of rewards is not very satisfying and may result in reduced performance. Third, development of a good pay-for-performance program requires the company to spell out exactly what is expected of employees. Knowing what is expected and how it relates to the success of the organization gives employees a better sense of ownership and involvement in the mission of the company.

Do Companies Tie Pay to Performance So That Performance Improves?

The vast majority of firms claim that they base their pay on performance.[46] Two recent polls consistently found that about 90 percent of large public and private sector organizations claim to have at least a portion of their compensation designed to tie pay to performance.[47] Another survey reported that 23 of 50 states and 13 of 24 foreign countries in the Organization for Economic Cooperation and Development have adopted pay-for-performance systems.[48] Even nonprofit organizations are interested in such programs, with 34 percent claiming to have pay-for-performance components in their compensation package.[49] This is up from just 10 percent of the nonprofit firms professing to have pay-for-performance components only five years earlier!

Even though companies in increasing numbers report that they tie pay to performance, many admit that they do not do it very well![50] This leads us to the more pessimistic side of the pay-for-performance question.

PAY FOR PERFORMANCE: THE NEGATIVE EVIDENCE

Perhaps the biggest movement toward a pay-for-performance system was mandated by the Civil Service Reform Act of 1978. This act required that 50 percent of any pay

---

[44]Thomas Rollins, "Pay for Performance: Is It Worth the Trouble?" *Personnel Administrator* 33, no. 5 (1988), pp. 42–47.

[45]Frederick W. Cook & Co., "Improving Merit Pay Effectivness," Compensation Conference, The Conference Board, 1988.

[46]Bruce R. Ellig, *Executive Compensation: A Total Pay Perspective* (New York: McGraw-Hill, 1982); Edward E. Lawler, *Pay and Organizational Development* (Reading, Mass.: Addison-Wesley, 1981).

[47]Laurie Hays, "All Eyes on DuPont's Incentive Pay Plan," *The Wall Street Journal,* December 5, 1988, p. B1; Compflash, "Dramatic Growth in Use of Incentives Attributed to Global Competition," *Compflash* 88, no. 11 (1988), p. 1.

[48]Government Accounting Office, *Pay for Performance: State and International Public Sector Pay-for-Performance Systems* (Washington, D.C.: GAO, 1990).

[49]Ibid.

[50]A. Bennett, "Paying Workers to Meet Goals Spreads, but Gauging Performance Proves Tough," *The Wall Street Journal,* September 10, 1991, p. B1.

increase was to be automatic, and that the remaining 50 percent was to be performance based. Here was an excellent opportunity to determine whether basing pay on performance (in part) would lead to improvements in productivity. One study of managers in the Social Security Administration, an agency covered by the act, found that merit pay had no impact on organizational performance.[51] Using a combination of objective (e.g., average number of days to pay certain claims) and subjective performance measures, there were no significant effects on performance from going to a merit pay system. Findings in the public sector are not entirely clear-cut, though. Another government project under the Civil Service Reform Act reported improvements in both perceptions of fairness and perceptions of a strengthened link between pay and performance when a pay-for-performance system was implemented in four Navy labs.[52]

Two other recent studies also portray a gloomy outlook for firms trying to implement pay-for-performance components. One survey of 16 organizations found 76 percent of employees receiving raises within 2 percent (above or below) of the budget.[53] Little differentiation in actual raises occurs, even though firms report a policy of paying for performance.[54] A closer look at the distribution of performance ratings in one company illustrates one major reason that pay for performance may not always be successful. Over a three-year period, a team of researchers traced the performance ratings of 800 employees in a large West Coast transit organization.[55] Ninety-eight percent of the time—over three different rating periods—employees were rated as *average or better* (3,510 ratings of 3,561). Despite the best of intentions, pay-for-performance systems may not work. In this example, either the vast majority of employees were average or better (which is statistically unlikely), or supervisors were not making the tough decisions to give poor performers the ratings they deserved. This highlights what some experts contend is a major problem with research on pay for performance: most of the evidence arguing against a pay-for-performance system is based on problems in implementing the system.[56] Unfortunately, eliminating some of these road blocks poses a serious problem. As examples consider the following.[57] First, it appears, as we have already noted, that supervisors

[51]Jane L. Pearce, William B. Stevenson, and James L. Perry, "Managerial Compensation Based on Organizational Performance: A Time Series Analysis of the Effects of Merit Pay," *Academy of Management Journal* 28, no. 2 (1985), pp. 261–78.

[52]U.S. Office of Personnel Management, *Results of Title VI Demonstration Projects: Implications for Performance Management and Pay-for-Performance* (Washington, D.C.: U. S. Office of Personnel Management, 1991).

[53]Kenneth Teel, "Are Merit Raises Really Based on Merit?" *Personnel Journal,* March 1986, pp. 88–92.

[54]G. Milkovich and A. Wigdor, eds., *Pay and Performance: Evaluating Performance Appraisal and Merit Pay* (Washington, D.C.: National Academy Press, 1991).

[55]Hills et al., "Merit Pay: Just or Unjust Desserts."

[56]Clay W. Hamner, "How to Ruin Motivation with Pay," *Compensation Review,* Third Quarter 1975, pp. 88–98; Herbert H. Meyer, "The Pay-for-Performance Dilemma," *Organizational Dynamics,* Winter 1975, pp. 71–78; CompFlash, "Companies Praise Pay-for-Performance Programs."

[57]Cook & Co., "Improving Merit Pay Effectiveness"; Rollins, "Pay for Performance: Is It Worth the Trouble?"

find it difficult to make the tough rating choices and give poor evaluations when they are deserved. Second, even if managers were willing to make the tough decisions, many appraisal forms require fine distinctions in performance levels that may be difficult for managers to understand and use. Third, even in companies that embrace the pay-for-performance concept, cost controls and modest budget increases make it difficult to reward outstanding employees. Fourth, the way appraisals are timed almost guarantees a large time gap (sometimes as long as a year) between performance and the reward supposedly linked to it. Any basic psychology book tells us that effective reinforcement of behavior should occur as soon after the behavior occurs as possible. Otherwise, the reinforcement value diminishes. Fifth, even when the pay-for-performance link is actually strong, perception by employees may not match the objective reality.[58] Finally, some people argue that the idea of rewarding individual performance may run contrary to organizational needs for group cohesiveness. Emphasis on individuals, the key to merit pay plans, may foster independence and lessen the motivation to help and work with others.

The next section of this chapter looks at ways to improve the chances that a pay-for-performance system will work. This involves both general issues in designing a performance measurement system and in designing the corresponding compensation system.

MEASURING AND PAYING FOR PERFORMANCE: DESIGN ISSUES

According to the pay model developed in Chapter 1, we should have three objectives in designing compensation systems to measure employee contributions. First, the system must be efficient. The design should contribute to improved productivity and savings in labor costs. In large part this objective is the focus of Chapter 10 where we discuss the different types of alternative reward systems and their impacts on productivity/labor costs. The second objective in designing the system concerns compliance with legal requirements. Chapter 13 and 14 deal specifically with this objective. In this section, we deal with the third objective of the compensation system: making sure it is equitable or fair.

Two types of fairness are concerns for employees. The first type is fairness in the amount that is distributed to employees. Not surprisingly, this type of fairness is labeled *distributive justice*.[59] Does an employee view the amount of compensation received as fair? As we discussed earlier in the section on equity theory, perceptions of fairness here depend on the amount of compensation actually received relative to inputs (e.g., productivity) compared against some relevant standard. Notice that several of the components of this equity equation are frustratingly removed from the control of the typical supervisor or manager working with employees. A manager has little influence over the size of an employee's pay check. Rather, our take-home pay is influenced to a large degree by external market conditions, pay policy decisions of the organization, and the occupational

---

[58]R. Heneman, D. Greenberger, and S. Strasser, "The Relationship between Pay-for-Performance Perceptions and Pay Satisfaction," *Personnel Psychology* 41 (1988), pp. 745–59.

[59]John Thibaut and Laurens Walker, *Procedural Justice: A Psychological View* (New York: John Wiley, 1975).

EXHIBIT 8.4 Stages in Measuring and Paying for Performance

Establish performance standards and reward allocation norms	$\rightarrow$	Collect performance data	$\rightarrow$	Determine how to allocate: When and how much	$\rightarrow$	Implement appeals mechanism	$\rightarrow$	Communicate allocations

---

choice we make. Even decisions about how much of a pay increase to give are typically constrained by budget limitations. Managers do have somewhat more control, though, over the second type of equity. Employees are also concerned about the fairness of *procedures* used to determine the amount of rewards they receive; they expect *procedural justice*. Evidence suggests that organizations that use fair procedures and supervisors who are viewed as fair in the means they use to allocate rewards are perceived as more trustworthy and command higher levels of commitment.[60] Some research even suggests that employee satisfaction with pay may depend more on the procedures used to determine pay than on the actual level distributed![61] This concern for fairness in procedures is something that organizations and supervisors can directly influence in a cost-effective way. For the remainder of this chapter, we outline the stages in measuring performance and subsequently determining compensation (see Exhibit 8.4). Issues of procedural fairness or justice for each of the stages are considered.

These stages correspond to the sequence of events most people might expect to occur in the appraisal and reward process. The first stage includes developing performance standards or expectations. What will be expected of workers for satisfactory or higher performance? Will rewards be allocated on the basis of that performance or on some other basis (e.g., allocate the same amount to each employee regardless of performance). Once the standards and allocation norms are determined, decisions are made about how much performance data will be collected and how they will be collected. These performance data are then used in the actual appraisal and both are input to a final appraisal rating for each employee. Following this, the organization must decide when compensation increases will be given and how much they will be. Any employee complaints about the level of rewards or process used should go to some form of appeals board. Finally, policies and procedures are established to communicate how this entire process operates. Each of these stages can add to or subtact from perceptions of procedural fairness.

Establishing Performance Standards and Reward Allocation Norms

Performance Standards. Based on research from a number of different areas, there appear to be at least four rules for making sure that performance standards are perceived as fair. First, the standards should represent all the concerns of the employees to be

---

[60]Folger and Konovsky, "Effects of Procedural and Distributive Justice on Reactions to Pay Raise Decisions."

[61]S. Alexander and M. Ruderman, "The Role of Procedural and Distributive Justice in Organizational Behavior," *Social Justice Research* 1 (1987), pp. 177–98.

evaluated later.[62] One major task to ensure that employee concerns are covered is to make sure that an updated job description is used as the foundation for deciding what performance dimensions should be measured. Second, the level of performance on each dimension should not be so hard as to be viewed as impossible. Apparently, though, employees will accept as fair those standards that are challenging.[63] Third, employees should participate in forming the performance standards.[64] Finally, employees perceive the whole process as fairer when they are informed about the standard early during the rating time period rather than at some later point.

Allocation Norms.   What does an employee get in return for meeting performance expectations? Rules for allocating rewards need to be spelled out. Exhibit 8.5 identifies five allocation rules and gives examples of what they entail. The natural inclination is to assume that the size of an increase will depend on how well an employee performs. Better performers receive larger increases. We know, though, that companies do not always pay for performance.

Apparently each of these five rules is used under different circumstances. The equity rule, not surprisingly, is used most frequently when the organization is committed to paying for performance and achieving increased productivity.[65] The equality rule is more appropriate when social harmony is an important outcome, that is, when a company needs

---

EXHIBIT 8.5   Rules for Allocation of Rewards

Rule	Example
1. Equity rule	Salary increases based on inputs (performance)
2. Equality rule	All receive the same increase regardless of performance (across-the-board increases)
3. Reciprocity rule	Golden rule (treat others as you would like to be treated)
4. Need rule	More to those with greater need
5. Contract rule	Allocate according to prior agreements

SOURCE: Adapted from Gerald Leventhal, " The Distribution of Rewards and Resources in Groups and Organizations," in *Equity Theory: Toward a General Theory of Social Interaction,* eds. Leonard Berkowitz and Elaine Walster, Advances in Experimental Social Psychology, volume 9 (New York: Academic Press, 1976), pp. 92–131.

---

[62]G. S. Leventhal, "Fairness in Social Relationships," in *Contemporary Topics in Social Psychology,* ed. J. W. Thibaut, J. G. Spence, and R. C. Carson (Morristown, N.J.: General Learning Press, 1976), pp. 211–39.

[63]Locke et al., "Goal Setting and Task Performance."

[64]Hamner, "How to Ruin Motivation with Pay"; Nathan B. Winstanley, "Are Merit Increases Really Effective?" *Personnel Administrator* 4 (1982), pp. 23–31; Robert H. Rock, "Pay-for-Performance: Accent on Standards and Measures," *Compensation Review* 16, no. 3 (1984), pp. 15–23.

[65]Jerald Greenberg, "Looking Fair vs. Being Fair: Managing Impressions of Organizational Justice," in *Research in Organizational Behavior,* vol. 12, ed. B. Staw and L. Cummings (Greenwich, Conn.: JAI Press, 1990).

employees to work together cooperatively.[66] No research studies have identified occasions when the reciprocity rule might be used, but we might speculate that supervisors with high moral and ethical standards might "do unto others as they would have done onto themselves." Basing increases on need (need rule), interestingly, used to be a fairly common argument for justifying higher wages for men than women. After all, the argument went, men have a family to support whereas women are working only for "pin money." Compensation administrators today are more sensitive to the fallacies evident in this argument. Apparently, though, a need-based allocation mechanism is still used when the recipient is a close personal friend of the person allocating the increase.[67] Finally, the contract rule indicates that rewards are allocated based on preestablished agreements. Union contracts fall in this category. Rules for allocating pay increases are clearly specified in the contract language. Less formal examples, however, might appear in different types of incentive systems. Employees are told up front that the compensation they receive will be strictly tied to the number of units produced or the cost savings achieved. The schedule of payouts for different levels of performance is agreed to in advance.

Collecting Performance Data

Procedural justice also means that supervisors should collect information about employee behavior in a fair manner. Best efforts should be made to ensure accurate data.[68] This includes specifying in advance the rules that will be used for collecting performance data.[69] For example, one study found that employees consider the appraisal process as more fair when the supervisor uses a diary to collect performance data.[70] Combining these suggestions, it appears that the employee and supervisor should discuss how the supervisor will keep track of performance, and that recorded observations (such as in a diary) are viewed favorably.

Performance Appraisal Interview

Given that the majority of performance evaluations are based on subjective judgments of supervisors, not on objective criteria (e.g., units produced), many employees believe that ratings are, or have the potential to be, biased. Substantial evidence exists to support this position. For example, several studies have shown that raters can agree reasonably well

---

[66]G. S. Leventhal, "Fairness in Social Relationships" in *Contemporary Topics in Social Psychology,* ed. J. W. Thibaut, J. T. Spence, and R. C. Carson (Morristown, N.J.: General Learning Press, 1976), pp. 211–39.

[67]M. J. Lerner, "The Justice Motive in Human Relations and the Economic Model of Man: A Radical Analysis of Facts and Fictions," in *Cooperation and Helping Behavior: Theories and Research,* ed. V. Derlega and J. Grezlak (New York: Academic Press, 1982), pp. 121–45.

[68]Winstanley, "Are Merit Increases Really Effective?"; J. Greenberg, "Using Diaries to Promote Procedural Justice in Performance Approach," *Social Justice Review* 4 (1988), pp. 17–27.

[69]Leventhal, "Fairness in Social Relationships."

[70]Greenberg, "Using Diaries to Promote Procedural Justice in Performance Approach."

in their relative ratings of employees, but they do not discriminate particularly well across rating dimensions.[71] Dunnette and Borman have noted that "this means that different raters and/or methods tend to rank ratees similarly but that different facets or dimensions of job performance are poorly differentiated."[72]

Chapter 10 covers in great detail the appraisal interview and forms to best ensure bias-free results. We should note here, though, that efforts to *appear* fair in the actual interview seem to depend on whether subordinates are allowed to participate (provide their view of performance) and believe that they have some input into the final decision.[73] Employees who perceive that the appraisal system adheres to written standards (i.e., that people are evaluated on what is outlined in writing) are more satisfied with the overall pay system.[74] The behavior of the supervisor conducting the appraisal also is important. Subordinates who perform well view the process as fairer when they are told by supervisors that the appraisal results are based on performance. Subordinates who do badly want to know that the supervisor is concerned about their welfare (e.g., "I am sorry to have to give you such a low rating").[75] A bit of compassion goes a long way!

How to Allocate: When and How Much?

When to Appraise?   When should appraisals be conducted? One survey indicates that employees prefer appraisals once per year.[76] The number probably should be more often for new (probationary) employees and employees who are having a difficult time meeting performance expectations.

How Much of an Increase Should Be Given?   How large should pay increases be? There are three obvious actors with vested interests in the answer to this question, and each must be considered in arriving at an effective level of merit increase. First, the size of an increase is important to the company. Organizations appear to pay attention to three factors in deciding on pay increases. Research suggests that salary raises are smaller when budgets are smaller and are larger when performance is higher and when the job is central to the organization's mission, other things being equal.[77]

---

[71]R. F. Burnaska and T. D. Hollman, "An Empirical Comparison of the Relative Effects of Rater Response Biases on Three Rating Scale Formats," *Journal of Applied Psychology* 59 (1974), pp. 307–12; B. A. Freedman and E. F. Cornelius, "Effect of Rater Participation in Scale Construction on the Psychometric Characteristics of Two Rating Scale Formats," *Journal of Applied Psychology* 61 (1976), pp. 210–16.

[72]Marvin Dunnette and Martin Borman, "Personnel Selection and Classification Systems," *Annual Review of Psychology* 30 (1979), p. 488.

[73]F. Landy, J. Barnes, and K. Murphy, "Correlates of Perceived Fairness and Accuracy of Performance Evaluation," *Journal of Applied Psychology* 63 (1978), pp. 751–54.

[74]M. Miceli, I. Jung, J. Near, and D. Greenberger, "Predictors and Outcomes of Reactions to Pay-for-Performance Plans," *Journal of Applied Psychology* 76 (1991), pp. 508–21.

[75]J. Greenberg, "Using Explanations to Manage Impressions of Performance Appraisal Fairness," Paper presented at the 1988 Academy of Management Meetings, Anaheim, Calif., 1988.

[76]J. Laumeyer and T. Beebe, "Employees and Their Appraisal," *Personnel Administrator,* December 1988, pp. 76–80.

[77]Ibid.

A second participant in the salary increase process is an employee's supervisor. Recent research on salary increment decision making indicates that supervisors in general tend to follow an adjustment approach to allocating salary raises. This type of system allocates larger raises to employees who are underpaid relative to peers at the same performance level.[78] Future research will need to determine what factors affect the type of allocation scheme supervisors select and identify ways to ensure that procedures used by supervisors are consistent with organizational goals.

The final actor in the salary increase process is, of course, the employee receiving the pay increase. Considerable research indicates that employees have clear views about what constitutes a sufficient pay increase. People appear to interpret raises in one of two ways.[79] One group evaluates raises relative to the cost of living. If purchasing power declines, the raise is insufficient. After all, a 6 percent increase during periods of 9 percent inflation is hardly reason for celebration in the struggle to increase personal purchasing power. A second group looks at raises as a form of recognition. These employees become concerned about the level of their raises in comparison to raises of others in the company. High relative raises act as feedback that performance is considered good by the powers that be.[80]

The total of this research indicates that appropriate pay size is not a fixed value. Although we have made some progress in identifying the factors that organizations consider important in establishing pay increase guidelines (Chapter 14), huge gaps in our understanding of supervisory and subordinate reactions to these pay guidelines still exist. To the extent that either party is unhappy with the allocation scheme or pay raise level devised by the organization, unintended and potentially counterproductive consequences may be the result.

Appeals Mechanisms

One of the important roles that unions serve in organizations is to protect members from unfair decisions. The grievance process lets employees challenge decisions they see as unjust. Apparently such an appeals mechanism, whether mandated by a union contract or implemented by management unilaterally, represents an important element of justice.[81] Opportunities should exist for appraisal decisions to be modified.

---

[78]M. H. Birnbaum, "Perceived Equity of Salary Policies," *Journal of Applied Psychology* 68 (1983), pp. 49–59.

[79]Linda A. Krefting, Jerry M. Newman, and Frank Krzystofiak, "What Is a Meaningful Pay Increase?" *New Perspectives on Compensation,* ed. Luis R. Gomez-Mejia and David B. Balkin (Englewood Cliffs, N.J.: Prentice Hall, 1987), pp. 135–40.

[80]Krefting and Mahoney, "Determining the Size of a Meaningful Pay Increase"; Frank Krzystofiak, Jerry M. Newman, and Linda A. Krefting, "Determining the Size of a Meaningful Pay Increase," *Proceedings of the Midwest Academy of Management* (1982), pp. 191–99; Frank Krzystofiak, Jerry Newman, and Linda Krefting, "Pay Meaning, Satisfaction, and Size of a Meaningful Pay Increase," *Psychological Reports* 51 (1982), pp. 660–62.

[81]G. S. Leventhal, J. Karuza, and W. R. Fry, "Beyond Fairness, A Theory of Allocation Preferences," in *Justice and Social Interaction,* ed. G. Mikula (New York: Springer Verlag, 1980), pp. 167–218.

Communications

Many organizations adopt a policy of *pay secrecy*. Secrecy may make it easier for allocators to use whatever allocation rules they wish, largely because there is less likelihood of review by others.[82] Open pay policies, though, lead allocators to gravitate toward an equality standard, that is, tending to give equal raises for everyone.[83] Apparently allocators expect that this will generate fewer complaints from subordinates. Open pay policies also lead allocators to be more responsive to pay raise demands, but only for employees perceived by the allocator as crucial to achieving unit performance goals.[84]

Hamner argues that the secrecy surrounding pay increases may lead employees to believe that there is no direct relationship between pay and performance.[85] The alternative is to explain how pay raises are determined and to announce all raises/promotions resulting from this stated policy.[86]

SUMMARY

On a superficial level, the idea of pay for performance sounds like a viable policy to improve employee performance in organizations. After all, numerous studies have been summarized showing that employees who believe that pay depends on performance actually perform at a higher relative level. Three key problems exist in translating this philosophy into a working practice. First, employees must value pay. Although there is reasonable evidence to suggest that pay, at least indirectly, can satisfy individual needs, it should not be assumed that pay is the preeminent motivator capable of solving all organizational motivation problems. In essence, pay alone will not lead to achievement of high performance expectations. This leads to the second point. If pay is to assume a role as motivator of performance, other detractors from this goal must be eliminated. This means that an organization must develop sound HR systems (e.g., selection, planning, evaluating performance, training) to complement the wage and salary system. Supervisors also must be trained to interact with subordinates about job expectations and to provide feedback about job performance. Compensation does not, and never will be able to, exist in a vacuum. Even the best designed compensation system will falter when other HR systems are inadequately designed to meet organizational needs.

The third problem in developing a pay-for-performance system centers on the fact that employees must believe that pay is tied to performance. This implies more than a policy statement to this effect. Organization practices must convey that pay is actually tied to performance. This precipitates a number of thorny issues: (1) a reasonable amount of salary increases must be allocated to merit so that performance differences translate

---

[82]J. Pfeffer, *Power in Organizations* (Marshfield, Mass.: Pitman, 1981).

[83]Leventhal et al., "Beyond Fairness," pp. 167–218.

[84]K. Bartol and D. Martin, "Effects of Dependence, Dependency Threats, and Pay Secrecy on Managerial Pay Allocations," *Journal of Applied Psychology* 74 (1989), pp. 105–13.

[85]Hamner, "How to Ruin Motivation with Pay."

[86]J. Greenberg, "Cultivating an Image of Justice: Looking Fair on the Job," *Academy of Management Executive* 2, no. 2 (1988), pp. 155–57.

into meaningful differences in pay raises, (2) supervisors must be trained to discriminate among subordinates in performance, (3) supervisors must be willing and able (i.e., trained) to provide feedback to employees about performance, (4) this feedback must be accompanied by a supportive environment in which supervisors view their roles partially as facilitators of employee performance (i.e., that performance is essentially a team effort), and (5) these practices must be adhered to consistently over time.

It is not surprising that organizations fail to tie pay to performance effectively. When confronted with the choice between making a commitment to all that pay for performance implies and adopting a far more tranquil strategy with fewer payoffs, the choice is frequently made to avoid the more costly long-term strategy. If this is the choice, we should stop deluding ourselves that pay motivates performance and search for other strategies to motivate it.

REVIEW QUESTIONS

1. How would VIE theory be used to argue that tying pay to performance will increase performance? What might VIE theory predict about performance for unionized employees who receive increases based strictly on seniority?

2. John Krefting, supervisor, is very pleased with the performance of Sally Frost, one of his best workers. To reward her, he begins to give her more challenging tasks, grooming her for a future promotion. Three months later Frost quits. Use equity theory to give possible explanations for why she quit. How do perceptions play a role in this process?

3. Cite four reasons why pay for performance may not work in an organization.

4. How does procedural justice differ from distributive justice? Defend the position that supervisors have considerable control over procedural justice in their departments but little control over distributive justice. How might you use the principles of procedural justice to avoid having Sally Frost quit (see Question 2)?

5. Identify the five rules that might be used for allocating rewards. How might company policy, value systems, and labor status (union versus nonunion) dictate which of these rules is used most frequently to allocate rewards?

Clinton Pharmaceutical is a medium-sized pharmaceutical company located in Sherwood, New Jersey. Most of Clinton's profits over the past 20 years have been generated by high volume production of drugs used by veterinarians in the care of domesticated animals. Since there is only a small markup in this market, Clinton must make its profit from high volume. With somewhat loose quality control laws for drugs distributed to veterinarians, Clinton historically has been able to achieve unit production levels that are high for the pharmaceutical industry.

Unfortunately, in the past two years productivity has significantly deteriorated at Clinton. Records for the past five years are provided in Exhibit 1. In addition, turnover and absenteeism are up (Exhibits 2 and 3).

John Lancer, president of Clinton Pharmaceutical, is deeply concerned. The key to Clinton's success has always been its high productivity and resulting low unit production costs. For some reason profits have been down 18 percent during the past two years (1988 = −13 percent; 1989 = −23 percent). Mr. Lancer has an annual stockholders' meeting in two weeks and he is determined he will go in with some answers. Maybe they can't correct the drop-off in time for the meeting, but heads will roll if he doesn't get some answers. All department heads subsequently are sent detailed letters outlining the profit picture and requesting explanations.

Ralph Simpson is the top human resources person at Clinton Pharmaceutical. As director of Human Resources Management, he was informed by John Lancer three weeks ago that a marked drop in profits had occurred over the past year. Mr. Simpson offers the data in Exhibit 4 as a possible explanation for the profit decline.

EXHIBIT 1 Clinton Pharmaceutical Productivity Trends, 1988–1992*

1988	1989	1990	1991	1992
127,000	123,000	122,786	104,281	100,222

*Dollars gross revenue generated per employee in constant dollars.

EXHIBIT 2 Turnover Percentages, All Occupations, 1988–1992

1988	1989	1990	1991	1992
14%	12.5%	19.0%	20.2%	21.1%

EXHIBIT 3 Absenteeism, Average Days per Employee, 1988–1992

1988	1989	1990	1991	1992
*	*	9.6	9.7	10.2

*Records not available.

Discussion Questions

1. Do Exhibits 1, 2, and 3 suggest any problems that might explain or be related to the profit declines?

2. Given the discussion of motivation theory in your text, do the data in Exhibit 4 suggest that productivity declines may be due to motivation problems? What other human resource management explanations are plausible?

EXHIBIT 4 Attitude Survey toward Compensation: Level and Administration

---

$N = 1,427$ (87 percent response rate)
Questions 1–15

Column A Scaling	*Column B Scaling*	*Column C Scaling*

1 = Very important to me	1 = Very satisfied	1 = Very dependent
2 = Important to me	2 = Satisfied	2 = Dependent
3 = Neither important nor unimportant	3 = Neutral	3 = Unsure
4 = Unimportant to me	4 = Dissatisfied	4 = Rarely dependent
5 = Very unimportant to me	5 = Very dissatisfied	5 = Never dependent

Indicate how important the following rewards available to Clinton employees are to you in column A.
Indicate how satisfied you are with the level Clinton delivers in column B.
How dependent are these rewards on your performance (column C)?

	A	*B*	*C*
1. A good salary	2	2	4
2. An annual raise equal to or greater than the cost of living	1	2	5
3. A profit sharing plan	5	3	3
4. Paid sick days	5	3	5
5. Vacation	3	1	5
6. Life insurance	4	1	5
7. Pension	4	1	5
8. Medical plan	3	1	5
9. Opportunity for advancement	2	5	5
10. Job security	1	2	2
11. Good supervisors	2	2	5
12. Opportunity to develop new skills	2	5	5
13. Good coworkers	3	3	5
14. Steady hours	3	2	2
15. Feedback about performance	1	5	3

Subjective Performance Evaluation and Merit Pay

Chapter Outline

The Harper

According to one version of Aesop's fables, a man who used to play upon the harp, and sing to it, in little alehouses, and made a shift in those narrow confined walls to please the dull sots who heard him, from hence entertained an ambition of shewing his parts on the public theater, where he fancied he could not fail of raising a great reputation and fortune in a very short time. He was accordingly admitted upon trial; but the spaciousness of the place, and the throng of the people, so deadened and weakened both his voice and instrument, that scarcely either of them could be heard, and where they could, his performance sounded so poor, so low, and so wretched, in the ears of his refined audience, that he was universally hissed off the stage.

Moral: As beauty is in the eyes of the beholder, so too is a performance evaluation in the eyes of the rater.

Chapter 8 discussed the relative merits of tying pay to performance. As we noted, many companies would like to pay for performance but are unsure how to do so. Part of the problem is simply that performance is hard to define and even harder to measure.[1] This chapter looks at the different ways that human resource experts have tried to improve the performance measurement process.

THE ROLE OF PERFORMANCE APPRAISAL IN COMPENSATION DECISIONS

Some experts argue that individual salary determination has greater potential to influence an organization's success than many of the compensation issues we discussed earlier in this book. A large factor in this salary determination process is performance. By the year 2000, employees may have between 10 to 15 percent of their pay determined by their level of performance. This is up from 5 percent in 1980 and 6.8 percent in 1991.[2] If we also add in other forms of compensation tied to performance (group performance and company performance), another 10 to 15 percent of total compensation depends on some accurate measure of performance.[3] At times, performance can be expressed in terms of objective, quantifiable results. Indeed, some good estimates suggest that between 13 (for hourly workers) and 70 percent of the time (for managerial employees), employee performance is tied to these objective, quantifiable measures.[4] In many jobs, though, objective performance standards are not feasible. Either job output is not readily quantifiable or the components that are quantifiable do not reflect important job dimensions. A secretarial job could be reduced to words per minute and errors per page of typing. But many secretaries, and their supervisors, would argue that this captures only a small portion of the job. Courtesy in greeting clients and in answering phones, initiative in solving problems without running to the boss, dependability under deadlines—all of these intangible qualities can make the difference between a good and a poor secretary. Such subjective goals are less easily measured, though. The end result all too often is a performance appraisal process that is plagued by errors.

COMMON ERRORS IN APPRAISING PERFORMANCE

Efforts to accurately evaluate employee performance can be sidetracked by a number of different types of errors that raters commonly make. These rating errors are listed in Exhibit 9.1.

Obviously, the potential for errors causes employees to lose faith in the performance appraisal process. One poll, in fact, found that 30 percent of employees believed their

---

[1]Amanda Bennett, "Paying Workers to Meet Goals Spreads, but Gauging Performance Proves Tough," *The Wall Street Journal,* June 7, 1990, pp. B1, B8.

[2]Ibid.

[3]Ibid.

[4]Susan E. Jackson, Randall S. Schuler, and J. Carlos Rivero, "Organizational Characteristics as Predictors of Personnel Practices," *Personnel Psychology* 42 (1989), pp. 727–86.

EXHIBIT 9.1   Common Errors in the Appraisal Process

Halo error	An appraiser giving favorable ratings to all job duties based on impressive performance in just one job function. For example, a rater who hates tardiness rates a prompt subordinate high across all performance dimensions *exclusively because of this one characteristic.*
Horn error	The opposite of a halo error. Downgrading an employee across all performance dimensions *exclusively because of poor performance on one dimension.*
First impression error	Developing a negative (positive) opinion of an employee early in the review period and allowing that to negatively (positively) influence all later perceptions of performance.
Recency error	The opposite of first impression error. Allowing performance (either good or bad) at the end of the review period to play too large a role in determining an employee's rating for the entire period.
Leniency error	Consistently rating someone higher than is deserved.
Severity error	The opposite of leniency error. Rating someone consistently lower than is deserved.
Central tendency error	Avoiding extremes (both high and low) in ratings across employees.
Clone error	Giving better ratings to individuals who are like the rater in behavior and/or personality.
Spillover error	Continuing to downgrade an employee for performance errors in prior rating periods.

---

performance appraisals were ineffective. Employees, quite naturally, will be reluctant to have pay systems tied to such error-ridden performance ratings. At the very least, charges that the evaluation process is political will abound.[5] To counter such problems, companies and researchers alike have expended considerable time and money to identify ways performance ratings can be improved.

STRATEGIES TO IMPROVE THE ACCURACY OF PERFORMANCE RATINGS

Early research to improve the accuracy of performance ratings centered on identifying the best appraisal format. If only the ideal format could be found, so the argument goes, raters would be guided by the format to make more accurate ratings. More recent attention has focused less on the rating format and more on the raters themselves. One branch of this work identifies different possible categories of raters (e.g., supervisor, peers, subordinates, self) and asks if the role that each assumes in the firm leads to more or less accurate ratings. The second branch of this research about raters attempts to identify how raters process information used to derive appraisal ratings. Such information, including an understanding of how irrelevant information plays a role in the evaluation of employees, may yield strategies to lessen the flaws in the total process. Finally, data also suggest

---

[5]Clinton Longnecker, Henry Sims, and Dennis Gioia, "Behind the Mark: The Politics of Employee Appraisal," *Academy of Management Executive* 1, no. 3 (1987), pp. 183–93.

that raters can be trained to increase the accuracy of their ratings. The following sections discuss these different approaches to improve rating accuracy.

Performance Ranking and Rating Formats

Evaluation formats can be divided into two general categories.[6] One category involves ranking procedures. *Ranking formats* require the rater to compare employees against each other to determine the relative ordering of the group on some performance measure (usually some measure of overall performance). Exhibit 9.2 illustrates three different methods of ranking employees.

EXHIBIT 9.2   Three Ranking Formats

Straight Ranking Method

Rank	Employee's Name
Best	1. _____
Next best	2. _____
Next best	3. _____

Alternation Ranking

Rank	Employee's Name
Best performer	1. _____
Next best	2. _____
Next best	3. _____
Etc.	4. _____
Next worst	3. _____
Next worst	2. _____
Worst performer	1. _____

(Alternate identifying best performer then worst performer, best of those left then worst of those left, etc.)

Paired Comparison Ranking Method

	John	Pete	Sam	Tom	Number of Times Ranked Higher
Bill	x	x	x	x	4
John		x	x	x	3
Pete			x	x	2
Sam				x	1

X indicates the person in the row who is ranked higher than the person in the column. The highest ranking goes to person with most "ranking wins."

---

[6]Daniel Ilgen and Jack Feldman, "Performance Appraisal: A Process Focus," *Research in Organizational Behavior* 5 (1983), pp. 141–97.

The *straight ranking procedure* is just that: Employees are ranked relative to each other. *Alternation ranking* recognizes the raters are better at ranking people at extreme ends of the distribution. Raters are asked to indicate the best employee amd then the worst employee. Working at the two extremes permits a rater to get more "practice" prior to making the harder distinctions in the vast middle ground of employees. Finally, the *paired comparisons ranking* method simplifies the ranking process by forcing raters to make ranking judgments about only discrete pairs of people. Each individual is compared separately with all others in the work group. The person who "wins" the most paired-comparisons is ranked top in the group, and so on. Unfortunately, as the size of the work group goes above 10 to 15 employees, the number of paired comparisons becomes unmanageable.

The second category of appraisal formats involves ratings, rather than rankings, of employees. The various *rating formats* share two underlying commonalities. First, in contrast to ranking formats, rating formats require raters to evaluate employees on some absolute standard rather than relative to other employees. Second, each performance standard has attached to it a measurement scale indicating varying levels of performance on that dimension. Appraisers rate employees by checking the point on the scale that best represents the appraisee's performance level. Possible performance variation is described along a continuum from good to bad. The types of descriptors used in anchoring this continuum provide the major difference in rating scales. These descriptors include adjectives, behaviors, and outcomes. When adjectives are used as anchors, the format is called a *standard rating scale*. Exhibit 9.3 shows a typical rating scale with adjectives as anchors (well above average to well below average).

When behaviors are used as anchors, a second type of rating scale results: behaviorally anchored rating scales (BARS). Although there are variants on this scale and small differences in construction and explanation (e.g., behavioral observation scale, behavioral expectation scale), BARS seems to be the most common behavioral format. By anchoring scales with concrete behaviors, firms adopting a BARS format hope to make evaluations less subjective. When raters try to decide on a rating, they have a common definition (in the form of a behavioral example) for each of the performance levels. This directly addresses a major criticism of standard rating scales: Different raters carry with them into

---

EXHIBIT 9.3   Rating Scales Using Absolute Standards

Standard Rating Scale with Adjective Anchors					
Communications skills:	Written and oral ability to clearly and convincingly express thoughts, ideas, or facts in individual or group situations.				
Circle the number that best describes the level of employee performance	1 Well above average	2 Above average	3 Average	4 Below average	5 Well below average

the rating situation different definitions of the scale levels (e.g., different raters have different ideas about what "average work" is). Exhibit 9.4 illustrates a behaviorally anchored rating scale.

Overall performance for rating formats is some weighted average (weighted by the importance the organization attaches to each dimension) of the ratings on all dimensions. The appendix to this chapter gives examples of rating scales and the total appraisal form for some well-known organizations. As a brief illustration, though, consider Exhibit 9.5.

The employee evaluated in Exhibit 9.5 is rated slightly above average. An alternative method for obtaining an overall rating is to allow the rater discretion in rating both performance on the individual dimensions and in assigning an overall evaluation. In this case, the weights from the far right column of Exhibit 9.5 would not be used and the overall evaluation would be based on a subjective and internal assessment by the rater.

The third type of standard, outcomes, is used more frequently in yet another type of appraisal format: management by objectives (MBO). Management by objectives is both a planning and appraisal tool that has many different variations across firms.[7] As a first step, organization objectives are identified from the strategic plan of the company. Then each successively lower level in the organizational hierarchy is charged with identifying work objectives that will support attainment of organizational goals. Exhibit 9.6 illustrates a common MBO objective. Notice that the emphasis is on outcomes achieved by employees. At the beginning of a performance review period, the employee and supervisor discuss performance objectives (column 1).[8] Months later, at the end of the review period, the two again meet to record results formally (of course, multiple informal discussions should have occurred before this time). Results are then compared against objectives, and a performance rating is then determined based on how well objectives were met.

A review of firms using MBO indicates generally positive improvements in performance for both individuals and the organization. This performance increase is accompanied by managerial attitudes toward MBO that become more positive over time, particularly when the system is revised periodically to reflect feedback of participants. Managers are especially pleased with the way that MBO provides direction to work units, improves the planning process, and increases superior/subordinate communication. On the negative side, MBO appears to require more paperwork and increases both performance pressure and stress.[9]

Exhibit 9.7 shows some of the common components of an MBO format and the percentage of experts who judge this component vital to a successful evaluation effort.

A final type of appraisal format does not easily fall into any of the categories yet discussed. In an *essay* format, supervisors answer open-ended questions in essay form

---

[7]Mark L. McConkie, "A Clarificaiton of the Goal Setting and Appraisal Processes in MBO," *Academy of Management Review* 4, no. 1 (1979), pp. 29–40.

[8]Ibid.

[9]J. S. Hodgson, "Management by Objectives: The Experiences of a Federal Government Department," *Canadian Public Administration* 16, no. 4 (1973), pp. 422–31.

EXHIBIT 9.4 Rating Scale with Behavioral Anchors

Communications Skills:	Written and oral ability to clearly and convincingly express thoughts, ideas or facts in individual or group situations.

Exceeds Standards

1	2
Through clarity and logic of communications is able to persuade others to adopt policies and practices, even those which may have been unpopular initially. Makes complex ideas understandable for all levels and types of audiences. Would be a top choice for presenting an unpopular subject to a hostile audience.	Clearly and logically presents ideas in a way that makes even complex subjects easy to grasp for a wide variety of audiences. Frequently is able to persuade others to adopt policies and practices, even those which may have been unpopular initially. Not normally among the first people considered to present an unpopular subject to a hostile audience.

Meets Standards

3	4	5
Typically presents ideas clearly and logically without assistance from others. Recognizes when content of message is not understood and is able to explain ideas in a different manner to clarify. Communications ability may not have the power to convert unsympathetic listeners.	Ideas are clear and logical, but success may come only after pretesting arguments with others and clarifying content of message. Recognizes when content of message is not understood and usually is able to rephrase in a way that clarifies.	With help of others can develop clear and logical communications. Occasionally, may not be clear when ideas are first presented in casual conversations or in written drafts, but on own or with help, recognizes where message is not understood. Struggles to find ways to clarify message and is usually successful.

Does Not Meet Standards

6	7
Occasionally unclear in formal presentations and in final papers, either because of failure to seek input from others or because of inability to act upon that input. May not be able to recognize when listeners or readers do not understand message. May not be able to clarify message even when gap in understanding is recognized. Gives appearance of trying to improve these skills.	Frequently unclear in communications of both casual and great importance. Shows little ability or interest in understanding where misunderstanding is or in correcting same.

Rating	Documentation of Rating (optional except for 6 & 7):
____	

EXHIBIT 9.5 **An Example of Employee Appraisal**

Employee: Kelsey T. Mahoney

Job Title: Supervisor, Shipping and Receiving

Performance Dimension	Dimension Rating					Dimension Weight
	Well Below Average 1	Below Average 2	Average 3	Above Average 4	Well Above Average 5	
Leadership ability				×		0.2 (× 4) = 0.8
Job knowledge					×	0.1 (× 5) = 0.5
Work output				×		0.3 (× 4) = 1.2
Attendance		×				0.2 (× 3) = 0.6
Initiative		×				0.2 (× 3) = 0.6

Sum of rating × weight = 3.7
Overall rating = 3.7

EXHIBIT 9.6 **Example of MBO Objective for Communications Skill**

1. Performance Objective	*2. Results*
By July 1 of this year, Pat will complete a report summarizing employee reactions to the new performance appraisal system. An oral presentation will be prepared and delivered to all nonexempt employees in groups of 15 to 20. All oral presentations will be completed by August 31, and reactions of employees to this presentation will average at least 3.0 on a 5-point scale.	Written report completed by July 1. All but one oral presentation completed by August 31. Last report not completed until September 15 because of unavoidable conflicts in vacation schedules. Average rating of employees (reaction to oral presentation) was 3.4, exceeding minimum expectations.

describing employee performance. Since the descriptors used could range from comparisons with other employees to the use of adjectives describing performance, types of behaviors, and goal accomplishments, the essay format can take on characteristics of all the formats discussed previously.

Exhibit 9.8 reports the relative popularity for some of these formats in industry.

EXHIBIT 9.7 **Components of a Successful MBO Program**

	Total Number of Responses*	Percentage of Authorities in Agreement
1. Goals and objectives should be specific.	37	97
2. Goals and objectives should be defined in terms of measurable results.	37	97
3. Individual goals should be linked to overall organization goals.	37	97
4. Objectives should be reviewed "periodically."	31	82
5. The time period for goal accomplishment should be specified.	27	71
6. Wherever possible, the indicator of the results should be quantifiable; otherwise, it should be at least verifiable.	26	68
7. Objectives should be flexible; changed as conditions warrant.	26	68
8. Objectives should include a plan of action for accomplishing the results.	21	55
9. Objectives should be assigned priorities of weights.	19	50

*In this table the total number of responses actually represents the total number of authorities responding; thus, percentages also represent the percentage of authorities in agreement with the statements made.

SOURCE: Mark L. McConkie, "A Clarification of the Goal Setting and Appraisal Process in MBO," *Academy of Management Review* 4, no. 1 (1979), pp. 29–40. © 1979, Academy of Management Review.

EXHIBIT 9.8 **Usage of Performance Evaluation Formats**

	Usage by Percentage of Type of Employee	
Type of System	Nonexempt	Exempt
1. Standard rating scale	52%	32%
2. Essay	30	3
3. Management by objectives or other objective-based system	19	73
4. Behaviorally anchored scale	23	24
5. Other	33	32

NOTE: Percentages total more than 100% because of multiple systems in different companies.

SOURCE: Based on a survey of 256 firms from a population of 1,300 large organizations completed by Drake, Beam, and Morin, (New York: Drake, Beam, and Morin, 1983).

Evaluating Performance Appraisal Formats. Appraisal formats are generally evaluated against five criteria: (1) employee development potential (amount of feedback about performance that the form offers), (2) administrative ease, (3) personnel research potential, (4) cost, and (5) validity. Admittedly, different organizations attach different weights to these dimensions. For example, a small organization in its formative years is likely to be very cost conscious. A large organization with pressing affirmative action commitments might place relatively high weight on validity and nondiscrimination and show less concern about cost issues. A progressive firm concerned with employee development might demand a format allowing substantial employee feedback. Less enlightened organizations might be concerned solely with costs. These criteria are explained below.[10]

Employee Development Criterion. Does the method communicate the goals and objectives of the organization? Is feedback to employees a natural outgrowth of the evaluation format, so that employee developmental needs are identified and can be attended to readily?

Administrative Ease Criterion. How easily can evaluation results be used for administrative decisions concerning wage increases, promotions, demotions, terminations, and transfers? Comparisons among individuals for personnel action require some common denominator for comparison. Typically this is a numerical rating of performance. Evaluation forms that do not produce numerical ratings cause administrative headaches.

Personnel Research Criterion. Does the instrument lend itself well to validating employment tests? Can applicants predicted to perform well be monitored through performance evaluation? Similarly, can the success of various employees and organizational development programs be traced to impacts on employee performance? As with the administrative criterion, though, evaluations typically need to be quantitative to permit the statistical tests so common in personnel research.

Cost Criterion. Does the evaluation form require a long time to develop initially? Is it time-consuming for supervisors to use in rating their employees? Is it expensive to use? All of these factors increase the format cost.

Validity Criterion. By far the most research on formats in recent years has focused on reducing error and improving accuracy. Success in this pursuit would mean that decisions based on performance ratings (e.g., promotions, merit increases) could be made with increased confidence. In general, the search for the "perfect format" to eliminate rating errors and improve accuracy has been unsuccessful. The high acclaim, for example, accompanying the introduction of BARS has not been supported by research.[11]

Exhibit 9.9 provides an evaluation of the five most common rating formats in terms of their performance on the criteria just discussed.

---

[10]Bruce McAfee and Blake Green, "Selecting a Performance Appraisal Method," *Personnel Administrator* 22, no. 5 (1977), pp. 61–65.

[11]H. John Bernardin, "Behavioral Expectation Scales v. Summated Ratings: A Fairer Comparison," *Journal of Applied Psychology* 62 (1977), pp. 422–27; H. John Bernardin, Kim Alvares, and C. J. Cranny, "A Recomparison of Behavioral Expectation Scales to Summated Scales," *Journal of Applied Psychology* 61 (1976), pp. 284–91; C. A. Schriesheim and U. E. Gattiker, "A Study of the Abstract Desirability of Behavior-Based v. Trait-Oriented Performance Rating," *Proceedings of the Academy of Management* 43 (1982), pp. 307–11; and F. S. Landy and J. L. Farr, "Performance Rating," *Psychological Bulletin* 87 (1980), pp. 72–107.

EXHIBIT 9.9   An Evaluation of Performance Appraisal Formats

	Employee Development Criterion	Administrative Criterion	Personnel Research Criterion	Economic Criterion	Validity Criterion
Ranking	Poor—ranks typically based on overall performance, with little thought given to feedback on specific performance dimensions.	Poor—comparisons of ranks across work units to determine merit raises are meaningless. Other administrative actions similarly hindered.	Average—validation studies can be completed with rankings of performance.	Good—inexpensive source of performance data. Easy to develop and use in small organizations and in small units.	Average—good reliability but poor on rating errors, especially halo.
Standard rating scales	Average—general problem areas identified. Some information on extent of developmental need is available, but no feedback on necessary behaviors/outcomes.	Average—ratings valuable for merit increase decisions and others. Not easily defended if contested.	Average—validation studies can be completed, but level of measurement contamination unknown.	Good—inexpensive to develop and easy to use.	Average—content validity is suspect. Rating errors and reliability are average.
Behaviorally anchored rating scales	Good—extent of problem and behavioral needs are identified.	Good—BARS good for making administrative decisions. Useful for defense if contested because job relevant.	Good—validation studies can be completed and measurement problems on BARS less than many other criterion measures.	Average—expensive to develop but easy to use.	Good—high content validity. Some evidence of interrater reliability and reduced rating errors.
Management by objectives	Excellent—extent of problem and outcome deficiencies are identified.	Poor—MBO not suited to merit income decisions. Level of completion and difficulty of objectives hard to compare across employees.	Poor—nonstandard objectives across employees and no overall measures of performance make validity studies difficult.	Poor—expensive to develop and time-consuming to use.	Excellent—high content validity. Low rating errors.
Essay	Unknown—depends on guidelines or inclusions in essay as developed by organization or supervisors.	Poor—essays not comparable across different employees considered for merit or other administrative actions.	Poor—no quantitative indices to compare performance against employment test scores in validation studies.	Average—easy to develop but time-consuming to use.	Unknown—unstructured format makes studies of essay method difficult.

Possibly the best way to view rating formats is as a tool to help raters (1) identify what types of employee performance the company thinks are relevant, (2) focus observation on these types of behavior, and (3) translate these behavioral observations into evidence about performance.

Suggestions for Choosing Rating Formats. Historically, the selection of a performance appraisal format has been guided primarily by fads and fashions. Organizations have been disposed to jump on the proverbial "bandwagon" by adopting the latest "in" format. Little consideration was given to the organization's needs, employee needs, or the types of jobs being evaluated. These factors are vital in the selection of a performance appraisal format. Because these factors vary across organizations and within organizations, across jobs and individuals, a contingency approach to format selection may be the most appropriate strategy. The argument is made that no single evaluation format may be entirely appropriate across all jobs and individuals in an organization. It may be better to adopt different appraisal formats for different situations. Advocates of this contingency approach argue that the nature of the task and/or past performance of the individual may warrant the use of an array of formats rather than a single format.

Keeley suggests as a first contingency approach that the choice of an appraisal format depends on the type of tasks being performed.[12] He argues that tasks can be ordered along a continuum from those that are very routine in nature to those for which the appropriate behavior for goal accomplishment is very uncertain. In Keeley's view, different appraisal formats require assumptions about the extent to which correct behavior for task accomplishment can be specified. The choice of an appraisal format requires a matching of formats with tasks that meet the assumptions for that format. At one extreme of the continuum are behavior-based evaluation procedures that define specific performance expectations against which employee performance is evaluated. Keeley argues that behaviorally anchored rating scales fall into this category. The behavioral anchors define specific performance expectations representing different levels of performance possible by an employee. Only for highly routine, mechanistic tasks is it appropriate to specify behavioral expectations. For these routine tasks it is possible to identify the single sequence of appropriate behaviors to accomplish a goal. Consequently, it is possible to identify behavioral anchors for a performance scale that illustrate varying levels of attainment of the proper sequence of activities.

When tasks become less routine, however, it becomes more difficult to specify a single sequence of procedures that must be followed to accomplish a goal. Rather, multiple strategies are both feasible and appropriate to reach a final goal. Under these circumstances, Keeley argues that the appraisal format should focus on evaluating the extent to which the final goal is accomplished.[13] Thus, for less certain tasks, a management by objective (MBO) strategy would be appropriate. As long as the final goal can be specified, performance can be evaluated in relation to that goal without specifying or evaluating

---

[12]Michael Keeley, "A Contingency Framework for Performance Evaluation," *Academy of Management Review* 3 (July 1978), pp. 428–38.

[13]Ibid.

the behavior used to reach that goal. The focus is exclusively on the degree of goal accomplishment.

At the other extreme of the continuum are tasks that are highly uncertain in nature. A relatively low consensus exists about the characteristics of successful performance. Moreover, the nature of the tasks is so uncertain that it may be difficult to specify expected goals. For this type of task, Keeley argues that judgment-based evaluation procedures—as exemplified by standard rating scales—may be most appropriate. Subjective estimates are made by raters about the levels of employee performance on tasks for which neither the appropriate behavior nor the final goal is well specified. The extent of this uncertainty makes this type of appraisal very subjective and may well explain why trait-rating scales are openly criticized for the number of errors that result in performance evaluation.

A second contingency approach bases choice of rating method on the level of employee performance.[14] High performers are given tasks that have relatively uncertain behavioral requirements and perhaps even uncertain goal specification. Presumably this is both a reward to the employee and an affirmation by the supervisor that performance need not be monitored closely. In contrast, average and below average performers are assigned to tasks that are increasingly more specified in terms of behavioral requirements. In turn, the level of task specificity defines the appropriate evaluation format. Exhibit 9.10 outlines the issues in this contingency approach.

Who Should Conduct Ratings?

A second way that firms have tried to improve the accuracy of performance ratings is to focus on who might conduct the ratings and which personnel might be the most accurate. The three general contenders are an employee's supervisor, peers, or the employee himself or herself.

Supervisors as Raters.   Some estimates indicate that more than 80 percent of the input for performance ratings comes from supervisors.[15] There is good reason that supervisors play such a dominant role. Supervisors assign (or jointly determine) what work employees are to perform. This makes a supervisor knowledgeable about the job and the dimensions to be rated. Also, supervisors frequently have considerable prior experience in rating employees, thus giving the supervisors some pretty firm ideas about what level of performance is required for any given level of performance rating. Supervisor ratings also tend to be more reliable than those from other sources.[16] On the negative side, though, unless supervisors are diligent, they may not actually observe employee performance on a daily basis. Rating an employee without sufficient knowledge begs for claims of unfair treatment.

---

[14]Larry L. Cummings and Donald P. Schwab, *Performance in Organizations* (Glenview, Ill.: Scott, Foresman, 1973).

[15]Jackson, Schuller, and Rivero, "Organizational Characteristics as Predictors of Personnel Practices."

[16]E. Pulakos and W. Borman, *Developing the Basic Criterion Scores for Army-Wide and MOS-Specific Ratings* (Alexandria, Va.: U.S. Army Research Institute, 1987).

EXHIBIT 9.10 A Contingency Evaluation Approach Based on Past Employee Performance

Program	Past Employee Performance	Type of Tasks Assigned to Employee	Appropriate Evaluation Format
Developmental Action Program (DAP)	Consistently high performance in past with demonstrated potential for growth.	Tasks for which there is considerable discretion in way goals are accomplished.	1. MBO. 2. BARS.
Maintenance Action Program (MAP)	1. Average acceptable performance with low potential for growth, or 2. Above average performance working on job with low discretion.	Tasks for which: 1. Clearly defined and communicated goals are established, and 2. The method for carrying out tasks is frequently improved by the technology or the supervisor, and 3. Close direction and frequent evaluation is possible.	1. Conventional trait rating. 2. BARS. 3. Weighted checklist. 4. Forced choice.
Remedial Action Program (RAP)	Employees who are clearly below acceptable performance standards.	Highly structured tasks for which it is possible to: 1. Provide feedback about why performance is inadequate, 2. Provide behavioral critical incidents to point out examples of poor and acceptable performance, 3. Develop a structured program for correction with performance measures and time perspectives clearly explained and frequently reviewed.	1. BARS.

SOURCE: L. L. Cummings and D. P. Schwab, *Performance in Organization* (Glenview, Ill.: Scott Foresman, 1973). Reprinted with permission.

Peers as Raters.   One of the major strengths of using peers as raters is that they work more closely with the ratee and probably have an undistorted perspective of typical performance, particularly in group assignments (as opposed to what a supervisor might observe in a "casual" stroll around the work area). Balanced against this positive are at least two powerful negatives. First, peers may have little or no experience in conducting appraisals, leading to rather mixed evidence about the reliability of this rating source. Second, in a situation in which teamwork is promoted, placing the burden of rating one's peers on coworkers can either create group tensions (in the case of low evaluations) or yield unreasonably high evaluations.

Self as Rater.   Some organizations have experimented with self-ratings. Obviously, self-ratings are performed by someone who has the most complete knowledge about the ratees performance! Unfortunately, though, self-ratings are generally more lenient and possibly more unreliable than ratings from other sources. One compromise in the use of self-ratings is to use them for developmental rather than administrative purposes. Firms are increasingly asking employees to rate themselves as the first step in the actual appraisal process. Forcing employees to think about their performance in advance may lead to more realistic assessments, which are also more in tune with a supervisor's own perceptions.

Understanding How Raters Process Information

A third approach to reducing errors in the appraisal process centers on understanding how raters gather, store, and use performance data about ratees. The 1980s ushered in an explosion of research on these topics. Many experts believe this is a potentially more fruitful research direction to help improve performance rating than previous efforts directed at rating formats.[17] This research already has yielded models of how people review information and make judgments.[18] Combine this with systematic research testing parts of these models and there is quickly developing a body of information about why we commit rating errors—information that will help us design strategies to lessen these errors.

Models of the Appraisal Process.   It appears that the performance appraisal process involves several stages. First, the rater observes the behavior of a ratee. Second, this behavior is encoded as part of a total picture of the ratee (e.g., one way of saying this is that we form stereotypes about people). Third, we store this information in memory, which is subject to both short- and long-term decay. Simply put, we forget things! Fourth, when it comes time to evaluate a ratee, the rater reviews the performance dimensions and retrieves stored observations/impressions to determine their relevance to the performance dimensions. Finally, the information is reconsidered and integrated with other available information as the rater makes the final ratings.[19] Quite unintentionally, when people process this information, errors occur. And they can occur at any of the stages.

Errors in the Rating Process.   Ideally, raters should attend exclusively to performance-related factors when they observe employee behavior. In fact, all of the processing stages should be guided by *performance relevancy*. Unless a behavior (or personality trait)

---

[17]Bernardin, "Behavioral Expectation Scales v. Summated Readings: A Fairer Comparison," pp. 422–27; Bernardin, Alvares, and Cranny, "A Re-comparison of Behavioral Expectation Scales to Summated Scales," pp. 284–91; Schriesheim and Gattiker, "A Study of the Abstract Desirability of Behavior-Based v. Trait-Oriented Performance Rating," pp. 307–11; and Landy and Farr, "Performance Rating," pp. 72–107.

[18]Daniel Ilgen and Jack Feldman, "Performance Appraisal: A Process Focus," *Research in Organizational Behavior* 5 (1983), pp. 141–97.

[19]Landy and Farr, "Performance Rating"; A. S. Denisi, T. P. Cafferty, and B. M. Meglino, "A Cognitive View of the Performance Appraisal Process: A Model and Research Propositions," *Organizational Behavior and Human Performance* 33 (1984), pp. 360–96; Jack M. Feldman, "Beyond Attribution Theory: Cognitive Processes in Performance Appraisal," *Journal of Applied Psychology* 66, no. 2 (1981), pp. 127–48; and W. H. Cooper, "Ubiquitous Halo," *Psychological Bulletin* 90 (1981), pp. 218–44.

affects performance, it should not influence performance ratings! Fortunately, studies show that performance actually does play an important role, perhaps the major role, in determining what rating a supervisor gives a subordinate.[20] Employees who are technically proficient and who do not create problems on the job tend to receive higher ratings than others who score lower on these dimensions.[21] On the negative side, though, many other factors appear to influence ratings which shouldn't; that is, they cause errors in the evaluation process.[22]

Errors in Observation (Attention).   Generally, researchers have varied two types of input information to see what raters pay attention to when they are collecting information for performance appraisals. First, it appears that raters are influenced by general appearance characteristics of the ratees. Males are rated higher than females (other things being equal). A female ratee is observed not as a ratee but as a female ratee. A rater may form impressions based on stereotypic beliefs about women rather than the reality of the work situation. Performance ratings are then influenced by the gender of the ratee, quite apart from any performance information. Interestingly, it seems that females are rated less accurately only when the rater has a traditional view of women's "proper" role. Raters with nontraditional stereotypes of "women's place" are not prone to such errors.[23] Race also matters when performance ratings are made. Blacks (whites) are rated higher when the rater is of the same race.[24] In general, it seems that supervisors who see ratees

[20]Leo Leventhal, Raymon Perry, and Philip Abrami, "Effects of Lecturer Quality and Student Perception of Lecturer Experience on Teacher Ratings and Student Achievement," *Journal of Educational Psychology* 69, no. 4 (1977), pp. 360–74; Angelo Denisi and George Stevens, "Profiles of Performance, Performance Evaluations, and Personnel Decisions," *Academy of Management* 24, no. 3 (1981), pp. 592–602; Wayne Cascio and Enzo Valenzi, "Relations among Criteria of Police Performance," *Journal of Applied Psychology* 63, no. 1 (1978), pp. 22–28; William Bigoness, "Effects of Applicant's Sex, Race, and Performance on Employer Performance Ratings: Some Additional Findings," *Journal of Applied Psychology* 61, no. 1 (1976), pp. 80–84; and Dorothy P. Moore, "Evaluating In-Role and Out-of-Role Performers, *Academy of Management Journal* 27, no. 3 (1984), pp. 603–18; W. Borman, L. White, E. Pulakos, and S. Oppler, "Models of Supervisory Job Performance Ratings," *Journal of Applied Psychology* 76, no. 6 (1991), pp. 863–72.

[21]Borman, White, Pulakos, and Oppler, "Models of Supervisory Job Performance Ratings," pp. 863–72.

[22]H. J. Bernardin and Richard Beaty, *Performance Appraisal: Assessing Human Behavior at Work* (Boston: Kent Publishing, 1984).

[23]G. Dobbins, R. Cardy, and D. Truxillo, "The Effects of Purpose of Appraisal and Individual Differences in Stereotypes of Women on Sex Differences in Performance Ratings: A Laboratory and Field Study," *Journal of Applied Psychology* 73, no. 3 (1988), pp. 551–58.

[24]Edward Shaw, "Differential Impact of Negative Stereotyping in Employee Selection," *Personnel Psychology* 25 (1972), pp. 333–38; Benson Rosen and Thomas Jurdee, "Effects of Applicant's Sex and Difficulty of Job on Evaluations of Candidates for Managerial Positions," *Journal of Applied Psychology* 59 (1975), pp. 511–12; Gail Pheterson, Sara Kiesler, and Philip Goldberg, "Evaluation of the Performance of Women as a Function of Their Sex, Achievement, and Personal History," *Journal of Personality and Social Psychology* 19 (1971), pp. 114–18; W. Clay Hamner, Jay Kim, Lloyd Baird, and William Bigoness, "Race and Sex as Determinants of Ratings by Potential Employers in a Simulated Work Sampling Task," *Journal of Applied Psychology* 59, no. 6 (1974), pp. 705–11; and Neal Schmitt and Martha Lappin, "Race and Sex as Determinants of the Mean and Variance of Performance Ratings," *Journal of Applied Psychology* 65, no. 4 (1980), pp. 428–35.

as similar to themselves tend to be positively influenced in making performance ratings, independent of actual performance.[25]

Second, researchers also look at change in performance over time to see if this influences performance ratings. Both the pattern of performance (performance gets better or worse over time) and the variability of performance (consistent versus erratic) influence performance ratings, even when the overall level of performance is controlled.[26] Workers who start out high in performance and then get worse are rated lower than workers who stay consistently low across time.[27] Not surprisingly, workers with an ascending pattern of performance are seen as highly motivated; those who are more variable in their performance are tagged as having less motivation. All of us have seen examples of workers (and students) who intuitively recognize this type of error and try to use it to their advantage. The big surge of work at the end of an appraisal period is often designed to "color" a rater's perceptions.

Errors in Storage and Recall.   Research suggests that raters store information in the form of traits.[28] More importantly, perhaps, people also tend to recall information in the form of trait categories. For example, a rater observes a specific behavior, that is, an employee resting during what are obviously work hours. The rater stores this information not as the specific behavior, but rather in the form of a trait, such as "that worker is lazy." Specific instructions to recall information about the ratee, as for a performance review, elicit the trait—lazy. Further, in the process of recalling information, a rater may remember events that didn't actually occur simply because they are consistent with the trait category.[29] The entire rating process then may be heavily influenced by these trait categories that we adopt, regardless of their accuracy!

Errors in storage and recall also appear to arise from memory decay. At least one study indicates that rating accuracy is a function of the delay between performance and subsequent rating. The longer the delay, the less accurate the ratings.[30]

---

[25]D. Turban and A. Jones, "Supervisor-Subordinate Similarity: Types, Effects and Mechanisms," *Journal of Applied Psychology* 73, no. 2 (1988), pp. 228–34.

[26]Denisi and Stevens, "Profiles of Performance, Performance Evaluations, and Personnel Decisions"; William Scott and Clay Hamner, "The Influence of Variations in Performance Profiles on the Performance Evaluation Process: An Examination of the Validity of the Criterion," *Organizational Behavior and Human Performance* 14 (1975), pp. 360–70; and Edward Jones, Leslie Rock, Kelly Shaver, George Goethals, and Laurence Ward, "Pattern of Performance and Ability Attributions: An Unexpected Primacy Effect," *Journal of Personality and Social Psychology* 10, no. 4 (1968), pp. 317–40.

[27]B. Gaugler and A. Rudolph, "The Influence of Assessee Performance Variation on Assessor's Judgments," *Personnel Psychology* 45 (1992), pp. 77–98.

[28]Landy and Farr, "Performance Rating"; Bernardin and Beaty, *Performance Appraisal: Assessing Human Behavior at Work.*

[29]N. Cantor and W. Mischel, "Traits v. Prototypes: The Effects on Recognition and Memory," *Journal of Personality and Social Psychology* 35 (1977), pp. 38–48; R. J. Spiro, "Remembering Information from Text: The 'State of Schema' Approach," in *Schooling and the Acquisition of Knowledge*, ed. R. C. Anderson, R. J. Spiro, and W. E. Montague (Hillsdale, Calif.: Erlbaum, 1977); and T. K. Srull and R. S. Wyer, "Category Accessibility and Social Perception: Some Implications for the Study of Person Memory and Interpersonal Judgments," *Journal of Personality and Social Psychology* 38 (1980), pp. 841–56.

[30]Robert Heneman and Kenneth Wexley, "The Effects of Time Delay in Rating and Amount of Information Observed on Performance Rating Accuracy," *Academy of Management Journal* 26, no. 4 (1983), pp. 677–86.

Errors in Evaluation.   The context of the actual evaluation process also can influence evaluations.[31] Several researchers indicate that the purpose of evaluation affects the rating process.[32] Supervisors who know that ratings will be used to determine merit increases are less likely to differentiate among subordinates than when the ratings will be used for other purposes.[33] Being required to provide feedback to subordinates about their ratings also yields less accuracy than a secrecy policy.[34] Presumably, anticipation of an unpleasant confrontation with the angry ratee "persuades" the rater to avoid confrontation. How? By giving ratings that are higher than justified.

Training Raters to Rate More Accurately

Although there is some evidence that training is not effective,[35] or is less important in reducing errors than other factors,[36] most research indicates that rater training is an effective method to reduce appraisal errors.[37] Rater training programs can be divided into three distinct categories:[38] (1) rater error training, in which the goal is to reduce psychometric errors (i.e., leniency, severity, central tendency, halo) by familiarizing raters with their existence, (2) performance dimension training, which exposes supervisors extensively to the performance dimensions to be used in rating, and (3) performance standard training designed to provide raters with a standard of comparison or frame of reference for making ratee appraisals.

Several generalizations about ways to improve rater training can be summarized from this research. First, lecturing to ratees about ways to improve ratings generally is ineffective. Second, individualized or small group discussion sections are more effective in conveying proper rating procedures. Third, when these sessions are combined with extensive practice and feedback sessions, the rating accuracy is significantly improved.

---

[31]Robert Liden and Terence Mitchell, "The Effects of Group Interdependence on Supervisor Performance Evaluations," *Personnel Psychology* 36, no. 2 (1983), pp. 289–99.

[32]See, for example, Dobbins, Cardy, and Truxillo, "The Effects of Purpose of Appraisal and Individual Differences in Stereotypes."

[33]Winstanley, "How Accurate Are Performance Appraisals?" *Personnel Administrator* 25 (August 1980), pp. 41–44; Landy and Farr, "Performance Rating"; and Heneman and Wexley, "The Effects of Time Delay in Rating and Amount of Information Observed on Performance Rating Accuracy."

[34]Cummings and Schwab, *Performance in Organizations*.

[35]H. J. Bernardin and E. C. Pence, "Effects of Rater Training: Creating New Response Sets and Decreasing Accuracy," *Journal of Applied Psychology* 6 (1980), pp. 60–66.

[36]Sheldon Zedeck and Wayne Cascio, "Performance Appraisal Decision as a Function of Rater Training and Purpose of the Appraisal," *Journal of Applied Psychology* 67, no. 6 (1982), pp. 752–58.

[37]H. J. Bernardin and M. R. Buckley, "Strategies in Rater Training," *Academy of Management Review* 6, no. 2 (1981), pp. 205–12; D. Smith, "Training Programs for Performance Appraisal: A Review," *Academy of Management Review* 11, no. 1 (1986), pp. 22–40; B. Davis and M. Mount, "Effectiveness of Performance Appraisal Training Using Computer Assisted Instruction and Behavioral Modeling," *Personnel Psychology* 3 (1984), pp. 439–52; H. J. Bernardin, "Effects of Rater Training on Leniency and Halo Errors in Student Ratings of Instructors," *Journal of Applied Psychology* 63, no. 3 (1978), pp. 301–8; and J. M. Ivancevich, "Longitudinal Study of the Effects of Rater Training on Psychometric Error in Ratings," *Journal of Applied Psychology* 64, no. 5 (1979), pp. 502–8.

[38]Bernardin and Buckley, "Strategies in Rater Training."

Fourth, longer training programs (more than two hours) generally are more successful than shorter programs. Fifth, performance dimension training and performance standard training (as explained above) generally work better than rater error training, particularly when the two superior methods are combined. Finally, the greatest success has come from efforts to reduce halo errors and improve accuracy. Leniency errors have proved the most difficult form of error to eliminate. This shouldn't be surprising! Think about the consequences to a supervisor of giving inflated ratings versus accurate or even deflated ratings. The latter two courses are certain to result in more complaints and possibly reduced employee morale. The easy way out is to artificially inflate ratings.[39] Unfortunately, the positive outcome for supervisors may come back to haunt them; with everyone receiving relatively high ratings, there is less distinction between truly good and poor performers. Obviously, it is also more difficult to pay for real performance differences.

ELEMENTS OF GOOD APPRAISAL

Several researchers have indicated that errors can also be prevented in the planning and actual conduct of appraisal interviews.[40] Exhibit 9.11 provides a detailed discussion of the elements of a good appraisal, the essence of which can be distilled into eight requirements:[41] (1) maintain a diary of employee performance to document performance and to jog the memory,[42] (2) conduct a performance diagnosis to determine in advance whether the problem arises because of motivation, skill deficiency, or external environmental constraints[43]—in turn this tells the supervisor whether the problem requires "motivation building," training, or efforts to remove external constraints, (3) seek genuine participation between superior and subordinate in the appraisal process—not unilateral "discussion," (4) stress that supervisors and their employees are working together as a team to achieve results, (5) use goal setting to focus work efforts and provide a basis for

---

[39]Longnecker, Sims, and Gioia, "Behind the Mask: The Politics of Employee Appraisal."

[40]Bernardin and Buckley, "Strategies in Rater Training"; Winstanley, "How Accurate Are Performance Appraisals?"; Bernardin and Pence, "Effects of Rater Training: Creating New Response Sets and Decreasing Accuracy"; J. M. Ivancevich, "Subordinates' Reactions to Performance Appraisal Interviews: A Test of Feedback and Goal Setting Techniques," *Journal of Applied Psychology* 67 (1982), pp. 581–87; D. Cederblom, "The Performance Appraisal Review: A Review, Implications and Suggestions," *Academy of Management Review* 7 (1982), pp. 219–27; S. Snell and K. Wexley, "Performance Diagnosis: Identifying the Causes of Poor Performance," *Personnel Administrator*, April 1985, pp. 117–27; J. M. Ivancevich and J. T. McMahon, "The Effects of Goal Setting, External Feedback, and Self-Generated Feedback on Outcome Variables: A Field Experiment," *Academy of Management Journal* 25 (1982), pp. 359–72; and A. S. Denisi and W. A. Blencoe, "Level and Source of Feedback and Determinates of Feedback Effectiveness," *Proceedings of Academy of Management* 41 (1982), pp. 175–79.

[41]Winstanley, "How Accurate Are Performance Appraisals?"; Bernardin and Buckley, "Strategies in Rater Training"; Ivancevich, "Subordinates' Reactions to Performance Appraisal Interviews: A Test of Feedback and Goal Setting Techniques"; Cederblom, "The Performance Appraisal Interview: A Review, Implications and Suggestions."

[42]A. DeNisi, T. Robbins, and T. Cafferty. "Organization of Information Used for Performance Appraisals: Role of Diary-keeping," *Journal of Applied Psychology* 74, no. 1 (1989), pp. 124–29.

[43]Snell and Wexley, "Performance Diagnosis: Identifying the Causes of Poor Performance."

EXHIBIT 9.11   Tips on Appraising Employee Performance

Preparation for the Performance Interview

1. Keep a weekly log of individual's performance. Why?
   A. It makes the task of writing up the evaluation simpler. The rater does not have to strain to remember six months or a year ago.
   B. It reduces the chances of some rating errors (e.g., recency, halo).
   C. It gives support/backup to the rating.
2. Preparation for the interview should *not* begin a week or two before it takes place. There should be continual feedback to the employee on his/her performance so that (*a*) problems can be corrected before they get out of hand, (*b*) improvements can be made sooner, and (*c*) encouragement and support are ongoing.
3. Allow sufficient time to write up the evaluation. A well-thought-out evaluation will be more objective and equitable. Sufficient time includes (*a*) the actual time necessary to think out and write up the evaluation, (*b*) time away from the evaluation, and (*c*) time to review and possibly revise.
4. Have employees fill out an appraisal form prior to the interview. This prepares employees for what will take place in the interview and allows them to come prepared with future goal suggestions, areas they wish to pursue, and suggestions concerning their jobs or the company.
5. Set up an agreed-upon, convenient time to hold the interview (at least one week in advance). Be sure to pick a nonthreatening day.
6. Be prepared!
   A. Know what you are going to say. Prepare an outline (which includes the evaluation and future goal suggestions).
   B. Decide on developmental opportunities *before* the interview. Be sure you know of possible resources and contacts.
   C. Review performance interview steps.
7. Arrange the room in such a way as to encourage discussion.
   A. Do not have barriers between yourself and the employee (such as a large desk).
   B. Arrange with secretary that there be no phone calls or interruptions.

Performance Appraisal Interview (Steps)

1. Set the subordinate at ease. Begin by stating the purpose of the discussion. Let the individual know that it will be a two-way process. Neither superior nor subordinate should dominate the discussion.
2. Give a general, overall impression of the evaluation.
3. Discuss each dimension separately. Ask the employee to give his/her impression on own performance first. Then explain your position. If there is a problem on some, try *together* to determine the cause. When exploring causes, urge the subordinate to identify three or four causes. Then, jointly determine the most important ones. Identifying causes is important because it points out action plans which might be taken.
4. Together, develop action plans to correct problem areas. These plans will flow naturally from the consideration of the causes. Be specific about the who, what, and when. Be sure to provide for some kind of follow-up or report back.
5. Close the interview on an optimistic note.

Communication Technique Suggestions

1. Do not control the interview—make it two-way. Do this by asking open-ended questions rather than submitting your own solutions. For example, rather than saying, "Jim, I'd like you to do these reports over again," it would be better to say, "Jim, what sort of things might we do here?" Avoid questions that lead to one-word responses.
2. Stress behaviors and results rather than personal traits. Say, "I've noticed that your weekly report has been one to two days late in the last six weeks," rather than, "You tend to be a tardy, lazy person."
3. Show interest and concern. Instead of saying, "Too bad, but we all go through that," say, "I think I know what you're feeling. I remember a similar experience."
4. Allow the subordinate to finish a sentence or thought. This includes being receptive to the subordinate's own ideas and suggestions. For example, rather than saying, "You may have something there, but let's go back to the real problem," say, "I'm not certain I understand how that relates to this problem. Why don't you fill me in on it a bit more?"

These last four suggestions emphasize problem analysis rather than appraisal. Of course, appraisal of past performance is a part of problem analysis, but these suggestions should lead to a more participative and less defensive subordinate role. These suggestions will also help improve creativity in problem solving. The subordinate will have a clearer understanding of why and how he/she needs to change work behavior. There should be a growth of climate of cooperation, which increases motivation to achieve performance goals.

comparison of results versus goals, (6) focus discussion, with performance and ways to improve it as the target, (7) use minimal criticism, and focus on the future and strategies to achieve future goals, (8) eliminate multipurpose appraisal systems; experts suggest that it may be dysfunctional to talk with a ratee about both developmental needs and the size of a merit increase in the same meeting. Some experts believe interviews with different purposes should be separated in time.

EQUAL EMPLOYMENT OPPORTUNITY AND PERFORMANCE EVALUATION

Equal employment opportunity (EEO) and affirmative action have influenced human resource decision making for almost 30 years. Although there are certainly critics of these programs, there has been at least one important trend traceable to the civil rights vigil in the workplace. Specifically, EEO has forced organizations to document decisions and to ensure that their evaluations are firmly tied to performance or expected performance. Nowhere is this more apparent than in the performance appraisal area. Performance appraisals are subject to the same scrutiny as employment tests. Consider the use of performance ratings in making decisions about promotions. In this context, a performance appraisal takes on all the characteristics of a test used to make an initial employment decision. If employees pass the test (i.e., are rated highly in the performance evaluation process), they are predicted to do well (i.e., have promotion potential) at higher level jobs. This interpretation of performance evaluation as a test, subject to validation requirements, was made in *Brito* v. *Zia Company*.[44] In this case, Zia Company used performance ratings based on a rating format to lay off employees. The layoffs resulted in a disproportionate number of minorities being discharged. The court held the following:

> Zia, a government contractor, had failed to comply with the testing guidelines issued by the Secretary of Labor, and that Zia had not developed job-related criteria for evaluating employees' work performance to be used in determining employment promotion and discharges which is required to protect minority group applicants and employees from the discriminatory effects of such failure.[45]

Since the *Brito* case there has been growing evidence that the courts have very specific standards and requirements for performance appraisal.[46] The courts stress six issues as important in setting up a performance appraisal system.[47] First, the courts are

---

[44]*Brito* v. *Zia Company*, 478 F. 2d. 1200 (1973).

[45]Ibid.

[46]G. L. Lubben, D. E. Thompson, and C. R. Klasson, "Performance Appraisal: The Legal Implications of Title VII," *Personnel* 57, no. 3 (1980), pp. 11–21; H. Feild and W. Halley, "The Relationship of Performance Appraisal System Characteristics to Verdicts in Selected Employment Discrimination Cases," *Academy of Management Journal* 25, no. 2 (1982), pp. 392–406; *Albermarle Paper Company* v. *Moody*, U.S. Supreme Court, no. 74-389 and 74-428, 10 FEP Cases 1181 (1975); also *Moody* v. *Albermarle Paper Company*, 474 F. 3d. 134.

[47]Feild and Hally, "The Relationship of Performance Appraisal System Characteristics to Verdicts in Selected Employment Discrimination Cases"; and Gerald Barrett and Mary Kernan, "Performance Appraisal and Terminations: A Review of Court Decisions Since *Brito* v. *Zia* with Implications for Personnel Practices," *Personnel Psychology* 40 (1987), pp. 489–503.

favorably disposed to appraisal systems that give specific written instructions on how to complete the appraisal. Presumably, more extensive training in other facets of evaluation would also be viewed favorably by the courts. Second, organizations tend to be able to support their cases better when the appraisal system incorporates clear criteria for evaluating performance. Performance dimensions and scale levels that are written, objective, and clearly understood tend to be viewed positively by courts in discrimination suits.[48] In part, this probably arises because behaviorally oriented appraisals have more potential to provide workers feedback about developmental needs. Third, as pointed out by every basic personnel book ever printed, and reinforced by this text, the presence of adequately developed job descriptions provides a rational foundation for personnel decision making of every form. The courts reinforce this by ruling more consistently for the defendant (company) when its appraisal systems are based on sound job descriptions. Fourth, courts also approve of appraisal systems that require supervisors to provide feedback about appraisal results to the employees affected. Absence of secrecy permits employees to identify weaknesses and to challenge undeserved appraisals. Fifth, the courts seem to like evaluation systems that incorporate a review of any performance rating by a higher level supervisor(s). Finally, and perhaps most important, the courts consistently have suggested that the key to fair appraisals depends on consistent treatment across ratees, regardless of race, color, religion, sex, and national origin. The focal question then becomes whether similarly situated individuals are treated similarly. This standard is particularly evident in a recent court case involving performance appraisal and merit pay.[49] A black male filed suit against General Motors, claiming race discrimination in both the timing and amount of a merit increase. The court found this case without merit. General Motors was able to show that the same set of rules was applied equally across all individuals.

What will be the probable thrust of future EEO cases dealing with performance appraisal? If performance evaluations continue to be treated as tests, a number of trends can be predicted. First, the courts will continue to require that performance standards are content valid (i.e., they must be related to the job being evaluated). This means that dimensions on which performance is to be rated must be derived from job analysis, reflecting content of the job in question. Second, it is also likely the courts will insist that performance evaluations be as free as possible from errors (e.g., halo, leniency, severity, central tendency) based on subjective judgments. Partial support for these predictions comes from a Supreme Court case, *Albermarle Paper Co.* v. *Moody*.[50] In this case, Albermarle used a rating system based on overall job performance to evaluate employee performance. The Court found this inappropriate:

> Albermarle's supervisors were asked to rank employees by a "standard" that was extremely vague and fatally open to divergent interpretations. Each job grouping contained a number of different jobs, and the supervisors were asked, in each grouping, to "determine which

[48]D. Martin and K. Bartol, "The Legal Ramifications of Performance Appraisal: An Update," *Employee Relations* 17, no. 2 (1991).

[49]*Payne* v. *General Motors,* 53 Fair Employment Practice Cases (BNA) 471 (D, C, Kan. 1990).

[50]*Albermarle Paper Company* v. *Moody;* also *Moody* v. *Albermarle Paper Company.*

ones (employees) they felt, irrespective of the job that they were actually doing, but in their respective jobs, did a better job than the person they were rating against. . . ." There is no way of knowing precisely what criteria of job performance the supervisor was considering, the same criteria or whether, indeed, any of the supervisors actually applied a focused and stable body of criteria of any kind.[51]

A third possible requirement for performance evaluation could be that the process be empirically validated (i.e., some demonstration that the performance ratings for employees predict, in the case of promotions, performance on the job after promotion). If this requirement is mandated, current organizational practices will have to be dramatically altered. In a survey of company performance appraisal practices, not one of 217 companies using performance appraisal results to make promotion decisions had completed an empirical study to determine whether the ratings were a good predictor of later job performance after promotion.[52]

If EEO affects the performance evaluation area to any serious extent, two formats appear most likely to survive: behaviorally anchored ratings scales and management by objectives. Each requires close attention to job content in establishing performance dimensions or objectives. Each focuses on assessment of concrete observable performance dimensions. And each has the latitude to provide employees with specific feedback about performance, lessening the chances of charges based on subjective biases.

TYING PAY TO SUBJECTIVELY APPRAISED PERFORMANCE

Think, for a moment, about what it really means to give employees merit increases. Bill Peterson makes $40,000 per year. He gets a merit increase of 5 percent, the approximate average increase over the past few years.[53] Bill's take-home increase (adjusted for taxes) is a measly $27 more than he used to make. Before we console Bill, though, consider Jane Krefting, who is a better performer than Bill, and receives an 8 percent merit increase. Should she be thrilled by this pay for performance differential and motivated to continue as a high achiever? Probably not. After taxes, her paycheck (assuming a base salary similar to Bill's) is only $15 dollars per week more than Bill's check.

The central issue involving merit pay is "how do we get employees to view raises as a reward for performance." Chapter 8 illustrated this difficulty in theoretical terms. Now it is addressed from a pragmatic perspective. Very simply, organizations frequently grant increases that are not designed or communicated to be related to performance. Perhaps the central reason for this is the way merit pay is managed. Many companies view raises not as motivational tools to shape behavior but as budgetary line items to control costs.[54] Frequently this results in pay increase guidelines with little motivational

---

[51]Schlei and Grossman, *Employee Discrimination Law*, p. 173.

[52]Robert I. Lazer, "The Discrimination Danger in Performance Appraisal," in *Contemporary Problems in Personnel*, ed. W. Hammer and F. Schmidt (Chicago: St. Clair Press, 1977), pp. 239–45.

[53]G. Milkovich and C. Milkovich, "Strengthening the Pay-for-Performance Relationship," *Compensation and Benefits Review*. In press.

[54]Ibid.

impact. The three pay increase guidelines that particularly lead to low motivation will be discussed briefly before outlining a standard that *attempts* to link pay to performance.[55]

Two types of pay increase guidelines with low-motivation potential provide equal increases to all employees regardless of performance. The first, a general increase, typically is found in unionized firms. A contract is negotiated that specifies an across-the-board (equal) increase for each year of the contract. Similar increases occur because of cost-of-living adjustments (COLA), but these would be triggered by changes in the consumer price index (CPI) (Chapter 17).

The third form of guideline comes somewhat closer to tying pay to performance. Longevity (seniority) increases tie pay increases to a preset progression pattern based on seniority. For example, a pay grade might be divided into 10 equal steps, and employees move to higher steps based on seniority. To the extent that performance improves with time on the job, this method has the rudiments of paying for performance.

By far the most prevalent form of pay guideline for exempt employees is one intended to link pay and performance.[56] Invariably this guideline takes one of two forms. The simpler version (Exhibit 9.12) specifies pay increases permissible for different levels of performance.

Increases expressed in the form of ranges (as in Exhibit 9.12) may be warranted if the goal is to give supervisors some discretion in the amount of increases. A variant on this guideline would permit the time between increases to vary. Better performers might receive increases every 8 months; the poorest performers might have to wait 15 months to two years for their next increase.

A more complex guideline ties pay not only to performance but also to position in the pay range. Exhibit 9.13 illustrates such a system for a food market firm. The percentages in the cells of Exhibit 9.13 are changed yearly to reflect changing economic conditions. Despite these changes, though, two characteristics remain constant. First, as would be expected in a pay-for-performance system, lower performance is tied to lower pay increases. In fact, in many organizations, the poorest performers receive no merit increases. The second relationship is that pay increases at a decreasing rate (percentage)

EXHIBIT 9.12 Performance-Based Guideline

	1	2	3	4	5
Performance level	Outstanding	Very satisfactory	Satisfactory	Unsatisfactory	Marginally unsatisfactory
Merit increase	6–8%	5–7%	4–6%	2–4%	0%

---

[55]*Compensating Salaried Employees during Inflation: General vs. Merit Increases,* Report no. 796 (New York: The Conference Board, 1981).

[56]Jackson, Schuller, and Rivero, "Organizational Characteristics as Predictors of Personnel Practices."

as employees move through a pay range. For the same level of performance, employees low in the range receive higher percentage increases than employees who have progressed farther through the range. In part this is designed to forestall the time when employees reach the salary maximum and have salaries frozen. In part, though, it is also a cost-control mechanism tied to budgeting procedures, as discussed in Chapter 15.

Performance- and Position-Based Guideline

Given a salary increase matrix, merit increases are relatively easy to determine. As Exhibit 9.13 indicates, an employee at the top of a pay grade who receives a "competent" rating would receive a 4 percent increase in base salary. A new trainee starting out below the minimum of a pay grade would receive a 10 percent increase for a "commendable" performance rating.

Designing Merit Guidelines

Designing merit guidelines involves answering four questions. First, what should the poorest performer be paid as an increase? Notice that this figure is seldom negative! Wage increases are, unfortunately, considered an entitlement. Wage cuts tied to poor performance are very rare. Most organizations, though, are willing to give no increases to very poor performers.

The second question involves average performers. How much should they be paid as an increase? Most organizations try to ensure that average performers are kept whole (wages will still have the same purchasing power) relative to cost of living. This dictates that the midpoint of the merit guidelines equals the percentage change in the local or national cost-of-living index (usually the CPI). Following this guideline, the 6 percent increase for an average performer in the second quartile of Exhibit 9.13 would reflect the change in CPI for that area. In a year with lower inflation, all the percentages in the matrix probably would be lower.

Third, how much should the top performers be paid? In part, budgetary considerations (Chapter 15) answer this question. But there is also growing evidence that employees vary as to the size of increases that they consider meaningful (Chapter 8). Continuation

---

EXHIBIT 9.13   Performance Rating Salary Increase Matrix

Position in Range / Performance Rating	Unsatisfactory	Improvement Needed	Competent	Commendable	Superior
Fourth quartile	0%	0%	4%	5%	6%
Third quartile	0%	0%	5%	6%	7%
Second quartile	0%	0%	6%	7%	8%
First quartile	0%	2%	7%	8%	9%
Below minimum of range	0%	3%	8%	9%	10%

of this research may help determine the approximate size of increases needed to "make a difference" in employee performance.

Finally, matrices can differ in the size of the differential between different levels of performance. Exhibit 9.13 basically rewards successive levels of performance with 1 percent increases (at least in the portion of the matrix in which any increase is granted). A larger jump between levels would signal a stronger commitment to recognizing performance with higher pay increases. Most companies balance this, though, against cost considerations. Larger differentials cost more. When money is tight, this option is less attractive.

PROMOTIONAL INCREASES AS A PAY-FOR-PERFORMANCE TOOL

Let's not forget that firms have methods of rewarding good performance other than raises. One of the most effective is a promotion accompanied by a salary increase, generally reported as being in the 8 to 12 percent range. This method of linking pay to performance has at least two characteristics that distinguish it from traditional annual merit pay increases. First, the very size of the increment is approximately double a normal merit increase. A clearer message is sent to employees, both in the form of money and promotion, that good performance is valued and *tangibly rewarded*. Second, promotion increases represent, in a sense, a return to employees for commitment and exemplary performance over a sustained period of time. Promotions are not generally annual events. They complement annual merit rewards by showing employees that there are benefits to both single-year productivity and to continuation of such desirable behavior.

SUMMARY

The process of appraising employee performance can be both time-consuming and stressful. These costs are compounded if the appraisal system is poorly developed or if a supervisor lacks appropriate training to collect and evaluate performance data. Development of a sound appraisal system(s) requires an understanding of organizational objectives balanced against the relative merits of each type of appraisal system. For example, despite its inherent weaknesses, an appraisal system based on ranking of employee performance may be appropriate in small organizations that, for a variety of reasons, choose not to tie pay to performance. In contrast, a sophisticated management-by-objective appraisal system may not be appropriate for such a company.

Training supervisors effectively to appraise performance requires an understanding of organizational objectives. We know relatively little about the ways in which raters process information and evaluate employee performance. However, a thorough understanding of organizational objectives combined with a knowledge of common errors in evaluation can make a significant difference in the quality of appraisals.

REVIEW QUESTIONS

1. LeBoy Corporation manufactures specialty equipment for the auto industry (e.g., seat frames). One job involves operation of machines that form heat-treated metal into

different shaped seats. The job is fairly low-level and routine. Without any further information, which of the six types of appraisal formats (see Exhibit 9.9) do you think would be most appropriate for this job? Justify your answer.

2. Employees in your department have formed semiautonomous work teams (they determine their own production schedule and individual work assignments). Individual performance is assessed using four performance dimensions: quantity of work, quality of work, interpersonal skills, and teamwork. Should the supervisor have a role in the rating process? What role, if any, should other members of the work team have in the assessment process?

3. What do you think should be included in the design of a performance appraisal process to lessen the probability that your company would be accused of discrimination in performance appraisal?

4. If you wanted to ensure that employees had good feedback about performance problems and strengths, which appraisal format would you recommend using? Why?

5. Assume that you had one employee fall into each of the cells in Exhibit 9.13 (25 employees in the company). How much would base salary increase in dollars if the current average salary in the company is $15,000? (Assume that ratings are randomly distributed by salary level, so that you can use $15,000 as your base salary for calculation in each of the cells.)

3M'S POSITION-TAILORED PERFORMANCE REVIEW

MAIL TO:	Manager's Name J. J. Mc Habe	Manager's Address	Date Prepared

Employee Name John T. Doe		Personnel Action Code	Employee Number 1234567
Position Title Sales		Country Canada	Date PDQ Completed 01/04/83
Functional Area Engineering		Date Entered Present Position / /	Appraisal Period From / / To / /

Section I–Overall Performance

Check the box below that best summarizes this employee's overall job performance in terms of the job requirements. Your rating should take into account

1. The degree to which the job requirements have been satisfied.
2. The difficulty of the job requirements.
3. The employee's methods for satisfying job requirements.

☐	Excellent	Achievements consistently far exceed the position's key objectives.
☐	Better than satisfactory	Achievements consistently meet and frequently exceed the position's key objectives or requirements.
☐	Satisfactory	Achievements consistently meet the position's key objectives or requirements. Accomplishments may exceed work requirements in some areas.
☐	Needs further improvement	Achievements partially meet the position's key objectives or requirements. With improvement, performance should become satisfactory.
☐	Unsatisfactory	Achievements do not meet the position's key objectives or requirements.

Major job responsibilities during appraisal period: List, in order of importance, what this employee was supposed to do during this appraisal period.

Time spent in major functions

80%	Representing
70%	Coordinating
60%	Administration
50%	Consulting
40%	Monitoring business indicators
30%	Controlling
20%	Supervising
12%	Other
10%	Planning and organizing

Accomplishments for this appraisal period: List significant accomplishments or results achieved during this appraisal period related to the major job responsibilities listed above. Explain any lack of results.

<table>
<tr><td colspan="2">
**3M'S POSITION-TAILORED
PERFORMANCE REVIEW**
</td><td>
John T. Doe
PDQ Completed 01/04/83
</td></tr>
</table>

Section II–Performance Factors

This section contains nine job performance factors, definitions of these factors, and examples of each factor. Rate this employee's job performance by:

1. Reading the definitions and examples of each factor.
2. Rating the employee on each factor by placing an X in the appropriate box of the shaded column. If a factor is not applicable, write "NA" in the Comments section for that factor.

The Comments section for each factor can be used to expand upon the ratings made.

---

1. **Economics management:** Uses information, finances, equipment, and supplies to maximize long-term profit; achieves forecasts and objectives.

   - Determining plans and performance objectives of an organization the size of 3M, worldwide.
   - Determining plans and performance objectives of an organization the size of a sector.
   - Determining plans and performance objectives of an organization the size of a group or international geographic area.
   - Forecasts manpower requirements.
   - Reviews and, if necessary, revises budget allocations.

	Far exceeds requirements
	Exceeds requirements
	Meets all requirements
	Partially meets requirements
	Does not meet requirements

   Comments:

---

2. **Emphasizing goals and productivity:** Setting and attainment of high performance standards for self and group in line with company goals.

   - Developing implementation strategy for long-range plans.
   - Planning and coordinating the introduction of new products or services.
   - Determining plans to phase out unprofitable products/services.
   - Setting selling prices.
   - Making additions to headcount that are within the approved budget.

	Far exceeds requirements
	Exceeds requirements
	Meets all requirements
	Partially meets requirements
	Does not meet requirements

   Comments:

---

3. **Organizing and facilitating work:** Plans, organizes, and ensures effective job performance through oral and written communication and delegation of tasks to subordinates.

   - Hiring an individual for an approved position.
   - Determining reductions in employee headcount, should this become necessary.
   - Revising the structure of an organization having 400 or more employees.
   - Evaluating an organization of 200–400 employees to determine the best allocation and utilization of resources.
   - Scheduling work of subordinates so that it flows evenly and steadily.

	Far exceeds requirements
	Exceeds requirements
	Meets all requirements
	Partially meets requirements
	Does not meet requirements

   Comments:

---

4. **Managing subordinates:** Emphasizes cooperation and teamwork among subordinates; motivates subordinates.

   - Allocating and scheduling resources to ensure that they will be available when needed.
   - Developing operational policies and procedures under which managers are expected to perform.
   - Establishing parameters to guide the planning of organizations in excess of 800 employees.
   - Giving guidance to other organizations for planning beyond one year.
   - Recommending changes in policy and procedures.

	Far exceeds requirements
	Exceeds requirements
	Meets all requirements
	Partially meets requirements
	Does not meet requirements

   Comments:

3M'S POSITION-TAILORED PERFORMANCE REVIEW	John T. Doe PDQ Completed 01/04/83

5. Knowledge of job: Has and regularly updates knowledge of job-related concepts and/or skills.

- Determining implementation methods for meeting operational objectives established by others.
- Makes use of assigned administrative or technical staff.
- Defines areas of responsibility for managerial personnel.
- Interacts face-to-face with subordinates on an almost daily basis.
- Assigns priorities for others on no less than a quarterly basis.

	Far exceeds requirements
	Exceeds requirements
	Meets all requirements
	Partially meets requirements
	Does not meet requirements

Comments:

6. Problem solving and decision making: Monitors and analyzes situations, identifies problems, and makes appropriate decisions to resolve problems.

- Develops executive level management talent.
- Reviews subordinates' work almost continually.
- Reviews subordinates' work methods for possible increases in productivity.
- Motivates subordinates to change or improve performance.
- Analyzes subordinates' weaknesses and training needs.

	Far exceeds requirements
	Exceeds requirements
	Meets all requirements
	Partially meets requirements
	Does not meet requirements

Comments:

7. Appraisal and development of subordinates: Evaluates subordinates objectively on a regular basis and is active in the setting and attainment of objectives for subordinates.

- Guides subordinates on technical aspects of the job.
- Monitors subordinates' progress toward objec. of unit and adjusts activ. as necessary to reach them.
- Provides complete instructions to subordinates when giving assignments.
- Delegates work, assigns responsibility to subordinates, and establishes appropriate controls.
- Maintains a smooth working relationship among various individuals who need to work cooperatively.

	Far exceeds requirements
	Exceeds requirements
	Meets all requirements
	Partially meets requirements
	Does not meet requirements

Comments:

8. Equal opportunities: Utilizes skills and talents of subordinates and ensures equal opportunities for all subordinates.

	Far exceeds requirements
	Exceeds requirements
	Meets all requirements
	Partially meets requirements
	Does not meet requirements

Comments:

9. Other:

	Far exceeds requirements
	Exceeds requirements
	Meets all requirements
	Partially meets requirements
	Does not meet requirements

Comments:

3M'S POSITION-TAILORED PERFORMANCE REVIEW	John T. Doe PDQ Completed 01/04/83

Section III–Development Plan

This section helps develop the jobholder's skills as they pertain to this position.

Relative strengths	Specific recommendations for better utilizing strengths	Target date
	Manager:	
	Employee:	
	Human resources:	

Relative weaknesses	Specific recommendations for improving current job performance	Target date
	Manager:	
	Employee:	
	Human resources:	

3M'S POSITION-TAILORED **PERFORMANCE REVIEW**	John T. Doe PDQ Completed 01/04/83

Section IV–Overall Comments

Comments of J. J. Mc Habe

Comments of reviewer

Comments of John T. Doe

Section V–Signatures

This performance review has been reviewed and discussed with the employee:

Employee Signature: John T. Doe	Manager Signature: J. J. Mc Habe	Reviewer Signature
Date	Date	Date

outokumpu american brass

Salaried Personnel Performance Appraisal

Name		OAB Employee #	OAB Service Date
(Last)	(First)	(MI)	Appraisal Date _____ / _____ / _____
Location		Function	Department
Classification Title		Pay Grade	Time in present position _____ years _____ months

Performance Rating (check one)

			Comment (if any)
Exceeds Standards	1	—	
	2	—	
Meets Standards	3	—	
	4	—	
	5	—	
Does Not Meet Standards	6	—	
	7	—	

A copy of this form is to be provided to the employee upon completion of the appraisal process.

Submit the original to the Human Resources Department

Employee Signature: _____

(your signature does not imply agreement)

Completed by: _____

Reviewed by: _____

Job Knowledge:	The ability to effectively understand, utilize and demonstrate technical concepts and operating procedures applicable to all aspects of the job. People differ in the breadth of knowledge across jobs, the depth of knowledge within jobs, and the ability to innovatively use this knowledge to complete tasks.

Exceeds Standards

1	2
Displays broad knowledge and innovative ability on technical concepts and operating procedures for even the most complex tasks. Most people in the department consider this person the expert on a wide variety of department jobs.	Broad knowledge of technical and operating procedures for all aspects of own and closely related jobs. If you needed to know both standard and alternative procedures for performing any aspect of this job you would think of this person as the source.

Meets Standards

3	4	5
Broad knowledge of standard technical and operating procedures for all aspects of own job. If you needed to know existing or alternative procedures for any aspect of this job, this person could be expected to provide correct information.	Generally knowledgeable about all standard technical and operating aspects of own job. Might be expected to occasionally double check procedures with others on the most complex of tasks.	Generally understands standard job components but may not be versed in all the more complex aspects. Wouldn't normally expect others to go to this person for technical and/or operating information because of these knowledge gaps. Would expect this person to go to others for information rather than perform inadequately because of knowledge gaps.

Does Not Meet Standards

6	7
Technical and/or operating information about some standard aspects of job may be faulty, leading to occasional improper performance of job. May show desire to improve but progress has been minimal thus far.	Regularly makes mistakes because of faulty knowledge on many standard and more complex aspects of job. Shows little sign of improvement despite prior counseling.

Rating	Documentation of Rating (optional except for 6 & 7):
____	

329

Interpersonal Skills:

The ability to show understanding, support, courtesy, tact and cooperation in interactions with coworkers, subordinates, customers, and visitors. People differ in the extent they are recognized and sought out to show this skill, the frequency and nature of lapses in this skill, and the ability to recognize and correct lapses as they occur.

Exceeds Standards

1	2
The understanding support and tact shown by these employees make them the choice for difficult negotiations with others; reaction to sensitive business ideas; ability to resolve conflict between individuals. Is recognized company-wide for consistency in interpersonal skills.	This person is seen by others as genuinely interested in their welfare. Able to make others feel comfortable when asked to conduct discussions of even the most sensitive and stressful subjects. Is recognized department wide for consistency in interpersonal skills.

Meets Standards

3	4	5
This person could be expected to show courtesy, tact and understanding in interactions with coworkers, subordinates, customers and visitors even under sensitive and stressful circumstances.	This person occasionally might have lapses in courtesy, tact and understanding in sensitive and stressful situations, but lapses would be confined to internal employees and not customers / visitors. Person could be expected to recognize and seek to repair damage to relationship immediately.	This person occasionally might have lapses in courtesy, tact and understanding, but lapses would be confined to internal employees. Would be expected to seek to repair damage to relationship immediately if recognized.

Does Not Meet Standards

6	7
Lapses in courtesy, tact and understanding are not uncommon and not confined to just internal employees. Could be expected to attempt to repair damage to relationship, when it is recognized or pointed out. Seems genuinely interested in improving.	Lapses in courtesy, tact and understanding are not uncommon and not confined to just internal employees. Could be expected to show little remorse and not feel damage repair is personal responsibility.

Rating	Documentation of Rating (optional except for 6 & 7):
___	

330

Organization & Planning:	Ability to systematically make plans and set objectives, structure tasks to achieve objectives, establish priorities and make schedules.	

Exceeds Standards		Meets Standards			Does Not Meet Standards	
1	2	3	4	5	6	7
Can be relied upon to have a plan for accomplishing tasks, even when working from unclear directions or vague strategic goals. Plan shows clear recognition of problems and constraints. Tasks have reasonable timeframes and accurately reflect company or supervisory priorities.	Once understands overall responsibilities as explained by supervisor, could be expected to develop a clear plan for tasks to be completed without being prompted. Plan usually shows clear recognition of problems and constraints. Tasks have reasonable timeframes and accurately reflect supervisor's priorities.	Supervisor explains overall responsibilities. Without prompting, this employee could be expected to develop an effective plan of attack with only occasional assistance from supervisor in one or more of the following: defining tasks to be performed, establishing priorities and timeframes, identifying constraints.	Supervisor explains overall responsibilities. Occasionally requires prompting to develop plan for completing tasks. Supervisor provides occasional assistance in: defining tasks to be performed, establishing priorities and timeframes, identifying constraints.	Supervisor explains overall responsibilities. Occasionally requires prompting to develop plan for completing tasks. Supervisor occasionally (on complex tasks) must monitor planning and organizing to ensure no gaps in: defining tasks to be performed, establishing priorities and timeframes, identifying constraints.	Supervisor explains overall responsibilities and must assist employee in outlining tasks to be performed. Planning and organization still show gaps and possible errors. Employee misses deadlines because of poor plan of attack or prioritization of tasks.	Without direct intervention by supervisor this employee could be expected to work without any clear plan for completing tasks; has only vague ideas about priorities, time tables and constraints.

Rating	**Documentation of Rating** (optional except for 6 & 7):
___	

Communications Skills:	Written and oral ability to clearly and convincingly express thoughts, ideas or facts in individual or group situations.

Exceeds Standards		Meets Standards			Does Not Meet Standards	
1	2	3	4	5	6	7
Through clarity and logic of communications is able to persuade others to adopt policies and practices, even those which may have been unpopular initially. Makes complex ideas understandable for all levels and types of audiences. Would be a top choice for presenting an unpopular subject to a hostile audience.	Clearly and logically presents ideas in a way that makes even complex subjects easy to grasp for a wide variety of audiences. Frequently is able to persuade others to adopt policies and practices, even those which may have been unpopular initially. Not normally among the first people considered to present an unpopular subject to a hostile audience.	Typically presents ideas clearly and logically without assistance from others. Recognizes when content of message is not understood and is able to re-explain ideas in a different manner to clarify. Communications ability may not have the power to convert unsympathetic listeners.	Ideas are clear and logical, but success may come only after pretesting arguments with others and clarifying content of message. Recognizes when content of message is not understood and usually is able to rephrase in a way that clarifies.	With help of others can develop clear and logical communications. Occasionally, may not be clear when ideas are first presented in casual conversations or in written drafts, but on own or with help, recognizes where message is not understood. Struggles to find ways to clarify message and is usually successful.	Occasionally unclear in formal presentations and in final papers, either because of failure to seek input from others or because of inability to act upon that input. May not be able to recognize when listeners or readers do not understand message. May not be able to clarify message even when gap in understanding is recognized. Gives appearance of trying to improve these skills.	Frequently unclear in communications of both casual and great importance. Shows little ability or interest in understanding where misunderstanding is or in correcting same.

Rating	Documentation of Rating (optional except for 6 & 7):
____	

Judgement: Ability to obtain and evaluate information from all relevant sources. Uses information effectively to arrive at conclusions which are appropriate to the situation.

Exceeds Standards

1	2
Readily perceives existent or potential problems, collects information relevant to solution from affected sources. Makes effective decisions which reflect sensitivity to Financial, Operating and Human Resource constraints of both short and long term nature.	Readily perceives existing problems. Usually able to identify potential problems before they occur. With occasional direction from others is able to identify and obtain information from parties who will be affected by decision. Decisions effective from short term perspective and usually reflect consideration of long term concerns.

Meets Standards

3	4	5
Good at perceiving existing problems. May need help to identify potential problem areas, but responds quickly when identified. Understands importance of getting input from affected parties, and able to identify many of these sources on own. Usually needs help, though, to identify input sources. Decisions are typically quite good from a short term perspective and at least reflect consideration of long term issues.	Responsive to claims by others that potential or current problems exist. Frequently is aware of these concerns on own. Seeks and obtains help in identifying appropriate sources for input information. First pass at problem solution may be incomplete, but is diligent in seeking input from others before errors result. Final decisions are typically good from a short term perspective and at least reflect consideration of long term issues.	Responsive to claims by others that potential or current problems exist. Not always perceptive on own, though, that problems exist or are developing. First pass at problem solution may be incomplete, but is diligent in seeking input from others before errors result. Final decisions are acceptable but sometimes not optimal, either in short or long term perspective.

Does Not Meet Standards

6	7
Occasionally fails to recognize existing or potential problems and may let them magnify before acting on advice of others. Once acts, though, can be spurred by others to seek information from some, but not always all, relevant sources. Not always diligent in getting input to final decision. Decisions regularly are unacceptable from short and/or long term perspective.	Shows little effort to recognize or deal with problems unless forced by others. Decisions lack input of relevant sources and are usually unacceptable.

Documentation of Rating (optional except for 6 & 7):

Rating _____

Initiative-Dependability:

Ability to fulfill responsibilities on time and according to expectations of supervisor. Includes recognition and quality completion of necessary tasks beyond the scope of initial instructions.

Exceeds Standards

1	2	3
Recognizes tasks which need to be performed to complete overall mission. Undertakes such tasks, even if beyond initial instructions of supervisor, checking for approval where appropriate. Completes these and other assigned tasks on time, even if efforts beyond the norm are required.	Receives task assignments from supervisor and regularly finds ways to exceed requirements. Completes tasks on time and according to directions of supervisor, even if efforts beyond the norm are required.	Receives task assignments from supervisor and occasionally finds ways to exceed requirements. Completes tasks on time and according to directions of supervisor, even if efforts beyond the norm are required.

Meets Standards

4	5
Receives task assignments and occasionally finds ways to exceed requirements. Completes top priority tasks on time, and few modifications are needed. Usually completes important tasks on time and without reminders. This work may have minor flaws which employee might catch and correct immediately, causing deadline to be narrowly missed. Occasionally exerts efforts beyond those normally required.	Rarely would expect this person to complete tasks beyond those assigned by supervisor. Completes top priority tasks accurately and on time, but occasionally may need to be reminded to do so. Less important tasks are completed, but sometimes reminders are needed when deadlines are drawing close. May leave these tasks to last minute such that, to meet deadline, minor flaws are not corrected. Corrects flaws immediately when noted. Wouldn't be expected to regularly and willingly exert efforts beyond those normally required.

Does Not Meet Standards

6	7
Does work assigned but occasionally misses important deadlines, and more often misses lesser deadlines, unless closely supervised. Work regularly does not meet supervisor expectations, but employee can be expected to try to make corrections. Only reluctantly exerts efforts beyond those normally required.	Can not be counted on to meet deadlines except under very close supervision. Even then, work does not meet minimum expectations. Employee begrudgingly corrects work if demanded, but errors may still exist. Only works beyond normal hours when directly instructed.

Rating	Documentation of Rating (optional except for 6 & 7):
___	

334

Teamwork:	Ability to contribute to group performance, to draw out the best from others, to foster activities building group morale, even under high pressure situations.

Exceeds Standards		Meets Standards			Does Not Meet Standards	
1	2	3	4	5	6	7
Seeks out or is regularly requested for group assignments. Groups this person works with inevitably have high performance and high morale. Employee makes strong personal contribution and is able to identify strengths of many different types of group members and foster their participation. Wards off personality conflicts by positive attitude and ability to mediate unhealthy conflicts, sometimes even before they arise. Will make special effort to insure credit for group performance is shared by all.	Seen as a positive personal contributor in group assignments. Works well with all types of people and personalities, occasionally elevating group performance. Good ability to resolve unhealthy group conflicts that flare up. Will make special effort to insure strong performers receive credit due them.	Seen as a positive personal contributor in group assignments. Works well with most types of people and personalities. Is never a source of unhealthy group conflict and will encourage the same behavior in others.	When group mission requires skill this person is strong in, employee seen as strong contributor. On other occasions will not hinder performance of others. Works well with most types of people and personalities and will not be the initiator of unhealthy group conflict. Will not participate in such conflict unless provoked on multiple occasions.	Depending on the match of personal skill and group mission, this person will be seen as a positive contributor. Will not be a hindrance to performance of others and avoids unhealthy conflict unless provoked.	Unlikely to be chosen for assignments requiring teamwork except on occasions where personal expertise is vital to group mission. Not responsive to group goals, but can be enticed to help when personal appeals are made. May not get along with other members and either withdraw or generate unhealthy conflict. Seeks personal recognition for team performance and/or may downplay efforts of others.	Has reputation for non contribution and for creating conflicts in groups. Cares little about group goals and is very hard to motivate towards goal completion unless personal rewards are guaranteed. May undermine group performance to further personal aims. Known to seek personal recognition and/or downplay efforts of others.

Rating	Documentation of Rating (optional except for 6 & 7):
___	

335

Quantity / Quality:	Amount of high quality work completed in a variety of situations relative to expectations.

Exceeds Standards

1	2	3
Consistently exceeds expectations in both quality and quantity of work for tasks requiring widely different skills.	Output often exceeds standards and is of the highest quality, even across tasks requiring widely different skills.	Consistently exceeds expectations in both quality and quantity of work for tasks in area of known competence. For tasks requiring less developed skills, meets expectations for both quantity and quality.

Meets Standards

4	5
Consistently meets, and occasionally exceeds, expectations in both quality and quantity of work for tasks in area of known competence. For tasks requiring less developed skills, may initially not meet expectations, but will quickly develop to a satisfactory level.	Meets expectations in quality and quantity of work for tasks in area of known competence. On rare occasions when expectations aren't met initially, employee makes effort to correct problem immediately. For tasks requiring less developed skills, may initially not meet expectations but will quickly develop to a satisfactory level.

Does Not Meet Standards

6	7
Does not consistently meet expectations in quality and quantity of work for tasks in area of known competence. May attempt to correct problem, but still fall below expectations. Shows little interest and capability to achieve acceptable quantity / quality standards in areas of less developed skills.	Frequently marginally misses quality / quantity expectations on a wide variety of tasks or misses by a wide margin on a few tasks, even after prior counseling.

Rating	Documentation of Rating (optional except for 6 & 7):
_____	

336

Management of Human Resources	The ability to effectively select, utilize and develop subordinates. Also requires recognition and compliance with accepted and required personnel policies and procedures. (RATING IN THIS AREA REQUIRED ONLY FOR SUPERVISORY POSITIONS)

Exceeds Standards		Meets Standards			Does Not Meet Standards	
1	2	3	4	5	6	7
Widely recognized in the company as very good at selecting good people, placing them in jobs which utilize their skills effectively, and providing developmental experiences which increase their value to the organization. Is conscientious in keeping current and following accepted and required personnel policies and procedures. Insists on same from subordinates.	Employees within the department would characterize this person as one of the top people in selecting, utilizing and developing subordinates. Complaints by subordinates about treatment rarely occur, and are never traceable to improper behavior by this person. Is conscientious in keeping current and following accepted and required personnel policies and procedures. Insists on same from subordinates.	Good at utilizing and developing better employees. Less conscientious with average employees. Occasionally has employees who don't meet expectations. Likely to consult HR staff and others for strategies to assist these employees. Such strategies are typically successful. Complaints by subordinates about treatment rarely occur, handled appropriately when they do. Conscientious in keeping current and following accepted and required personnel policies and procedures. Subordinates don't always follow these guides as closely.	Has a mixed group of employees in terms of effectiveness. Is concerned about placement and development and will respond to suggestions if offered, but not particularly proactive except for top subordinates. Complaints by subordinates about treatment are handled quickly and effectively. Few lapses of the same type arise later. Will attempt to comply with accepted and required personnel policies and procedures, but both self and subordinates have occasional lapses which are quickly corrected when pointed out.	Mixed group of employees in terms of effectiveness. Concerned about placement and development and will respond to suggestions offered, but not particularly proactive except for top subordinates. Complaints about treatment sometimes follow patterns previously observed, but are handled quickly and usually effectively, at least in short run. Attempts to comply with accepted and required personnel policies & procedures, but both self and subordinates have occasional lapses which are quickly corrected when pointed out.	Seems concerned about selecting and developing good employees, but is a continuing source of complaints. Shows the same pattern of mistakes over time. Corrects problems with help from HR department, but does not seem to have sense of ways to avoid problems in the future. Lapses in compliance with accepted and required personnel policies and procedures are not uncommon for self and subordinates. Responds, at least in short run, to notification about infractions.	Regularly has complaints from employees about treatment. Will respond only when complaint is voiced and pursued outside department. Not unusual to trace violations of accepted personnel policies and procedures back to this department. Shows little talent and/or motivation for changing treatment of employees.

Rating	Documentation of Rating (optional except for 6 & 7):
___	

Performance Against Standards
The ability to achieve objectives as agreed upon by supervisor and employee.
(RATING IN THIS AREA IS OPTIONAL FOR NON-EXEMPT EMPLOYEES)

Exceeds Standards

1	2	3
Exceeds expectations on all objectives	Exceeds expectations on all priority objectives and most remaining objectives. Any problems are generally traceable to external constraints not under control of employee.	Meets or exceeds expectations on all objectives. Exceeds expectations on one, but not all, priority objectives.

Meets Standards

4	5
Meets expectations on all priority objectives. May occasionally fall below standards on one or a few remaining objectives, but this is balanced against performance exceeding expectations on an equal number of other objectives.	On average, performance meets expectations, but there is variability across objectives. Performance which does not meet standards on one objective is balanced against high performance on another objective of approximately equal importance.

Does Not Meet Standards

6	7
On average, performance does not meet expectations. Either the employee generally meets standards on most objectives with a few (more than 1) sub marginal ratings, or, on average, good performance (exceeds standards) does not balance out occasions of poor performance. Does not meet standards on at least one priority objective.	On average, does not meet standards for a majority of objectives. More than one objective not met.

Rating _____

Documentation of Rating (optional except for 6 & 7):

1ˢᵗ PRIORITY (ONE OF TOP THREE OR FOUR IN THIS BUSINESS UNIT) OBJECTIVE & DESIRED RESULTS	ACTUAL RESULTS & COMMENTS	RATING EXCEED, MET, NOT MET OR DEFERRED)

2ⁿᵈ PRIORITY OBJECTIVE & DESIRED RESULTS	ACTUAL RESULTS & COMMENTS	RATING EXCEED, MET, NOT MET, DEFERRED)

3rd PRIORITY OBJECTIVE & DESIRED RESULTS	ACTUAL RESULTS & COMMENTS	RATING EXCEED, MET, NOT MET, AND DEFERRED

4th PRIORITY OBJECTIVE & DESIRED RESULTS	ACTUAL RESULTS & COMMENTS	RATING EXCEED, MET, NOT MET, AND DEFERRED)

OTHER OBJECTIVES & DESIRED RESULTS	ACTUAL RESULTS & COMMENTS	RATING
INCLUDE HERE TASKS PERFORMED BUT NOT ANTICIPATED AT START OF PLAN YEAR		EXCEED, MET, NOT MET, DEFERRED

WHAT TRAINING PROGRAMS OR OTHER ACTIVITIES WILL BE SCHEDULED TO INCREASE THIS PERSON'S JOB RELATED SKILLS?

EMPLOYEE COMMENTS (OPTIONAL): EMPLOYEE COMMENTS MUST BE REVIEWED AND INITIALED BY ALL SUPERVISORS INVOLVED IN THE PROCESS.

REVIEWER'S INITIALS

1	2	3	4
___	___	___	___

Your Turn: Policy Implications of Merit Pay Guides

GEMCAR is a manufacturer of decals and hood ornaments for all varieties of American cars. During the past four years, profits have plummeted 43 percent. This decline is attributed to rising costs of production and is widely believed to have triggered the resignation of GEMCAR's longtime president, C. Milton Carol. The newly-hired CEO is Winston McBeade, a former vice-president of finance and of human resources management at Longtemp Enterprises, a producer of novelty watches. As his first policy statement in office, Mr. McBeade declared a war on high production costs. As his first official act, Mr. McBeade proposed implementing a new merit pay guide (see Exhibits 1 and 2 for former and revised pay guides). What can you deduce about Mr. McBeade's "philosophy" of cost control from both the prior and newly revised merit guides? What implications does this new philosophy have for improving the link between pay and performance and, hence, productivity?

Exhibit 1 Merit Pay Guide for Last Year

Position in Salary Range	Performance: *Well Below Average*	*Below Average*	*Average*	*Above Average*	*Well Above Average*
Above Grade Maximum (red circle)	0 0	2 0	3 10	4 5	5 15
Q4	0 0	3 0	4 5	5 10	6 15
Q3	0 0	4 0	5 10	6 25	7 10
Q2	2 	5 2	6 9	7 9	8 10
Q1	2 0	6 3	7 6	8 5	9 9

Notes: 1. Cost of living rose 5 percent last year.
2. The number at the lower right corner of each cell represents the number of employees falling into that cell during the previous year.

EXHIBIT 2   Revised Pay Guide

		Performance				
		Well Below Average	*Below Average*	*Average*	*Above Average*	*Well Above Average*
Position in Salary Range	Above grade maximum (red circle)	0	0	0	0	0
	Q4	0	0	2	4	6
	Q3	0	0	3	5	7
	Q2	0	0	4	6	8
	Q1	0	0	5	7	9

NOTE: Cost of living is expected to rise 5 percent this year.

10 Alternatives to Traditional Reward Systems

Chapter Outline

One way to look at the relationship between an organization and its employees is in the form of a contract. The organization offers inducements (or rewards) that should be designed to satisfy employee *needs*. In return, employees provide contributions of their own in the form of work output.[1] For an organization to achieve its business objectives, it must identify ways to ensure that this work output that is the employee's part of the

---

[1]C. Barnard, *The Function of the Executive* (Cambridge, Mass.: Harvard University Press, 1938); and J. March and H. Simon, *Organizations* (New York: John Wiley, 1958).

contract will support business objectives. In turn, the employer's side of the contract requires the design of *effective reward administration and performance measurement systems*. An effective reward system is designed to satisfy employee needs and reinforce job behaviors consistent with organizational objectives. An effective performance measurement system is designed to translate business objectives into some set of performance expectations and then measure employee performance against those expectations.

Thus far this book has presented a traditional view of reward administration systems in organizations. Jobs are evaluated according to some criteria of internal worth to the organization (Chapter 4). The external worth of jobs is assessed through salary surveys indicating what other firms pay for their jobs (Chapter 7). Based on some combination of internal and external measures of worth, jobs are assigned to pay grades. Movement within those grades is based on individual performance (Chapter 9) or some other measure of personal characteristics (e.g., job tenure).

Although this characterization of compensation still dominates organizational practices, alternative reward systems do exist in firms, and these alternatives are becoming more and more prevalent. Exhibit 10.1 summarizes a number of interesting statistics, all of which show a rising trend toward the use of alternative reward systems.

Columns 1–5 in Exhibit 10.1 show the longevity of alternative reward systems in organizations. Profit sharing plans (16.9 percent of the companies with current plans have had them for 25 years or longer) and individual incentive plans (13.3 percent of companies report histories of more than 25 years with them) have the longest histories in companies. Column 6 indicates the percentage of companies currently using the different types of plans, and column 7 reports the expected increase in adoption. Profit sharing and individual incentive plans currently are most popular, with about 30 percent of the firms using such plans. The greatest future interest, though (in percentage terms), is in pay-for-knowledge systems, small group incentives, and gain-sharing plans.

EXHIBIT 10.1   Alternative Reward Systems and Their Longevity in Organizations—Years' Experience with Different Plans (Percentage of companies)

Type of Plan	1 25 + Years	2 16–25 Years	3 11–15 Years	4 6–10 Years	5 1–5 Years	6 Current	7 Projected
				Use (%) Increase			
Individual incentive plan	13.3%	12.2%	10.2%	22.1%	42.3%	28%	31%
Small group incentive plan	6.2	8.4	6.2	17.4	61.8	14	70
Gain-sharing plan	2.8	.7	4.9	18.7	72.9	13	68
Profit sharing plan	16.9	17.4	14.5	21.5	29.5	32	20
Pay-for-knowledge plan	6.7	0.0	1.7	23.4	68.4	5	75
All-salaried workforce	13.7	20.9	15.8	25.9	23.7	11	29

SOURCE: Carla O'Dell, *Major Findings from People, Performance and Pay* (Houston, Tex.: American Productivity Center, 1986).

Along with this growth in alternative reward systems has been a relative decline in some of the more traditional compensation practices. For example, in a sample of 1,598 respondents from 857 companies, a significant number indicated plans either to eliminate or significantly reduce participation in across-the-board increases (36 percent), cost of living increases (28 percent), and merit increases (25 percent).[2] Although this survey anticipates a decline in the use of traditional merit increases, there is still widespread use of individual performance appraisals and efforts to link these appraisals to individual merit increases (see Chapter 9 for this discussion).

In the next section, we discuss why alternative reward systems are becoming popular. Subsequent sections describe the different types of plans along with their relative strengths and weaknesses for satisfying employee needs and motivating performance consistent with organizational objectives.

EXPLORING THE POPULARITY OF ALTERNATIVE REWARD SYSTEMS

Exhibit 10.1 lists the various innovations that we group as alternative reward systems. In one way or another, all of these alternatives represent experiments by organizations to better tie individuals to them and to better link rewards given to employees to performance of the organization. Such programs are becoming increasingly popular for several reasons. First, increasing domestic and international competition forces companies to be even more cost conscious than in prior eras. Most of these reward systems attempt to control costs by better linking rewards to performance increases. One study of 4,500 organizations found that the single factor that best explained why organizations adopted alternative reward systems was increases in domestic and foreign competition.[3] Second, the rate of technological change seems to be increasing, with new products and new methods of production introduced at what sometimes appears to be a bewildering pace. Organizations that fail to capitalize on new technologies and to recognize new product opportunities face an uncertain future. Their competitors threaten to steal market share and/or erode profits. If this happens, workers face possible layoffs and terminations. To avoid this scenario, compensation experts are focusing on ways to design reward systems so that workers will be able and willing to move quickly into new jobs and new ways of performing old jobs. The ability and incentive to do this comes partially from reward systems that more closely link worker interests with the objectives of the company.

ALTERNATIVE REWARD SYSTEMS

All-Salaried Work Force

Exhibit 10.1 indicates that 11 percent of organizations have moved to an all-salaried work force. The mechanics of this are self-evident. Both exempt employees (exempt from

---

[2]Carla O'Dell, *Major Findings from People, Performance and Pay* (Houston, Tex.: American Productivity Center, 1986).
[3]Ibid.

provisions of the Fair Labor Standards Act; see Chapter 13), who traditionally are paid a salary rather than an hourly rate, and nonexempt employees receive a prescribed amount of money each pay period that does not primarily depend on the number of hours worked. Companies adopt this type of plan to lessen the "we versus them" attitude that sometimes separates management and workers. By paying all workers under the same system and avoiding having "second-class" citizens, such companies hope that an all-salaried work force will more readily share the aspirations of management and work toward the objectives of the firm.

Firms that adopt an all-salaried plan still are subject to provisions of the Fair Labor Standards Act. Employers must still pay nonexempt employees time and one half for any hours worked over 40 during the week. Hence, the advantages of a salaried work force are not in cost savings but rather in perceptions of greater loyalty and commitment to the organization.

Pay-for-Knowledge Systems

Pay-for-knowledge plans (i.e., skill-based pay plans) exist in approximately 5 to 8 percent of companies in the United States.[4] These plans vary compensation as a function of the number of different jobs or skills that employees are able to perform competently (Chapter 4 covers this in greater detail). An example is the General Foods Maxwell House coffee plant in Houston. Since 1985, maintenance workers there have been classified into four skill groups: (1) maintenance workers, (2) machine adjusters, (3) refrigeration mechanics, and (4) instrument and electrical maintenance personnel. Each of the four groups has multiple proficiency levels, and compensation increases are tied to learning multiple jobs at ever-higher levels of proficiency. For example, the maintenance worker position is divided into five levels. Each of the first four levels is worth 15 cents extra (paid as a separate check on a quarterly basis), and the last level is worth 40 cents more.[5]

The General Foods example is fairly typical. Most plans have about 10 skill units, but maximums are reported as high as 100 different skill units.[6] Most companies limit the number of skills a person is allowed to learn (mean = 4) for fear that an employee will become a "jack of all trades, master of none."

Perhaps the most interesting feature of pay-for-knowledge plans is the way they reverse the drive for specialization that has been a hallmark of American industry since the turn of the century. Pay-for-knowledge systems encourage diversification in workers. The major impetus for paying workers to broaden their skill base appears to be the flexibility it offers for firms to quickly change business and product/service emphasis in response to changing technologies and changing consumer demand.[7] Two by-products of this greater flexibility are increased work force stability and greater job security for

---

[4]"Pay For Knowledge," *The Wall Street Journal,* December 16, 1986, p. 1.

[5]Bureau of National Affairs, *Changing Pay Practices: New Developments in Employee Compensation* (Washington, D.C.: BNA; 1988).

[6]Nina Gupta, T. Schweizer, and G. Douglas Jenkins, "Pay for Knowledge Compensation Plans: Hypotheses and Survey Results," *Monthly Labor Review,* October 1987, pp. 40–43.

[7]Bureau of National Affairs, *Changing Pay Practices.*

employees.[8] Workers with multiple job skills can be moved quickly into jobs for which there is high demand. If the sale of pocket calculators drops for Hewlett-Packard while personal computer sales boom, workers with skills in both areas can be reassigned easily. Supporters of pay-for-knowledge systems also claim that workers will be more satisfied with their jobs and company, more motivated, more productive, and have less absenteeism/turnover.[9] In reality, the positive impact of pay-for-knowledge systems may be less impressive, but early feedback is still very encouraging.[10] One study of 20 plants with pay-for-knowledge systems did find increased commitment, satisfaction, and worker productivity. Management also reported labor cost reductions.[11] Interestingly, these companies also reported broad scale improvements in labor-management relationships. Presumably the work force stability and job security resulting from a pay-for-knowledge system contributed to a perception that management was concerned about the welfare of labor, even during periods of fluctuating product demand.

On the negative side of the ledger, pay-for-knowledge systems are more costly, both in terms of compensation costs and training costs. In fact, the General Foods program referred to previously costs about $50,000 per year in increased training costs, and this is for a group of only 135 workers. Critics of pay-for-knowledge systems are also skeptical about claims of increased productivity and reduced labor costs.[12] How, they ask, can workers trained in several different jobs perform all of them better than a group of workers trained in only one job area? This flaunts a major tenant of industrial engineering (i.e., specialization improves efficiency). Perhaps more experience with pay-for-knowledge systems and more reports on their effectiveness will resolve this question.

Incentive Plans

So far the alternative reward systems we have discussed (all-salaried work force and pay-for-knowledge plans) have not been, fundamentally, pay-for-performance plans. Both of these plans focus more on *characteristics* of the individuals (exempt versus nonexempt distinction, number of skill competencies) than on their *performance*. Why would an organization choose to consciously do this, to pay for something other than performance? After all, Chapter 8 illustrated the potential motivation and performance advantages of tying compensation as closely as possible to performance. The answer is simple. Organizations are limited in their ability to tie pay to performance by their ability to measure performance. Some jobs don't have easily definable performance outcomes. How do we measure the performance of an engineer whose job involves making cars more aerodynamic? What is the increased dollar value of a car with a better drag coefficient (wind resistance)? Other jobs have a defined output, but no single individual is responsible for

---

[8]Ibid.

[9]Ibid.

[10]Gupta, Schweizer, and Jenkins, "Pay for Knowledge Compensation Plans: Hypotheses and Survey Results."

[11]Ibid.

[12]Ian Ziskin, "Knowledge-Based Pay! A Strategic Analysis," *ILRR Report* 24, no. 1 (August 1974), pp. 16–22.

EXHIBIT 10.2   The Link between Performance Measurement Problems and Pay

	Smallest Work Unit for Which Output Can Be Measured		
	Individual	*Small Group*	*Division or Company*
Base pay	May be based directly on performance (individual incentive system)	Determined by traditional job evaluation and market pricing	Determined by traditional job evaluation and market pricing
Extra compensation	None. All is function of individual performance. May have group or company plan if desire to tie pay to overall performance of organization	Small group incentive plan possible. Extra compensation then tied to group performance. May use subjective performance evaluation and give merit increases	Gain-sharing, profit sharing, or employee stock ownership plan possible

the entire product or service. Working on an assembly line in Detroit yields cars at the rate of one every minute or less, but the added value of any single worker is difficult to separate from the contributions of other employees.

To the extent that performance of individuals is difficult to measure objectively, organizations must resort to more subjective measures of individual worth. Considerable effort is channeled into developing evaluation systems that are perceived as accurate and fair. Even the best of these systems, though, is still subjective. Perhaps because these systems are more subjective, and employee acceptance is more tenuous, pay systems tied to them are less complex and less rigidly dependent on evaluation of performance. And as performance becomes more difficult to measure, organizations are, not surprisingly, less willing to tie pay directly to performance. Exhibit 10.2 illustrates this point.

In contrast, when output is concrete and measurable, performance evaluation is straightforward. A supervisor simply determines whether quantity standards are being met. The major debate in this type of setting, as noted later, concerns the difficulty of the performance standards. What level of output should an employee be expected to achieve to receive a specific reward level? When performance can be measured this objectively, pay systems may be quite sophisticated. When to adopt such systems and how to develop them become key issues.

ISSUES IN THE ADOPTION AND DESIGN OF PERFORMANCE-BASED PAY PLANS

Adoption Issues

There has long been a recognition that incentive plans tend to be more prevalent in industries sharing four characteristics:[13]

---

[13]Robert B. McKersie, Carroll F. Miller, and William E. Quarterman, "Some Indicators of Incentive Plan Prevalence," *Monthly Labor Review*, May 1964, pp. 271–76.

1. High labor costs.
2. High cost competition in product markets.
3. Slow or nonexistent advancements in technology.
4. High potential for production bottlenecks.

Consider, for example, the clothing industry. Labor represents a large proportion of total costs for production of clothing. The market is extremely cost competitive, particularly when international production of clothing along the Pacific Rim is considered. The technology for making clothing has not advanced very quickly, and there is a reasonably high potential for bottlenecks in the production of the final good. Similar kinds of problems face the steel industry, which in recent years has been accused of being negligent in its adoption of new technologies. These factors, combined with severe competition from overseas steel markets, have made the advantages of incentive systems appear attractive.

In contrast, the automobile industry has traditionally been relatively restrained in its use of incentive systems. Although it faces problems similar to the steel industry in terms of foreign competition, technological advances tended in the past to keep labor costs down to a level where price competition with foreign produces was at least feasible. This, combined with the United Auto Workers' stand against incentive systems, had resulted in relatively infrequent adoption of incentive systems. As we will see in Chapter 17, though, the Big Three all adopted profit sharing plans in the 1980s. A large part of this change in position can be explained by the need of automakers to control costs and to assume a more competitive stance in the international automobile market.

Incentive system adoption also may be influenced by several additional factors: (1) organizational strategy, (2) managerial value system, (3) organizational design and work relationships, (4) unit and individual performance standards, (5) unit and individual performance, and (6) employee attraction issues.

Organizational Strategy. Organizations differ in the amount of risk they are willing to assume and to reinforce in their employees. Some organizations pride themselves on stability and growth through "tried and true" methods, that is, growth through internally generated diversification or through further penetration of existing markets.[14] These organizations are also likely to have compensation systems that promote stable employment relationships. Rewards are based on seniority. Any incentive system used in this type of organization is likely to take a long-term perspective on profits and is apt to foster interdependence between divisions through goals emphasizing *both* divisional and organizational performance.[15]

In contrast, some firms adopt a more risk-taking approach to growth, actively prospecting for acquisitions and generally pursuing external diversification programs.[16] These

---

[14]M. Leonitiades, *Strategies for Diversification and Change* (Boston: Little, Brown, 1980).

[15]Arch Patton, "Why Incentive Plans Fail," *Harvard Business Review,* May–June 1972, pp. 58–66; Jeffrey Kerr, "Diversification Strategies and Managerial Rewards: An Empirical Study," *Academy of Management Journal* 28, no. 1 (1985), pp. 155–79; and Jerry M. Newman, "Selecting Incentive Plans to Complement Organizational Strategy," in *Current Trends in Compensation Research and Practice,* ed. L. Gomez-Mejia and D. Balkin (Englewood Cliffs, N.J.: Prentice Hall, 1987), pp. 14–24.

[16]Leonitiades, *Strategies for Diversification and Change.*

organizations encourage more entrepreneurial behavior by employees.[17] Entrepreneurial behavior is reinforced by designing bonus and incentive systems that promote autonomy and competitive drive. Bonuses may assume a much larger role in these organizations than in those characterized by more conservative values.[18] Incentives are likely to stress short-term performance on relatively objective measures of divisional performance. Concern for shaping cooperative behavior between units is conspicuously absent. Autonomy and competition are valued, and the compensation system reflects these concerns.[19]

Management Values.   A related factor influencing compensation design is the existing management value system. Incentive systems are more readily accepted when management values promote stable work relationships. Trust between workers and management must be strong to weather the conflict that incentive plans sometimes foster.[20] This trust evolves, in part, as workers experience a work environment in which cyclical employment patterns are avoided and fears of job loss diminish. In turn, this stability lessens fears that introduction of an incentive system is a "management plot" to increase production and lay off workers. Trust also evolves when management is willing to empower their workers by listening to their recommendations and involving them in the design and implementation of the system.[21]

Organizational Design and Work Relationships.   A compensation system also complements the way organizational units are designed to interact. Autonomous units with sole responsibility for particular goods or services are ideal for objective, results-oriented performance measures. Independent units can be held accountable for successfully meeting targets; and incentive systems can tie rewards to these performance targets.[22]

Firms that stress interdependence, though, are finding it difficult to adapt traditional incentive systems to more team-oriented production methods. As of yet, there has been little success in finding incentive systems that reward individual performance while still reinforcing the advantages of teamwork.

Unit and Individual Performance Standards.   Research indicates that inappropriate choice of performance standards is the single biggest cause of certain incentive system failures. If performance can't be measured validly and objectively, the potential advantage

---

[17]Pitts, "Incentive Compensation and Organization Design," *Personnel Journal,* 53 (1974), 338–48; and M. S. Salter, "Tailor Incentive Compensation to Strategy," *Harvard Business Review* 51, no. 3 (1973), pp. 94–102.

[18]Kerr, "Diversification Strategies and Managerial Rewards."

[19]Newman, "Selecting Incentive Plans to Complement Organizational Strategy."

[20]Patton, "Why Incentive Plans Fail"; Kerr, "Diversification Strategies and Managerial Reward"; Pitts, "Incentive Compensation and Organization Design"; and Robert McKersie, "The Promise of Gainsharing," *ILR Report* 24, no. 1 (1986), pp. 7–11.

[21]McKersie, "The Promise of Gainsharing."

[22]Pitts, "Incentive Compensation and Organization Design"; Newman, "Selecting Incentive Plans to Complement Organizational Strategy"; and Organizational Analysis and Practice, *Strategic Issues in Reward Systems: An Analysis of Incentive Systems* (Ithaca, N.Y.: Organizational Analysis and Practice, 1982).

[23]Organizational Analysis and Practice, *Strategic Issues in Reward Systems;* and Jude T. Rich and John A. Larson, "Why Some Long-Term Incentives Fail," *Compensation Review* 16, no. 1 (1984), pp. 26–37.

of incentive systems is greatly reduced.[23] Employee trust in management fairness plummets.

Unit and Individual Performance.   In general, incentive systems may lead employees to work smarter and more independently. Cost consciousness and higher productivity may be the end result. On the negative side, incentive systems may lead to deteriorating product quality (particularly if quantity is rewarded and quality is neglected). Another negative side effect is increased mistrust of any management activities that give even the slightest sign that either performance standards or payout rates will be adversely changed. The positive outcomes of incentive compensation tend to follow more from work environments in which employees are satisfied with their jobs, believe that they have some control over the amount of incentive they receive, and believe that the performance-reward connection is strong. Employees who don't hold these beliefs may resort to less desirable work behaviors.[24]

Employee Attraction Issues.   Compensation, as noted earlier, is intended to attract, retain, and motivate workers. Incentive systems are useful on the last of these objectives: motivating workers when performance is below par. However, it is not clear that incentives are nearly so effective in helping to attract or retain employees. One survey indicates that 72 percent of blue-collar workers and 56 percent of white-collar workers would prefer straight wages over any type of incentive plan.[25] What lesson might we learn from this? If the goal is to make the firm more attractive to applicants, an incentive compensation plan might not help achieve this. At the very least, such a plan has implications for the type of workers who will be attracted to apply, those who are motivated primarily by economic rewards.

Design Issues

Should rewards be paid to individual employees for individual performance? Or should larger groups be the unit of focus? What should be the standard that triggers incentives? And what should be the form (frequency) of incentives? These issues are discussed in this section.

Group or Individual Plans: Level of Aggregation?   *Level of aggregation* refers to the size of the work unit for which performance is measured (e.g., individual, work group, department, plant, organization) and to which rewards are distributed. The issue is important for two reasons. First, *contrasting motivational forces* are unleashed by an organization's decision to aggregate. What type of employee behavior best fits organizational needs? Individual incentive systems are generally associated with more competition,

---

[24]J. George, A. Brief, and J. Webster, "Organizationally Intended and Unintended Coping: The Case of an Incentive Compensation Plan," *Journal of Occupational Psychology* 64 (1991), pp. 193–205.

[25]Bureau of National Affairs, *Changing Pay Practices: New Developments in Employee Compensation* (Washington, D.C.: Bureau of National Affairs, 1988).

increased pressure on individuals to perform and to accept responsibility for their own actions, increased risk-taking behavior, and lower acceptance of management values/job demands that don't directly affect incentive output.[26] Alternatively, group incentive plans reinforce behaviors that promote collective rather than individual success. The perceived connection between pay and performance may be lessened, but this may be offset by an increase in cooperation and joint effort among employees working for a shared reward based on aggregate performance. Exhibit 10.3 lists the advantages and disadvantages of individual incentive plans. The trend in recent years has been away from individual incentive plans and toward group plans.[27] In part this can be traced to the increased interest in promoting teamwork and cooperation. Exhibit 10.4 identifies other factors that influence the decision about type of incentive plan to adopt, individual or group.

Of course, combinations of these plans are also possible. One of the most popular is to measure performance at the plant or total organization level but to distribute rewards

---

EXHIBIT 10.3   Advantages and Disadvantages of Individualized Incentive Plans

Advantages

1. Substantial contribution to raise productivity, to lower production costs, and to increase earnings of workers.
2. Less direct supervision is required to maintain reasonable levels of output than under payment by time.
3. In most cases, systems of payment by results, if accompanied by improved organizational and work measurement, enable labor costs to be estimated more accurately than under payment by time. This helps costing and budgetary control.

Disadvantages

1. Greater conflict may emerge between employees seeking to maximize output and managers concerned about deteriorating quality levels.
2. Attempts to introduce new technology may be resisted by employees concerned about the impact on production standards.
3. Reduced willingness of employees to suggest new production methods for fear of subsequent increases in production standards.
4. Increased complaints that equipment is poorly maintained, hindering employee efforts to earn larger incentives.
5. Increased turnover among new employees discouraged by the unwillingness of experienced workers to cooperate in on-the-job training.
6. Elevated levels of mistrust between workers and management.

SOURCE: T. Wilson, "Is It Time to Eliminate the Piece Rate Incentive System?" *Compensation and Benefits Review* 24, no. 2 (1992), pp. 43–49; Pinhas Schwinger, *Wage Incentive Systems* (New York: Halsted, 1975).

---

[26]Organizational Analysis and Practice, *Strategic Issues in Reward Systems;* Pinhas Schwinger, *Wage Incentive Systems* (New York: Halsted, 1975); Kerr, "Diversification Strategies and Managerial Rewards"; and Salter, "Tailor Incentive Compensation to Strategy."

[27]Hewitt Associates, *An Overview of Productivity-Based Incentive Systems,* Document P3022/2625, May 1985.

EXHIBIT 10.4   Factors Influencing Aggregation Levels

Characteristic	Individual Level of Incentives Appropriate	Group Level of Incentives—Unit, Department, Organization— Appropriate
Performance measurement	Good measures of individual performance exist. Task accomplishment not dependent on performance of others.	Output is group collaborative effort. Individual contributions to output cannot be assessed.
Organizational adaptability	Individual performance standards are stable. Production methods and labor mix relatively constant.	Performance standards for individuals change to meet environmental pressures on relatively constant organizational objectives. Production methods and labor mix must adapt to meet changing pressures.
Organizational commitment	Commitment strongest to individual's profession or superior. Supervisor viewed as unbiased and performance standards readily apparent.	High commitment to organization built upon sound communication of organizational objectives and performance standards.
Union status	Nonunion. Unions promote equal treatment. Competition between individuals inhibits "fraternal" spirit.	Union or nonunion. Unions less opposed to plans that foster cohesiveness of bargaining unit and which distribute rewards evenly across group.

---

at the individual level, based on some supervisory evaluation of individual performance. One variation currently used by 3M is described in the appendix at the end of this chapter.

A second reason that the issue of aggregation is important centers on *technical constraints*. The nature of an organization's technology, both in production and in information processing, constrains choice of a compensation system. In general, individual incentive systems are less appropriate when[28]

1. Individual contributions of workers are difficult to measure either because of interdependent work flows or because of machine-controlled work pace.
2. Work stoppages are regular and uncontrollable.
3. The management information and cost accounting systems are relatively primitive.

The key to these constraints is that performance must be measurable and the agent (who completed the work) must be identifiable. Usually these constraints become more severe the lower the level of analysis (e.g., individuals).[29] After all, any organization

---

[28]Organizational Analysis and Practice, *Strategic Issues in Reward Systems;* and Schwinger, *Wage Incentive Systems*.

[29]Newman, "Selecting Incentive Plans to Complement Organizational Strategy."

can provide performance data (e.g., profits) for the entire organization. When the unit of analysis is smaller, though, it becomes more and more difficult to decide on objective measures of performance and to attribute that performance to specific individuals or groups.

Form of Incentive.   Incentives can be categorized by the type of performance objectives they are linked to. When short-term (e.g., one-year duration) objectives are stressed, some companies choose to use bonuses. A bonus is a lump sum payment to an employee in recognition of goal achievement. Typically the goal is not expressed in standard output but represents a major step toward achievement of organizational goals. For example, AT&T has devised a bonus system linked to customer satisfaction. As a major organizational objective, numerous measures of customer satisfaction have been devised (e.g., number of orders with missed promise dates; number of sales orders with defects). Employee bonuses are heavily influenced by level of customer satisfaction. In bonus systems, the payout is frequently a percentage of base pay (see Exhibit 10.5 for an illustration).

One industry in which bonuses are particularly popular is the highly competitive high technology industry. A Hay survey of 33 high-tech companies showed that the top 7 percent of managerial, professional, and technical employees were eligible for bonuses. In smaller high-tech organizations (less than $100 million sales versus $1 billion sales for the larger companies), 47 percent of all managerial, professional, and technical employees received bonuses. These percentages are generally higher than for other manufacturing industries (e.g., large manufacturing firms average approximately 3 percent participation rates).[30]

Much of the popular press has criticized U.S. business for taking too short a perspective on organizational goals. Emphasizing short-term profits to the detriment of longer term objectives, so this argument runs, frequently hurts us in international competition. Japanese firms, for example, take a more long-range perspective on business prospects, and this helps in capturing market share. It is true that short-term incentive plans are more prevalent in U.S. companies than long-term plans. For example, one study found that 75 percent of firms ($n = 110$) had short-term plans, but only 55 percent had long-term incentive plans.[31] However, there is increasing emphasis on designing incentive plans that both meet organizational objectives *and* are consistent with incentive plans of differing durations.[32] This focus shifts discussions away from the less productive question of whether to use short-term or long-term incentive plans toward the more relevant question of what the nature of the mix and objectives of each type of plan should be. Organizational success then becomes a function of identifying consistent short- and long-term goals and ensuring that both are met.

---

[30]CompFlash, "Survey Shows Bonuses Are the Way to Go," *AMA CompFlash* 85–07 (1985), p. 4.

[31]CompFlash, "Short-Term Plans Outnumber Long-Term Plans," *AMA CompFlash* 85–06 (1985), p. 1.

[32]Bruce R. Ellig, "Incentive Plans: Short-Term Design Issues," *Compensation Review* 16, no. 3 (1984), pp. 26–36; and Peat Marwick, "Capital Accumulation and Long-Term Incentive Practices in the 500 Top Industrial Companies," *Compensation Briefs Research Report* (February 1986).

EXHIBIT 10.5   Illustration of a Bonus Payment System in a Large Retail Store

Time Frame for Goal Attainment	*Performance Standard*	*Bonus*
June 1989–June 1990	Increase sales volume by 6 percent and reduce customer complaints by 10 percent	20 percent of base pay as of June 1990

Frequency of Incentives.   Instrumental conditioning experiments indicate that rewards work best when administered immediately after task completion. This conjures up images of monkeys pressing bars and immediately receiving bananas from a chute. Obviously, this kind of compensation system would not be very popular or practical with humans. The most frequent concession is to pay incentives on standard time schedules: weekly, monthly, quarterly, and yearly. Unfortunately, though, task cycles are not conveniently equal to calendar cycles.[33] Employees end up receiving incentives at times far removed from the accomplishments triggering the rewards. A more viable strategy would be to adopt a performance contract mechanism. Upon completion of agreed-upon work at an agreed-upon date, an incentive will be paid. If the time frame is too short to make payment practical, regular feedback about incentive accumulations should be provided until payment can be made.

The frequency question also can be considered from an entirely different perspective. How does an organization with stringent cost constraints still employ an incentive system? Consider a bank hard hit by deregulation during the early 1980s. Bank officers want to offer tellers an incentive payment based on their ability to sell new bank products, but they face constraints on their ability to pay incentives if the employees are too successful in their promotional efforts. Organizations are adopting *incentive lottery programs* to cover just these circumstances. Employees who exceed standard output (e.g., opening 30 new savings accounts per month) earn "lottery tickets" that apply toward a large payoff rather than receiving a minuscule incentive payment with little or no motivational impact (e.g., 20 cents per new account). The cost of both the traditional program and the lottery program are identical. A lottery, though, capitalizes on the reward value of taking a risk.[34]

INDIVIDUAL INCENTIVE PLANS

All incentive plans have one common feature: an established standard against which worker performance is compared to determine the magnitude of the incentive pay. For individual incentive systems, this standard is compared against individual worker

---

[33]P. Clark, *Organizational Design* (London: Travistock, 1972).

[34]Karen Evans, "On the Job Lotteries: A Low Cost Incentive That Sparks Higher Productivity," *Personnel,* April 1988.

performance. From this basic foundation, a number of seemingly complex and divergent plans have evolved. Before discussing the more prevalent of these plans, however, it is important to note that each varies along two dimensions and can be classified into one of four cells illustrated in Exhibit 10.6.

The first dimension on which incentive systems vary is in the *method of rate determination*. Plans either set up a rate standard based on units of production per time period or in time period per unit of production. On the surface, this distinction may appear trivial but, in fact, the deviations arise because tasks have different cycles of operation.[35] Short-cycle tasks, those that are completed in a relatively short period of time, typically have as a standard a designated number of units to be produced in a given time period. For long-cycle tasks, this would not be appropriate. It is entirely possible that only one task or some portion of it may be completed in a day. Consequently, for longer cycle tasks, the standard is typically set in terms of time required to complete one unit of production. Individual incentives are based on whether or not workers complete the task in the designated time period.

The second dimension on which individual incentive systems vary is the specified relationship between production level and wages. The first alternative is to tie wages to output on a one-to-one basis, so that wages are some constant function of production. In contrast, some plans vary wages as a function of production level. For example, one common alternative is to provide higher dollar rates for production above the standard than for production below the standard.

EXHIBIT 10.6   Individual Incentive Plans

		Method of Rate Determination	
		Units of production per time period	*Time period per unit of production*
Relationship between production level and pay	*Pay constant function of production level*	*(1)* Straight piecework plan.	*(2)* Standard hour plan.
	Pay varies as function of production level	*(3)* Taylor differential piece-rate system. Merrick multiple piece-rate system.	*(4)* Halsey 50–50 method. Rowan plan. Gantt plan.

---

[35]Thomas Patten, *Pay: Employee Compensation and Incentive Plans* (New York: Macmillan, 1977); and Schwinger, *Wage Incentive Systems*.

Each of the plans discussed in this section has as a foundation a standard level of performance determined by some form of time study or job analysis completed by an industrial engineer or trained personnel administrator. (Exhibit 10.7 provides an illustration of a time study.) The variations in these plans occur in either the way the standard is set or the way wages are tied to output. As in Exhibit 10.6, there are four general categories of plans.

1. *Cell 1.* The most frequently implemented incentive system is a straight piecework system (Exhibit 10.8). Rate determination is based on units of production per time period, and wages vary directly as a function of production level. A standard is developed reflecting the units of output a worker is expected to complete in, say, an hour. Workers are paid for each unit of output. Consequently, workers who consistently exceed the established standard receive higher than average wages.

The major advantages of this type of system is that it is easily understood by workers and, perhaps consequently, more readily accepted than some of the other incentive systems. The major disadvantages center on the difficulty in setting a standard. For example, the industrial engineer charged with establishing a standard for the drilling operation in

---

EXHIBIT 10.7   Example of a Time Study

Task: Drilling operation.

Elements:
1. Move part from box to jig.
2. Position part in jig.
3. Drill hole in part.
4. Remove jig and drop part in chute.

Notes and remarks	Observation number	Elements (1)	(2)	(3)	(4)
	1	.17	.22	.26	.29
	2	.17	.22	.27	.34
	3	.16	.21	.28	.39
	4	.18	.21	.29	.29
	5	.19	.20	.30	.36
	6	.25	.21	.31	.31
	7	.17	.23	.29	.33
Observed time		.17 (mode)	.21 (mode)	.29 (median)	.33 (mean)
Effort rating	(130%)	1.30	1.30	1.30	1.30
Corrected time		.2210	.2730	.3370	.4290
Total corrected time					1.2600

Allowances:
fatigue	5%
personal needs	5%
contingencies	10%
Total	20% (of total corrected time of 1.2600)

Total corrected time of 1.2600)   .2520

Total allotted time for task   1.5120

SOURCE: From Stephen J. Carroll and Craig E. Schneier, *Performance Appraisal and Review Systems* (Glenview, Ill.: Scott, Foresman, 1982). Copyright © 1982 by Scott, Foresman and Company. Reprinted by permission.

EXHIBIT 10.8   Illustration of a Straight Piece Rate Plan

Piece rate standard (e.g., determined from time study): 10 units/hour
Guaranteed minimum wage (if standard is not met): $5/hour
Incentive rate (for each unit over 10 units): $.50/unit

Examples of Worker Output		*Wage*
10 units or less		$5.00/hour (as guaranteed)
20 units	20 × $.50 =	$10/hour
30 units	30 × $.50 =	$15/hour

Exhibit 10.7 may be expected to observe numerous drillers performing the task. The time study expert would then derive a standard indicating the number of holes it should be possible to drill in a given time period by workers performing at a normal rate. The accuracy of the industrial engineer's measurements, the workers chosen to observe, and the definition of a normal rate of speed all influence the final standard.[36] An inappropriate standard can result in labor dissension (too high a standard) or excessive labor costs (too low a standard). Either outcome is likely to result in deteriorating labor-management relations. Consequently, great care must be taken to ensure that both management and the workers have a role in establishing standards. Very frequently in unionized firms, this is formally ensured through inclusion of standards as a negotiable issue in the contract language.

2. *Cell 2.* Two relatively common plans set standards based on time per unit and tie incentives directly to level of output: (1) standard hour plans and (2) Bedeaux plans. A *standard hour plan* is a generic term for plans setting incentive rate based on completion of a task in some expected time period. A common example can be found in any neighborhood gasoline station or automobile repair shop. Let us assume that you need a new transmission. The estimate you receive for labor costs is based on the mechanic's hourly rate of pay, multiplied by a time estimate for job completion derived from a book listing average time estimates for a wide variety of jobs. If the mechanic receives $30 per hour and a transmission is listed as requiring four hours to remove and replace, the labor costs would be $120. All this is determined in advance of any actual work. Of course, if the mechanic is highly experienced and fast, the job may be completed in considerably less time than indicated in the book. However, the job is still charged as if it took the quoted time to complete. This is the basic mechanism of a standard hour incentive plan. If a task can be completed in less than the designated time, a worker is still paid at a rate based on the standard time allotted for that job times an hourly rate. Standard hour plans are more practical than a straight piecework plan for long-cycle operations and jobs that are nonrepetitive and require numerous skills for completion.[37]

---

[36]Stephen Carroll and Craig Schneier, *Performance Appraisal and Review Systems* (Glenview, Ill.: Scott, Foresman, 1982).

[37]Patten, *Pay: Employee Compensation and Incentive Plans;* Schwinger, *Wage Incentive Systems.*

A *Bedeaux plan* provides a variation on straight piecework and standard hour plans. Instead of timing an entire task, a Bedeaux plan requires division of a task into simple actions and determination of the time required by an average skilled worker to complete each action. After the more fine time analysis of tasks, the Bedeaux system functions similarly to a standard hour plan. Workers receive a wage incentive for completing a task in less than standard time. This incentive is a direct function of the time saved in completing the task.

3. *Cell 3*. The two plans included in cell 3 provide for variable incentives as a function of units of production per time period. Both the Taylor plan and the Merrick plan provide different piece rates, depending on the level of production relative to the standard. To illustrate this, consider the contrasts of these plans with a straight piece rate plan. A straight piece rate plan varies wages directly with output. If workers reach standard production, they receive the standard wage. Eighty percent of standard production results in 80 percent of standard wage. Plotting a graph with percentage of standard production on one axis and percentage gain in base hourly rate on the other, the slope for a straight piece rate system would be 1.00. Both the Taylor and Merrick plans would have variable slopes, depending on production levels of workers. For example, the Taylor plan establishes two piecework rates. One rate goes into effect when a worker exceeds the published standard for a given time period. This rate is set higher than the regular wage incentive level. A second rate is established for production below standard, and this rate is lower than the regular wage.

The Merrick system operates in the same way, except that three piecework rates are set: (1) high—for production exceeding 100 percent of standard; (2) medium—for production between 83 percent and 100 percent of standard; and (3) low—for production less than 83 percent of standard.[38] Exhibit 10.9 compares these two plans.

Both systems are designed to reward highly the efficient worker and penalize the inefficient worker. Quite obviously, there are infinite variations on the number and type of piecework rates that could be established. Although these two plans are designed to encourage the highly efficient, they are not as penalty-laden for less efficient workers as their now defunct predecessors.

4. *Cell 4*. The three plans included in cell 4 provide for variable incentives linked to a standard expressed as time period per unit of production. The three plans include the Halsey 50–50 method, the Rowan plan, and the Gantt plan.

The *Halsey 50–50 method* derives its name from the shared split between worker and employer of any savings in direct cost. An allowed time for a task is determined via time study. The savings resulting from completion of a task in less than the standard time are allocated 50–50 (most frequent division) between the worker and the company.

The *Rowan plan* is similar to the Halsey plan in that an employer and employee both share in savings resulting from work completed in less than standard time. The major distinction in this plan, however, is that a worker's bonus increases as time required to complete the task decreases. For example, if the standard time to complete a task is 10 hours and it is completed in 7 hours, the worker receives a 30 percent bonus. Completion

---

[38]Schwinger, *Wage Incentive Systems.*

EXHIBIT 10.9   Illustrations of the Taylor and Merrick Plans

Piece rate standard: 10 units per hour
Standard wage: $5.00/hour
Piecework rate:

Output	Taylor Rate per Unit	Taylor Wage	Merrick Rate per Unit	Merrick Wage
7 units/hour	$.50/unit	$3.50	$.50/unit	$3.50
8 units/hour	$.50/unit	$4.00	$.50/unit	$4.00
9 units/hour	$.50/unit	$4.50	$.60/unit	$5.40
10 units/hour	$.50/unit	$5.00	$.60/unit	$6.00
11 units/hour	$.70/unit	$7.70	$.70/unit	$7.70
12 + units	calculations at same rate as for 11 units			

of the same task in 6 hours would result in a 40 percent bonus above the hourly wage for each of the 6 hours.

The *Gantt plan* differs from both the Halsey and Rowan plans in that standard time for a task is purposely set at a level requiring high effort to complete. Any worker who fails to complete the task in standard time is guaranteed a preestablished wage. However, for any task completed in standard time or less, earnings are pegged at 120 percent of the time saved. Consequently, workers' earnings increase faster than production whenever standard time is met or exceeded.

GROUP INCENTIVE PLANS (GAIN-SHARING AND PROFIT SHARING PLANS)

In one sense, group incentive plans are similar to individual incentive plans. An attempt is made to tie pay to performance by giving workers an additional payment when there has been an increase in profits or a decrease in costs to the firm. All plans begin by comparing inputs to outcomes. In this case, labor inputs are compared to some measure of production outputs. In a basic sense, incentives are awarded when some base period calculation of labor inputs and production outputs is exceeded, either by reducing labor inputs, increasing production outcomes, or both. It should be stressed, though, that these improvements don't necessarily result because employees individually or collectively decide to work harder. Rather, improvements probably arise because employees work smarter, identifying means to perform tasks more efficiently without working harder.

Deviation from individual incentive plans obviously arises because incentives are based on some measure of group performance rather than individual performance. Incentives are based on a comparison of present profits or costs against historical cost accounting data on the same figures. When the organization achieves greater profits or lower costs relative to a base year, groups participating in the incentive plan receive a portion of the accrued funds.

Complexity is introduced into these formulas, though, because different organizations have different goals. Different strategies and management value systems yield different solutions to some of the common questions that organizations must answer. The following issues must be considered before selecting one of the several different types of gain-sharing plans.[39]

1. *Strength of reinforcement.* What role should base pay assume relative to incentive pay? Incentive pay tends to encourage only those behaviors that are rewarded. For example, try returning an unwanted birthday present to a store that pays its sales force solely for new sales! Tasks that carry no rewards are only reluctantly performed (if at all!).

2. *Productivity standards.* What standard will be used to calculate whether employees will receive an incentive payout? Almost all group incentive plans use a historical standard. A historical standard involves choosing a prior year's performance to use for comparison with current performance. Which baseline year should be used? If a comparison year that was too good (or too bad) is used, the standard will be too hard (easy) to achieve, with obvious motivational and cost effects. One possible compromise is to use a moving average of several years (e.g., the average for the past five years, with the five-year block changing by one year on an annual basis).

One of the major problems with historical standards is the problem that changing environmental conditions can cause.[40] For example, consider the company that sets a target of 6 percent return on investment based on historical standards. When this level is reached, it triggers an incentive for eligible employees. Yet in a product market in which the average for that year is 15 percent return on investment, it is apparent that no incentive is appropriate for our underachiever.[41] Such problems are particularly insidious during economic swings and for organizations that face volatile economic climates. Care must be taken to ensure that the link between performance and rewards is sustained. This means that environmental influences on performance, not controllable by plan participants, should be factored out when identifying incentive levels.

3. *Sharing the gains: split between management and workers.* Part of the plan must address the relative cuts between management and workers of any profit or savings generated. This issue also necessitates discussion of whether an emergency reserve (gains withheld from distribution in case of future emergencies) will be established in advance of any sharing of profits.

4. *Scope of the formula.* Formulas can vary in the scope of inclusions for both the labor inputs in the numerator and productivity outcomes in the denominator.[42] For example, the standard could be as narrowly defined as reducing labor costs or it could incorporate a wide range of alternative organizational goals. Efforts to improve quality could be reinforced by focusing on reductions in customer complaints, increases in market share, or some other measure selected to reflect management concerns. Great care must be exercised, though, to ensure that the behaviors reinforced actually affect the desired bottom line goal. Getting workers to expend more effort, for example, might not always be the desired behavior. Increased effort may bring unacceptable levels of accidents. Or

[39]Max Bazerman and Brian Graham-Moore, "PG Formulas: Developing a Reward Structure to Achieve Organizational Goals," in *Productivity Gainsharing,* ed. Brian Graham-Moore and Timothy Ross (Englewood Cliffs, N.J.: Prentice Hall, 1983).

[40]Rich and Larson, "Why Some Long Term Incentives Fail."

[41]Patton, "Why Incentive Plans Fail."

[42]Newman, "Selecting Incentive Plans to Complement Organizational Strategy."

it may be preferable to encourage cooperative planning behaviors that result in smarter, rather than harder, work.

5. *Perceived fairness of the formula.* Not all incentive systems cover all employees in a firm.[43] In fact, it is common to limit eligibility to individuals in key positions whose income exceeds certain minimum standards.[44] When multiple plans with different goals and covering different employee groups are implemented, coordination to ensure equity becomes increasingly important.

6. *Ease of administration.* Sophisticated plans with involved calculations of profits or costs can become too complex for existing company information systems. Increased complexities also require more effective communications and higher levels of trust among participants.

7. *Production variability.* One major cause of problems in group incentive plans is failure to set targets properly.[45] Management loses credibility when it bases new targets on historical standards that are impossibly difficult (or easy) to achieve. If standards are based on historical financial and/or production data that are stable, greater confidence is possible.[46] Instability in past years causes problems. Such problems are particularly insidious during economic swings and for organizations that face volatile economic climates. Care must be taken to ensure that the link between performance and rewards is sustained. This means that environmental influences on performance, not controllable by plan participants, should be factored out when identifying incentive levels.

One survey of 50 executives in different companies identified the "formula" for a successful gain-sharing plan in slightly different terms.[47] Exhibit 10.10 illustrates these ingredients.

Exhibit 10.11 summarizes three different formulas that can be used as the basis for gain-sharing plans. The numerator, or input factor, is always some labor cost variable, expressed in either dollars or actual hours worked. Similarly, the denominator is some output measure such as net sales or value added. Each of the plans determines employees' incentive based on the difference between the current value of the ratio and the ratio in some agreed-upon base year. The more favorable the current ratio relative to historical standard, the larger the incentive award.[48] The three primary types of gain-sharing plans, differentiated by their focus on either cost savings (the numerator of the equation) or some measure of profits (the denominator of the equation), are noted below.

Gain-Sharing Plans (Cost-Savings Plans)

Scanlon Plan. A Scanlon plan is designed to lower labor costs without lowering the level of a firm's activity. Incentives are derived as a function of the ratio between labor

[43]John Belcher, "Design Options for Gain Sharing" (American Productivity Center, Houston, Texas, 1987).

[44]Ellig, "Incentive Plans: Short Term Design Issues."

[45]Rich and Larson, "Why Some Long Term Incentives Fail."

[46]Patton, "Why Incentive Plans Fail."

[47]Jay Schuster and Patricia Zingheim, "Designing Incentives for Top Financial Performance," *Compensation and Benefits Review* 18, no. 3 (1986), pp. 39–48.

[48]Ibid.

EXHIBIT 10.10   Determinants of a Successful Gain-Sharing Plan

Factor	What the Best Companies Do	What the Rest Do
Eligibility	To be eligible a person must impact on some measurable factor of importance to the company	Based on job level
Compensation Mix	At risk is larger percentage of total pay with 200–300% of base pay typical	At risk pay is no more than 100% of base pay
Basis of reward formula	Performance	More attuned to what competitors give than any measure of performance
Time period	Plan length geared to time necessary to achieve objectives	Calendar or fiscal year yardstick
Distribution of rewards	20% receive no award 20% receive minimum 20% receive more than minimum but less than maximum 40% receive fully competitive cash incentive	Many more receive maximum award

SOURCE: Adapted from J. Schuster and P. Zingheim, "Designing Incentives for Top Financial Performance," *Compensation and Benefits Review* 18, no. 3 (1986), pp. 39–48.

EXHIBIT 10.11   Three Gain-Sharing Formulas

	Scanlon Plan (Single Ratio Variant)	Rucker Plan	Improshare
Numerator of ratio (input factor)	Payroll costs	Labor cost	Actual hours worked
Denominator of ratio (outcome factor)	Net sales (plus or minus inventories)	Value added	Total standard value hours

Adapted from M. Bazerman and B. Graham-Moore, "P. G. Formulas: Developing a Reward Structure to Achieve Organizational Goals," in *Productivity Gainsharing,* ed. B. Graham-Moore and T. Ross (Englewood Cliffs, N.J.: Prentice Hall, 1983).

---

costs and sales value of production (SVOP).[49] The SVOP includes sales revenue and the value of goods in inventory. To illustrate how these two figures are used to derive incentives under a Scanlon Plan, consider Exhibit 10.12.

In practice, the $50,000 savings in Exhibit 10.12 is not all distributed to the work force. Rather, 25 percent is distributed to the company, 75 percent of the remainder is

---

[49]A. J. Geare, "Productivity from Scanlon Type Plans," *Academy of Management Review* 1, no. 3 (1976), pp. 99–108.

Exhibit 10.12   Examples of a Scanlon Plan

1989 Data (base year) for Alcon, Ltd.

SVOP	= $10,000,000
Total wage bill	= 4,000,000
Total wage bill	

$$\frac{\text{Total wage bill}}{\text{SVOP}} = 4,000,000 \div 10,000,000 = .40 = 40\%$$

Operating Month, August 1987

SVOP	= $950,000
Allowable wage bill	= .40 ($950,000) = $380,000
Actual wage bill (August)	= 330,000
Savings	= 50,000

$50,000 available for distribution as a bonus.

distributed as bonus, and 25 percent of the remainder is withheld and placed in an emergency fund to reimburse the company for any future months in which a "negative bonus" is earned (i.e., when the actual wage bill is greater than the allowable wage bill). The excess remaining in the emergency pool is distributed to workers at the end of the year. Appendix A illustrates a variant of the Scanlon plan adopted at Dresser Rand's Painted Post facility.

Rucker Plan.   The Rucker plan involves a somewhat more complex formula for determining worker incentive bonuses than does a Scanlon plan. Essentially, a ratio is calculated that expresses the value of production required for each dollar of total wage bill. Consider the following illustration.[50]

1. Assume that accounting records show that the company put $.60 worth of electricity, materials, supplies, and so on into production to produce $1 worth of product. The value added is $.40 for each $1 of sales value. Assume also that records show that 45 percent of the value added was attributable to labor; a productivity ratio (PR) can be allocated from the formula:

2. PR $\times$ 0.45 = 1. Solving yields PR = 2.22.

3. If the wage bill equals $100,000, the *expected* production value is the wage bill ($100,000) $\times$ PR (2.22) = $222,222.22.

4. If *actual* production value equals $280,000, then the savings (actual production value minus expected production value) equals $57,777.78.

5. Since the labor contribution to value added is 45 percent, the bonus to the work force should be 0.45 $\times$ $57,777.78 = $26,000 (rounded).

6. The savings are distributed as an incentive bonus according to a formula identical to the Scanlon plan formula: 75 percent of the bonus is distributed to

[50]Ibid.

workers and 25 percent is kept as an emergency fund to cover poor months. Any excess in the emergency fund at the end of the year is then distributed to workers.

Implementation of the Scanlon/Rucker Plans.   Two major components are vital to the implementation and success of a Rucker- or Scanlon-type plan: (1) a productivity norm and (2) the development of effective worker committees. Development of a productivity norm requires both effective measurement of base year data and acceptance by workers and management of this standard for calculating bonus incentives. Effective measurement requires an organization to keep extensive records of historical cost relationships and make them available to workers or union representatives to verify cost accounting figures. Acceptance of these figures, assuming that they are accurate, requires that the organization choose a base year that is neither a "boom" nor a "bust" year. The logic is apparent. A boom year would reduce opportunities for workers to collect bonus incentives. A bust year would lead to excessive bonus costs for the firm. The base year chosen also should be fairly recent, allaying worker fears that changes in technology or other factors would make the base year unrepresentative of a given operational year.

The second ingredient of Scanlon/Rucker plans is a series of worker committees (also known as *productivity committees* or *bonus committees*). The primary function of these committees is to evaluate employee and management suggestions for ways to improve productivity and/or cut costs. Operating on a plant-wide basis in smaller firms, or a departmental basis in larger firms, these committees have been highly successful in eliciting suggestions from employees. It is not uncommon for the suggestion rate to be above that found in companies with standard suggestion incentive plans.[51]

It is the climate that the Scanlon/Rucker plans foster that is perhaps the most vital element of success. Numerous authorities have pointed out that these plans have the best chance for success in companies with competent supervision, cooperative union-management attitudes, strong top management interest and participation in the development of the program, and management openness to criticism and willingness to discuss different operating strategies. It is beyond the scope of this discussion to outline specific strategies adopted by companies to achieve this climate, but the key element is a belief that workers should play a vital role in the decision-making process.

Differences between Individual Incentive Plans and Scanlon/Rucker Plans.   Scanlon and Rucker plans differ from individual incentive plans in their primary focus. Individual incentive plans focus primarily on using wage incentives to motivate higher performance through increased effort. Although this is certainly a goal of the Scanlon/Rucker plans, it is not the major focus of attention. Rather, given that increased output is a function of group effort, more attention is focused on organizational behavior variables. The key is to promote faster, more intelligent, and acceptable decisions through participation. This participation is won by developing a group unity in achieving cost savings, a goal that is not stressed, but often stymied, in individual incentive plans.

---

[51]Ibid.

Differences between Scanlon and Rucker Plans.   Even though Scanlon and Rucker plans share a common attention to groups and committees through participation as a linking pin, there are two important differences between the two plans. First, Rucker plans tie incentives to a wide variety of savings, not just the labor savings focused on in Scanlon plans.[52] Second, this greater flexibility may help explain why Rucker plans are more amenable to linkages with individual incentive plans.

Improshare.   *Improshare* (IMproved PROductivity through SHARing) is a relatively new gain-sharing plan that has proven easy to administer and to communicate.[53] First, a standard is developed that identifies the expected hours required to produce an acceptable level of output. This standard comes either from time and motion studies conducted by industrial engineers or from a base period measurement of the performance factor. Any savings arising from production of agreed-upon output in fewer than expected hours are shared by the firm and by the worker.[54]

One survey of 104 companies with an Improshare plan found a mean increase in productivity during the first year of 12.5 percent.[55] By the third year, the productivity gain rose to 22 percent. A significant portion of this productivity gain was traced to reduced defect rates and downtime (e.g., repair time).

The calculation of an Improshare plan is presented in Exhibit 10.13.

Exhibit 10.14 compares these three types of gain-sharing programs on the dimensions discussed earlier.[56]

Profit Sharing Plans

The second general category of group incentive plans includes all profit sharing plans, whether the profit shared is distributed currently or deferred until later (typically at retirement, disability, severance, or death).[57] Although provisions of the Employee Retirement Income Security Act (ERISA) have taken some of the incentive out of implementing incentive plans, recent estimates still suggest that about 37 percent of the private nonfarm work force receives some kind of profit sharing.[58]

Profit sharing, as is evident from the name, focuses on profitability as the standard for group incentives. Both the financial research literature and the human resources management literature currently are debating what is the best measure of profitability.[59] Exhibit 10.15 illustrates measures used by different organizations.

---

[52]Patten, "Pay: Employee Compensation and Incentive Plans"; Schwinger, *Wage Incentive Plans.*

[53]Graham-Moore and Ross, *Productivity Gainsharing.*

[54]Newman, "Selecting Incentive Plans to Complement Organizational Strategy."

[55]R. Kaufman, "The Effects of Improshare on Productivity," *Industrial and Labor Relations Review* 45, no. 2 (1992), pp. 311–322.

[56]Ibid.

[57]Robert McCaffery, *Managing the Employee Benefits Process* (New York: AMACOM, 1983).

[58]Bureau of National Affairs, "Incentive Pay Schemes Seen as a Result of Economic Employee Relation Change," *BNA Daily Report,* October 9, 1984, pp. cc–1.

[59]Bruce R. Ellig, "Incentive Plans: Over the Long Term," *Compensation Review* 16, no. 2 (1984), pp. 39–54; and Ellig, "Short Term Design Issues."

EXHIBIT 10.13 Calculation of an Improshare Payout

Assume: 1. 60 production workers.
2. 50 nonproduction workers.
3. 40-hour work week for all employees.
4. Company produces three products, A, B, and C.

Step 1: Calculate Employee Hour Standards for Each Product for *Production Workers Only*.
Product A (25 workers needed, each working 40 hours) and total production = 200

$$\frac{25 \times 40}{200} = 5 \text{ hours}$$

Product B (20 workers, 40 hours each, turning out 400 units of B)

$$\frac{20 \times 40}{400} = 2 \text{ hours}$$

Product C (15 workers, 40 hours each, turning out 600 units of C)

$$\frac{15 \times 40}{600} = 1 \text{ hour}$$

Step 2: Incorporate the Time of Nonproduction Workers, That Is, Those Who Do Not Directly Contribute to Production of Goods.

$$\text{Base productivity factor (BPF)} = \frac{\text{Total production and nonproduction hours}}{\text{Total standard value hours}}$$

Calculation of the numerator yields: 60 workers + 50 workers × 40 hours = 4,400
Calculation of the denominator (standard value hours):

Product A—5 hours/unit × 200 units = 1,000 standard value (SV) hours

Product B—2 hours/unit × 400 units = 800 standard value (SV) hours

Product C—1 hour/unit × 600 units = 600 standard value (SV) hours

Total standard value hours = 2,400

$$\text{Base productivity factor (BPF)} = \frac{(60 \text{ workers} + 50 \text{ workers}) \times 40 \text{ hours}}{2,400}$$

$$= \frac{4,400}{2,400} = 1.833$$

The BPF indicates the number of hours (a standard) it should take to produce one unit of goods. To calculate the bonus for a future time period, calculate how many units were produced during that period, the number of hours it should have taken to produce those goods (BPF × Number of units), and the *actual number* of hours it took to produce those goods.

Assume that production during some future time period of Product A = 400
B = 300
C = 400

(*continued*)

EXHIBIT 10.13   *(concluded)*

Step 3: Calculate the Number of Hours It Should Have Taken to Complete This Level of Production.

$$\text{Product A—5 hours} \times 400 \text{ units} \times 1.833 = 3,667$$

$$\text{Product B—2 hours} \times 300 \text{ units} \times 1.833 = 1,100$$

$$\text{Product C—1 hour} \times 600 \text{ units} \times 1.833 = \;\;\;733$$

Total number of hours that Improshare says production should take = 5,500

Step 4: Calculate Bonus.

$$\text{Actual hours taken (from company records)} = 4,400$$

$$\text{Earned hours} = 1,100$$

$$\text{Bonus hours (Earned hours} \times \text{Some negotiated \%)} = 1,100 \times 0.5 = 550$$

$$\text{Bonus percentage} = \frac{\text{Bonus hours}}{\text{Actual hours}} = 12.5\% \text{ (applied to worker wages)}$$

SOURCE: Adapted from Department of Defense, "Guide for the Design and Implementation of Productivity Gain Sharing Programs," Department of Defense Document DoD 5010.31-G (1985).

Profit sharing plans typically can be found in one of three combinations. First, current distribution plans provide full payment to participants soon after profits have been determined, usually quarterly or annually. As might be expected, the incentive value of profit distribution declines as the time between performance and payoff increases and as the size of the payoff declines relative to previous years. Second, deferred plans have a portion of current profits credited to employee accounts, with cash payment made at time of retirement, disability, severance, or death.[60] Because of certain tax advantages, this is the fastest-growing type of profit sharing system, with approximately 80 percent of the companies with some form of profit sharing plans using the deferred option.[61] The median range of profits distributed varies from 14 percent to about 33 percent.[62] Third, combination plans incorporate aspects of both current and deferred options. A portion of profits is immediately distributed to employees with the remaining amount set aside in designated accounts. About 20 percent of all companies with profit sharing plans have this option.

Profit sharing plans and the other group incentive plans discussed have certain similarities. Both types of plan foster a climate in which cost-cutting suggestions are more acceptable to employees. Furthermore, both types of plan are designed to pay out incentives when the organization is most able to afford them. However, the similarities

---

[60]Schwinger, *Wage Incentive Systems*.

[61]McCaffery, *Managing the Employee Benefits Process*.

[62]Patten, "Pay: Employee Compensation and Incentive Plans"; Schwinger, *Wage Incentive Systems*.

EXHIBIT 10.14 A Comparison among Gain-Sharing Plans

Behavioral and Organizational Issues in Choosing a Plan

	Strength of reinforcement	*Scope of formula*	*Perceived fairness of formulation*	*Ease of administration*	*Production variablity*
Scanlon	Reinforcement hindered because incentives tied to group performance.	Narrowly concerned with labor costs and sales.	Simplicity of formula and broad base of cooperation yield perception of fairness.	Simplicity makes administration easy.	Rapid peaking of production cycles not easy to deal with.
Rucker	Reinforcement only hindered because incentives tied to group performance.	Even more narrow than Scanlon in that sales value of production is corrected for inflation.	Complexity slightly reduces perceived fairness. Requires somewhat less cooperative effort than Scanlon.	Value added concept and formula exclusions difficult to administer.	Formula for calculating value added specifically deals with changing economic conditions.
Improshare	Reinforcement only hindered because incentives tied to group performance.	Narrow measures of labor hours saved.	Lack of employee involvement in development of plan may reduce perceived fairness.	Simplicity makes administration easy.	Management must closely monitor inventory to ensure variability in economic conditions is reflected in production changes.

EXHIBIT 10.15   Common Performance Measures Used in Incentive Plans

Measure	Definition	Organization
1. Operating margin (percent)	*Total sales and revenues less total costs and expenses* divided by total sales and revenues.	American Motors, American Airlines.
2. Operating return on assets	*Operating income* divided by average total assets.	General Motors, Borg-Warner, Federated Department Stores, Texas Instruments.
3. Earnings per share	*Income available to common stockholder* divided by average number of common shares outstanding.	Jewel Company, Winn Dixie Stores.

end here. Although a cash or current distribution profit sharing plan carries some motivational incentive, thus resembling Scanlon/Rucker plans, deferred payment plans more closely resemble a pension fund. The incentive value of working to increase current profits when rewards are distributed much later is, at best, minimal. To balance this disadvantage, profit sharing plans have two distinct advantages. First, they do not require elaborate cost accounting systems to calculate incentives to be allocated to employees. Second, and perhaps more important, profit sharing plans have been implemented in organizations that cover the entire spectrum in size. Admittedly, there is a definite tendency for smaller organizations to opt for a current distribution plan and for larger organizations to choose the deferred option, but until there is more evidence that Scanlon/Rucker plans can be adapted successfully to larger organizations, profit sharing plans seem to represent the major alternative for organizations of any size. Appendix B outlines the profit sharing plan used at 3M as part of its management compensation package.

EFFECTIVENESS OF GAIN-SHARING PLANS

Although there are many case studies of gain-sharing programs in the literature, very few of them report hard data collected in a well-controlled study.[63] Many of the better studies, however, do report positive results from such plans. The General Accounting Office, for example, interviewed 36 companies with gain-sharing programs. Estimates indicated an average of 17 percent savings from these programs.[64] Another study reports an extensive literature search on gain-sharing studies.[65] Of the 33 programs with sufficient detail for comparison, virtually all reported only post hoc analyses; hence, it was virtually impossible

---

[63]C. Peck, *Gainsharing for Productivity* (New York: The Conference Board, 1991), #967.

[64]General Accounting Office, "Productivity Sharing Programs: Can They Contribute to Productivity Improvement?" Washington, D.C.: General Accounting Office, undated ms.

[65]R. J. Bullock and E. E. Lawler, "Gainsharing: A Few Questions and Fewer Answers," *Human Resource Management* 23, no. 1 (1984), pp. 23–40.

to make any but the most preliminary conclusions. The data are encouraging, though: (1) some level of productivity increase, rise in quality, or cost reduction was reported by 75 percent of the companies; (2) 75 percent of the companies indicated an increase in ideas, suggestions, and innovations by employees; (3) among participants, the programs were generally popular, with 64 percent reporting improved morale or quality of work life; and (4) about 50 percent of the participants reported improved communications, either between superiors and subordinates, labor and management, or both. Another recent study compares a company 18 months after implementation of a gain-sharing plan with the firm's status before implementation. Employee satisfaction, perceptions of cooperation between workers and management, and productivity all increased significantly.[66]

Why do gain-sharing programs work? Unfortunately there is almost no information available to answer this question.[67] The most plausible speculation, though, suggests that gain-sharing programs succeed because they change the culture of the firm. Employees at all levels develop a broader perspective about the organization's objectives and greater commitment to achieving them.[68] Another way of asking the same question is to ask "Why do gainsharing programs sometimes fail?" Exhibit 10.16 reviews some of the factors associated with failure.

EXHIBIT 10.16   Factors in Gain-Sharing Failures

Organizational Variables
1. Low trust of management.
2. Low accountability required of workers.
3. Low participation in decision making.
4. Poor communications within and across departments.
5. Low commitment of workers to organization.
6. Wage follower in industry.

External Environment
1. Unstable employment.
2. Unstable input (e.g., raw materials) or customer markets.
3. Highly competitive product market.
4. Highly regulated by government.

Financial Information
1. Poor tracking of financial information in firm.
2. Variable corporate profits over time.

SOURCE: Adapted from T. Ross, "Why Gainsharing Sometimes Fails," in *Gainsharing: Plans for Improving Performance,* ed. B. Graham-Moore and T. Ross (Washington, D.C.: BNA, 1990), pp. 100–15.

---

[66]T. Ross, L. Hatcher, and R. Ross, "Attitude Change vs. Performance Improvement: One Look at the Long-Term Results," in *Gainsharing: Plans for Improving Performance,* ed. B. Graham-Moore and T. Ross (Washington, D.C.: BNA, 1990), pp. 266–77.
[67]Ibid.
[68]Ibid.

SUMMARY

The decision to establish an alternative reward system can be highly confusing. The sheer number and complexity of plans may appear overwhelming at first. But as we noted earlier, organizational characteristics and compensation policy objectives serve well to narrow the list of suitable alternatives. The major caution to recognize is that these alternative reward systems are not a panacea for all productivity problems. Rather a program should be considered within the broader spectrum of changes that could be made to affect employee behavior.

REVIEW QUESTIONS

1. List and explain at least four reasons that an organization might choose to develop an incentive plan at the group rather than individual level.

2. Assume that an organization wishes to increase its commitment to quality. It currently sells paint to retailers in the northeastern United States. Too many cans of paint have been returned because the wholesalers claim the color does not match the color chips shown to customers for the purpose of paint selection. Outline the issues that you would have to consider in setting up an individual incentive system geared to reducing the number of bad batches missed by quality control inspectors.

3. Calculate the Improshare bonus percentage to each worker given the following information:
   a. 90 production workers.
   b. 30 nonproduction workers.
   c. All employees work 40 hours per week.
   d. Company produces two products, A and B.
   e. Product A requires 60 production workers to turn out 400 units/week.
   f. Product B requires 30 production workers to turn out 300 units/week.
   g. Assume production during some future time period of A, 600 units, B, 400 units.
   h. This production took 2,300 hours total (production and nonproduction workers).

4. How do profit sharing plans differ from Scanlon/Rucker type plans?

5. What might be the problems in implementing an individual incentive plan in a company with a long history of labor strikes and grievances?

APPENDIX A
GAINSHARING AT DRESSER RAND

HISTORY

Let's start with some background on the history of gainsharing and the Painted Post Gainsharing Plan.

Gainsharing plans have been on the American industrial scene for almost 50 years. One of the first gainsharing plans developed was by the late Joseph Scanlon. Scanlon was a one-time prize fighter; cost accountant; later, he went to work in a steel mill where he became a local union president. Scanlon eventually joined the United Steelworkers of America staff as its Research Director.

In 1938, the steel mill where Scanlon worked was on the verge of bankruptcy. The men were desperately anxious to protect their jobs. Scanlon, who had worked on the management side as an accountant and on the union side as union president, realized that the productivity of the plant was exceedingly low.

Scanlon convinced the president of the company to join him in a visit to the office of Mr. Clinton S. Golden, Vice President of the Steelworkers, to talk things over. Mr. Golden encouraged them to go back and devise a plan whereby the union and management could work together to save the company. As a result, the first plan of its type was worked out between the management and the union. A new principle was introduced—the principle of employee participation. Later on, Scanlon became a professor at the Massachusetts Institute of Technology, but he died an untimely death in 1956.

Scanlon's work is being carried on by a small group of mostly university professors who are committed to cooperation and team work in American industry. One of those professors, Dr. Michael Schuster of Syracuse University, was commissioned by Ingersoll-Rand management to conduct a feasibility study to see if gainsharing was an idea that might help Painted Post.

The results of the feasibility study were positive. A recommendation was made to implement a productivity gainsharing program at Painted Post. The Plan is modeled after plans used in many other companies, but has several unique features which are special to Painted Post. Painted Post was the first Ingersoll-Rand location to attempt a gainsharing plan. It was started July 1, 1985. If you would like more details regarding gainsharing, stop into the Plant Personnel Office.

Now let's get down to the Plan itself. The basic purpose of the Plan is to tap the huge reservoir of know-how, skill, and experience which is present in every work force. The Plan permits and encourages all employees to participate in the solution to productivity, quality, and cost problems.

In addition, each employee will share in the success of the Plan through the bonus program. In short, the Plan gives each employee a financial stake in the business.

Key Features of the Painted Post Gainsharing Plan

1. A productivity, quality, and cost reduction formula to recognize employees for their efforts. Employees can earn a bonus by:

   - Increasing productivity
   - Improving quality
   - Saving on shop supplies

   This element of the Plan gives employees a triple opportunity to be productive and, at the same time, conscious of quality, material, and shop supplies.

2. An expansion of the Employee Involvement Teams (EIT) to provide employees with an opportunity to solve problems that can increase productivity and quality, while reducing the costs of material and shop supplies.

3. A Bonus Committee composed of four union and four management representatives that are responsible for the overall administration of the program.

4. The program recognizes Painted Post employees for performance efforts that exceed the plant's 1984 levels.

5. Team work and employee participation are the key ingredients of the plan. Both require your support and commitment in order for the program to be successful.

THE EMPLOYEE INVOLVEMENT TEAMS

The success of the Painted Post Gainsharing Plan will largely be determined by the extent to which all employees, hourly and salary, get involved in making Painted Post a successful business once again. The vehicle for doing this is through an expanded and modified process of employee involvement. ALL EMPLOYEES MUST GET INVOLVED IF WE ARE TO MAKE THIS GAINSHARING PLAN A SUCCESS.

You know more about your work operations than anyone else. You know best how they can be improved, what shortcuts can be taken, how materials can be saved and scrap minimized, how work can be performed more efficiently.

The best suggestions are those which recognize the problem and propose a solution.

There will be Employee Involvement Teams (EITs) in each department of the plant, and where possible on the second shift as well. The primary purpose of the EIT teams should be in the areas of cost reduction, quality, and productivity. The teams will have the option of seeking their own projects. The Steering Committee will also form task forces, task teams, and project teams to work on specific projects, which, in the view of the Steering Committee, might contribute to reducing costs, increasing quality, or reducing production inefficiencies and bottlenecks. Other companies have found that expansion of the EITs will allow us to:

- Use our creative powers in our daily tasks to make suggestions which will improve productivity and quality that will result in better earnings and bonuses.
- Communicate clearly with each other—management to employees and employees to management.
- Join fully and cooperatively in the common effort to increase productivity, quality, and earnings.
- Keep an open-minded attitude to change.

When an EIT team has developed a solution to a problem and the supervisor agrees with the solution, it may be implemented immediately if the cost of the solution is less than $200 and it does not impact on another department. The reason for this is that we want all employees to take greater responsibility for the success of the business.

If, after discussion and analysis, the employees feel the idea is still a good one, and the supervisor or area manager does not, the employees may ask for a review by the EIT Steering Committee. The reason for this is that no one employee, hourly or salaried, can be permitted to stand in the way of a good idea being heard.

The only bad idea is one that is not suggested. You may think your suggestion is not important enough to bring up. **WRONG**. It may prove to be the catalyst needed by your fellow employee to trigger another idea.

There will be an Employee Involvement Steering Committee which will coordinate all employee involvement activities. The EIT Steering Committee will have the following functions:

- Oversee the operation of the EIT teams.
- Encourage the teams to take on significant projects.
- Review ideas that have been rejected by supervisors or managers.
- Coordinate review of ideas that cut across more than one department.
- Provide regular communications on the activities of the EITs.
- Act as a mechanism that will create greater trust, confidence, and team work.

THE BONUS COMMITTEE

The Bonus Committee is made up of four union and four company representatives. It is one of the most effective means of communication between employees and management. The committee meets once each quarter to review the bonus computation for the previous quarter and analyze why it was, or was not, favorable. Accurate minutes will be kept by the Bonus Committee.

THE GAINSHARING BONUS

The productivity bonus is paid to recognize employees for their efforts. **The bonus is not a gift.** It will be paid when it has been earned by exceeding 1984 performance levels for labor costs, quality, and shop supplies.

The program utilizes three measurement points when calculating the bonus payout:

Productivity (as measured in labor costs)

Quality (as measured by spoilage, scrap, and reclamations)

Shop supplies

The Painted Post Gainsharing Plan permits gains in productivity to be enhanced by savings in scrap and reclamation expenses and shop supplies. Thus, a bonus is determined by the following formula:

$$\text{Gainsharing bonus} = \underset{\text{(Labor costs)}}{\text{Productivity}} \pm \underset{\text{(Spoilage, scrap, \& reclamation)}}{\text{Quality}} \pm \text{Shop supplies}$$

However, if quality falls below the stated target, it will reduce the bonus earned from a productivity gain. Conversely, if productivity falls below the stated target, it will reduce a bonus that could have been earned from a quality improvement.

Thus, employees are required to focus on three very important indicators of plant performance. This measurement system ensures that productivity gains are not achieved at the expense of quality and prudent shop supply usage. At Painted Post, the dual importance of productivity and quality must be recognized by all employees.

The Role of Quality

Maintaining and increasing the quality of Painted Post products is achieved with this measurement formula in two ways.

First, only "good product" is to be recognized in accounting for sales.

Second, "bad product" will be scrapped and will adversely affect spoilage, scrap, and reclamation, as well as labor costs.

Thus, there is a double benefit for employees to produce good quality products, and a severe penalty for failure to do so.

CALCULATION OF THE GAINSHARING BONUS

Employees will receive a bonus when they exceed their own levels of performance in 1984. Bonuses from the Painted Post Gainsharing Plan are not based upon management or employee opinion of how much work should be done and of what quality. Instead, the bonus is based upon improvements in how the work force actually performed in 1984. Following is an example of how the gainsharing bonus will be calculated.

PAINTED POST
Gainsharing Calculation Example

Net sales	$ 9,000,000
Inventory change sales value	+ 1,000,000
Sales value of production	10,000,000
Labor Bonus Pool	
Target labor and fringe (16.23%)	1,623,000
Actual labor and fringe	1,573,000
Labor/fringe savings bonus	50,000
Actual percent of sales value	15.73%
Waste Savings Bonus Pool	
Target spoiled and reclamation (3.34%)	$334,000
Actual spoiled and reclamation	294,000
Waste savings bonus	40,000
Actual percent of sales value	2.94%
Operating Supplies Bonus Pool	
Target operating supplies (4.00%)	$400,000
Actual operating supplies	370,000
Operating supplies savings bonus	30,000
Actual percent of sales value	3.70%
Distribution	
Total all savings bonus pools	$ 120,000
Less: Current quarter reserve provision	40,000
Apply to prior quarter loss	–0–
Available for distribution	80,000
Employee share (65%)	52,000
Participating payroll	1,000,000
Employee share—percentage of participating payroll	5.20%
Reserve balance	$40,000

The reserve is established in order to safeguard the Company against any quarters with lower than normal output. At the end of each plan year, whatever is left in the reserve will be paid out with 65 percent going to the employees and 35 percent to the Company.

On the next several pages we examine the bonus formula in detail. Please read this information carefully. It is very important for every employee to understand how we arrive at a bonus.

PAINTED POST GAINSHARING PLAN
XXXX Quarter 19XX
(Example 1)

Net Sales are the combination of the following: $9,000,000
  Gas compressor sales
  Air compressor transfers
  V & R transfers
  Transfers to repair centers
  Transfers to DRCS
  In short, **New Sales** is what Painted Post receives for what it does.

± Inventory Change Sales Value   + 1,000,000
  Inventory is work in progress and finished goods that have not been
  shipped.

SALES VALUE OF PRODUCTION $10,000,000
  The actual quarterly sales plus or minus the inventory increases or
    decreases.

  Incidentally, if we can get some price increases, that should
    increase the sales value of production and help us to earn a
    bonus.

PAINTED POST GAINSHARING PLAN
XXXX Quarter 19XX
(Example 2)

SALES VALUE OF PRODUCTION $10,000,000
Target Labor and Fringe (16.23%)   1,623,000
  The historical relationship between payroll cost (less pension) and
    sales for the year 1984. Payroll costs were adjusted to reflect the
    1985 contract changes.

  This is the amount of labor we would expect if we had $10,000,000
    in sales. It is the target we must beat if we are to earn a bonus.

Actual Labor and Fringes   1,573,000
  The actual monies paid during the quarter for wages and fringes.

LABOR COSTS SAVINGS $ 50,000
  The difference between what we would have expected in labor costs
    from what actually occurred.

  Can we do better than the past and earn a bonus?

  Answer: There is nothing the Painted Post work force can't do
    when it tries.

PAINTED POST GAINSHARING PLAN
XXXX Quarter 19XX
(Example 3)

Target Spoilage and Reclamation (3.34%) $334,000
  The historical relationship between spoilage, scrap, and reclamations
  and sales for the year 1984.

  This is the cost of spoilage, scrap, and reclamation we would expect if
  we had $10,000,000 in sales.

Actual Spoilage and Reclamation   294,000
  The actual costs of spoilage, scrap, and reclamations for the quarter.

QUALITY SAVINGS $ 40,000
  The difference between what we would have expected in quality costs
  and what actually occurred.

  Can we reduce the costs of quality?

  Answer: Painted Post has one of the most highly skilled work forces
  anywhere.
    We can improve our quality and probably increase our sales as a
  result.

PAINTED POST GAINSHARING PLAN
XXXX Quarter 19XX
(Example 4)

Target Operating supplies (4.00%) $400,000
  The historical relationship between operating supplies and sales for the
  year 1984.

  This is the cost of shop supplies we would expect if we had
  $10,000,000 in sales.

Actual Operating Supplies   370,000
  The actual costs of operating supplies for the quarter.

OPERATING SUPPLIES SAVINGS $ 30,000
  The difference between what we would have expected in operating
  supply costs and what actually occurred.

  Does anyone know where savings might be found in operating
  supplies?

  Answer: Everyone knows.

(continued)

PAINTED POST GAINSHARING PLAN
XXXX Quarter 19XX
(Example 5)

TOTAL ALL SAVINGS BONUS POOLS		$120,000
Labor	+ $ 50,000	
Quality	+ 40,000	
Supplies	+ 30,000	
	$120,000	
Less 1/3 as current Qtr. Reserve Provision		40,000
Apply to prior quarter loss		–0–
Available for Distribution		80,000
Employee share of savings 65%		52,000
Participating Payroll		1,000,000
Employee Share—% of Participating Payroll		5.20%
(Participating payroll is total wages for all hours worked.)		
RESERVE BALANCE		40,000

The Reserve is established to provide some safeguard for the Plan against quarters with lower than normal efficiency where we fail to meet our stated labor costs, spoilage, scrap and reclamation, and shop supplies goals. At the end of the gainsharing year, the money remaining in the Reserve Account will be distributed.

Questions and Answers

Q: What should an employee do if he or she has a question about the plan or an idea that might increase the bonus?

A: Questions or ideas should be referred to the employee's supervisor, the EIT Steering Committee, the Plant Personnel office, or the Gainsharing Committee.

Q: Will being absent or tardy affect my bonus?

A: Employees will only receive a bonus for actual hours worked. The employee who has lost time will not be paid a bonus for that period of absences.

Q: What about other pay-for-time-not-worked benefits?

A: Bonuses will be excluded from all pay-for-time-not-worked benefits, such as vacations, holidays, death in family, jury duty, etc.

Q: What if there is ever a question as to the accuracy of the calculation of the bonus formula?

A: If there is ever a question as to the accuracy of the information, the company has agreed to permit Price Waterhouse to conduct an audit.

Q: How long will the program last?

A: The Gainsharing Plan will exist for the life of the present collective bargaining agreement. Since the plan is an annual plan, each year the nature of the plan will be reviewed. The Union and the Company will have the right to meet to review the plan if either becomes dissatisfied with it.

APPENDIX B
PROFIT-SHARING AT 3M

Prologue

". . . In years of unusual company prosperity, incomes under a properly designed plan may go up, allowing the employee to participate in the company's prosperity; and during lean years, incomes automatically decrease. It seems to me that those in important positions should recognize that it is proper to expect their incomes to vary somewhat in relation to the prosperity of their division, subsidiary, and/or the prosperity of the company as a whole."

William L. McKnight
Chairman 1949–1966

3M's management compensation system is designed to reinforce the manager's responsibility to improve profitability. The formula is based on a simple philosophy; the individual manager's income should vary with the business unit's profitability. This booklet explains how "profit-sharing" converts this philosophy into practice.

Salary Surveys

Our management compensation system starts with a review of competitive pay rates in the marketplace. For 3M, the "marketplace" is not the average U.S. corporation, but rather, respected companies that are similar to us in management philosophies and human resource principles. In other words, the "peer" companies with which we compete for talent.

The survey process involves asking our peers for information about base salaries, discretionary bonuses, and any special incentive programs. These components are added together to provide the basis for 3M's salary range structure.

As you'll see, as a manager part of your total cash compensation is paid to you as base salary, and the remainder as profit-sharing. The relationship of your total pay to the market rate determined by survey is illustrated by this diagram.

MARKET	3M RANGE MIDPOINT
BONUS/ SPECIALS	PROFIT-SHARING (VARIABLE)
BASE SALARY	BASE SALARY
PEERS	3M

The diagram helps to illustrate a very important concept. Your profit-sharing is not an "over and above" payment, nor is it a bonus. Rather, it is a variable portion of your total cash compensation that will fluctuate with the success of your business unit.

Definitions

Before explaining how a profit-sharing plan is developed, we must discuss two important terms.

As noted earlier, profit-sharing is a variable part of your cash compensation. In order to calculate the variable payment, it is first necessary to assign a fixed number of profit-sharing "shares." These shares are not owned, nor do they have a market value; they are a device to calculate profit-sharing. Then, after the end of each quarter, the number of shares is multiplied by the profit-sharing "rate." The rates vary with profitability; hence, your profit-sharing payment will increase or decrease, depending upon profitability.

The Rate Calculation section of this booklet describes how profit-sharing rates are determined.

Your Initial Plan

When you are first appointed to management, 5 percent to 10 percent of your new total compensation is normally allocated to profit-sharing. Let's go through an example to show how the initial plan is developed. The example assumes you work for an operating division; if you are a staff manager, you will normally receive company shares instead of the division shares referred to in the example.

Let's assume that when you are appointed, your total cash compensation is $45,600 per year, and you receive a promotional increase of approximately 15 percent. The computation works like this.

$45,600	Total compensation
×1.15	15% promotional increase
$52,520	New total compensation
×0.05	5% allocated to profit-sharing
$ 2,600	Amount allocated to profit-sharing

The next step is to determine your number of shares. To do this, your profit-sharing dollar allocation is divided by your division's four-quarter profit-sharing rate (the sum of the most recent four quarter's rates). In our example, the four-quarter rate is $0.17391. Accordingly,

$$\frac{\$2,600 \text{ Dollar Allocation}}{\$0.17391 \text{ Division Rate}} = 14,950 \text{ Division Shares}$$

Your annualized profit-sharing compensation plan would then be:

Base Salary	$49,920 Paid Monthly
Divison Profit-Sharing	
14,950 Shares at $0.17391	2,600 Paid Quarterly
	$52,520 Total Compensation

Generally, your initial share assignment is division shares only, since, as a new manager, your most significant contributions will be at the division level. However, as your responsibilities increase, you may be assigned group and company shares. As a staff manager, you will receive company shares which will be increased as responsibilities increase.

Rate Calculations

The 3M profit-sharing system provides for profit-sharing at the division, group, and company level. All three types of profit-sharing rates are described in this section.

All profit-sharing rates are calculated quarterly. Quarterly profit is determined as follows:

$$
\begin{array}{l}
\text{Year-to-date profit, current quarter} \\
- \ \underline{\text{Year-to-date profit, previous quarter}} \\
= \ \text{Current quarter profit}
\end{array}
$$

Division Rates.   A division's quarterly profit-sharing rate is determined by dividing the division's current quarter profit by the number of 3M common shares outstanding at the end of the previous quarter. As an example, let's assume your division had a $5,000,000 profit and there were 115 million shares of 3M common stock outstanding.

$$
\frac{\$\ 5,000,000\ \text{Quarterly Profit}}{115,000,000\ \text{3M Common Stock}} =
\begin{array}{l}\$0.04348\ (\text{Division Profit-} \\ \text{Sharing rate per share})\end{array}
$$

Since the number of outstanding shares of 3M common stock remains relatively constant, the quarterly rate will increase if division profit increases. This creates the opportunity for you to earn more than your planned income; remember, your share allocation was based on the four-quarter rate at the time your shares were assigned. Conversely, if profit declines, the quarterly rate declines and you will be paid less than your planned income.

Group Rates.   Group quarterly profit-sharing rates are calculated using the same formula as division rates. That is, group quarterly profit is divided by the number of 3M common shares outstanding. For example, if your group's quarterly income was $18,750,000 your group rate would be:

$$
\frac{\$18,750,000\ \text{Group Profit}}{115,000,000\ \text{3M Common Stock}} =
\begin{array}{l}\$0.16304\ (\text{Group Profit-} \\ \text{Sharing rate per share})\end{array}
$$

The assignment of group shares is determined using the most recent four-quarter group rate in the manner described for division share assignments.

Company Rates.   The formula used to calculate company quarterly profit-sharing rates differs from the division/group formula.

The formula is: Current quarter 3M consolidated net income, minus 2.5% of the previous quarter's Stockholders' Equity (Assets minus Liabilities), divided by the previous quarter's number of 3M common shares outstanding. Using representative numbers, the quarterly calculation looks like this:

Reserve for Return on Stockholders' Equity

Total Assets	$6,593,000,000
Less Total Liabilities	2,585,000,000
Stockholders' Equity	$4,008,000,000
	× 2 1/2%
Minimum Reserve	$ 100,200,000
Income Available for Profit-Sharing	
Consolidated Net Income	$ 186,450,000
Less Minimum Reserve	100,200,000
Adjusted Net Income	$ 86,250,000

Company Share Rate

$$\frac{\$86,250,000 \text{ Profit-Sharing Income}}{115,000,000 \text{ 3M Common Stock}} = \substack{\$0.750 \text{ (Company Profit-} \\ \text{Sharing rate per share)}}$$

By establishing the minimum reserve, this formula recognizes the fact that the shareholders own the company and are entitled to a reasonable return before profits are shared with management. And, the inclusion of assets and liabilities in the calculation provides an incentive for managers to use assets wisely in their efforts to increase profits.

The assignment of company shares uses the same four-quarter rate method described for division share assignments.

Another Example

Now that you understand rate calculations, let's go through another example that will build on the first.

Your initial plan was designed to pay you a total of $52,520, of which $2,600 was to be profit-sharing. However, since that plan became effective, your division's four-quarter rate increased from $0.17391 to $0.20000. As a result, your plan is now paying at an annual rate of $52,910, as follows:

Base Salary	$49,920 Paid Monthly
Division Profit-Sharing	
14,950 shares @ $0.20000	2,990 Paid Quarterly
	$52,910 Total

Your manager has decided that:

- You have earned a 6 percent merit increase.
- You should have 10 percent of your total pay in profit-sharing (up from 5 percent).

- You should receive some group and company shares.
- The value of the group/company profit-sharing should be 10 percent of your profit-sharing.

Assuming that the four-quarter group and company rates are $0.65216 and $3.000 respectively, your new plan would look like this.

Base Salary	$50,460 Paid Monthly
Division Profit-Sharing:	
25,200 shares @ $0.2000	5,040 Paid Quarterly
Group Profit-Sharing:	
425 shares @ $0.65216	277 Paid Quarterly
Company Profit-Sharing:	
100 shares @ $3.000	300 Paid Quarterly
	$56,077 Total Planned Pay

It's important to note that your 6 percent increase was calculated at a value determined by the current four-quarter rate, and not from the rate used when your shares were originally assigned. In other words, $56,077 is 106 percent of $52,910.

The addition of group/company shares and a change in the percent allocated to profit-sharing is most often timed to correspond with a merit or promotional increase. Other changes to your plan, called "conversions," are explained in the last section of this booklet.

You've noted that your profit-sharing allocation was not divided equally between division, group, and company profit-sharing. The reasons are explained in the next section.

Profit-Sharing Mix

Our example illustrated an important feature of the 3M profit-sharing system. Because your most important contributions will always be at the division level (as long as you have a division job), division profit-sharing will always be the most important. However, as your responsibility level increases, the value of the group/company portion may increase, to about 40 percent of the total profit-sharing allocation. When group shares are used, the value of group and company profit-sharing will normally be kept approximately equal (up to 20 percent for each). The desired mix is achieved by adjusting the number of shares (without subtracting division shares), generally at the time of an increase.

Profit-Sharing/Base Salary Balance

It is also important to maintain a proper relationship between profit-sharing and base salary. As you advance in management, more dollars are assigned to profit-sharing, increasing your potential for an increase or decrease in earnings as a result of business unit profitability. For example, as a new or first-level manager, no more than 15 percent of your total planned compensation will be assigned to profit-sharing, whereas senior managers may have up to 40 percent of their total planned compensation in profit-sharing. At the time of compensation plan changes, increases are planned so as to retain the desired balance between base salary and profit-sharing in your plan (without reducing base salary).

Participation Limits

Profit-sharing is intended to provide significant increases in total cash compensation during periods of improving profitability; however, profit growth rates vary by division, and sometimes dramatically. As a consequence, managers in divisions experiencing rapid or even explosive growth can significantly outearn their counterparts in divisions with lower profit growth or even declining profits. When profit growth is more related to the business/product cycle of the division than to relative managerial effectiveness, excessive earnings are not justified. To maintain internal equity while still permitting increased earnings through profit-sharing, participation limits have been established.

Participation limits are calculated as a percent of your base salary, and they vary by salary grade. Participation limits are calculated on a year-to-date basis. It is important to emphasize that participation limits do not stop profit-sharing; they only restrain the rate at which you participate in profit growth.

Suppose, using our last example, your division is extremely successful. The division, group, and company four-quarter profit-sharing rates have jumped to $0.75000, $1.00000, and $3.500 respectively. At those rates, the annualized value of your profit-sharing has increased by approximately 350 percent.

Type	Planned	Now Paying
25,200 Division Shares	$5,020	$18,900
425 Group Shares	277	425
100 Company Shares	300	350
	$5,597	$19,675

However, at your salary grade, the participation limit is 35 percent. Here's how it works.

Base Salary	$50,420
	× 35%
100% participation up to	$17,647
50% participation in the next	$17,647
25% participation in the remainder	

So, in our example you would receive:

100% participation	$17,647
50% participation in excess ($2,028)	1,014
Total	$18,661

Normally, after participation limits are reached, the plan will be revised to provide the desired balance between base salary and profit-sharing without a loss in planned total compensation. The resulting new plan effectively captures the level of compensation attained and allows for full participation in future profit growth.

Conversions

Occasionally, events such as the sale or transfer of commodities, the acquisition or divestiture of a subsidiary or business, or the reorganization of a division will affect division profits, resulting in an increase or decrease in the profit-sharing rate that does not reflect operating results. If the event results in a net change of 3 percent in a division's rate or a 6 percent change in a group rate, the Compensation Department will automatically "convert" your plan.

Conversion is simply restating the number of shares you have in your plan, based on the four-quarter profit-sharing rates. For example, the number of division shares you are assigned will decrease if your division rate increased because of added profit, and they will increase if your division lost profit. The intent, of course, is to cancel the influence of the event and allow the profit-sharing rate to reflect normal changes in business operations.

Summary

The 3M Management Profit-Sharing Compensation system has and continues to:

- Focus management attention on profits and the effective use of assets,
- Provide a measure of variable compensation,
- Allow managers to participate in the growth and decline of the profits of their division, group, and the company.

If there are any questions still unanswered, you should contact your manager, your Human Resource Manager, or the Compensation Department.

YOUR TURN:
J. MARTIN GAMES: COSTING OUT AN INDIVIDUAL INCENTIVE SYSTEM

A competitor to GTM Toys has decided to implement an individual incentive plan to improve productivity. As a first step in this process, the company hired an industrial engineer to do time studies for the three assembler positions involved in assembling The Dunk-it Basketball Game. General descriptions of the three positions follow:

Position 1: Remove basketball hoop and miniature backboard from feeder lines and attach hoop to backboard with available screws.

Position 2: Remove net from number 2 feeder line and attach to hoop.

Position 3: Assemble Dunk-it Basketball Game box and enclose foam rubber basketball and assembled hoop.

Time studies indicate that each of the jobs should take an allotted time (with allowance for fatigue and other contingencies) (see Exhibit 1). Current pay and productivity for the three position incumbents is also available (see Exhibit 2).

What is the likely response of the three position

EXHIBIT 1 Time Study

Position	Allotted Time (Minutes, Seconds)		Established Standard (Units/Hour)
1	–0–	45	80
2	–0–	36	100
3	–0–	54	66

EXHIBIT 2 Productivity and Wage Data

Position	Incumbent	Wages/Hour	Units/Hour
1	Arnold	$7.50	71
2	Ramirez	$7.50	88
3	Friedman	$7.50	59

incumbents if they are put on a straight piecework schedule as noted in Exhibit 1 and they continue to perform at the level noted in Exhibit 2?

EXHIBIT IV.1 The Pay Model

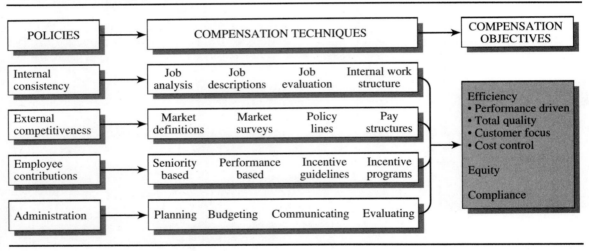

PART IV Employee Benefits

The area of employee benefits represents more of a mystery than any other topic covered thus far in this book. The reason is simple. Benefit practices today frequently are based on faith rather than facts. Consider, for example, the compensation objectives noted in the pay model, Exhibit IV.1.

Does effective employee benefits administration facilitate organization performance? Or do employee benefits impact on an organization's ability to attract, retain, and motivate employees? Conventional wisdom says that employee benefits can affect retention, but there is little research to support this conclusion. A similar lack of research surrounds each of the other potential payoffs to a sound benefits program.

Is it any wonder, then, that firms are becoming increasingly concerned about the steadily rising costs of benefits? They represent a labor cost with no apparent returns.

Balanced against this is the perception of employee benefits as an entitlement. Employees believe they are entitled to continued benefits as a term of employment. Efforts to reduce benefit levels or eliminate parts of the package altogether would meet with employee resistance and dissatisfaction.

Somewhere between these two perspectives is the probable truth about employee benefits. Operating on this assumption, this part of the book takes the perspective that organizations must control costs of benefits wherever possible and increasingly seek ways to maximize the returns from benefit expenditures. As a first step in this direction, Chapter 11 identifies issues that organizations should face in developing and maintaining a benefits program. A model of the benefits determination process also is presented to provide a structure for thinking about employee benefits.

Chapter 12 provides a summary of the state of employee benefits today. It is hoped that this will provide the groundwork for innovative and effective benefit packages of tomorrow.

The Benefits Determination Process

Chapter Outline

Item 1: Oneida Silversmith employees can rent, at reduced rates, cottages and campsites on company-owned property on New York's Lake Oneida.[1]

Item 2: Ingersoll Rand Company, Woodcliffe Lake, N.J., lets staffers plant gardens on its grounds and even plows, fertilizes, and waters the plots.[2]

---

[1]Andrea Stone, "Innovative Benefit Programs Perk Up," *USA Today,* January 31, 1986, p. 30.
[2]*The Wall Street Journal,* June 10, 1980, p. 1.

Item 3: Other benefits from assorted companies: tear gas classes, weekly barbecue, on-site barber shop, on-site department store, company pro shop.[3]

Item 4: Half of payroll costs may go for employee benefits by decade's end, up from 37 percent currently, some consultants predict.[4]

Are items 1 to 3 isolated cases of liberal employee benefits, or do they foreshadow a reality predicted by the doomsayers in item 4? How can employee benefits expand so rapidly, especially when we compare them with the following brief chronicle of "benefits" of the past:[5]

- A carriage shop published a set of rules for employees in 1880 that stated, in part: "Working hours shall be from 7 A.M. to 9 P.M. every day except the Sabbath. . . . After an employee has been with this firm for five years he shall receive an added payment of five cents per day, provided the firm has prospered in a manner to make it possible. . . . It is the bounden duty of each employee to put away at least 10 percent of his monthly wages for his declining years so he will not become a burden upon his betters."

- In 1915, employees in the iron and steel industry worked a standard 60 to 64 hours per week. By 1930 that schedule had been reduced to 54 hours.

- The Blue Cross concept of prepaid medical costs was not introduced until 1929.

- Prior to 1935, only one state (Wisconsin) had a program for holidays. In most companies, employees were told not to report for work on holidays and to enjoy the time off, but their paychecks were smaller the following week.

In comparison to these "benefits" from the past, today's reality seems staggering. Although esoteric benefits are the rarity, private sector organizations still expend on average $12,402 per employee on benefits costs (1990), up from $7,000 in 1983.[6] Between 1980 and 1987 benefit payments increased by 97 percent.[7]

Employee benefits—that part of the total compensation package, other than pay for time worked, provided to employees in whole or in part by employer payments (e.g., life insurance, pension, workers' compensation, vacation).

---

[3]Hewitt Associates, "Innovative Benefits" (Lincolnshire, Ill.: Hewitt Associates, 1982).

[4]*The Wall Street Journal,* June 10, 1980, p. 1.

[5]Robert W. McCaffery, *Managing the Employee Benefits Program* (New York: American Management Association, 1983).

[6]U.S. Chamber of Commerce, *Employee Benefits, 1983* (Washington, D.C.: U.S. Chamber of Commerce, 1984); U.S. Chamber of Commerce, *Employee Benefits, 1990* (Washington, D.C.: U.S. Chamber of Commerce, 1991).

[7]Employee Benefits Research Institute, *EBRI Databook on Employee Benefits* (Washington, D.C.: EBRI Institute, 1990).

EXHIBIT 11.1   Changes in Benefit Costs: 1959, 1969, 1990

	1959	*1969*	*1990*
Percentage of payroll (total)	24.7	31.1	38.4
Legally required benefits	3.5	5.3	8.8
Pension, insurance, and other agreed upon payments	8.5	10.4	15.9
Rest periods and lunch breaks	2.2	3.1	2.4
Payment for time not worked (holidays, vacations, etc.)	8.4	10.1	10.5
Miscellaneous	2.1	2.2	0.8

Costs are reported as a percentage of payroll.
SOURCE: Adapted from U.S. Chamber of Commerce Annual Benefits Surveys.

Employee benefits can no longer realistically be called *fringe benefits*. Benefits represent an ever-escalating percentage of total payroll, as illustrated in Exhibit 11.1.[8]

These average figures vary considerably by industry. The clothing industry is on the low end, paying benefits averaging only 30 percent of payroll. The rubber goods industry is on the high end, with benefits averaging 48.6 percent of payroll (1990).[9] By any standard, though, benefits represent a huge cost for the private sector. Costs are rapidly approaching $1 trillion today!! As a more tangible example of the cost to industry, General Motors estimates that it pays more for employee medical benefits alone than it does for all the steel necessary to produce its yearly output of automobiles![10]

Probably the most important statistic in Exhibit 11.1 is the trend shown in cost of benefits. Benefits rose from 25 percent of payroll in 1959 to 38 percent of payroll in 1990. Over one 20-year period (1955–1975), employee benefit costs rose at a rate almost four times those of employee wages or the consumer price index.[11] A similar comparison for the period 1964–1987 shows that the rate of growth has slowed (benefit costs rose only twice as fast as wage costs), but organizations still express extreme concern for controlling the cost of benefits.[12] Experts agree that this concern is legitimate, and the problem is expected to worsen. The aging of the work force alone is expected to dramatically increase both pension and health care costs for companies.[13] Before exploring

---

[8]U.S. Chamber of Commerce, *Employee Benefits, 1980* (Washington, D.C.: U.S. Chamber of Commerce, 1981); U.S. Chamber of Commerce, *Employee Benefits, 1988* (Washington, D.C.: U.S. Chamber of Commerce, 1988).

[9]Ibid.

[10]Hallie Kintner and Ernest B. Smith, "General Motors Provides Health Care Benefits to Millions," *American Demographics*, May 1987, pp. 44–45.

[11]John Hanna, "Can the Challenge of Escalating Benefits Costs Be Met?" *Personnel Administration* 27, no. 9 (1977), pp. 50–57.

[12]U.S. Chamber of Commerce, *Employee Benefits, 1988*.

[13]Kintner and Smith, "General Motors Provides Health Care Benefits to Millions"; Health Care Institute, "1985 Health Care Cost Containment Survey" (Walnut Creek, Calif.: Health Research Institute).

ways to rationally plan and administer benefits programs in a cost-effective manner, we outline the reasons for this growth in employee benefits in the next section.

WHY THE GROWTH IN EMPLOYEE BENEFITS?

Wage and Price Controls

During both World War II and the Korean War, the federal government instituted strict wage and price controls. The compliance agency charged with enforcing these controls was relatively lenient in permitting reasonable increases in benefits. With strict limitations on the size of wage increases, both unions and employers sought new and improved benefits to satisfy worker demands.

Unions

The climate fostered by wage and price controls created a perfect opportunity for unions to flex the muscles they had recently acquired under the Wagner Act of 1935. Several National Labor Relations Board rulings during the 1940s conferred legitimacy upon negotiations over employee benefits. Absent the leverage to raise wages very much, unions fought for the introduction of new benefits and the improvement of existing benefits. Success on this front during the war years led to further postwar demands. Largely through the efforts of unions, most notably the auto and steelworkers, several benefits common today were given their initial impetus: pattern pension plans, supplementary unemployment compensation, extended vacation plans, and guaranteed annual wage plans.[14]

Employer Impetus

It would be a mistake to assume that the war years provided the only incentive fostering a receptive benefits climate. In fact, many of the benefits in existence today were provided at employer initiative. Much of this employer receptivity can be traced to pragmatic concerns about employee satisfaction and productivity. Rest breaks often were implemented in the belief that fatigue increased accidents and lowered productivity. Savings and profit sharing plans (e.g., Proctor & Gamble's profit sharing plan initiated in 1885) were implemented to improve performance and provide increased security for worker retirement years. Indeed, many employer-initiated benefits were designed to create a climate in which employees perceived that management was genuinely concerned for their welfare.

---

[14]McCaffery, *Managing the Employee Benefits Program.*

Cost Effectiveness of Benefits

Another important impetus for the growth of employee benefits is their cost effectiveness in three situations. The first cost advantage is that most employee benefits are not taxable. Provision of a benefit rather than an equivalent increase in wages avoids payment of federal and state personal income tax. Remember, though, that recurrent tax reform proposals continue to threaten the favorable tax status granted to many benefits. In the last several years, several standard benefits have had their tax exempt status threatened, including these:

1. Portions of employer health contributions.
2. Group life insurance premiums.
3. Dependent life insurance.
4. Educational assistance.
5. Legal services.
6. Cafeteria pay plans.[15]

Already there has been one minor casualty, with the Deficit Reduction Act (Defra) of 1984 limiting the types of benefits that can be included in cafeteria or flexible benefit plans (e.g., no parking fees paid, limits on vacation homes). Obviously, taxation of any or all of these benefits would reduce or eliminate their advantage over allocating the corresponding amount to direct wages.

A second cost effectiveness component of benefits arises because many group-based benefits (e.g., life, health, and legal insurance) can be obtained at a lower rate than could be obtained by employees acting on their own. Group insurance also has relatively easy qualification standards, giving security to a set of employees who might not otherwise qualify (e.g., an employee with a heart condition who becomes eligible for group life insurance at a nonprohibitive rate after being denied individual insurance).

Third, a well-conceived benefits plan that meets employee needs may yield advantages far beyond the dollar cost. In an economic sense, if the utility of the cash value of a benefit is less than the utility of the benefit itself, the organization is better off providing the benefit.

Government Impetus

Obviously, the government has played an important role in the growth of employee benefits. Three employee benefits are mandated by either the state or federal government: worker's compensation (state), unemployment insurance (federal), and social security (federal). In addition, most other employee benefits are affected by such laws as the Employee Retirement Income Security Act (ERISA—affects pension administration) and various sections of the Internal Revenue Code.

---

[15]Carson E. Beadle, "Taxing Employee Benefits: The Impact on Employers and Employees," *Compensation Review* 17, no. 2 (1985), pp. 12–19.

THE VALUE OF EMPLOYEE BENEFITS

Exhibit 11.2 shows the relative importance that employees attached to different types of benefits across three different studies.[16]

In general, the three studies reported in Exhibit 11.2 show fairly consistent results. For example, medical payments regularly are listed as one of the most important benefits employees receive. These rankings take on added significance when we note that health care costs are the most rapidly growing and the most difficult to control of all the benefit options offered by employers.[17] In 1990, health care costs alone were estimated at $3,197 per employee, up 26 percent from 1988 and a whopping 46 percent from 1987.[18]

These costs would not seem nearly so outrageous if we had evidence that employees place high value on the benefits they receive. Unfortunately, there is evidence that employees frequently are not even aware of, or undervalue, the benefits provided by their organization. For example, in one study employees were asked to recall the benefits they received. The typical employee could recall less than 15 percent of them! In another study, MBA students were asked to rank order the importance attached to various factors

---

EXHIBIT 11.2   Ranking of Different Employee Benefits

	Study		
	1	*2*	*3*
Medical	1	1	3
Pension	2	3	8
Paid vacation and holidays	3	2	—
Sickness	4	—	5
Dental	5	—	6
Profit sharing	6	—	2
Long-term disability	7	—	7
Life insurance	8	—	4

NOTE: Dashes indicate that the item was not rated.

---

[16]This table was compiled from three different sources. Some of the reward components rated in some of the studies were not traditional employee benefits and have been deleted from the rankings here. The three studies were *Wall Street Journal,* "The Future Look of Employee Benefits," September 8, 1988, p. 23 (Source: Hewitt Associates); Kermit Davis, William Giles, and Hubert Feild, *How Young Professionals Rank Employee Benefits: Two Studies* (Brookfield, Wis.: International Foundation of Employee Benefit Plans, 1988); and Kenneth Shapiro and Jesse Sherman, "Employee Attitude Benefit Plan Designs," *Personnel Journal,* July 1987, pp. 49–58.

[17]Mary Fruen and Henry DiPrete, "Health Care in the Future" (Boston, Mass.: John Hancock, 1986); HRM Update, "Health Plan Increases" (New York: The Conference Board, May 1988); Kintner and Smith, "General Motors Provides Health Care Benefits to Millions"; Health Research Institute, "1985 Health Care Cost Containment Survey"; North West National Life Insurance Co., "Ten Ways to Cut Employee Benefit Costs" (1988).

[18]U.S. Chamber of Commerce, *Employee Benefits, 1990.*

influencing job selection.[19] Presumably, the large percentage of labor costs allocated to payment of employee benefits would be partially justified if benefits turned out to be an important factor in attracting good MBA candidates. Of the six factors ranked, employee benefits received the lowest ranking. Opportunity for advancement (1), salary (2), and geographic location (3) all ranked considerably higher than benefits as factors influencing job selection. Compounding this problem, these students also were asked to estimate the percentage of payroll spent on employee benefits. Slightly less than one half (46 percent) of the students thought that benefits represented 15 percent or less of payroll. Nine of 10 students (89 percent) thought benefits accounted for less than 30 percent of payroll. Only 1 in 10 students had a reasonably accurate (38 percent of payroll) or inflated perception of the magnitude of employee benefits.[20]

The ignorance about the value of employee benefits inferred from those studies is further compounded by complacency. Benefits are taken for granted. Employees view them as a right with little comprehension of, or concern for, employer costs.[21]

One possible salvation from this money pit comes from recent reports that employees are not necessarily looking for more benefits but rather greater choice in the benefits they receive.[22] In fact, up to 70 percent of employees in one study indicated they would be willing to pay more out of pocket for benefits if they were granted greater choice in the design of their own benefits package. This leads us to the issues of benefits planning, design, and administration. All three offer an opportunity to improve benefits effectiveness.

KEY ISSUES IN BENEFITS PLANNING, DESIGN, AND ADMINISTRATION

Benefits Planning and Design Issues

First, and foremost, the benefits planning process must address this vital question: "What is the relative role of benefits in a total compensation package?"[23] For example, if a major compensation objective is to attract good employees, we need to ask, "What is the best way to achieve this?" The answer is not always, nor even frequently, "Let's add another benefit." Consider a company that needs to fill some entry-level jobs that pay minimum wage. One temptation might be to set up a day care center to attract more mothers with preschool children. Certainly this is a popular response today, judging from all the press that day care needs are receiving. A more prudent compensation policy would ask the question: "Is day care the most effective way to achieve my compensation objective?" Sure, day care may be popular with working mothers. But can the necessary workers be

---

[19]Richard Huseman, John Hatfield, and Richard Robinson, "The MBA and Fringe Benefits," *Personnel Administration* 23, no. 7 (1978), pp. 57–60.

[20] Ibid.

[21]Foegen, "Are Escalating Employee Benefits Self-Defeating?" *Pension World* 14, no. 9 (September 1978).

[22]Employee Benefit Research Institute, *America in Transition: Benefits for the Future* (Washington, D.C.: EBRI, 1987).

[23]Jerry Rosenbloom and G. Victor Hallman, *Employee Benefit Planning* (Englewood Cliffs, N.J.: Prentice Hall, 1981).

attracted to the company using some other compensation tool that better meets company goals?

As a second example, how do we deal with undesirable turnover? We might be tempted to design a benefits package that improves progressively with seniority, thus providing a reward for continuing service. This would only be the preferred option, though, if other compensation tools (e.g., increasing wages, introducing incentive compensation) are less effective.

In addition to integrating benefits with other compensation components, the planning process also should include strategies to ensure external competitiveness and adequacy of benefits. Competitiveness requires an understanding of what other firms in your product and labor markets offer as benefits. Firms conduct benefits surveys much as they conduct salary surveys. Either our firm must have a package comparable to that of survey participants, or there should be a sound justification of why deviation makes sense for the firm.

In contrast, ensuring that benefits are adequate is a somewhat more difficult task. Most organizations evaluating adequacy consider the financial liability of employees with and without a particular benefit (e.g., *employee medical expenses with and without medical expense benefits*). There is no magic formula for defining benefits adequacy.[24] In part, the answer may lie in the relationship between benefits adequacy and the third plan objective: cost of effectiveness. More organizations need to consider whether employee benefits are cost justified. Consider, for example, the health care area. Employer costs of providing medical and dental coverage increased 199 percent between 1980 and 1990. Health care increases continue to exceed other cost increases. During the 1980s, health care costs alone rose 117 percent, compared to *only* a 59 percent jump by the general consumer price index. The end result is higher deductibles and greater sharing of premium payments with employees. At the extreme, some experts have even suggested limiting health coverage solely to catastrophic illness. Any cost savings would then be shared with employees. Such cost-benefit analyses must become a stronger feature in both planning and administration of benefits.

Benefits Administration Issues

Three major administration issues arise in setting up a benefits package: (1) Who should be protected or benefited? (2) How much choice should employees have among an array of benefits? (3) How should benefits be financed?[25]

Every organization has a variety of employees with different employment statuses. Should these individuals be treated equally with respect to benefits coverage? Exhibit 11.3 illustrates that companies do indeed differentiate treatment based on employment status. For example, part-timers receive, proportionately, far fewer benefits than do full-time employees.

---

[24]M. Meyer, *Profile of Employee Benefits,* report no. 813 (New York: The Conference Board, 1981), p. 2.

[25]Rosenbloom and Hallman, *Employee Benefit Planning,* pp. 427–31.

EXHIBIT 11.3   Benefits Comparison: Part-Timers versus Full-Timers

	Percent of Firms Giving Benefits to	
	Part-Timers	*Full-Timers*
Benefit		
All benefits	17.0	100
Health	22.0	99
Retirement	31.6	85
Vacation	33.2	98

SOURCE: U.S. Chamber of Commerce, *Employee Benefits, 1990* (Washington, D.C.: U.S. Chamber of Commerce, 1991).

As a second example, should retired automobile executives be permitted to continue purchasing cars at a discount price, a benefit that could be reserved solely for current employees? In fact, a whole series of questions needs to be answered:

1. What probationary periods (for eligibility of benefits) should be used for various types of benefits? Does the employer want to cover employees and their dependents more or less immediately upon employment or provide such coverage for employees who have established more or less "permanent" employment with the employer? Is there a rationale for different probationary periods with different benefits?

2. Which dependents of active employees should be covered?

3. Should retirees (as well as their spouses and perhaps other dependents) be covered, and for which benefits?

4. Should survivors of deceased active employees (and/or retirees) be covered? And if so, for which benefits? Are benefits for surviving spouses appropriate?

5. What coverage, if any, should be extended to employees who are suffering from disabilities?

6. What coverage, if any, should be extended to employees during layoff, leaves of absence, strikes, and so forth?

7. Should coverage be limited to full-time employees?[26]

The answers to these questions depend on the policy decisions regarding adequacy, competition, and cost effectiveness discussed in the last section.

The second administrative issue concerns choice (flexibility) in plan coverage. In the standard benefits package, employees typically have not been offered a choice among employee benefits. Rather, a package is designed with the "average" employee in mind

---

[26]Ibid.

EXHIBIT 11.4   **Example of Possible Options in a Flexible Benefits Package**

	Package			
	A	*B*	*C*	*D*
Health	No	No	No	Yes
Dental	No	No	No	Yes
Vision	No	Yes	Yes	Yes
Life insurance	1 × AE*	2 × AE	2 × AE	3 × AE
Dependent care	Yes	No	No	No
401–K savings	No	No	No	No
Cash back	Yes	No	No	No

*AE = Average earnings

and any deviations in needs simply go unsatisfied. The other extreme is represented by "cafeteria-style," or flexible benefit plans. Under this concept, employees are permitted great flexibility in choosing benefits options of greatest value to them. Picture an individual allotted x number of dollars walking down a cafeteria line and choosing menu items (benefits) according to their attractiveness and cost. The flexibility in this type of plan is apparent. Exhibit 11.4 illustrates a typical choice among packages offered to employees under a flexible benefits system.

Even companies that are not considering a flexible benefits program are offering greater flexibility and choice. Such plans might provide, for example, (1) optional levels of group term life insurance, (2) the availability of death or disability benefits under pension or profit sharing plans, (3) choices of covering dependents under group medical expense coverage, (4) a variety of participation, cash distribution, and investment options under profit sharing, thrift, and capital accumulation plans.[27]

Exhibit 11.5 summarizes some of the major advantages and disadvantages of flexible benefits. Judging from recent acceleration in use of flexible benefits, it seems that employers consider the advantages noted in Exhibit 11.5 to far outweigh the disadvantages.[28] A recent survey of 1,100 employers found that 27 percent of the firms offered flexible benefits package, with another 11 percent planning such a move.[29] Many companies cite

---

[27]Kenneth Shapiro, "Flexibility in Benefit Plans," *Hay Compensation Conference Proceedings* (Philadelphia: Hay Management Consultants, 1983).

[28]Commerce Clearing House, *Flexible Benefits* (Chicago: Commerce Clearing House, 1983); American Can Company, *Do It Your Way* (Greenwich, Conn.: American Can Co., 1978); L. M. Baytos, "The Employee Benefit Smorgasbord: Its Potential and Limitations," *Compensation Review,* First Quarter 1970, pp. 86–90; "Flexible Benefit Plans Become More Popular," December 16, 1986, p. 1; Richard Johnson, *Flexible Benefits: A How to Guide* (Brookfield, Wis.: International Foundation of Employee Benefit Plans, *The Wall Street Journal,* 1986).

[29]Christopher Conte, "Flexible Benefit Plans Grow More Popular as Companies Seek to Cut Costs," *The Wall Street Journal,* March 19, 1991, p. A1.

EXHIBIT 11.5 Advantages and Disadvantages of Flexible Benefit Programs

Advantages
1. Employees choose packages that best satisfy their unique needs.
2. Flexible benefits help firms meet the *changing* needs of a *changing* work force.
3. Increased involvement of employees and families improves understanding of benefits.
4. Flexible plans make introduction of new benefits less costly. The new option is added merely as one among a wide variety of elements from which to choose.
5. Cost containment—the organization sets the dollar maximum. Employee chooses within that constraint.

Disadvantages
1. Employees make bad choices and find themselves not covered for predictable emergencies.
2. Administrative burdens and expenses increase.
3. Adverse selection—employees pick only benefits they will use. The subsequent high benefit utilization increases its cost.
4. Subject to nondiscrimination requirements in Section 125 of the Internal Revenue code.

---

the cost savings from flexible benefits (46 percent of those that adopt) as a primary motivation.[30]

A key consideration in the continued popularity of flexible benefit plans may well be the increased scrutiny of the Internal Revenue Service. Section 125 of the Internal Revenue Code outlines a series of requirements that a company must meet in setting up a flexible benefits package.[31] The most important of these restrictions is a nondiscrimination clause, that is, a plan may not give significantly higher benefits to highly compensated executives relative to average employees. In fact, the average benefits for nonhighly compensated employees must equal or exceed 75 percent of the average benefits for highly compensated executives.

The final administrative issue involves the question of financing benefits plans. Alternatives include the following:

1. Noncontributory (employer pays total costs).
2. Contributory (costs shared between employer and employee).
3. Employee financed (employee pays total costs for some benefits—by law the organization must bear the cost for some benefits).

Exhibit 11.6 presents the arguments for each of these three methods of financing. In general, organizations prefer to make benefits options contributory, reasoning that a "free good," no matter how valuable, is less valuable to an employee. Furthermore, employees have no personal interest in controlling the cost of a free good.

---

[30]Ibid.
[31]Johnson, *Flexible Benefits: A How to Guide.*

EXHIBIT 11.6 Advantages of Different Types of Benefit Financing Plans

---

Arguments for Noncontributory Financing

1. *Coverage for all eligible employees:* Under a noncontributory plan, all eligible employees who have completed the probationary period, if any, are covered by the plan. This feature can avoid employee and public relations problems that might arise under a contributory plan. For example, otherwise eligible employees may not elect coverage under a contributory plan and hence, they and/or their dependents may not be covered when a loss or retirement occurs.
2. *Tax efficiency:* In most cases, employer contributions to an employee benefit plan do not result in current gross income to the covered employees for federal income tax purposes, even though these contributions are normally deductible by the employer as a reasonable and necessary business expense.
3. *Group purchasing advantages:* To the extent that all eligible employees are covered, as opposed to less than all under a contributory plan, the employer may be able to secure more favorable group rates or other conditions of coverage than would otherwise be the case.
4. *Union or collective bargaining pressures:* Labor unions generally favor noncontributory plans.
5. *Ease and economy of administration:* Since payroll deduction is not necessary under a noncontributory plan, benefit and accounting records are easier to maintain.

Arguments for Contributory Financing

1. *More coverage and/or higher benefits possible:* Given a certain level of employer contribution toward the cost of an employee benefit plan, employee contributions may make possible a more adequate plan, or they may enable a plan to be installed in the first place.
2. *Possible enhanced employee appreciation of the plan:* When employees contribute to a plan, they will have greater appreciation for the benefits that they are helping to finance. They will not take such benefits for granted.
3. *Possible lessening of abuses of benefits:* In a vein similar to the previous argument, employees will be less likely to abuse an employee benefit plan if they know that such abuses may increase their own contribution rates.

Arguments for Employee-Pay-All Financing

1. *Separate optional plans offered:* Some employers offer employees the opportunity of purchasing additional, supplementary coverage at group rates, without individual underwriting, which is separate from the benefits of the regular employee benefit plan. This coverage might include, for example, additional accident insurance, life insurance, or hospital-indemnity coverage to supplement Medicare. This additional coverage is normally on an employee-pay-all basis.
2. *Benefits not otherwise available:* Employee-pay-all financing may be the only basis on which an employer believes it can offer the coverage. In the future, such a plan might be shifted to a contributory or even to a noncontributory basis.

SOURCE: Jerry Rosenbloom and G. Victor Hallman, *Employee Benefit Planning* (Englewood Cliffs, N.J.: Prentice Hall, 1991), pp. 427, 429–34. Reprinted by permission of Prentice Hall, Englewood Cliffs, N.J.

COMPONENTS OF A BENEFITS PLAN

Exhibit 11.7 outlines a model of the factors influencing benefits choice, from both the employer and employee perspective. The remainder of this chapter briefly examines each of these factors.

EXHIBIT 11.7   Factors Influencing Choice of Benefits Package

---

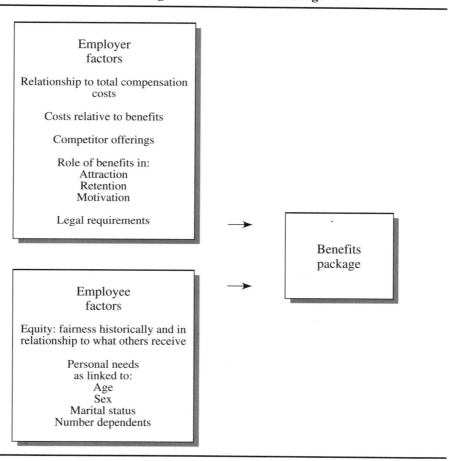

Employer
factors

Relationship to total compensation
costs

Costs relative to benefits

Competitor offerings

Role of benefits in:
Attraction
Retention
Motivation

Legal requirements

Employee
factors

Equity: fairness historically and in
relationship to what others receive

Personal needs
as linked to:
Age
Sex
Marital status
Number dependents

Benefits
package

Employer Factors

As Exhibit 11.7 indicates, a number of factors affect employer preference in determining desirable components of a benefits package.

Relationship to Total Compensation Costs.   A good compensation manager considers employee benefit costs as part of a total package of compensation costs. Frequently employees think that just because an employee benefit is attractive, the company should provide it. A good compensation manager thinks somewhat differently: "Is there a better use for this money? Could we put the money into some other compensation component and achieve better results?" Benefit costs are only one part of a total compensation package. Decisions about outlays have to be considered from this perspective.

Costs Relative to Benefits.   A major reason for the proliferating costs of benefits programs is the narrow focus of benefits administrators. Too frequently the costs/benefits of a particular benefit inclusion are viewed in isolation, without reference to total package costs or forecasts of rising costs in future years. To control spiraling benefits costs, administrators should adopt a broader, cost-centered approach. As a first step, this approach would require policy decisions on the level of benefits expenditures acceptable both in the short and long term. Historically, benefits managers negotiated or provided benefits on a "package" basis rather than a cost basis. The current cost of a benefit would be identified and, if the cost seemed reasonable, the benefit would be provide for (or negotiated with) employees. The crucial error in this process was a failure to recognize that rising costs of this benefit were expected to be borne by the employer. The classic example of this phenomenon is health care coverage. An employer considering a community-based medical plan like Blue Cross during the early 1960s no doubt agreed to pay all or most of the costs of one of the Blue Cross options. As costs of this plan skyrocketed during the 60s and 70s, the employer was expected to continue coverage at the historical level. In effect, the employer became locked into a level of coverage rather than negotiating a level of cost. In subsequent years, then, the spiraling costs were essentially out of the control of the benefits manager.

This cost-centered approach would require benefits administrators, in cooperation with insurance carriers and armed with published forecasts of anticipated costs for particular benefits, to determine the cost commitments for the existing benefits package. Budget dollars not already earmarked may then be allocated to new benefits that best satisfy organizational goals. Factors affecting this decision include an evaluation of benefits offered by other firms and the competitiveness of the existing package. Also important is compliance with various legal requirements as they change over time (Chapter 12). Finally, the actual benefit of a new option must be explored in relation to employee preferences. Those benefits that top the list of employee preferences should be evaluated in relation to current and future costs. Because future cost estimates may be difficult to project, it is imperative that benefits administrators reduce uncertainty. If a benefit forecast suggests that future cost containment may be difficult, the benefit should be offered to employees only on a cost-sharing basis. Management determines what percentage of cost it can afford to bear within budget projections, and the option is offered to employees on a cost-sharing basis, with projected increases in both employer and employee costs communicated openly. In the negotiation process, then, employees or union representatives can evaluate their preference for the option against the forecasted cost burden. In effect, this approach defines the contribution an employer is willing to make in advance. And it avoids the constraints of a defined benefit strategy that burdens the employer with continued provision of that defined benefit level despite rapidly spiraling costs.

Competitor Offerings.   Two important considerations establish external equity in a benefits program. One of the issues that must be confronted is the absolute level of benefits payments relative to important product and labor market competitors. A policy decision must be made about the position (market lead, market lag, or competitive) the organization wants to maintain in its absolute level of benefits relative to the competition. Many employers adopt a benefit that a competitor has initiated only to find some time later that it is inappropriate given the makeup of the organization. A classic example is the employer who installs an education reimbursement plan in an organization with an aging work force. Data suggest that this composition of employees is less likely to use this benefit and consequently places relatively low value on it.

One of the best strategies to determine *external equity* is to conduct a benefits survey. Alternatively, many consulting organizations, professional associations, and interest groups collect benefits data that can be purchased. Perhaps the most widely used of these surveys is the annual benefits survey conducted by the U.S. Chamber of Commerce. To illustrate typical inclusions in a survey, the survey used by the U.S. Chamber of Commerce is reproduced in Exhibit 11.8.[32]

Role of Benefits in Attraction, Retention, and Motivation. Given the rapid growth in benefits and the staggering cost implications, it seems only logical that employers would expect to derive commensurate return on this investment. In fact, there is at best only anecdotal evidence that employee benefits are cost justified. This evidence falls into three categories.[33] First, employee benefits are widely claimed to help in the retention of workers. Benefit schedules are specifically designed to favor longer term employees. For example, retirement benefits increase with years of service, and most plans do not provide for full employee eligibility until a specified number of years of service has been reached. Equally, amount of vacation time increases with years of service, and, finally, employees' savings plans, profit sharing plans, and stock purchase plans frequently provide for increased participation or benefits as company seniority increases. By tying these benefits to seniority, it is assumed that workers are more reluctant to change jobs.

There is also some research to support this common assumption that benefits increase retention. Two studies uncovered a negative relationship between fringe benefit coverage and job change patterns.[34] Higher benefits reduced mobility. A more detailed follow-up study, though, found that only two specific benefits curtailed employee turnover: pensions and medical coverage.[35] Virtually no other employee benefit had a significant impact on turnover. Some people argue, though, that this reduction in turnover because of benefits may not always be good. One poll found that 3 Americans in 10 have, at one time or

[32]U.S. Chamber of Commerce, *Employee Benefits, 1990.*

[33]Donald P. Crane, *The Management of Human Resources,* 2nd ed. (Belmont, Calif.: Wadsworth, 1979); Foegen, "Are Escalating Employee Benefits Self-Defeating?" pp. 83–84, 86.

[34]Olivia Mitchell, "Fringe Benefits and Labor Mobility," *Journal of Human Resources* 17, no. 2 (1982), pp. 286–98; Bradley Schiller and Randal Weiss, "The Impact of Private Pensions on Firm Attachment," *Review of Economics and Statistics* 61, no. 3 (1979), pp. 369–80.

[35]Olivia Mitchell, "Fringe Benefits and the Cost of Changing Jobs," *Industrial and Labor Relations Review* 37, no. 1 (1983), pp. 70–78.

EXHIBIT 11.8

Please return the completed questionnaire to:
ECONOMIC POLICY DIVISION/EMPLOYEE BENEFITS SURVEY
U.S. CHAMBER OF COMMERCE/WASHINGTON, D.C. 20062

CONFIDENTIAL

EMPLOYEE BENEFITS SURVEY — 1990

For Office
Coding—
Leave Blank

—————— A 1

——————— 6
———————
———————

——— 27

—— 30

— 32

— 33

INSTRUCTIONS

1. **It is confidential** — Data from individual firms will not be disclosed. Data will be published only in the form of totals for groups of companies. Only the researchers will see your questionnaire(s).

2. **Company coverage** — If you have several divisions that operate in different industries and separate data is available for each division you may prefer to fill out separate forms for each division. You may either copy this form or call Martin Lefkowitz at (202) 463-5620 for either additional forms or more information.

3. **Employees covered in survey** — We are surveying *both* hourly-paid and salaried employees, if this break-out is available. If the break-out is available, please fill out separate surveys for hourly-paid and salaried employees. The hourly-paid employee survey begins on the next page and the salaried employee survey begins on page 5. If a separate breakout is not available for hourly and salaried employees please use the survey on the following page for reporting the combined totals for all employees on pages 2 through 4.

HOURLY-PAID EMPLOYEE SURVEY AND/OR COMBINED TOTAL OF SALARIED AND HOURLY PAID EMPLOYEES IF NOT AVAILABLE SEPARATELY

When filling out the questionnaire surveying hourly-paid workers, *include data for workers whose pay varies with the number of hours worked.* In addition, include data for *salaried* employees if their pay varies if they work overtime or less than full-time; but do not include them if they receive their regular pay regardless of hours worked.

Organizations having difficulty making this employee separation between hourly-paid and salaried workers should include all nonsupervisory employees and all working supervisors in this hourly-paid employee survey, *regardless of method of payment.* However, please *exclude* all officers of company.

4. **Approximate or incomplete data** — If you are unable to give exact data for the various items, please give estimates — *your best estimate is much better than a zero.* Guidelines for making estimates are included in the survey forms. If you cannot break down the data on payments exactly as they are outlined, please give the data that is available. Also, please indicate the items or benefits for which payments were made, but for which you cannot give separate figures.

EXHIBIT 11.8 *(continued)*

Show actual data or best estimate for employees covered in survey.

A. GROSS PAYROLL FOR EMPLOYEES IN SURVEY:

- For this item, report *actual* wages. Report pay prior to employee deductions for all income and payroll taxes, pay deferral programs, such as 401K plans, and other insurance and deductions. Report on line A-1 the straight-time wages for all hours, including pay for time *not* worked, plus payments in lieu of vacations and holidays.

- Report premium and bonus payments on lines other than line A-1. Thus, if your firm paid $15,000 in overtime pay and the overtime rate is time and one-half, put $10,000 on line A-1, and $5,000 in premium pay on line A-2.

Total amount for 1990

1. Straight-time for employees in survey (include payment for time not worked, holidays, vac., etc.).. $_____ 34
2. Overtime premium pay (premium only, put straight time on line 1) .... $_____ 46
3. Holiday premium pay (premium only, put straight time on line 1) .... $_____ 58
4. Shift differential (premium only, put straight time on line 1) .... $_____ 70
5. Earned incentive or production bonus (including commissions)................................ $_____ 82
6. Other (Specify: _____) .... $_____ 94
7. TOTAL GROSS PAYROLL .... $_____ 106

B. LEGALLY-REQUIRED PAYMENTS (*employer's* share only):

1. Old-Age, Survivors, Disability, and Health Insurance (employer FICA taxes) and Railroad Retirement Tax .... $_____ 118
2. Unemployment Compensation (federal and state taxes) .... $_____ 130
3. Workers' Compensation (estimate cost if self-insured)...................................... $_____ 142
4. State sickness benefits insurance .... $_____ 154
5. Other (Specify: _____) .... $_____ 166
6. TOTAL .... $_____ 178

C. RETIREMENT AND SAVINGS PLAN PAYMENTS (*employer's* share only):

- ITEM C-4 (PENSION AND INSURANCE PREMIUMS)—For pension and insurance premiums, report *net* payments after deducting any dividends or credits returned to employer by insurer.

1. Defined benefit pension plan contributions
   (a defined benefit plan is one that is insured by the Pension Benefit Guaranty Corporation involving a promise to pay a fixed level of benefits on retirement)............................ $_____ 190
2. Defined contribution plan payments
   (a defined contribution plan is one that provides for an individual account for each participant and for benefits based on the amount contributed to the participant's account)
   a. 401K or similar payments (employers share only).................................... $_____ 202
   b. Profit-sharing payments .... $_____ 214
      (employer contributions are based on current profits of the business, fluctuating with current profit levels)
   c. Stock bonus and employee stock ownership plans (ESOP) .... $_____ 226
3. Money purchase plans .... $_____ 238
4. Pension plan premiums (net) under insurance and annuity contracts (insured and trusteed) ...... $_____ 250
5. Costs of plan administration
   (please estimate the administrative costs paid separately or as part of contributions to the plan).. $_____ 262
6. Other (Specify: _____) .... $_____ 274
7. TOTAL .... $_____ 286
8. Please report the number of employees participating in your company's retirement and savings plan programs.. _____ 298

D. LIFE INSURANCE AND DEATH BENEFITS (*employer's* share only):

- Exclude premiums for life insurance purchased under a pension plan. Such premiums should be reported under item C-4.

1. Life insurance premiums (net)... $_____ 304
2. Death benefits not covered by insurance .... $_____ 316
3. TOTAL .... $_____ 328

EXHIBIT 11.8 *(continued)*

E. MEDICAL AND MEDICALLY-RELATED BENEFIT PAYMENTS (*employer's* share only):

1. Hospital, surgical, medical, and major medical insurance premiums (net) .... $_____ 340
2. Self-insured hospital, surgical, medical, and major medical payments............................ $_____ 352
3. Short-term disability, sickness or accident insurance (company plan or insured plan) .... $_____ 364
4. Long-term disability or wage continuation (insured, self-administered, or trust) .... $_____ 376
5. *Retiree* (payments for retired employees) hospital, surgical, medical, and major medical insurance premiums (net) .... $_____ 388
6. Self-insured *retiree* (payments for retired employees) hospital, surgical, medical, and major medical payments .... $_____ 400
7. Dental insurance premiums .... $_____ 412
8. Vision care and prescription drugs .... $_____ 424
9. Physical and mental fitness programs .... $_____ 436
10. Medically-related benefits for *former* workers and family members, such as the continuation of health benefit payments after termination of employment (do not include payments to retirees and/or for maternity leave) .... $_____ 448
11. Other (Specify: _____) .... $_____ 460
12. TOTAL .... $_____ 472

F. PAID REST PERIODS, COFFEE BREAKS, LUNCH PERIODS, WASH-UP TIME, TRAVEL TIME, CLOTHES-CHANGE TIME, GET-READY TIME, ETC.

● This should be reported if time is paid for, whether or not there is a formal work rule providing for such time off. A simple rule of thumb is that if employees typically take two 10-minute rest periods per day, this would amount to approximately 4% of gross payroll; if two 15-minute breaks are taken, the figure would come to 6% of gross payroll (Item A-7). $_____ 484

G. PAYMENTS FOR TIME NOT WORKED:

1. Payments for or in lieu of vacations (for estimating purposes, each day of paid vacation = .00385 x straight-time pay) .... $_____ 496

    If unable to estimate a dollar figure, please indicate the average number of days of vacation an employee receives a year. _____

2. Payments for or in lieu of holidays (for estimating purposes, each paid holiday = .00385 x straight-time pay).. $_____ 508

    If unable to estimate a dollar figure, please indicate the average number of paid holidays an employee receives a year. _____

3. Sick leave pay.. $_____ 520
4. Parental leave (maternity and paternity leave payments) .... $_____ 532
5. Payments required under guaranteed workweek or work year—only that part that represents payment for time not worked .... $_____ 544
6. Payments for State or National guard duty; jury, witness, and voting pay allowances; payments for time lost due to death in family; or other personal reasons .... $_____ 556
7. Other (Specify: _____) .... $_____ 568
8. TOTAL .... $_____ 580

H. MISCELLANEOUS BENEFIT PAYMENTS (*employer's* share only):

1. Discounts on goods and services purchased from company by employees......................... $_____ 592
2. Employee meals furnished by company.. $_____ 604
3. Child care: a. On-site child care... $_____ 616
                 b. Third-party provided care.. $_____ 628
4. Parking.. $_____ 640
5. Employee education expenditures (tuition refunds, seminar attendance, etc.) .... $_____ 652
6. Payments for legal counselling .... $_____ 664
7. Payments to union stewards or officials for time spent in settling grievances or in negotiating agreements .... $_____ 676
8. Christmas or other special bonuses (not tied to profits), service awards, suggestion awards, etc..... $_____ 700
9. Other (Specify: _____) .... $_____ 712
10. TOTAL .... $_____ 724

CONFIDENTIAL

EXHIBIT 11.8 *(concluded)*

I. EMPLOYEE PAYROLL DEDUCTIONS (*employee's* share only):
- For this question, report deductions from *employee* pay. Employer contributions are reported in questions B-E.

1. Old-Age, Survivors, Disability, and Health Insurance (employee FICA taxes) and Railroad
   Retirement Taxes... $_____ 736
2. Retirement and Savings Plan payments (including 401K and similar programs)................... $_____ 748
3. Life insurance premiums .... $_____ 760
4. Medical and Medically-Related Benefits Payments .... $_____ 772
5. Other (Specify: _____). Do not include deductions for
   income tax.. $_____ 784
6. TOTAL .... $_____ 796

J. EMPLOYEE HOURS
- These figures include hours worked or paid for (including time actually worked, *plus*
  holidays, vacation, sick leave, and other time paid for but not worked).

1. Total hours of a **typical full-time employee**   _____ × 52 = _____ 808
   during 1990:   average number of hours   total hours
                                                      per week per employee   during 1990
                                                                                       per employee

2. Total hours of **all** employees in survey during 1990:
   - The total number of hours worked or paid for of all employees covered in the survey,
     corresponds to earnings given on line A-1.

   _____ × _____ = _____ 812
   total hrs. during 1990   full-time equivalent   total hours of
   per employee   employees included   all employees
                               in your survey data   in 1990
                               for 1990

PRIMARY STANDARD INDUSTRIAL CLASSIFICATION CODE (SIC Code)   =   _____

- If you do not know your SIC Code, please give a description of the major type of business and/or the principal lines or products manufactured or handled.

SUPPLEMENTAL QUESTIONS

Please answer the following questions:

	For Office Coding— Leave Blank
	___ ___ ___ B1

1. Does your firm have a fixed benefit plan or a cafeteria plan (a cafeteria plan is one that allows
   employees to choose between benefits and/or benefit plans)?   (Check appropriate box)
   Fixed Benefit Plan.. F ☐
   Cafeteria Plan... C ☐
   Mixed benefit package (part of benefits package is fixed and part is cafeteria)............... M ☐   6

2. What is the estimated percentage of part-time workers as the percentage of your total workforce (part-time workers are those who work less hours than the normal work week)?........ _____ 7

3. If you provide benefits to part-time employees, which benefits do you provide?
   All (If you checked this line "yes" please skip to question 4) .... Yes ☐ No ☐ 12
   Health .... Yes ☐ No ☐ 13
   Retirement... Yes ☐ No ☐ 14
   Vacations .... Yes ☐ No ☐ 15
   Bonuses... Yes ☐ No ☐ 16
   Others (please specify: _____)

4. Please estimate the total annual cost for administering your benefit costs that are not included
   in the above cost data on employee benefits.
   a. Estimated annual internal costs of administering benefits programs not included in the
      above data on benefit costs... $_____ 17
   b. Estimated annual cost of outside consultants, attorneys and other persons consulted
      regarding the administration of benefits programs.. $_____ 29

5. What administrative costs associated with COBRA (the law that requires your firm to make
   available health insurance to former employees) during 1990? $_____ 41

6. What is the biggest problem you face in providing health benefits to former employees? Check
   only one of the following)
   a) general administrative burden (paperwork, recordkeeping, and billing) .... a ☐
   b) burdensome claims costs .... b ☐
   c) premium payments and notification from COBRA beneficiaries........................... c ☐
   d) keeping track of changes in the law .... d ☐   53

Please list the name, title and phone number of the person who is responsible for filling out this questionnaire in case our researchers have any questions.

_____ _____ (____) _____
Name   Title   Phone Number

another, stayed in a job they wanted to leave simply because they could not give up their health care coverage.[36] This job lock probably is not a desirable outcome for employers.

Second, employee benefits also are lauded for their presumed impact on employee satisfaction. One survey by the International Survey Research Corporation casts doubt on this claim, though. Today only 50 percent of workers consider their benefits adequate. This is down from 83 percent in the early 80s.[37] The lowest satisfaction marks go to disability, life, and health insurance.[38] Why have satisfaction ratings fallen? One view holds that benefits satisfaction falls as cost-cutting companies attempt to reduce coverage and also shift more of the costs to employees.[39] A second view is more pessimistic, arguing that benefits plans fail to meet either employer or employee needs. In this view, simply pumping more money into benefits is inappropriate. Rather, employers must make fundamental changes in the way they approach the benefits-planning process. Companies must realize that declining satisfaction with benefits is a result of long-term changes in the work force. Ever-increasing numbers of women in the labor force, coupled with increasing numbers of dual career families and higher educational attainments, suggest changing values of employees.[40] Changing values, in turn, necessitate a reevaluation of benefits packages.

Finally, employee benefits also are valued because improved retention and increased satisfaction will, some organizations hope, have bottom line effects on profitability. This is consistent with the old adage: "A happy worker is a productive worker."

Unfortunately, the research supporting these declarations is relatively scant, particularly in relation to the huge costs incurred in the name of employee benefits. There are some glimmers of potential, though. Employee stock ownership plans (ESOPs described in more detail in Chapter 12) reportedly improve company productivity.[41] Presumably owning stock motivates employees to be more productive. After all, part of the reward returns to them in the form of dividends and increased stock value. Similar productivity improvements are reported for employee assistance programs (e.g., alcohol and drug treatment programs for employees), with reports of up to 25 percent jumps in productivity after implementation of EAP programs.[42]

Legal Requirements.   Employers obviously want a benefits package that complies with all aspects of the law. Exhibit 11.9 shows part of the increasingly complex web of legislation in the benefits area. Greater details on the three legally mandated benefits (workers' compensation, social security, and unemployment insurance) are provided in Chapter 12.

---

[36]New York Times and CBS poll, as reported in the *Human Resource Management News* (Chicago: Remy Publishing, 1991).

[37]Conte, "Flexible Benefit Plans Grow More Popular," p. A1.

[38]*The Wall Street Journal,* April 30, 1985, p. 1.

[39]George Dreher, Ronald Ash, Robert Bretz, "Benefit Coverage and Employee Cost: Critical Factors in Explaining Compensation Satisfaction," *Personnel Psychology* 41 (1988), pp. 237–54.

[40]Ibid.

[41]"ESOPs Key to Performance," *Employee Benefit News* 5 (1987), p. 16.

[42]Lynn Densford, "Bringing Employees Back to Health," *Employee Benefit News* 2 (February 1988), p. 19.

EXHIBIT 11.9   **Impact of Legislation on Selected Benefits**

Legislation	Impact on Employee Benefits
Fair Labor Standards Act, 1938	Created time and one-half overtime pay. Benefits linked to pay (e.g., social security) increase correspondingly during those overtime hours.
Employee Retirement Income Security Act, 1974	If an employer decides to provide a pension (it is not mandated!), specific rules must be followed. Plan must vest (employee has right to both personal and company contributions into pension) after five-years of employment. Pension Benefit Guaranty Corporation, as set up by this law, provides workers some financial coverage when a company and its pension plan goes bankrupt.
Tax reform, 1982, 1986	Permit individual retirement accounts (IRAs) for eligible employees. Established 401-K programs, a matched contributions saving plan (employer matches part or all of employee contribution) that frequently serves as part of a retirement package.
Health Maintenance Act, 1973	Required employers to offer alternative health coverage (e.g., health maintenance organizations) options to employees.
Discrimination legislation (Age Discrimination in Employment Act, Civil Rights Act, Pregnancy Disability Act, various state laws)	Benefits must be administered in a manner that does not discriminate against protected groups (on basis of race, color, religion, sex, national origin, age, pregnancy).
Consolidated Omnibus Budget Reconciliation Act (COBRA), 1984	Employees who resign or are laid off through no fault of their own are eligible to continue receiving health coverage under employer's plan at a cost borne by the employee.

Absolute and Relative Compensation Costs.   Any evaluation of employee benefits must be placed in the context of total compensation costs. Cost competitiveness means the total package must be competitive—not just specific segments. Consequently, decisions on whether to adopt certain options must be considered in light of the impact on total costs and in relationship to expenditures of competitors (as determined in benefits surveys such as the Chamber of Commerce survey discussed later in this chapter).

Employee Factors

Employee preferences for various benefit options are determined by individual needs. Those benefits perceived to best satisfy individual needs are most highly desired. In part these needs arise out of feelings of perceived equity or inequity.

Equity.   To illustrate the impact of equity, consider the example of government employees working in the same neighborhood as auto workers. Imagine the dissatisfaction with government holidays created when government employees leave for work every morning knowing that their autoworker neighbors are home in bed for the whole week between Christmas and New Year's Day. The perceived unfairness of this difference need not be rational. But it is, nevertheless, a factor that must be considered in determining employee needs. Occasionally this comparison process leads to a "bandwagon" effect in which new benefits offered by a competitor are adopted without careful consideration, simply because the employer wants to avoid hard feelings. This phenomenon is particularly apparent for employers with strong commitments to maintaining a totally or partially nonunion work force. Benefits obtained by a unionized competitor or a unionized segment of the firm's work force are frequently passed along to nonunion employees. Although the effectiveness of this strategy in thwarting unionization efforts has not been demonstrated, many nonunion firms would prefer to provide the benefit as a safety measure.

Personal Needs of Employees.   A major assumption in empirical efforts to determine employee preferences is that preferences are somehow systematically related to what are termed *demographic differences*. The demographic approach assumes that demographic groups (e.g., young versus old, married versus unmarried) can be identified for which benefits preferences are fairly consistent across members of the group. Furthermore, it assumes that meaningful differences exist between groups in terms of benefit preferences.

There is some evidence that these assumptions are only partially correct. One study extensively reviewed patterns of group preferences for particular benefits.[43] As one might expect, older workers showed stronger preferences than younger workers for pension plans.[44] Also, families with dependents had stronger preferences for health/medical coverage than families with no dependents.[45] The big surprise in all these studies, though, is that many of the other demographic group breakdowns fail to result in differential benefit preferences. Traditionally, it has been assumed that benefit preferences ought to differ among males versus females, blue collar versus white collar, married versus single, young versus old, and families with dependents versus those with none. Few of these expectations have been borne out by these studies. Rather, the studies have tended to be more valuable in showing preference trends that are characteristic of all employees. Among the benefits available, health/medical and stock plans are highly preferred benefits, but such options as early retirement, profit sharing, shorter hours, and counseling services rank among the least preferred options. Beyond these conclusions, most preference studies have shown wide variation in individuals with respect to benefit preferences.

The weakness of this demographic approach has led some organizations to undertake a second and more expensive empirical method of determining employee preference: surveying individuals about needs. One way of accomplishing this requires development

---

[43]William F. Glueck, *Personnel: A Diagnostic Approach* (Plano, Tex.: Business Publications, 1978).

[44]Ludwig Wagner and Theodore Bakerman, "Wage Earners' Opinions of Insurance Fringe Benefits," *Journal of Insurance,* June 1960, pp. 17–28; Brad Chapman and Robert Otterman, "Employee Preference for Various Compensation and Benefits Options," *Personnel Administrator* 25 (November 1975), pp. 31–36.

[45]Stanley Nealy, "Pay and Benefit Preferences," *Industrial Relations,* October 1963, pp. 17–28.

EXHIBIT 11.10 Questionnaire Formats for Benefits Surveys

A. Ranking method

Rank order the following benefits from 1 (high) to 4 (low) in terms of their value to you.

_____ Health/medical coverage
_____ Extended holiday schedule
_____ Pension plan
_____ Life insurance

B. Likert-type scale

How important are each of the following benefits to you (check one for each benefit).

	(1) Very Important	(2) Important	(3) Neutral	(4) Unimportant	(5) Very Unimportant
Health/medical coverage	_____	_____	_____	_____	_____
Extended holiday schedule	_____	_____	_____	_____	_____
Pension plan	_____	_____	_____	_____	_____
Life insurance	_____	_____	_____	_____	_____

of a questionnaire on which employees evaluate various benefits. For example, Exhibit 11.10 illustrates two types of questionnaire formats.

While other strategies for scaling are available (e.g., paired comparison), the most important factor to remember is that a consistent method must be used in assessing preferences on a questionnaire. Switching between a ranking method and a Likert-type scale may, by itself, affect the results.[46]

A third empirical method of identifying individual employee preferences is commonly known as a *flexible benefit plan* (also called, at various times, a *cafeteria-style plan* or a *supermarket plan*). As previously noted, employees are allotted a fixed amount of money and permitted to spend that amount in the purchase of benefit options. From a theoretical perspective, this approach to benefits packaging is ideal. Employees directly identify the benefits of greatest value to them, and by constraining the dollars employees have to spend, benefits managers are able to control benefits costs.

ADMINISTERING THE BENEFITS PROGRAM

The job description for an employee-benefits executive found in Exhibit 11.11 indicates that administrative time is spent on three functions that require further discussion: (1) communicating about the benefits program, (2) claims processing, and (3) cost containment.[47]

---

[46]George T. Milkovich and Michael J. Delaney, "A Note on Cafeteria Pay Plans," *Industrial Relations,* February 1975, pp. 112–16.

[47]McCaffery, *Managing the Employee Benefits Program.*

EXHIBIT 11.11   Job Description for Employee-Benefits Executive

---

Position

The primary responsibility of this position is the administration of established company benefits programs. Develops and recommends new and improved policies and plans with regard to employee benefits. Ensures compliance with ERISA requirements and regulations.

Specific Functions

1. Administers group life insurance, health and accident insurance, retirement programs, and savings plans.
2. Processes documents necessary for the implementation of various benefits programs and maintains such records as are necessary.
3. Recommends and approves procedures for maintenance of benefits programs and issues operating instructions.
4. Participates in the establishment of long-range objectives of company benefits programs.
5. Conducts surveys and analyzes and maintains an organized body of information on benefits programs of other companies.
6. Informs management of trends and developments in the field of company benefits.
7. Gives advice and counsel regarding current developments in benefits programs.
8. Acts as liaison between company and banks, insurance companies, and other agencies.
9. Conducts special studies as requested by management.

   In addition, the employee-benefits executive may be responsible for various employee services, such as recreation programs, advisory services, credit unions, and savings bond purchase programs.

SOURCE: Robert McCaffery, *Managing the Employee Benefits Program* (New York: American Management Association, 1983), p. 25.

EMPLOYEE BENEFITS COMMUNICATION

The most frequent method for communicating employee benefits today is probably still the employee benefits handbook.[48] A typical handbook contains a description of all benefits, including levels of coverage and eligibility requirements. To be most effective, this benefits manual should be accompanied by group meetings and videotapes.[49] Although some organizations may supplement this initial benefits discussion with periodic refreshers (e.g., once per year), a more typical approach involves one-on-one discussions between the benefits administrator and an employee seeking information on a particular benefit. There are also a number of excellent newsletters published by firms to update employees on changes in benefits.

In recent years, the dominance of the benefits handbook has been challenged by personalized benefits statements generated by computer software programs specially designed for that purpose. These tailor-made reports provide a breakdown of package components and list selected cost information about the options. Many experts predict

---

[48]Towers, Perrin, Forster, and Crosby, "Corporate Benefit Communication . . . Today and Tomorrow," 1988.

[49]Ibid.

that the future of benefits communications includes interactive computer programs by which employees can enter questions into the computer and have the computer provide basic benefits counseling.[50]

Despite such innovative plans to communicate employee benefit packages, failure to understand benefits components and their value is still one of the root causes of employee dissatisfaction.[51] We believe an effective communications package must have three elements. First, an organization must spell out its benefit objectives and ensure that any communications achieve these objectives. Exhibit 11.12 outlines typical benefits objectives.

Second, the program should make use of the most effective presentation mediums. Exhibit 11.13 indicates the effectiveness ratings for a variety of communications tools.

And, finally, the content of the communications package must be complete, clear, and free of the complex jargon that so readily invades benefits discussions. The amount of time/space devoted to each issue should vary closely with both perceived importance of the benefit to employees and with expected difficulty in communicating option alternatives.[52]

EXHIBIT 11.12   Typical Benefits Objectives

Objective	Respondents Indicating This Is a Primary Objective (%)
1. Increase employee understanding of plan objectives	82*
2. Increase employee appreciation of the benefits program	81
3. Increase employee knowledge of the cost of providing benefits	41
4. Obtain employee cooperation in controlling benefit costs	36
5. Encourage employees to take responsibility for their own financial security	16
6. Maintain the company's commitment to open employee communications	16

*Multiple responses permitted

SOURCE: Towers, Perrin, Forster, and Crosby (1988), "Corporate Benefit Communication . . . Today and Tomorrow."

[50]Ibid.

[51]Reported in "Yoder-Heneman Creativity Award Supplement," *Personnel Administration* 26, no. 11 (1981), pp. 49–67.

[52]"How Do You Communicate? It May Not Be Nearly As Well As You Think," *Benefits*, December 1988, pp. 13–15; Kevin Greene, "Effective Employee Benefits Communication," in *New Perspectives on Compensation*, ed. David Balkin and Luis Gomez-Mejia (Englewood Cliffs, N.J.: Prentice Hall, 1987).

EXHIBIT 11.13   Effectiveness of Different Communications Tools

Communciations Tool	Rating
Memos	3.4
Special brochures	3.8
Employee handbooks	3.3
Small group meetings	4.2
Personalized benefit statements	4.3
Letters to employee's home	3.5
Company-wide publications	3.3
"Live" slide shows	3.8
Large group meetings	3.6
Bulletin boards	3.1
Videotapes	4.0
Employee annual reports	2.4
Slides/audiotapes	3.7
Individual discussions with supervisors	3.4
Benefit newsletters	3.6
Telephone hotlines	3.6
Electronic communications	3.3
Films	3.5

5 = Highly effective; 1 = Highly ineffective.

SOURCE: Towers, Perrin, Forster, and Crosby (1988), "Corporate Benefit Communication . . . Today and Tomorrow."

CLAIMS PROCESSING

As noted by one expert, claims processing arises when an employee asserts that a specific event (e.g., disablement, hospitalization, unemployment) has occurred and demands that the employer fulfill a promise of payment.[53] As such, a claims processor must first determine whether the act has, in fact, occurred. If it has, the second step involves determining whether the employee is eligible for the benefit. If payment is not denied at this stage, the claims processor calculates payment level. It is particularly important at this stage to ensure coordination of benefits. If multiple insurance companies are liable for payment (e.g., working spouses covered by different insurers), a good claims processor can save from 10 to 15 percent of claims cost by ensuring that the liability is jointly paid.[54]

Although these steps are time-consuming, most of the work is quite routine in nature. The major job challenges come in those approximately 10 percent of all claims when payment is denied. A benefits administrator must then become an adroit counselor ex-

---

[53]Bennet Shaver, "The Claims Process," in *Employee Benefit Management*, ed. H. Wayne Snider (New York: Risk and Insurance Management Society, 1980), pp. 141–52.

[54]Thomas Fannin and Theresa Fannin, "Coordination of Benefits: Uncovering Buried Treasure," *Personnel Journal*, May 1983, pp. 386–91.

EXHIBIT 11.14   A Basic Primer of Cost Containment Terminology

---

Deductibles—the requirement that the first x amount of dollars in a year be paid by the claimant when an employee makes a claim for insurance coverage.

Coinsurance (copayment)—a proportion of insurance premiums paid by the employee.

Benefit cutbacks—corresponding to wage concessions, negotiations by some employers with employees to eliminate or reduce employer contributions to selected options.

Defined contribution plans—limits of employers' responsibility for employee benefits in terms of dollar contribution maximum.

Defined benefits plans—limits of employers' responsibility for employee benefits in terms of a specific benefit and the options included. As the cost of these options rises in future years, the employer is obligated to provide the benefit as negotiated despite its increased cost.

Dual coverage—in families in which both spouses work, coverage of specific claims from each employee's benefit package. Employers cut costs by specifying payment limitations under such conditions.

Benefit ceiling—a maximum payout for specific claims (e.g., limiting liability for extended hospital stays to $150,000).

---

plaining the situation to the employee in a manner that conveys the equitable and consistent procedures used.

COST CONTAINMENT

Cost containment is easily the largest issue in benefits planning and administration today. Escalating costs of the 1960s, 1970s, and 1980s, combined with disappointing evidence that benefits have little impact on shaping positive employee behaviors, have molded the cost-cutting drives of the 1990s. Increasingly, employers are auditing their benefits options for cost containment opportunities. The terminology of cost containment is becoming a part of every employee's vocabulary; Exhibit 11.14 defines some common cost containment terms.

SUMMARY

Given the rapid escalation in the cost of employee benefits over the past 15 years, organizations would do well to evaluate the effectiveness of their benefits adoption, retention, and termination procedures. Specifically, how does an organization go about selecting appropriate employee benefits? Are the decisions based on sound evaluation of employee preferences balanced against organizational goals or legal compliance and competitiveness? Do the benefits chosen serve to attract, retain, and/or motivate employees? Or are organizations paying billions of dollars of indirect compensation without any tangible benefit? This chapter has outlined a benefits determination process that identifies major issues in selecting and evaluating particular benefit choices. The next chapter catalogs the various benefits available and discusses some of the decisions confronting a benefits administrator.

REVIEW QUESTIONS

1. Your CEO is living proof that a little bit of knowledge is dangerous. He just read in *The Wall Street Journal* that employee benefits cost, on average, 38 percent of payroll. To save money, he suggests the company fire its two benefits administrators, do away with all benefits, and give employees a 38 percent pay hike. What arguments could you provide to persuade the CEO this is not a good idea?

2. Assume that an organization (Company A) develops a benefits program in the following way. First it identifies the major demographic groups in the organization. Then the company offers benefits known to be highly desired by people in those demographic groups in general (i.e., more senior employees prefer larger allocations to pensions). What kinds of problems could arise using this type of strategy to design a benefits program?

3. Why is it more difficult to control costs under a defined benefits program versus a defined contributions program?

4. How is the concept of external equity similar or different in discussing pay versus benefits?

5. Describe how a flexible benefits program might increase worker satisfaction with benefits at the same time that costs are being reduced.

YOUR TURN:
MONDAILLE HYDRAULICS

Mondaille Hydraulics manufactures pumps for construction equipment and residential homes. In six months contract negotiations are scheduled with the bargaining representative for all blue collar workers, Local 1099 of the United Auto Workers. The president of your company, Forrest Sutton, is convinced that he must get concessions from the workers if Mondaille is to compete effectively with increasing foreign competition. In particular, Mr. Sutton is displeased with the cost of employee benefits. He doesn't mind conceding a small wage increase (maximum 3 percent), but he wants the total compensation package to cost 3 percent less for union employees during the first year of the new contract. Your current costs are shown in Exhibit 1.

Your labor relations assistant has surveyed other companies obtaining concessions from UAW locals.

You also have data from a consulting firm that indicates employee preferences for different forms of benefits (Exhibit 2). Based on all this information, you have two possible concession packages that the union just might accept, labeled Option 1 and Option 2 (Exhibit 3).

1. Cost out these packages given the data in Exhibits 1 and 2 and the information contained from various insurance carriers and other information sources (Exhibit 4).
2. Which package should you recommend to the president? Why?
3. Which of the strategies do you think need not be negotiated with the union before implementation?

EXHIBIT 1 Current Compensation Costs

Average yearly wage	$24,336.00
Average hourly wage	12.17
Dollar value of yearly benefits, per employee	10,284.00
Total compensation (wages plus benefits)	34,620.00
Daily average number of hours paid	8.0

Benefits (by Category)	Dollar/Cost/ Employee/Year
1. Legally required payments (employer's share only)	$2,141.00
a. Old-age, survivors, disability, and health insurance (FICA) taxes	1,509.00
b. Unemployment compensation	292.00
c. Workers' compensation (including estimated cost of self-insured)	311.00
d. Railroad retirement tax, railroad unemployment and cash sickness insurance, state sickness benefits insurance, etc.	29.00
2. Pension, insurance, and other agreed-upon payments (employer's share only)	$3,129.00
a. Pension plan premiums and pension payments not covered by insurance-type plan (net)	1,460.00
b. Life insurance premiums; death benefits; hospital, surgical, medical, and major medical insurance premiums, etc. (net)	1,427.00
c. Short-term disability	83.00
d. Salary continuation or long-term disability	57.00
e. Dental insurance premiums	51.00

(continued)

EXHIBIT 1   (*concluded*)

Benefits (by Category)	Dollar/Cost/ Employee/Year
f. Discounts on goods and services purchased from company by employees	27.00
g. Employee meals furnished by company	–0–
h. Miscellaneous payments (compensation payments in excess of legal requirements, separation or termination pay allowances, moving expenses, etc.)	24.00
3. Paid rest periods, lunch periods, wash-up time, travel time, clothes-change time, get-ready time, etc. (60 minutes)	$727.00
4. Payments for time not worked	$2,703.00
a. Paid vacations and payments in lieu of vacation (16 days average)	1,558.00
b. Payments for holidays not worked (9 days)	973.00
c. Paid sick leave (10 days maximum)	172.00
d. Payments for state or national guard duty; jury, witness, and voting pay allowances; payments for time lost due to death in family or other personal reasons, etc.	66.00
5. Other items	$157.00
a. Profit-sharing payments	–0–
b. Contributions to employee thrift plans	71.00
c. Christmas or other special bonuses, service awards, suggestion awards, etc.	–0–
d. Employee education expenditures (tuition refunds, etc.)	40.00
e. Special wage payments ordered by courts, payments to union stewards, etc.	46.00
Total	$10,284.00

EXHIBIT 2   Benefit Preferences

Benefit Type or Method of Administering	Importance to Workers
Pensions	87
Hospitalization	86
Life insurance	79
Paid vacation	82
Holidays	82
Long-term disability	72
Short-term disability	69
Paid sick leave	70
Paid rest periods, lunch periods, etc.	55
Dental insurance	51
Christmas bonus	31
Profit sharing	21
Education expenditures	15
Contributions to thrift plans	15
Discount on goods	5
Fair treatment in administration	100

Note: 0 = Unimportant; 100 = Extremely important.

EXHIBIT 3 Two Possible Concession Packages

Option 1

Implement COPAY for Benefit	*Amount of COPAY*
Pension	$200.00
Hospital, surgical, medical, and major medical premiums	250.00
Dental insurance premiums	15.00

Reduction of Benefit

Eliminate 10-minute paid break (workers leave work 10 minutes earlier)
Eliminate one paid holiday per year
Coordination with legally required benefit; social security coordinated with Mondaille pension

Option 2

Improved claims processing
   Unemployment compensation
   Workers' compensation
   Long-term disability
Require probationary period (one year) before eligible for
   Discounts on goods
   Employee meal paid by company
   Contributions to employee thrift plans
Deductible ($100 per incident)
   Life insurance; death benefits; hospital, etc.
   Dental insurance

COPAY	*Amount of COPAY*
Hospital, surgical, medical and major medical premiums	$200.00

EXHIBIT 4   **Analysis of Cost Implications for Different Cost-Cutting Strategies: Mondaille Hydraulics**

Cost-Saving Strategy	Savings as Percent of Benefit-Type Cost
COPAY	Dollar for dollar savings equal to amount of COPAY
Deductible ($100 per incident)	
Life insurance premiums, death benefits, hospital, etc.	6%
Dental insurance	30
Require probationary period before eligible (one year)	
Discount on goods and services	10
Employee meals furnished by company	15
Contributions to employee thrift plans	10
Improved claims processing	
Unemployment compensation	8
Workers' compensation	3
Long-term disability	1
Coordination with legally required benefits	
Coordinate social security with Mondaille Pension Plan	15

CHAPTER

12 Benefits Options

Chapter Outline

Human resources (HR) professionals share three widely held views about benefits administration. First, the number of employee benefits and the laws affecting them have been escalating rapidly. Second, a good benefits administrator can save an organization substantial sums of money through proper benefits plan design and effective administration of benefits. Third, proficiency in benefits plan administration requires years of experience. The first two of these statements were endorsed in Chapter 11. The third statement, however, requires qualification. Admittedly, the number of benefits options and choices can, at times, be quite overwhelming. Even trained HR professionals can err in their evaluation of a benefits package. For example, one study asked both college graduates

---

EXHIBIT 12.1   Categorization of Employee Benefits

Type of Benefit

1. Legally required payments (employers' share only)
   a. Old age, survivors, disability, and health insurance (employer FICA taxes) and railroad retirement tax.
   b. Unemployment compensation.
   c. Workers' compensation (including estimated cost of self-insured).
   d. State sickness benefits insurance.
2. Retirement and saving plan payments (employers' share only)
   a. Defined benefit pension plan contributions (401–K type).
   b. Defined contribution plan payments.
   c. Profit sharing.
   d. Stock bonus and employee stock ownership plans (ESOP).
   e. Pension plan premiums (net) under insurance and annuity contracts (insured and trusted).
   f. Administrative and other cost.
3. Life insurance and death benefits (employers' share only)
4. Medical and medically related benefits payments (employers' share only)
   a. Hospital, surgical, medical, and major medical insurance premiums (net).
   b. Retiree (payments for retired employees) hospital, surgical, medical, and major medical insurance premiums (net).
   c. Short-term disability, sickness, or accident insurance (company plan or insured plan).
   d. Long-term disability or wage continuation (insured, self-administered, or trust).
   e. Dental insurance premiums.
   f. Other (vision care, physical, and mental fitness benefits for former employees).
5. Paid rest periods, coffee breaks, lunch periods, wash-up time, travel time, clothes-change time, get-ready time, etc.
6. Payments for time not worked
   a. Payments for or in lieu of vacations.
   b. Payment for or in lieu of holidays.
   c. Sick leave pay.
   d. Parental leave (maternity and paternity leave payments).
   e. Other.
7. Miscellaneous benefit payments
   a. Discounts on goods and services purchased from company by employees.
   b. Employee meals furnished by company.
   c. Employee education expenditures.
   d. Child care.
   e. Other.

and HR recruiters to rank order 11 different benefits equated for costs to a company.[1] The HR recruiters' role was to estimate the graduates' responses. Surprisingly, at least to the recruiters, the college graduates placed high value on medical/life insurance, company stocks, and pensions. Less importance was placed on holidays and scheduling conveniences (e.g., flextime, four-day work week). The recruiters systematically underestimated the value of most of the top benefits and overestimated the value of the leisure and work-schedule benefits. Despite the surprises, though, and despite the obvious magnitude of benefits information, some basic issues can still be identified as equally relevant across different organizations. These commonalities serve as a foundation for aspiring benefits plan administrators. After categorizing benefits, these issues will be discussed as they relate to each benefit category. Exhibit 12.1 provides the most widely accepted categorization of employee benefits. In its annual report based on a nationwide survey of employee benefits, the U.S. Chamber of Commerce identified seven categories of benefits.[2] Since this breakdown is familiar to benefits plan administrators, it will be used to organize this chapter and illustrate important principles affecting administration of each benefit type.

Exhibit 12.2 provides data from both the private sector (both small and large firms) and the public sector on employee participation in selected benefits programs.[3] Notice the high rate of participation for such common benefits as life/health insurance and pension

EXHIBIT 12.2 Percentage of Participation in Selected Benefits

Benefit Type	Small Firms (100 or fewer) 1985	Large Firms 1980	Large Firms 1985	Large Firms 1989	State and Local Government 1987
Paid holiday	?	99	98	97	81
Paid vacation	59	100	99	97	72
Sickness and accident insurance	34	54	52	43	14
Long-term disability	?	40	48	45	31
Health insurance	42	97	96	92	94
Life insurance	33	96	96	94	85
Retirement	18				93
Defined benefit plan	?	84	80	63	
Defined contribution plan	?	?	41	48	9

SOURCE: Selected volumes from Bureau of Labor Statistics: *Employee Benefits in Medium and Large Firms; Employee Benefits in State and Local Government; National Federation of Independent Businesses; Small Business Employee Benefits,* 1985.

---

[1]Kermit Davis, William Giles, and Hubert Feild, "Compensation and Fringe Benefits: How Recruiters View New College Graduates' Preferences," *Personnel Administrator,* January 1985, pp. 43–50.

[2]U.S. Chamber of Commerce, *Employee Benefits, 1987* (Washington, D.C.: Chamber of Commerce, 1988).

[3]U.S. Department of Labor, *Employee Benefits in Medium and Large Firms, 1986,* Bulletin 2281 (1987).

plans in all except small firms. These participation rates are exceeded only by those of legally required benefits. In general, a higher percentage of employees are covered in the private sector. The one major exception is with pension coverage. Typically, state and local government employees are more likely to have some form of retirement coverage than are their private sector counterparts.

LEGALLY REQUIRED BENEFITS

Virtually every employee benefit is *somehow affected* by statutory or common law (many of the limitations are imposed by tax laws). In this section, the primary focus will be on benefits that are *required* by statutory law: workers' compensation, social security, and unemployment compensation.

Workers' Compensation

Workers' compensation is an insurance program paid for by the employer that is designed to protect employees from expenses incurred for a work-related injury or disease. An injury or disease qualifies for workers' compensation if it results from an accident that arose out of, and while in, the course of employment. Workers' compensation benefits are given for the following:[4]

1. Permanent total disability and temporary total disability.
2. Permanent partial disability—loss of use of a body member.
3. Survivor benefits in cases of fatal injuries.
4. Medical expenses.
5. Rehabilitation.

Of these five categories, temporary total disability is both the most frequent type of claim and one of the two most costly (along with permanent partial disability).[5]

Workers' compensation can consist of either monetary reimbursement or payment of medical expenses. The amount of compensation is based on fixed schedules of minimum and maximum payments. Disability payments are often tied to the employee's earnings, modified by such economic factors as the number of dependents.

The employee receives workers' compensation, regardless of fault in an accident. Detailed recordkeeping of work accidents, illnesses, and deaths are required by state statute.

States require that employers obtain workers' compensation insurance through a private carrier or, in some states, through participation in a state fund. The employer is liable for premium payments; the employee does not pay for this insurance.

---

[4]Ronald G. Ehrenberg, "Workers' Compensation, Wages, and the Risk of Injury," in *New Perspectives in Workers Compensation,* ed. John Burton (Ithaca, N.Y.: ILR Press, 1988).
[5]Ibid.

Some states provide "second injury funds." These funds relieve an employer's liability when a preemployment injury combines with a work-related injury to produce a disability greater than that caused by the latter alone. For example, if a person with a known heart condition is hired and then breaks an arm in a fall triggered by a heart attack, medical treatments for the heart condition would not be paid from workers' compensation insurance; treatment for the broken arm would be compensated.

Exhibit 12.3 summarizes the most common features of the various state laws.[6]

The cost of workers' compensation, as well as level of protection, varies widely from state to state. In some states, employers pay more for workers' compensation than they do for state income tax. In 1988 more than $38 billion were paid out in workers' compensation claims.[7] Between 1950 and 1980, workers' compensation benefits as a percentage of payroll almost doubled, from 0.36 to 0.70 percent.[8] Some employers argue that these high costs are forcing them to uproot established businesses in states with high costs to relocate in lower cost states.[9]

Why these rapid cost increases? At least three factors seem to play a role.[10] First, medical costs continue to skyrocket. More than 30 percent of workers' compensation costs can be traced to medical expenses. Second, some employees use workers' compensation as a surrogate for more stringent unemployment insurance programs. Rising numbers of employees, fearing recession and possible layoffs, fake new illnesses or stall reporting back after existing illnesses. Finally, workers' compensation also faces a serious threat from inclusion of new illnesses for coverage under the law. The most common new inclusions are stress-related ailments. The number of claims for stress-induced illness doubled between 1979 and 1984.[11]

EXHIBIT 12.3 Commonalities in State Workers' Compensation Laws

Issue	*Most Common State Provision*
Type of law	Compulsory (*N* = 47 states).
	Elective (*N* = 3 states).
Self-insurance	Self-insurance permitted (*N* = 47 states).
coverage	All industrial employment.
	Farm labor, domestic servants, and casual employees usually exempted.
	Compulsory for all or most public sector employees (*N* = 47 states).
Occupational diseases	Coverage for all diseases arising out of and in the course of employment. No compensation for "ordinary diseases of life."

---

[6]U.S. Chamber of Commerce, *Analysis of Workers' Compensation Laws, 1985*, Publication no. 6803 (Washington, D.C.: Chamber of Commerce, 1985).

[7]Employee Benefits Research Institute, *EBRI Databook on Employee Benefits* (Washington D.C.: EBRI, 1990).

[8]Robert Lampman and Robert Hutchens, "The Future of Workers' Compensation," in *New Perspectives*, ed. J. Burton.

[9]Ibid.

[10]Ibid.

[11]Ibid.

Unfortunately, these cost problems appear to be spiraling. Several studies indicate that the number of workers' compensation claims depends directly on the size of benefits specified in the state law.[12] When benefits rise, more people find reasons to file claims. Equally disturbing, though, when the number of claims rise, state legislators have a tendency to vote for more generous benefits![13]

If this cost spiral is to be broken, legislators and benefits administrators need to better understand how the system works. First we provide a brief history of workers' compensation. This is followed by a discussion of program objectives and an evaluation of success against these objectives.

The first workers' compensation state laws to survive the constitutionality question were passed in 1911. By 1920, all but six states had passed some form of workers' compensation law; all 50 states currently have one. The passage of these first laws is attributable to two related events. First, prior to the passage of the first state laws (1907–1908), the accident rate in industry attained an unacceptable level: "approximately 30,000 workers died from occupational-related accidents."[14]

In addition to this high accident rate, workers had no protection for work-related accidents. The only source of remedy for workers was the courts, and prevailing law heavily favored employer rights over those of employees. As accident rates mounted, however, public support grew for some form of worker compensation.

The result of this rising sentiment, tempered by more than 60 years of experience and modification, is the modern workers' compensation system. According to the National Commission on State Workmen's Compensation Laws, the existing workers' compensation system is designed to achieve five major objectives.[15] The following paragraphs outline these objectives and assess the degree to which they have been achieved.

First, workers' compensation is designed to pay prompt and reasonable compensation to victims of work accidents. Little can be said about the promptness of payments, since few jurisdictions collect or report such data. The reasonableness of compensation, however, is more easily assessed. Most states attempt to provide an injured worker with 50 to 67 percent of lost income. According to one authority, though, this compensation level frequently is not achieved in practice.[16] Numerous states set maximum weekly benefits that fall below the target policy. Of even more concern, many jurisdictions provide for benefits that are below the poverty threshold.

Second, workers' compensation attempts to eliminate delays, costs, and wastes of personal injury litigation. The existing system is based on the no-fault concept, presumably eliminating the need to undertake costly battles to establish guilt or innocence. This goal has been largely achieved, despite some administrative problems in minimizing delays and costs.

---

[12]Ehrenberg, "Workers' Compensation Wages"; J. Paul Leigh, "Analysis of Workers' Compensation Using Data on Individuals," *Industrial Relations* 24, no. 2 (1985), pp. 247, 256.

[13]Ibid.

[14]Robert J. Paul, "Workers' Compensation: An Adequate Employee Benefit?" *Academy of Management Review*, October 1976, p. 113.

[15]Ibid.

[16]Ibid.

Third, the law attempts to reduce the number of accident cases. Although data on accident reduction records are not widely available, workers' compensation has two components that act as incentives for developing a safe work environment. First, since most employers are experience rated (insurance premiums vary directly with the number of accidents experienced), they have a monetary incentive to reduce accidents.[17] Second, most laws require accurate records on accident data that can be analyzed and provide input into design of safer work environments. Unfortunately, many employers do not respond to this component of the law. Consequently, the resulting accident data are often sketchy and of little value in accident prevention.

Perhaps the most convincing evidence that workers' compensation laws have not met public expectations about accident prevention can be inferred from passage of the Occupational Safety and Health Act (OSHA) of 1970.[18] The provisions of OSHA are designed to improve working conditions in industry, thereby reducing worker accidents and job-related illnesses. Passage of the act suggests that the reactive approach (i.e., react to injuries after the fact through compensation) is insufficient incentive to stem job-related accidents.

Fourth, workers' compensation requires firms to provide prompt and adequate medical treatment. This provision has been a major success for the workers' compensation law. Most jurisdictions provide full medical treatment for injured workers without legal limitation on the time or cost of treatment.

Fifth, the law provides for rehabilitation of workers unable to return to their former jobs. Prior to the early 1970s, this provision was the least effective aspect of existing workers' compensation programs. However, massive reforms of the law during the 1970s resulted in additional rehabilitative benefits for disabled employees enrolled in a retraining program.

Social Security

When social security became effective in 1937, only about 60 percent of all workers were eligible.[19] Today most working Americans and their families are protected by social security. Whether a worker retires, becomes disabled, or dies, social security benefits are paid to replace part of the lost family earnings. Indeed, ever since its passage, the Social Security Act has been designed and amended to provide a foundation of basic security for American workers and their families. Exhibit 12.4 identifies initial coverage of the law and subsequent broadening of this coverage over the years.[20]

---

[17]Ibid.

[18]James Ledvinka, *Federal Regulation of Personnel and Human Resource Management* (Belmont, Calif.: Wadsworth Publishing, 1982).

[19]Employee Benefit Research Institute, *Fundamentals of Employee Benefit Programs* (Washington, D.C.: EBRI, 1990).

[20]William J. Cohen, "The Evolution and Growth of Social Security," in *Federal Policies and Worker Status Since the Thirties,* ed. J. P. Goldberg, E. Ahern, W. Haber, and R. A. Oswald (Madison, Wis.: Industrial Relations Research Association, 1976), p. 62.

EXHIBIT 12.4   Social Security through the Years

1935:   **Original provisions of the law**
        Federal old-age benefits program.
        Public assistance for the aged, blind, and dependent children who would not otherwise qualify for
            social security.
        Unemployment compensation.
        Federal state program for maternity care, crippled children's services, child-welfare services.
        Public health services.
        Vocational rehabilitation services.

        Changes in the law since 1935
1939:   Survivor's insurance added to provide monthly life insurance payments to the widow and
            dependent children of a deceased worker.
1950–
1954:   Old-age and survivor's insurance was broadened.
1956:   Disability insurance benefits provided to workers and dependents of such employees.
1965:   Medical insurance protection to the aged and later (1973) the disabled under age 65 (medicare).
1972:   Cost-of-living escalator tied to the consumer price index—guaranteed higher future benefits for all
            beneficiaries.
1974:   Existing state programs of financial assistance to the aged, blind, and disabled were replaced by
            SSI (supplemental security income) administered by the Social Security Administration.

The money to pay these benefits comes from the social security contributions made by employees, their employers, and self-employed people during working years. As contributions are paid in each year, they are immediately used to pay for the benefits to current beneficiaries. Herein lies a major problem with social security. Although the number of retired workers continues to rise (because of earlier retirement and longer life spans), no corresponding increase in the number of contributors to social security has offset these costs. Combine these increases with other cost stimulants (e.g., liberal cost-of-living adjustments), and the outcome is not surprising. To maintain solvency, there has been a dramatic increase in both the maximum earnings base and the rate at which that base is taxed. Exhibit 12.5 illustrates the trends in tax rate, maximum earnings base, and maximum tax for social security.

The combined impact of these schedules for employers is twofold. Consider, for example, employees who earned $45,000 in 1992. They will have deducted from their wage $3,442 (7.65 percent of $45,000). The first obvious impact on employers is that they must also pay $3,442. In addition, employers also should integrate this social security contribution with any existing private pension benefits. A targeted level of pension benefits that neglects social security contributions results in retirement incomes that exceed employer intentions.

It is generally agreed that current funding levels will produce a massive surplus throughout the 1990s. Current baby boomers will reach their peak earnings potential and subsidize a much smaller generation born during the 1930s. Forecasts project a $70 billion surplus in 1996 alone! As Exhibit 12.6 starkly projects, though, this surplus is expected to turn into a substantial shortfall sometime after the year 2015. By that time, baby boomers will be at retirement age and too few workers will be contributing to the fund

EXHIBIT 12.5   Tax Rates, Maximum Earnings Base, and Maximum Social Security Tax

| Year | Taxation Rate on Covered Earnings | | Total × Maximum Earnings Base | | Maximum Social Security Tax (dollars) |
	For Retirement Survivors' and Disability Insurance (percent)	For Hospital Insurance (percent)	(percent)	(dollars)	
1978	5.05	1.00	6.05	× $17,700	$1,070.85
1979	5.08	1.05	6.13	× 22,900	1,403.77
1980	5.08	1.05	6.13	× 25,900	1,587.67
1981	5.35	1.30	6.65	× 29,700	1,975.05
1982	5.40	1.30	6.70	× 32,400	2,170.80
1983	5.40	1.30	6.70	× 35,700	2,391.90
1984	5.40	1.30	7.00	× 37,800	2,646.00
1985	5.70	1.35	7.05	× 39,600	2,791.80
1986	5.70	1.45	7.15	× 42,000	3,003.00
1987	5.70	1.45	7.15	× 43,800	3,131.70
1988	6.06	1.45	7.51	× 45,000	3,379.50
1989	6.06	1.45	7.51	× 48,000	3,604.80
1990	6.20	1.45	7.65	× 51,300	3,924.45
1991	6.20	1.45	7.65	× 53,400	4,085.10
2000	6.20	1.45	7.65	× (to be set later)	—

SOURCE: *Social Security Bulletin, Annual Statistical Supplement* (1990).

to balance the outflow. One proposed solution is to set aside current surpluses rather than using the money to finance part of the general debt. Unfortunately, there is no evidence that Congress has this much self-control.

Benefits under Social Security.   The majority of benefits under social security fall into one of four categories: (1) old age or disability benefits paid to the covered worker, (2) benefits for dependents of retired or disabled workers, (3) benefits for surviving family members of a deceased worker, and (4) lump sum death payments. To qualify for these benefits, a worker must work in a covered employment and earn a specified amount of money (about $500 today) for each quarter year of coverage. Forty quarters of coverage will insure any worker for life. The amount received under the four benefits categories noted above varies, but in general is tied to the amount contributed during eligibility quarters. The average monthly benefit rose from $571 in 1990 to $602 in 1991.[21]

---

[21]"Social Security Benefits to Rise 5.4% Next Year," *The Wall Street Journal.* October 19, 1990, p. A2.

EXHIBIT 12.6   Social Security: Projected Surpluses and Shortfalls

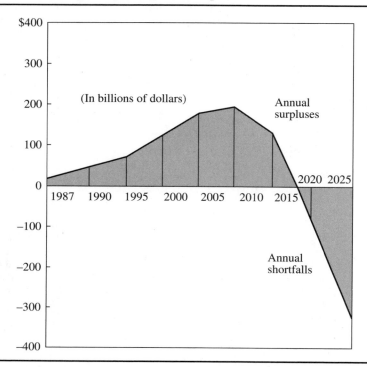

SOURCE: Social Security Administration (1988).

Unemployment Insurance

The earliest union efforts to cushion the effects of unemployment for their members (c. 1830s) were part of benevolence programs of self-help. Working members made contributions to their unemployed brethren.[22] With passage of the unemployment insurance law (as part of the Social Security Act of 1935), this floor of security for unemployed workers became less dependent upon the philanthropy of fellow workers. Since unemployment insurance laws vary by state, this review will cover some of the major characteristics of different state programs.

Financing.   Unemployment compensation paid out to eligible workers is financed exclusively by employers who pay federal and state unemployment insurance tax. The tax amounts to 6.2 percent of the first $7,000 earned by each worker. The state unemployment

---

[22]Raymond Munts, "Policy Development in Unemployment Insurance," in *Federal Policies and Worker Status Since the Thirties*, ed. Goldberg, Ahern, Haber, and Oswald.

commission (or its equivalent) receives 5.4 percent of this 6.2 percent, and the remainder goes to the federal government for administrative costs and to repay federal government loans to the extended unemployment compensation account. All states allow for experience rating, that is, charging lower percentages to employers who have terminated fewer employees. The tax rate may fall to 0 percent in some states for employers who have had no recent experience with former employees collecting chargeable unemployment insurance or may rise to 10 percent for organizations with large numbers of layoffs.

Eligibility.   To be eligible for benefits, an unemployed worker must (1) be able, available, and actively seeking work; (2) not have refused suitable employment; (3) not be unemployed because of a labor dispute (except Rhode Island and New York); (4) not have left a job voluntarily; (5) not have been terminated for gross misconduct; and (6) have been previously employed in a covered industry or occupation, earning a designated minimum amount for a specified period of time.

Coverage.   All workers except a few agricultural and domestic workers are currently covered by unemployment insurance (UI) laws. These covered workers (97 percent of the work force), though, must still meet eligibility requirements to receive benefits.

Duration.   Until 1958, the maximum number of weeks any claimant could collect UI was 26 weeks. However, the 1958 and 1960–1961 recessions yielded large numbers of claimants who exhausted their benefits, leading many states to temporarily revise upward the maximum benefits duration. The most recent modification of this benefits' duration (1982) involves a complex formula that ensures extended benefits in times of high unemployment. Extended benefits will be paid when either of two conditions prevails: (1) when the number of insured unemployed in a state reaches 6 percent or (2) when the unemployment rate is higher than 5 percent and at least 20 percent higher than in the same period of the two preceding calendar years, and remains that way for 13 weeks.[23]

Weekly Benefits Amount.   Those unemployed workers who do meet eligibility requirements are entitled to a weekly benefit amount designed to equal 50 percent of the claimants' lost wages. A recent study indicates, though, that most states don't reach this 50 percent target level.[24] Nor do benefits appear to cover even the minimum nondeferrable expenditures (e.g., minimum outlay for food and housing) faced by the average recipient.[25] Recognizing this problem, some states recently raised their benefits levels.

Controlling Unemployment Taxes.   Every unemployed worker's unemployment benefits are "charged" against the firm or firms most recently employing a currently

---

[23]C. Arthur Williams, John S. Turnbull, and Earl F. Cheit, *Economic and Social Security,* 5th ed. (New York: John Wiley, 1982).

[24]Elchanan Cohn and Margaret Capen, "A Note on the Adequacy of UI Benefits," *Industrial Relations* 26, no. 1 (1987), pp. 106–111.

[25]Ibid.

unemployed worker. The more money paid out on behalf of a firm, the higher is the unemployment insurance rate for that firm. Efforts to control these costs quite logically should begin with a well-designed HR planning system. Realistic estimates of HR needs will reduce the need for hasty hiring and morale-breaking terminations. Additionally, though, a benefits administrator should attempt to audit prelayoff behavior (e.g., tardiness, gross misconduct, absenteeism, illness, leaves of absence) and compliance with UI requirements after termination (e.g., job refusals, insufficient duration of covered work).

RETIREMENT AND SAVINGS PLAN PAYMENTS

The last chapter noted that a high relationship exists between employee age and preference for a pension plan. Although this need for old age security may become more pronounced as workers age, it is evident among younger workers also.

This security motive and certain tax advantages have fostered the rise of pension programs. As Exhibit 12.2 indicated, the vast majority of employers choose to provide this benefit as part of their overall package. Pension programs provide income to an employee at some future time as compensation for work performed now. Two types of pension plans will be discussed to varying degrees here: (1) defined benefit and (2) defined contribution plans. As you read these descriptions, keep in mind that defined benefit plans may be a dying breed. In 1991, 10,064 defined benefit plans were terminated, and only 370 new ones were adopted.[26] During the same interval, defined contribution plans remained about even, with approximately 12,000 additions by companies and 12,000 terminations by others.[27]

Defined Benefit Plans

In a defined benefit plan an employer agrees to provide a specific level of retirement pension that is expressed as either a fixed dollar or percentage of earnings amount that may vary (increase) with years of seniority in the company. The firm finances this obligation by following an actuarially determined benefits formula and making current payments that will yield the future pension benefit for a retiring employee.

Defined benefit plans generally follow one of three different formulas. The most common approach (54 percent) is to calculate average earnings over the last three to five years of service for a prospective retiree and offer a pension that is a function of this earnings average and years of seniority. Plans that are considered generous typically target for pensions equal to 50 to 80 percent of final average earnings. At the low end of the "generosity" scale are plans that target for 30 to 50 percent of final average pay. The second formula (14 percent of companies) for a defined benefits plan uses average career earnings rather than earnings from the last few years: other things being equal, this would reduce the level of benefit for pensioners. The final formula (28 percent of companies)

---

[26]CompFlash, "A Vanishing Breed: Defined-Benefit Pension Plans," *CompFlash* (Saranac Lake, N.Y.: American Management Association, 1992), p. 6.

[27]"Defined Benefit," *The Wall Street Journal,* February 11, 1992, p. A1.

commits an employer to a fixed dollar amount that does not depend on any earnings data. This figure generally rises with seniority level.

The level of pension a company chooses to offer depends on the answer to several questions. First, what level of retirement compensation would a company like to set as a target, expressed in relation to preretirement earnings? Second, should social security payments be factored in when considering the level of income an employee should have during retirement? About one third of the plans monitored by the Department of Labor have a provision for integration with social security benefits.[28] One integration approach reduces normal benefits by a percentage (usually 50 percent) of social security benefits.[29] Another feature employs a more liberal benefits formula on earnings that exceed the maximum income taxed by social security. Regardless of the formula used, about two thirds of U.S. companies do not employ the cost-cutting strategy. Once a company has targeted the level of income it wants to provide employees in retirement, it makes sense to design a system that integrates private pension and social security to achieve that goal. Any other strategy is not cost effective.

Third, should other postretirement income sources (e.g., savings plans that are partially funded by employer contributions) be integrated with the pension payment? Fourth, a company must decide how to factor seniority into the payout formula. The larger the role played by seniority, the more important pensions will be in retaining employees. Most companies believe that the maximum pension payout for a particular level of earnings should be achieved only by employees who have spent an entire career with the company (e.g., 30 to 35 years). As Exhibit 12.7 vividly illustrates, job hoppers are hurt financially by this type of strategy.

EXHIBIT 12.7 **The High Cost of Job-Hopping (Pensions Based on One Percentage Point for Each Year of Service Multiplied by Final Salary)**

		Years of Service	Percentage Point Credit		Final Salary		Annual Pensions
Employee A	1st job	10	10%	×	$ 35,817	=	$ 3,582
	2nd job	10	10	×	64,143	=	6,414
	3rd job	10	10	×	114,870	=	11,487
	4th job	10	10	×	205,714	=	20,571
					Total pension:		$42,054
Employee B	1st job	40	40	×	205,714	=	82,286
					Total pension:		$82,286

NOTE: Figures assume starting salary of $20,000 and 6% annual inflation rate.
Pay increases match inflation rate.
SOURCE: Federal Reserve Bank of Boston.

---

[28]Robert Frumkin and Donald Schmitt, "Pension Improvements since 1974 Reflect Inflation, New U.S. Law," *Monthly Labor Review* 102, no. 4 (April 1979), pp. 18–22.

[29]Jerry S. Rosenbloom and G. Victor Hallman, *Employee Benefit Planning* (Englewood Cliffs, N.J.: Prentice Hall, 1981).

Defined Contribution Plans

Defined contribution plans require specific contributions by an employer, but the final benefit received by employees is unknown, depending on the investment success of those charged with administering the pension fund.

There are two popular forms of defined contribution plans. A 401–(K) plan, so named for the section of the Internal Revenue Code describing the requirements, is a savings-type plan in which employees are allowed to defer income up to a $7,000.00 maximum. Employers match employee savings, typically at the level of 50 cents for each dollar deferred. The maximum deferral level rises from $7,000.00, depending on changes in the consumer price index (e.g., 1991 = $8,475).

The second type of plan is an employee stock ownership plan (ESOP). In a basic ESOP, a company makes a tax deductible contribution of stock shares or cash to a trust. The trust then allocates company stock (or stock bought with cash contribution) to participating employee accounts. The amount allocated is based on employee earnings. When an ESOP is used as a pension vehicle (as opposed to an incentive program), the employees receive cash at retirement based on the stock value at that time. ESOPs have one major disadvantage that limits their utility for pension accumulations. Many employees are reluctant to "bet" most of their future retirement income on just one investment source. If the company's stock takes a downturn, the result can be catastrophic for employees approaching retirement age. Despite this disadvantage ESOPs continue to be popular. One public opinion poll found that about one half of employees would trade their next pay increase for a share in ownership of the company.[30] Further evidence of ESOP popularity comes from the growth of participation by employees. In 1975 about 250,000 employees were enrolled in ESOPs. That number exceeded 11,500,000 by 1989.[31]

Finally, profit sharing can also be considered a defined contribution pension plan if the distribution of profits is delayed until retirement. Chapter 10 explains the basics of profit sharing.

The advantages and disadvantages of these two generic categories of pensions (defined benefit and defined contribution) are outlined in Exhibit 12.8.

Possibly the most important of the factors noted in Exhibit 12.8 is the differential risk borne by employers on the cost dimension. Defined contribution plans have known costs from Year 1. The employer agrees to a specific level of payment that changes only through negotiation or through some voluntary action. In contrast, defined contribution plans commit the employer to a specific level of benefit. Errors in actuarial projections can add considerably to costs over the years. Perhaps for this reason, defined contribution plans have been more popular for new adoptions over the past 15 years.

Not surprisingly, both of these deferred compensation plans are subject to stringent tax laws. For deferred compensation to be exempt from current taxation, specific re-

---

[30]Employee Benefit Research Institute, *Fundamentals of Employee Benefit Programs* (Washington, D.C.: EBRI, 1990).

[31]Ibid.

EXHIBIT 12.8   Relative Advantages of Different Pension Alternatives

Defined Benefit Plan	*Defined Contribution Plan*
1. Provides an explicit benefit that is easily communicated.	Unknown benefit level is difficult to communicate.
2. Company absorbs risk associated with changes in inflation and interest rates that affect cost.	Employees assume these risks.
3. More favorable to long service employees.	More favorable to short-term employees.
4. Employer costs unknown.	Employer costs known up front.

quirements must be met. To qualify (hence, labeled a *qualified* deferred compensation plan), an employer cannot freely choose who will participate in the plan. This requirement eliminated the common practice of discriminating in favor of executives and other highly compensated employees. The major advantage of a qualified plan is that the employer receives an income tax deduction for contributions made to the plan even though employees may not yet have received any benefits. The disadvantage arises in recruitment of high-talent executives. A plan will not qualify for tax exemptions if an employer pays high levels of deferred compensation to entice executives to the firm, unless proportionate contributions also are made to lower level employees.

The appendix to this chapter illustrates one example of the language used in describing pension benefits.

ERISA

Private pension plans ran into serious criticism in the recession of the early 1970s for a number of reasons. Many people who thought they were covered were the victims of complicated rules, insufficient funding, irresponsible financial management, and employer bankruptcies. Some pension funds, including both employer-managed and union-managed funds, were accused of mismanagement; other pension plans required long vesting periods. The Employee Retirement Income Security Act (ERISA) was passed in 1974 in response to these criticisms.

ERISA *does not require* that employers offer a pension plan. But if a company decides to have one, it is rigidly controlled by ERISA provisions. These provisions were designed to achieve two goals: (1) to protect the interest of workers who are covered today by private retirement plans, and (2) to stimulate the growth of such plans.

The actual success of ERISA in achieving these goals has been mixed at best. In the first two full years of operation (1975–1976), more than 13,000 pension plans were terminated. A major factor in these terminations, along with the recession, was ERISA. Employers complained about the excessive costs and paperwork of living under ERISA. Some disgruntled employers even claimed that ERISA was an acronym for Every Ridiculous Idea Since Adam. To examine the merits of these claims, let us take a closer look at the major requirements of ERISA.

General Requirements.   ERISA requires that employees be eligible for pension plans beginning at age 21. Employers may require one year of service as a precondition for participation. The service requirement may be extended to three years if the pension plan offers full and immediate vesting.

Vesting and Portability.   These two concepts are sometimes confused but have very different meanings in practice. *Vesting* refers to the length of time an employee must work for an employer before he or she is entitled to employer payments into the pension plan. The vesting concept has two components. First, any contributions made by the employee to a pension fund are immediately and irrevocably vested. The vesting right becomes questionable only with respect to the employer's contributions. As mandated by ERISA, and amended by the tax reform act of 1986, the employer's contribution must vest at least as quickly as one of the following two formulas: (1) full vesting after five years, or (2) 20 percent after three years and twenty percent each year thereafter (full in 7 years).

  The vesting schedule an employer uses is often a function of the demographic makeup of the work force. An employer who experiences high turnover may wish to use the five-year service schedule. By so doing, any employee with less than five years' service at time of termination receives no vested benefits. Or the employer may use the second schedule in the hope that earlier benefits accrual will reduce undesired turnover. The strategy adopted, therefore, depends on organizational goals and work force characteristics.

  Portability of pension benefits becomes an issue for employees moving to new organizations. Should pension assets accompany the transferring employee in some fashion?[32] ERISA does not require mandatory portability of private pensions. On a voluntary basis, though, the employer may agree to let an employee's pension benefits transfer to the new employer. For an employer to permit portability, of course, the pension rights must be vested.

Fiduciary Responsibility.   Today more than $400 billion exist in private pension accounts in the United States. Unrestrained investment of these funds by a company representative could lead to substantial abuse.[33] Consequently, ERISA stipulates that the fiduciary entrusted with investment decisions is legally obligated to follow a "prudent man" rule. Included in the operational definition of a prudent man are certain prohibitions against investments made in self-interest.

Pension Benefit Guaranty Corporation.   Despite the wealth of constraints imposed by ERISA, the potential still exists for an organization to go bankrupt or in some way fail to meet its vested pension obligations. To protect individuals confronted by this problem,

---

[32]Susan M. Philips and Linda P. Fletcher, "The Future of the Portable Pension Concept," *Industrial and Labor Relations Review* 30 (1977), p. 197.

[33]Mark Gertner, "ERISA and the Investment Decision-Making Process: The Past, the Present, and the Future," *Employee Benefits Journal,* June 1985, pp. 28–35.

employers are required to pay insurance premiums to the Pension Benefit Guaranty Corporation (PBGC) established by ERISA. In turn, the PBGC guarantees payment of vested benefits to employees formerly covered by terminated pension plans.

LIFE INSURANCE

One of the most common employee benefits (about 95 percent of medium to large private sector firms) offered by organizations is some form of life insurance. Typical coverage would be a group term insurance policy with a face value of one to two times the employee's salary.[34] Most plan premiums are paid completely by the employer (87 percent of employers).[35] Slightly more than 80 percent include retiree coverage. The term policy provides protection against loss of life for a specified period but provides no cash surrender value or investment value. About two thirds of all policies include accidental death and dismemberment clauses. To discourage turnover, almost all companies make this benefit forfeitable at termination.

Life insurance is one of the benefits heavily affected by movement to a flexible benefits program. Flexibility is introduced by providing a core of basic life coverage (e.g., $25,000) and then permitting employees to choose more coverage (e.g., in increments of $10,000 to $25,000) as part of their optional package.

MEDICAL AND MEDICALLY RELATED PAYMENTS

General Health Care

The American health system today costs in excess of $800 billion annually.[36] Health care costs represented 5.9 percent of gross national product in 1965, 10.5 percent in 1983, and is expected to reach 14 percent in 1992. One of every $7 spent by Americans in 1992 was spent on health care![37] More costly technology, increased numbers of elderly, and a system that does not encourage cost savings have all contributed to the rapidly rising costs of medical insurance. In the past 10 years, though, employers have begun to take steps designed to curb these costs. After a discussion of the types of health care systems, these cost-cutting strategies will be discussed. Exhibit 12.9 provides a brief overview of the three most common health care options.

An employer's share of health care costs is contributed in one of five health care systems: (1) a community-based system, such as Blue Cross, (2) a commercial insurance plan, (3) self-insurance, (4) a health maintenance organization (HMO), or (5) a preferred provider organization (PPO).

Of these five, plans 1 through 3 (labeled as traditional coverage in Exhibit 12.9) operate in a similar fashion. Two major distinctions exist, however. The first distinction

---

[34]Employee Benefit Research Institute, *Fundamentals of Employee Benefit Programs.*
[35]Ibid.
[36]Kathy Sawyer, "Health Care Spending May Reach 14% of GNP," *Washington Post,* December 30, 1991, p. A6.
[37]Ibid.

EXHIBIT 12.9   How Health Insurance Options Differ on Key Dimensions

Issue	Traditional Coverage	Health Maintenance Organization (HMO)	Preferred Provider Organization (PPO)
Who is eligible?	May live anywhere.	May be required to live in HMO–designated service area.	May live anywhere.
Who provides health care?	Doctor and health care facility of patient's choice.	Must use doctors and facilities designated by HMO.	May use doctors and facilities associated with PPO. If not, may pay additional copayment/deductible.
How much coverage on routine, preventative level?	Does not cover regular checkups and other preventative services. Diagnostic tests may be covered in part or full.	Covers regular checkups, diagnostic tests, other preventative services with low or no fee per visit.	Same as with HMO. If doctor and facility are on approved list. Copayments and deductibles are assessed at much higher rate for others not on list.
Hospital care.	Covers doctors and hospital bills.	Covers doctors and hospital bills if HMO–approved hospital.	Covers doctors and hospitals if PPO–approved.

is in the manner payments are made. With Blue Cross, the employer-paid premiums guarantee employees a direct service, including room, board, and any necessary health services covered by the plan. Coverage under a commercial insurance plan guarantees fixed payment for hospital service to the insured, who in turn reimburses the hospital. And, finally, a self-insurance plan implies that the company provides coverage out of its own assets, assuming the risks itself within state legal guidelines. A Johnson and Higgins Survey claims that self-funding is on the rise, with 46 percent of the companies surveyed claiming some level of self-funding. The most common strategy is to have stop-loss coverage, with an insurance policy covering costs in excess of some predetermined level (e.g., $50,000.00).[38]

The second distinction is in the way costs of medical benefits are determined. Blue Cross operates via the concept of community rating. In effect, insurance rates are based on the medical experience of the entire community. Higher use of medical facilities results in higher premiums. In contrast, insurance companies operate from a narrower experience rating base, preferring to charge each company separately according to its medical facility usage. Finally, of course, the cost of medical coverage under a self-insurance program

---

[38]"Self Funding: Many Companies Try It for Health Benefits," *The Wall Street Journal,* June 2, 1987, p. 1.

is directly related to usage level, with employer payments going directly to medical care providers rather than to secondary sources in the form of premiums.

As a fourth delivery system, health maintenance organizations offer comprehensive benefits for a fixed fee. HMOs offer routine medical services at a specific site. Employees make prepayments in exchange for guaranteed health care services on demand. By emphasizing preventative treatment and early diagnosis, HMOs reduce the need for hospitalization to about one half the national average.[39] By law, employers of more than 25 employees are required to provide employees the option of joining a federally qualified HMO. If the employee opts for HMO coverage, the employer is required to pay the HMO premium or an amount equal to the premium for previous health coverage, which ever is less.

Finally, preferred provider organizations represent a new form of health care delivery in which there is a direct contractual relationship between and among employers, health care providers, and third-party payers.[40] An employer is able to select providers (e.g., selected doctors) who agree to provide price discounts and submit to strict utilization controls (e.g., strict standards on number of diagnostic tests that can be ordered). In turn, the employer influences employees to use the preferred providers through financial incentives. Doctors benefit by increasing patient flow. Employers benefit through increased cost savings. And employees benefit through wider choice of doctors than might be available under an HMO.

Health Care: Cost Control Strategies. Basically, three general strategies are available to benefit managers for controlling the rapidly escalating costs of health care.[41] First, organizations can motivate employees to change their demand for health care through changes in either the design or the administration of health insurance policies.[42] Included in this category of control strategies are (1) deductibles (the first x dollars of health care cost in each year are paid by the employee), (2) coinsurance rates (premium payments are shared by company and employee), (3) maximum benefits (defining a maximum payout schedule for specific health problems), (4) coordination of benefits (ensure no double payment when coverage exists under both the employee's plan and spouse's plan), (5) auditing of hospital charges for accuracy, (6) requiring preauthorization for selected visits to health care facilities, and (7) mandatory second opinion whenever surgery is recommended.[43] In general, Exhibit 12.10 indicates a rapid rise in utilization of selected cost management strategies.

---

[39]Janice Ross, "Attacking Soaring Health Benefit Costs," *Pension World* 14, no. 1 (1978), p. 51.

[40]Thomas Billet, "An Employer's Guide to Preferred Provider Organizations," *Compensation Review* 16, no. 4 (1984), pp. 58–62.

[41]Regina Herzlinger and Jeffrey Schwartz, "How Companies Tackle Health Care Costs: Part I," *Harvard Business Review* 63 (July–August 1985), pp. 69–81.

[42]David Rosenbloom, "Oh Brother, Our Medical Costs Went Up Again," Paper presented at the Health Data Institute, March 16, 1988.

[43]Herzlinger and Schwartz, "How Companies Tackle Health Care Costs: Part I"; Regina Herzlinger, "How Companies Tackle Health Care Costs: Part II," *Harvard Business Review* 63.

EXHIBIT 12.10   Selected Cost Control Strategies and Their Utilization over Time (in percentages)

Provision	1984	1986	1988
Preadmission testing	87	83	84
Precertification of length of stay	17	31	61
Second surgical opinion	54	83	81
Home health care	68	70	77
Hospice care	39	52	66
Wellness program	15	28	52
Annual physical	18	41	36
Ambulatory surgical facilities	81	89	89

SOURCE: The Wyatt Company, *1988 Group Benefits Survey* (Washington D.C.: The Wyatt Company, 1988).

The second general cost control strategy involves changing the structure of health care delivery systems and participating in business coalitions (for data collection and dissemination). Under this category falls the trend toward HMOs and PPOs. Even under more traditional delivery systems, though, there is more negotiation of rates with hospitals and other health care delivery agents.

The final cost strategy involves promotion of preventative health programs. No-smoking policies and incentives for quitting smoking are popular inclusions here. But there is also increased interest in healthier food in cafeterias and vending machines, on-site physical fitness facilities, and early screening to identify possible health problems before they become more serious.[44] One review of physical fitness programs found that fitness led to better mental health and improved resistance to stress. There also was some evidence of increased productivity, increased commitment, decreased absenteeism, and decreased turnover.[45]

Short- and Long-Term Disability

A number of benefit options provide some form of protection for disability. For example, workers' compensation covers disabilities that are work related. Even social security has provisions for disability income to those who qualify. Beyond these two legally required sources, though, there are two private sources of disability income: employee salary continuation plans and long-term disability plans.

Many companies have some form of salary continuation plan that pays out varying levels of income depending on duration of illness. At one extreme is short-term illness

---

[44]W. Robert Nay, "Worksite Health-Promotion Programs," *Compensation and Benefits Review* 17, no. 5 (1985), pp. 57–64.

[45]Loren Falkenberg, "Employee Fitness Programs: Their Impact on the Employee and the Organization," *Academy of Management Review* 12, no. 3 (1987), pp. 511–22.

covered by sick leave policy and typically reimbursed at a level equal to 100 percent of salary.[46] After such benefits run out, disability benefits become operative. The benefit level is typically 50 to 67 percent of salary, and may be multitiered.[47]

A long-term disability plan might begin when the short-term plan expires, typically after 26 weeks.[48] Long-term disability is usually underwritten by insurance firms and provides 50 to 66 percent of an employee's wages for a period varying between two years and life. Only about 35 percent of all U.S. businesses are estimated to provide long-term disability insurance.[49]

Dental Insurance

A rarity 20 years ago, dental insurance is now quite prevalent. Dental insurance is a standard inclusion for somewhere between 79 and 91 percent of the major U.S. employers.[50] This translates into more than 100 million workers with some form of dental insurance.

In many respects, dental care coverage follows the model originated in health care plans. The dental equivalent of HMOs and PPOs are standard delivery systems. For example, a dental HMO enlists a group of dentists who agree to treat company employees in return for a fixed monthly fee per employee.[51]

Fortunately for employees, dental insurance costs have not spiraled like health care costs. In 1990, a family of four could be insured for $527 for a year of dental coverage.[52] In part, these relatively modest costs are due to stringent cost control strategies (e.g., plan maximum payouts are typically $1,000 or less per year), but the excess supply of dentists in the United States also has helped keep costs competitive.[53] Dental costs remain relatively stable around 0.8 to 1.0 percent of payroll.[54]

Vision Care

Vision care dates back only to the 1976 contract between the United States Auto Workers and the Big 3 automakers. Since then, this benefit has spread to other auto-related industries and parts of the public sector. Most plans are noncontributory and usually cover

---

[46]Employee Benefit Research Institute, *Fundamentals of Employee Benefit Programs*.

[47]Ibid.

[48]Ibid.

[49]Ibid.

[50]Carroll Roarty, "Biting Dental Insurance Costs," *Personnel Administrator* 33 no. 11 (1988), pp. 68–71; Employee Benefit Research Institute, *Fundamentals of Employee Benefit Programs*.

[51]"Dental Insurance Program Gains Favor among Firms," *The Wall Street Journal,* September 21, 1984, p. 31.

[52]Albert Kan, "Dental Care Bites Employers, but the Costs Can Be Managed," *The Wall Street Journal* January 22, 1991, p. A1.

[53]Harry Sutton, "Prescription Drug and Dental Programs," *Compensation and Benefits Review* 18, no. 4 (1986), pp. 67–71.

[54]Ibid.

partial costs of eye examination, lenses, and frames. About 35 percent of medium and large organizations have some form of vision care program.[55]

PAID TIME OFF DURING WORK HOURS

Paid rest periods, lunch periods, wash-up time, travel time, clothes-change time, and get-ready time benefits are self-explanatory.

PAYMENT FOR TIME NOT WORKED

Included within this category are several self-explanatory benefits:

1. Paid vacations and payments in lieu of vacation.
2. Payments for holidays not worked.
3. Paid sick leave.
4. Other (payments for national guard or army or other reserve duty, jury duty and voting pay allowances, and time lost due to death in family or other personal reasons).

Judging from employee preferences discussed in the last chapter and from observation of negotiated union contracts, pay for time not worked continues to be a high-demand benefit. Twenty years ago it was relatively rare, for example, to grant time for anything but vacations, holidays, and sick leave. Now many organizations have a policy of ensuring payments for civic responsibilities and obligations. Any pay for such duties (e.g., national guard and jury duty) is usually nominal, so companies often supplement this pay, fre-

---

EXHIBIT 12.11   Payment for Time Not Worked

Paid Leave Type	Average Private Sector, 1989	Average State and Local Government, 1987
Rest period	26 minutes/day	29 minutes/day
Holidays	9/year	11/year
Vacation	9.0 days for 1 year service	12 days for 1 year service
	20 days for 20 years service	21.4 days for 20 years
Funeral leave	3 days/occurrence	3.7 days/occurrence
Military leave	12 days/year	17.2 days/year
Jury duty	as needed	as needed
Sick leave	15.4 days/year with full pay after 1 year service	13 days/year with full pay after 1 year service

SOURCE: U.S. Department of Labor Bulletins 2363 (1989); *Employee Benefits in Medium and Large Firms, 1988;* Bureau of Labor Statistics, *Employee Benefits in State and Local Governments, 1987*, Bulletin 2309.

---

[55]Employee Benefit Research Institute, *Fundamentals of Employee Benefit Programs.*

quently to the level of 100 percent of wages lost. There is also increasing coverage for parental leaves. Maternity and, to a lesser extent, paternity leaves are much more common than 25 years ago.

Exhibit 12.11 outlines the average paid leave time for covered employees.

MISCELLANEOUS BENEFITS

Child Care

As of 1988, approximately 3,500 companies offered day care as a benefit.[56] About 23 percent of all children under five with working mothers are enrolled in organized child care facilities.[57] Over the next 15 years, more and more companies are projected to open day care centers for the preschool children of employees. In part, these centers are intended as a tool to attract and retain employees. Indeed, Traveler's Insurance reports reduced turnover (at a child care cost of $1,200 per child per year), and Mutual Insurance believes that child care is an excellent recruitment tool.[58]

Legal Insurance

Prior to the 1970s, prepaid legal insurance was practically nonexistent. In recent years, however, prepaid legal insurance has become an increasingly popular benefit, with recent estimates placed at 30 million enrollees.[59] Tremendous variety exists in the structure, options, delivery systems, and attorney compensation mechanisms. Across these plans, though, there are still some commonalities. A majority of plans provide routine legal services (e.g., divorce, real estate matters, wills, traffic violations) but exclude provisions covering felony crimes, largely because of the expense and potential for bad publicity. Employees with legal problems either select legal counsel from a panel of lawyers chosen by the firm (closed-panel mechanism) or freely choose their own lawyers with claims reimbursed by an insurance carrier.

SUMMARY

Since the 1940s, employee benefits have been the most volatile area in the compensation field. From 1940 to 1980, these dramatic changes came in the form of more and better forms of employee benefits. The result should not have been unexpected. Employee benefits are now a major, and many believe prohibitive, component of doing business. Look for the decade of the 1990s to be dominated by cost-saving efforts to improve the competitive position of American industry. A part of these cost savings will come from

---

[56]Jaclyn Fierman, "Child Care: What Works—and Doesn't," *Fortune*, November 21, 1988, pp. 165–76.

[57]Employee Benefit Research Institute, *Fundamentals of Employee Benefit Programs.*

[58]Sue Shellenbargen, "Employers Report Gains from Babysitting Aid," *The Wall Street Journal*, July 22, 1991, p. B1.

[59]William Giese, "Cover Story," *USA Today*, July 9, 1987, p. 1.

tighter administrative controls on existing benefit packages. But another part, as already seen in the auto industry, may come from a reduction in existing benefits packages. If this does evolve as a trend, benefits administrators will need to develop a mechanism for identifying employee preferences (in this case "least preferences") and use those as a guideline to meet agreed-upon savings targets.

REVIEW QUESTIONS

1. Name six practices you could implement in health care coverage for a company that could result in cost savings.

2. Why are people concerned about funding social security payments if there is currently a surplus (tax exceeds payouts)?

3. Why are defined contribution pension plans gaining in popularity in the United States and defined benefit plans losing popularity?

4. Your company has a serious turnover problem among employees with less than five years' seniority. The CEO wants to use employee benefits to lessen this problem. What might you do, specifically, in the areas of pension vesting, vacation and holiday allocation, and life insurance coverage in efforts to reduce turnover?

5. Assume that you are politically foolhardy and decide to challenge your CEO's decision in Question 4 to use benefits as a major tool for reducing turnover. Before she fires you, what arguments might you try to use to persuade her? (*Hint:* Are there other compensation tools that might be more effective in reducing turnover? Might the changes in benefits have unintended consequences on more senior employees? Could you make a cost argument against such a strategy? Is turnover of these employees necessarily bad (and how would you demonstrate that this turnover isn't a problem)?

APPENDIX:
ILLUSTRATION OF A BENEFITS PROGRAM: PFIZER BENEFITS PROGRAM

Your Benefits at Pfizer

At first glance, the Pfizer Employee Benefits Program—like all such programs—may appear to be an assortment of unrelated plans. Actually, each Pfizer benefit has been developed and improved to take care of you—*and* in many cases your dependents—in certain types of situations when extra financial assistance is needed.

There are four major types of coverage in the Pfizer Employee Benefit Program: survivors' assistance, disability protection, health care, and retirement income—all of which are outlined in this brochure. In addition, you and your family may enjoy many other benefits throughout your active Pfizer career. These include: holidays, vacations, educational assistance, matching gifts, scholarships, military leave and active duty training allowances, and adoption benefits—highlights of which are also shown in this brochure.

All in all, the Pfizer Employee Benefits Program gives you and your family a full range of financial protection and security—above and beyond your regular earnings as an employee. Actually, these benefits represent a substantial *addition* to your earnings and many allow certain tax advantages.

In addition to your Pfizer benefits, social security provides income and medical benefits to you and/or your qualified dependents upon disability, death, or retirement. Workers' compensation also provides cash, income, medical, and death benefits to you and certain family members if you qualify as the result of a job-related accident.

As you can see, the various benefits in the Pfizer Program and those provided by law work together to give you and your family well-rounded protection when it's needed most.

Each plan in the Benefit Program has been carefully designed with the welfare of our employees in mind. The plans are continually reviewed to make certain they remain up-to-date and to ensure that they are accomplishing the job they were intended to do. In fact, we feel that the program is one of the best to be found anywhere today.

Survivor Benefits	*Coverage*
Life Insurance . . . pays benefits to your beneficiary whatever the cause of your death.	**Basic**—Approximately *two times* your annual compensation—maximum benefit of *$500,000*—until your normal retirement date—reduced amounts thereafter. Part of your Life Insurance continues into retirement—at no cost to you. **Supplemental**—Choice of approximately one, two or three times your annual compensation, up to a maximum benefit of *$500,000*.
Accidental Death and Dismemberment Coverage . . . pays *additional* benefits to your beneficiary if you die—or to you if you suffer dismemberment as a result of an accident.	Amounts equal to your Basic and Supplemental Life Insurance for: • loss of life • loss of any two limbs or entire sight of both eyes (one-half of the coverage for loss of one limb or entire sight of one eye).
Business Travel Accident Insurance . . . pays *additional* benefits to your beneficiary if you are killed on a covered Company business trip—or to you, if you lose sight or limb.	*Six* times your annual compensation— *Minimum $50,000/maximum $500,000*—for loss of life, any two limbs or entire sight of both eyes. *One-Half* of insurance amount— *Minimum $50,000/maximum $250,000*—for loss of one limb or entire sight of one eye.

Disability Benefits	*Coverage*		
Short Term Disability . . . helps continue part of our pay for temporary absences from work because of illness or injury.	Service	Full Salary	Half Salary
	Less than 10 years	6 months	0
	10 but less than 15 years	6 months	3 months
	15 or more years	6 months	6 months
Long Term Disability Plan . . . helps continue part of your pay if you become ill or are injured and cannot work.	*60%* of your insured monthly compensation *up* to a maximum monthly benefit of *$3,600* including Workers' Compensation, Social Security disability benefits and any other Pfizer Group Plan Benefits.		

(continued)

Health Care Benefits	*Coverage*
For you and each of your covered dependents: **Comprehensive Medical Plan** . . . provides coverage for a broad range of medical services. Three types of expenses are covered by the Plan—Type A, Type B and Type C.	*TYPE A EXPENSES*—100% of reasonable and customary charges, with no deductible required, for certain cost-effective services such as second surgical opinions, outpatient surgery and outpatient diagnostic x-rays and lab tests. *TYPE B EXPENSES*—100% of reasonable and customary charges for semi-private hospital room and board and special services or intensive care charges *after* the deductibles are met. Most hospital benefits are payable for as long as each hospital confinement lasts—except for confinements for treatment of alcoholism and drug abuse. For those conditions, hospital benefits are payable for up to a lifetime maximum of 365 days. *TYPE C EXPENSES*—80% of reasonable and customary charges for all other covered services and supplies not included as Type A or Type B expenses *after* the deductibles are met.

Health Care Benefits	*Coverage*

	DEDUCTIBLES
	• Calendar year Plan deductible of $200 per individual/$500 per family for most Type B and Type C expenses.
	• Hospital deductible of $100 per confinement—in addition to the calendar year Plan deductible, if not previously satisfied—up to a maximum of three hospital deductibles per person per calendar year.
	• Services received in a hospital emergency room
	   —$25 deductible per visit for treatment or outpatient surgery within 72 hours of an accident;
	   —$25 per visit deductible *and* calendar year Plan deductible (if not previously satisfied) for all other services performed in a hospital emergency room.
	
	EMPLOYEE OUT-OF-POCKET MAXIMUM
	• An out-of-pocket calendar year maximum of $2,000 per family applies to all covered expenses not reimbursed by the Plan, including the deductibles. Thereafter, the Plan will pay 100% of additional covered charges incurred during the remainder of that calendar year. (Expenses for the treatment of alcohol and drug abuse may not be applied toward the out-of-pocket maximum.)
	
	PLAN MAXIMUMS
	• Unlimited lifetime dollar maximum for most covered charges.
	• $50,000 per person combined lifetime maximum for outpatient psychiatric visits and outpatient treatment of alcoholism and drug abuse.
	• $50,000 per person maximum for hospice care.

Dental Plan . . . pays benefits for a wide variety of dental procedures—*including orthodontia*—with no deductible at all.	*100%* of reasonable and customary charges for most forms of preventive and diagnostic care—*and* *50%* of reasonable and customary charges for repair or replacement of natural teeth—*up to* *$1,000* per person each calendar year—*with* *$10,000* in lifetime benefits per peron—*plus* *$1,000* in lifetime benefits per person for orthodontia alone.

Retirement Benefits	*Coverage*
Retirement Annuity Plan . . . is designed to pay an income for life to you and—in the case of your death—to your surviving spouse.	The pension plan has two formulas and the one which produces the *higher* benefit for you is used. One formula provides a benefit based on 1.4% of your Pfizer Career Earnings for service up to 35 years. The other formula provides a benefit based on 1.75% of your Pfizer Career Earnings for service up to 35 years less a portion of your projected Primary Social Security benefit. Career Earnings are determined by multiplying the *average* of your earnings for your highest consecutive five calendar years prior to January 1, 1987 times years of service prior to January 1, 1987 and then adding your actual earnings from 1987 to the date you retire. If you are *not* married when your retirement benefit commences, you will receive a straight life annuity payable only to you, unless you choose an optional payment method. If you are *married* when payments begin, your benefits will be in the form of a 50% joint and survivor annuity *unless* your spouse signs a waiver and consent form permitting you to choose a payment option other than a joint and survivor annuity.

Retirement Benefits	*Coverage*
	Normal retirement is age 65. *Early* retirement is any time after age 50 with at least 10 years of service if your age and service equals 65 or more. If you retire early, your pension will be reduced *unless* your age plus service equals 90 or more, and you are at least age 60 when you retire. *Late* retirement is anytime after age 65. *Vesting*—i.e., your right to a pension—occurs after 5 years of service.
Savings and Investment Plan . . . affords you the opportunity to accumulate finds towards retirement through your contributions and Company contributions made on your behalf. Contributions may be made on a before-tax basis, after-tax basis or a combination of both. Company contributions vest at a rate of 20% per year.	Contributions from 2%–15% of your regular earnings, up to the maximum permitted by current laws and regulations, may be made to the Plan. The Company matches these contributions dollar for dollar on the first 2% of your pay that is contributed to the Plan and 50¢ for every dollar on the next 4% of your pay that is contributed to the Plan. You can invest in one, two or all three investment funds. All Company matching contributions are invested in Pfizer common stock. *Vesting* is full and immediate for the value of your own contributions and at 20% for each year in which you participate in the Plan on the value of Company contributions; *up to 100%* after 5 years. If you are married, your spouse will *automatically* be your primary beneficiary *unless* your spouse signs a waiver and consent form permitting you to name someone else as a primary beneficiary.

YOUR TURN:
KRAMER TOOL COATING COMPANY

Background

Kramer Tool Coating company (KTC) is a high technology firm that coats cutting tools by bombarding them with ions of a patented substance. Because of the high cost of the ion chambers needed for this process, KTC has yet to make a profit in its 10 years of existence. Forecasts project, however, that KTC will make money next year, and by 10 years from now (barring drastic changes in cutting tool technology) will boast a return after taxes of $30 million.

KTC is unionized by an independent union comprising workers who used to be employed at a nearby company unionized by the United Auto Workers. When that company went bankrupt, KTC hired 20 of its most skilled individuals. These people are now key members in the independent union. Remembering the bankruptcy, these employees have been reluctant to press for too much, too fast, lest history repeat itself. But it is evident now that the company is past its danger point. The new contract will be the first to include any but the bare minimum of benefits. The old package included the legally required benefits (e.g., workers' compensation, unemployment insurance, social security) and a relatively low-cost health care package.

The Situation

The union insists that the next package include a substantial growth in employee benefits. Hard ne-gotiation has determined that the union is willing to forgo substantial wage increase demands in exchange for some inroads in the following areas: (1) life insurance, (2) dental insurance, (3) package of short-term (sick days) and long-term disability coverage, and (4) a contributory 401–(K) pension plan. Life insurance and dental insurance coverage as proposed by the union cost approximately the same amount. Similarly, the disability package and the pension package are about equally expensive. You believe the union will settle for one of the two insurance packages and either the pension or disability coverage. Basically, you are indifferent in terms of costs.

Your Task

The president wants a recommendation about which way to have the labor lawyer negotiate. Consider how current and long-term corporate goals might influence your decision making. Also, do you want any other cost data or projections before making a decision? Are there any benefits that, if adopted, might make another of the requested benefits less necessary? What other information might you want to collect?

Exhibit v.1 The Pay Model

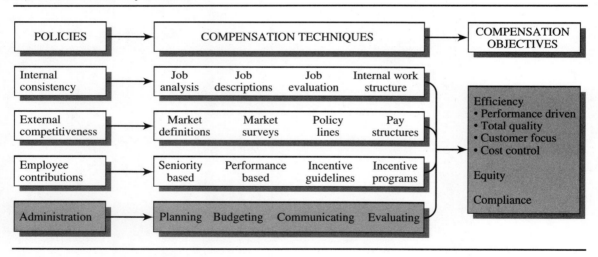

PART V Compliance

We have now completed the discussion of three strategic policies in the pay model used in this book. The first, which focused on determining the structure of pay, dealt with internal consistency. The second was determining the pay level based on external competitiveness, and the third dealt with determining the pay for employees according to their contributions. Strategic decisions regarding consistency, competitiveness, and contributions are directed at achieving the objectives of the pay system. Specific objectives vary among organizations; helping achieve competitive advantage and treating employees fairly are basic ones.

Before discussing the fourth strategic decision, the nature of administration, we need to consider the significant role that government and legislation play in the management of compensation. Laws and regulations are the most obvious intervention by government into compensation management. Laws serve to regulate pay decisions. Minimum wage legislation is an obvious example. Others include the Equal Pay Act and Title VII of the Civil Rights Act, which prohibit pay discrimination.

But government is more than a source of laws and regulations. It is a major player in the marketplace, and consequently affects both the demand and supply for labor. As a major employer, as a consumer of goods and services, and through its fiscal and monetary policies, government affects the demand for labor. Similarly, it affects the supply of labor by setting licensing standards, appropriating funds for education and training programs that affect skills, and by competing for human resources directly.

This part of the book has two chapters devoted to examining government as a major force in the design and management of pay systems (see Exhibit V.1). Chapter 13 examines government's role in general and also several laws. Pay discrimination is considered in Chapter 14.

CHAPTER 13 The Government's Role in Compensation

Chapter Outline

Fifty years ago, President Roosevelt railed against the pay for corporate executives, calling it "entrenched greed."[1] In response, Congress passed legislation requiring corporations to report to stockholders the pay of the top five highest-earning officers in the company, reasoning that the glare of publicity would bring executive salaries closer in line to those of rank-and-file employees. In the 1990s, the public is still railing against the pay for corporate executives, particularly when they read that Michael Eisner, chief executive officer at Disney, received more than $7 million in cash in one year, an amount 10 times

---

[1]George T. Milkovich and Bonnie Rabin, "Firm Performance: Does Executive Compensation Really Matter?" in *Executive Compensation*, ed. Fred Foulkes (Boston: Harvard Business School Press, 1991).

what a Disney theme park ride operator can expect to earn in a lifetime. The following year, Mr. Eisner received $40 million. In 1973, the pay of Time-Warner CEO Steve Ross was 150 times that of an average U.S. manufacturing worker, but in 1989 he earned more than 9,000 times that amount: $200 million or so.[2] In response, new legislation has been proposed to force companies to divulge more information to stockholders about the full amount of executive compensation, including the value of stock options. Whether or not these proposals ever become law, they illustrate the continuing process by which society attempts to address perceived problems through legislation.[3] A problem is defined ("executives are overpaid") and corrective legislation is proposed (Corporate Responsibility Act). If enough support develops, often as a result of compromises and trade-offs, the proposed legislation becomes law. Employers, along with other stakeholders, all attempt to influence the form any legislation will take. Once passed, laws are enforced by agencies through rulings, regulations, inspections, and investigations. Companies respond to legislation by auditing and perhaps altering their practices, and perhaps again lobby for legislative change. Consequently, the regulatory climate—the laws and regulations issued by governmental agencies created to enforce the laws—represents a significant influence on compensation decisions.

GOVERNMENT INFLUENCES ON PAY

The government influences compensation practices and wages both directly and indirectly. Its direct effect on wages is through legislation. For example, the minimum wage law sets a floor on what an employer must pay, the Equal Pay Act requires that pay differences among employees doing the same job cannot be based on the sex of the employee. But the government also indirectly affects compensation, as shown in Exhibit 13.1. Governmental actions can affect both the demand and supply of labor; consequently, wages are also affected. Protective legislation often restricts the supply of labor in an occupation. Requiring plumbers to be licensed restricts the number of people who can legally offer plumbing services. Although these licensing requirements are initiated in the name of consumer protection, they also constrain the labor supply, which puts upward pressure on wages.

Legislation aimed at protecting specific groups also tends to restrict that group's full participation in the labor supply. Compulsory schooling laws, for example, restrict the supply of 15-year-olds available to sell hamburgers. In the past, laws intended to protect women from harsh working conditions also limited the hours they could work and the amount of physical labor they could perform. Although the intent may have been well-meaning, such laws restricted women's access to many good-paying occupations. Other indirect effects of government on labor supply and hence wages include government-sponsored training and social welfare programs (e.g., aid to families with dependent children).

---

[2]Graef Crystal, *In Search of Excess* (New York: Norton, 1991).
[3]"Executive Pay Bills Draw Mixed Reaction," *ACA News*, February 1992, pp. 1, 6.

EXHIBIT 13.1 Indirect Government Influences on Pay

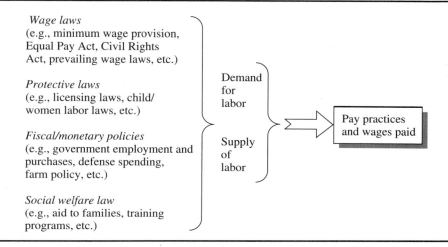

Wage laws
(e.g., minimum wage provision, Equal Pay Act, Civil Rights Act, prevailing wage laws, etc.)

Protective laws
(e.g., licensing laws, child/women labor laws, etc.)

Fiscal/monetary policies
(e.g., government employment and purchases, defense spending, farm policy, etc.)

Social welfare law
(e.g., aid to families, training programs, etc.)

Demand for labor

Supply of labor

Pay practices and wages paid

Government actions also affect the demand for labor in several ways, most directly as a major employer. Employment at all levels of government has grown from around 6 million employees in 1946 to 18.4 in 1991.[4] In spite of continuing calls for governmental cutbacks, government employment continues to increase, particularly at the state and local level. Yearly growth rates of 5 percent were common in the 1970s and 1980s, and even though the entire U.S. economy stagnated in 1991, local government employment managed to expand by 2 percent. In many state capitals and county seats the government is the dominant employer; consequently, it is a major force in determining the wages paid.

In addition to being a major employer, government is a major consumer. Federal expenditures as a percent of the gross national product have risen from 7.3 percent in 1902 to 23.5 percent in 1991.[5] A decision by the government to purchase 10 B-757 aircraft from Boeing has a dramatic effect on the demand for labor in Seattle, where Boeing is located.

Government fiscal and monetary policies that affect the economy indirectly affect market forces which, in turn, influence wages. Foreign trade policies, money supply decisions, farm policy—all these governmental actions have indirect effects on wages paid. Restricted farm exports mean that farmers will have less money, which means that manufacturers of farm equipment and fertilizer will hire fewer people. Lowered interest rates mean that more people can afford to purchase houses, which means jobs not only

---

[4]"Current Labor Statistics: Employment Data," *Monthly Labor Review,* February 1992, pp. 80–83.

[5]*Economic Report of the President,* transmitted to Congress February 1992 (Washington, D.C.: U.S. Government Printing Office, 1992).

for builders but also for employees of appliance, furniture, and carpet manufacturers. Lower tax rates mean more cash for all taxpayers, which, at least according to some economic theorists, translates into a boost for all employers and an increased demand for labor. Tax subsidies for hiring certain disadvantaged youth have the intent of stimulating a weak demand for such employees. So government's effect on wages is wide-ranging and pervasive.

GOVERNMENT AND THE PAY MODEL

Regulatory compliance is one of the objectives of the pay model used in this book. The compensation techniques and the results of those techniques must all comply with the laws.

However, employers frequently try to influence the type of legislation that is passed.[6] They lobby through their governmental relations units or through a consortium of employers, such as Business Roundtable or American Compensation Association. They testify before committees drafting legislation. To influence legislation, compensation managers must establish links with the firm's law department as well as with professional societies.

Employers also influence court interpretation of legislation through defending their practices during litigation, although this is a costly procedure and not one many employers seek. An example of employer influence on legislation is the Equal Pay Act, in which Congress chose skill, effort, responsibility, and working conditions as factors to define equal work.[7] These factors were chosen largely because Congress became aware of them through lobbying efforts and testimony as the criteria commonly used by employers and unions to evaluate jobs. Compensation professionals need to put greater emphasis on proactive activities intended to shape the legislation and regulations or to defend sound pay practices in the courts.

Let us now look at some specific compensation legislation.

MINIMUM WAGES AND COMPENSABLE TIME

The main legislation in this category is the Fair Labor Standards Act and the Portal-to-Portal Act. The Fair Labor Standards Act is the older and has the broader coverage.

Fair Labor Standards Act of 1938 (FLSA)

FLSA covers all employees (with some exceptions discussed later) of companies engaged in interstate commerce or in production of goods for interstate commerce. FLSA has four major provisions:

---

[6]James Ledvinka, *Federal Regulation of Personnel and Human Resource Management* (Boston: Kent Publishing Company, 1982).

[7]Equal Employment Opportunity Commission, *Legislative History of Titles VII and XI of Civil Rights Act of 1964* (Washington, D.C.: U.S. Government Printing Office, 1968).

1. Minimum wage.
2. Hours of work.
3. Child labor.
4. Equal pay.

Minimum Wage.   When first enacted in 1938, the minimum wage was $.25 per hour. A new minimum of $4.25 per hour, coupled with a lower training wage for teenagers in the first 90 days on the job, took effect in 1991. Forty-seven states also have minimum wage laws (shown in Exhibit 13.2), which cover employees exempt from FLSA. Coverage of the minimum wage provision does not extend to all employees. For example, current regulations allow the Department of Labor to authorize exemptions for workers with handicaps, apprentices, and learners. The bulk of such exemptions are utilized in the restaurant industry.[8]

Effects of Minimum Wage Provisions.   Minimum wage legislation was intended to provide an income floor for workers in society's lowest paid and least productive jobs. Who benefits by changes in the minimum wage rates? Some evidence suggests that adult women have been the primary beneficiaries, because higher rates have attracted them into full-time from part-time employment. Other evidence suggests that all workers have benefited: as the pay rate at the lowest end of the scale moves up, so have pay rates above it, in order to maintain pay differentials among jobs.[9]

The shift in the pay structure resulting from an increased minimum wage is greater in some industries than others. For example, the lowest rates paid in the steel, chemical, oil, and pharmaceutical industries are well above minimum wage; any legislative change would have little direct impact on employers in these industries. Retailing and service firms, however, employ many clerks and sales personnel at or near the minimum wage. Hence, pay of all personnel is increased to maintain pay differentials. The resulting higher labor bill increases the possibility of substituting capital for jobs (e.g., introducing automated inventory control systems, or prepacked frozen french fries) or holding down employment level (e.g., fewer sales personnel) to control labor costs.

Employment Effects.   Some economists believe that employment opportunities for inexperienced and unskilled youth are hurt by the minimum wage. Employers may reason that the skills this group possesses are not commensurate with their costs. If a higher wage is to be paid, the employer will try to find more experienced or skilled workers. The high rate of unemployment among teenagers is consistent with this argument.

So people working at or near the minimum wage who continue to work definitely do benefit from mandated minimum wage increases, and other workers in higher level jobs in those same companies may also benefit. Yet as labor costs increase, fewer workers

---

[8]July 16, 1982, Federal Register (47 FR 31010).

[9]Simon Rottenberg, ed., *The Economics of Legal Minimum Wages* (Washington, D.C.: American Enterprise Institute, 1981).

EXHIBIT 13.2   **Minimum and Subminimum Hourly Wage Rates under State Laws (Subminimum Wage Rates Applicable Only to Learners or Apprentices)**

	Minimum Wage Rate	Subminimum Wage Rate		Minimum Wage Rate	Subminimum Wage Rate
Alabama	None	None	Montana	$4.25	None
Alaska	$4.75	75%[1]	Nebraska	$4.25	75%[1]
Arizona	None	None	Nevada	$4.25	None
Arkansas	$3.65	None	New Hampshire	$3.95	75%[1]
California	$4.25	85%[2,3]	New Jersey	$4.25	None
Colorado	$3.00[3]	None	New Mexico	$3.35	None
Connecticut	$4.27	85%[4]	New York	$4.25	$4.25
D.C.	$3.50–$5.45	[18]	North Carolina	$3.80	90%[1]
Delaware	$4.25	None	North Dakota	$4.25	85%[11]
Florida	None	None	Ohio	$4.25	[12]
Georgia	$3.25	None	Oklahoma	$4.25	None
Hawaii	$3.85	None	Oregon	$4.75	None
Idaho	$4.25	None	Pennsylvania	$4.25	85%[1]
Illinois	$4.25	70%[5]	Puerto Rico	$0.24–$6.50	[18]
Indiana	$3.35	None	Rhode Island	$4.45	[13]
Iowa	$4.65	None	South Carolina	None	None
Kansas	$2.65	80%[6]	South Dakota	$4.25	$3.61[14]
Kentucky	$4.25	None	Tennessee	None	None
Louisiana	None	None	Texas	$3.35	None
Maine	$4.25	None	Utah	$4.25	$4.00[15]
Maryland	$4.25	85%[7]	Vermont	$4.25	85%[16]
Massachusetts	$4.25	[8]	Virginia	$3.65	$3.61
Michigan	$3.35	None	Washington	$4.25	85%[1,3]
Minnesota	$4.25[9]	[10]	West Virginia	$3.80	None
Mississippi	None	None	Wisconsin	$4.25	75%[17]
Missouri	$4.25	None	Wyoming	$1.60	None

[1]Percentage rate of the statutory minimum for learners and/or apprentices

[2]Percentage rate, for first 160 hours of employment

[3]By state wage board order(s)

[4]Percentage rate, for first 200 hours of employment

[5]Percentage rate, for up to six months

[6]Percentage rate, for up to two months

[7]For initial, and second, 90-day employment of eligible employee

[8]Scale of rates, for specified occupations

[9]$4.00 an hour, for employer whose annual gross volume is less than $362,500

[10]At minor's rate, for first 300 hours of employment

[11]For up to 240 hours or 60 days, whichever comes first

[12]Eighty percent for learners, for period not exceeding 180 days and 85 percent for apprentices, for period of up to 90 days

[13]At rate determined by director of labor, for up to 90 days

[14]For employees age 18 or 19, for up to 90 days

[15]For first 160 hours of employment

[16]Percentage rate for retail, wholesale, and service establishments by wage order, for up to 240 hours or 30 days for learners

[17]Percentage rate, for student learners age 14 to 18

[18]Specific rates established by wage orders for various categories of employees

SOURCE: *Labor Relations Reporter: State Labor Laws*, 801, March 9, 1992.

will be hired if the increased costs cannot be passed on to consumers or offset by increased productivity.

Hours of Work.   The overtime provisions of the FLSA require payment at one and a half times the standard for working more than 40 hours per week.[10] There is a "union contract exemption" covering employees working under guaranteed annual employment agreements. Many union contracts provide for overtime after a shorter work week, some as short as 25 hours. If a compensation plan includes incentives, productivity bonuses, attendance bonuses, commissions, and so on, these payments must be included in the regular rate of pay when computing overtime. Gifts, special occasion bonuses, and payments to a profit sharing plan do *not* need to be included, because they are at the employer's discretion. When a pay form is promised to employees if certain conditions are met (profits hit a certain level, employees show up), then those payments must be included as part of an employee's regular rate on which overtime is based.[11]

The overtime provision is aimed at sharing available work. It seeks to make hiring more workers a less costly option than scheduling overtime for current employees. But overtime pay for current employees is often the least costly option. This is due to (1) an increasingly skilled work force, with higher training costs per employee and (2) higher fringe benefits, the bulk of which are fixed per employee. These factors have lowered the point at which it pays employers to schedule longer hours and pay the overtime premium, rather than hire, train, and pay fringes for more employees. Models to examine the break-even points between working overtime and hiring additional workers compare added expense of time-and-a-half wages to the added fringe benefits and training costs required for new hires.

Several amendments to increase the overtime penalty have been proposed over the years. These typically seek to increase the penalty, reduce the standard workweek to less than 40 hours, or repeal some of the exemptions. Only about 58 percent of all employees are covered by the overtime provision at present.

Effects of the Overtime Provision.   Some researchers have investigated overtime's effect on worker satisfaction. Generally, as hours of work increase, both pay satisfaction and job satisfaction decrease. But any negative effects of overtime vary with the reason for using overtime. For example, is overtime scheduled because of a growing workload, or because of inefficient work scheduling? If overtime is required because of what employees consider to be incompetent management, they are probably going to resent the requirement.

The hours-of-work provision requires that records of actual time worked by employees in covered jobs be kept. This brings up two issues of interest: (1) What is and is not included in "actual time worked"? and (2) Which jobs are covered?

---

[10] 29 Code of Federal Regulations, Chap. V, Secs. A.3–A.5.

[11] Gina Ameci, "Overtime Pay: Avoiding FLSA Violations," *Personnel Administrator,* February 1987, pp. 29–30.

Exempt and Nonexempt.   Whether jobs are classified as exempt or nonexempt by the FLSA is of major importance. Nonexempt jobs must be paid time and a half for hours worked overtime and extensive records must be kept and filed with the Department of Labor. Overtime pay is not required for exempt jobs, nor is recordkeeping of hours worked. The exceptions to FLSA are the most complex part of the act. Some of the exemptions are shown in Exhibit 13.3. Professional, executive, and administrative jobs are exempt. So are many jobs in the transportation industry.

Some exemptions suspend only certain provisions of the act; others suspend all provisions. Some apply to all employees of certain businesses, others to only certain employees. To compound the confusion, exemptions may overlap. Repeated amendments to the act have made the distinction between exempt and nonexempt difficult to determine. One writer observed, "As soon as the distinction between exempt and nonexempt begins to emerge clearly from court cases, the act is amended, setting off a new round of court cases."[12]

The Wage-Hour Division of the Department of Labor, which is charged with enforcement of the FLSA, provides strict criteria that must be met in order for jobs to be considered professional and exempt from minimum wage and overtime provisions. Professionals must

Do work requiring knowledge generally acquired by prolonged, specialized study, or engage in original and creative activity in a recognized artistic field.

Consistently exercise discretion or judgment.

Do work that is primarily intellectual and nonroutine.

Devote at least 80 percent of their work hours to such activities.[13]

There are also criteria for exempt status for executives. Executives must

Primarily undertake management duties.

Supervise two or more employees.

Have control (or at least great influence) over hiring, firing, and promotion.

Exercise discretionary powers.

Devote at least 80 percent of their work hours to such activities.[14]

Child Labor.   The child labor provision of FLSA regulates the type and hours of work for employees under age 18.[15] The age varies, depending on the type of work and whether or not the employer is the child's parents. Workers under 16 may not work more than three hours on any school day or eight hours on nonschool days. They cannot work more than 18 hours a week when school is in session or 40 hours when it is not. Workers age 16 and 17 have no hourly restrictions; however, workers under age 18 are restricted from working in hazardous jobs such as meat packing, meat cutting, or logging.

---

[12]Ledvinka, *Federal Regulation*.
[13]29 Code of Federal Regulations, Chap. V, Sec. 541.3.
[14]Ibid., Sec. 541.1
[15]Ibid., Secs. 541.2, and 541.500.

EXHIBIT 13.3   **Some Exemptions to the Minimum Wage and Overtime Provisions of the Fair Labor Standards Act**

Section 13 (a)(1)	Outside salesmen, professional executive, and administrative personnel ("including any employee employed in the capacity of academic administrative personnel or teacher in elementary or secondary schools")
Section 13(a)(3)	Employees of certain seasonal amusements or recreational establishments.
Section 13(a)(5)	Fishing and first processing at sea employees.
Section 13(a)(6)	Agricultural employees employed by farms utilizing fewer than 500 man-days of agricultural labor, employed by a member of their immediate family, certain local seasonal harvest laborers and seasonal hand harvest laborers 16 years of age or under, and employees principally engaged in the range production of livestock.
Section 13(a)(7)	Employees exempt under Section 14 of the Act (certain learners, apprentices, students and handicapped workers).
Section 13(a)(12)	Seamen on foreign vessels.
Section 13(a)(15)	Babysitters employed on a casual basis and persons employed to provide companion services.
Section 7(b)	Certain employees under collectively bargained guaranteed annual wage plans and wholesale or bulk petroleum distribution employees.
Section 7(i)	Certain commission salesmen in retail or service establishments.
Section 13(b)(1)	Motor carrier employees.
Section 13(b)(2)	Railroad employees.
Section 13(b)(3)	Airline employees.
Section 13(b)(6)	Seamen.
Section 13(b)(12)	Agricultural employees.
Section 13(b)(15)	Maple sap employees.
Section 13(b)(29)	Employees of amusement or recreational establishments located in a national park or national forest or on land in the National Wildlife Refuge System.

In turn-of-the-century America, 25 percent of the workers in our factories, textile mills, and coal mines were children. These children had no protection from the dangers of the workplace. Today's children do. Unfortunately, the tidal wave of immigration to the United States in the last 10 years has brought children who speak no English, who are unaware of legal protections, and whose families depend on the meager earnings of every member. Once again, garment manufacturing districts of some large cities are creating contemporary sweatshops, duplicating conditions that led to the original passage of child labor laws. Violations soared in the 1980s, from 9,000 in the early 1980s to almost 40,000 in 1990. Many of the violations concerned children working too late in the evening or too many hours at restaurants and supermarkets. Although working too late at the supermarket is a far cry from the dangers in sweatshops, the number of violations is a cause for concern. States vary in their responses to the situation. Some states have liberalized their laws, particularly in allowing young teenagers to work later into the evening (until 7 P.M. for 14- and 15-year-olds). Other states have called for greater restrictions, on the grounds that educational achievement suffers if young students work part-time. The Department of Labor has stepped up its enforcement of child labor laws, and financial penalties for violations have been increased.

The fourth major provision of FLSA, equal employment, will be discussed in the next chapter. Equal employment was not covered in the original 1938 FLSA. It was added as an amendment in 1963, called the *Equal Pay Act,* and is today of major importance. The whole topic of wage discrimination merits a separate chapter. (See Chapter 14.)

Portal-to-Portal Act of 1947

Recall that FLSA requires records of time actually worked by covered employees. But when does the workday begin? Is it when the employee arrives at the actual job site? Or on the employer's premises? Think of working in an underground coal mine. Underground travel time to get to the actual site where coal is being extracted is under the control of the employer and may be substantial. According to current interpretation of FLSA and the courts, this travel time should be part of the hours worked and included in calculating pay and overtime rates. But in *Anderson* v. *Mt. Clemens Pottery,* the courts extended this "travel time" concept to manufacturing, ruling that time spent walking between the plant gate and the work bench as well as time spent on certain "make-ready" activities was all compensable working time.[16] The flood of lawsuits for wages owed that followed prompted Congress to pass the Portal-to-Portal Act. The act provides that time spent on activities between beginning or after completion of the "principal activity" is compensable only if payment is required under a contract or has customarily been counted as work time prior to the *Mt. Clemens* case.

The next group of laws set pay for work done to produce goods and services contracted by the federal government. These are called "prevailing wage" laws.

PREVAILING WAGE LAWS

A government-defined prevailing wage is the minimum wage that must be paid for work done on covered government projects or purchases. The original purpose was to prevent the government from undercutting local workers. For example, if a government project of the magnitude of Hoover Dam were to pay low wages to construction workers, its sheer force of size could drive down the entire wage structure in the area. So the government requires that surveys identify the prevailing wage in an area. That prevailing wage then becomes the mandated minimum wage on the government-financed project.

Contractors object to this requirement because it frequently means that they have to match a wage rate that only a minority of area workers are receiving. A 1982 regulation permitted a weighted average formula to calculate prevailing wage if a majority of area employees do not happen to work at a single rate.[17]

A number of laws contain prevailing wage provisions. They vary on the government expenditures they target for coverage. The following are the main prevailing wage laws:

1. Davis-Bacon (1931), which covers mechanics and laborers on public construction projects with expenditures over $2,000.
2. Walsh-Healey Public Contracts Act (1936), which extends the provisions of Davis-Bacon to manufacturers or suppliers of goods for government contracts over $10,000.

---

[16]*Anderson* v. *Mt. Clemens Pottery Co.,* 6 WH Cases 595, USDC E. Michigan.
[17]May 28, 1982, Federal Register (47 FR 23644).

3. Service Contract Act (1965), which extends coverage to suppliers of services to the federal government in excess of $2,500 (e.g., cleaning, catering).

4. National Foundation Arts and Humanities Act (1965), which covers professionals, laborers, and mechanics working on projects that receive funding from the Foundation. Only those employees directly engaged in producing or furnishing for the federal contract are covered; other employees of the manufacturer/supplier are not.

In addition to a prevailing wage, the Walsh-Healey Act also requires the following:

1. One and a half times the regular pay rate for hours over 8 per day or 40 per week must be paid.

2. Sanitary and nonhazardous working conditions must be maintained.

3. Payroll records must be kept.

4. Employees must be above 16 years.

Walsh-Healey predates the FLSA. The FLSA duplicates some Walsh-Healey requirements and extends them to additional employees.

In 1990, two counties and one city in California passed prevailing wage ordinances that require private employers to pay wages and benefits determined by the California Labor Code on construction projects that cost above a certain amount ($250,000 or $500,000, depending on county).[18] Although similar in intent to federal legislation, these local laws break legal ground because they seek to set wages on private construction

EXHIBIT 13.4   Federal Laws: Equal Employment Opportunity

Regulation	*Major Provisions*
Equal Pay Act	A 1963 amendment to FLSA; equal pay required for male and female workers doing "substantially similar work" in terms of skill, effort, responsibility, and working conditions. Exemptions allowed for seniority, merit pay, and piece work systems.
Title VII of Civil Rights Act	(1) Prohibits discrimination in all employment practices on basis of race, sex, color, religion, national origin, or pregnancy. (2) Bennett Amendment links Title VII and the Equal Pay Act by providing that it is not unlawful to differentiate on the basis of sex in determining pay if such differentiation is authorized by the Equal Pay Act.
Age Discrimination Act	Protects employees aged 40 and over against age discrimination.
Pregnancy Discrimination Act	Disability and medical benefits plans cannot single out pregnancy for differential treatment. Pregnancy must be covered to same extent that other medical conditions are covered.

---

[18]Deborah O. Cantrell, "Wage Laws under Legal Challenge," *Personnel Journal*, August 1991, pp. 93–98.

projects in addition to government-funded projects. In addition, they require that only apprentices from programs approved by the state can be hired. A legal challenge filed by the U.S. Chamber of Commerce alleges that by mandating wage and benefit levels without regard to what employees want or employers can afford, these local laws run counter to the concept of collective bargaining that is sanctioned in federal labor law. A federal judge overturned one of the ordinances in 1991, but appeals are likely.

Much of the legislation discussed so far was originally passed in the 1930s and 1940s in response to social issues of that time. In the 1960s, the equal rights movements pushed different social problems to the forefront. The Equal Pay Act and the Civil Rights Act were passed. Because of their substantial impact on human resource management and compensation, they are discussed at length in the next chapter. Additional rights legislation includes the Pregnancy Discrimination Act and the Age Discrimination in Employment Act (Exhibit 13.4).

EQUAL RIGHTS LEGISLATION

Age Discrimination in Employment Act of 1967

The Age Discrimination in Employment Act (ADEA), passed in 1967 and amended in 1978, 1986, and 1990, protects workers age 40 and over from employment discrimination due to age.[19] To date this act has been applied principally to retirement, promotion, and layoff policies, but it applies to all personnel decisions. The purpose of the act is to "promote employment of older persons on their ability rather than age; to prohibit arbitrary age discrimination in employment; to help employers and workers find ways of meeting problems arising from the impact of age on employment." The law forbids limiting or classifying employees in any way that would adversely affect their status because of age, reducing any employee's wage rate to comply with the act, or discriminating in compensation or terms of employment because of age.

The 1986 amendment forbids mandatory retirement (formerly legal at age 70) for all except fire fighters, police officers, and tenured professors(!), an exception of acute personal interest to the author. Congress will review these exceptions in 1993. A 1991 panel recommended removing the age barrier for college faculty. A 1992 panel recommended removing it for police, fire, and correctional departments. It also recommended using physical and psychological tests for retirement evaluations instead of chronological age. The committee found that physical fitness and mental abilities showed much stronger links to job performance than did age. Moreover, older public safety workers often move into supervisory positions in which their accumulated knowledge aids younger workers on the front lines, according to Frank Landy, the director of the panel.[20] According to publicly available records, Professor Landy is old enough to be covered by the ADEA.

---

[19]29 U.S.C. Sec. 621–634 (1970 and Supp. V. 1975) as amended by Public Law 95–256 (1978).
[20]"Mandatory Retirement: Public Safety Hazard," *Science News,* January 25, 1991, p. 54.

The 1990 amendment to the act, called the *Older Workers Benefit Protection Act,* extends ADEA coverage to all employee benefits. It was passed as a correction to a 1989 Supreme Court ruling that found legal a state law allowing disability retirements only through age 60.[21] The case involved an employee who became disabled at age 61 and was forced to take early retirement, which provided no medical insurance and whose monthly payments were less than half the amount that disability payments would have been. The Supreme Court found such age-based benefits acceptable, but the public did not, and so a new law was swiftly passed.

The law also contains an "equal benefit or equal cost" principle, which means that benefits for older employees can be less only if the cost of providing the benefit increases with age. For example, assume that the employer pays $500 for life insurance for each employee. For an employee under age 25, $500 will buy $200,000 worth of insurance. But for an employee age 60, $500 will buy only $50,000 worth of insurance. The employer can provide either the same level of insurance (equal benefit) or pay the same amount per employee for insurance (equal cost).[22]

Performance and Age

Age discrimination focuses attention on the compensation issue of paying for performance and the relationship between performance and age. For example, the career stage literature often assumes a "decline" stage in later years, although the age of decline varies. However, the literature on aging does not support such an assumption. Variations in performance exist at all ages, including among older workers. A pay system that purports to pay for performance must be sure that performance appraisal systems are not biased by age or that appraisers do not assume a lower performance level simply because a worker is older.[23]

In most cases it is difficult to document age discrimination because age is so closely correlated to seniority, and it is not illegal to vary treatment of employees on the basis of seniority. Another difficulty in pinpointing age discrimination is the frequently higher base position of an older worker. For example, older workers have lower promotion rates than younger workers, but this difference reflects the lower number of possible positions available into which older workers could be promoted. Additionally, lower salary increases for older workers may reflect their higher position in the pay ranges for particular jobs. The chapters on employee contributions discuss various ways of linking pay and performance. But the best advice in regard to the regulatory compliance objective is to avoid assuming performance differences on the basis of age, sex, race, or other illegal criteria. The focus should be on accurate performance appraisal.

---

[21]*Public Employees Retirement System of Ohio* v. *Betts,* 109 S. Ct. 2854 (1989).

[22]Peter Gray, Henry Rose, and Robert Nobile, "Employment Issues in the 1990s," prepared by the law firm of Epstein Becker and Green, New York, and presented at Cornell ILR Human Resources Executive Development Program, July 1991.

[23]*Mistressa* v. *Sandia Corp.,* U.S. District Court 21, FEP Cases 1671, 1978.

Pregnancy Discrimination Act of 1978

This act is actually an amendment to Title VII of the Civil Rights Act. It requires employers to extend to pregnant women the same disability and medical benefits provided other employees. The Pregnancy Discrimination Act forbids exclusion of pregnancy from the list of disabilities for which the employer compensates absent employees. It does not require an employer to offer a disability plan, nor does it prevent a dollar limit being placed on reimbursement of medical costs. The law merely places disability benefits for pregnant employees on an equal footing with those of nonpregnant employees.

In *McNulty* v. *Newport News Shipbuilding* (1983), the Supreme Court applied the Pregnancy Discrimination Act to pregnancy benefits received by spouses of male employees. The Court ruled that a limitation on pregnancy coverage for spouses is legal only if the same limitation also applied to other medical coverage for spouses. No limitation can be put on pregnancy expenses that is not applied to other medical conditions. For example, an employer may cover 100 percent of an employee's personal medical expenses but only 75 percent of medical expenses for spouses and dependents if they impose the same limits on all spouses and dependents, regardless of sex.

WAGE AND PRICE CONTROLS

Wage control programs typically aim at maintaining low inflation at low levels of unemployment. They frequently focus on limiting the size of the pay raises as well as the rate of increases in the prices charged for goods and services.

Control programs can vary in their stringency. In 1942, for example, wages were frozen at a level that prevailed on September 15 of that year. The government established "going rates" for key occupations and then permitted pay increases up to the minimum of a going rate bracket. Benefits could be instituted only if employers could show that they were customary in an area. Despite these restrictions, because of the demand and supply imbalances created by World War II, the average wage increased 24 percent between January 1941 and July 1945.

Another freeze was ordered in 1951, but by then many union members had labor contracts that provided automatic wage increases tied to the cost of living as well as annual "productivity" raises.[24] Once stabilization officials decided to permit the continued operation of these contracts, they were forced to sanction similar raises for other groups of employees.

Rather than an across-the-board wage freeze, the Council of Economic Advisers (CEA) in the early 1960s tried a more moderate approach. It tied wage rate and benefit increases to overall productivity increases, reasoning that acceptance of this guide would maintain stability of labor cost per unit of output for the overall economy. But productivity is only one of many factors related to pay, and any national productivity rate is meaningless when applied to a specific employer's productivity.

---

[24]Solomon Fabricant, "Which Productivity? Perspectives on a Current Question," *Monthly Labor Review*, June 1962, pp. 18–24.

In 1971 the Nixon administration, facing a 6 percent inflation rate and an unemployment level just over 5 percent, imposed freeze and control measures that rivaled those of World War II. These policies were able to slow inflation to just over 3 percent through most of 1971 and 1972. But once the controls were relaxed, prices rose rapidly: more than 6 percent in 1973 and 11 percent in 1974. Some economists interpret the rapid growth of postcontrol inflation as proof that the controls were effective and should have remained in place. Others interpret the same data to indicate that wage-price controls merely redistributed inflation over time but did not eliminate it.

In the late 1970s, the Council on Wage and Price Stability tried less encompassing voluntary wage guidelines. Employers were provided formulas to determine their own compliance with pay standards. Government purchases favored employers who complied and penalized noncompliance. However, even though flexibility had been a goal of the program, an absolute standard soon developed, along with a bureaucracy to consider exceptions to the standard.

So wage controls or guidelines can vary in the broadness of application and in the stringency of the standard. The standard for allowable pay increases can range from absolute denial during a freeze to increases equal to some productivity or price change measure.

Eventually any freeze or outside control exerted at an arbitrary point in time cannot help but be inequitable to some employers and employees, since the wage-setting process is ongoing. Both unions and managers are united in their concern for the difficulty in maintaining employee equity under wage controls.

How can compensation managers best protect their employees and managers facing government intervention in the wage-setting process? Those companies that seem to suffer the least disruptions are the ones that have sound and flexible compensation systems in place, with well-thought-out policies that demonstrably have been followed in the past. Such companies can document what they have done and why they did it, and are far more able to handle government intervention than employers that have no formal pay system and cannot justify their behavior. The same is true with any other area of government interest, be it meeting FLSA pay and recordkeeping requirements, or complying with equal rights legislation. A system based on work- and business-related logic is an employee's and an employer's best protection.

REGULATION OF BENEFITS

We have already mentioned the requirements that benefits packages must be nondiscriminatory on the basis of sex, race, religion, and national origin. Additional governmental effects on benefit options are discussed in Chapter 12. Government has its impact in two ways. The first is by legally requiring that some specific benefits be provided, either at employer expense or as an expense shared between employer and employee. Workers' compensation, social security, and unemployment insurance are all legally required. Workers' compensation and unemployment insurance are completely employer-financed, whereas employees and employers jointly contribute to social security.

The second way the government influences benefits is through its tax policy. Benefits are, in general, tax free to employees and a tax-deductible expense to employers, providing certain conditions are met. These conditions change frequently, almost with every legislative session, but their general aim is to ensure that a benefit package is structured to be available to all employees rather than to a select few, and to be sure that tax-free cash is not funneled to employees under the guise of benefits, thus escaping the long arm of the Internal Revenue Service. These issues are discussed in the benefits chapters.

SUMMARY

Compliance with laws and regulations can be a constraint and/or an opportunity for a compensation manager. The regulatory environment certainly constrains the decisions that can be made. Once laws are passed and regulations published, employers must comply. But a proactive compensation manager can influence the nature of regulations and their interpretation. Astute professionals must be aware of legislative and judicial currents, to protect both employers' and employees' interests, and to ensure that compensation practices conform to judicial interpretation.

How can a compensation manager best undertake these efforts? First, join professional associations to stay informed on emerging issues and to act in concert to inform and influence public and legislative opinion. Second, constantly review compensation practices and the results of their application. The equitable treatment of all employees is the goal of a good pay system, and that is the same goal of legislation. When interpretations of equitable treatment differ, informed public discussion is required. Such discussion cannot occur without the input of informed compensation managers.

Most of the legislation specifying minimum wages and compensable time was originally passed in the 1930s and 1940s, to correct harsh conditions faced by employees, including children. Prevailing wage laws specify a higher minimum for work on government projects, a minimum that is equal to the "prevailing rate" in an area, which usually translates into a union rate far above the minimum. In the 1960s, legislation addressing equal rights issues had a profound impact on all of U.S. society, including employment relationships. This chapter discussed age discrimination. The many other laws enacted to prevent race and gender discrimination are discussed in the next chapter.

REVIEW QUESTIONS

1. What is the nature of government's role in compensation?
2. Explain why changes in minimum wage can have differential effects on employees.
3. How could a compensation manager examine the effect of minimum wage on a specific employer's labor bill?
4. Your employer's production manager has recommended adding a third shift of workers. What advice can you give?
5. What kinds of proactive activities can an employer undertake to enhance the regulatory environment?
6. Could the pay objective of regulatory compliance ever conflict with other objectives? Could it conflict with the employer's notion of consistency or competitiveness? An employee's notion of equity? If so, how would you deal with such situations?

Your Turn:
Amending the Minimum Wage

Over the years, a number of changes have been proposed to the minimum wage provision of the Fair Labor Standards Act. Prepare a brief report outlining the effects of ONE of the proposed changes listed below. Find out if there is currently any legislative activity regarding this change. You may have to use your library's information service to track current activity.

In your report, answer these questions:

WHAT PROBLEM will this change address? Whom will it help? Whom will it hurt? Do you think such a change is a good idea? If you were a legislator, would you vote for such an amendment?

A different student should research each proposed change. Reports should then be presented to the class. Presenters should be prepared to answer questions and defend their votes. After discussion, the entire class will vote on the proposals.

Proposed Changes

a. A youth differential allowing a lower rate for jobs held by unskilled, inexperienced workers.

b. Elimination of the bulk of exemptions.

c. Elimination of the entire minimum wage provision.

d. Index the minimum wage to reflect changes in the Consumer Price Index. (Chapter 15 contains a discussion of the Consumer Price Index.)

e. Index the minimum wage to reflect changes in average hourly earnings in private business.

f. Reduce noncompliance by permitting class action lawsuits, increasing penalties, and targeting enforcement efforts.

g. Limit student certification exemptions to high school students.

Chapter Outline

The . . . wage curve . . . is not the same for women as for men because of the more transient character of the service of the former, the relative shortness of their activity in industry, the differences in environment required, the extra services that must be provided, overtime limitations, extra help needed for the occasional heavy work, and the general sociological factors not requiring discussion herein. Basically then we have another wage curve . . . for women below and not parallel with the men's curve.[1]

It has been suggested that the concept of discrimination is vague. In fact it is clear and simple and has no hidden meanings. To discriminate is to make a distinction, . . . and these differences in treatment which are prohibited . . . are those based on the five forbidden criteria: race, color, religion, sex, and national origin. [Floor debate preceding passage of Title VII, Interpretive Memorandum, Senators Clark and Case, floor managers, Title VII, 110 Congressional Record 7218 (1964)][2]

The pay practice described above, taken from a 1939 job evaluation manual, is now prohibited by law. Discriminatory practices such as paying women and minorities less than white men for equal work contributed to the need for legislation. Legislation, in turn, requires interpretation by regulatory agencies and courts. And despite the assurances offered during the heat of congressional debates, definitions of pay discrimination and the interpretation of the laws enacted to prohibit it have been neither clear nor simple. The laws pertaining to pay discrimination, their interpretation, and implications for pay systems are the subject of this chapter.

PAY DISCRIMINATION: WHAT IS IT?

More than 20 years have passed since the laws intended to prohibit pay discrimination were enacted; although a number of issues have been settled, some remained unresolved. To better understand pay discrimination, it is useful to begin by distinguishing between *access* and *valuation* discrimination.

Access discrimination focuses on the staffing and allocation decisions made by employers (e.g., recruiting, hiring, promoting, training, and layoffs). Access discrimination denies particular jobs, promotions, or training opportunities to qualified women or minorities. *Valuation discrimination* focuses on the pay women and minorities receive for the jobs they perform. The Equal Pay Act makes it clear that it is discriminatory to pay minorities or women less than males when performing equal work (i.e., working side by side, in the same plant, doing the same work, producing the same results). This definition of pay discrimination hinges on the standard of equal pay for equal work.

But many believe that this definition does not go far enough.[3] They believe that valuation discrimination can also occur when men and women hold entirely different jobs

---

[1]The job evaluation manual was introduced as evidence in *Electrical Workers (IUE)* v. *Westinghouse Electric Corp.*, 632 F.2d 1094, 23 FEP Cases 588 (3rd Cir. 1980), cert. defined, 452 U.S. 967, 25 FEP Cases 1835 (1981).

[2]Interpretive memorandum, Title VII, 110 Cong. Rec. 7213 (1964).

[3]B.F. Reskin and H.I. Hartmann, eds., *Women's Work, Men's Work: Segregation on the Job* (Washington, D.C.: National Academy Press, 1986).

(i.e., when job segregation or access discrimination has forced women or minorities into a limited range of jobs). For example, office and clerical jobs are typically staffed by women, and craft jobs (electricians, welders) are typically staffed by men. Is it illegal to pay employees in one job group less than employees in the other, if the two job groups contain work that is not equal in content or results, but is "in some sense of comparable worth" to the employer?

In this case, the proposed definition of pay discrimination hinges on the standard of equal pay for work of comparable worth. Existing federal laws do not support this standard. However, several states have enacted laws that require a comparable worth standard for state and local government employees.[4] The province of Ontario, Canada, has extended such legislation to the private sector. We shall examine its experience later in this chapter.

So two standards for defining pay discrimination need to be considered: equal pay for equal work, and equal pay for work of comparable worth. For an understanding of the legal foundations of each, let us turn to the legislation and key court cases.

THE EQUAL PAY ACT

The major laws prohibiting pay discrimination are the Equal Pay Act (EPA) of 1963 and Title VII of the Civil Rights Act of 1964.[5] The EPA was the first modern statute directed at eliminating discrimination in the job market. It forbids wage discrimination between employees on the basis of sex when employees perform equal work on jobs in the same establishment requiring equal skill, effort, and responsibility and performed under similar working conditions. Pay differences between equal jobs can be justified when that differential is based on (1) a seniority system, (2) a merit system, (3) a system measuring earnings by quality or quantity of production, or (4) any factor other than sex.[6]

---

[4]Toby Parcel, "Comparable Worth, Occupational Labor Markets and Occupational Earnings: Results from the 1980 Census," *Pay Equity: Empirical Inquiries* (Washington, D.C.: National Academy of Science, 1989); Elaine Sorensen, "Measuring the Effect of Occupational Sex and Race Composition on Earnings," *Pay Equity: Empirical Inquiries;* "General Accounting Office to Conduct Pay Equity Study of the Federal Workforce" (Washington, D.C.: National Committee on Pay Equity, March 16, 1989); Alice Cook, *Comparable Worth: A Case Book of Experiences in States and Localities, 1986 Supplement* (Honolulu: Industrial Relations Center, University of Hawaii at Manoa), and *Survey of State-Government Level Pay Equity Activity 1988* (Washington, D.C.: National Committee on Pay Equity, no date); and *Pay Equity Implementation Series* (Toronto, Ontario, Canada: The Pay Equity Commission). This is a series of guidelines addressing questions regarding implementation of the province's pay equity legislation.

[5]The 14th Amendment also provides equal treatment under the law and some cases involving pay discrimination have been heard under it, especially since *Mescall* v. *Burrus,* 603 F.2d 1266, 1271 (7th Cir. 1979); most, however, have been brought jointly with a Title VII claim.

[6]29 U.S.C. § 206 (d) (1979). Since the EPA is an amendment to the Fair Labor Standards Act, it originally exempted the same occupational groups as did the FLSA. However, with the passage of the Education Amendments of 1972, EPA exemptions for bona fide executives, administrators, professionals, and outside salespeople were eliminated [29 U.S.C. § 213(a) (1970)].

Reducing wages of the higher paid employee in order to achieve compliance is also prohibited. The act embraces the "equal work" definition of pay discrimination. It permits comparisons among equal jobs only, and defines equal work by four factors: (1) skill, (2) effort, (3) responsibility, and (4) working conditions. As noted during our discussion of job evaluation (Chapters 4 and 5), these factors, or some variation of them, are commonly used in most job evaluation plans.

Pay differences are permitted under the EPA's four *affirmative defenses*. Differences in pay among men and women doing equal work are legal if these differences are based on (1) seniority, (2) quality of performance, (3) quality or quantity of production, or (4) some factor other than sex.

The act is deceptively simple, yet numerous court cases have been required to clarify its provisions, particularly its definition of *equal*:

Equal work: How equal is equal?

Equal skill: effort, responsibility, and working conditions.

Factors other than sex.

Definition of *Equal*

After years of judicial indecision, the Court established guidelines to define equal work in the *Schultz* v. *Wheaton Glass Company* case. Wheaton Glass Company maintained two job classifications for selector packers in its production department, male and female. The female job class carried a pay rate 10 percent below that of the male job class. The company claimed that the male job class included additional tasks such as shoveling broken glass, opening warehouse doors, doing heavy lifting, and the like, that justified the pay differential. The plaintiff claimed that the extra tasks were infrequently performed, and not all men did them.[7] Further, these extra tasks performed by some of the men were regularly performed by employees in another classification ("snap-up boys"), and these employees were paid only 2 cents an hour more than the women. Did the additional tasks performed by some members of one job class render the jobs unequal? The court decided not. It ruled that the equal work standard required only that jobs be *substantially* equal, not identical. The extra duties performed by the men did not justify paying the men 10 percent more than the women were paid. "Substantially equal work" based on the *Wheaton Glass Company* case has become the standard for assessing whether or not jobs are equal.

Additionally, the courts have generally held that the *actual work performed* is the appropriate information to use when deciding if jobs are substantially equal. This was established in several cases in which it was found that the duties employees actually performed were different from those in the written descriptions of the job.

---

[7]Plaintiffs are those who bring suit to obtain a remedy for injury to their rights. Defendants are those (usually the employer) who explain practices to answer the suit.

Definitions of the Four Factors

The Department of Labor provides these definitions of the four factors:[8]

1. Skill: Experience, training, education, and ability as measured by the performance requirements of a particular job.
2. Effort: Mental or physical. The amount or degree of effort (not type of effort) actually expended in the performance of a job.
3. Responsibility: The degree of accountability required in the performance of a job.
4. Working conditions: The physical surroundings and hazards of a job including dimensions such as inside versus outside work, heat, cold, and poor ventilation.

Guidelines to clarify these definitions have evolved through court decisions. For an employer to support a claim of *unequal* work, the following conditions must be met:

1. The effort/skill/responsibility must be substantially greater in one of the jobs compared.
2. The tasks involving the extra effort/skill/responsibility must consume a *significant amount* of time for *all* employees whose additional wages are in question.
3. The extra effort/skill/responsibility must have *a value commensurate* with the questioned pay differential (as determined by the employer's own evaluation).

The courts have also dealt with equal working conditions.[9] In *Brennan* v. *Corning Glass Works,* the court ruled that time of day did not constitute dissimilar working conditions. Shift differentials are not illegal, but if they are paid, the employer must clearly state that their purpose is to compensate workers for unusual conditions, and they must be separate from the base wage for the job.

Factors Other than Sex

Under the Equal Pay Act, *unequal* pay for equal work may be justified through the four affirmative defenses: seniority, merit, performance-based incentive system, or a factor other than sex. Factors other than sex include shift differentials; temporary assignments;

---

[8]U.S. Department of Labor, *Women Workers Today* (Washington, D.C., 1976); U.S. Department of Labor, *The Earnings Gap between Women and Men* (Washington, D.C., 1976); U.S. Department of Labor, Interpretative Bulletin, *Equal Pay for Equal Work under the Fair Labor Standards Act* (Washington, D.C., August 31, 1971); and U.S. Department of Labor, *Brief Highlights of Major Federal Laws and Orders on Sex Discrimination in Employment* (Washington, D.C., February 1977).

[9]Elizabeth A. Cooper and Gerald V. Barrett, "Equal Pay and Gender: Implications of Court Cases for Personnel Practices," *Academy of Management Review* 9, no. 1 (1984), pp. 84–94.

bona fide training programs; differences based on ability, training, or experience; and others.[10]

Factors other than sex have been interpreted as a broad exception that may include business reasons advanced by the employer. In *Kouba* v. *Allstate*,[11] Allstate Insurance Company paid its new sales representatives a minimum salary during their training period. After completing the training, the sales reps received a minimum salary or their earned sales commissions, whichever was higher. The minimum salary paid during training needed to be high enough to attract prospective agents to enter the training program, yet not so high as to lessen the incentive to earn sales commissions after training. Allstate agreed that the minimum salary needed to be calculated individually for each trainee, and the trainee's past salary was a necessary factor used in the calculation. But Allstate's approach resulted in women trainees generally being paid less than male trainees, since women had held lower paying jobs before entering the program. Allstate maintained the pay difference resulted from acceptable business reasons, a factor other than sex.

Lola Kouba didn't buy Allstate's arguments. She argued that acceptable business reasons were limited to "those that measure the value of an employee's job performance to his or her employer." But the court rejected Kouba's argument. It said that Allstate's business reasons for a practice must be evaluated for reasonableness. A practice will not automatically be prohibited simply because wage differences between men and women result.

The court did not say that Allstate's "business" reasons were justified. It did say that Allstate's argument could not be rejected *solely because the practice perpetuated historical differences in pay*. Rather, Allstate needed to justify the business relatedness of the practice.

The case was settled out of court, so no legal clarification of Allstate's rationale was ever provided. Thus, the definition of "factor other than sex" remains somewhat murky. It does seem that pay differences for equal work can be justified for demonstrably business-related reasons. But what is and is not demonstrably business related has not yet been cataloged.

Reverse Discrimination

Several cases deal with the important issue of reverse discrimination against men when pay for women is adjusted. In these cases, men have claimed that they were paid less than women doing similar work, simply because they were men. In one case, the University of Nebraska created a model to calculate salaries based on values estimated for a faculty member's education, field of specialization, years of direct experience, years

---

[10]*Bona fide* is interpreted here as (1) established, either formally or informally, (2) systematically applied in a nondiscriminatory fashion, and (3) communicated to all covered employees. H.R. Rep. No. 309, 88th Cong. 1st Sess. 3 (1963).

[11]*Kouba and EEOC* v. *Allstate Insurance Company*, 691 F.2d 873 (1982).

of related experience, and merit.[12] Based on these qualifications, the university granted raises to 33 women whose salaries were less than the amount computed by the model. However, the university gave no such increases to 92 males whose salaries were also below the amount the model set for them based on their qualifications. The court found this system a violation of the Equal Pay Act. It held that, in effect, the university was using a new system to determine a salary schedule, based on specific criteria. To refuse to pay employees of one sex the minimum required by these criteria was illegal.

In another case, the male faculty at Northern Illinois University (NIU) sued to have a model the university developed to adjust women faculty salaries applied to them, also.[13] The NIU model was used to allocate a *one-time salary adjustment* to overcome the results of past discrimination against women, and was not a permanent change in the compensation system. Therefore, the court ruled that it did not need to be applied to men. NIU's approach differed from Nebraska's. NIU made a one-time payment to women to correct past discrimination. Nebraska, on the other hand, developed a new way to calculate salaries and therefore must apply it to all faculty members equally.

More recently, male flight attendants at Northwest Airlines sued to recover back pay comparable to that awarded by Northwest to female attendants who had charged the airline with sex discrimination. The 265 male attendants charged that the airline violated the Civil Rights Act of 1964 by not paying them the back pay when the airline settled with the female attendants. Under a 1992 settlement, the male attendants will share $1 million.

So what does this have to do with compensation management? Viewed collectively, the courts have provided reasonably clear directions. The design of pay systems must incorporate a policy of equal pay for substantially equal work. The determination of substantially equal work must be based on the actual work performed (the job content) and must reflect the skill, effort, and responsibility required, and the working conditions. It is legal to pay men and women who perform substantially equal work differently if the pay system is designed to recognize differences in performance, seniority, quality and quantity of results, or certain factors other than sex, in a nondiscriminatory manner. Further, to minimize vulnerability to reverse discrimination suits, if a new pay system is designed, it must be equally applied to all employees. If, on the other hand, a one-time adjustment is made to correct past problems, it need apply only to the affected group.

But what does this tell us about discrimination on jobs that are *not substantially equal*—dissimilar jobs? For example, suppose that almost all women employees work in one job classification: office/clerical. Further suppose that the employer granted cost of living increases semiannually to all job classes *except* the office/clericals. The office/clerical jobs are not "substantially equal" to the other jobs, so the Equal Pay Act

---

[12]*Board of Regents of University of Nebraska* v. *Dawes,* 522 F.2d 380, 11 FEP Cases 283 (8th Cir. 1976); 424 U.S. 914, 12 FEP Cases 343 (1976); K. M. Weeks, "Equal Pay: The Emerging Terrain," *College and University Law,* Summer 1985, pp. 41–60.

[13]*Ende* v. *Board of Regents of Northern Illinois University,* 37 FEP Cases 575 (7th Cir. 1985). Peter Saucier wonders whether affirmative action plans are "a factor other than sex" in "Affirmative Action and the Equal Pay Act," *Employee Relations Law Journal* 11, no. 2 (Winter 1985/86), pp. 453–66.

does not apply. Can the office/clerical employees still charge their employer with pay discrimination? Yes, under Title VII of the Civil Rights Act.

TITLE VII OF THE CIVIL RIGHTS ACT OF 1964

Title VII prohibits discrimination on the basis of sex, race, color, religion, or national origin in any employment condition, including hiring, firing, promotion, transfer, compensation, and admission to training programs.[14] Title VII was amended in 1972 and 1978. The 1972 amendments strengthened enforcement and expanded coverage to include employees of government and educational institutions, as well as private employers of more than 15 persons. The pregnancy amendment of 1978 made it illegal to discriminate based on pregnancy, childbirth, or related conditions.

Since 1964 the courts have evolved two theories of discrimination behavior under Title VII: (1) disparate treatment and (2) disparate impact. Exhibit 14.1 contrasts the two theories.

Disparate Treatment.   Disparate or unequal treatment includes those practices in which an organization treats minorities or women less favorably than others are treated, either openly or covertly. Under this definition, a practice is unlawful if it applies different standards to different employees, for example, based on seniority for women but performance for men (different standards). The mere fact of unequal treatment may be taken as evidence of the employer's intention to discriminate.

Disparate Impact.   Personnel practices that have a differential *effect* on members of protected groups are illegal under the disparate or unequal impact theory of Title VII, unless the differences can be justified as necessary to the safe and efficient operation of the business or are work related. The major case that established this interpretation of

---

Exhibit 14.1   Discriminatory Behavior

Disparate Treatment	Disparate Impact
1. Different standards for different individuals or groups.	1. Same standards have differing consequences.
2. Intent to discriminate may be inferred by behaviors.	2. Discrimination shown by general statistical impact; discriminatory intent need not be present.
3. Employer can justify actions by absence of discriminatory intent and exercise of reasonable business judgment.	3. Employer can justify pay differences through business necessity.

---

[14]29 U.S.C. § 206 (d) (1) (1970). Its coverage is broader, also. Employers, employment agencies, labor organizations, and training programs involving 15 or more employees and some 120,000 educational institutions fall under its jurisdictions.

Title VII is *Griggs* v. *Duke Power Co.*,[15] in which the Court struck down employment tests and educational requirements that screened out a higher proportion of blacks than whites. Even though the practices were applied equally—both blacks and whites had to pass the tests—they were prohibited because (1) they had the consequence of excluding a protected group (blacks) disproportionately and (2) they were not related to the jobs in question.

Under the disparate impact theory of discrimination, whether or not the employer intended to discriminate is irrelevant. Thus, a personnel decision can, on its face, seem neutral, but if the results of it are unequal, the employer must demonstrate that the decision is either work related or a business necessity.

CIVIL RIGHTS ACT OF 1991

The two standards of discrimination—disparate treatment and disparate impact—appeared well established when applied to access discrimination issues. But a 1989 Supreme Court ruling, *Wards Cove Packing* v. *Atonio,* upset the apple cart by ruling that plaintiffs must specify which employment practice had the adverse impact and then link that practice to the resulting imbalance.[16] But as you recall from your introductory human resource management course, trying to isolate the effect of a single personnel practice is like separating the strands of a spider web. Pick up a single strand and find the whole world attached. The Civil Rights Act of 1991 redressed the issue by reestablishing the standards for discrimination in widespread use before 1989. Nevertheless, the two standards remain difficult to apply to pay issues, since pay differences are legal for dissimilar work.

To understand the evolving status of pay discrimination under Title VII, we examine two basic questions.

1. Can pay discrimination exist in different pay rates for dissimilar jobs?
2. What constitutes pay discrimination in dissimilar jobs?

PAY DISCRIMINATION AND DISSIMILAR JOBS

The Supreme Court, in *Gunther* v. *County of Washington*, determined that pay discrimination may occur in establishing pay differences for dissimilar jobs.[17] In this case, four jail matrons in Washington County, Oregon, claimed that their work was comparable to that performed by male guards. The women matrons guarded one-tenth the number of prisoners for which the male guards were responsible. The rest of their job responsibilities were of a clerical nature.

Both the county's own wage survey and its assessment of job worth had indicated that the matrons should be paid about 95 percent as much as the guards. Instead, their pay was only about 70 percent that of the guards. Lower courts refused to consider the

[15]*Griggs* v. *Duke Power Co.,* 401 U.S. 414 (1971).

[16]*Wards Cove Packing* v. *Atonio,* 57 U.S.L.W. 4583 (1989).

[17]*Gunther* v. *County of Washington,* U.S. Sup Ct 451 U.S. 161 (1981).

matrons' case on the grounds that their evidence did not meet the equal work requirement of the Equal Pay Act. The Supreme Court overturned the lower courts and stated that a Title VII pay case was not bound by the definitions of equal work or the affirmative defenses of the Equal Pay Act, ruling that "to hold that sex-based wage discrimination violates Title VII only if it also violates the EPA would be denying relief to victims of discrimination who did not hold the same jobs as a higher paid man." The Court also went out of its way to state what it was *not* ruling on:

> We emphasize at the outset the narrowness of the question before us in this case. Respondents' claim is not based on the controversial concept of "comparable worth," under which the plaintiff might claim increased compensation on the basis of a comparison of the intrinsic worth or difficulty of their job with that of other jobs in the same organization or community. Rather, respondents seek to prove, by direct evidence, that their wages were depressed because of intentional sex discrimination, consisting of setting the wage scale level lower than its own survey of outside markets and the worth of the jobs warranted.

(The case was returned to a lower court for additional evidence of discrimination, and was eventually settled out of court.)

Although the *Gunther* case established that charges of pay discrimination on dissimilar (not equal) jobs could be brought under Title VII, it did not consider what might constitute pay discrimination in dissimilar jobs under Title VII. To examine this question, we discuss three possible approaches: (1) where the employer exhibited a pattern of discrimination in many of its personnel practices beyond wage setting, (2) where the employer used market data to justify pay differences, and (3) where the employer conducted a pay equity study using job evaluation to determine jobs of "comparable worth."

Proof of Discrimination: Pattern of Personnel Practices

Under this approach, employees seek to prove that discrimination pervades the entire employment relationship, including the pay system. In *Taylor* v. *Charley Brothers Company*,[18] a wholesale distributor maintained two separate departments based on what products were handled, not on what work was done. For example, warehouse workers who handled frozen food were in department 1; those who handled health and beauty aids were in department 2. Charley Brothers hired only men for the first department; women applicants were not even considered for positions in that department. If female applicants specifically requested department 1, they were told that the work there required greater physical strength, but they were not told that it also paid more. Additional evidence indicated that no males were considered for jobs in department 2, and that both company officials and union officials discouraged female employees from bidding for jobs in department 1. Clearly, the company's hiring and job assignment policies violated Title VII in that women were denied equal access to jobs, but did its pay policies discriminate, too? The Court held that both the EPA and Title VII were violated: Charley Brothers

---

[18]*Taylor* v. *Charley Brothers Company*, 25 FEP Cases 602 (W. D. Pa. 1981).

intentionally discriminated in its entire pay system. Women were paid substantially less than men in the all-male department simply because they worked in a department populated only by women, not because the jobs they performed were inherently worth less than jobs performed by men. The Court took as evidence of the company's intent to discriminate the fact that it never had undertaken any type of evaluation of any of the jobs, that it segregated women within the one department, and that officials of the company made various discriminatory remarks.[19] Sufficient proof of Charley Brothers' intention to discriminate was shown through the pattern of its personnel practices, including pay, regardless of the dissimilarity of the jobs involved.

Most cases are less clearcut than the Charley Brothers case. Consider, for example, a case that focuses on the way in which pay rates for two obviously dissimilar jobs are determined. Examples include the pay rates for nurses versus tree trimmers or nurses versus sanitarians or even professors of nursing versus professors of business administration. If these jobs are dissimilar and if no pattern of discrimination in hiring, promotion, or other personnel decisions exists, then what constitutes pay discrimination?

Proof of Discrimination: Use of Market Data

In the case of *Lemons* v. *The City and County of Denver,*[20] nurse Mary Lemons claimed that her job, held predominantly by women, was illegally paid less than the jobs held predominantly by men (tree trimmers, sign painters, tire servicemen, etc.). Lemons claimed that the nurse's job required more education and skill. Therefore, to pay the male jobs more than the nurses' jobs simply because the male jobs commanded higher rates in the local labor market was discriminatory. She argued that the market reflected historical underpayment of "women's work." The court disagreed, adding that "market disparities are not among those Title VII seeks to adjust." Thus, the situation identified by *Lemons*—pay differences in dissimilar jobs—did not by itself constitute proof of intent to discriminate.

The courts have continually upheld employers' use of market data to justify pay differences for different jobs. *Spaulding* v. *University of Washington*[21] developed the argument in greatest detail. In this case, the predominantly female faculty of the Department of Nursing claimed that it was illegally paid less than faculty in other departments. The statisticians for Spaulding presented a model of faculty pay comparisons in "comparable" departments that controlled for the effects of level of education, job tenure, and other factors. They asserted that any pay difference not accounted for in their model was discrimination. But the courts have been dubious of statistics. Such an approach to defining discrimination has been likened to the owner of a missing piece of jewelry concluding that it must be in the kitchen, "because I've looked through every other room

---

[19]The union was also accused of discrimination against female employees. The courts accepted as evidence discriminatory statements made by union leaders but did not hold them liable for their behaviors, since they had not made the hiring and allocation decisions.

[20]*Lemons* v. *City and County of Denver*, 620 F. 2d 228 (1980).

[21]*Spaulding* v. *University of Washington*, 35 FEP Cases 217 (9th Cir. 1984).

in the house." Far better to define discrimination directly, rather than concluding that it is "whatever is left."[22] The *Spaulding* judge observed that the model "unrealistically assumed the equality of all master's degrees, ignored job experience prior to university employment, and ignored detailed analysis of day-to-day responsibilities." Without such data, "we have no meaningful way of determining just how much of the proposed wage differential was due to sex and how much was due to academic discipline."

But the court went beyond criticizing the model. It ruled on the use of competitive market data as a policy. The court held that every employer who is constrained by market forces must consider market values in setting labor costs. "Naturally, market prices are inherently job-related." Employers who rely on the market deal with it as a given and do not meaningfully have a "policy" about it in the relevant Title VII sense, according to the court. Allowing reliance on the market to constitute a facially neutral policy for disparate impact purposes "would subject employers to liability for pay disparities with respect to which they have not, in any meaningful sense, made an independent business judgment."

Is There a "Market Policy"?   Recall from the market survey discussion (Chapter 7) all the decisions that go into designing and conducting a survey. What employers constitute the "relevant market"? Does the relevant market vary by occupation? Do different market definitions yield different wage patterns? Clearly, judgment is involved in answering these questions. Yet the courts have thus far neglected to examine those judgments for possible bias. Perhaps the pattern of judgment does indeed constitute a "policy" in a Title VII sense.

Spaulding and other court cases have tended to view the market as a "given" that allows little room for discretion. If that is so, then according to Rynes and Milkovich, the employer's role is to "find out precisely what that rate is. If, on the other hand, a *range* of possible wages exists for any given job, then . . . the observed, or measured, market wage will depend on where the wage data is collected, . . . (and) *sampling* becomes critical."[23]

Should market survey procedures be subject to the same issues that surround other statistical procedures (e.g., availability analysis for fairness in hiring and promotion, or validity and job relatedness of tests)? Although Rynes and Milkovich do not take a position on this question, they point out that "judgment enters into virtually every step of the wage survey process, and each successive judgment may modify the eventual results." Clearly, not all employers are the "price takers" that the courts have assumed.[24]

---

[22]Orley Ashenfelter and Ronald Oaxaca, "The Economics of Discrimination: Economists Enter the Courtroom," *American Economic Review*, May 1987, pp. 321–25; and Victor Fuchs, *Women's Quest for Economic Equality* (Cambridge, Mass.: Harvard University Press, 1988).

[23]Sara L. Rynes and George T. Milkovich, "Wage Surveys: Dispelling Some Myths about the 'Market Wage,' " *Personnel Psychology*, Spring 1986, pp. 71–90.

[24]Sara L. Rynes, Caroline L. Weber, and George T. Milkovich, "The Effects of Market Survey Rates, Job Evaluation and Job Gender on Job Pay," *Journal of Applied Psychology* 74, no. 1 (1989), pp. 114–23.

Proof of Discrimination: Jobs of "Comparable Worth"

A third approach to attempting to determine pay discrimination on jobs of dissimilar content hinges on finding a standard by which to compare the value of jobs. The standard must be two things. First, it must permit jobs with dissimilar content to be declared equal or "in some sense comparable."[25] Second, it must permit pay differences for dissimilar jobs that are not comparable. Job evaluation has been proposed as that standard.[26] If an employer's own job evaluation study shows jobs of dissimilar content to be of equal value to the employer, then isn't failure to pay them equally proof of intent to discriminate? The issue has been considered in *AFSCME* v. *State of Washington*.[27]

In 1973, the state of Washington commissioned a study of the concept of comparable worth (discussed later in this chapter) and its projected effect on the state's pay system. The study concluded that by basing wages on the external market, the state was paying women approximately 20 percent less than it was paying men in jobs deemed of comparable value to the state. The state took no action on this finding, alleging it could not afford to do so, so AFSCME, the employees' union, sued to force implementation of a compensation system based on comparable worth as outlined in the study. The union alleged that since the state was aware of the adverse effect of its present policy, failure to change it constituted discrimination.

But an appeals court ruled that the state was not obligated to correct the disparity. An employer's merely being aware of adverse consequences for a protected group did not constitute discrimination. "The plaintiff must show the employer chose the particular policy because of its effect on members of a protected class."

AFSCME v. *State of Washington* differs from previous cases that used market data in that this is the first case in which the evidence that the jobs were in any sense "equal" was developed by the employer. But even though the state had commissioned the study, it had not agreed to implement the study's results. Therefore, the employer had not, in the court's view, admitted that the jobs were equal or established a pay system that purported to pay on the basis of "comparable worth" rather than markets. Rather than appeal, the parties settled out of court. The state revamped its pay system and agreed to make more than $100 million in "pay equity" adjustments by 1992.

So where does this leave us? Clearly, Title VII prohibits intentional discrimination in compensation if it is based on sex or other proscribed factors, whether or not the employees in question hold the same or different jobs. Discrimination may be proved by direct evidence of an employer's intent (e.g., an overall pattern of behavior that demonstrates disparate treatment). However, "job evaluation studies and comparable worth

---

[25]Reskin and Hartmann, *Women's Work, Men's Work;* and Judith Olans Brown, Phyllis Tropper Baumann, and Elain Millar Melnick, "Equal Pay for Jobs of Comparable Worth: An Analysis of the Rhetoric," *Harvard Civil Rights—Civil Liberties Law Review,* Winter 1986, pp. 127–70.

[26]*Job Evaluation: A Tool for Pay Equity* (Washington, D. C.: National Committee on Pay Equity, November 1987); and Rynes, Weber, and Milkovich, "Effects of Market Survey Rates, Job Evaluation, and Job Gender on Job Pay."

[27]*American Federation of State, County, and Municipal Employees* v. *State of Washington,* 578 F. Supp 846 (W.D. Wash. 1983).

statistics alone are insufficient to establish the requisite inference of discriminatory motive."[28] The disparate impact standard, in which no proof of discriminatory intent is required, appears to be inappropriate for broad challenges to general compensation policies.

Title VII rulings make it clear that pay discrimination is not limited only to equal jobs; it may also occur in setting different rates for different jobs. It is also clear that the courts are not about to rule the use of external market rates illegal. Competitive market pricing, by itself, does not appear to constitute a policy that has disparate impact. Further, to prevail in a disparate treatment allegation, plaintiffs need to demonstrate a pattern of discrimination practices that is specific and deliberate—"regularly and purposefully treat(ing) women differently and generally less favorably than men."[29] Simply demonstrating pay differences on jobs that are not equal is insufficient to prove discrimination.

What additional implications for the design and administration of pay systems can be drawn? These court decisions imply that pay differentials between dissimilar jobs will not be prohibited under Title VII if the differences can be shown to be based on the content of the work, its value to the organization's objectives, and the employer's ability to attract and retain employees in competitive external labor markets. The courts appear to recognize that "the value of a particular job to an employer is but one factor influencing the rate of compensation for a job."[30]

ECONOMIC EQUALITY AS A SOCIAL ISSUE

Clearly, present interpretation of federal law in the United States does not mandate a comparable worth theory of discrimination. Why then does the issue persist? It is part of a continuing evolution of the role of women in society. Women have still not achieved economic parity with men.[31] Some people believe that elimination of gender-related pay differentials on equal jobs and opening access to all jobs is sufficient.[32] But many others do not.[33] They believe that despite the equal pay standard, women continue to face severe handicaps in the labor market. To paraphrase Mark Twain, they are "surrounded by insurmountable opportunities." These opportunities present themselves as differences in occupational attainment and a persistent gap in the wages received by women compared to men.

---

[28]David A. Cathcart and Pamela L. Hemminger, *Developments in the Law of Salary Discrimination* (Los Angeles: Gibson, Dunn and Crutcher, 1985).

[29]*Taylor* v. *Charles Brothers Company*.

[30]*AFSCME* v. *Washington*.

[31]Fuchs, *Women's Quest for Economic Equality*.

[32]Myron Lieberman, "The Conversion of Interests to Principles: The Case of Comparable Worth," *Journal of Collective Negotiations* 15, no. 2 (1986), pp. 145–52.

[33]Jerald Greenberg and Claire L. McCarty, "Comparable Worth: A Matter of Justice," in *Research in Personnel and Human Resources Management*, vol. 8, ed. K. M. Rowland and G. R. Ferris (Greenwich, Conn.: JAI Press, 1990); and Claudia Goldin, *Understanding the Gender Gap* (New York: Oxford University Press, 1990).

EXHIBIT 14.2   Changes in the Wage Gap 1979–1991: Median Weekly Earnings as Percent of White Male Earnings

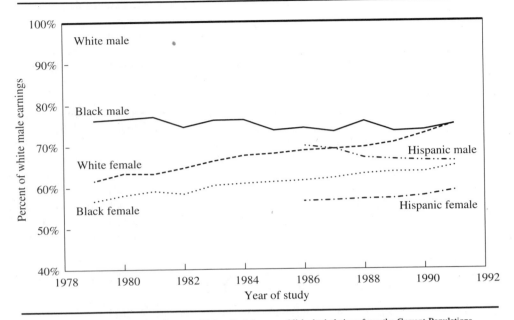

SOURCE: U.S. Department of Labor, Bureau of Labor Statistics, unpublished tabulations from the Current Populations Survey.

The Earnings Gap

According to the Bureau of Labor Statistics, white women working full-time in 1991 had a median weekly wage equal to 73 percent of the weekly wage earned by white men. The ratio for black males was also 73 percent, for black females 63 percent, for Hispanic males 65 percent, and for Hispanic females 58 percent. Exhibit 14.2 shows how the wage gap has persisted over time. Although the size of the differences has fluctuated over time, it has been extremely persistent, and always to the advantage of white males. That relatively constant pattern occurred despite the passage of the Equal Pay Act in 1963, the Civil Rights Act of 1964, and the executive orders that mandated affirmative action in firms doing business with the federal government. What do we know about why that gap exists? Respected economists agree that many complex and subtly interrelated factors are involved (which is why we never sit next to economists at parties).[34]

Some of the more important factors, shown in Exhibit 14.3, include the following:

---

[34]See Dave Barry, *Dave Barry Slept Here* (New York: Random House, 1989), p. 25.

EXHIBIT 14.3   Possible Determinants of Pay Differences

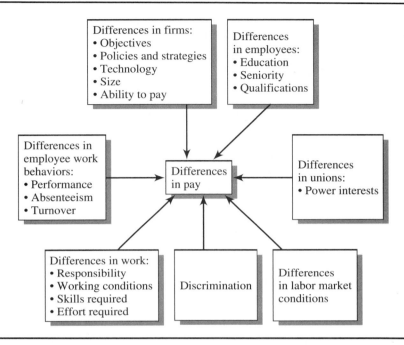

SOURCE: George T. Milkovich, "The Emerging Debate," in *Comparable Worth: Issues and Alternatives,* ed. E. Robert Livernash (Washington, D.C.: Equal Employment Advisory Council, 1980).

1. Differences in the occupational attainment and the jobs held by men and women.
2. Differences in personal work-related characteristics and work behaviors.
3. Differences among industries and firms.
4. Differences in union membership.
5. The presence of discrimination.

First let us examine some data, then some conflicting beliefs.

Differences in Occupational Attainment

One of the most important factors that accounts for much of the remaining gap is the difference in the nature of jobs held by men and women. A variety of data illustrates these differences.

The Bureau of Labor Statistics reports that half of all working women in the United States are employed in only 20 percent of the 427 occupations. In addition, among the 427 occupational classes, 80 percent of women work in classes in which at least 70 percent of employees are women. Forty percent of Canadian women work in just 10 job categories. The difference in occupational attainment is the major factor accounting for the earnings gap.[35]

Supporters of comparable worth believe these differences are a reflection of discrimination in society.[36] Discrimination and gender stereotyping in counseling and courses taken in high school, admission to colleges, and the hiring and promotion practices of employers have all worked, the argument goes, to allocate or crowd women into a limited number of occupations. Because these occupations are typed as women's work, they are devalued. That is, women's jobs pay less because wage discrimination acts on an entire occupation, not only on individual women workers.

On the other hand, the opponents of comparable worth believe that wages are determined primarily by supply and demand; that is, by choices of women and employers. Wages and employment levels are flexible and labor markets adjust, so that the supply available, made up of choices of workers to undertake training required and seek job opportunities, adjusts to equal the demand. If we just get markets competitive and working efficiently, the argument goes, the goal of maximizing profits will eventually lead employers to eliminate discrimination.[37]

According to this view, women make choices about which occupations to train for and when to leave and enter the work force. From this efficient market perspective, women earn less because the jobs they choose have low productivity and low wages, but those jobs permit women to enter and leave the work force readily; require relatively less training; and are not onerous or dangerous.[38]

Recent data indicate that these occupational patterns are changing. Women are gaining access to a wider array of occupations. Those occupations with the biggest changes tend to be the ones that are growing the fastest. When a strong demand for employees exists,

[35]Linda Subich, Gerald Barrett, Dennis Doverspike, and Ralph Alexander, "The Effects of Sex Role-Related Factors on Occupational Choice and Salary," *Pay Equity: Empirical Inquiries* (Washington, D. C.: National Academy of Science, 1989); Randall K. Filer, "Occupational Segregation, Compensating Differentials and Comparable Worth," *Pay Equity: Empirical Inquiries*; and Elaine Sorensen, "The Crowding Hypothesis and Comparable Worth," *Journal of Human Resources* 25, no. 1, pp. 55–89.

[36]Paula England, "Do Men's Jobs Require More Skill than Women's?" *ILR Report* 19, no. 2 (Spring 1983), pp. 20–23.

[37]G. G. Cain, *The Economic Analysis of Labor Market Discrimination: A Survey,* Special Report 37 (Madison: University of Wisconsin, March 1985); Solomon W. Polachek, "Women in the Economy: Perspectives on Gender Inequality," *Comparable Worth: Issue for the 80's,* vol. 1 (Washington, D.C.: U.S. Commission on Civil Rights, 1985); and Claudia Goldin, *Occupational Segregation by Sex: The Roles of Supervisory Costs and Human Capital, 1890–1940* (Cambridge, Mass.: National Bureau of Economic Research, 1984).

[38]G. Johnson and G. Solon, *Pay Differences between Women's and Men's Jobs* (Cambridge, Mass.: National Bureau of Economic Research, 1984); W. F. Oi, "Neglected Women and Other Implications of Comparable Worth," *Contemporary Policy Issues* (April 1986), pp. 21–32; and J. Roback, *A Matter of Choice: A Critique of Comparable Worth by a Skeptical Feminist* (New York: Priority Press, 1986).

fewer barriers to women's entry exist. Both the wage gap and occupational segregation diminishes.[39] Exhibit 14.4 data are from some selected companies. For example in 1979, only 10 percent of lawyers were women; by 1986 it was 15 percent; and by 1991 it was almost 25 percent. The earnings ratio among women lawyers had increased from 55 to 81 percent. Similar increases occurred for janitors and accountants. However, the earnings ratio for registered nurses and food preparation supervisors has fallen since 1986.

It is a fact that (1) women tend to be employed in female-dominated occupations and (2) that wages in these occupations are relatively lower. It is also a fact that (3) women tend to hold the lower paying jobs in each occupation. So although the percentage

EXHIBIT 14.4   Female/Male Earnings Ratio

| | Full-Time Workers Selected Occupations | | | | | |
| | 1979 | | 1986 | | 1991 | |
Occupation	*Percent Female*	*Earnings Ratio*	*Percent Female*	*Earnings Ratio*	*Percent Female*	*Earnings Ratio*
Registered nurses	94.6%	82	92.7%	91	93.3%	85
Bookkeepers, accounting and auditing clerks	88.1	66	93.0	74	91.2	81
Nursing aides, orderlies, and attendants	85.1	72	88.3	81	88.0	90
Administrative support occupations, misc.	62.9	62	82.4	70	78.1	76
Social workers	60.6	83	60.0	73	66.1	90
Computer operators	56.6	69	63.8	73	64.5	74
Supervisors, food preparation, and service occupations	41.6	72	48.2	67	59.3	61
Secondary school teachers	39.7	83	49.1	86	52.0	89
Accountants and auditors	34.0	60	44.7	72	53.5	71
Computer programmers	28.0	80	39.7	81	34.6	86
Janitors and cleaners	15.3	74	21.0	69	22.3	83
Supervisors, production occupations	12.9	62	15.1	67	16.6	73
Lawyers	10.4	55	15.2	63	24.6	81

SOURCE: 1991, U.S. Department of Labor, Bureau of Labor Statistics, unpublished tabulations from the Current Populations Survey: 1991 annual averages.

[39]Judith Fields and Edward Wolff, "The Decline of Sex Segregation and the Wage Gap, 1970–80," *Journal of Human Resources* 26, no. 4, pp. 608–22.

of women employed is increasing dramatically, new workers are more likely to hold lower paying jobs. Thus, the influx of women into the work force has also tended to hold down women's earnings.

Based on a recent survey of the research conducted on the earnings gap, no study has been able to explain more than half of the difference between male/female earnings without one or more variables designed to measure differences in occupations and the nature of the work performed. So we know that the nature of the jobs performed is a critical factor.

The Glass Ceiling

Even at the top, women and blacks have frequently complained of a "glass ceiling," an invisible barrier that permits them to get close to the top positions but keeps them out of the highest jobs. A 1991 report by the Department of Labor confirms what other surveys have shown: Few women and even fewer minorities hold top management jobs in U.S. companies.[40] Among 94 contractors reviewed, women represented only 6.6 percent and minorities only 2.6 percent of executive-level positions (assistant vice president or above). In some of the companies studied, no women or minorities were employed above entry level.

Potential barriers to the movement of women and minorities into top management that were identified in the report include executive recruiting practices that bypass women and minority candidates, a lack of mentoring, and few assignments to high visibility jobs, projects, or training programs. Such barriers can block advancement at different levels of management. The department advocates a voluntary "glass ceiling" effort that identifies and removes barriers to the movement of more women and minorities into top management, at whatever level of management those barriers exist.

Reactions to the Department of Labor plan have been mixed. Although some management groups applaud its apparent understanding of the diversity in companies' promotion practices, other business groups question the need for any initiative. They say that women and minorities have simply not been in the "pipeline" long enough to reach top management levels. On the other hand, women's groups suggest that more than voluntary efforts and publicity are needed to overcome the sometimes subtle, sometimes overtly discriminatory, influences that have kept women and minorities out of the executive suite.

A 1989 Supreme Court case addressed promotions to top management. In *Price Waterhouse* v. *Hopkins* (109 S. Ct. 1775), a female plaintiff claimed that although she had generated more billable hours and business than any other partnership candidate, her promotion was denied, at least in part, because she had violated traditional sex role stereotypes. In comments written for the partnership decision, several partners stated that the plaintiff was "macho," "overcompensated for a woman," and "should dress more femininely." The Court agreed that under Title VII, sex, racial, or ethnic stereotypes should not influence promotion decisions. Businesses may be liable unless they can provide

---

[40]U.S. Department of Labor, *A Report on the Glass Ceiling Initiative* (Washington, D.C., 1991).

evidence that such stereotypes have no influence on high-level promotion decisions. Unfortunately, stereotypes die hard.

A survey of human resource managers identifies these barriers to the top:

- Assigning women and minorities to staff positions that are not viewed as training grounds for top management.
- Discounting women's and minorities' qualifications and performance.
- Providing lower returns to women and minorities (in terms of responsibility, authority, and overall compensation) for their promotions.
- Limiting access of women and minorities to informal networks of higher level managers.
- Using a restricted range of referrals and outside sources when hiring executives.[41]

Most of these barriers have also been identified by human resource management research. For example, a 1990 review of research on hiring decisions found that in 29 of 34 studies, whites were judged more qualified than minorities who had identical qualifications.[42] Research on performance appraisals also suggests that despite comparable performance, women and minorities do not receive performance ratings equal to those of white men. A common thread running through all this research is that the qualifications and performance of women and minorities are likely to be discounted when the work involved has traditionally been done by white men, when it involves supervision of white men, and when the qualifications for the work are relatively general or subjectively defined. These characteristics—traditionally the domain of white men, supervision of white men, and subjectively defined qualifications—describe many managerial positions, especially those at higher levels.

Differences in Personal Work-Related Characteristics

Differences in employee attributes and behaviors are an important factor explaining the earnings gap. These include differences in experience and seniority within a firm, continuous time in the work force, education, and the like.

Experience and Seniority. To illustrate with some data, consider experience and seniority differences among full-time workers. On average, men work 6 percent more hours

[41]*Women in Corporate Management: The Results of a Catalyst Survey* (New York: Catalyst, 1990).

[42]T. Cox, Jr., and S. M. Nkomo, "Invisible Men and Women: A Status Report on Race as a Variable in Organization Behavior Research," *Journal of Organizational Behavior* 11 (1990), pp. 419–31; G. N. Powell, "One More Time: Do Female and Male Managers Differ?" *Academy of Management Executive* 4 (1990) pp. 68–75; S. J. Spurr, "Sex Discrimination in the Legal Profession: A Study of Promotion," *Industrial and Labor Relations Review* 43, no. 4 (1990), pp. 406–17; J. H. Greenhaus, S. Parasuraman, and W. M. Wormely, "Effects of Race on Organizational Experiences, Job Performance Evaluations, and Career Outcomes," *Academy of Management Journal* 33 (1990) pp. 64–86; Renae Broderick and Carolyn Milkovich, *Breaking the Glass Ceiling* (Ithaca, N.Y.: Industrial and Labor Relations School, Cornell University, 1991).

per week than women. By the time men and women have been out of school for 6 years, women on average have worked 1.6 years, or 30 percent less than men. After 16 years out of school, women average half as much labor market experience as men.[43]

But these characteristics are changing and are likely to continue to change. A study of almost 400 members of the class of 1988 at the College of Commerce and Business Administration at the University of Illinois found striking similarities between females and males in their career choices and expected work force participation. However, the young women still expect lower salaries than their male classmates, and the size of the expected differential increases with the time horizon.[44]

Research shows that the male/female differential is reduced by about half when women are compared to men with the same years of work experience. So difference in experience is a critical factor.

Education.   So, too, are differences in the level of education and in educational specialty. Currently men and women graduate from college in nearly equal numbers. As you might expect, if the occupations women enter are changing, so too are the college majors chosen by women. And college major is the strongest factor affecting income of college graduates. A major in engineering or business brings the highest income for both men and women; majors in education the lowest.[45] In 1964, 42.5 percent of all bachelors degrees earned by women were in education; in 1981 only 18 percent of women's degrees were in this area. Fields attracting women today are those traditionally chosen by men, with the sharpest growth in professional degrees. In 1964, women earned only 5 percent of the medical degrees, 4 percent of the law degrees, and 3 percent of the MBAs. By 1984, 25 percent of the medical degrees, 32 percent of the law degrees, and 25 percent of the MBAs were earned by women. We are observing significant shifts in the education/training choices made by women.

Age.   We also know that the earnings gap varies by age of workers. The gap is larger for older than younger workers. The ratio almost disappears at ages 16–19; it is about 96 percent. At age 20–24 it is 89 percent, and, for those 55-64 years of age, it is at 65 percent.

Combining Factors.   Although many researchers studied the effects of differences in jobs and occupations and personal characteristics such as experience and education, few studies have looked at their effects on pay difference *over time*. Given that employees' pay at any point in time is a result of many factors that unfold over time, this is a serious omission. One longitudinal study examined starting and current salaries of men and women

---

[43]Fuchs, *Women's Quest for Economic Equality*.

[44]Francine Blau and Marianne Ferber, "Career Plans and Expectations of Young Women and Men," *Journal of Human Resources* 26, no. 4, pp. 581–607.

[45]Estelle James, N. Absalam, J. Conaty, and Duc-le To, "College Quality and Future Earnings" (Working paper, Department of Economics, SUNY Stony Brook, Stony Brook, NY, 1989).

hired between 1976 and 1986, using data from within a single Fortune 500 firm.[46] Controlling for education degree, college major, and prior experience, males had a 12 percent higher starting salary than females. Among college graduates, college major was a key determinant of gender differences in starting salaries. When all the variables in the study's model were included, the current salary differential among male college graduates and female college graduates was less than 3 percent. The implication is that women received greater pay *increases* after they were hired than men did, but differences in starting salary remain important and persistent contributors to gender-related pay differences.

Differences in Industries and Firms

Other factors affecting earnings differences between men and women are the industry and the firms in which they are employed. Studies report that employees in some jobs can get about a 20 percent pay increase simply by switching industries in the same geographic area while performing basically similar jobs.[47]

There is some evidence that within the same occupations, industries that employ higher percentages of women (e.g. retail, insurance) tend to pay a lower average wage than those firms in industries employing higher percentages of men. In other words, office and clerical workers, most likely women, tend to be paid less in retailing than in manufacturing or chemicals.

Differences in the firm's compensation policies and objectives within a specific industry is another factor that accounts for some of the earnings gap. As noted in Chapters 6 and 7, some firms within an industry adopt pay strategies that place them among the leaders in their industry; other firms adopt policies that may offer more employment security coupled with bonuses and gain-sharing schemes. The issue here is whether within an industry some firms are more likely to employ women than other firms and whether that likelihood leads to earnings differences.

We also know that the size of a firm is systematically related to differences in wages. Female employment is more heavily concentrated in small firms. Wages of men in large firms are 54 percent higher than wages of men in small firms. That gap was only 37 percent for women in small versus large firms.

Differences in Union Membership

Finally, we also know that belonging to a union will affect differences in earnings. Belonging to a union in the public sector seems to raise female wages more than it raises

[46]Barry A. Gerhart and George T. Milkovich, "Salaries, Salary Growth, and Promotions of Men and Women in a Large, Private Firm," *Pay Equity: Empirical Inquiries.*

[47]Reuben Gronau, "Sex-related Wage Differentials and Women's Interrupted Labor Careers—the Chicken or the Egg," *Journal of Labor Economics* 6, 31 (1988), pp. 277–301; and Barry Gerhart and Nabil El Cheikh, "Earnings and Percentage Female: A Longitudinal Study" (Working paper 89-04, Center for Advanced Human Resource Studies, Cornell University).

male wages. Little research has been devoted to studying the gender effect of union membership in the private sector.

Presence of Discrimination

So we know that many factors affect pay; discrimination may possibly be one of them.[48] But we are not in agreement as to what constitutes evidence of discrimination. Although the earnings gap is the most frequently cited example, closer inspection reveals the weaknesses in this statistic.

RESEARCH ON THE EARNINGS GAP: A MIXED BAG

Unfortunately, many studies of the earnings gap have little relevance to understanding discrimination in pay-setting practices. Three examples of these limitations are discussed: the use of unexplained residuals as evidence of pay discrimination, inferring employer-level behavior from aggregate rather than employer-specificdata, and problems with proxies.

Unexplained Residual Approach

A standard statistical approach for determining whether discrimination explains part of the gap is to try to relate pay differences to the factors just discussed above (e.g., occupation, type of work, experience, education, and the like). The procedure typically used is to regress some measure of earnings on those factors thought to legitimately influence earnings. If the average wage of men with a given set of values for these factors is not significantly different from the average wage of women with equal factors, then discrimination is not assumed to occur.

The standard statistical approach is to interpret the residual portion of the gap as discrimination.[49] This residual approach brings to mind an observation made by Carl Sagan, Cornell astronomer who hosted a PBS series designed to educate the public about the cosmos. He observed that although space exploration and research have increased our knowledge of the universe, much remains to be learned. He cautioned, "Just because we can't identify a light doesn't make it a space ship." Many people looking at the earnings gap fall into the same trap. Just because we can't explain all the differences in pay between men and women doesn't make it discrimination.

Must this residual earnings disparity be considered a function of discrimination? Consider studies on the earnings of white men. Studies that attempt to explain differences in white men's earnings, using such factors as jobs held and experience, education, time worked and age, are able to account for about 60 to 70 percent of the differences. How can we logically conclude that residual unexplained portion is discrimination among white

---

[48]Donald J. Treiman and H. J. Hartmann, eds., *Women, Work and Wages* (Washington, D.C.: National Academy Press, 1981).

[49]Felice N. Schwartz, "The Riddle of the Ring," *Across the Board*, April 1992, pp. 32–36.

men? Statistical studies are just one type of evidence that people need to consider when deciding whether pay differences are attributable to discrimination.

If they do not tell us what portion of the gap is discrimination, what do these analyses show? They show that the gap is not fully explained by a number of factors: differences in characteristics of men or women employees, differences in jobs they hold, the occupations they are in, the firms in which they are employed, the industry, and so on. But these studies do not eliminate the possibility that the discrepancy is caused by unmeasured variables other than discrimination. Nor can they rule out that wage and earnings differences are the result of voluntary behaviors.

Inferring from Aggregated Data

Many studies of the earnings gap have little relevance to understanding pay discrimination because actual pay decisions are decentralized: made by individual employers, unions, and employees. Most analysis of the earnings gap is conducted at aggregate levels. Studies using aggregate data often do not adequately include factors actually used in wage determination. This is not always because researchers are not aware of these factors; the omissions are due in large part to two problems. First, there is a lack of adequate publicly available data, and second, the proxies used are often too abstract.[50]

Consider a study that treats all employee experiences as equal (measured as age minus years of education minus five years) and all fields of education as equal (measured as years of education completed). Common sense and your own experience tell you that there are differences in the types of experience (whether it is continuous with one employer and the type of training received) and that there are differences in the specialties and quality of education (a four-year degree in social work is not equivalent to a four-year degree in electrical engineering). Anyone knowledgeable in pay determination believes that these differences are important in attracting and retaining the work force necessary for an effective organization. Hence, these differences also affect pay differences. Consider the earnings differential between Mr. and Mrs. Jones. Both have college degrees (his in psychology, hers in computer science), both are in sales (he in shoes and she in computers), and both work for private sector employers (he for J.C. Penney and she for IBM). They probably earn very different salaries, but most aggregate data would report them to have similar skills and education, and similar jobs.

Problems with Proxies

Years of education often serve as a proxy for all the differences in a person's skills and abilities and quality of the education received. Employee performance may be measured as absenteeism, and differences in firms may be measured as differences in industries,

---

[50]Barbara R. Bergmann, "Occupational Segregation, Wages, and Profits when Employers Discriminate by Race or Sex," *Eastern Economic Journal* 1 (1974), pp. 103–16; C. Selden, E. Mutari, M. Rubin, and K. Sacks, *Equal Pay for Work of Comparable Worth* (Chicago: American Library Association, 1982); and Ashenfelter and Oaxaca, "The Economics of Discrimination."

treating each firm within an industry as the same. One study even used number of children as a proxy for time spent away from the job.[51] We have reached that point as parents when we better understand a counter point, that the number of teenagers one has will increase the time spent on the job and away from home.

Another problem with the proxies used is that mere possession of a qualification or skill does not mean it is work related. Examples of cab drivers, secretaries, and house painters with college degrees are numerous.

Even if the legitimate factors fully explain pay differences between men and women, discrimination still could have occurred. First, the factors themselves may be tainted by discrimination. For example, past discrimination against women in the admission to engineering schools may have affected their earnings. Or women may be better qualified on some factors that were omitted in the analysis.

In sum, statistical analysis needs to be treated as part of a pattern of evidence and needs to reflect the wage behaviors of specific firms. If we infer behaviors from unexplained residuals, we can be misled by grossly aggregated data and poor proxies. As one reviewer has written, "It is not the quantity of studies that is lacking; it is the quality."[52]

WAGES FOR "WOMEN'S WORK"

Why are jobs held predominantly by women, almost without exception, paid less than jobs held predominantly by men? Are women's jobs fairly valued, by the same standards that are used to value other jobs, or have they been systematically undervalued and/or underpaid?[53] Do job evaluation systems give adequate recognition to job-related contributions in those jobs held primarily by women? The state of Washington conducted a study that concluded that the job of a licensed practical nurse required skill, effort, and responsibility equal to that of a campus police officer. In 1978 the state paid the licensed practical nurse, on average, $739 a month. The campus police officer was paid, on average, $1,070 a month. These salary differences were not related to productivity-related job content characteristics included in the study.[54]

It is this type of wage difference (e.g., nurses' versus police officers' wages) that is controversial. Some argue that pay differences are the result of consistent undervaluing of work done by women, and it ought to be illegal.[55] If jobs require comparable skill, effort, and responsibility, the pay must be comparable, no matter how dissimilar the job

---

[51]Barbara Norris, "Comparable Worth, Disparate Impact, and the Market Rate Salary Problem: A Legal Analysis and Statistical Application," *California Law Review* 71, no. 2 (March 1983), pp. 730–40.

[52]Donald P. Schwab, "Using Job Evaluation to Obtain Pay Equity," in *Comparable Worth: Issue for the 80's,* vol. 1.

[53]Sharon Toffey Shepela and Ann T. Viviano, "Some Psychological Factors Affecting Job Segregation and Wages," in *Comparable Worth and Wage Discrimination,* ed. H. Remick (Philadelphia: Temple University Press, 1984).

[54]Helen Remick, "Beyond Equal Pay for Equal Work: Comparable Worth in the State of Washington," in *Equal Employment Policy for Women,* ed. Ronnie Steinberg-Ratner (Philadelphia: Temple University Press, 1980), pp. 405–48; and Ronnie J. Steinberg, " 'A Want of Harmony': Perspectives on Wage Discrimination and Comparable Worth," in *Comparable Worth and Wage Discrimination.*

[55]Paula England, "Socioeconomic Explanations of Job Segregation," in *Comparable Worth and Wage Discrimination.*

content may be. Others respond that pay differences between men and women are the result of many factors, not the least of which are market factors, for which no acceptable substitute is available.[56] And they question who or what, if not market-based factors, will determine wages for such dissimilar jobs as nurses and police officers. But critics respond that current pay differentials based on market forces are discriminatory. The market is faulty, they argue, because it reflects historic *access discrimination,* when employers simply refused to hire women for most jobs. Women were restricted to only a few job categories, resulting in an oversupply of people to fill these jobs and artificially holding down wages for women's jobs relative to the rates paid for other jobs. Pay systems that value jobs today based on their market rates, these critics assert, incorporate and perpetuate this past discrimination against women and minorities. Therefore, they argue, jobs held predominantly by women ought to be paid at the market rate for "comparable" jobs held predominantly by men.[57]

COMPARABLE WORTH

Comparable worth has been debated off and on since World War II. The National Academy of Science (NAS) suggests that a comparable worth standard requires that whatever characteristics of jobs are considered worthy of compensation by a single employer (excluding market considerations) should be equally regarded, irrespective of the sex of the job incumbent. The courts do not seem inclined to interpret present laws in a manner that encompasses comparable worth. Consequently, comparable worth proponents continue to lobby for either new legislation or voluntary action on the part of employers that would include the comparable worth standard.

Much of this political activity is occurring in state and local governments. In California, for example, the largest sex- and race-based discrimination suit ever filed, affecting nearly 70,000 present and former state workers, went to trial in 1989. The California State Employees Association alleged that the state discriminated by paying job classes dominated by women and minorities less than other job classes. However, a judge dismissed key portions of the suit after finding the evidence ambiguous and the statistical methodology faulty. The union's "expert witnesses" had matched jobs for comparison purposes solely on the basis of job titles, not on job duties. Too bad they hadn't read Chapter 7.

By the early 1990s, almost half the states had begun or completed "pay equity adjustments" for state civil services. Some states specify that wages must be equal for those performing "comparable work," others require pay equity for performing work of a "comparable character." Coverage of these statutes varies from state to state.

Action at the federal level focuses on rhetoric and commissioning studies. A proposal for a "pay equity study" of federal government employees has aroused opposition from business groups, who believe that the study will be structured to conclude that pay

---

[56]George H. Hildebrand, "The Market System," in *Comparable Worth: Issues and Alternatives,* ed. E. R. Livernash (Washington, D.C.: Equal Employment Advisory Council, 1980).

[57]Bergmann, "Occupational Segregation, Wages, and Profits When Employers Discriminate by Race or Sex."

adjustments are necessary. Extending this conclusion to the private sector is seen as the next logical step, one that concerns them.

The Mechanics

Establishing a comparable worth plan typically involves the following four basic steps:

1. *Adopt a single job evaluation plan for all jobs within a unit.* If employees are unionized, separate plans can be prepared for each bargaining unit and take precedence over previous agreements. The key to a comparable worth system is a single job evaluation plan that serves as the standard for establishing pay for the company jobs with dissimilar content.
2. *All jobs with equal job evaluation results should be paid the same.* Although each factor in the job evaluation may not be equal, if the total points are equal, the wage rates must also be equal.
3. *Identify general representation (percentage male and female employees) in each job group.* A job group is all positions with similar duties and responsibilities, requires similar qualifications, is filled by similar recruiting procedures, and is paid under the same pay schedule. Typically, a female-dominated job class is defined as 60 percent or more female incumbents; a male-dominated job class has 70 percent or more male incumbents.
4. *The wage-to-job evaluation point ratio should be based on the wages paid for male-dominated jobs* since they are presumed to be free of pay discrimination.

These steps are based on the state of Minnesota's law that mandates comparable worth for all public sector employees (e.g., the state, cities, school districts, libraries).

Consider Exhibit 14.5. The solid dots represent jobs held predominantly by women (i.e., female representation greater than or equal to 60 percent). The circles represent jobs held predominantly by men (i.e., greater than or equal to 70 percent men). The policy line (solid) for the women's jobs is below and less than the policy line for male jobs (dotted line). A comparable worth policy would use the results of the single job evaluation plan and price all jobs as if they were male-dominated jobs (dotted line). Thus, all jobs with 100 job points would receive $600, all those with 200 points would receive $800, and so on.

Proponents of comparable worth are of two minds when it comes to job evaluation. Some see it as the primary technique for establishing jobs of comparable worth, as illustrated above.[58] Others see it as too subjective to rely on.[59] How dollars are actually

---

[58]Helen Remick, ed., *Comparable Worth and Wage Discrimination* (Philadelphia: Temple University Press, 1984).

[59]Ruth G. Blumrosen, "Wage Discrimination, Job Segregation and Title VII of the Civil Rights Act of 1964," *University of Michigan Journal of Law Reform* 12, no. 397 (1979), pp. 17–23; Richard W. Beatty and James R. Beatty, "Some Problems with Contemporary Job Evaluation Systems," in *Comparable Worth and Wage Discrimination;* Robert Madigan, "Comparable Worth Judgments," *Journal of Applied Psychology* 70, no. 1 (1985), pp. 137–47; Robert Grams and Donald Schwab, "An Investigation of Systematic Gender-Related Error in Job Evaluation," *Academy of Management Journal* 28, no. 2 (June 1985), pp. 279–90; and Mark Lengnick-Hall, "The Effects of Group Processes on Bias in Job Evaluation," Paper presented at 1989 Academy of Management Meetings, Washington, D.C.

EXHIBIT 14.5   Job Evaluation Points and Salary

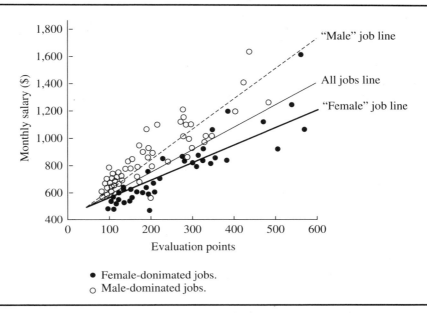

attached to job evaluation points is still being debated. Recent applications (see step 4) use market rates for male-dominated jobs to convert the job evaluation points to salaries. The point-to-salaries ratio of male-dominated jobs is then applied to female-dominated jobs.

Some question the use of male-dominated jobs rather than all job data to establish the relationship between job evaluation points and pay rates. They argue that using only male-dominated jobs will artificially inflate other job rates. The approach presumes that clerical work is subject to identical union and market forces as are police, firefighters, and craft workers. Arbitrators and legislators are struggling with this issue.

Since past pay legislation has outlawed lowering any wage to make pay equal, a comparable worth policy may require employers to pay all employees at the highest market line or point-to-dollar ratio that exists for any segment of its employees (steps 3 and 4). This translates into the rate paid for jobs held predominantly by men (Exhibit 14.5, the dotted line). Such an arrangement raises a host of issues:

- Would the unions give up their right to negotiate contracts independent of the pay arrangements in the other segments of the organization; for example, would unions B, C, D, E, etc., have to agree to the same point/dollar relationship as union A, which signed the first agreement?

- If the individual unions negotiated jointly for the same point/pay relationship, would there be any need for more than one union?

- How would an organization entice people into jobs where there were shortages because of distasteful work if there were not premium pay for the same points, or more pay for fewer points?
- If one unit in a firm pays only base salary, will it have to increase its pay level if another unit in the same firm introduces an incentive plan suitable for the business sector in which it competes?
- Must a state pay the same dollars for the same points to employees who work and live in a low-cost rural area as it does to employees in the high-cost large cities?
- Must a high-tech company raise the pay of its accountants (male dominated) to equal the pay of its engineers (also male dominated) for the same points?[60]

Underlying these points is a more basic one, which is whether legally mandating a job evaluation approach is defensible. Many employers do not use job evaluation at all. A myriad of approaches is used to determine pay ranging from market pricing to skill-based pay to gain sharing to maturity curves. A mandated job evaluation approach simply does not fit all circumstances.

Single versus Multiple Plans.   A key issue in designing a comparable worth system is the use of a single job evaluation plan across job families. In practice, the overwhelming majority of employers that use job evaluation use more than one plan to cover all jobs. A partner of Hay Associates observed:

> We, ourselves, do not know of a single case, in all the years before and after the legislation of 1963 and 1964, where a large and diverse organization in the private sector concluded that a single job evaluation method, with the same compensable factors and weightings, was appropriate for its factory, office, professional, management, technical, and executive personnel in all profit center divisions and all staff departments.[61]

Rosen, Rynes, and Mahoney add:

> The problem of making global assessments of a position's overall contribution to organizational goals and objectives cannot be underestimated. As work increases in complexity and interdependence, it becomes progressively more difficult to define common criteria of worth and to assess the unique contribution of any given position to the organization.[62]

Yet the use of a single plan seems crucial to comparable worth. The NAS study concludes, "Whatever characteristics of jobs are considered worthy of compensation by a single employer should be equally regarded, irrespective of the sex of the job incumbent."[63]

---

[60] Alvin O. Bellak, "Comparable Worth: A Practitioner's View," in *Comparable Worth: Issue for the 80s,* vol. 1.

[61] Ibid.

[62] Benson Rosen, Sara Rynes, and Thomas A. Mahoney, "Compensation, Jobs, and Gender," *Harvard Business Review,* July/August 1983, pp. 170–90.

[63] Treiman and Hartmann, *Women, Work and Wages;* Donald P. Schwab, "Job Evaluation and Pay Setting: Concepts and Practices," in *Comparable Worth: Issues and Alternatives.*

How to conduct such an evaluation in a bias-free manner is difficult to imagine. There is no way to discern with certainty what the absolute point value of any particular job is; such a value does not exist. People who advocate such approaches credit job evaluation with more explanatory power than it possesses. By relying solely on job evaluation, they are putting all their eggs in a loosely woven basket.[64]

Ontario's Experience

The province of Ontario, Canada, has accumulated the most extensive experience with comparable worth. The Ontario Pay Equity Act, in effect since 1988, covers both the private and public sectors. Employers are required to compare female-dominated job classes to male-dominated job classes. In jobs of equal value, the pay in the female class is raised if it is lower than the pay for the male job class. If there is no male job class of the same value, comparisons are made to a male job class of less worth if that class is also paid more than the female class. Pay adjustments can be phased in over time, with the timetable based on the employer's size. The law differs from the comparable worth approach described earlier in this chapter in that it requires that job evaluation plans be negotiated with all unions in the facility. Therefore, a single employer may have a number of different plans—one for each bargaining unit plus a different plan for nonunionized employees. The use of multiple plans reduces the number of possible comparisons for women who believe that their jobs are undervalued.

Ontario has wrestled with the issue of possible comparisons.[65] The law requires comparisons between female-dominated job classes and male-dominated job classes in the same bargaining unit. If the comparison is to a male class of lower value, the law says that the female job class should be paid equal to the highest wage in that lesser-valued male class. But what if that highest wage is earned by a management trainee who is only temporarily doing that job? Or what if that wage results from production-related bonuses or incentives? If no comparisons in the same bargaining unit exist, women may compare throughout the workplace. But if other jobs are valued under a different job evaluation system, it's hard to prove equal value.[66]

Employers say that the complex nature of the legislation and a flood of guidelines from the commission has slowed its implementation. Others say that the law is too vague, which sounds like a plea for more guidelines. On the other hand, lack of appropriate comparisons has left a large percentage of Ontario's working women unaffected by the act. Women who work in female-dominated workplaces such as libraries, day care centers, and nursing homes are not covered because there are no male-dominated job classes at

---

[64]Greg Hundley, "The Effects of Comparable Worth in the Public Sector on Public/Private Occupational Relative Wages," *Journal of Human Resources* (forthcoming); Erica Groshen, "The Structure of the Female/Male Wage Differential," *Journal of Human Resources* 26, no. 3, pp. 457–72.

[65]*Newsnotes,* National Committee on Pay Equity, Fall 1991, pp. 6–7.

[66]Patricia McDermott, "Pay Equity in Ontario: A Critical Legal Analysis," *Osgoode Hall Law Journal,* Summer 1990, pp. 381–407.

their workplace. An amendment has been proposed that offers alternative comparisons when no male-dominated job class exists in the same workplace.[67]

According to a report evaluating compliance with the law, the private sector is closer to compliance than the public sector in terms of developing plans and posting them. However, the size of pay equity adjustments was higher in the public sector. The law requires employers to allocate at least 1 percent of payroll each year to equity increases until the pay gaps are eliminated. Not surprisingly, most employers are refusing to allocate more than the mandated 1 percent.[68]

Who Gains? Who Pays?   An issue concerning any comparable worth proposal is whether it will benefit those who were its intended beneficiaries. A report released by Ontario's Pay Equity Commission claims that women in professional and managerial positions have benefitted the most.[69] Lower-paid female dominant job classes, such as clerical or production workers, who were the targeted beneficiaries, were either compared to other low-paying male job classes or not compared at all, because no comparable male job class could be found within the organization. The report also found a negative effect on union-management relationships and employee morale, as well as widespread confusion among employers about their obligations under the act.

Employers claim that administrative costs to comply with the legislation have been higher than anticipated—in many cases much higher than the resulting wage adjustments. That's because pay equity can't be done piecemeal. Some employers must adjust their entire pay system. At Eaton's department store, for example, female salesclerks selling women's and children's apparel typically earn only straight wages, but men selling furniture, menswear, or major appliances earn commissions. How can these two systems be reconciled? A heavily unionized workplace will probably have to adjust clerical salaries far above market wage, since the legal comparator will now be salaries that have been skewed due to union negotiating strength. A potential problem in any work site is what happens if clerk X's salary is adjusted to match maintenance worker Y's rate, which also happens to be the rate paid to clerk X's supervisor. Other employers have paid huge consulting fees to find out that their systems are evenhanded. A Toronto consultant cites one company that spent $13,000 analyzing its wages but paid only a few hundred dollars in pay increases.[70]

---

[67]"Proportional value," which is similar to the comparable worth approach advocated by Remick, and "proxy comparisons," which apply only to the public sector and which provide far more direction on whom to compare with, have been proposed.

[68]"What Works . . . Experiences with Implementation of the Pay Equity Legislation," Report prepared for Pay Equity Commission (Toronto: Avesbury Research and Consulting Limited, 1991).

[69]"An Evaluation of Pay Equity in Ontario: The First Year," Report prepared for Pay Equity Commission, (Toronto: SPR Associates, 1991).

[70]"Under Ontario's Pay-Equity Law: Administrative Costs Outweigh Pay Increases," *Compflash*, March 1992, p. 6.

Union Developments

Unions support "pay equity" as a concept. Some interpret pay equity to mean comparable worth; others use pay equity as a more all-encompassing, less well-defined term. Some unions, such as the American Federation of State, County, and Municipal Employees (AFSCME) and the Communication Workers of America (CWA) actively support comparable worth and have negotiated comparable worth-based pay increases, lobbied for legislation, filed legal suits, and attempted to educate their members and the public about comparable worth.[71]

Collective bargaining has produced more comparable worth pay increases than any other approach. The amount of union support for comparable worth is directly related to its effects on the union's membership. The public sector faces little competition for its services and is frequently better able to absorb a wage increase, since public employees are in a better position to pressure lawmakers than are taxpayers. This probably accounts for the relative success of public employees' unions in bargaining comparable worth pay adjustments. But trade-offs between higher wages and fewer jobs make unions in industries facing stiff foreign competition (e.g., International Ladies' Garment Workers' Union and the United Steel Workers) reluctant to aggressively support comparable worth.

Nationally, the AFL-CIO has adopted a resolution calling for its affiliated unions to

1. Treat sex-based pay inequities in contract negotiations like all other inequities that must be corrected.
2. Initiate joint union-employer pay equity studies, as AFSCME has already done with a number of public employers.
3. Take all other appropriate action to bring about true equality in pay for work of comparable value and to remove all barriers to equal opportunity for women.

The beauty of "equity adjustments," from a union's perspective, is that because they are a separate budget item, they do not appear to come at the expense of overall pay increases for all union members.[72]

---

[71]Sara Rynes, T. Mahoney, and B. Rosen, "Union Attitudes toward Comparable Worth," in *Pay Equity in Comparable Worth;* Karen Shallcross Koziara, "Comparable Worth: Organizational Dilemmas," *Monthly Labor Review,* December 1985, pp. 13–16; Barbara N. McLennan, "Sex Discrimination in Employment and Possible Liabilities of Labor Unions," *Labor Law Journal,* January 1982, pp. 26–35; *Breaking the Pattern of Injustice* (Washington, D.C.: American Federation of State, County, and Municipal Employees, 1983); *Pay Equity: A Union Issue for the 1980s* (Washington, D.C.: American Federation of State, County, and Municipal Employees, 1980); *Ourself: Women and Unions* (Washington, D.C.: Food and Beverage Trades Department, AFL-CIO, 1981); and Lisa Portman, Joy Ann Grune, and Eve Johnson, "The Role of Labor," in *Comparable Worth and Wage Discrimination.*

[72]Marvin J. Levine, "Comparable Worth in the 1980s: Will Collective Bargaining Supplant Legislative Initiatives and Judicial Interpretations?" *Labor Law Journal,* June 1987, pp. 323–34.

International Developments

Canada has gone further than any nation toward requiring a comparable worth pay standard. Although the province of Ontario extends its law to the private sector, the Canadian Human Rights Act, in effect since 1978, requires that equal pay for work of equal value be paid to federal employees, approximately 10 percent of the country's work force.

The International Labour Organization (ILO) has had a directive since 1951 promoting "equal pay for work of equal value," but this has been generally interpreted to mean equal pay for equal work. The European Community (EC) issued an equal pay directive in 1975, specifying elimination of all discrimination on grounds of sex for the "same work or for work to which equal value is attributed." The 12 member states are free to choose the methods most suitable for complying with the directive. As a result of complaints and subsequent court decisions, both Denmark and the United Kingdom were required to change their laws to incorporate the directive's provisions. In Denmark in 1986, the wage gap in average hourly earnings was 82 percent. In the United Kingdom it was 74 percent.

But although passage of laws may not be sufficient, it also may not be necessary. Sweden's Act on Equality between Men and Women at Work, in force since 1980, prohibits sex discrimination but does not specify equal pay for work of equal value. Yet the ratio of women's wages in 1985 was 91 percent. The narrowness of the gap has been attributed in part to the Swedish unions' practice of negotiating the largest increases for the lowest-paid workers, which narrows the wage structure and also the wage gap.[73]

Costs

Opposition to comparable worth legislation is almost a reflex action for many employers. Legislation constrains their ability to act, to redesign pay systems, and to meet changing conditions. In addition, legislation usually translates into increased costs. Nevertheless, some employers that oppose a mandated approach to comparable worth are investigating how it could be implemented and its expected costs.

Private sector data on costs of comparable worth adjustments are not available, for competitive reasons. When adjustments have been made in the public sector, there is a wide variation in the magnitude of costs. Hawaii, for example, appropriated $1 million in 1987 for "equity adjustments," even though a task force found only minimal inequities.[74] In Iowa, $32 million worth of comparable worth adjustments affected 60 percent of the state's employees. In contrast, $20 million of adjustments were shared by about 30 percent of Michigan state employees.

In Minnesota, where coverage extends to all local cities, counties, and school districts, costs statewide have averaged 1.7 percent of payroll for school districts, 4.1 percent for cities, and 3.8 percent for counties. At the state level, adjustments totaling $22.2 million,

---

[73]"Closing the Wage Gap: An International Perspective" (National Committee on Pay Equity: Washington, D.C., October 1988).

[74]Survey of State-Government Level Pay Equity Act.

approximately 3.7 percent of payroll, were negotiated for clerical and health care workers. The case at the end of this chapter is adapted from an arbitration hearing in a Minnesota city. The local police believed their pay raises should be comparable to pay raises police officers in other municipalities were receiving, even though the city's "pay equity analysis" dictated a wage freeze.

How generalizable are these figures? One writer estimated costs at .7 percent to 5 percent of payroll but did not report the underlying models used to arrive at those estimates.[75] A simple model shown in Exhibit 14.6 allows us to make an initial estimate of the cost of comparable worth adjustments. Perlman and Grune estimate a 50–20 percent pay difference in male-female jobs that have the same job evaluation points in most firms.[76] We can use their 20 percent figure as the size of the wage adjustment required and further assume that 25 percent of the firm's entire payroll is earned by people whose wages need to be increased. Based on the formula in Exhibit 14.6, the adjustment is a 5 percent increase in the employer's total wage bill. In organizations in which wage differences are less than 20 percent or a smaller percent of the total wage bill is paid to female-dominated jobs, the percentage would be smaller.

A 5 percent increase in total wage costs may not be too high a price for some employers—those that can pass the costs on in the form of higher prices or increased taxes, or those whose overall labor costs are a very small portion of total costs (e.g., petroleum firms). Conversely, those employers facing greater competition and with a higher percentage of employees receiving adjustments will find a 5 percent increase in their wage costs intolerable.

Obviously, the model in Exhibit 14.6 oversimplifies the real costs involved. It calculates the cost for only a single period; it does not include additional costs resulting from benefits tied to pay level (e.g., pensions, overtime pay, social security).

EXHIBIT 14.6 Preliminary Calculations of Comparable Worth's Addition to Wage Bill

---

Percent Increase $= DF$

where

D = Percent differential between wage for female-dominated occupations and comparable male-dominated occupations

F = Percent of total wages presently paid to members of female-dominated occupations

If $D = 20\%$ $F = 30\%$, comparable worth adds 6 percent to total wage bill.

If $D = 15\%$ $F = 20\%$, comparable worth adds 3 percent to total wage bill.

---

[75]Cook, *Comparable Worth: A Case Book of Experiences in States and Localities, 1986 Supplement*. See also Richard Arvey and Katherine Holt, "The Cost of Alternative Comparable Worth Strategies," *Compensation and Benefits Review,* September-October 1988, pp. 37–46.

[76]Nancy Perlman and Joy Ann Grune, "Comparable Worth Testimony of the National Committee on Pay Equity," Presented before the U.S. House of Representatives, Subcommittees on Civil Service, Human Resources, and Compensation and Employee Benefits, 1982.

Some advocates of comparable worth try to gain support by using the term *pay equity*—no one wants to be against equity. Others say comparable worth penalizes women who have made the efforts to get the training and experience that allowed them to move into higher paying jobs. The concept can evoke strong feelings. But the pay determination process has always had a political aspect. Unionized workers have frequently been able to obtain higher wages than have comparable unorganized workers. So if women can convince employers to adopt comparable worth, why shouldn't they? The issue then becomes whether it should be mandated. Or should it be part of the ongoing collective bargaining process?

The bottom line is that there simply is no intrinsic economic worth to any one job or group of jobs or job structure.[77] Why should a nurse be paid more than a ditch digger? Why should a ditch digger be paid more than a nurse? Within limits, workers are paid what is required—to get people to do work, which is determined through the confluence of many forces: the markets, unions, individual preferences, and so on. Who is to say another system is "fairer"? Fairer to whom?[78]

SUMMARY

Pay discrimination laws require special attention for several reasons. First, these laws regulate the design and administration of pay systems. Second, the definition of pay discrimination, and thus the approaches used to defend pay practices, are in a state of flux. Many of the provisions of these laws simply require sound pay practices that should have been employed in the first place. And sound practices are those with three basic features:

1. They are work related.
2. They are related to the mission of the enterprise.
3. They include an appeals process for employees who disagree with the results.

Achieving compliance with these laws rests in large measure on the shoulders of compensation managers. It is their responsibility to ensure that the pay system is properly designed and managed.

Should comparable worth be legally mandated? Not surprisingly, opinions vary. But how much, if any, comparable worth policy will diminish the earnings differential remains an unanswered question. The earnings differential is attributable to many factors. Discrimination, whether it be access or valuation, is but one factor. Others include market force, industry and employer differences, and union bargaining priorities. Compensation managers need to examine critically traditional pay practices to ensure that they are complying with regulations. Certainly, the focus needs to be on pay discrimination.

Is all this detail on interpretation of pay discrimination really necessary? Yes. Without understanding the interpretation of pay discrimination legislation, compensation managers

---

[77]June O'Neill, "An Argument against Comparable Worth," in *Comparable Worth: Issue for the 80's,* vol. 1.

[78]Greenberg and McCarty, "Comparable Worth: An Issue of Fairness."

risk violating the law, exposing their employers to considerable liability and expense, and losing the confidence and respect of all employees when a few are forced to turn to the courts to gain nondiscriminatory treatment.

REVIEW QUESTIONS

1. What is the difference between access and valuation discrimination?
2. Differentiate between disparate impact and disparate treatment, using pay practices as your examples. (Your illustrative practices may be legal or illegal.)
3. What is the relationship between the Equal Pay Act and Title VII of the Civil Rights Act?
4. What are the reasons given to indicate a need for a comparable worth standard? Why hasn't a comparable worth standard been embraced by all employers?
5. What are the pros and cons of labor market data in setting wages? Can you defend their use?
6. How would you design a pay system that was based on comparable worth?

Your Turn:
Wayzata Police Officers

Background

The following information is based on an actual interest arbitration case that took place in Wayzata, Minnesota, to decide issues contained in the collective bargaining agreement between the city of Wayzata and the Law Enforcement Union. The relevant issue is salary increases for patrol officers.

The union has requested an increase of 5 percent in the first year and 5 percent in the second year. It bases its proposal on external wage comparisons with other police departments in the Wayzata geographical district and other cities that have been determined demographically comparable. Such market comparisons suggest that the requested salary increases are justified.

The city proposes a wage freeze in the first year, based upon applicable comparisons with other cities and the requirements of Minnesota's Comparable Worth Legislation (CWL). The city argues that CWL considerations manifest a clear legislative intent to downgrade the use of market wage rates and that any raise to be awarded should in no event exceed the 3.25 percent increase already granted to the public works employees.

The debate revolves primarily around the meaning and application of CWL. Applicable statutory provisions read as follows:

1. Every political subdivision of this state shall establish equitable compensation relationships between female-dominated, male-dominated, and balanced classes of employees.

2. The arbitrator shall consider the equitable compensation relationship standards established under this (comparable worth law) together with other standards appropriate to interest arbitration. The arbitrator shall consider both the results of a job evaluation study and any employee objections to the study.

3. Job positions bear reasonable relationships to one another if

a. The compensation for positions that require comparable skill, effort, responsibility, working conditions, and other relevant work-related criteria is comparable.

b. The compensation for positions that require differing skill, effort, responsibility, working conditions, and other relevant work-related criteria is proportional to the skill, effort, responsibility, working conditions, and other relevant work-related criteria required.

Additional Information

The Consumer Price Index (CPI; see Chapter 15 for more detail) indicates an overall increase of 4.3 percent during the past year and a 5.3 percent increase from June of the past year to June of the current year. The increase in CPI during the next year is projected to be between 4.4 percent and 5.2 percent.

Wayzata uses a quantitative job analysis system to support its job evaluation. Exhibit 1 shows the police officers' job evaluation points-to-wages ratio, in comparison to ratios for others jobs. It shows an extremely high points-to-wages ratio for this job.

Discussion

Divide the class into thirds. One third is the union team and presents the union arguments. One third presents the city's position. The final third of the class makes up the arbitration panel who will issue a discussion.

Issues for the Union

As expert witness for the union, you will want to evaluate the current system for job evaluation. Will a quantitative job evaluation process produce results useful in a comparable worth setting? Will it effectively/sufficiently differentiate between a wide range of jobs? Should there be a mechanism through which

EXHIBIT 1 **Wayzata Pay Equity Analysis: Market Line Generated Using Regression Analysis, with Additional Lines Showing 90% of Market and 110% of Market**

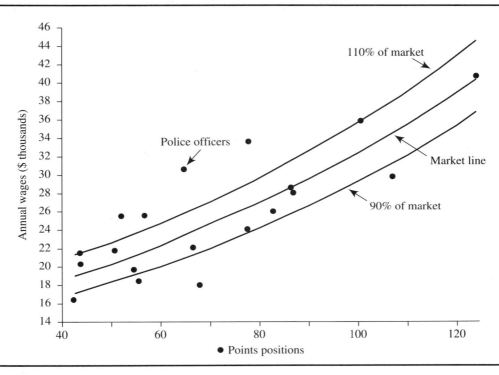

Issues for the City

How might you respond to the union's criticisms regarding the quantitative job evaluation process as applied to the police officers' jobs? Is it realistic to expect that job evaluation be an objective measure for which we can achieve reliability and validity, or is it better characterized as a subjective process designed and continually modified to value work so that it "works" for the system and its participants? How important is employee participation in the process? Why? How does the language of the CWL treat market wage rates or external relationships as

employees can offer feedback on the final outcome (i.e., job descriptions and job evaluation scores)? What questions and issues are relevant to the determination of salaries in a comparable worth state?

Do not focus on this particular job evaluation method. Rather, focus on job evaluation per se and whether a quantitative job evaluation method developed to cover a wide range of jobs can adequately evaluate the police officers' jobs. Is job evaluation really "measurement" or merely rules for negotiation? Wayzata is a wealthy community; emphasize your market comparisons with other police departments.

a determinant of compensation relationships? Are the revenues and expenditures incurred by the city relevant to the determination of police officers' pay raises? How should market data be handled, and what are relevant comparisons?

Issues for the Arbitrator

As the arbitrator, you have the legal duty to decide how to weight the usefulness of the job evaluation system against the legislative intent of CWL. What conclusions might the legislation lead you to in terms of the relevance of market data for determining compensation relationships? What types of data might constitute "other standards" appropriate to interest arbitration? How will your decision about police officers' wages impact the wages of female-dominated professions valued comparably? Should police officers be treated specially by receiving awards greater than those for comparable jobs outside law enforcement? Should the financial burden to the city of raising wages for female-dominated classes be a consideration in your decision about police officers' wages? Does the projected rise in price levels as indicated by the CPI make a difference?

EXHIBIT VI.1   The Pay Model

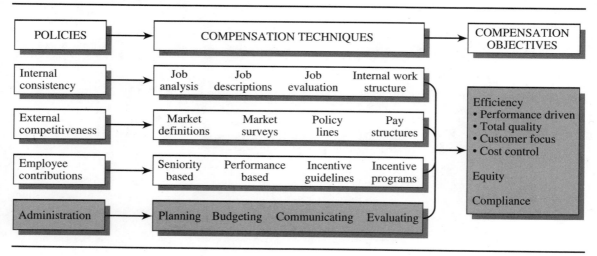

PART VI

Managing the System

Let us return to the pay model shown previously and in Exhibit VI.1. We have covered three basic strategic decisions—consistency, competitiveness, and contribution—along with the specific techniques and decisions required to achieve objectives such as achieving competitive advantage, fair treatment of employees, and compliance with regulations. We have also examined in the preceding two chapters the role of government in design of pay systems and in pay discrimination. Now we take up the fourth, and last, basic strategic decision shown in the pay model, the administration of the system. Many facets of pay administration have already been examined. Yet several important issues remain. These are covered in this final part of the book.

The most important remaining issue concerns managing costs. In fact, one of the key reasons for being systematic about pay decisions is to control costs. Some basic questions that need to be answered include these: What are the labor costs associated with recommended pay decisions? How can the labor costs be contained? How are these costs to be budgeted and managed?

In addition to these questions, other administration issues also need to be considered. The best-designed system in the world will founder if it is ineffectively implemented and managed. How will line managers and employees participate in administering the system? How does the system help achieve the organization objectives? What should line managers and employees be told about the system? Why? Can the effectiveness of the pay system be evaluated?

The objective of Part VI is to answer these questions and discuss the techniques involved in administering the pay system. Techniques for managing costs, budgeting, and administration are discussed in Chapter 15. Chapter 16 examines compensation systems designed for employee groups working in special circumstances. These include executives, international employees, sales personnel, scientists and engineers, and first-level supervisors. As noted throughout the book, unions often play a significant role in the pay determination process. The book therefore concludes with a separate chapter, 17, devoted to the role of unions in compensation management.

15 Budgets and Administration

Chapter Outline

John Russell, former American Compensation Association Board member, was approached by his Missouri community to develop a salary plan for the city. He worked on it diligently and submitted the plan.

Subsequently, he decided to run for the position of alderman on the city council and was elected. His salary program was then brought before the council for a vote. Mr. Russell voted against his own program. He explained his behavior by commenting, "I never realized how tight the budget was!"

Today, managers of compensation should not share Mr. Russell's dilemma. They are business partners. The financial status of the organization, the competitive pressures it faces, and budgeting are integral to managing compensation. The cost implications of decisions such as updating the pay structure, merit increases, or gain-sharing proposals are critical for making sound decisions. Consequently, budgets are an important part of managing compensation; they are also part of managing human resources and the total organization.[1] Creating a compensation budget involves trade-offs among the basic pay policies—how much of the increase in external market rates should be budgeted according to employee contributions to the organization's success compared to automatic across-the-board increases. Trade-offs also occur over short- versus long-term incentives, over pay increases contingent on performance versus seniority, and over direct pay (cash) compared to benefits. Budgeting also involves trade-offs between how much to emphasize compensation compared to other aspects of human resource management. In such cases, managers must decide the financial resources to deploy toward compensation compared to staffing (e.g., work force size and job security) compared to training (e.g., work force skills) and so on. The human resource budget implicitly reflects the organization's human resource strategies; it becomes an important part of the human resource plan. Finally, budgeting in the total organization involves allocating financial resources to human resources and/or technology, capital improvements, and the like. So from the perspective of a member of the city council, John Russell ended up making different resource allocation decisions than he might have made from the perspective of the compensation manager. Today's managers of compensation need to be business partners. They need to understand and demonstrate how compensation decisions help achieve organization success while treating employees fairly.

The four basic pay policies dealing with consistency, competitiveness, contribution, and administration serve to guide and regulate pay decisions. In turn, the compensation systems (techniques) are designed to be consistent with these policies and to achieve specific pay objectives. Pay systems are intended to serve as mechanisms that assist managers to make better decisions about pay. How the pay systems are used by managers involves the administration of pay.

---

[1]Harry J. Holzer, "Wages, Employer Costs, and Employee Performance in the Firm," Paper presented at ILR-Cornell Research Conference on "Do Compensation Policies Matter?" Ithaca, N.Y., 1989; Michael Guthman, "Managing Total Labor Costs," *Compensation and Benefits Review,* November–December 1991, pp. 52–60.

ADMINISTRATION AND THE PAY MODEL

Consider making pay decisions without a formal system. Under such an arrangement, each manager would have total flexibility to pay whatever seemed to work at the moment. Total decentralization of compensation decision making, carried to a ridiculous extreme, would result in a chaotic array of rates. Employees could be treated inconsistently and unfairly. The objective of individual managers and some employees may be served, but the overall fair treatment of employees and the organization's objectives may be ignored.

This may seem like textbook hyperbole to make a point, but it is not. At the beginning of this century, the "contract system" set up highly skilled workers as managers as well as workers. The employer agreed to provide the "contractor" with floor space, light, power, and the necessary raw or semifinished materials. The contractor both hired and paid labor. Bethlehem Steel operated under such a "decentralized" contract system. Skilled workers and plan captains had wide discretion; pay inconsistencies for the same work were common. Some contractors demanded kickbacks from employees' pay checks; many hired their relatives and friends. Dissatisfaction and grievances became widespread, resulting in legislation and an increased interest in unions.[2]

Lest we pass the "contract system" off as ancient history dredged up by overzealous compensation professors, read on. Some contemporary experts at the end of the century are promoting network organizations such as Benetton and Apple Computer, which rely on networks of independent parties to perform the essential functions of their businesses. Networking is linked to the concept of outsourcing. *Outsourcing* means that organizations secure a growing range of services and supplies from independent, external vendors. Ultimately, some see outsourcing driven to its logical extreme as individual contractors or small teams. "All individual workers will be self-employed business units."[3] Look back to the turn of the century, replace the term *contract system* with *outsourcing*, and the similarities emerge. Will dissatisfaction, unfair treatment, cost sharing, and risk shifting to employees again be the result?

To avoid this result, any management system, including the compensation system, needs to be goal directed. Compensation is managed to achieve the three pay model objectives: efficiency, equity, and compliance. Properly designed pay techniques help managers achieve these objectives. Rather than goal-directed tools, however, pay systems often degenerate into bureaucratic burdens or blindly follow the fads and fashions of the day. Techniques become ends in themselves rather than focusing on objectives. Operating managers may complain that pay techniques are more a hindrance than a help, and these managers are frequently correct. So any discussion of administration must again raise the questions: What does this technique do for us? How does it help us better achieve our

---

[2] Sanford M. Jacoby, "Industrial Labor Mobility in Historical Perspective," *Industrial Relations*, Spring 1983, pp. 261–82; T. J. Schlereth, *Victorian America: Transformations in Everyday Life, 1876–1915* (New York: Harper Collins, 1991); E. L. Otey, *Employers' Welfare Work* 123 (Washington, D.C.: Bureau of Labor Statistics, May 15, 1913).

[3] W. Davidson and S. Davis, "Management and Organization Principles for the Information Economy," *Human Resource Management*, Winter 1990, pp. 365–84.

objectives? Are employees fairly treated? Although it is possible to design a system that includes internal consistency, external competitiveness, and employee contributions, the system will not achieve its objectives without competent administration.

Although many pay administration issues have been discussed throughout the book, a few remain to be called out explicitly. Therefore, this chapter covers a variety of compensation administration issues, including (1) managing labor costs, (2) inherent controls, (3) forecasting and budgeting, (4) communication and appeals, (5) structuring the compensation function, and (6) auditing and evaluating the pay system.

MANAGING LABOR COSTS

You already know many of the factors that affect labor costs. As shown in Exhibit 15.1,

$$\text{Labor costs} = \text{Employment} \times \left(\begin{array}{c} \text{Average cash} \\ \text{compensation} \end{array} + \begin{array}{c} \text{Average benefit} \\ \text{cost} \end{array} \right)$$

Using this model, there are three main factors to control in order to manage labor costs: employees (i.e., employee numbers, hours worked), average cash compensation (i.e., wages, bonuses), and average benefit costs (i.e., health and life insurance, pensions). The cash and benefits factors are this book's focus. However, if our objective is to better manage labor costs, it should be clear that all three factors need attention. Controlling benefit costs were discussed at length in Chapters 11 and 12. Here we concentrate on controlling employment and the average salary.

Controlling Employment: Head Count and Hours

Managing the number of employees (head count) or the hours worked is the most obvious and perhaps most common approach to managing labor costs. Obviously, paying the same to fewer employees is less expensive. Employers who reduce their work forces get headlines. There is even some evidence that announcement of layoffs and plant closings have favorable effects on stock prices because the stock market reacts positively to events

---

EXHIBIT 15.1   Managing Labor Costs

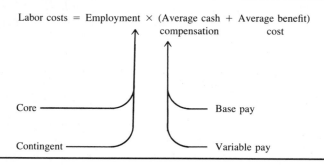

designed to improve cash flow and control costs. Obviously, the adverse effects of work force reduction, such as loss of trained and talented employees, and loss of unrealized potential productivity, need to be factored into decisions to downsize.

To manage labor costs better, many employers attempt to buffer themselves and employees by establishing different relationships with different groups of employees. As Exhibit 15.2 depicts, the two groups are commonly referred to as *core employees,* with whom a strong and long-term relationship is desired, and *contingent workers,* whose employment agreements may cover only short, specific time periods.[4] Rather than expand/contract the core work force, many employers achieve flexibility and control labor costs by expanding/contracting the contingent work force.

The logic underlying the "network" organization referred to earlier is to shrink the core and expand the contract or contingent work force. Hence, the fixed portion of labor costs becomes smaller and the variable portion longer. And one can expand/contract the variable portion more easily than the core.

The pay for core employees has been the main focus of this book. What is known about the compensation of contingent employees? Not enough. Contingent workers are not a homogeneous group; their ranks include part-time and full-time employees,

EXHIBIT 15.2   Core and Contingent Employees

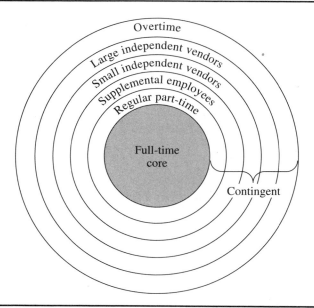

[4]Richard S. Belous, "How Human Resource Systems Adjust to the Shift toward Contingent Workers," *Monthly Labor Review,* March 1989, pp. 7–12.

temporaries, consultants, "life-of-project" workers, leased employees, and subcontractors. One fourth of the U.S. work force is estimated to be contingent; this group is growing twice as fast as the overall civilian labor force. The Bureau of Labor Statistics reports that part-time workers earn less per hour and often do not receive employee benefits such as health insurance. However, given the wide mix of employees classified as contingent, we need to be cautious in generalizing. Nevertheless, contingent workers appear to be cheaper than core employees, all things considered. And the historical mistreatment of these employees raises a flag of concern for the future.

Rather than defining employment in terms of number of workers, hours of work is often used. For nonexempt employees, hours over 40 per week are more expensive (1.5 × regular wage). Hence, another approach to managing labor costs is to examine overtime hours versus adding to the work force.

Note that the three factors—employment, cash compensation, and benefits cost—are not independent. Overtime hours require higher wages, for example. Other examples of interdependence are the apparent lower wages (and lack of benefits) for some contingent workers, or a program that sweetens retirement packages to make early retirement attractive. Sweetened retirements drive head count down and usually affect the most expensive head count: older, more experienced employees. Hence, the average wage and health care costs for the remaining (younger) work force will probably be lowered too.[5]

Controlling Average Cash Compensation

Controlling the average cash compensation, as shown in Exhibit 15.1, includes managing the adjustment in average salary level for the jobs performed and in variable compensation such as annual bonuses, gain sharing, and the like.

Average Salary Level.   A wide variety of approaches is used to manage adjustments to average salary level. Here we discuss two basic approaches: (1) "top down," in which upper management determines pay and allocates it "down" to each subunit and to individual employees for the plan year, and (2) "bottom up," in which individual employees' pay for the next plan year is forecasted and summed up to create an organization salary budget.

CONTROL SALARY LEVEL: TOP DOWN

Top down, unit level budgeting involves estimating the pay increase budget for an entire organization unit.[6] Once the total budget is determined, it is then allocated to each manager, who plans how to distribute it among subordinates. There are many approaches

---

[5]Nicholas Damico and Barbara Graham, "Early Retirement Incentive Window Plans: New Hurdles," *Benefits Law Journal,* Spring 1992, pp. 89–101.

[6]Robert Meehan and G. Victor Lemesis, "Compensation Plan Analysis," *HR Magazine,* February 1990, pp. 69–72.

EXHIBIT 15.3   Planned Level Rise

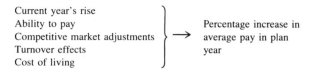

---

to unit level budgeting in use. A typical one, controlling the planned pay-level rise, will be considered. A planned pay-level rise is simply the percentage increase in average pay for the unit that is planned to occur.

As shown in Exhibit 15.3, the decision about how much to increase the average pay level planned for the next period is influenced by several factors: how much the average level was increased this period, ability to pay, competitive market pressures, turnover effects, cost-of-living, and so on.

Current Year's Rise

This is the percentage by which the average wage changed in the past year; mathematically:

$$\text{Percent level rise} = 100 \times \frac{\text{Average pay at year end} - \text{Average pay at year beginning}}{\text{Average pay at the beginning of the year}}$$

Ability to Pay

Obviously, the employer's financial circumstances affect the decision regarding how much to increase the average pay level. Financially healthy employers may wish to maintain their competitive positions in the labor market, and some may even share outstanding financial success through bonuses and profit sharing.

Conversely, financially troubled employers will be constrained and may not be able to maintain competitive market positions. Note that the conventional response in these circumstances has been to reduce employment [Labor costs = Employment × (Cash compensation + Benefits)]. However, other options are to reduce the rate of increase in average pay by controlling adjustments in base pay and/or variable pay.

Competitive Market Adjustments

In Chapter 7, we discussed how managers determine an organization's competitive position in relation to its competitors. Recall that a distribution of market rates for benchmark jobs was collected and analyzed into a single "average" wage for each benchmark. This "average market wage" became the "going market rate" and was compared to the average wage paid by the organization for its benchmark jobs.[7] The market rates adjust differently each year in response to a variety of pressures.

Turnover Effects

Variously referred to as *churn* or *slippage,* the turnover effect recognizes the fact that when people leave (through layoffs, quitting, retiring), they typically are replaced by workers earning a lower wage.[8] Depending on the degree of turnover, the effect can be substantial. Turnover effect can be calculated as Annual turnover × Planned average increase. For example, let us assume that an organization's labor cost equals $1 million a year. If the turnover rate is 15 percent and the planned average increase is 6 percent, the turnover effect is 0.9 percent, or $9,000 (0.009 × $1,000,000). So instead of budgeting $60,000 to fund a 6 percent increase, only $51,000 is needed. Note that from a total labor cost perspective, the lower average pay will also reduce those benefit costs linked to base pay, such as pensions. So the turnover effect influences both average pay and benefits costs in the total labor cost equation.

Cost of Living

Although there is little research to support it, employees undoubtedly compare their pay increases to changes in their costs of living, and unions consistently argue that increasing living costs justify adjustments in pay.[9]

A Distinction.   It is important to distinguish among three related concepts: the cost of living, changes in prices in product and service markets, and changes in wages in labor markets. As Exhibit 15.4 shows, changes in wages in labor markets are measured through wage surveys. These changes are incorporated into the system through market adjustments in the budget and updating the policy line and range structure. The second concept, price changes of goods and services in product and service markets, is measured by several government indexes, one of which is the consumer price index. The third concept, the cost of living, is more difficult to measure. Employees' expenditures on goods and services depend on many things: marital status, number of dependents and ages, personal preferences, and so on. Different employees probably experience different costs of living, and the only accurate way to measure them is to examine the personal financial expenditures of each employee.

The three concepts are interrelated. Wages from the labor market are costs of producing goods and services, and changes in wages create pressures on prices. Similarly,

---

[7]Beth Enslow, "Benchmarking Bonanza," *Across the Board,* April 1992, pp. 16–22; Mark Lerner, "Measuring Pay Costs in Your Organization against Pay in Other Organizations," *Personnel,* August 1988, pp. 70–73.

[8]Martin G. Wolf, "A Model to Improve Cashflow Payroll Cost Forecasting," *Compensation and Benefits Review,* January–February 1988, pp. 50–57.

[9]Daniel J. B. Mitchell, "Should the Consumer Price Index Determine Wages?" *California Management Review,* Fall 1982, pp. 5–19.

EXHIBIT 15.4   Three Distinct but Related Concepts and Their Measures

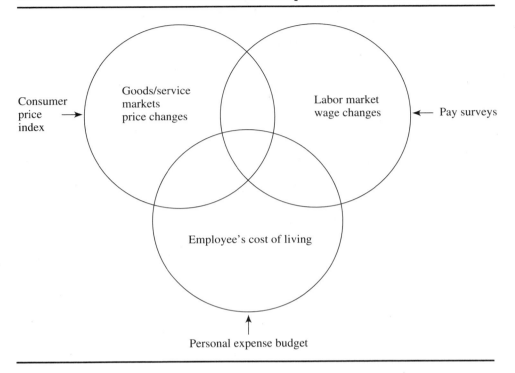

changes in the prices of goods and services create needs for increased wages in order to maintain the same lifestyle. Many people refer to the consumer price index (CPI) as a "cost of living" index, and many employers choose, as a matter of pay policy or in response to union pressures, to tie wages to it. But in doing so, employers are confounding the concepts of living costs and labor market costs. The CPI does not necessarily reflect an individual employee's cost of living.

What Is the CPI?   The CPI measures changes over time in prices of a hypothetical market basket of goods and services.[10] The present index is based on a 1972–73 study of the actual buying habits of 38,000 individuals. From this study, 265 categories of major expenditures were derived, and weights were assigned based on each category's percentage of total expenditures. For example, the index gives a weighting of 5.02 percent to auto purchases. This means that of the total money spent by all 38,000 people in the 1972–73 study, 5.02 percent of it was spent to buy new cars. This weighting plan measures

---

[10]"How Reliable Is the Consumer Price Index?" *Business Week*, April 29, 1991, pp. 70–71.

both the price of cars and the frequency of new car purchases. To determine the new car component for today's CPI, today's price of a new car identically equipped to the one purchased in 1972–73 is multiplied by the factor weight of 5.02 percent. The result is called today's *market basket price* of a new car.

There is even an index for those readers who plan to lead the "good life." The annual Moet index tracks price changes for a dozen "upper crust" items. In 1992, the biggest increase was for Beluga caviar, $47 for a 30-gram jar—up 41 percent from 1991. Other items include Rolex watches for $11,700, up 12 percent, and Rolls Royce Cornich, up 12 percent to $205,500.

The CPI is the subject of public interest because changes in it trigger changes in labor contracts, social security payments, federal and military pensions, and food stamp eligibility, as well as employers' pay budgets. One source estimates that more than one half of the U.S. population is affected by payout changes tied to the CPI.[11] Tying budgets or payouts to the CPI is called *indexing*. Note that the cost of living is one of the factors, shown in Exhibit 15.3, that influences the percentage increase of average salary level. It also may affect cost of benefits faced by employers either through health insurance coverage or pension costs.

The CPI gets no respect these days. One of the main reasons is that the rigid "market basket" bears less and less resemblance to the real world purchases of workers. It includes the price of Macintosh apples, but if prices change, I switch varieties to golden delicious, or crispens. I've even been known to substitute an orange or a banana. Substitutes are not easily handled in the CPI. Another criticism is that it is difficult to include discount prices. Thus, a trip to the car dealer, which the Bureau of Labor Statistics makes, does not really capture the difference between sticker and real prices. And pricing services, especially medical care, is difficult in light of the rapidly changing types and qualities of service.

Geographical Differences in the CPI.   In addition to the national CPI, separate indexes are calculated monthly for five metropolitan areas and bimonthly for 23 other metropolitan areas and various regions. These local CPIs typically are more variable than the national indexes. They do not, as some mistakenly believe, indicate whether prices are absolutely higher in a particular area. Changes in the CPI indicate only whether prices have increased more or less rapidly in an area since the base period. For example, a CPI of 210 in Chicago and 240 in Atlanta does not necessarily mean that it costs more to live in Atlanta. It does mean that prices have risen faster in Atlanta since the base year than they have in Chicago, since both cities started with bases of 100.

An Example.   Let us assume that the managers take into account all these factors—current year's rise, ability to pay, market adjustments, turnover effects, and changes in the cost of living—and decide that the planned rise in average salary for the next period is 6.3 percent. This means that the organization has set a target of 6.3 percent as the

---

[11]Jerry Newman, "The Consumer Price Index: Issues and Understanding," Paper presented at the American Compensation Association National Conference, Scottsdale, Ariz., October 22, 1981.

increase in average salary that will occur in the next budget period. It does not mean that everyone's increase will be 6.3 percent. It means that at the end of the budget year, the average salary calculated to include all employees will be 6.3 percent higher than it is now.

The next question is how do we hand out that 6.3 percent budget in a way that is best designed to accomplish managers' objectives for the pay system and thus the organization.

Distributing the Budget to Subunits. A variety of methods to determine what percentage of the salary budget each manager should receive exists. Some use a uniform percentage, in which each manager gets an equal percentage of the budget based on the salaries of each subunit's employees. Others vary the percentage allocated to each manager based on pay-related problems, such as turnover or performance, which have been identified in that subunit.

Once salary budgets are allocated to each subunit manager, they become a constraint: a limited fund of money that each manager has to allocate to subordinates. Typically, merit increase guidelines are used to help managers make these allocation decisions.

Merit Increase Grids

Merit increase grids as devices to recognize employee performance were discussed in a previous chapter. Here we reconsider them as budget devices. First, they control the reward schedules to help ensure that different managers grant consistent increases to employees with similar performance ratings and in the same position in their ranges. Second, grids help control costs. Examples of grids are included in Chapter 9. Once a grid to deliver a 6.3 percent budget is determined, for example, it is used by managers to plan each employee's increase. (The logic and calculations for alternative merit grids are available in the appendix to this chapter.)

CONTROL SALARY LEVEL: BOTTOM UP

Bottom-up budgeting requires managers to forecast the pay increase they will recommend for each of their subordinates during the upcoming plan year. Exhibit 15.5 shows an example of the process involved. Each of the steps within this compensation forecasting cycle is described here.

1. *Instruct managers in compensation policies and techniques*. Train managers in the concepts of a sound pay-for-performance policy and in standard company compensation techniques such as the use of pay increase guidelines and budgeting techniques. Also communicate the salary ranges and market data.
2. *Study pay increase guidelines*. Review with the managers the purpose of increase guidelines and how to use them.
3. *Distribute forecasting instructions and worksheets*. Furnish managers with the forms and instructions necessary to preplan increases.

EXHIBIT 15.5   Compensation Forecasting and Budgeting Cycle

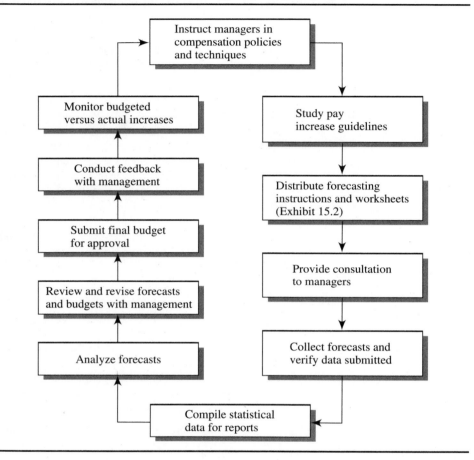

Exhibit 15.6 is an example of the forecasting worksheets that might be provided. In this exhibit, we see Sarah Ross's performance rating history, past raises, and timing of these raises. Some argue that providing such detailed data and recommendations to operating managers makes the system too mechanical. It removes the manager from planning and making judgments about individual employee pay. On the other hand, such histories ensure that managers are at least aware of this information and that pay increases for any one period should be part of a continuing message to individual employees, not some ad hoc response to short-term changes.

EXHIBIT 15.6 **A Pay History**

Name Sarah Ross	YEAR END EXPERIENCE 2	EMPLOYMENT DATE 08-22-89	YEAR AND SERVICE 21/04	YEAR FIRST DEGREE 89	HIGHEST DEGREE BS	HIGHEST DISCIPLINE Acctg.	SOC SEC NO 458-56-5332
Position Accountant	CLASSIF LEVEL 26	EMPL MO LEVEL	DATE ASSIGNED TO POSITION 08-22-89	DATE ASSIGNED TO CLASS LEVEL OF POSITION 08-22-89			

Previous Salary Change

DATE	PERFORMANCE RATING	AMOUNT	%	MONTHS INTERVAL	ANNUAL VALUE	FIC	SALARY	SALARY RANGE					
								UPPER BAND OR RANGE MAX		BAND MIDPOINT	LOWER BAND OR RANGE MIN		
02 01 90	2.0						23040						
12 01 90	3.0	1920	8.3	10	10		24960						

Forecast Salary Change

09 01 91		2496	10.0	10	12		27456	30018	28016	25214

4. *Provide consultation to managers.* Offer advice and salary information services to manager upon request.

5. *Collect forecasts and verify data submitted.* Audit the increases forecasted to ensure that they do not exceed the pay guidelines and are consistent with appropriate ranges.

6. *Compile statistical data for reports.* Prepare statistical data in order to feed back the outcomes of pay forecasts and budgets.

7. *Analyze forecasts.* Examine each manager's forecast and recommend changes based on noted inequities among different managers.

8. *Review and revise forecasts and budgets with management.* Consult with managers regarding the analysis and recommended changes.

9. *Submit final budget for approval.* Obtain top management approval of forecasts.

10. *Conduct feedback with management.* Present statistical summaries of the forecasting data by department and establish unit goals.

11. *Monitor budgeted versus actual increases.* Control the forecasted increases versus the actual increases by tracking and reporting periodic status to management.

The result of the forecasting cycle is a budget for the upcoming plan year for each organization's unit as well as estimated pay treatment for each employee. The budget does not lock in the manager to the exact pay change recommended for each employee. Rather, it represents a plan, and deviations due to unforeseen changes such as performance improvements, unanticipated promotions, and the like are common.

This approach to pay budgeting requires managers to plan the pay treatment for each of their employees. It places the responsibility for pay management on the managers.

The compensation professional takes on the role of adviser to operating management's use of the system.

VARIABLE PAY AS A COST CONTROL

Variable pay depends on performance and is *not* "rolled into" (added to) employees' base pay. Thus, the compounding effects of merit pay and across-the-board increases do not occur. As discussed in Chapter 10, variable pay takes many forms: annual bonuses, spot awards, gain sharing, and so forth. The essence of variable pay is that it must be reearned each period, in contrast to conventional merit pay increases or across-the-board increases that are added to base pay each year and that increase the base on which the following year's increase is calculated.

From a labor cost perspective, conventional increases impact not only the average pay level but also the costs of all benefits contingent on base pay (e.g., pension). Consequently, the greater the ratio of variable pay to base pay, the more variable (flexible) the organization's labor costs. Reconsider the general labor cost model in Exhibit 15.1; note that the greater the ratio of contingent to core workers and variable to base pay, the greater the variable component of labor costs, and the greater the options available to managers to control these costs. Although variability in pay and employment may be an advantage for managing labor costs, it may be less appealing from the standpoint of managing equitable treatment of employees. The inherent financial insecurity built into variable plans may adversely affect employees' financial well-being and subsequently their attitudes toward their work and their employers. All to say, managing labor costs is only one objective for managing compensation; others in the pay model include sustaining competitive advantage (productivity, total quality, customer service, and costs) and equitable treatment of employees.

INHERENT CONTROLS

Pay systems have two basic processes that serve to control pay decision making: (1) those inherent in the design of the techniques and (2) the formal budgeting process.

Think back to the several techniques already discussed: job analysis and evaluation, skill-based plans, policy lines, range minimums and maximums, performance evaluation, gain sharing, and salary increase guidelines. In addition to their primary purposes, they also regulate managers' pay decisions by guiding what managers do. Controls are imbedded in the design of these techniques to ensure that decisions are directed toward the pay system's objectives. A few of these controls are examined below.

Range Maximums and Minimums

These ranges set the maximum and minimum dollars to be paid for specific work. The maximum is an important cost control: Ideally, it represents the highest value the organization places on the output of the work. Under job-based structures, skills and knowledge possessed by employees may be more valuable in another job, but the range maximum represents all that the work produced in a particular job is worth to the organization. For example, the job of airline flight attendant is in a pay range with a maximum that is the highest an airline will pay a flight attendant, no matter how well the attendant performs the job. Pressures to pay above the range maximum occur for a number of reasons—for example, when employees with high seniority reach the maximum or when promotion opportunities are scarce. If employees are paid above the range maximum, these rates are called *red circle rates*. Most employers "freeze" red circle rates until the ranges are shifted upward by market update adjustments so that the rate is back within the range again. If red circle rates become common throughout an organization, then the design of the ranges and the evaluation of the jobs need to be reexamined.

Range minimums are just that: the minimum value placed on the work. Often rates below the minimum are used for trainees. Below minimum payment may also occur for outstanding employees who receive a number of rapid promotions.

Banding several adjacent salary grades, discussed in Chapter 7, has the effect of widening ranges and hence removing the controls imposed by range maximums. As banding becomes more common, the issue of what guidelines to offer managers becomes more important.

Compa-Ratios

Range midpoints reflect the pay policy line of the employer in relationship to external competition. To assess how managers actually pay employees in relation to the midpoint, an index called a *compa-ratio* is often calculated.

$$\text{Compa-ratio} = \frac{\text{Average rates actually paid}}{\text{Range midpoint}}$$

A compa-ratio of less than 1.00 means that, on average, employees in that range are paid below the midpoint. Translated, this means that managers are paying less than the intended policy. There may be several valid reasons for such a situation. The majority of employees may be new or recent hires; they may be poor performers; or promotion may be so rapid that few employees stay in the job long enough to get into the high end of the range.

A compa-ratio greater than 1.00 means that, on average, the rates exceed the intended policy. The reasons for this are the reverse of those mentioned above: a majority of workers with high seniority, high performance, low turnover, few new hires, or low promotion rates. Compa-ratios may be calculated for individual employees, for each range, for organization units, or for functions.

Other examples of controls designed into the pay techniques include the mutual signoffs on job analysis and job descriptions required of supervisors and subordinates. Another is slotting new jobs into the pay structure via job evaluation, which helps ensure that jobs are compared on the same factors.

Similarly, a performance evaluation system used organization-wide is intended to ensure that all employees are evaluated on similar factors.

Analyzing Costs

Costing out wage proposals is commonly done prior to recommending pay increases. It is also used in preparation for collective bargaining. For example, it is useful to bear in mind the dollar impact of a 1 cent per hour wage change, or a 1 percent change in payroll as one goes into bargaining.[12] Knowing these figures, negotiators can quickly compute the impact of a request for a 9 percent wage increase.

Use of Computers

If you've been thinking to yourself during these various budgetary calculations that "there's got to be an easier way," you're right. Commercial computer software is available to analyze almost any aspect of compensation information you can think of.

Computers can provide analysis and data that will improve the administration of the pay system. For example, computers can easily check the accuracy of past estimates in comparison to what actually occurred (e.g., the percentage of employees that actually did receive a merit increase, and the amount). Alternate wage proposals can be quickly simulated and their potential effects compared, using spreadsheet programs.

But computers have wider applications to compensation administration besides costing. In fact, every aspect of compensation may benefit from computer applications. For example, we discussed computerized job analysis and job evaluation and its advantages over conventional methods. Software is also available to evaluate salary survey data and incentive and gain-sharing results.[13]

INTERNATIONAL WAGE COMPARISONS

In Chapter 7 we discussed the numerous difficulties in measuring a market wage rate. Many large companies face difficulties of even greater magnitude when they try to compare their labor costs with those of foreign competitors. Comparisons among societies as different as the United States and Japan, for example, can be very misleading. Even if wages appear the same, expenses for health care, living costs, and typical company-provided perquisites such as dormitories and commuting allowances all complicate the picture. Comparing between a specific U.S. firm and a specific Japanese firm may be even more misleading. Accurate data are difficult to obtain. Statistics may not be publicly available or may not completely specify what is or is not included. A number of different comparisons may all be valid, but all may paint different pictures. Exhibit 15.7, for example, shows three different wage comparisons between Caterpillar, Inc. in the United States and Komatsu, Ltd., a Japanese competitor. These comparisons were offered by various parties during a 1992 strike by the United Auto Workers (UAW) against Caterpillar in Peoria, Illinois.

---

[12]Stephen Holoviak, *Costing Labor Contracts* (New York: Praeger, 1984); Myron Gable and Stephen Holoviak, "Determining the Cost of Supplemental Benefits," *Compensation and Benefits Review,* September–October 1985, pp. 22–23; and Robert E. Allen and Timothy J. Keaveny, "Costing Out a Wage and Benefit Package," *Compensation Review,* Second Quarter 1983, pp. 27–39.

[13]*Software for Compensation Professionals* (Scottsdale, Ariz.: American Compensation Association, 1991).

EXHIBIT 15.7 Comparing Labor Costs

> Caterpillar compared its hourly U.S. labor costs with those of its own joint venture in Japan, under the theory that the Japanese venture has costs similar to those of Komatsu:
>
> | Caterpillar | Shin Caterpillar Mitsubishi |
> | --- | --- |
> | $22.26/hour cash compensation plus $10/hour in benefits | About $20.25/hour plus $5/hour in benefits |
>
> The UAW examined cash compensation at Cat and Komatsu, but didn't include the added cost of benefits:
>
> | Caterpillar | Komatsu |
> | --- | --- |
> | $20.91/hour | $19.66/hour |
>
> Add in recent wage increases and changes in exchange rates, and there's little difference in annual cash compensation:
>
> | Caterpillar | Komatsu |
> | --- | --- |
> | $39,350 | $39,700 |

Source: Robert L. Rose and Masayoshi Kanabayashi, "Comparing U.S.–Japan Labor-Cost Data Can Be Murky," *The Wall Street Journal*, June 4, 1992, p. B4.

As the exhibit shows, when benefits costs are eliminated, wages at Caterpillar and Komatsu are not far apart. But Caterpillar says benefits costs add $10 an hour to its U.S. costs. According to the Japanese government, Komatsu's health care plan covers 60 percent of expenses and costs Komatsu approximately $2,430 per employee. In contrast, Caterpillar's plan covers all expenses and costs Caterpillar $6,500 for each worker. But because these estimates are based in part on salaries as well as exchange rates, they are already out of date. Thus, international comparisons are only valid for a broad overview.

COMMUNICATION AND APPEALS

Earlier in this book, we stressed that employees must believe that the pay system is fair.[14] Employees' perceptions about the pay system are shaped through the treatment they

---

[14]R. Folger and M. A. Konovsky, "Effects of Procedural and Distributive Justice on Reactions to Pay Raise Decisions," *Academy of Management Journal* 32 (1989), pp. 115–30; J. Greenberg, "Reactions to Procedural Injustice in Payment Distributions: Do the Ends Justify the Means?" *Journal of Applied Psychology* 72 (1987), pp. 55–61; R. Folger and J. Greenberg, "Procedural Justice: An Interpretive Analysis of Personnel Systems," in *Human Resources Management,* vol. 3, ed. K. M. Rowland and G. R. Ferris (Greenwich, Conn.: JAI Press, 1985), pp. 141–83; Denise Rousseau and Judi McLean Parks, "The Contracts of Individuals and Organizations," in *Research in Organizational Behavior,* vol. 15, ed. L. Cummings and Barry Staw (Greenwich, Conn.: JAI Press, 1992); and William Gorden, Carolyn Anderson, and Stephen Bruning, "Employee Perceptions of Corporate Partnership," *Employee Responsibilities and Rights Journal* 5, no. 1 (1992), pp. 75–85.

receive by managers, the formal communication programs about pay and their performance evaluations (Chapter 8), and employee participation in various aspects of the design of the system. Additionally, there should be some way for employees to appeal the results of their treatment by the system. Communication and appeals procedures or "speak ups" are our next topics.

Communication or Marketing?

Salaries of the executives in publicly held corporations are published in annual financial reports. Similarly, collective bargaining agreements spell out in detail pay rates for covered employees. And if you know which budget books to examine, you can even find the salaries of most public officials. But these groups constitute only a fraction of all employees. Most employees are not told what their coworkers are being paid. The literature on compensation management usually exhorts employers to communicate pay information; however, there is no standard approach on what to communicate to individuals about their own pay or that of their colleagues.

Some organizations have adopted a marketing approach. Similar to selling products to consumers, the pay system is a product, and employees and managers are the customers. Marketing approaches include consumer attitude surveys about the product, snappy advertising about the pay policies, and elaborate videotapes expounding policies and strengths. The marketing approach aims to directly manage expectations and attitudes about pay. In contrast, the communication approach tends to provide technical details. The market approach focuses on the quality and advantages of overall policies and is silent on specifics such as range maximums, increase guides, and the like.

The research on pay communication is dated and lags behind current practices. A variety of approaches exists; unfortunately, little is known about their effects.

Two reasons are usually given for communicating pay information. The first is that considerable resources have been devoted to designing a fair and equitable system that is intended to motivate effective performance and encourage productivity. For managers and employees to gain an accurate view of the pay system and perhaps influence their attitudes about it, they need to be informed.

The second reason is that, according to some research, employees seem to misperceive the pay system.[15] For example, they tend to overestimate the pay of those with lower level jobs and to underestimate the pay of those in higher level jobs. In other words, they tend to think that the pay structure is more compressed than it actually is. If differentials are underestimated, their motivational value in encouraging employees is diminished.[16]

---

[15]Thomas A. Mahoney and William Weitzel, "Secrecy and Managerial Compensation," *Industrial Relations* 17, no. 2 (1978), pp. 245–51; "Administering Pay Programs . . . An Interview with Edward E. Lawler III," *Compensation Review*, First Quarter 1977, pp. 8–16; and Julio D. Burroughs, "Pay Secrecy and Performance: The Psychological Research," *Compensation Review*, Third Quarter 1982, pp. 44–54.

[16]David M. Hegedus and E. Alan Hartman, "The Effects of Intra- and Inter-Organizational Movement on Rate of Movement and Salary," Paper presented at 1989 Annual Meeting Academy of Management, Washington, D.C.

Further, there is some evidence to suggest that the goodwill engendered by the act of being open about pay may also affect perceptions of pay equity.[17] Interestingly, the research also shows that employees in companies with open pay communication policies are as inaccurate in estimating pay differentials as those in companies in which pay secrecy prevails. However, employees under open pay policies tend to express higher satisfaction with their pay and with the pay system.

What to Communicate.   The first point to be made about pay communication is that if the pay system is not based on work-related or business-related logic, then the wisest course is probably to avoid formal communication until the system is put in order. However, avoiding *formal* communication is not synonymous with avoiding communication. Employees are constantly getting intended and unintended messages through the pay treatment they receive.

The second point is that achieving a fair and equitable pay system requires active involvement and feedback from managers and employees. An open policy helps ensure that employees understand how their pay is determined. The third point is that providing accurate pay information may cause some initial short-term concerns among employees. Over the years, employees probably have rationalized a set of relationships between their pay and the perceived pay and efforts of others. Receiving accurate data may require those perceptions to be adjusted.

Exhibit 15.8 is one major employer's communications policy. Many employers communicate the range for an incumbent's present job and for all the jobs in a typical career path or progression to which employees can logically aspire.

In addition to ranges, some employers communicate the typical pay increases that can be expected for poor, satisfactory, and top performance. The rationale given is that employees exchange data (not always factual) and/or guess at normal treatment, and the rumor mills are probably incorrect. Providing accurate data may have a positive effect

---

EXHIBIT 15.8   Typical Communications Policy

Program Communications

A. **To supervisors.** New ranges and guides should be published to affected supervisors upon approval together with a memo explaining the change and outlining the program review, the changes made, the effective data, the new ranges and guides, and any instructions for communication to employees.

B. **Supervisors should communicate to affected employees.** Employees should understand that our salary ranges are reviewed periodically and that they are competitive with the market. They should be told the dollar value for their salary range and the A–B–C performance definitions. They should know the supervisor's evaluation of their performance—the reasons for that position in the range. Guides are not discussed.

---

[17]Ed Lawler III, "The New Pay," in *Current Issues in Human Resource Management,* ed. Sara L. Rynes and George T. Milkovich (Plano, Tex.: Business Publications, 1986), pp. 404–12.

on employee work attitudes and behaviors. One potential danger in divulging increase schedule data is the inability to maintain that schedule in the future for reasons outside the control of the compensation department (e.g., economic or product market conditions). Nevertheless, pay increase data, coupled with performance expectations, should enhance employee motivation, which is a prime objective of the pay system.

Perhaps the most important information to be communicated is the work-related and business-related rationale on which the system is based. Some employees may not agree with these rationales or the results, but at least it will be clear that pay is determined by something other than the whims or biases of their supervisors.

STRUCTURING THE COMPENSATION FUNCTION

Compensation professionals seem to be constantly reevaluating where within the organization the responsibility for the design and administration of pay systems should be located. The organizational arrangements of the compensation function vary widely.

Centralization-Decentralization

An important issue related to structuring the function revolves around the degree of decentralization (or centralization) in the overall organization structure. *Decentralized* refers to a management strategy of giving separate organization units the responsibility to design and administer their own systems. This contrasts with a *centralized* strategy, which locates the design and administration responsibility in a single corporate unit. Some firms, such as Chevron and Pacific Gas and Electric, have relatively large corporate staffs whose responsibility it is to formulate pay policies and design the systems. Administration of these policies and systems falls to those working in various units, often personnel generalists. Such an arrangement runs the risk of formulating policies and practices that are well tuned to overall corporate needs but less well tuned to each unit's particular needs and circumstances. The use of task forces, with members drawn from the generalists in the affected units, to design new policies and techniques helps diminish this potential problem.

Other highly decentralized organizations, such as TRW and AT&T, have relatively small corporate compensation staffs (three or four professionals). Their primary responsibility is to manage the systems by which executives and the corporate staff are paid. These professionals operate in a purely advisory capacity to other organization subunits. The subunits, in turn, may employ compensation specialists. Or the subunits may choose to employ only personnel generalists rather than compensation specialists, and may turn to outside compensation consultants to purchase the expertise required on specific compensation issues.

Decentralizing certain aspects of pay design and administration has considerable appeal. Pushing these responsibilities (and expenses) close to the units and managers affected by them may help ensure that decisions are business related. However, decentralization is not without dilemmas. For example, it may be difficult to transfer employees from one business unit to another. Problems adhere to policies that emphasize internal consistency and concerns for potential pay discrimination crop up. So, too, do problems of designing pay systems that support a subunit's objectives but run counter to the overall corporate objectives.

Flexibility within Corporatewide Principles

The answer to these and related problems of decentralization can be found in developing a set of corporatewide principles or guidelines that all must meet. Those principles may differ for each major pay technique. As examples, Exhibits 15.9 and 15.10 are the corporate guides for incentive plans for IBM and TRW business units. IBM's business units worldwide have the flexibility to design incentive plans tailored to each unique business unit's strategies and cultures. The only guidance is to ensure that the principles presented in Exhibit 15.9 (adhere to IBM's basic beliefs, improve financial and business objectives, and so on) are met.

Keep in mind that the pay system is one of many management systems used in the organization. Consequently, it must be congruent with these other systems. For example, it may be appealing, on paper at least, to decentralize some of the compensation functions. However, if financial data and other management systems are not also decentralized, the pay system will not fit and may even be at odds with other systems.

A final issue related to structuring the responsibility for pay design and administration involves the skills and abilities required in compensation professionals. The grandest strategy and structure may seem well designed, well thought out in the abstract, but could be a disaster if people qualified to carry it out are not part of the staff. Our earlier example in which the business subunits were staffed by personnel generalists who were not trained or prepared to design pay systems tailored to the unit's needs illustrates the point. So all three aspects of management—strategy, structure, and staffing—must be considered.

EXHIBIT 15.9   Example of Corporatewide Principles: IBM

Variable Pay Program

Variable pay enhancements to IBM's merit pay system should be developed consistent with the following principles, objectives, and design considerations.

Principles—All variable pay programs must
- Adhere to IBM's basic beliefs
- Improve IBM's financial/business performance
- Support human resources strategy and meritocracy
- Consider local environment/compensation practices
- Be cost effective/neutral
- Maintain/enhance IBM reputation

Objectives
- Contain or reduce costs/enhance affordability
- Stimulate improved performance
- Share business success/risk
- Sharpen focus on business strategy/results

EXHIBIT 15.10   Example of Corporatewide Principles: TRW

Group Incentive Plan Guidelines

- The design of a group incentive plan must be consistent with the organization's business and human resources strategies, and management and employee values.
- Performance measures must directly influence financial performance. Standards of performance must be at or above target financial levels or at least above the organization's historical levels. Historical performance measurements should be set at a realistic baseline.
- The plan must also address how product quality and customer satisfaction will be enhanced through attainment of the plan's objectives.
- The plan must be designed to be self-funding (i.e., plan-generated compensation is the result of increased profits or decreased costs).
- The plan must provide an equitable return to both the employees and the company. Payouts should be timed to logical milestones within the organization, but as close to the performance event as possible.
- All elements of the plan must be in compliance with applicable national and local laws and regulations.
- The plan should be written for a defined period and contain procedures for responding to changes in the business, work, and economic environment that may affect the plan's performance measures.
- Communication and employee involvement programs must be developed to support the plan. These programs should provide employees with information on how they can influence organization performance. Reports on the organization's progress toward attainment of performance goals should be provided on a timely basis.
- All plans must be approved by the cognizant Group Human Resources director or vice president in conjunction with a review of the plan by Sector Human Resources or Company Compensation for direct reporting groups.

In view of the importance of a well-trained staff, both the American Compensation Association (ACA) and the Society of Human Resource Managers (SHRM) have professional development programs to entice readers into the compensation field.[18]

CONTROLS AS GUIDELINES: LET MANAGERS BE FREE

One of the major attacks on traditional compensation plans is that these plans often degenerate into bureaucratic nightmares that interfere with the organization's ability to respond to competitive pressures. Some recommend reducing the controls and guidelines inherent in any pay plan. Hence, banding eliminates or at least reduces the impact of

---

[18]Schedules and course registration information are available from American Compensation Association, 14040 N. Northsight Blvd., Scottsdale, AZ 85260, and from Society of Human Resource Managers, 606 N. Washington Street, Alexandria, VA 22314.

range maximums and minimums. Replacing merit grids with awards and bonuses eliminates the link between the pay increase and the employees' salary position in the range and performance rating. Replacing job evaluation with skill-based plans opens up the freedom to assign employees to a wider variety of work, regardless of their pay and the value of the work they perform.

Such approaches are consistent with the oft-heard plea that managers should be free to manage pay. Or, as some more bluntly claim, pay decisions are too important to be left to compensation professionals. There is a ring of truth to all this. Our experience with many companies is that their pay systems are managed like the worst bureaucratic nightmares in Kafka's *Trial*.

Yet permitting managers to be free to pay employees as they judge best rests on a basic premise: managers will use pay to achieve the organization's objectives—efficiency, equity, and compliance with regulations—rather than their own. Clearly, some balance between hidebound controls and chaos is required to ensure that pay decisions are directed at the organization goals, yet permit sufficient flexibility for managers and employees to respond to unique situations. Achieving the balance becomes part of the art of managing compensation.

SUMMARY

We have now completed the discussion of the pay administration process. Administration includes control: control of the way managers decide individual employees' pay as well as control of overall costs of labor. As we noted, some controls are designed into the fabric of the pay system (inherent controls, range maximums and minimums, etc.). The salary budgeting and forecasting processes impose additional controls. The formal budgeting process focuses on controlling labor costs and generating the financial plan for the pay system. The budget sets the limits within which the rest of the system operates.

Other aspects of administration we examined in this chapter included the fair treatment of employees in communications and appeals processes. The basic point was that pay systems are tools, and like any tools, they need to be evaluated in terms of usefulness in achieving an organization's objectives.

REVIEW QUESTIONS

1. How does the administration of the pay system affect the pay objectives?
2. What difference does it make how a compensation function is structured?
3. Give some examples of uses of inherent controls.
4. Why is it important to manage labor costs?
5. Are there any circumstances for which being a contingent worker may be desirable?
6. Merit increase guidelines have been discussed in this book as both a technique for recognizing performance and a cost control technique. Explain this dual nature.

APPENDIX
MERIT GRIDS

Merit grids combine 3 variables: level of performance, distribution of employees within their job's pay range, and merit increase percentages.
Example:

1. Assume a performance rating scale of A through D; 30 percent of employees get A, 35 percent get B, 20 percent get C, and 15 percent get D. Change to decimals.

A	B	C	D
.30	.35	.20	.15

2. Assume a range distribution as follows: 10 percent of all employees are in the top (fourth) quartile of the pay range for their job, 35 percent are in the third quartile, 30 percent in second quartile, and 25 percent in lowest quartile. Change to decimals.

1	.10
2	.35
3	.30
4	.25

3. Multiply the performance distribution by the range distribution to obtain the percent of employees in each cell. Cell entries = Performance × Range.

	A	*B*	*C*	*D*
1	.30 × .10 = .03	.35 × .10 = .035	.20 × .10 = .02	.15 × .10 = .015
2	.30 × .35 = .105	.35 × .35 = .1225	.20 × .35 = .07	.15 × .35 = .0525
3	.30 × .30 = .09	.35 × .30 = .105	.20 × .30 = .06	.15 × .30 = .045
4	.30 × .25 = .075	.35 × .25 = .1225	.20 × .25 = .05	.15 × .25 = .0375

   Cell entries tell us that 3 percent of employees are in top quartile of pay range AND received an A performance rating, 10.5 percent of employees are in second quartile of pay range AND received an A performance rating, etc.

4. Distribute increase percentage among cells, varying the percentages according to performance and range distribution, for example, 6 percent to those employees in cell A1, 5 percent to those employees in cell B1.

5. Multiply increase percentages by the employee distribution for each cell. Sum of all cells should equal the total merit increase percentage.

Example:

$$6\% \times \text{cell A1} = .06 \times .03 = .0018$$
$$5\% \times \text{cell B1} = .05 \times .035 = .00175$$

etc.   _____

Targeted Merit Increase Percentage = Sum

6. Adjust increase percentage among cells if needed in order to stay within budgeted increase.

You have the opportunity to deal with a compensation matter that has come up in the emergency room at Sacramento Medical Center (SMC). The hospital is going through a major change in administration, and the new administrators have raised questions about the emergency room nursing staff, particularly its pay.

Andersen Consulting firm conducted an analysis of the Medical Center and reported the following:

- Emergency room nurses (EMNs) all receive the same pay, $19 per hour. (There are 10 EMNs.)
- EMNs and their supervisors (three lead emergency nurses) believe strongly that they should be paid more than nurses in pediatrics, long-term care, cardiology, and other specialties. However, nurses in the other specialties don't all agree, though some do say that the EMN's job is different and requires different knowledge and so on.
- Currently the only way EMNs receive pay increases is as a result of changes in cost of living allowance (COLAs). Andersen Consulting reports that some EMNs believe that "EMNs aren't paid what they are worth at Sacramento Medical Center"; "It doesn't make any difference to the

hospital how we perform our jobs"; "They don't care if we keep up with the latest technology and new ideas or not!"

- The best EMNs at SMC seem to quit after three years. Some go to other regional hospitals; others transfer to other nursing assignments within SMC.
- The labor cost budget is tight, but SMC has been able to keep it under control.

1. Analyze the situation of EMNs at SMC based on the information presented above and the material discussed in the text. Please be very sure to consider *each* piece of information and discuss the implications for EMNs' behaviors and labor costs.

2. What changes would you recommend SMC consider making and why? How will these changes affect your compensation objectives?

3. List three pieces of *additional* data you'd recommend collecting to be able to better analyze this situation. Explain how or why each piece would be useful (e.g., why bother?). Organize your answer using models discussed in the book.

Compensation of Special Groups

Chapter Outline

So far we have described compensation programs as if they were fairly uniform across all jobs in an organization. Compensation is determined by analyzing jobs; determining the job's internal worth from a job evaluation; using salary surveys to determine what other competitors pay for the job; reconciling discrepancies; and making provisions to recognize that variation in performance across individuals in the same job should be recognized by compensation differences. Not all jobs follow all these stages, though. Indeed, all we have to do is open a newspaper to see that some jobs and some people are singled out for special compensation treatment in an organization. Why does Jim Kelly (quarterback, Buffalo Bills) have a contract for more than $20 million over three years? Why does Michael Eisner (chief executive officer, Walt Disney Company) regularly make more than $10 million per year? Are the value of these jobs and the incumbents in them determined in the same way as compensation is determined for other jobs and their incumbents in a company? The answer is probably no. But why? To answer this question, it is useful to work backward. What jobs get special compensation treatment in a company? Are they basically the same kinds of jobs across companies? If they are the same kinds of jobs, is there any common characteristic(s) the jobs share that would cause companies to devise special compensation packages?

When we begin to look at company practices with these questions in mind, a pattern begins to emerge. Special treatment, in the form either of add-on packages not received by other employees or of compensation components entirely unique in the organization, tends to focus on a few specific groups. This chapter argues that special groups share two characteristics. First, special groups tend to be placed in positions that have built-in conflict that arises because different factions place incompatible demands on members of the group. And second, the way that this conflict is resolved has important consequences for the success of the company. Facing conflict is not sufficient. The way incumbents deal with that conflict must have important consequences for the success of the firm. When both of these conditions are met, we tend to find distinctive compensation practices adapted to meet the needs of these special groups. Exhibit 16.1 describes the nature of the conflicts faced by such special groups as supervisors, top management, boards of directors, professional employees, sales staff, and employees in foreign subsidiaries. As an example of facing conflict that has consequences for the success of the firm, consider the contrast in compensation treatment for engineers in two different organizations. One is a high technology firm with a strong research and development component. The other

EXHIBIT 16.1   Conflicts Faced by Special Groups

Special Groups	*Type of Conflict Faced*
Supervisors	Caught between upper management and employees. Must balance need to achieve organization's objectives with importance of helping employees satisfy personal needs. If unsuccessful, either corporate profit or employee morale suffers.
Top management	Stockholders want healthy return on investment. Government wants compliance with laws. Executive must decide between strategies that maximize short-term gains at expense of long-term gains versus directions that focus on long run.
Board of directors	Face possibility that disgruntled stockholders may sue over corporate strategies that don't "pan out."
Professional employees	May be torn between goals, objectives, and ethical standards of their profession (e.g., should an engineer leak information about a product flaw, even though that information may hurt corporate profits) and demands of an employer concerned more with the profit motive.
Sales staff	Often go for extended periods in the field with little supervision. Challenge is to stay motivated and continue making sales calls even in the face of limited contact with or scrutiny from manager.
Employees in foreign countries	Work in foreign countries with different cultural, legal, and social customs. Geographic distance from headquarters makes it more difficult to balance needs of company against realities of a foreign environment.

organization is a firm in which engineers are not central to its mission. A survey concerning just such differences in employee composition and organizational strategy found that research and development organizations with heavy concentrations of engineers had evolved unique compensation systems that were responsive to the special needs of the engineering contingent. Organizations with a different focus and with fewer engineers merged this group's compensation with the standard package offered other employees.

COMPENSATION STRATEGY FOR SPECIAL GROUPS

Supervisors

Remember that supervisors are caught between the demands of upper management in terms of production and the needs of employees in terms of rewards and reinforcements. The major challenge in compensating supervisors centers on equity. Some incentive must be provided to entice nonexempt employees to accept the challenges of being a supervisor. For many years, the strategy was to treat supervisors like lower-level managers. But in so doing, sometimes the existing job evaluation system left these supervisors making less money than the top paid employees they supervised. As you might imagine, this created little incentive to take on the extra work involved. More recently, organizations have devised several strategies to attract workers into supervisory jobs. The most popular method is to key base salary of supervisors to some amount exceeding the top paid subordinate in the unit (5 percent to 30 percent represents the typical size of the differential).[1]

Another method to maintain equitable differentials is simply to pay supervisors for scheduled overtime. Over the past few years, this option has become slightly more popular, as Exhibit 16.2 demonstrates. Companies that do pay overtime are about evenly split between paying straight-time versus time and one half for overtime hours.

Finally, some organizations (about 20 percent) develop special supervisory incentive and bonus plans. More than a third of companies offer some type of bonus plan for these employees, with profit sharing plans the most common form.[2]

EXHIBIT 16.2 Percentage of Firms Paying Supervisors Overtime

	1989	*1990*	*1991*
Percentage of firms paying for overtime	34%	36%	38%

Source: Wyatt Data Services (1992).

---

[1]E. C. Miller, "Supervisory Overtime, Incentive and Bonus Practices," *Compensation Review* 10, no. 4 (1978), pp. 12–25.

[2]"The Salary Scene," *Compflash* (Saranac Lake, N.Y.: American Management Association, 1991), p. 2.

Corporate Directors

A board of directors generally comprises 10 to 20 individuals who meet on a regular basis to serve a variety of roles in the interest of the corporation and its shareholders. Historically, directors frequently have been given the role of "rubber stamping" decisions made by top management. Such boards were "stacked" with people affiliated in some way with the organization (e.g., retired corporate officers, suppliers, attorneys). Modern corporate boards have changed considerably. Membership now includes more outside directors (approximately two thirds) than inside directors (e.g., chief executive officers, corporate officers). Outside members now include unaffiliated business executives, representatives from important segments of society, and major shareholders. The days of rubber stamped decisions are quickly passing. Boards now face increased responsibility for decision making and increased responsibility for the success of the firm. They face the increased risk that disgruntled shareholders might bring suit against them for making unprofitable or unpopular corporate decisions. Oftentimes compensation has not kept up with this increased responsibility that directors face. Indeed, there is a growing concern that board members are paid too much to perform rubber stamp duties that previously described the job but too little to assume the risks, responsibilities, and pressures of today's corporate director.

According to a recent survey, the average outside director in an industrial firm earns $42,935, about $6,000 more than a director in a service firm.[3] Exhibit 16.3 shows other forms of compensation that directors receive. If any trend exists in the compensation of

EXHIBIT 16.3   Other Compensation for Directors

Percentage of Directors Receiving Type of Compensation	*Type of Compensation*
	Insurance
78	Liability for wrongful decisions
36	Travel/accident
16	Life
17	Accidental death
9	Medical
2	Dental
49	Deferred compensation
33	Matching donations
31	Pension
10	Discounted company products
2	Physical exams

Source: E. Arreglado, *Corporate Director's Compensation*, no. 969 (New York: The Conference Board, 1991), p. 24.

---

[3]"At the Top," *Compflash* (Saranac Lake, N.Y.: American Management Association, 1992), p. 1.

corporate directors, it is toward increased variable compensation. About 33 percent of all companies provide directors with some form of stock compensation.[4] The compensation goal is to make sure that directors make decisions with the best interests of stockholders at heart. This is also true for executives. An obvious way to achieve this is to make sure that the directors also are stockholders!

Chief Executive Officers

How would you like to make $1.4 million per year? That is the 1991 average compensation (salary plus bonus) for U.S. chief executive officers (CEOs).[5] Add in such long-term incentives as stock options, and the annual figure rises to *$2.8 million dollars.*[6] Exhibit 16.4 shows the total compensation for the *highest paid executive* during each of the past 10 years. Many critics argue that this level of compensation for executives is excessive.[7] Are the critics right? One way to answer the question is to look at the different ways people say that executive compensation is determined and ask "does this seem reasonable?"

Possible Explanations for CEO Compensation.   One approach to explain why executives receive such large sums of money involves social comparisons.[8] According to this approach, executive salaries bear a consistent relative relationship to compensation of

---

EXHIBIT 16.4   Highest Paid Executives, 1982–1991

Year	CEO	Company	Total Pay (millions)
1991	Anthony O'Reilly	H. J. Heinz	$75.1
1990	Stephen Wolf	UAL	18.3
1989	Craig McCaw	Cellular	53.9
1988	Michael Eisner	Disney	40.1
1987	Charles Lazarus	Toys "R" Us	60.0
1986	Lee Iacocca	Chrysler	20.5
1985	Victor Posner	DWG	12.7
1984	T. Boone Pickens	Mesa Petroleum	22.8
1983	William Anderson	NCR	13.2
1982	Federick Smith	Federal Express	51.5

SOURCE: *Business Week,* March 30, 1992, pp. 52–58.

---

[4]E. Arreglado, *Corporate Director's Compensation,* no. 969 (New York: The Conference Board, 1991), p. 27.

[5]Graef S. Crystal, *In Search of Excess* (New York: W. W. Norton, 1991). Based on 200 major companies in seven industries.

[6]Ibid.

[7]Ibid.

[8]Herber A. Simon, *Administrative Behavior,* 2nd ed. (New York: Macmillan, 1957).

lower-level employees. When salaries of lower-level employees rise in response to market forces, top executive salaries also rise to maintain the same relative relationship. In part, the data in Exhibit 16.5 support this explanation. Managers who are in the second level of a company earn about two thirds of a CEO's salary, and those in the next level down earn slightly more than half of a CEO's salary.

These ratios have been reasonably stable for more than a decade. The relative relationship breaks down, however, in a comparison of CEO salary to that of lower-level workers. In 1980, the average CEO had a salary that was 42 times that of an ordinary worker. By 1990, that ratio more than doubled to *85 times the wages of ordinary workers*. As a point of reference, the corresponding differential in Japan is less than 20![9] Both these facts suggest that a social comparison explanation is not sufficient to explain why executive wages are as high as they are.

A second approach to understanding executive compensation focuses less on the *difference* in wages between executive and other jobs and more on explaining the *level* of executive wages. The premise in this economic approach is that the worth of a CEO should correspond closely to some measure of company success (e.g., profitability, sales). Intuitively, this explanation makes sense. There is also empirical support. Numerous studies during the past 30 years have demonstrated that executive pay bears some relationship to company success.[10]

One recent study combined both social comparison and economic explanations to try to better understand CEO salaries. Both of these explanations turned out to be significant. Size and profitability affected level of compensation, as did social comparisons. In this study, the social comparison of wages was between CEOs and members of the board of directors. It seems that CEO salaries rose, on average, 51 percent for every

---

EXHIBIT 16.5   Ratio of Subordinate Salaries to CEO Salaries across Industries, 1990 versus 1986

Position Relative to CEO	Manufacturing		Banking		Insurance		Construction		Utilities	
	1990	*1986*	*1990*	*1986*	*1990*	*1986*	*1990*	*1986*	*1990*	*1986*
Second level	65	68	66	68	65	67	71	77	65	58
Third level	52	53	55	52	53	54	52	61	52	54

SOURCE: *Top Executive Compensation* (New York: The Conference Board, 1986 and 1990).

---

[9]This comparison needs to be interpreted with some caution. One counter argument (the Hay Group, Compflash, April 1992, p. 3) notes that American companies are generally much larger than their foreign counterparts. When compared to like-sized companies in other countries, the U.S. multiple is comparable to the international average.

[10]Marc J. Wallace, "Type of Control, Industrial Concentration, and Executive Pay," *Academy of Management Proceedings,* 1976, pp. 284–88; W. Lewellan and B. Huntsman, "Managerial Pay and Corporate Performance," *American Economic Review* 60 (1970), pp. 710–20.

$100,000 that was earned by directors on the board.[11] Recognizing this, some CEOs are said to lobby to have persons who are highly paid in their primary jobs appointed to the board of directors.

A third view of CEO salaries involves the political motivations that are an inevitable part of the corporate world. Sometimes, this argument runs, CEOs make decisions that aren't in the economic best interest of the firm and its shareholders. One variant on this view suggests that the normal behavior of a CEO is self-protective: they will make decisions to solidify their position and to maximize the rewards they personally receive.[12] As evidence of this self-motivated behavior, consider the following description of how executives ensure their high compensation.[13] The description comes from the experience of a well-known executive compensation consultant, now turned critic, who specialized for years in the design of executive compensation packages.

1. *If the CEO is truly underpaid:* A compensation consultant is hired to survey true competitors of the company. The consultant reports to the board of directors that the CEO is truly underpaid. Salary is increased to a competitive or higher level.

2. *If the CEO is not underpaid and the company is doing well:* A compensation consultant is hired. A list of companies is recommended to the consultant as appropriate for surveying. Companies tend to be selected because they are on the top end in terms of executive compensation. The consultant reports back to the board that its CEO appears to be underpaid. Salary is increased.

3. *If the CEO is not underpaid and the company is doing poorly:* A compensation consultant is hired. The CEO laments to the consultant that wages are so low for top management that there is a fear that good people will start leaving the company and going to competitors. Of course, no one ever asks why the company is underperforming if it has such a good management team. Anyway, the result is that the consultant recommends a wage increase to avoid future turnover.

In each of these scenarios, CEO wages rise. Inevitably, someone points out that such practices lead to outcomes like those experienced in 1990: Profits slid 7 percent but executive compensation *rose 7 percent*.[14]

The result of the continued rise in CEO compensation has been increasing cries from both shareholders and the general public that executive compensation should be tied to the success of the firm. One study found 83 percent agreement with this practice, but only 38 percent belief that firms actually did this.[15] One tangible piece of evidence that

---

[11]Charles O'Reilly, Brian Main, and Graef Crystal, "CEO Compensation as Tournament and Social Comparison: a Tale of Two Theories," *Administrative Science Quarterly* 33 (1988), pp. 257–74.

[12]Kathyrn M. Eisenhardt, "Agency Theory: An Assessment and Review," *Academy of Management Review* 14 (1989), pp. 57–74.

[13]Crystal, *In Search of Excess.*

[14]"The Flap over Executive Pay," *Business Week,* May 6, 1991, pp. 90–96.

[15]Compflash, "At the Top," *Compflash* (Saranac Lake, N.Y.: American Management Association, 1990), p. 1.

the complaints are having an effect is that the CEO of IBM took a 40 percent cut in base pay in 1992, largely because of the poor performance Big Blue has shown over the last several years!

In response to calls for better links between executive pay and executive performance, at least two trends appear evident. The first trend began at least a decade ago. The trend involves the adoption of some form of long-term incentive plan.[16] One survey of 500 large industrial firms found that 72 percent had three or more long-term incentive plans. The most common of these plans is some type of stock option. In its simplest form, the plan gives an executive the option to purchase shares of the company stock at some future date for an amount equaling the fair market price at the time the option is granted. There is a built-in incentive for an executive to increase the value of the firm. The executive exercises the option to buy the stock at the agreed-upon price. Stock prices rise. Because of the rise in the stock price, the executive profits from the increased value of the stock purchased.

Although this sounds like an effective tool to motivate executives, it has many critics.[17] The major complaint is that stock options don't have a downside risk. If stock prices rise, the stock options are exercised. If stocks don't improve, the executive suffers no out-of-pocket losses. Some argue that executive compensation should move toward requiring executives to own stock, not just having the option to buy.[18] With the threat of possible financial loss and the hope of possible substantial gains, motivation may be higher. Some early evidence supports this position. In three industries in which executives had large stock holdings, firms outperformed industries in which executives had little or no stock investment.

The second trend in response to complaints about excessive executive compensation is increasing government regulation. In 1992, the Securities and Exchange Commission (SEC) entered the controversy.[19] The SEC now permits stockholders to propose and vote to limit executive compensation. This and other proposed rule changes signal renewed interest in, and closer scrutiny of, all components of executive compensation. The following discussion outlines these different components.

Components of an Executive Compensation Package.   Most executive compensation packages have five basic elements: (1) base salary, (2) short-term (annual) incentives or bonuses, (3) long-term incentives and capital appreciation plans, (4) employee benefits, and (5) perquisites. Because of the changing nature of tax legislation, each of these at one time or another has received considerable attention in designing executive compensation packages. Exhibit 16.6 traces the trend in these components over time.

One obvious trend is apparent from these data. Companies are placing more and more emphasis on long-term incentives at the expense of base salary. Such a change in

---

[16]Amanda Bennett, "Big Firms Rely More on Options but Fail to End Pay Criticism," *The Wall Street Journal,* March 11, 1992, p. A 1.

[17]Ibid.

[18]Ira T. Kay, "Beyond Stock Options: Emerging Practices in Executive Incentive Programs" *Compensation and Benefits Review* 23, no. 6 (1991), pp. 18–29.

[19]Michelle Osborn, "SEC: Executive Pay Is an Issue for Shareholders," *USA Today,* p. B1.

EXHIBIT 16.6   Percentage Breakdown of Executive Compensation Components

Compensation Component	Percentage during 1970s	Percentage during 1980s	Percentage during 1990s
Base salary	60	40	38
Benefits	*	15	10
Perks	*	5	3
Short-term incentive	25	20	23
Long-term incentive	15	20	26

*Unreported

SOURCE: Various issues of *The Wall Street Journal*, data from TPF&C, Wyatt Co; Michael Bishko, "Compensationg Your Overseas Executives, Part 1: Strategies for the 1990s," *Compensation and Benefits Review*, May–June 1990.

EXHIBIT 16.7   Base Salary of Top Executives

Industry	Organization Level of Executive				
	CEO	Second Highest	Third Highest	Fourth Highest	Fifth Highest
Manufacturing	$463,000	$290,000	$231,000	$207,000	$195,000
Commercial banking	375,000	258,000	218,000	175,000	153,000
Communications	525,000	350,000	306,000	267,000	254,000
Diversified services	375,000	245,000	195,000	175,000	148,000
Energy and natural resources	460,000	312,000	275,000	200,000	180,000
Insurance	350,000	212,000	185,000	155,000	142,000
Utilities	345,000	221,000	173,000	157,000	155,000

SOURCE: E. Arreglado, *Top Executive Compensation* (New York: The Conference Board, 1991).

emphasis signals the growing importance attached to making decisions that ensure the long-run growth and survival of a company.

Base Salary.   As noted earlier, being competitive is a very important factor in the determination of executive base pay. But this competition does not extend across industries. As Exhibit 16.7 shows, base salaries vary significantly across industries.

Although formalized job evaluation still plays an occasional role in determining executive base pay, other sources are much more important. Particularly important is the opinion of a compensation committee, usually comprising the company's board of directors (or a subset of the board). Frequently this compensation committee takes over some of the data analysis tasks previously performed by the chief personnel officer, even going so far as to analyze salary survey data and performance records for executives of comparably sized firms.[20]

Bonuses.   Annual bonuses often play a major role in executive compensation and are primarily designed to motivate better performance. Most striking is the rapid rise in popularity of this type of compensation. Only five years ago only 36 percent of companies gave annual bonuses. Today bonuses are given to 87 percent of top executives![21] The size of these bonuses as a percentage of base pay varies from a low of 35 percent in utility firms to a high of 60 percent or more in energy and manufacturing companies.[22]

There are two constraints on the use of bonuses to compensate executives beyond their base salary levels. First, legal or company policy prohibitions prevent several industries from extensive use of bonuses. The following are types of organizations that typically rely almost exclusively on base salary for total direct compensation: (1) firms with tight control of stock ownership, (2) not-for-profit institutions, and (3) firms operating in regulated industries.[23]

The second constraint on bonus systems is usually tied to organization level of the executives. Eligibility is typically limited to those few executives at the top whose performance is judged to have potentially significant impacts on overall company performance.

Long-Term Incentive and Capital Appreciation Plans.   Exhibit 16.8 illustrates the increased popularity of one form of long-term incentives, stock option plans. Generally, the data indicate increased use of these long-term incentives. Boards of directors are shifting their focus for executive compensation to long-term achievements, sometimes even at the expense of short-term profits.

Exhibit 16.9 identifies other types of long-term incentives and describes their main features.[24]

Executive Benefits.   Since many benefits are tied to income level (e.g., life insurance, disability insurance, pension plans), executives typically receive higher benefits than most

---

[20]Ernest C. Miller, "How Companies Set the Base Salary and Incentive Bonus Opportunity for Chief Executive and Chief Operating Officers. . . A Compensation Review Symposium," *Compensation Review* 9 (Fourth Quarter 1976), pp. 30–44; Monci Jo Williams, "Why Chief Executives' Pay Keeps Rising," *Fortune,* April 1, 1985, pp. 66–72, 76.

[21]Arreglado, *Top Executive Compensation: 1990 Edition* (New York: The Conference Board, 1991).

[22]Ibid.

[23]William H. Cash, "Executive Compensation," *Personnel Administrator* 22, no. 7 (1977), pp. 11–19.

[24]Other tax reform issues are discussed in Gregory Wiber, "After Tax Reform, Part I: Planning Employee Benefit Programs," *Compensation and Benefits Review* 19, no. 2 (1987), pp. 16–25; and Irwin Rubin, "After Tax Reform, Part 2," *Compensation and Benefits Review* 20, no. 1 (1988), pp. 26–32.

EXHIBIT 16.8 Trends over Time in the Use of Stock Options (in percentages)

Industry	1982	1984	1985	1988	1989
Manufacturing	80	84	82	84	84
Retail trade	63	77	73	—	—
All trade	—	—	—	77	77
Construction (publicly held)	61	62	—	—	—
Insurance: stock	48	43	45	68	76
Commercial banking	44	50	61	74	72
Gas and electric utilities	20	20	24	—	—
All utilities	—	—	—	38	48
Diversified services	—	—	100	70	67
Communication	—	—	—	83	88
Energy	—	—	—	78	81
Total	62	66	68	75	75

SOURCE: Various issues of *Top Executive Compensation* (New York: The Conference Board).

EXHIBIT 16.9 Long-Term Incentives for Executives

Type	Description	Comments
Incentive stock options	Purchase of stock at a stipulated price, conforming with Internal Revenue Code (Section 422A).	No taxes at grant. Company may not deduct as expense.
Nonqualified stock options	Purchase of stock at a stipulated price, not conforming with Internal Revenue Code.	Excess over fair market value taxed as ordinary income. Company may deduct.
Phantom stock plans	Cash or stock award determined by increase in stock price at a fixed future date.	Taxed as ordinary income. Does not require executive financing.
Stock appreciation rights	Cash or stock award determined by increase in stock price during any time chosen (by the executive) in the option period.	Taxed as ordinary income. Does not require executive financing.
Restricted stock plans	Grant of stock at a reduced price with the condition that it may not be sold before a specified date.	Excess over fair market value taxed as ordinary income.
Performance share/unit plans	Cash or stock award earned through achieving specific goals.	Taxed as ordinary income. Does not require executive financing.

SOURCE: *1990 Executive Compensation Report*, Sibson & Co.

other exempt employees. Beyond the typical benefits outlined in Chapter 12, however, many executives also receive additional life insurance, exclusions from deductibles for health-related costs, and supplementary pension income exceeding the maximum limits permissible under ERISA guidelines for qualified (i.e., eligible for tax deductions) pension plans.

Of course, various sections of ERISA and the tax code restrict employer ability to provide benefits for executives that exceed a certain level above those of other workers. The assorted clauses require that a particular benefits plan (1) cover a broad cross section of employees (generally 80 percent), (2) provide definitely determinable benefits, and (3) meet specific vesting (see Chapter 12) and nondiscrimination requirements. The nondiscrimination requirement specifies that the average value of benefits for low-paid employees must be at least 75 percent of the average value for high-paid employees.[25]

Executive Perquisites.   Perquisites, or "perks," probably have the same genesis as the expression "rank has its privileges." Indeed, life at the top has its rewards designed to satisfy several types of executive needs. One type of perk could be classified as "internal," providing a little something extra while the executive is inside the company: luxury offices, executive dining rooms, special parking. A second category also is company related but for business conducted externally: company-paid membership in clubs/associations and payment of hotel, resort, airplane, and auto expenses.

The final category of perquisites should be totally isolated from the first two because of the differential tax status. This category, called *personal perks,* includes such things as low-cost loans, personal and legal counseling, free home repairs and improvements, personal use of company property, and expenses for vacation homes.[26]

Since 1978, various tax and regulatory agency rulings have slowly been requiring companies to place a value on perks.[27] If this trend continues, the taxable income of executives with creative perk packages may increase considerably.

Exhibit 16.10 identifies different types of perks and the percentages of companies that offer them.

Scientists and Engineers in High Technology Industries

Scientists and engineers are classified as professionals. According to the Fair Labor Standards Act, this category includes any person who has received special training of a scientific or intellectual nature and whose job does not entail more than a 20 percent time allocation for supervisory responsibilities.

The compensation of scientists and engineers focuses on rewarding incumbents for their special scientific or intellectual training. Here lies one of the special compensation problems that scientists and engineers face. Consider the electrical engineer who graduates with all the latest knowledge in the field. For the first few years after graduation, this knowledge is a valuable resource on engineering projects in which new applications of

---

[25]Dennis Blair and Mark Kimble, "Walking through the Discrimination Testing Wage for Welfare Plans," *Benefits Quarterly* 3, no. 2 (1987), pp. 18–26. Author's note: At press time, Section 89 of the Tax Code was under serious attack. If repealed, the nondiscrimination laws would change again.

[26]Michael F. Klein, "Executive Perquisites," *Compensation Review,* 12, Fourth Quarter, 1979, pp. 46–50.

[27]R. L. VanKirk and L. S. Schenger, "Executive Compensation: The Trend Is Back to Cash," *Financial Executive,* May 1978, pp. 83–91.

EXHIBIT 16.10 Popular Perks Offered to Executives

Type of Perk	Percentage of Companies Offering Perk
Physical exam	91
Company car	68
Financial counseling	64
Company plane	63
Income tax preparation	63
First-class air travel	62
Country club membership	55
Luncheon club membership	55
Estate planning	52
Personal liability insurance	50
Spouse travel	47
Chauffeur service	40
Reserved parking	32
Executive dining room	30
Home security system	25
Car phone	22
Financial seminars	11
Loans at low or no interest	9
Legal counseling	6

SOURCE: Hewitt Associates, 1990.

the latest theories are a primary objective. Gradually, though, this engineer's knowledge starts to become obsolete. Team leaders begin to look to the newer graduates for fresh, new ideas. The salaries of scientists and engineers reflect a high correlation between pay increases and knowledge obsolescence. Early years bring higher than average (relative to employees in other occupations) increases. After 10 years, however, increases drop below average and become downright puny in the 15 to 20 year time frame. Partly because of these salary plateaus, many scientists and engineers make career changes (e.g., move into management) or temporarily leave business and reenter academia to update their technical knowledge. In recent years, some firms have tried to deal with the plateau effect and to accommodate the different career motivations of mature scientists and engineers. The result has been the creation of dual career ladders, as exemplified in Exhibit 16.11.

Notice that dual career ladders provide exactly that: two different ways to progress in an organization, each reflecting different types of contributions to the organization's mission. The first, or managerial, ladder ascends through increasing responsibility for supervision or direction of people. The second, or professional, ladder ascends through increasing positions of a professional nature that do not mainly entail the supervision of employees. Scientists and engineers (SEs) have the opportunity at some stage in their careers to consider a management ladder or continue along the scientific ladder. Dual career ladders offer greater advancement opportunities for SEs. Maximum base pay in the technical track can approximate that of upper management positions.

EXHIBIT 16.11 IBM Dual Ladder

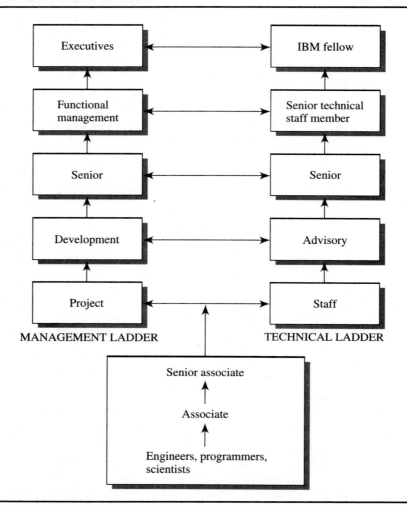

A second problem in designing the compensation package of scientists and engineers centers on the question of equity. The very nature of scientific knowledge and its dissemination requires relatively close association among SEs across organizations. SEs tend to compare themselves for equity purposes with the graduates who entered the labor market at the same time period. Partially because of this and partially because of the volatile nature of both jobs and salaries in SE occupations, organizations rely very heavily on external market data in determining SE base pay.[28] The form of these data involves the construction of maturity curves.

Maturity curves reflect the relationship between SE compensation and years of experience in the labor market. Generally, surveying organizations ask for information about salaries as a function of years since the incumbent last received a degree. This degree information is intended to measure the half-life of technical obsolescence. In fact, a plot of these data with appropriate smoothing to eliminate aberrations typically shows curves that are steep for the first five to seven years and then rise more gradually as technical obsolescence erodes the value of jobs. Exhibit 16.12 illustrates such a graph with somewhat greater sophistication built into it, that is, different graphs are constructed for different levels of performance. To construct such graphs, the surveying organization must also ask for data broken down by broad performance levels. Notice in the illustration that the high performers begin with somewhat higher salaries and the differential continues to broaden over the first few years.

Scientists and engineers receive compensation beyond base pay. In general, high technology firms place a great emphasis on the use of performance-based incentives.[29] Common forms of incentives include profit sharing and stock ownership incentives. Other incentives link payment of specific cash amounts to completion of specific projects on or before agreed-upon deadlines. Post hoc bonuses are also paid for such achievements as patents, publications, election to professional societies, and attainment of professional licenses.

Finally, organizations have devoted considerable creative energy to development of "perks" to satisfy the unique needs of SEs. Such perks include flexible work schedules, large offices, campus-like work environments, and lavish athletic facilities. The strategic importance of SEs to the firms dictates that both mind and body be kept active.

Sales Force

The sales force spans the all-important boundary between the organization and consumers of the organization's goods or services. Besides the sales function, or even as part of selling, the sales force must be sensitive to changing consumer tastes and provide rapid feedback to appropriate departments. The role requires individuals with high initiative who can work under low supervision for extended periods of time. The standard compensation system is not designed for this type of job. Indeed, much of the value for sales jobs is determined by factors largely external to the organization and driven by market forces.[30] The challenge is to incorporate these factors in the design of a sales compensation plan.

---

[28]Jo C. Kail, "Compensating Scientists and Engineers," in *New Perspectives on Compensation,* ed. David B. Balkin and Luis R. Gomez-Mejia (Englewood Cliffs, N. J.: Prentice Hall, 1987), pp. 247–281.

[29]George T. Milkovich, "Compensation Systems in High Technology Companies," in *New Perspectives on Compensation,* ed. Balkin and Gomez-Mejia, pp. 269–277.

[30]John K. Moynahan, *The Sales Compensation Handbook* (New York: Amacom, 1991).

EXHIBIT 16.12   Maturity Curve Showing Years since Last Degree Relative to Salary

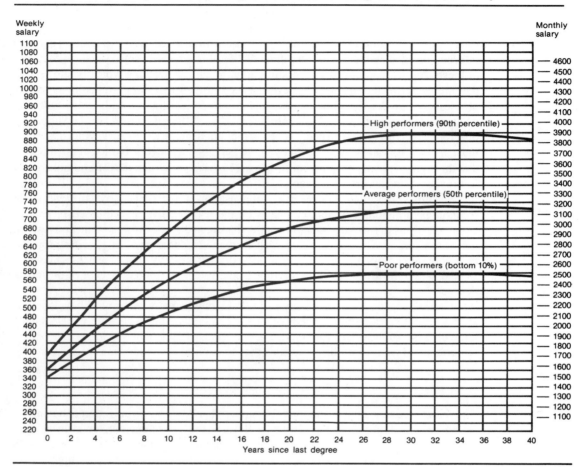

Designing a Sales Compensation Plan.   Four major factors influence the design of sales compensation packages: (1) the nature of people who enter the sales profession, (2) organizational strategy, (3) competitor practices, and (4) product to be sold.

The Nature of People Who Enter the Sales Profession.   Popular stereotypes of salespeople characterize them as heavily motivated by financial compensation. A recent study supports this stereotype, with salespeople ranking pay significantly higher than five other

EXHIBIT 16.13 **Average Annual Compensation Change: Mid-Level Salesperson**				
1986	*1987*	*1988*	*1989*	*1990*
$42,758	$36,469	$38,869	$37,073	$39,666

SOURCE: Various issues of *Sales & Marketing Management.*

forms of reward.[31] As a source of satisfaction, pay rated a mean of 83.7 on a scale to 100. Promotional opportunities, sense of accomplishment, personal growth, recognition, and job security were all less highly regarded. These values almost dictate that the primary focus of sales compensation should be direct financial rewards (base pay + incentives). Exhibit 16.13 shows the level of, and change in, average annual compensation for a mid-tier salesperson over the past five years. In general, compensation has not changed much, perhaps reflecting the stagnation in the economy.

Organizational Strategy.   A sales compensation plan should link desired behaviors of salespeople to organizational strategy. Salespeople must know when to stress customer service and when to stress volume sales. When volume sales are the goal, salespeople should know which products to push the most. Strategic plans signal which behaviors are important. For example, emphasis on customer service to build market share, or movement into geographic areas with low potential, may limit sales volume. Ordinarily, sales reps under an incentive system will view customer service as an imposition, taking away from money-making sales opportunities. And woe be to the sales supervisor who assigns a commission-based salesperson to a market with low sales potential. Sales reps asked to forgo incentive income for these low sales tasks should be covered under a compensation system with a high base pay and small incentive component.

Alternatively, an organization may want to motivate aggressive sales behavior. A straight commission-based incentive plan focuses sales efforts in this direction, to the possible exclusion of supportive tasks (e.g., processing customer returns). These incentive plans include both a statement about the size of the incentive and a discussion of the performance objective necessary to achieve it. Typical performance measures include overall territory volume, market share, number of product placements in retail stores, number of new accounts, gross profit, percentage of list price attainment (relative to other salespeople in organization), consistency of sales results, expense-control productivity per square foot (especially popular in retail stores), and bad debt generated by sales.[32] Each measure, of course, corresponds to a different business goal. For example, an organization might use some volume measure such as number of units, orders, invoices,

---

[31] N. Ford, O. Walker, and G. Churchill, "Differences in the Attractiveness of Alternative Rewards among Industrial Salespeople: Additional Evidence," *Journal of Business Research* 13, no. 2 (1985), pp. 123–38.

[32] Moynahan, *The Sales Compensation Handbook.*

or cash received if the business goal is to increase sales growth. Alternatively, if the goal is profit improvement, the appropriate measurement would be gross margin on sales or price per unit. Percentage account erosion would be stressed if improved account retention became a major focus of attention, and sales per account might be stressed when account penetration becomes a major organizational goal.

Competitor Practices. In selecting an appropriate pay level, organizations should recognize that external competitiveness is essential. The very nature of sales positions means that competitors will cross paths, at least in their quest for potential customers. This provides the opportunity to chat about relative compensation packages, an opportunity that salespeople will frequently take. To ensure that the comparison process is favorable, the organization identifies a compensation level strategy that should explicitly indicate target salaries for different sales groups and performance levels.

Product to Be Sold. The very nature of the product or service to be sold may influence the design of a compensation system. Consider a product which, by its very technical nature, takes time to understand and fully develop an effective sales presentation for. Such products are said to have high barriers to entry, meaning that salespeople require considerable training to become effective in selling them. Compensation in this situation usually includes a large base pay component, minimizing the risk a sales representative faces and encouraging entry into the necessary training program. At the opposite extreme are products with lower barriers to entry, for which the knowledge needed to make an effective sales presentation is relatively easy to acquire. These product lines are sold more often using a higher incentive component, thus paying more for actual sales than for taking the time to learn any necessary skills to sell them.

Products or services that sell themselves, when sales ability isn't so crucial, inspire different compensation packages than products or services for which the salesperson is more essential to sales. Base compensation tends to be more important with easily sold products. Not surprisingly, incentives become more important when willingness to work hard may make the difference between success and failure. Few jobs fit the ideal specifications for either of the two extremes, represented by straight salary or straight commission plans. A combination plan is intended to capture the best of both these plans. A guaranteed straight salary can be linked to performance of nonsales functions (e.g., customer service), and a commission for sales volume yields the incentive to sell. A plan combining these two features signals the intent of the organization to ensure that both types of activities occur in the organization.

One survey of organizations indicates that sales plans with an incentive component will continue to be popular into the foreseeable future. About 90 percent of all companies surveyed indicated that sales incentive plans will have as large or larger budget in the future as in the past.[33] Other forms of rewards, however, continue to play a role, albeit a small one, in the total compensation package of salespeople. For example, some

---

[33]A. Urbanski, "Incentives Get Specific," *Sales and Marketing Management* 136, no. 5 (1986), pp. 47–102.

companies develop formal recognition programs for high sales performers (e.g., 44 percent of those surveyed). More popular forms of recognition, though, focus on more tangible incentives, offering merchandise and travel for outstanding performance (61 percent of those surveyed). Of course, standard benefits are also provided, with additional features such as company cars and expense accounts thrown in to recognize the distinctive feature of the jobs performed by this special group.

Employees in Foreign Subsidiaries

Placing a U.S. employee in a foreign subsidiary can be both expensive and, at times, prone to failure. The average annual cost to send an employee overseas for a year or more approaches **one quarter of a million dollars**.[34] This figure is about five times higher than for a domestic relocation.

One of the many decisions multinational organizations face involves the type of personnel to hire at their foreign locations. They may choose among a mix of U.S. expatriates (USEs), third-country nationals (TCNs), and local country nationals (LCNs). One obvious choice is to staff the subsidiary with individuals whose citizenship corresponds to the country in which the subsidiary is located (LCNs). Hiring these LCNs has its advantages. Relocation expenses are saved. Concerns about the employee "fitting in" with the local culture are avoided. Employment of LCNs satisfies the host country's demands for hiring of locals. Only rarely do organizations decide that hiring of LCNs is inappropriate.

Usually, reasons for hiring USEs or TCNs can be traced to one of the following: (1) the foreign assignment represents an opportunity to develop the international perspective of selected USEs, (2) the position is sufficiently confidential that information is entrusted only to a proven domestic veteran, (3) the particular talent demanded for a position is not available in the local pool, (4) the talent is available but in insufficient quantities, or (5) hiring of LCNs has yielded a history of expensive "pirating" by other local firms. When one of these situations arises, the foreign subsidiary either transfers USEs to the foreign subsidiary or hires a TCN, an individual whose home country is neither the United States nor the host country. Depending on the location of the foreign subsidiary, the decision can have substantial cost implications, as Exhibit 16.14 suggests.

The compensation package offered each of these three groups must meet three criteria. First, the compensation must be high enough to attract qualified applicants. Ensuring reasonable compensation, though, sometimes is more difficult than in a more familiar domestic environment. Companies operating in foreign countries report that it is quite difficult to obtain local data on competitive compensation rates.[35] Second, the compensation costs must be tolerable to the organization so that the foreign operation remains comparatively profitable. And, most important, the compensation package must be equitable for the three groups. This latter concern yields special compensation treatment for personnel in foreign subsidiaries. For example, equity for USEs becomes an issue

---

[34]Mike Fergus, "Employees on the Move," *HRMagazine* 36, no. 5 (May 1990), pp. 44–46.

[35]Peter J. Dowling, "Hot Issues Overseas," *Personnel Administrator*, January 1989, pp. 66–72.

EXHIBIT 16.14   Cross-Country Cost Comparisons for Local Country Nationals and U.S. Expatriates

	Belgium	France	United Kingdom	Germany
Local national	$221,000	$204,000	$139,000	$199,000
U.S. expatriate	217,000	193,000	217,000	246,000

SOURCE: Jack B. Anderson, "Compensating Your Overseas Executives, Part 2: Europe in 1992," *Compensation and Benefits Review* 22, no. 4 (1990), pp. 25–35.

both in keeping them whole relative to salary of their U.S.–based counterparts and in providing an incentive wage for accepting employment in an unfamiliar, and perhaps less comfortable, environment. Equity concerns for both LCNs and TCNs center on the appropriate compensation standard for comparative purposes. Should, for example, TCNs be paid according to their home country norms, U.S. norms, or local country norms? North American firms show a preference (51 percent) for following home country wage practices for executive TCNs. European- (33 percent) and Japanese-based companies (19 percent) are less likely to use this standard, preferring instead to link executive salaries to competitive practices in the home country of the operation.[36]

Three standards for setting wages are generally used: using home country wage levels, host country wage levels, or some combination of the two. Using the home country salary as a basis of equitable comparison probably best corresponds to the equity standard each of these three groups employs; in addition it probably facilitates home country repatriation. A host country standard probably helps to establish a psychological bond with the local environment, facilitating the transition to a foreign work environment. Finally, wages based on some combination of different country standards are typically employed to facilitate transfer within certain geographic areas, most notably among the Common Market countries. More explicit statements on the compensation packages for the three groups of employees are covered below.

U.S. Expatriates.   Maintaining equity for USEs while serving in a foreign subsidiary typically requires a three-component compensation package, including a base salary, incentive, and equalization. The three parts of the package are guided by the principle of keeping the workers whole. This means that compensation is allocated for psychological and real costs borne by the USE in excess of costs that would have been incurred in the home country.

Base salary of USEs depends on job worth, typically assessed using the same job evaluation system and surveys employed for domestic workers.

---

[36]Hewitt Associates, *Europe 1992: Business Outlook and Human Resource Planning in Multinational Companies* (Lincolnshire, Ill.: Hewitt Associates, 1992).

The second component, the incentive component, referred to as a *foreign service premium,* is paid because the foreign assignment requires the expatriate to (1) work with less supervision than an American counterpart; (2) live and work in strange and, in some cases, uncongenial surroundings; and (3) represent the U.S. employer in the host country. The size of the premium is a function of both the expected hardship to be endured in the host country during employment and the type of expatriate employed. As the hardship increases, the size of the foreign service premium increases. For example, an assignment in Brussels would yield little or no foreign service premium, but one in Beijing might warrant a considerably larger incentive. Balanced against this hardship component are also considerations of the role played by the USE. For example, career international employees are less likely to receive a foreign service premium, in large part because their choice of an international career eliminates the need to provide transfer incentives. Foreign service premiums also are less prevalent in organizations where foreign service assignments are viewed as a necessary career progression stage, preparatory to assumption of top-level positions in the multinational organization. For more traditional international assignments with neutral career implications, though, incentives may be necessary to attract these boundary spanners to the geographic frontiers of the organization. When foreign service premiums exist, though, they have the potential of creating perceptions of unfair treatment. Local nationals working alongside USEs receiving such premiums may perceive such continued compensation as inequitable. From an employee relations perspective, some firms believe that it makes sense to offer one-time transfer incentives granted at the time a foreign service assignment is accepted. This eliminates the difference in base wages that trigger perceptions of unfairness.[37]

A third component of the USE compensation package includes four equalization allowances. The intent of these allowances is to keep the worker whole financially while serving in an overseas assignment. The first income source is a tax equalization allowance. Income earned in foreign countries has two potential sources of income tax liability. With few exceptions (Saudi Arabia is one), foreign income tax liabilities are incurred on foreign-earned income. The United States also taxes foreign-earned income above a certain dollar level (more than $95,000 in foreign income triggers U.S. taxes). Tax equalization allowances provide for employer payment of tax liabilities at a rate sufficient to ensure that a USE does not have any negative tax impact from employment in a foreign country. In some countries this cost can be substantial. The marginal tax rate in both Belgium and the Netherlands can exceed 70 percent.[38]

A second allowance covers housing in the host country. These payments are intended to compensate for the difference between U.S. housing costs and comparable foreign housing. The alternative to providing this allowance is to provide an expatriate housing complex. Obviously, this option is considered only when the USE contingent is large enough to warrant such outlays. A fourth equalization allowance, offered by many organizations, pays for language training of the expatriate and family members who also

[37]Compflash, "International Issues," *Compflash,* August 1991, p. 5.

[38]Peter Dowling and Randall Schuler, *International Dimensions of Human Resource Management* (Boston: PWS-KENT, 1990).

make the move. In addition, some companies provide educational allowances to ensure that the quality of children's education is equivalent to that in the home country.

Finally, cost of living allowances (COLAs) are intended to equalize the differential for a market basket of goods an USE might be expected to purchase. These adjustments tend to be a major source of complaints in expatriate compensation. High-quality and readily available goods in the United States may be extremely costly or unavailable in the foreign subsidiary. No COLA can compensate for the changes in life style necessitated by differences in quality and type of goods available. Despite the inherent difficulties of comparing apples and oranges, most companies use some index of living costs abroad, typically provided either by a consulting firm or by the State Department. For example Runzheimer International provides comparative cost of living data for different cities around the world. A $75,000 cost outlay for a typical family of four in the United States would translate into a cost of $40,800 in Warsaw, $73,000 in Rome, $151,000 in Seoul, or a whopping $207,000 in Tokyo.[39]

Third Country Nationals. TCN's compensation could be determined from a local standard, a standard in the TCN's home country or a U.S. standard. Any of the three have legitimacy, particularly when the TCN is working alongside a USE receiving U.S.– based compensation and an LCN receiving compensation pegged to local rates. Typically the organization must ask two questions before selecting an appropriate standard. First, is the person hired by the corporation as part of an international reservoir of talent or by the subsidiary to satisfy local needs? As part of an international contingent, the appropriate standard might be the home country or the U.S. standard. If the hire is to satisfy local needs, the standard might be the local pay scale. As a second question, does the individual plan to retire in the home or the local country? As an indicator of the allegiances for the TCN, the answer would either dictate home country or local pay scales, respectively.

It is not uncommon to base compensation decisions on the basis of original employment. A TCN hired in the country of employment would be treated the same as a local national. Recruitment from the country of origin would necessitate compensation linked to that country's wage standards.[40]

Local Country Nationals. Although there is a growing trend to pay USEs, TCNs, and LCNs on the same scale, the prevalent compensation standard for LCNs continues to be the local pay scale. The major difficulty arises when compensation is pegged to the value of the U.S. dollar. If the dollar changes in value relative to local currency, the compensation system must be flexible to ensure that the fluctuation does not penalize or provide windfall salary levels.

---

[39]"Stacking Up the Cities for U.S. Expatriates," *The Wall Street Journal,* May 4, 1990, p. B1.

[40]C. Ian Sym-Smith and Mark S. White, "Compensation Programs for International Organizations," in *Handbook of Wage and Salary Administration,* ed. Milton Rock (New York: McGraw Hill, 1984), pp. 55:1–55:15.

Conclusions.   Special groups are portrayed here as having jobs with high potential for conflict, resolution of which is central to the goals of the organization. Probably because of these elements, special groups receive compensation treatment that differs from other employees. Unfortunately, most of this compensation differentiation is prescriptive in nature, and little is known about the specific roles assumed by special groups and the functions compensation should assume in motivating appropriate performance. Future practice and research should focus on these issues.

REVIEW QUESTIONS

1. Is it possible for occupational groups other than those discussed in this chapter to assume the status of a special group for the purpose of compensation? If your answer is no, explain why not. If your answer is yes, explain why. Use as your example the job of a lawyer in an industry going through deregulation (elimination or revision of some of the rules governing the way firms in the industry do business).

2. For each of the special groups discussed in this chapter, explain how the issue of equity is especially important. Who are the comparison groups against which special group members might compare themselves to determine whether compensation is fair?

3. Identify possible explanations for paying executives such high levels of compensation. Which of the possible explanations identified in this book seem least likely? Why?

4. Why are external market wages so important in the determination of wages for both professional (scientist and engineer) and sales personnel?

5. Employees in foreign subsidiaries provide a perfect opportunity to illustrate how rewards other than wages influence the way we structure compensation packages. Explain how compensation might differ depending on the way the firm communicates the importance of the assignment to an employee's career.

Altoun, a small country in Central Africa, represents 12 percent of the market for Enfantmil, an American competitor in the infant formula market. Enfantmil represents the major product (81 percent of gross revenues) of TEJAK enterprises, a small firm located in Columbus, South Carolina. Enfantmil is the brainchild of Erinn E. Andrews, the founder of TEJAK and a Ph.D. in nutrition from the University of Michigan. Domestic employment for TEJAK is 436; current employment in Altoun is 28. The Altoun subsidiary is in charge of marketing and distribution to all of that country (128,000 square miles). TEJAK salaries for Altounian employees (including foreign service premium but excluding other allowances) follow:

Position	Number	Status	Current Foreign Compensation
General manager	1	USE	$88,000
Marketing manager	1	USE	$59,000
Distribution manager	1	LCN	$14,000
Drivers	3	LCN	$ 3,000
Drivers	3	TCN	$ 8,000
Handlers/labor	14	LCN	$ 1,200
Clerical	4	LCN	$ 1,400
Legal	1	LCN	$17,500

USE = U.S. expatriate; LCN = local country national; TCN = third country national.

Jim Higgins, the general manager in Altoun, has reported that two problems exist in these compensation figures (as far as he can determine). First, his marketing manager, Pete Foy, has been complaining for months that his salary is not sufficient to compensate for living in Altoun. He has made threats, which Mr. Higgins believes, that he will exercise his option to return to the United States when his current contract expires in three months. The second problem Mr. Higgins faces is a complaint by Altounian truck drivers that their salaries are much lower than those received by the three Greek drivers. Drivers are scarce in Altoun, and Mr. Higgins can't afford to lose anyone who knows how to drive the large delivery trucks used to transport Enfantmil. As compensation manager for TEJAK, you have the responsibility to recommend salary increases and rationales to Mr. Higgins. The following data are available to you.

Domestic salaries (U.S.) for selected comparable positions
Marketing manager	$49,000
Driver	$27,000

Greek salaries for selected comparable positions
Marketing manager	$16,000 (U.S. dollars)
Driver	$12,500 (U.S. dollars)

Altounian salaries for selected comparable positions
Marketing manager	No available data
Driver	$3,000 (U.S. dollars)

The following are applicable tax rates (average for salaries quoted).

	Income Level (in percentages)				
	$3,000	$8,000	$12,500	$49,000	$59,000
U.S. tax rate	–0–	–0–	–0–	20	21
Greek tax rate	–0–	5	15	41	68
Altounian tax rate	4	24	57	70	70

Legal Framework

U.S.	By law, $95,000 of foreign income excluded from U.S. taxes
Greek	By law, $10,000 of foreign income excluded from Greek taxes
Altounian	All foreigners are required to pay full taxes on income earned in Altoun

The following are TEJAK allowances:

	Type of Employee		
	US	*LCN*	*TCN*
Housing	*	–0–	*
Education and language training	–0–	–0–	–0–
Cost of living allowance	8%†	–0–	–0–
Tax equalization allowance	30%†	–0–	–0–

*Appropriate housing provided
†Percentage of current foreign compensation

1. Does Mr. Foy have a legitimate complaint about his wages, or is this just another example of his squeaky wheel mentality? If corrections are necessary, where should they be made and how large should they be?

2. Is the LCN salary appropriate? By what basis of comparison is this judgment made (i.e., who should the comparison be made against and what should the comparison dollar amount be)?

3. If you think you need further information to answer this question completely, indicate what information you need and provide a justification.

Union Role in Wage and Salary Administration

Many experts believe that unions are currently facing their most critical challenge of the last 50 years.[1] Between 1954 and 1987, union membership fell 50 percent.[2] During roughly that same period, the union success rate in certification elections (winning rights

---

[1]Thomas A. Kochan, Harry C. Katz, and Robert B. McKersie, *The Transformation of American Industrial Relations* (New York: Basic Books, 1986), pp. 221–23.
[2]Kirkland Ropp, "State of the Unions," *Personnel Administrator* 32, no. 7 (1987), pp. 36–41.

to represent previously nonunion workers) fell from 60 percent to approximately 45 percent.[3]

One popular explanation for this decline is that management is taking an increasingly hard stance against unions in general and union demands in particular. Much of this management opposition to unions is spurred by increasing pressure from both domestic and international competitors. Management increasingly resists wage increases that would give nonunion competitors, both domestic and foreign, a competitive price advantage. The end result of these competitive pressures is a declining union–nonunion wage differential. In fact, one study shows that a 10 percent rise in import share (a popular measure of international competition) has the effect of lowering the union wage differential by approximately 2 percent.[4]

Such competitive pressures during the 1980s and early 1990s have triggered lower than normal wage increases in unionized firms and even some wage concessions. Accompanying these wage trends is an increasing pessimism about the continued viability of unions in American industry. One survey of union employees covering changing attitudes during the 1983–1984 period reported a decline from 53 percent to 41 percent in positive answers to the question: "Are unions necessary for equitable labor relations?"[5] More recent surveys report similar attitudes toward unions (Exhibit 17.1).

Despite these pessimistic statistics, though, it would be a mistake to conclude that the impact of unions on wage and salary administration is minor. Even in a nonunion firm, the actions taken by wage and salary administrators are influenced by external union

EXHIBIT 17.1   Attitudes in the Labor Management Arena

Question	Percentage of Response	
	Yes	*Other*
Are workers better off with a union?		
Overall response	49	51
Union respondents	83	17
Management respondents	46	54
Do you view unions favorably?	44	56
Do you view management favorably?	64	36
Do you favor right to work laws?	70	30
(bans mandatory union membership)		

Source: Media General Associated Press Poll, 1989.

---

[3]Richard B. Freeman, *On the Divergence of Unionism among Developed Countries* (Working paper no. 2817, National Bureau of Economic Research, 1989).

[4]David A. Macpherson and James B. Steward, "The Effect of International Competition on Union and Non-Union Wages," *Industrial and Labor Relations Review* 43, no. 4, (1990), pp. 434–46.

[5]R. Wayne Mondy and Shane Preameaux, "The Labor Management Power Relationship Revisited," *Personnel Administrator,* May 1985, pp. 51–54.

activity. This chapter outlines the general factors affecting wages in unionized firms and then illustrates the specific impact of unions in wage determination. Four specific areas of union impact are discussed: (1) on general wage and benefit levels, (2) on the structure of wages, (3) on nonunion firms (known as *spillover*), and (4) on wage and salary policies and practices in unionized firms. The final discussion focuses on union response to the changing economic environment of the 1980s and the alternative compensation systems that have evolved in response to these changes.

GENERAL FACTORS AFFECTING WAGES IN UNIONIZED FIRMS

Some interesting economic realities have made compensation decision making a crucial factor in organizational success for the 1990s. First, it is increasingly apparent that international competition has a significant impact on the profitability of U.S. enterprises. Our ability to compete, in both domestic and foreign markets, continues to decline.[6] As our product prices become noncompetitive in the international market, the result, as any executive in the auto industry during the past decade can attest, can be catastrophic.

The United States also is experiencing significant changes in the composition of industries. Fewer manufacturing and more service jobs are being created. Most of these new jobs come from small firms. In fact, between 1980 and 1986, 63 percent of all new positions were generated in small firms.[7] Both these small firms fighting to survive and larger firms striving to combat foreign competition seek ways to control labor costs. To understand the direction these efforts take in unionized settings, it would help first to understand the factors affecting wage determination in unionized organizations. These factors include (1) productivity, (2) changes in the cost of living, (3) ability of an employer to pay, and (4) comparability among wage rates (equity).[8] Not surprisingly, each of these issues has received considerable attention lately, and the outcome of this attention may well be dramatic changes in compensation of unionized employees.

Productivity

Although the United States has the highest per worker productivity of any country in the world, yearly increases in productivity have lagged far behind most other industrial countries over the past decade. Although this decline is undoubtedly due to a host of factors, including slow modernization rates in key manufacturing sectors, a portion of the blame for lower productivity continues to be directed at unions. The sources of these complaints are twofold. First, union contracts establish staffing practices or other work rules that artificially reduce output. Examples of such practices include minimum crew size requirements and provisions limiting subcontracting. Second, union-initiated strikes obviously restrict output during the term of the strike.

---

[6]Bureau of National Affairs, *Changing Pay Practices: New Developments in Employee Compensation* (Washington, D.C.: Bureau of National Affairs, 1988).

[7]Ibid.

[8]Daniel Quinn Mills, *Labor Management Relations* (New York: McGraw-Hill, 1989).

Alternatively, some experts suggest that output is enhanced by unions. This argument suggests that unions negotiate higher wages and provide an outlet to vent grievances against management. By improving satisfaction and lowering turnover, unions are argued to have positive impact on net productivity.[9]

No matter the outcome of these debates. Management is acting as if unions cause lower productivity. The result has been an increasingly tougher stand in negotiations and more agreements to tie wage increases to productivity increases. A whole host of compensation changes has resulted, including incentive systems, profit sharing plans, and merit-based pay plans. Later in this chapter we will discuss the nature of these changes and the role of unions in this process.

Cost of Living

Cost of living adjustments (COLAs) are designed to increase wages automatically during the life of the contract as a function of changes in the consumer price index. During the inflation-ridden 1970s, unions made a strong drive for these escalator clauses. Indeed, by 1978, COLA clauses had made broad inroads on the labor management scene, despite evidence that such contract clauses failed to keep workers "whole" with respect to inflation.[10] More recently, though, unions have exhibited less interest in bargaining for COLA clauses. This shift is probably traceable to deceleration of the consumer price index during the mid- and late-1980s. Historically, unions have clamored for COLAs during periods of high inflation and deemphasized them when inflation rates were more tolerable. Now that the inflation rate has moderated in the past several years, fewer unions consider COLA clauses a vital element of a total package. The number of workers covered by COLA clauses in negotiated contracts declined from 59 percent in 1980 to 49 percent in 1985.[11] Since 1987, the extent of COLA coverage has leveled off. Today, approximately 38 percent of the 5.9 million workers covered by major agreements have COLA clauses in their contracts.[12]

Despite the decreased current interest in them, escalator clauses deserve discussion, if only in anticipation of future bouts with inflation and renewed interest in this contractual safeguard. All COLAs have two common elements: some measure of change in living costs and a formula to adjust wages as a function of these changes in living costs. The most common measure of change in living costs is the consumer price index (CPI) prepared by the Bureau of Labor Statistics. Recall from Chapter 15 that the CPI provides an estimate of the change in cost of a market basket of goods (as many as 4,000 individual

[9]Richard Freeman, "Individual Mobility and Union Voice in the Labor Market," *American Economic Review,* May 1976, pp. 361–68.

[10]Victor J. Sheifer, "Collective Bargaining and the CPI: Escalation v. Catch-Up," *Proceedings of the 31st Annual Meeting, Industrial Relations Research Association Series,* 1978, pp. 257–63.

[11]Richard Henderson, "Contract Concessions: Is the Past Prologue?" *Compensation and Benefits Review* 18, no. 5 (1986), pp. 17–30.

[12]Bureau of Labor Statistics, "Major Collective Bargaining Settlements in Private Industry," *Current Wage Developments* 43, no. 3 (1990).

items may be priced every month to determine changes in the cost patterns). The cost of this market basket is compared against a base period cost to determine change.

The second element of an escalator clause is the formula for adjusting wages as the CPI changes. The most common formulas provide for a 1 cent increase in wages for each 0.3 or 0.4 percent rise in the consumer price index.[13]

Ability to Pay and Wage Comparability within Industries

The third factor affecting wage levels in unionized organizations is an employer's ability to pay. In profitable years, unions reason that part of the profits should accrue to the work force responsible for much of the organization's success. This argument plays a role in the eventual determination of bargained wage levels. What follows then is well-known by the U.S. consumer. Product prices are raised and labor cost increases are cited as a major reason. In the past, this pattern usually did not cause problems. Consumers continued to purchase what remained a competitively priced product compared to the same product offered by other firms in the industry.

In large part, this continued competitiveness can be explained by introducing the fourth factor affecting wage levels: comparability among wage rates. As one group of workers representing one firm received wage increases, product competitors agreed to similar demands by their work force. The result was labor cost and product price increases that rose relatively uniformly across firms in the industry. As long as unions were able to control wage increases within an industry (usually by organizing the whole industry), no employer suffered a disproportionate wage increase or the resulting noncompetitive product price! Employers were content to go along with this situation as long as they received a reasonable return on investment and their market share remained unaffected. What they failed to realize, and what must be considered in future wage negotiations, is the rapid internationalization of product markets. Increased imports during the 1980s and 1990s caused major retrenchments for such diverse industries as shoes, apparel, steel, autos, consumer electronics, and capital goods.[14] Spurred by the need to compete with international producers, several of these industries (e.g., auto and steel) negotiated major wage and work rule concessions.[15] The auto industry is a classic example. Japanese autoworkers receive compensation worth approximately one half that of their U.S. counterparts. As long as Japan assumed a small role in the auto market, U.S. auto manufacturers were concerned primarily about wages relative to domestic manufacturers. As Japan increased its market share due to competitive price/quality differentials, however, the comparative wage differential loomed larger and larger. This differential played a large role in United Auto Workers (UAW) concessions to both Ford and General Motors in 1982.

Is the auto industry unique, or are wage concessions a new, and potentially permanent, feature of the industrial relations scene? One view argues that current wage concessions

---

[13]Sheifer, "Collective Bargaining and the CPI: Escalation v. Catch-Up."

[14]John A. Fossum, *Labor Relations: Development, Structure, Process* (Homewood, Ill.: BPI/Irwin, 1989).

[15]Ibid.

represent "much ado about nothing."[16] As evidence, this faction points out that during the depression (1929–1933), average hourly earnings fell 22 percent. In contrast, the height of the "wage concession" period was marked by a *22 percent rise* in average hourly earnings (1981–1986).[17] A second view argues that wage concessions are real and have been a fixture of the industrial relations scene at different times during the entire 20th century.[18] For example, in 1908, the glass bottle blowers accepted a 20 percent wage cut in the hope of fighting automation. During the 1930s, concessions were a regular feature in the construction, printing, and shoe industries. Concessions were also made in the apparel and textile industries during the 1950s. Continuing into the 1980s, major contract concessions occurred in eight industries: air transport, food stores, shoe manufacturing, primary metals, metal cans, transportation equipment, textiles, and trucking.[19] The pattern of wage changes over the last decade is illustrated in Exhibit 17.2.

Notice that the magnitude of union wage settlements declined markedly in the early 1980s. In 1983, for example, a large number of contracts were characterized by wage reductions. Current wage patterns show fewer wage cuts but are still marked by low overall levels of increases. In part, this is obviously due to the declining inflation rate over this period.

It would be a mistake to assume that concessions come only in the form of straightforward wage reductions. Other concession strategies exist. Because of their increasing prominence, we discuss three further variations of concessions.

One further type of concession comes in the form of *lump-sum awards*. Although not traditionally cast as a concession, lump-sum awards do fit this category. Workers receive a lump sum of money at a specified time. The dollar amount is not factored into their base salary. For example, in September 1988, Revlon and the UAW began working

---

EXHIBIT 17.2   Types of First-Year Wage Adjustments in Major Agreements

	Percentage of Workers				
Wage Adjustment	*1980*	*1983*	*1988*	*1989*	*1990*
Wages decreased	–0–	15	2	<1	<1
No change	<1	22	20	20	4
Increase less than 4%	4	14	50	44	60
Increase more than 4%	95	48	28	37	35

SOURCE: Bureau of Labor Statistics, Department of Labor, *Current Wage Developments,* various issues.

---

[16]John Dunlop, "Have the 1980's Changed U.S. Industrial Relations," *Monthly Labor Review* 5 (1988), pp. 29–34.

[17]Ibid.

[18]Richard Freeman and James Medoff, *What Do Unions Do?* (New York: Basic Books, 1984).

[19]Robert Gay, "Union Contract Concessions and Their Implications for Union Wage Determination" (Working paper no. 38, Division of Research and Statistics, Board of Governors of the Federal Reserve System, 1984).

under a contract that awarded workers a lump sum equal to 100 hours of pay rather than a 5 percent increase in base salary. Lump-sum awards save companies money in two ways. Consider a worker with an initial salary of $10,000 dollars. A 5 percent increase would raise base wages to $10,500. Employee benefits tied to base wages (e.g., life insurance is typically provided as some percentage of base wages) would rise correspondingly. During the next year of the contract, any percent increase is applied to the new base of $10,500. Contrast this with a lump-sum award equal to 5 percent. Employees still receive $500, but it is given as a separate check, not added to base wages. Benefit costs are not affected and any future percentage raises are applied to a base of $10,000, not $10,500. The difference may be small for one worker during one year, but over many workers and across many years, the savings can be substantial. In 1990, fully 44 percent of all contracts provided for lump-sum payouts.[20]

An additional form of concession consists of a *back-loaded wage clause*. Approximately 27 percent of all workers covered by contracts negotiated in 1989 had back-loaded clauses included.[21] These contracts specify low increases during the early years of the contract and larger increases at the back end. Given the time value of money (a fixed dollar amount is worth more now than later), this reduces the overall cost of the wage packages for employers.

A final type of concession centers on reductions in benefit costs. According to a study by a Washington consulting firm, employee health insurance premiums represent a cost drain equal to about one fourth of net earnings for many American corporations.[22] Not surprisingly, this has led many employers to try shifting the costs of health insurance premiums more to employees. According to an analysis of union contracts by the Bureau of National Affairs, premium cost sharing was found in 19 percent of contracts in 1986 and 28 percent of contracts in 1989.[23] For example, the International Brotherhood of Electrical Workers was asked to increase both its annual deductibles for medical care and its deductible for prescription drugs in its 1991 contract negotiation with GTE Florida. The deductible rose from $260 to $265 for single health care coverage and from $780 to $795 for family coverage. The deductible for prescription drugs doubled to $8.[24]

Examples of other types of concessions are numerous. For example, the General Motors Stamping plant workers in Fairfield, Ohio, agreed to a 50 percent cut in paid vacations during the last contract negotiation in exchange for greater job security and other forms of management trade-offs.[25]

---

[20]U.S. Department of Labor, "Current Wage Developments," March 1991, pp. 4–5.

[21]Department of Labor, "Current Wage Developments," March 1990, p. 5.

[22]"Labor Leaders Agree on a Health Care Position," *Los Angeles Times,* February 20, 1991, p. D5.

[23]Bureau of National Affairs, *Basic Patterns in Union Contracts* (Washington, D.C.: Bureau of National Affairs, 1989).

[24]"Current Wage Developments," *Monthly Labor Review,* July 1991, p. 138.

[25]Ibid.

THE IMPACT OF UNIONS IN WAGE DETERMINATION

Union Impact on Wage and Benefit Levels

The first compensation issue concerns whether the presence of a union in an organization raises the level of wages and benefits of workers above what they would be if the company were not unionized. The commonly held belief among workers is that unions do have a wage impact. More than 80 percent of the respondents to a quality of employment survey believed that unions improved the wages of workers.[26] Efforts to determine whether this perception is accurate have been a focus of research for at least 40 years.

Unfortunately, comparing the union versus nonunion wage and benefit differential is no easy chore. Several measurement problems are difficult to overcome. The ideal situation for estimating union impact would compare numerous organizations that were identical except for the presence or absence of a union.[27] Any wage differences among these organizations could then be attributed to unionization. Unfortunately, few such situations exist. One alternative strategy adopted has been to identify organizations within the same industry that differ in level of unionization. For example, consider company A, which is unionized, and company B, which is not. It is difficult to argue with assurance that wage differences between the two firms are attributable to the presence or absence of a union. First, the fact that the union has not organized the entire industry weakens its power base (e.g., strike efforts to shut down the entire industry could be thwarted by nonunion firms). Consequently, any union impact in this example might underestimate the role of unions in an industry in which percentage of unionization is higher. A second problem in measuring union impact is apparent from this example. What if company B grants concessions to employees as a strategy to avoid unionization? These concessions, indirectly attributable to the presence of a union (the union in company A), would lead to underestimation of union impact on wages.

A second strategy for estimating union impact on wages is to compare two different industries that vary dramatically in the level of unionization.[28] This strategy suffers because nonunionized industries (e.g., agriculture, service) are markedly different from unionized industries in the types of labor employed and their general availability. Such differences have a major impact on wages independent of the level of unionization and make any statements about union impact difficult to substantiate.

One source of continuing data on unionized and nonunionized firms is the Bureau of Labor Statistics. Between 1969 and 1985, union wage premiums more than doubled from 17.6 to 35.6 percent.[29] Between 1979 and 1988, union versus nonunion pay

---

[26]Thomas A. Kochan, "How American Workers View Labor Unions," *Monthly Labor Review,* April 1979, pp. 23–31.

[27]Allan M. Carter and F. Ray Marshall, *Labor Economics* (Homewood, Ill.: Richard D. Irwin, 1982).

[28]Ibid.

[29]Michael L. Wachter and William H. Carter, "Norm Shifts in Union Wages: Will 1989 Be a Replay of 1969?" in *Brookings Papers on Economic Activity,* ed. William C. Brainard and George L. Perry (Washington, D.C.: The Brookings Institution, 1989), pp. 233–76.

differential increased in 6 industries and decreased in 9 (of 15 selected industries).[30] Historically, union wages have experienced multiple-year upswings followed by multiple-year downswings. The 1950s were characterized by a widening of the union wage impact, followed by constriction in the 1960s, an enlargement from 1969 to 1983, and another constriction from 1983 to the present.[31] Since 1983, the nonunion sector has been securing larger wage increases than the unionized sector, partially due to unions' acceptance of lump-sum payments in lieu of increases in base wage.[32]

Perhaps the best conclusion about union versus nonunion wage differences comes from a recent summary analysis of 114 different studies.[33] Two important points emerged:

1. Unions do make a difference in wages. Union workers earn somewhere between 8.9 percent and 12.4 percent more than their nonunion counterparts.

2. The size of the wage gap varies from year to year. During periods of higher unemployment, the impact of unions is large. When economies are strong, the union-nonunion gap is small. Part of the explanation for this time-based phenomenon is related to union resistance to wage cuts during recessions and the relatively slow responses of unions to wage increases during inflationary periods (because of rigidities or lags introduced by the presence of multiyear labor contracts).

In addition, research indicates that the presence of a union adds about 20 to 30 percent to employee benefits.[34] Unions also have an impact on the difference between wages for selected groups. Wage differentials between workers who are different in terms of race, age, service, skill level, and education appear to be lower under collective bargaining.[35]

Similar studies of union-nonunion wage differentials exist for employees in the public sector.[36] In a summary of 13 public sector union studies, Lewin concluded that the average wage effect of public sector unions is approximately +5 percent. As Lewin notes, this wage differential is smaller than typically assumed and certainly smaller than is estimated for the private sector. Of course, this 5 percent average masks some large variations in wage increases for different occupational groups in the public sector. The largest gains for public sector employees are reported for fire fighters, with some studies reporting as much as an 18 percent wage differential attributable to the presence of a union. At the

---

[30]Kay E. Anderson, Philip M. Doyle, and Albert E. Schwenk, "Measuring Union-Nonunion Earnings Differences," *Monthly Labor Review* 113 (1990), pp. 26–38.

[31]Wachter and Carter, "Norm Shifts in Union Wages: Will 1989 Be a Replay of 1969?"

[32]Anderson, Doyle, and Schwenk, "Measuring Union-Nonunion Earnings Differences."

[33]Stephen B. Jarrell and T. D. Stanley, "A Meta Analysis of the Union-Non Union Wage Gap," *Industrial and Labor Relations Review* 44, no. 1 (1990), pp. 54–67.

[34]Freeman and Medoff, *What Do Unions Do?*

[35]R. Freeman and J. Medoff, "The Impact of Collective Bargaining: Illusion or Reality?" in J. Steiber, R. McKersie, and D. Q. Mills, *U.S. Industrial Relations 1950–1980: A Critical Assessment* (Madison, Wis.: IRRA).

[36]David Lewin, "Public Sector Labor Relations: A Review Essay," in *Public Sector Labor Relations: Analysis and Readings,* ed. David Lewin, Peter Feuille, and Thomas Kochan (Glen Ridge, N.J.: Thomas Horton and Daughters, 1977), pp. 116–44.

other extreme, however, teachers' unions (primarily affiliates of the National Education Association and the American Federation of Teachers) have not fared as well, with reported impacts generally in the range of + 1 to + 4 percent.[37]

The Structure of Wage Packages

The second compensation issue involves the structure of wage packages. One dimension of this issue concerns the division between direct wages and employee benefits. There is evidence that union employees have employee benefit packages that are about 20 to 30 percent higher than nonunion employees have. Whether because of reduced management control, strong union-worker preference for benefits, or other reasons, unionized employees also have a higher percentage of their total wage bill allocated to employee benefits.[38] Typically, this shows up in the form of higher pension expenditures or higher insurance benefits.[39] One particularly well-controlled study found unionization associated with 24 percent higher levels of pension expenditures and 46 percent higher insurance expenditures.[40]

A second dimension of the wage structure issue is a relatively new phenomenon. Along with the concession bargaining movement have come two-tier pay plans. Basically a phenomenon of the union sector, two-tier wage structures differentiate pay based upon hiring date. A contract is negotiated that specifies that employees hired after a given target date will receive lower wages than their higher seniority peers working on the same or similar jobs. From management's perspective, wage tiers represent a viable alternative compensation strategy. Tiers can be used as a cost control strategy to allow expansion or investment or as a cost-cutting device to allow economic survival.[41] Two-tier pay plans initially spread because unions viewed them as less painful than wage freezes and staff cuts among existing employees. The trade-off was to bargain away equivalent wage treatment for future employees! Remember, this is a radical departure from the most basic precepts of unionization. Unions evolved and continue to endure, in part, based on the belief that all members are equal. Two-tier plans are obviously at odds with this principle. Lower-tier employees, those hired after the contract is ratified, receive wages 50 to 80 percent lower than employees in the higher tier.[42] The contract may specify that the wage

---

[37]For a discussion of the reasons for this smaller public sector union impact see Lewin, *Public Sector Labor Relations: An Analysis and Readings.*

[38]Bevars Mabry, "The Economics of Fringe Benefits," *Industrial Relations* 12 (1973), pp. 95–106.

[39]Robert Rice, "Skill, Earnings and the Growth of Wage Supplements," *American Economic Review* 56 (1966), pp. 583–93; George Kalamotousakis, "Statistical Analysis of the Determinants of Employee Benefits by Type," *American Economist,* Fall 1972, pp. 139–47; William Bailey and Albert Schwenk, "Employer Expenditures for Private Retirement and Insurance Plans," *Monthly Labor Review* 95 (1972), pp. 15–19.

[40]Loren Solnick, "Unionism and Fringe Benefits Expenditures," *Industrial Relations* 17, no. 1 (1978), pp. 102–7.

[41]James E. Martin and Thomas D. Heetderks, *Two-Tier Compensation Structures: Their Impact on Unions, Employer, and Employees* (Kalamazoo, Mich.: W. E. Upjohn Institute for Employment Research, 1990).

[42]Mollie Bowers and Roger Roderick, "Two-Tier Pay Systems: The Good, the Bad and the Debatable," *Personnel Administrator* 32, no. 6 (1987), pp. 101–12.

differential may be permanent, or the lower tier may be scheduled ultimately to catch up with the upper tier. Eventually, the inequity from receiving different pay for the same level of inputs may cause employee dissatisfaction.[43] Consider the Roman emperor who implemented a two-tier system for his army in 217 A.D.[44] He was assassinated by his disgruntled troops shortly thereafter. Although such expressions of dissatisfaction are unlikely today, Exhibit 17.3 indicates a number of problems related to two-tier programs.

The future of two-tier structures is uncertain. Some predict that they will continue to increase in popularity; others indicate a decline in contracts with two-tier structures.[45] This latter view is best supported by the Bureau of National Affairs annual surveys of employer bargaining objectives. Between 1988 and 1989, there was a 14 percent decline (from 95 to 81) in firms expecting to continue two-tier structures and a decrease from 18 to 12 percent of firms contemplating implementation of two-tier structures.[46] If these

---

EXHIBIT 17.3 Experiences with Two-Tier Systems (in percentages)

Have two tiers	28
Do not have two tiers	72

Reasons for Not Adopting Two-Tier System

1. Labor unrest	14
2. Morale problems	10
3. Productivity declines	2.3
4. Insufficient benefit from system	26
5. Other	27

Concessions Granted by Management to Obtain Two-Tier System

1. None	72
2. Increased employee security	7
3. Restricted subcontracting	2
4. Bonus	4
5. Reframe from shifting operations overseas	0
6. Increased salary to incumbents	10
7. Other	10

Based on a sample of 434 companies in 1986.

SOURCE: Towers, Perrin, Forster, and Crosby, "Survey of Company Experiences with Two-Tier Wage Systems," (Washington, D.C.: Towers, Perrin, Forster and Crosby, 1986).

---

[43]James Martin and Melanie Peterson, "Two-Tier Wage Structures: Implications for Equity Theory," *Academy of Management Journal* 30, no. 2 (1987), pp. 297–315.

[44]"Two-Tier Wage Systems Falter as Companies Sense Workers' Resentment," *The Wall Street Journal*, June 16, 1987, p. 1.

[45]Martin and Heetderks, *Two-Tier Compensation Structures: Their Impact on Unions, Employer, and Employees.*

[46]Bureau of National Affairs, "Agreements with Two-Tier Wage Plans Continue to Decline in 1987, Study Says," *Labor Relations Week,* March 2, 1988, pp. 201–2; and Bureau of National Affairs, "Employer Bargaining Objectives, 1989," *Collective Bargaining Negotiations and Contracts* 1131 (October 6, 1988), pp. 951–58.

trends persist, other cost-cutting compensation strategies (e.g., increased use of incentive plans) may replace two-tier systems.

Union Impact: The Spillover Effect

Although union wage settlements have declined in recent years, the impact of unions in general would be understated if we did not account for what is termed the *spillover effect*. Specifically, employers seek to avoid unionization by offering workers the wages, benefits, and working conditions won in rival unionized firms. The nonunion management continues to enjoy the freedom from union "interference" in decision making, and the workers receive the spillover of rewards already obtained by their unionized counterparts. Several studies document the existence and importance of this phenomenon, providing further evidence of the continuing role played by unions in wage determination.[47]

Role of Unions in Wage and Salary Policies and Practices

Perhaps of greatest interest to current and future compensation administrators is the role unions play in administering wages. The role of unions in administration of compensation is outlined primarily in the contract. The following illustrations of this role are taken from major collective bargaining agreements in effect between 1977 and 1992.[48]

1. *Basis for pay.* The vast majority of contracts specify that one or more jobs are to be compensated on an hourly basis and that overtime pay will be paid beyond a certain number of hours. Notice the specificity of the language in the following contract clause:

> Time and one half shall be paid for each or any of the following instances and each instance shall not be dependent on any other instance:
>
> > *a*. All hours worked in excess of eight (8)
> > hours per day.
> > *b*. The first eight (8) hours worked on a Saturday.
> > *c*. All work performed during an eating or rest period if required by the company.
> > *d*. All hours worked prior to the scheduled starting time of his shift provided
> > that the employee works the full scheduled shift or as required by the
> > company.[49]

---

[47]Loren Solnick, "The Effect of Blue Collar Unions on White Collar Wages and Fringe Benefits," *Industrial and Labor Relations Review* 38, no. 2 (1985), pp. 23–35; Lawrence Kahn, "The Effect of Unions on the Earnings of Nonunion Workers," *Industrial and Labor Relations Review* 31, no. 1 (1978), pp. 205–16.

[48]U.S. Department of Labor, *Major Collective Bargaining Agreements: Wage Administration Provisions* Bulletin 1425–17 (Washington, D.C.: Bureau of Labor Statistics, 1978); General Motors–UAW, "Agreement between General Motors Corporation and the UAW" (September 1984); Bureau of National Affairs, "Wage Patterns and Wage Data," in *Collective Bargaining Negotiations and Contracts,* 18.10-18.993 (Washington, D.C.: Bureau of National Affairs, 1984).

[49]Collective agreement between ITT Aimco Division–Tonawanda, N.Y., and International Association of Machinists and Aerospace Workers Local Lodge 1053, July 31, 1989–July 31, 1992.

Further, many contracts specify that a premium be paid above the worker's base wage for working nonstandard shifts:

> The . . . rates are based on day work and the following differentials are paid in addition thereto for the various shift classifications:
>> An individual scheduled to work days, afternoons, and nights on rotating shifts Monday through Friday, inclusive, shall receive a differential of twenty-eight cents ($.28) per hour for all hours worked.
>> An employee scheduled to work a straight night shift, including or excluding Sundays and holidays, shall receive a differential of thirty-two cents ($.32) per hour for all hours worked.[50]

Alternatively, agreements may specify a fixed daily, weekly, biweekly, or monthly rate. In addition, agreements often indicate a specific day of the week as payday and sometimes require payment on or before a certain hour. The following contract clause illustrates this requirement.

> The company will continue to pay wages earned on a weekly basis. The first shift will be paid on/or before 7:30 A.M. Friday; the second shift will be paid on/or before 3:30 P.M. Friday; and the third shift will be paid on/or before 11:30 P.M. Thursday.[51]

Much less frequently, contracts specify some form of incentive system as the basis for pay. The vast majority of clauses specifying incentive pay occur in manufacturing (as opposed to nonmanufacturing) industries. Many of these clauses provide for union-management discussion of incentives:

> It is agreed that all matters pertaining to piece work, incentive pay, and bonus are subject to discussion between the company and the union. . . .
> All work being performed on incentive basis shall have the allowance established prior to the start of the job; and this allowance and description of the job shall be furnished to the men performing the work at the beginning of the shift or job, except in cases where the allowance for the work to be performed is to be divided between individuals or groups, in which case the allowance shall be given to the individual or group prior to the end of the shift. If the allowance and the description are not furnished as required above, the job shall be considered day work.
> Incentive allowance rates will not be reduced after work has been started upon the particular job or after the completion of the particular job covered by the allowance, except when some reduction is made in the quantity of work originally specified or where the method of performing the work has been revised.[52]

2. *Occupation-wage differentials.* Most contracts recognize that different occupations should receive different wage rates. Within occupations, though, a single wage rate prevails.[53] The following contract clause illustrates this point.

---

[50]Collective Agreement between U.S. Vanadium Corp.–Niagara Falls, N.Y., and Oil, Chemical and Atomic Workers International Union Local 8-250, November 2, 1989–November 2, 1992.

[51]General Motors–UAW, "Agreement between General Motors Corporation and the UAW"; Bureau of National Affairs, "Wage Patterns and Wage Data," 1987.

[52]Ibid.

[53]Collective Agreement between U.S. Vanadium Corp.–Niagara Falls, N.Y., and Oil, Chemical and Atomic Workers International Union Local 8-250.

Effective Date of This Agreement	
Electrical technician	$15.61
Leader Machinist	15.42
Maintenance Mechanic A	14.92
Crane operator	13.35
Janitor	12.20

Although rare, some contracts do not recognize occupational/skill differentials. These contracts specify a single standard rate for all jobs covered by the agreements. Usually such contracts cover a narrow range of skilled groups.

3. *Experience/merit differentials.* Single rates are usually specified for workers within a particular job classification. Single-rate agreements do not differentiate wages on the basis of either seniority or merit. Workers with varying years of experience and output receive the same single rate. Alternatively, agreements may specify wage ranges. The following example is fairly typical.[54]

Labor-Grade	Minimum							Maximum
19	$9.66	$9.91	$10.15	$10.39	$10.92	$11.40	$11.92	$12.40
18	8.99	9.22	9.46	9.67	10.16	10.60	11.05	11.54
17	8.34	8.55	8.77	8.98	9.41	9.84	10.26	10.67

The vast majority of contracts requiring wage ranges specify seniority as the basis for movement through the range. *Automatic progression* is an appropriate name for this type of movement through the wage range, with the contract frequently specifying the time interval between movements. This type of progression is most appropriate when the necessary job skills are within the grasp of most employees. Denial of a raise is a significant exception and frequently is accompanied by the right of the union to submit any wage denial to the grievance procedure.

At the other extreme of management intervention, some agreements permit management to shorten the time between automatic progressions for workers with outstanding performance records. For example,

> Nothing in this provision shall prevent the employer from granting individual increases more frequently than each 16 weeks if, in its judgment, they are merited.[55]

A second strategy for moving employees through wage ranges is based exclusively on merit. Employees who are evaluated more highly receive larger or more rapid

---

[54]AVX Corporation and IBEW, expires December 1992.

[55]Ibid.

increments than do average or poor performers. Within these contracts, it is common to specify that disputed merit appraisals may be submitted to grievance. If the right to grievance is not explicitly *excluded,* the union has the implicit right to it.

The third method for movement through a range combines automatic and merit progression in some manner. A frequent strategy is to grant automatic increases to the midpoint of the range and permit subsequent increases only when merited on the basis of performance appraisal.

4. *Other differentials.* A number of remaining contractual provisions deal with differentials for reasons not yet covered. The first example deals with differentials for new and probationary employees. About one half of major agreements refer to differentials for these employees. The most common rate designation is below or at the minimum of the rate range. For example,

> New employees hired on or after the effective date of this Agreement, who do not hold a seniority date in any General Motors plant and are not covered by the provisions of Paragraph (98b) below, shall be hired at a rate equal to eighty five (85) percent of the maximum base rate of the job classification. Such employees shall receive an automatic increase to: (1) ninety (90) percent of the job classification at the expiration of one hundred and eighty (180) days, (2) ninety five (95) percent of the maximum base rate of the job classification at the expiration of three hundred and sixty-five (365) days, (3) the maximum base rate of the job classification at the expiration of five hundred and forty five (545) days.[56]

The second example of contractual differentials deals with different pay to unionized employees who are employed by a firm in different geographic areas. Very few contracts provide for different wages under these circumstances, despite the problems that can arise in paying uniform wages across regions with markedly different costs of living.

The final category in which differentials are mentioned in contracts deals with part-time and temporary employees. Few contracts specify special rates for these employees. Those that do, however, are about equally split between giving part-time/temporary employees wages above full-time workers (because they have been excluded from the employee benefits program) and below full-time workers.

5. *Vacations and holidays.* Vacation and holiday entitlements are among clauses frequently found in labor contracts. They, too, use very specific language, as the following example illustrates:

> Vacations will be allotted and computed on the following basis: (a) Employees hired before October 18, 1986, who are on the payroll July 1 of the current year with one to three years of continuous service prior to July 1 will be entitled to one and one-half weeks with 3 1/2 percent of yearly earnings. Employees hired on or after October 18, 1986, who are on the payroll July 1 of the current year with one to three years of continuous service prior to July 1 will be entitled to one week with 2 percent of yearly earnings.[57]

---

[56]Ibid.

[57]Collective Agreement between MRC Bearings–Jamestown and Falconer, N.Y., and International Union, United Automobile, Aerospace and Agricultural Implement Workers of America Local 338, October 21, 1989– October 16, 1992.

In our second example, as tenure with the company increases, the percentage of annual pay used as the basis for vacation pay also increases:

All employees who have passed their probationary period shall be paid for the following holidays when no work is performed on such holidays.

New Year's Day Thanksgiving Day
Memorial Day Day after Thanksgiving
Fourth of July Christmas Day
Labor Day Day before or after Christmas
Two (2) floating holidays

Any employee who is required to work on any of the holidays specified shall receive, in addition to the holiday as outlined above, double his straight time rate on all hours worked, with a minimum guarantee of eight (8) hours, work or pay.

In order to be eligible to receive holiday pay, an employee must appear on the payroll in the week preceding the holiday or the week following the holiday and also have been available for work on the regularly scheduled work day before the holiday and the regularly scheduled work day after the holiday.[58]

6. *Wage adjustment provisions.* Frequently in multiyear contracts, some provision is made for wage adjustment during the term of the contract. These adjustments might be specified in three major ways: (1) deferred wage increases, (2) reopener clauses, and (3) cost of living adjustments (COLA) or escalator clauses. A deferred wage increase is negotiated at the time of initial contract negotiations with the timing and amount specified in the contract. A reopener clause specifies that wages, and sometimes such nonwage items as pension/benefits, will be renegotiated at a specified time or under certain conditions. Finally, a COLA clause, as noted earlier, involves periodic adjustment based typically on changes in the consumer price index:

The amount of the cost-of-living allowance payable on each Effective Date of Adjustment will be determined by comparing the three month average CPI-W for the adjustment period to the Base. $.01 per hour for each full .4 of a point change that the three month average CPI-W for the adjustment period exceeds the base will be added to any cost-of-living allowance payable effective December 5, 1988. The cost-of-living allowance will be paid as a separate rate per hour for all hours for which employees receive pay from the company.[59]

An analysis of trends in wage negotiations by the Bureau of National Affairs confirms that unions have lost some power in securing these types of wage increases. As Exhibit 17.4 suggests, deferred increases, wage reopeners, and cost of living adjustments have all lost popularity in recent years.

Geographically, as Exhibit 17.5 indicates, deferred increases predominate in New England, and cost of living clauses and lump-sum payments are most common among

---

[58]Collective Agreement between Alside Supply Center–Rochester, N.Y., and United Automobile Workers District 65, November 1, 1989–October 31, 1992.

[59]Collective Agreement between The Goodyear Tire & Rubber Company–Niagara Falls, N.Y., and Oil, Chemical and Atomic Workers Local 8-277, December 10, 1988–December 9, 1991.

EXHIBIT 17.4   **Popularity of Different Wage Clauses
(Frequency Expressed as Percentage of Contracts)**

	1948	*1957*	*1966*	*1975*	*1983*	*1989*
Deferred increases	n.a.	33	72	88	94	77
Wage reopeners	40	36	13	8	7	9
COLA clauses	n.a.	18	15	36	48	26

n.a. Not tabulated until trend emerged.
SOURCE: Bureau of National Affairs, *Basic Patterns in Union Contracts* (Washington, D.C.: Bureau of National Affairs, 1989).

EXHIBIT 17.5   **Wage Clauses by Geographic Area
(Frequency Expressed as a Percentage of Contracts in Each Region)**

	Deferred Increases	*Active Cost of Living Escalators*	*Lump-Sum Payments*	*Reopeners*
All regions	77	26	22	9
Middle Atlantic	84	23	17	6
Midwest	92	29	13	8
New England	100	24	16	4
North Central	75	27	20	2
Rocky Mountain	50	20	20	—
Southeast	76	12	22	22
Southwest	54	8	8	31
West Coast	80	28	26	7
Multiregion	58	48	35	8

SOURCE: Bureau of National Affairs, *Basic Patterns in Union Contracts* (Washington, D.C.: Bureau of National Affairs, 1989).

contracts covering multiple regions. Wage reopeners are most frequent in the Southeast and Southwest.

UNIONS AND ALTERNATIVE REWARD SYSTEMS

It is unlikely that the internationalization of business and the increased cost pressures that organizations face signal the death of traditional long-term labor contracts. Rather, union response is likely to center on ensuring that industries buffeted by deregulation and intense competition are able to control labor costs. This signals continued moderation in annual wage increase demands, increased willingness to consider work rule changes, renewed interest in cooperative labor-management relations, and further experimentation with profit sharing and other wage proposals that increase cost competitiveness. This section covers the likely union response to these alternative compensation systems.

Lump-Sum Awards

As discussed earlier, lump-sum awards are one-time cash payments to employees that are not added to an employee's base wages. These awards are typically given in lieu of traditional merit increases, which are more costly to the employer. This higher cost results because merit increases are added to base wages and because several employee benefits (e.g., life insurance and vacation pay) are figured as a percentage of base wages.

One indication that lump-sum payments are popular is the increased negotiation of major settlements that include lump-sum clauses. For example, the 1987 UAW–GM agreement includes a lump-sum payment equal to 3 percent of pay in the second and third years of the three-year contract. These increases were in lieu of the traditional annual improvement factor. The Oil, Chemical and Atomic Workers also accepted a lump-sum award in its 1988 agreement. Its contract included a $900 lump-sum bonus and a 30 cent per hour increase in the first year of a two-year agreement with the major oil companies. Other major companies negotiating lump-sum bonuses include Boeing, Lockheed, General Electric Corporation, Westinghouse, General Dynamics, and John Hancock Mutual Life Insurance.

Unions typically dislike lump-sum awards for the same reason employers favor them: base wages fall behind and benefit levels are less generous. On the positive side, though, receiving a large cash outlay can be an effective consolation for what is basically a wage concession.

Employee Stock Ownership Plans (ESOP)

An alternative strategy for organizations hurt by intense competition is to obtain wage concessions in exchange for giving employees part ownership in the company. For example, in both the 1988 and previous contract the teamsters negotiated a provision permitting local trucking companies and teamster employees to set up ESOP plans.[60] The National Master Freight Agreement specifies that employees will receive 49 percent ownership in a trucking company in exchange for wage concessions of no more than 15 percent over five years. So far, these plans have not been very effective in keeping marginal firms from eventually declaring bankruptcy. Approximately 20 such contracts have been negotiated, but only three still exist. Most of the remaining firms went out of business.[61]

ESOPs have been more successful in the airline industry in which soaring fuel costs and fare wars have severely damaged several companies. Three firms (Western, Republic, and PSA) turned around heavy loss years and became profitable after negotiating ESOPs.[62] These plans specify that employees get 12 to 32 percent of the airlines stock in exchange for 10 to 20 percent wage concession. In 1987, ESOP meant $33 million in payment to

---

[60]Bureau of National Affairs, *Changing Pay Practices: New Developments in Employee Compensation* (Washington, D.C.: Bureau of National Affairs, 1988).

[61]Ibid.

[62]Given that all three of these airlines were acquired by other airlines between 1986 and 1987, it is not entirely clear whether ESOPs can be acclaimed as the sole reason for increased profitability over time.

Republic employees.[63] Although unions typically agree to stock ownership plans only to keep organizations afloat, occasionally such programs result in considerable rewards for union employees.

Pay-for-Knowledge Plans

Pay-for-knowledge plans do just that: pay employees more for learning a variety of different jobs or skills. For example, the 1986 Chrysler agreement with the UAW specifies that journeymen will get up to 50 cents per hour extra for learning new trades. By coupling this new wage system with drastic cuts in the number of job classifications, organizations have greater flexibility in moving employees quickly into high demand areas. Unions also may favor pay-for-knowledge plans because they make each individual worker more valuable and less expendable to the firm. In turn, this also lessens the probability that work can be subcontracted out to nonunion organizations.

Gain-Sharing Plans

In the 1970s and early 1980s, gain-sharing plans were viewed as very effective ways to align workers and management in efforts to streamline operations and cut costs. Any cost savings resulting from employees working smarter were split according to some formula between the organization and the workers. In the past few years, though, several companies have become disenchanted by gain-sharing plans. Parker Pen, Gould Battery, and Ingersol-Rand all recently terminated gain-sharing plans.[64] One of the main problems centers on early productivity improvement plateaus. Payouts are sometimes tied to continued increases in savings. When savings level off, the "gains" shared with workers drop correspondingly.[65] Not surprisingly, unions are not enthusiastic about making changes that continue to benefit the organization but that result in wage gains for employees only in the short term.

Rather than opposing gain sharing, though, the most common union strategy is to delay taking a stand until real costs and benefits are more apparent.[66] Politically, this may be the wisest choice for a union leader. As the data in Exhibit 17.6 indicate, there are numerous possible costs and benefits to union membership for agreeing to a gain-sharing plan. Until the plan is actually implemented, though, it is unclear what the impact will be in any particular firm.

---

[63]Ibid.

[64]John Zalusky, "Labor's Collective Bargaining Experience with Gainsharing and Profit-Sharing," Paper presented IRRA 39th Annual Meeting, December 1986, pp. 175–82.

[65]*Changing Pay Practices: New Developments in Employee Compensation,* 1988.

[66]T. Ross and R. Ross, "Gainsharing and Unions: Current Trends," in *Gainsharing: Plans for Improving Performance,* ed. B. Graham-Moore and T. Ross (Washington, D.C.: Bureau of National Affairs, 1990), pp. 200–13.

EXHIBIT 17.6 **Union Perceptions of Advantages/Disadvantages of Gain Sharing**

Percentage in Agreement

Advantages	*Disadvantages*
1. Increased recognition (95%)	1. Management may try to substitute for wage increases (94%)
2. Better job security (94%)	2. Management can't be trusted (88%)
3. More involvement in job activities (94%)	3. Peer pressure to perform may increase (77%)
4. More money (94%)	4. Don't trust/understand bonus calculations (76%)
5. More feeling of contributing to firm (86%)	5. Union influence is undermined (66%)
6. Increased influence of union (70%)	6. Increased productivity may reduce need for jobs (64%)

SOURCE: T. Ross and R. Ross, "Gainsharing and Unions: Current Trends," in *Gainsharing: Plans for Improving Performance,* ed. B. Graham-Moore and T. Ross (Washington, D.C.: Bureau of National Affairs, 1990).

Profit Sharing Plans

Unions have debated the advantages of profit sharing plans for at least 80 years.[67] In 1948, Walter Reuther, then president of the CIO (which became the AFL–CIO in 1955), championed the cause of profit sharing in the auto industry. The goal of unions is to secure sound, stable income levels for the membership. When this is achieved, subsequent introduction of a profit sharing plan allows union members to share the wealth with more profitable firms while still maintaining employment levels in marginal organizations. We should note, though, that not all unions favor profit sharing plans. As indicated by recent grumblings of employees at General Motors, inequality in profits between firms in the same industry can lead to wage differentials for workers performing the same work. Payouts to Ford employees on the profit sharing plan totaled $9,400 between 1984 and 1988. During the same period, General Motors employees received less than $1,500.[68] Most General Motors employees would argue that the difference in payout cannot be traced to the fact that Ford employees work harder or smarter. In fact, the difference in profitability, the UAW argues, is due to management decision making. Therefore, the argument runs, workers should not be penalized for factors beyond their control.

CANADIAN UNION EXPERIENCE

Canadian trade unions won the legal right to organize in 1944, nine years after U.S. trade unions won that same victory. Canadian union density followed an increasing pattern

---

[67]Zalusky, "Labor's Collective Bargaining Experience with Gainsharing and Profit-Sharing"; William Shaw, "Can Labor Be Capitalized?" *American Federationist* June 1910, p. 517.

[68]*Changing Pay Practices: New Developments in Employee Compensation,* 1988.

similar to that of the United States through the 1950s. But although U.S. union density began to decline in the 1960s, Canadian union density continued to rise before declining slightly in the 1980s. In 1989, 36.2 percent of the Canadian work force was unionized, more than double the 16.4 percent rate in the U.S. work force.[69]

Canadian unions have been more successful than their U.S. counterparts in maintaining both union membership and the number of union certifications, thanks to more liberal labor laws in Canada than in the United States.[70] Although many U.S. unions agreed to givebacks and concessions in the 1980s, Canadian unions were more resistant to concession bargaining and engaged in strikes to avoid wage concessions.[71] Further, Canada's national health insurance policy ensures health care for every Canadian citizen, making the issue of basic health insurance less contentious in Canada than it is in the United States.

In sum, the political and legal environments of Canada have been more favorable to union activity and have allowed greater union success relative to that in the United States, particularly in recent years. Whether or not Canadian unions will continue to hold strong or follow in the footsteps of their U.S. counterparts has been, and will continue to be, an issue of considerable debate.

SUMMARY

The United States no longer can view itself as the dominant economic power in the world. Other countries continue to make inroads in product areas traditionally the sole domain of U.S. companies. The impact of this increased competition has been most pronounced in the compensation area. Labor costs must be cut to improve the U.S. competitive stance. Alternative compensation systems to achieve this end are regularly being devised. Unions face a difficult situation. How should they respond to these attacks on traditional compensation systems? Many unions believe that crisis demands changing attitudes from both management and unions. Labor and management identify compensation packages that both parties can abide. Sometimes these packages include cuts in traditional forms of wages in exchange for compensation tied more closely to the success of the firm. We expect the remainder of the 1990s will be dominated by more innovation in compensation design and increased exploration between unions and management for ways to improve the competitive stance of U.S. business.

---

[69]Gary N. Chaison and Joseph B. Rose, "The Macrodeterminants of Union Growth and Decline," in *The State of the Unions,* ed. George Strauss, Daniel G. Gallagher, and Jack Fiorito (Madison, Wis.: Industrial Relations Research Association, 1991), pp. 3–45.

[70]Yonatan Reshef, "Union Decline: A View from Canada," *Journal of Labor Research* 11, no. 1 (1990), pp. 25–39; Martin J. Morand, "Canada: Our Model?" *Monthly Review* 42, no. 2 (1990), pp. 40–7; and "Canada's Controversial Labor Leader Speaks Out, Early and Often," *The Christian Science Monitor,* January 28, 1988, p. 11.

[71]Ibid.

REVIEW QUESTIONS

1. Assume, as local union president, that you have just received valid information that the bankruptcy of the company employing your workers is imminent. What types of wage concessions might your union be able to make? Which of these are likely to have the least negative impact on your union workers' wages in the short term (one year)? Which represent the greatest cost savings potential for the company in the short term? Which is most likely to create internal dissension between different factions of the union?

2. Assume that you are a researcher working for the AFL–CIO. Your boss just gave you the assignment of designing a study to show the wage impact of unions in the restaurant industry. What problems must you surmount in figuring out what is, and what is not, a wage difference that is due to the union?

3. Unions agree to alternative reward systems in response to severe financial problems within organizations . What are some of the current causes of these financial problems, and how do the alternative reward systems deal with the problems? Give specific examples of alternative reward systems and how they help solve financial problems within companies.

4. Suppose an employee has a $30,000 base wage. Assume that she receives a 5 percent performance award at the end of each year for five years. What are the five-year cost savings for distributing this award as an annual lump-sum bonus rather than as an annual merit increase?

5. Under what economic circumstances do unions favor COLA clauses? Why do fewer contracts specify COLA clauses today than 10 years ago?

The Company

General Technology (GT) is an international producer of burglar alarm systems. To crack the international market, GT must comply with quality standards as set by the International Organization for Standardization (ISO). Compliance requires that all products and processes pass a series of 17 strict criteria, the so-called ISO 9000 audit.

The Union

The Technology Workers of America (TWA) organized GT's Buffalo division in 1979. In the last contract, both parties agreed to have a three-person panel listen to all disputes between union and management concerning the proper classification of jobs.

Your Role

You are the neutral third party hired to hear the dispute described below. The union representative has voted in the union's favor, and management has sided with management's position. You will break the tie. How do you vote and why? Some experts would argue that enough evidence is presented here for you to make a decision. See if you can figure out what the logic was that led to this conclusion. Further, list what other information you would like to have and how that might influence your decision.

The Grievance

A job titled Technical Review Analyst I with responsibility for ISO 9000 audits is slotted as a tier 3 job.[1] Union believes that this job should be evaluated as a tier 4 job. Management contends that both this job and its counterpart in tier 4 (Senior Technical Review Analyst) should be graded in tier 3.

Summary of Important Points in the Union Case

The union asserts, and management agrees, that the only difference historically between auditors classified as Technical Review Analysts I (tier 3) and those classified as Senior Technical Review Analysts (tier 4) was the presence or absence of one task. That task was the performance of systems tests. Only tier 4 personnel performed this work, and this yielded the higher tier classification. With the introduction of ISO 9000 audits, the systems test component of the tier 4 job was eventually phased out and both tier 3 and tier 4 auditors were asked to perform the ISO 9000 audit. Both the union and management agree that the systems test work previously performed by tier 4 employees was easier (and less valuable to the company) than the new ISO 9000 work now being performed. The union maintains that this added responsibility from the ISO 9000 audit, which involves about 150 hours of training, is sufficiently complex to warrant tier 4 classification. As partial support, the union provided a list of attendees to one ISO 9000 training session and noted that many of the attendees from other companies are managers and engineers, asserting this as evidence of the complexity involved in the audit material and the importance attached to this job by other firms.

The union also presented evidence to support the assertion that tier 3 personnel performing ISO 9000 audits are doing work of substantially the same value as the old grade 310 work.[2] This grade, as agreed by both the union and the company, is equivalent to the new tier 4.

---

[1]Tier 1 is the low end and tier 5 is the highest for all skilled craft jobs. Different evaluation systems are used for management and for clerical employees.

[2]The former job evaluation system broke jobs down into many more grades. As of the last contract, jobs are now classified into one of five tiers or grades.

Summary of Important Points in Management Case

Management's case includes four major points. First, management argues that a Technical Review Analyst performing ISO 9000 audits has a job that is similar in complexity, responsibility, and types of duties to jobs previously classified as grade 308 and 309. Jobs in these old grades are now slotted into tier 3, per the contract.

Second, management presented evidence that many of the duties performed in the ISO 9000 audits were performed in a series of prior audits, variously labeled Eastcore MPA, QSA 1981, and QPS 1982. This long and varied history of similar duties, management contends, is evidence that ISO 9000 does not involve higher level or substantially different (and hence no more valuable) duties than have been performed historically.

Third, management presented both notes and a memorandum from W. P. Salkrist (the company job evaluation expert) in support of his argument that the audit job with ISO 9000 responsibilities should be classified as a tier 4 job. Prior to introduction of the ISO 9000 audit, neither the union nor management had found any reason to complain about the existing prior job evaluations of the tier 3 and tier 4 review analysts.

Fourth, management provided evidence that these jobs at other facilities, *with other local contract provisions and conditions,* were all classified into tier 3.[3]

---

[3]Union strongly contests the introduction of this information. In the past, management has vehemently argued that conditions at other facilities should not be introduced because local contracts were negotiated, with different trade-offs being made by the different parties. Union believes that this same logic should now apply if a consistent set of rules is to evolve.

Glossary of Terms

Ability   Refers to an individual's capability to engage in a specific behavior.

Ability to Pay   The ability of a firm to meet employee wage demands while remaining profitable; a frequent issue in contract negotiations with unions. A firm's ability to pay is constrained by its ability to compete in its product market.

Access Discrimination   Focuses on the staffing and allocation decisions made by employers. It denies particular jobs, promotions, or training opportunities to qualified women or minorities. This type of discrimination is illegal under Title VII of the Civil Rights Act of 1964.

Across-the-Board Increases   A general adjustment that provides equal increases to all employees.

Adjective Checklist   An individual (or job) rating technique. In its simplest form, it is a set of adjectives or descriptive statements. If the employee (job) possesses a trait listed, the item is checked. A rating score from the checklist equals the number of statements checked.

Age Discrimination in Employment Act (ADEA) of 1967 (Amended 1978, 1986, and 1990)   Makes nonfederal employees age 40 and over a protected class relative to their treatment in pay, benefits, and other personnel actions. The 1990 amendment is called the *Older Workers Benefit Protection Act*.

All-Salaried Work Force   Both exempt employees (exempt from provisions of the Fair Labor Standards Act), who traditionally are paid a salary rather than an hourly rate, and nonexempt employees receive a prescribed amount of money each pay period that does not primarily depend on the number of hours worked.

Alternation Ranking   A job evaluation method that involves ordering the job descriptions alternately at each extreme. All the jobs are considered. Agreement is reached on which is the most valuable, then the least valuable. Evaluators alternate between the next most valued and next least valued and so on until all the jobs have been ordered.

American Compensation Association (ACA)   A nonprofit organization for training compensation professionals.

Appeals Procedures   Mechanism created to handle pay disagreements. They provide a forum for employees and managers to voice their complaints and receive a hearing.

Base Pay   *See* Base Wage.

Base Wage   The basic cash compensation that an employer pays for the work performed. Tends to reflect the value of the work itself and ignore differences in contribution attributable to individual employees.

Basic Pay Policies   Include decisions on the relative importance of (1) internal consistency, (2) external competitiveness, (3) employee contributions, and (4) the nature of the administration of the pay system. These policies form the foundation on which pay systems are designed and administered and serve as guidelines within which pay is managed to accomplish the system's objectives.

Bedeaux Plan   Individual incentive plan that provides a variation on straight piecework and standard hour plans. Instead of timing an entire task, a Bedeaux plan requires determination of the time required to complete each simple action of a task. Workers receive a wage incentive for completing a task in less than a standard time.

Behaviorally Anchored Rating Scales (BARS)   Variants on standard rating scales, in which the various scale levels are anchored with behavioral descriptions directly applicable to jobs being evaluated.

Benchmark Conversion   Matching survey jobs by applying the employer's plan to the external jobs and then comparing worth of external job with its internal "match."

Benchmark (or Key) Jobs   A prototypical job, or group of jobs, used as reference points for making pay comparisons within or without the organization. Benchmark jobs have well-known and stable contents; their current pay rates are generally acceptable and the pay differentials among them are relatively stable. A group of benchmark jobs, taken together, contains the entire range of compensable factors and is accepted in the external labor market for setting wages.

BLS   *See* Bureau of Labor Statistics.

Bonus   A lump-sum payment to an employee in recognition of goal achievement.

"Bottom Up" Approach to Pay Budgeting   Under this approach individual employees' pay rates for the next plan year are forecasted and summed to create an organization's total budget.

Broadbanding   Collapsing a number of salary grades into a smaller number of broad grades with wide ranges.

Budget   A plan within which managers operate and a standard against which managers' actual expenditures are evaluated.

Bureau of Labor Statistics   A major source of publicly available pay data. It also publishes the consumer price index.

Cafeteria (Flexible) Benefit Plan   A benefit plan in which employees have a choice as to the benefits they receive within some dollar limit. Usually a common core benefit package is required (e.g., specific minimum levels of health,

disability, retirement, and death benefit) plus elective programs from which the employee may select a set dollar amount. Additional coverage may be available through employee contributions.

Capital Appreciation Plans   *See* Long-Term Incentives.

Career Paths   Refers to the progression of jobs within an organization.

Central Tendency   A midpoint in a group of measures.

Central Tendency Error   A rating error that occurs when a rater consistently rates a group of employees at or close to the midpoint of a scale irrespective of true score performance of ratees. Avoiding extremes (both high and low) in ratings across employees.

Churn   *See* Turnover Effect.

Civil Rights Act   Title VII of the Civil Rights Act of 1964 prohibits discrimination in terms and conditions of employment (including benefits) that is based on race, color, religion, sex, or national origin.

Claims Processing   Begins when employee asserts that a specific event (e.g., disablement, hospitalization, unemployment) has occurred and demands that the employer fulfill a promise for payment. As such, a claims processor must first determine whether the act has, in fact, occurred.

Classification   Job evaluation method that involves slotting job descriptions into a series of classes or grades that cover the range of jobs and that serve as a standard against which the job descriptions are compared.

Clone Error   Giving better ratings to individuals who are like the rater in behavior or personality.

Coinsurance   Employees share in the cost of a benefit provided to them.

Commission   Payment tied directly to achievement of performance standards. Commissions are directly tied to a profit index (sales, production level) and employee costs; thus, they rise and fall in line with revenues.

Comparable Worth   A doctrine that maintains that women performing jobs judged to be equal on some measure of inherent worth should be paid the same as men, excepting allowable differences, such as seniority, merit, and production-based pay plans, and other non-sex-related factors.

Compa-Ratio   An index that helps assess how managers actually pay employees in relation to the midpoint of the pay range established for jobs. It estimates how well actual practices correspond to intended policy. Calculated as the following ratio:

$$\text{Compa-Ratio} = \frac{\text{Average rates actually paid}}{\text{Range midpoint}}$$

Compensable Factors   Job attributes that provide the basis for evaluating the relative worth of jobs inside an organization. A compensable factor must be work related, business related, and acceptable to the parties involved.

Compensating Differentials   Economic theory that attributes the variety of pay rates in the external labor market to differences in attractive as well as negative characteristics in jobs. Pay differences must overcome negative characteristics to attract employees.

Compensation   All forms of financial returns and tangible services and benefits employees receive as part of an employment relationship.

Compensation Budgeting   A part of the organization's planning process; helps to ensure that future financial expenditures are coordinated and controlled. It involves forecasting the total expenditures required by the pay system during the next period as well as the amount of the pay increases. "Bottom up" and "top down" are the two typical approaches to the process.

Compensation Differentials   Differentials in pay among jobs across and within organizations, and among individuals in the same job in an organization.

Compensation Objectives   The desired results of the pay system. The basic pay objectives include efficiency, equity, and compliance with laws and regulations. Objectives shape the design of the pay system and serve as the standard against which the success of the pay system is evaluated.

Compensation System Controls   Basic processes that serve to control pay decision making. They include (1) controls inherent in the design of the pay techniques (e.g., increase guidelines, range maximums and minimums), and (2) budgetary controls.

Competitive Objective   The midpoints for each pay range. The pay policy line that connects the midpoints becomes a control device: compensation must be managed to conform to these midpoints if the organization is to maintain the pay policy it has specified.

Compliance Pay Objective   Involves conforming to various federal and state laws and regulations. To ensure

continuous compliance, pay objectives need to be adjusted as these laws and regulations change.

Comprehensive Occupational Data Analysis Program (CODAP)   The earliest attempt to quantify job analysis using task-oriented data.

Compression   Very narrow pay differentials among jobs at different organization levels as a result of wages for jobs filled from the outside (frequently these are entry-level jobs) increasing faster than the internal pay structure.

Congruency   The degree of consistency or "fit" between the compensation system and other organizational components such as the strategy, product-market stage, culture and values, employee needs, union status.

Consolidated Omnibus Budget Reconciliation Act (COBRA)   Employees who resign or are laid off through no fault of their own are eligible to continue receiving health coverage under employer's plan at a cost borne by the employee.

Consumer Price Index (CPI)   Published by the Bureau of Labor Statistics, U.S. Department of Labor, it measures the changes in prices of a fixed market basket of goods and services purchased by a hypothetical average family.

Content Theories   Motivation theories that focus on *what* motivates people rather than on *how* people are motivated. Maslow's need hierarchy theory and Herzberg's two-factor theory fall in this category.

Contingent Employees   Workers whose employment is of a limited duration (part-time or temporary).

Contributory Benefit Financing Plans   Costs shared between employer and employee.

Conventional Job Analysis Methods   Method (e.g., functional job analysis) that typically involve an analyst using a questionnaire in conjunction with structured interviews of job incumbents and supervisors. The methods place considerable reliance on analysts' ability to understand the work performed and to accurately describe it.

Cooperative Wage Study (CWS)   A study undertaken by 12 steel companies and the United Steel Workers to design an industrywide point plan (the Steel Plan) for clerical and technical personnel.

Coordination of Benefits   Efforts to ensure that employer coverage of an employee does not "double pay" because of identical protection offered by the government (private pension and social security coordination) or a spouse's employer.

Core Employees   Workers with whom a long-term full-time work relationship is anticipated.

Cost of Living   Actual individual expenditures on goods and services. The only way to measure it accurately is to examine the expense budget of each employee.

Cost of Living Adjustments (COLAs)   Across-the-board wage and salary increases or supplemental payments based on changes in some index of prices, usually the consumer price index (CPI). If included in a union contract, COLAs are designed to increase wages automatically during the life of the contract as a function of changes in the consumer price index (CPI).

Cost Savings Plans   Group incentive plans that focus on cost savings rather than on profit increases as the standard of group incentive (e.g., Scanlon, Rucker, Improshare).

CPI   *See* Consumer Price Index.

Culture   The informal rules, rituals, and value systems of an organization that influence the way employees behave.

Davis-Bacon Act of 1931   Requires most federal contractors to pay wage rates prevailing in the area.

Deductibles   Employer cost-saving tool by which the first X number of dollars of cost when a benefit is used (e.g., hospitalization) are borne by the employee. Subsequent costs up to some maximum are covered by the employer.

Deferred Compensation Program   Provide income to an employee at some future time as compensation for work performed now. Types of deferred compensation programs include stock option plans and pension plans.

Defined Benefits Plan   A benefits option or package in which the employer agrees to give the specified benefit without regard to cost maximums. Opposite of defined contribution plan.

Defined Contribution Plan   A benefits option or package in which the employer negotiates a dollar maximum payout. Any change in benefits costs over time reduces the amount of coverage unless new dollar limits are negotiated.

Direct Compensation   Pay received directly in the form of cash (e.g., wages, bonuses, incentives).

Direct Pay.   *See* Direct Compensation.

Disparate (Unequal) Impact Standard   Outlaws the application of pay practices that may appear to be neutral but have a negative effect on females or minorities, unless those practices can be shown to be business related.

Disparate (Unequal) Treatment Standard   Outlaws the application of different standards to different classes of employees unless they can be shown to be business related.

Dispersion   Distribution of rates around a measure of central tendency.

Distributive Justice   Fairness in the amount of reward distributed to employees.

DOLs   Original Department of Labor methodology of job analysis. It categorized data to be collected as (1) actual work performed and (2) work traits or characteristics. Actual work performed is further refined into three categories: worker functions (what the worker does), work fields (the methods and techniques employed), and products and services (output).

Double-Track System   A framework for professional employees in an organization whereby at least two general tracks of ascending compensation steps are available: (a) a managerial track to be ascended through increasing responsibility for supervision of people and (2) a professional track to be ascended through increasing contributions of a professional nature.

Drive Theory   A motivational theory that assumes that all behavior is induced by drives (i.e., energizers such as thirst, hunger, sex), and that present behavior is based in large part on the consequences or rewards of past behavior.

Dual Career Ladders   Two different ways to progress in an organization, each reflecting different types of contribution to the organization's mission. The first, or managerial ladder, ascends through increasing responsibility for supervision or direction of people. The professional track ascends through increasing contributions of a professional nature that do not mainly entail the supervision of employees.

Efficiency Pay Objective   Involves (1) improving productivity and (2) controlling labor costs.

Efficiency Wage Theory   A theory to explain why firms are rational in offering higher than necessary wages.

Employee Benefits   That part of the total compensation package, other than pay for time worked, provided to employees in whole or in part by employer payments (e.g., life insurance, pension, workers' compensation, vacation).

Employee Contributions Refers to comparisons among individuals doing the same job for the same organization.

Employee Equity *See* Employee Contributions.

Employee Retirement Income Security Act of 1974 (ERISA) An act regulating private employer pension and welfare programs. The act has provisions that cover eligibility for participation, reporting, and disclosure requirements, establish fiduciary standards for the financial management of retirement funds, set up tax incentives for funding pension plans, and establish the Pension Benefit Guaranty Corporation to insure pension plans against financial failures.

Employee Services and Benefits Programs that include a wide array of alternative pay forms ranging from payments for time not worked (vacations, jury duty) through services (drug counseling, financial planning, cafeteria support) to protection (medical care, life insurance, and pensions).

Employer of Choice The view that a firm's external wage competitiveness is just one facet of its overall human resource policy, and competitiveness is more properly judged on overall policies. So challenging work, high calibre colleagues, or an organization's prestige must be factored into an overall consideration of attractiveness.

Entry Jobs Jobs that are filled from the external labor market and whose pay tends to reflect external economic factors rather than an organization's culture and traditions.

Equal Employment Opportunity Commission (EEOC) A commission of the federal government charged with enforcing the provisions of the Civil Rights Act of 1964 and the EPA of 1963 as it pertains to sex discrimination in pay.

Equalization Component As a part of an expatriate compensation package, equalization is one form of equity designed to "keep the worker whole" (i.e., maintain real income or purchasing power of base pay). This equalization typically comes in the form of four types of allowances: tax equalization, housing, education and language training, and cost of living (COLA) allowances.

Equal Pay Act (EPA) of 1963 An amendment to the Fair Labor Standards Act of 1938 prohibiting pay differentials on jobs which are substantially equal in terms of skills, effort, responsibility, and working conditions, except when they are the result of bona fide seniority, merit,

or production-based systems, or any other job-related factor other than sex.

Equity Absolute or relative justice or "fairness" in an exchange such as the employment contract. Absolute fairness is evaluated against a universally accepted criterion of equity, while relative fairness is assessed against a criterion that may vary according to the individuals involved in the exchange, the nature of what is exchanged, and the context of the exchange.

Equity Pay Objective Fair pay treatment for all the participants in the employment relationship. Focuses attention on pay systems that recognize employee contributions as well as employee needs.

Equity Theory A theory proposing that in an exchange relationship (such as employment) the equality of outcome/input ratios between a person and a comparison other (a standard or relevant person/group) will determine fairness or equity. If the ratios diverge from each other, the person will experience reactions of unfairness and inequity.

ESOP (Employee Stock Ownership Plan) A plan in which a company borrows money from a financial institution using its stock as a collateral for the loan. Principal and interest loan repayment are tax deductible. With each loan repayment, the lending institution releases a certain amount of stock being held as security. The stock is then placed into an Employee Stock Ownership Trust (ESOT) for distribution at no cost to all employees. The employees receive the stock upon retirement or separation from the company. TRASOPs and PAYSOPs are variants of ESOPs.

Essay An open-ended performance appraisal format. The descriptors used could range from comparisons with other employees through adjectives, behaviors, and goal accomplishment.

Exchange Value The price of labor (the wage) determined in a competitive market; in other words, labor's worth (the price) is whatever the buyer and seller agree upon.

Executive Perquisites (Perks) Special benefits made available to top executives (and sometimes other managerial employees). May be taxable income to the receiver. Company-related perks may include luxury office, special parking, and company-paid membership in clubs/associations, hotels, resorts. Personal perks include such things as low-cost loans, personal and legal counseling, free home repairs and improvements, and so on. Since

1978, various tax and agency rulings have slowly been requiring companies to place a value on perks, thus increasing the taxable income of executives.

Exempt Jobs   Jobs not subject to provisions of the Fair Labor Standards Act with respect to minimum wage and overtime. Exempt employees include most executives, administrators, professionals, and outside sales representatives.

Expatriates   Employees assigned outside their base country for any period of time in excess of one year.

Expectancies   Beliefs (or subjective probability climates) individuals have that particular actions on their part will lead to certain outcomes or goals.

Expectancy (VIE) Theory   A motivation theory that proposes that individuals will select an alternative based on how this choice relates to outcomes such as rewards. The choice made is based on the strength or value of the outcome and on the perceived probability that this choice will lead to the desired outcome.

External Competitiveness   Refers to the pay relationships among organizations and focuses attention on the competitive positions reflected in these relationships.

External Equity   Fairness in relation to the amount paid in the relevant external market.

Extrinsic Rewards   Rewards that a person receives from sources other than the job itself. They include compensation, supervision, promotions, vacations, friendships, and all other important outcomes apart from the job itself.

Face Validity   The determination of the relevance of a measuring device on "appearance" only.

Factor Comparison   A job evaluation method in which jobs are assessed on the basis of two criteria: (1) a set of compensable factors and (2) wages for a selected set of jobs.

Factor Scales   Reflect different degrees within each compensable factor. Most commonly five to seven degrees are defined. Each degree may also be anchored by the typical skills, tasks and behaviors, or key job titles.

Factor Weights   Indicate the importance of each compensable factor in a job evaluation system. Weights can be derived either through committee judgment or statistical analysis.

Fair Labor Standards Act of 1938 (FLSA)   A federal law governing minimum wage, overtime pay, equal pay for men and women in the same types of jobs, child labor, and recordkeeping requirements.

Fair Wage Model   A model that attributes above-market pay rates in high-profit industries to employees' comparisons of wages with relative profit level.

Federal Insurance Contribution Act (FICA)   The source of social security contribution withholding requirements. The FICA deduction is paid by both employer and employee.

First Impression Error   Developing a negative (positive) opinion of an employee early in the review period and allowing that to negatively (positively) color all subsequent perceptions of performance.

Flat Rates   A single rate, rather than a range of rates, for all individuals performing each job. Ignores seniority and performance differences.

Flexible Benefits   *See* Cafeteria (Flexible) Benefit Plan.

Flexible Benefits Plan   Benefits package in which employees are given a core of critical benefits (necessary for minimum security) and permitted to expend the remainder of their benefits allotment on options that they find most attractive.

Forms of Compensation   Pay may be received directly in the form of cash (e.g., wages, bonuses, incentives) or indirectly through services and benefits (e.g., pensions, health insurance, vacations). This definition excludes other forms of rewards or returns that employees may receive, such as promotion, recognition for outstanding work behavior, and the like.

Forms of Pay   *See* Forms of Compensation.

Functional Job Analysis (FJA)   A conventional approach to job analysis that is followed by the U.S. Department of Labor. Five categories of data are collected: what the worker does; the methodologies and techniques employed; the machines, tools, and equipment used; the products and services that result; and the traits required of the worker. FJA constitutes a modification of the DOLs methodology and is widely used in the public sector.

Gain-Sharing or Group Incentive Plans   Incentive plans that are based on some measure of group performance rather than individual performance. Taking data on a past year as a base, group incentive plans may focus on cost savings (e.g., the Scanlon, Rucker, and Improshare plans) or on profit increases (profit sharing plans) as the standard to distribute a portion of the accrued funds among relevant employees.

Gantt Plan   Individual incentive plan that provides for variable incentives as a function of a standard expressed as time period per unit of production. Under this plan, a standard time for a task is purposely set at a level requiring high effort to complete.

General Schedule (GS)   A job evaluation plan used by the U.S. Office of Personnel Management for white collar employees. It has 18 "grades" (classes). Most jobs are in 15 grades; the top three are combined into a "supergrade" that covers senior executives.

Generic Job Analysis   Generalized, less detailed data collection at a job level used to write a broad job description that covers a large number of related tasks. The result is that two people doing the same broadly defined job could be doing entirely different, yet related, tasks.

Geographic Differentials   *See* Locality Pay.

Glass Ceiling   A subtle barrier that keeps women and minorities out of the very highest executive positions.

Global Approach   Substitutes a particular skill and experience level for job descriptions in determining external market rates. Includes rates for all individuals who possess that skill.

Group Incentive Plans   *See* Gain-Sharing or Group Incentive Plans.

Halo Error   An appraiser gives favorable ratings to all job duties based on impressive performance in just one job function. For example, a rater who hates tardiness rates a prompt subordinate high across all performance dimensions exclusively because of this one characteristic.

Halsey 50–50 Method   Individual incentive method that provides for variable incentives as a function of a standard expressed as time period per unit of production. This plan derives its name from the shared split between worker and employer of any savings in direct costs.

Hay System   A point factor system that evaluates jobs with respect to know-how, problem solving, and accountability. It is used primarily for exempt (managerial/professional) jobs.

Health Maintenance Act   Requires employers to offer alternative health coverage options (e.g., Health Maintenance Organizations) to employees.

Health Maintenance Organization (HMO)   A nontraditional health care delivery system. HMOs offer comprehensive benefits and outpatient services, as well as hospital coverages, for a fixed monthly prepaid fee.

Hierarchies (or Job Structures)   Jobs ordered according to their relative content and/or value.

Hit Rate   The ability of a job evaluation plan to replicate a predetermined, agreed-upon job structure.

Horn Error   The opposite of a halo error; downgrading an employee across all performance dimensions exclusively because of poor performance on one dimension.

Human Capital Theory   An economic theory proposing that the investment one is willing to make to enter an occupation is related to the returns one expects to earn over time in the form of compensation.

Improshare (IMproved PROductivity through SHARing)   A gain-sharing plan in which a standard is developed to identify the expected hours required to produce an acceptable level of output. Any savings arising from production of agreed-upon output in fewer than expected hours are shared by the firm and the worker.

Incentive   Inducement offered in advance to influence future performance (e.g., sales commissions).

Incentive Stock Options (ISOs)   A form of deferred compensation designed to influence long-term performance. Gives an executive the right to pay today's market price for a block of shares in the company at a future time. No tax is due until the shares are sold.

Increase Guidelines   Inherent compensation system controls. They specify amount and timing of pay increases on an organization-wide basis.

Indirect Compensation   Pay received through services and benefits (e.g., pensions, health insurance, vacations).

Individual-Based Systems   They focus on employee rather than job characteristics. Pay is based on the highest work-related skills employees possess rather than on the specific job performed.

Institutional Theory   Theory that organizations base their practices to a large extent on what other organizations are doing. Also called *benchmarking*.

Instrumentality   The perceived contingency that an outcome (performing well) has for another outcome (a reward such as pay).

Internal Consistency   Refers to the pay relationships among jobs or skill levels within a single organization and focuses attention on employee and management acceptance of those relationships. It involves establishing equal pay for jobs of equal worth and acceptable pay differentials for jobs of unequal worth.

Internal Equity   *See* Internal Consistency.

Internal Labor Markets   The rules or procedures that serve to regulate the allocation of employees among different jobs within a single organization.

Internal Pricing   Pricing jobs in relationship to what other jobs within the organization are paid.

Interrater Reliability   The extent of agreement among raters rating the same individual, group, or phenomena.

Inventories   Questionnaires in which tasks, behaviors, and abilities are tested. The core of all quantitative job analysis.

Job Analysis   The systematic process of collecting and making certain judgments about all of the important information related to the nature of a specific job. It provides the knowledge needed to define jobs and conduct job evaluation.

Job-Based Systems   Focus on jobs as the basic unit of analysis to determine the pay structure; hence, job analysis is required.

Job Classes or Grades   Each represents a grouping of jobs that are considered substantially similar for pay purposes.

Job Cluster   A series of jobs grouped for job evaluation and wage and salary administration purposes on the basis of common skills, occupational qualifications, technology, licensing, working conditions, union jurisdiction, workplace, career paths, and organizational tradition.

Job Competition Theory   Economic theory that postulates a "quoted" wage for a job irrespective of an individual's qualifications. Because the most qualified applicants will be hired first, later hires will be more costly because they will require more training or will be less productive.

Job Content   Information that describes a job. May include responsibility assumed and/or the tasks performed.

Job Description   A summary of the most important features of the job as it is performed. It identifies the job and describes the general nature of the work, specific task responsibilities, outcomes, and employee characteristics required to perform the job.

Job Evaluation   A systematic procedure designed to aid in establishing pay differentials among jobs within a single employer. It includes classification, comparison of the relative worth of jobs, blending internal and external market forces, measurement, negotiation, and judgment.

Job Evaluation Committee   Usually having a membership representing all important constituencies within the organization. It may be charged with the responsibility of (1) selecting a job evaluation system, (2) carrying out or at least supervising the process of job evaluation, and (3) evaluating the success with which the job evaluation has been conducted. Its role may vary among organizations.

Job Evaluation Manual   Contains information on the job evaluation plan and is used as a "yardstick" to evaluate jobs. It includes a description of the job evaluation method used, descriptions of all jobs, if relevant, a description of compensable factors, numerical degree scales, and weights. May also contain a description of available review or appeals procedure.

Job Family   Jobs involving work of the same nature but requiring different skill and responsibility levels (e.g., computing and account-recording is a job family; bookkeeper, accounting clerk, teller are jobs within that family).

Job Grade   *See* Pay Grade.

Job Hierarchy   A grouping of jobs based on their job-related similarities and differences and on their value to the organization's objectives.

Job Structure   Relationships among jobs inside an organization, based on work content and the job's relative contribution to achieving organization's objectives.

Job Value Approach to Pay Survey   Under this approach, the employer uses its internal job evaluation plan to assess the benchmark jobs provided in the survey.

Just Wage Doctrine   A theory of job value that posited a "just" or equitable wage for any occupation based on that occupation's place in the larger social hierarchy. According to this doctrine, pay structures should be designed and justified on the basis of societal norms, custom, and tradition, not on the basis of economic and market forces.

Key Jobs   *See* Benchmark (or Key) Jobs.

Knowledge Analysis   The systematic collection of information about the knowledge or skills required to perform work in an organization.

Knowledge Blocks   The different types of knowledge or competencies required to perform work.

Knowledge Systems   Linking pay to additional knowledge related to the same job (depth) (e.g., scientists and teachers) or to a number of different jobs (breadth) (e.g., technician).

Labor Demand   In economic models, the demand for labor is a curve that indicates how the desired level of employment varies with changes in the price of labor when other factors are held constant. The shape of the labor demand curve is downward sloping. Thus, an increase in the wage rate will reduce the demand for labor in both the short and long run.

Labor Supply   In economic models, the supply of labor is a curve or schedule representing the average pay required to attract different numbers of employees. The shape of the labor supply curve varies depending on the assumptions. In perfectly competitive markets, an individual firm faces a horizontal (elastic) supply of labor curve.

Lag Pay Level Policy   Setting a wage structure to match market rates at beginning of plan year only. The rest of the plan year, internal rates will lag behind market rates. Its objective is to offset labor costs, but it may hinder a firm's ability to attract and retain quality employees.

Lead Pay Level Policy   Setting a wage structure to lead the market throughout the plan year. Its aim is to maximize a firm's ability to attract and retain quality employees and to minimize employee dissatisfaction with pay.

Least Squares Line   In regression analysis, the line fitted to a scatterplot of coordinates that minimizes the squared deviations of coordinates around the line. This line is known as the *best fit line*.

Legally Required Benefits   Benefits that are required by statutory law: workers' compensation, social security, and unemployment compensation.

Leniency Error   Consistently rating someone higher than is deserved.

Leveling   Weighing market survey data according to the closeness of the job matches.

Level of Aggregation   Refers to the size of the work unit for which performance is measured (e.g., individual work group, department, plan, or organization) and to which rewards are distributed.

Level Rise   The percentage increase in the average wage rate paid.

Percent level rise = 100 ×

$$\frac{\text{Average pay year end} - \text{Average pay year beginning}}{\text{Average pay at the beginning of the year}}$$

Linear Regression   A statistical technique that allows an analyst to build a model of a relationship between variables that are assumed to be linearly related.

Local Country Nationals (LCNs)   Citizens of a country in which a U.S. foreign subsidiary is located. LCNs' compensation is tied either to local wage rates or to the rates of U.S. expatriates performing the same job. Each practice has different equity implications.

Locality Pay   Adjusting pay rates for employees in a specific geographic area to account for local conditions such as labor shortages, housing cost differentials, and so on.

Long-Term Disability (LTD) Plan   An insurance plan that provides payments to replace income lost through an inability to work that is not covered by other legally required disability income plans.

Long-Term Incentives   Inducements offered in advance to influence longer rate (multiyear) results. Usually offered to top managers and professionals to focus on long-term organization objectives.

Low-High Approach   Using the lowest- and highest-paid benchmark job in the external market to anchor an entire skill-based structure.

Lump-Sum Award   Payment of entire increase (typically merit increase) at one time. Amount is not factored into base pay so any benefits tied to base pay also don't increase.

Management by Objectives (MBO)   An employee planning, development, and appraisal procedure in which a supervisor and a subordinate, or group of subordinates, jointly identify and establish common performance goals. Employee performance on the absolute standards is evaluated at the end of the specified period.

Marginal Product of Labor   The additional output associated with the employment of one additional human resources unit, with other factors held constant.

Marginal Productivity Theory (MPT)   By contrast with Marxist "surplus value" theory, MPT focuses on labor demand rather than supply and argues that employers will pay a wage to a unit of labor that equals that unit's use (not exchange) value. That is, work is compensated in proportion to its contribution to the organization's production objectives.

Marginal Revenue of Labor   The additional revenue generated when the firm employs one additional unit of human resources, with other factors held constant.

Market Pay Lines   Summarize the distributions of market rates for the benchmark jobs under consideration. Several methods to construct the lines can be used: a single line connecting the distributions' midpoints (means or medians), or the 25th, 50th, and 75th percentiles. Often the lines are fitted to the data through a statistical procedure, such as regression analysis.

Market Pricing   Setting pay structures almost exclusively through matching pay for a very large percentage of jobs with rates paid in the external market.

Maturity Curves   A plot of the empirical relationship between current pay and years since a professional has last received a degree (YSLD), thus allowing organizations to determine a competitive wage level for specific professional employees with varying levels of experience.

Merit Pay   A reward that recognizes outstanding past performance. It can be given in the form of lump-sum payments or as increments to the base pay. Merit programs are commonly designed to pay different amounts (often at different times) depending on the level of performance.

Merit Pay Increase Guidelines   Tie pay increases to performance. They may take one of two forms: The simplest version specifies pay increases permissible for different levels of performance. More complex guidelines tie pay not only to performance but also to position in the pay range.

Merrick Plan   Individual incentive plan that provides for variable incentives as a function of units of production per time period. It works like the Taylor plan, but three piecework rates are set: (1) high—for production exceeding 100 percent of standard; (2) medium—for production between 83 percent and 100 percent of standard; and (3) low—for production less than 83 percent of standard.

Middle and Top Management   Employees, above the supervisory level, who have technical and administrative training and whose major duties entail the direction of people and the organization. They can be classified as special groups to the extent the organization devises special compensation programs to attract and retain these relatively scarce human resources. By this definition, not all managers above the supervisory level qualify for consideration as a special group.

Minimum Wage   A minimum wage level for most Americans established by Congress as part of the FLSA of 1938.

Motivation   An individual's willingness to engage in some behavior. Primarily concerned with (1) what energizes human behavior, (2) what directs or channels such behavior, and (3) how this behavior is maintained or sustained.

Multiskill Systems   Link pay to the number of *different jobs* (breadth) an employee is certified to do, regardless of the specific job he or she is doing.

National Electrical Manufacturing Association (NEMA)   A point factor job evaluation system that evolved into the National Position Evaluation Plan sponsored by NMTA associates.

National Metal Trades Association Plan (NMTA)   A point factor job evaluation plan for production, maintenance, and service personnel.

National Position Evaluation Plan   A point factor job evaluation system that evolved from the former plan. Today, the plan is sponsored by 11 management/manufacturing associations and is offered under the umbrella group, NMTA associates.

Need Theories   Motivation theories that focus on internally generated needs that induce behaviors designed to reduce these needs.

Nonexempt Employees   Employees who are subject to the provisions of the Fair Labor Standards Act.

Nonqualified Deferred Compensation Plans   A plan does not qualify for tax exemption if an employer who pays high levels of deferred compensation to executives does not make proportionate contributions to lower level employees.

Objective Performance-Based Pay Systems   Focus on objective performance standards (e.g., counting output) derived from organizational objectives and a thorough analysis of the job (e.g., incentive and gain-sharing plans).

Organizational Culture   The composite of shared values, symbols, and cognitive schemes that ties people together in the organization.

Organizational Values   Shared norms and beliefs regarding what is socially, organizationally, and individually right, worthy, or desirable. The composite of values contributes to form a common organizational culture.

Outlier   An extreme value that may distort some measures of central tendency.

Paired Comparison   A ranking job evaluation method that involves comparing all possible pairs of jobs under study.

Pay Bands   Combining separate job classifications into a smaller number of divisions, called *bands*. Created to increase flexibility.

Pay Discrimination   It is usually defined to include (1) access discrimination that occurs when qualified women and minorities are denied access to particular jobs, promotions, or training opportunities and (2) valuation discrimination that takes place when minorities or women are paid less than white males for performing substantially equal work. Both types of discrimination are illegal under Title VII of the Civil Rights Act of 1964. Others argue that valuation discrimination can also occur when men and women hold entirely different jobs (in content or results) that are of comparable worth to the employer. Existing federal laws do not support the "equal pay for work of comparable worth" standard.

Pay Equity   *See* Comparable Worth.

Pay-for-Knowledge System   A compensation practice whereby employees are paid for the number of different jobs they can adequately perform or the amount of knowledge they possess.

Pay Grade   One of the classes, levels, or groups into which jobs of the same or similar values are grouped for compensation purposes. All jobs in a pay grade have the same pay range—maximum, minimum, and midpoint.

Pay Increase Guidelines   The mechanism through which performance levels are translated into pay increases and, therefore, dictate the size and time of the pay reward for good performance.

Pay Level   An average of the array of rates paid by an employer.

Pay Level Policies   Decisions concerning a firm's level of pay vis-à-vis product and labor market competitors. There are three classes of pay level policies: to lead, to match, or to follow competition.

Pay Mix   Relative emphasis among compensation components such as base pay, merit, incentives, and benefits.

Pay Objectives   *See* Compensation Objectives.

Pay Plan Design   A process to identify pay levels, components, and timing that best match individual needs and organizational requirements.

Pay Policy Line   Represents the organization's pay-level policy relative to what competitors pay for similar jobs.

Pay Ranges   The range of pay rates from minimum to maximum set for a pay grade or class. They put limits on the rates an employer will pay for a particular job.

Pay Satisfaction   A function of the discrepancy between employee perceptions of how much pay they *should* receive and how much pay they *do* receive. If these perceptions are equal, an employee is said to experience pay satisfaction.

PAYSOPs (Payroll-Based Tax Credit Employee Stock Ownership Plans)   A new form of TRASOPs beginning in 1983 in which the tax credit allotted to plan sponsors who permit and match voluntary employee contributions is payroll based, not investment based.

Pay Structures   The array of pay rates for different jobs within a single organization; they focus attention on differential compensation paid for work of unequal worth.

Pay Techniques   Mechanisms or technologies of compensation management, such as job analysis, job descriptions, market surveys, job evaluation, and the like, that tie the four basic pay policies to the pay objectives.

Pay with Competition Policy   This policy tries to ensure that a firm's labor costs are approximately equal to those of its competitors. It seeks to avoid placing an employer at a disadvantage in pricing products or in maintaining a qualified work force.

Pension Benefit Guaranty Corporation   To protect individuals from bankrupt companies (and pension plans!), employers are required to pay insurance premiums to this agency. In turn, the PBGC guarantees payment of vested benefits to employees formerly covered by terminated pension plans.

Pension Plan   A form of deferred compensation. All pension plans usually have four common characteristics: (1) they involve deferred payments to a former employee (or surviving spouse) for past services rendered; they all specify (2) a normal retirement age at which time benefits begin to accrue to the employee, (3) a formula employed to calculate benefits, and (4) integration with social security benefits.

Percentage Pay Range Overlap   The degree to which adjacent pay ranges in a structure overlap is usually calculated in terms of the following percentage:

$$\text{Percentage overlap} = 100 \times \frac{\text{Maximum rate for lower pay grade} - \text{Minimum rate for higher pay grade}}{\text{Maximum rate for lower pay grade} - \text{Minimum rate for lower pay grade}}$$

Performance Evaluation (or Performance Appraisal)   A process to determine correspondence between worker behavior/task outcomes and employer expectations (performance standards).

Performance Ranking   The simplest, fastest, easiest to understand, and least expensive performance appraisal technique. Orders employees from highest to lowest in performance.

Performance Standards   An explicit statement of what work output is expected from employees in exchange for compensation.

Planned Compa-Ratio Budgeting   A form of top-down budgeting in which a planned compa-ratio rather than a planned level rise is established to control pay costs.

Planned Level Rise   The percentage increase in average pay that is planned to occur after considering such factors as anticipated rates of change in market data, changes in cost of living, the employer's ability to pay, and the efforts of turnover and promotions. This index may be used in top-down budgeting to control compensation costs.

Planned Level Rise Budgeting   A form of top-down budgeting under which a planned level rise rather than a planned compa-ratio is established as the target to control pay costs.

Point (Factor) Method   A job evaluation method that employs (1) compensable factors, (2) factor degrees numerically scaled, and (3) weights reflecting the relative importance of each factor. Once scaled degrees and weights are established for each factor, each job is measured against each compensable factor and a total score is calculated for each job. The total points assigned to a job determine the job's relative value and hence its location in the pay structure.

Policy Capturing Approach to Factor Selection   *See* Statistical Approach to Factor Selection.

Policy Line   A pay line that reflects the organization's policy with respect to the external labor market.

Portability   Transferability of pension benefits for employees moving to a new organization; ERISA does not require mandatory portability of private pensions. On a voluntary basis, the employer may agree to let an employee's pension benefit transfer to an individual retirement account (IRA), or, in a reciprocating arrangement, to the new employer.

Portal-to-Portal Act of 1947   Defines compensable working time to include only the "principal activity" unless the custom is otherwise.

Position Analysis Questionnaire (PAQ)   A structured job analysis technique that classifies job information into seven basic factors: information input, mental processes, work output, relationships with other persons, job context, other job characteristics, and general dimensions. The PAQ analyzes jobs in terms of worker-oriented data.

Position Description Questionnaire (PDQ)   A quantitative job analysis technique.

Preferred Provider Organization   Health care delivery system in which there is a direct contractual relationship between and among employers, health care providers, and third-party payers. An employer is able to select providers (e.g., selected doctors) who agree to provide price discounts and submit to strict utilization controls.

Pregnancy Discrimination Act of 1978   An amendment to Title VII of the Civil Rights Act. It requires employers to extend to pregnant employees or spouses the same disability and medical benefits provided other employees or spouses of employees.

Prevailing Wage Laws   A government-defined prevailing wage is the minimum wage that must be paid for work done on covered government projects or purchases. In practice, these prevailing rates have been union rates paid in various geographic areas. The main prevailing wage laws are (1) Davis-Bacon (1931), (2) Walsh-Healey Public Contracts Act (1936), and (3) McNamara-O'Hara Service Contract Act (1965).

Procedural Equity   Concerned with the process used to make and implement decisions about pay. It suggests that the way pay decisions are made and implemented may be as important to employees as the results of the decisions.

Procedural Justice   Fairness in the procedures used to determine the amount of reward employees will receive.

Process Theories   Motivation theories that focus on *how* people are motivated rather than on *what* motivates people (e.g., drive, expectancy, and equity theories).

Product Market   The market (or market segments) in which a firm competes to sell products or services.

Professional Employee   An employee who has specialized training of a scientific or intellectual nature and whose major duties do not entail the supervision of people.

Profit Sharing Plan   Focus on profitability as the standard for group incentive. These plans typically involve one of three distributions: (1) cash or current distribution plans provide full payment to participants soon after profits have been determined (quarterly or annually); (2) deferred plans have a portion of current profits credited to employee accounts, with cash payment made at time of retirement, disability, severance, or death; and (3) combination plans incorporate aspects of both current and deferred options.

Progression through the Pay Ranges   Three strategies to move employees through the pay ranges: (1) automatic or seniority-based progression, which is most appropriate when the necessary job skills are within the grasp of most employees; (2) merit progression, which is more appropriate when jobs allow variations in performance; and (3) a combination of automatic and merit progression. For example, employers may grant automatic increases up to the midpoint of the range and permit subsequent increases only when merited on the basis of performance appraisal.

Qualified Deferred Compensation Plan   To qualify for tax exemption, a deferred compensation program must provide contributions or benefits for employees other than executives that are proportionate in compensation terms to contributions provided to executives.

Quantitative Job Analysis (QJA)   Job analysis method that relies on scaled questionnaires and inventories that produce job-related data that are documentable, can be statistically analyzed, and may be more objective than other analysis.

Range Maximums   The maximum values to be paid for a job grade, representing the top value the organization places on the output of the work.

Range Midpoint   The salary midway between the minimum and maximum rates of a salary range. The midpoint rate for each range is usually set to correspond to the pay policy line and represents the rate paid for satisfactory performance on the job.

Range Minimums   The minimum values to be paid for a job grade, representing the minimum value the organization places on the work. Often rates below the minimum are used for trainees.

Range Overlap   The degree of overlap between adjoining grade ranges is determined by the differences in midpoints among ranges and the range spread. A high degree of overlap and narrow midpoint differentials indicate small differences in the value of jobs in the adjoining grades and permit promotions without much change in the rates paid. By contrast, a small degree of overlap and wide midpoint differentials allow the manager to reinforce a promotion with a large salary increase. Usually calculated as

$$\text{Percentage overlap} = 100 \times \frac{\text{Maximum rate for lower pay grade} - \text{Minimum rate for higher pay grade}}{\text{Maximum rate for lower pay grade} - \text{Minimum rate for lower pay grade}}$$

Ranges   *See* Pay Ranges.

Range Width or Spread   The range maximum and minimum are usually based on what other employers are doing and some judgment about how the range spread fits the organization, including the amount of individual discretion in the work. Usually calculated as

$$\frac{[\text{Range maximum} - \text{Range minimum}]}{\text{Range minimum}}$$

Ranking   A simple job evaluation method that involves ordering the job descriptions from highest to lowest in value.

Rating Errors   Errors in judgment that occur in a systematic manner when an individual observes and evaluates a person, group, or phenomenon. The most frequently described rating errors include halo, leniency, severity, and central tendency errors.

Recency Error   The opposite of first impression error. Performance (either good or bad) at the end of the review period plays too large a role in determining an employee's rating for the entire period.

Red Circle Rates   Pay rates that are above the maximum rate for a job or pay range for a grade.

Regression   A statistical technique for relating present pay differentials to some criterion, that is, pay rates in the external market, rates for jobs held predominantly by men, or factor weights that duplicate present rates for all jobs in the organization.

Reinforcement Theories   Theories such as expectancy and operant conditioning theory grant a prominent role to rewards (e.g., compensation) in motivating behavior. They argue that pay motivates behavior to the extent merit increases and other work-related rewards are allocated on the basis of performance.

Relative Value of Jobs   Refers to their relative contribution to organizational goals, to their external market rates, or to some other agreed-upon rates.

Relevant Markets   Those employers with whom an organization competes for skills and products/services. Three factors commonly used to determine the relevant markets are: the occupation or skills required, the geography (willingness to relocate and/or commute), and the other employers involved (particularly those who compete in the product market).

Reliability   The consistency of the results obtained. That is, the extent to which any measuring procedure yields the same results on repeated trials. Reliable job information does not mean that it is accurate (valid), comprehensive, or free from bias.

Reopener Clause   A provision in an employment contract that specifies that wages, and sometimes such nonwage items as pension/benefits, will be renegotiated under certain conditions (changes in cost of living, organization, profitability, and so on).

Reservation Wage   A theoretical minimum standard below which a job seeker will not accept an offer, no matter how attractive the other job attributes.

Resource Dependency   The theory that internal pay structures are based on the differential control jobs exert over critical resources.

Revenue Act of 1978   Primarily simplified pension plans, added tax incentives for individual retirement accounts (IRAs), and adjusted requirements for ESOPs. The act also provided that cafeteria benefit plans need not be included in gross income and reaffirmed the legality of deferring compensation and taxes due on it for an employee.

Reward System   The composite of all organizational mechanisms and strategies used to formally acknowledge employee behaviors and performance. It includes all forms of compensation, promotions, and assignments; nonmonetary awards and recognitions; training opportunities; job design and analysis; organizational design and working conditions; the supervisor; social networks; performance standards and reward criteria; performance evaluation; and the like.

Rowan Plan   Individual incentive plan that provides for variable incentives as a function of a standard expressed as time period per unit of production. It is similar to the Halsey plan, but in this plan a worker's bonus increases as the time required to complete the task decreases.

Rucker Plan   A group cost savings plan in which cost reductions due to employee efforts are shared with the employees. It involves a somewhat more complex formula than a Scanlon plan for determining employee incentive bonuses.

Salary   Pay given to employees who are exempt from regulations of the Fair Labor Standards Act, and hence do not receive overtime pay (e.g., managers and professionals). "Exempts" pay is calculated at an annual or monthly rate rather than hourly.

Salary Continuation Plans   Benefit options that provide some form of protection for disability. Some are legally required, such as workers' compensation provisions for work-related disability and social security disability income provisions for those who qualify.

Salary Sales Compensation Plan   Under this plan, the sales force is paid a fixed income not dependent on sales volume.

Sales Compensation   Any form of compensation paid to sales representatives. Sales compensation formulas usually attempt to establish direct incentives for sales outcomes.

Scaling   Determining the intervals on a measurement instrument.

Scanlon Plan   A group cost savings plan designed to lower labor costs without lowering the level of a firm's activity. Incentives are derived as the ratio between labor costs and sales values of production (SVOP).

Seniority Increases   These tie pay increases to a progression pattern based on seniority. To the extent performance improves with time on the job, this method has the rudiments of paying for performance.

Severity Error   The opposite of leniency error. Rating someone consistently lower than is deserved.

Short-Term Disability   *See* Workers' Compensation.

Short-Term Incentives   Inducements offered in advance to influence future short-range (annual) results. Usually very specific performance standards are established.

Short-Term Income Protection   *See* Unemployment Insurance.

Sick Leave   Paid time when not working due to illness or injury.

Signaling   The notion that an employer's pay policy communicates to both prospective and current employees what kinds of behaviors are sought. Applicants may signal their likely performance to potential employees through their personal credentials such as experience or educational degrees.

Simplified Employee Pension (SEP)   A retirement income arrangement intended to markedly reduce the paperwork for regular pension plans.

Single Rate Pay System A compensation policy under which all employees in a given job are paid at the same rate instead of being placed in a pay grade. Generally applies to situations in which there is little room for variation in job performance, such as an assembly line.

Skill-Based/Global Approach to Wage Survey This approach does not emphasize comparison of pay for specific jobs. Instead, it recognizes that employers usually tailor jobs to the organization or individual employee. Therefore, the rates paid to every individual employee in an entire skill group or function are included in the salary survey and become the reference point to design pay levels and structures.

Skill-Based Pay System *See* Pay-for-Knowledge System.

Skill Blocks *See* Knowledge Blocks.

Skill Requirement Includes experience, training, and ability as measured by the performance requirements of a particular job.

Slippage *See* Turnover Effect.

Social Information Processing Theory (SIP) Counters need theory by focusing on external factors that motivate performance. According to SIP theorists, workers pay attention to environmental cues (e.g., inputs/outputs of co-workers) and process this information in a way that may alter personal work goals, expectancies, and perceptions of equity. In turn, this influences job attitudes, behavior, and performance.

Social Security The Social Security Act of 1935 established what has become the federal old-age, survivors, disability, and health insurance system. The beneficiaries are workers that participate in the social security program, their spouses, dependent parents, and dependent children. Benefits vary according to (1) earnings of the worker, (2) length of time in the program, (3) age when benefits start, (4) age and number of recipients other than the worker, and (5) state of health of recipients other than the worker.

Special Groups Employee groups for whom compensation practices diverge from typical company procedures (e.g., supervisors, middle and upper management, non-supervisory professionals, sales, and personnel in foreign subsidiaries).

Spillover Effect This phenomenon refers to the fact that improvements obtained in unionized firms "spill over" to nonunion firms seeking ways to lessen workers' incentives for organizing a union.

Spillover Error Continuing to downgrade an employee for performance errors in prior rating periods.

Standard Hour Plan Individual incentive plan in which rate determination is based on time period per unit of production, and wages vary directly as a constant function of production level. In this context, the incentive rate in standard hour plans is set based on completion of a task in some expected time period.

Standard Rating Scales Characterized by (1) one or more performance standards being developed and defined for the appraiser and (2) each performance standard having a measurement scale indicating varying levels of performance on that dimension. Appraisers rate the appraisee by checking the point on the scale that best represents the appraisee's performance level. Rating scales vary in the extent to which anchors along the scale are defined.

Statistical Approach to Factor Selection A method that uses a variety of statistical procedures to derive factors from data collected through quantitative job analysis from a sample of jobs that represent the range of the work employees (or an employee group) perform in the company. It is often labeled as *policy capturing* to contrast it with the committee judgment approach.

Stock Appreciation Rights (SARs) SARs permit an executive all the potential capital gain of a stock incentive option (ISO) without requiring the purchase of stock and, thus, reduce an executive's cash commitment. Payment is provided on demand for the difference between the stock option price and current market price.

Stock Purchase Plan (Nonqualified) A plan that is, in effect, a management stock purchase plan. It allows senior management or other key personnel to buy stock in the business. This plan has certain restrictions: (1) the stockholder must be employed for a certain period of time, (2) the business has the right to buy back the stock, and (3) stockholders cannot sell the stock for a defined period.

Stock Purchase Plan (Qualified) A program under which employees buy shares in the company's stock, with the company contributing a specific amount for each unit of employee contribution. Also, stock may be offered at a fixed price (usually below market) and paid for in full by the employees.

Straight Piecework System Individual incentive plan in which rate determination is based on units of production per time period; wages vary directly as a constant function of production level.

Strategic Issues   Critical considerations in compensation design such as congruency between the pay system and the strategy, the organization's culture and values, employee needs, and the nature of the union relationships.

Strategy   The fundamental direction of the organization. It guides the deployment of all resources, including compensation.

Subjective Performance-Based Pay Systems   Focus on subjective performance standards (e.g., achievement of agreed-upon objectives) derived from organizational objectives and a thorough analysis of the job.

Substantive Equity   In contrast with procedural equity, refers to the equity of the outcomes (results such as pay level, structure, and employee differentials) of the pay system.

Supplemental Unemployment Benefits (SUB) Plan   Employer-funded plan that supplements state unemployment insurance payments to workers during temporary periods of layoffs. Largely concentrated in the automobile, steel, and related industries.

Surplus Value   The difference between labor's use and exchange value. According to Marx, under capitalism wages are based on labor's exchange value—which is lower than its use value—and, thus, provide only a subsistent wage.

SVOP (Sales Value of Production)   This concept includes sales revenue and the value of goods in inventory.

Tax Equalization Allowances   A method whereby an expatriate pays neither more nor less tax than the assumed home-country tax on base remuneration. The employer usually deducts the assumed home-country tax from monthly salary and reimburses the employee for all taxes paid in the country of assignment and any actual home-country tax on company remuneration only.

Taylor Plan   Individual incentive plan that provides for variable incentives as a function of units of production per time period. It provides two piecework rates that are established for production above (or below) standard, and these rates are higher (or lower) than the regular wage incentive level.

Third Country Nationals (TCNs)   Employees of a U.S. foreign subsidiary who maintain citizenship in a country other than the United States or the host country. TCNs' compensation is tied to comparative wages in the local country, the United States, or the country of citizenship. Each approach has different equity implications.

Thrift Savings Plans   The typical thrift plan is designed to help American workers in meeting savings goals. The most common plan involves a 50 percent employer match on employee contributions up to a maximum of 6 percent of pay.

Title VII of the Civil Rights Act of 1964   A major piece of legislation prohibiting pay discrimination. It is much broader in intent than the EPA, forbidding discrimination on the basis of race, color, religion, sex, pregnancy, or national origin.

"Top-Down" Approach to Pay Budgeting   Also known as unit-level budgeting. Under this approach, a total pay budget for the organization (or unit) is determined and allocated "down" to individual employees during the plan year. There are many approaches to unit-level budgeting. They differ in the type of financial index used as a control measure. Controlling to planned level rise and controlling to a planned compa-ratio are two typical approaches.

Total Compensation   The complete pay package for employees including all forms of money, benefits, services, and in-kind payments.

TRASOP (Tax Reduction Act Employee Stock Ownership Plan)   A form of Employee Stock Ownership Plan (ESOP) that meets specific requirements of the Tax Reform Act of 1975, as amended.

Turnover Effect   The downward pressure on average wage that results from the replacement of high-wage-earning employees with workers earning a lower wage.

Two-Tier Pay Plans   Wage structures that differentiate pay for the same jobs based on hiring date. A contract is negotiated that specifies that employees hired after a stated day will receive lower wages than their higher seniority peers working on the same or similar jobs.

Unemployment Benefits   *See* Unemployment Insurance.

Unemployment Compensation   *See* Unemployment Insurance.

Unemployment Insurance (UI)   State-administered programs that provide financial security for workers during periods of joblessness. These plans are wholly financed by employers except in Alabama, Alaska, and New Jersey, where there are provisions for relatively small employee contributions.

Unequal Impact   *See* Disparate (Unequal) Impact Standard.

Unequal Treatment   *See* Disparate (Unequal) Treatment Standard.

U.S. Expatriates (USEs)   American citizens working for a U.S. subsidiary in a foreign country. Main compensation concerns are to "keep the expatriates whole" relative to U.S.–based counterparts and to provide expatriates with an incentive wage for accepting the assignment in a foreign country.

Universal Job Factors   Factors that could theoretically be used to evaluate all jobs in all organizations.

Use Value   The value or price ascribed to the use or consumption of labor in the production of goods or services.

Valence   The amount of positive or negative value placed on specific outcomes by an individual.

Validity   The accuracy of the results obtained. That is, the extent to which any measuring device measures what it purports to measure.

Valuation Discrimination   Focuses on the pay women and minorities receive for the work they perform. Discrimination occurs when members of these groups are paid less than white males for performing substantially equal work. This definition of pay discrimination is based on the standard of "equal pay for equal work." Many believe that this definition is limited. In their view, valuation discrimination can also occur when men and women hold entirely different jobs (in content or results) that are of comparable worth to the employer. Existing federal laws do not support the "equal pay for work of comparable worth" standard.

Variable Pay   Tying pay to productivity or some measure that can vary with the firm's profitability.

Vesting   A benefit plan provision that guarantees that participants will, after meeting certain requirements, retain a right to the benefits they have accrued, or some portion of them, even if employment under their plan terminates before retirement.

VIE Theory   *See* Expectancy (VIE) Theory.

Wage   Pay given the employees who are covered by overtime and reporting provisions of the Fair Labor Standards Act. "Nonexempts" usually have their pay calculated at an hourly rate rather than a monthly or annual rate.

Wage Adjustment Provisions   Clauses in a multilayer union contract that specify the types of wage adjustments that have to be implemented during the life of the contract. These adjustments might be specified in three major ways: (1) deferred wage increases—negotiated at the time of contract negotiation with the time and amount specified in the contract, (2) cost-of-living adjustments (COLAs) or escalator clauses, and (3) reopener clauses.

Wage and Price Controls   Government regulations that aim at maintaining low inflation and low levels of unemployment. They frequently focus on "cost push" inflation, limiting the size of the pay raises and the rate of increases in the prices charged for goods and services. Used for limited time periods only.

Wage Survey   The systematic process of collecting information and making judgments about the compensation paid by other employers. Wage survey data are useful to design pay levels and structures.

Walsh-Healey Public Contracts Act of 1936   A federal law requiring certain employers holding federal contracts for the manufacture or provision of materials, supplies, and equipment to pay industry-prevailing wage rates.

Work or Task Data   Involve the elemental units of work (tasks), with emphasis on the purpose of each task, collected for job analysis. Work data describe the job in terms of actual tasks performed and their output.

Worker or Behavioral Data   Include the behaviors required by the job. Used in job analysis.

Workers' Compensation   An insurance program, paid for by the employer, designed to protect employees from expenses incurred for a work-related injury or disease. Each state has its own workers' compensation law.

YSLD   Years since a professional has last received a degree.

Name Index

Subject Index